4-14-75

FOUNDATIONS OF
INTERPERSONAL
ATTRACTION

FOUNDATIONS OF INTERPERSONAL ATTRACTION

Ted L. Huston

College of Human Development
The Pennsylvania State University
University Park, Pennsylvania

ACADEMIC PRESS   New York and London   1974

A Subsidiary of Harcourt Brace Jovanovich, Publishers

ACADEMIC PRESS, INC.
111 Fifth Avenue, New York, New York 10003

United Kingdom Edition published by
ACADEMIC PRESS, INC. (LONDON) LTD.
24/28 Oval Road, London NW1

Library of Congress Cataloging in Publication Data

Huston, Ted L.
    Foundations of interpersonal attraction.

    Includes bibliographies.
    1.   Interpersonal attraction.   I.   Title.
[DNLM: 1.   Love.   BF575.L8 H972f 1974]
HM132.H87   301.11'2   73-18964
ISBN 0–12–362950–0

To my mother and father
with affection and appreciation

Contents

Part IV   *Antecedents of Attraction: Affective Feedback, Attitudes, and Situational Factors*

List of Contributors

Numbers in parentheses indicate the pages on which the authors' contributions begin.

IRWIN ALTMAN (121), Department of Psychology, University of Utah, Salt Lake City, Utah

ELLIOT ARONSON (235), Department of Psychology, University of Texas, Austin, Texas

ELLEN BERSCHEID (355), Department of Psychology, University of Minnesota, Minneapolis, Minnesota

DONN BYRNE (143), Department of Psychology, Purdue University, Lafayette, Indiana

GERALD L. CLORE (143), Department of Psychology, University of Illinois, Champaign, Illinois

WILLIAM GRIFFITT (285), Department of Psychology, Kansas State University, Manhattan, Kansas

TED L. HUSTON (3), College of Human Development, The Pennsylvania State University, University Park, Pennsylvania

ALAN C. KERCKHOFF (61), Department of Sociology, Duke University, Durham, North Carolina

MELVIN LERNER (331), Department of Psychology, University of Waterloo, Waterloo, Ontario, Canada

GEORGE LEVINGER (99), Department of Psychology, University of Massachusetts, Amherst, Massachusetts

THOMAS LICKONA (31), Center for Early Childhood Education, State University of New York at Cortland, Cortland, New York

ALBERT J. LOTT (171), Department of Psychology, University of Rhode Island, Kingston, Rhode Island

BERNICE E. LOTT (171), Department of Psychology, University of Rhode Island, Kingston, Rhode Island

GEORGE J. McCALL (217), Department of Sociology and Anthropology, University of Missouri—St. Louis, St. Louis, Missouri

DAVID R. METTEE (235), Department of Psychology, University of Denver, Denver, Colorado

PAUL C. ROSENBLATT (79), Department of Family Social Science, University of Minnesota, St. Paul, Minnesota

ZICK RUBIN (383), Department of Psychology and Social Relations, Harvard University, Cambridge, Massachusetts

JAMES T. TEDESCHI (193), Department of Psychology, State University of New York at Albany, Albany, New York

ELAINE WALSTER (355), Department of Sociology, University of Wisconsin, Madison, Wisconsin

LADD WHEELER (309), Department of Psychology, The University of Rochester, Rochester, New York

Preface

This book is intended to provide students of interpersonal relationships with a source book that reviews, integrates, and elaborates basic material concerned with interpersonal attraction—the affectional component of social relationships. All interpersonal relationships can be characterized, in part, by the strength and nature of the affectional tie between the persons involved. The ubiquity of attraction phenomena, and the extensive data that have begun to emerge concerning its nature, antecedents, and interpersonal correlates, provided the original rationale and impetus behind the development of the book.

The title of the volume, with its inclusion of the term "foundations," was chosen not so much because I wish to imply that the chapter contributors provide answers to a series of foundational issues that, when taken together, furnish a solid base from which to erect sophisticated theories of attraction phenomena. The intention was more modest. My hope was—and is—that we have addressed ourselves to what will be regarded as a series of important—if not critical—issues and that we have provided a number of preliminary blueprints for laying such foundations and facilitating future research on attraction.

Some of the major issues addressed are: (a) the nature, measurement, and antecedents of various forms of attraction; (b) the similarities and differences in attraction when studied within beginning as compared to long-term relationships; (c) strategies for investigating attraction, especially those relating to extending the study of attraction to enduring relationships; (d) the status of the "reward hypothesis" in terms of predicting who is likely to be attracted to whom, and under what conditions; (e) the developmental, subcultural, and cross-cultural differences in the nature and role of attraction in social relationships; (f) the behavioral correlates of attraction, including both nonverbal (for instance, eye contact) and verbal (for example, self-disclosing) behaviors; and (g) the role in attraction of factors such as similarity, social power, cognitive processes, and a person's expressions of liking and disliking toward an individual.

The contributors draw from a variety of theoretical approaches in treating these and other issues, including attribution theory, cognitive–developmental theories, reinforcement and exchange theories, role theory, social comparison theory, and several "minitheories" of social interaction. The issues, theories, and research paradigms used to study attraction are blended in the 16 chapters comprising the book which is organized in the following manner. Part I, which consists of my introductory chapter, briefly highlights the history of attraction research, indicates the rationale behind the organization of the book (see pages 4–5), and lays out some central themes related to conceptualizing and researching attraction. All persons develop attachments through social interaction, but the nature and antecedents of such feelings differ depending on the age and cognitive—developmental level of the persons involved as well as on the sociocultural context in which the interaction takes place. Part II is devoted to detailing these issues. Parts III and IV consist of a series of contributions that provide conceptual frameworks for studying attraction. The focus of the fifth, and final, part of the book is devoted to romantic attraction, an area of inquiry that, until recently, has received only minimal attention by social scientists.

Several people have contributed to the development of this book, the editing of which was for me a challenging educational experience. The contributors expanded my understanding of attraction phenomena, confronted some of my cherished ideas, and led me to broaden my conceptual outlook.

I owe my deepest debt of gratitude to Gilbert Geis, who provided me with the inspiration and the confidence to initiate the project and the editorial assistance to carry it out. He is an unusually knowledgeable and sensitive man who brings out the best in those with whom he works. I would also like to thank several individuals in the Department of Psychology at the State University of New York at Albany, where I completed my doctorate, who provided a context facilitating the germination of this book. These people include: James Mancuso, Paul McGhee, Joseph Steger, Richard Teevan, and Fred Tesch. McGhee, Tesch, and Tom Lickona, as well as a number of the contributors to the volume provided me with valuable ideas when the book was in its formative stages. I have found much enjoyment in and profited greatly from my colleagues and associates in the College of Human Development at Penn State. I feel particularly indebted to Steve Danish and Carl Ridley, both of whom have provided stimulating conversation, and to several graduate students—especially Gerry Adams, Dennis Bagarozzi, Jane Eboch, Chuck Figley, Nancy Fitzgerald, and Barbara Kavanaugh—who have contributed in numerous ways to putting the book together. I would also like to thank Janice George and Sheron Sefchick for finding and implementing administrative support facilitating the processing of the manuscript.

Most of all I want to express my debt to my wife, Chris, and our two daughters, Meg and Kelly, the three of whom have not only put up with me while I was working on the book, but also while I was not. Their responsiveness in the former situation has increased my pleasure in working on the book; their responsiveness in the latter situation gives my life its sustenance.

TED L. HUSTON
University Park, Pennsylvania

PART I

Introduction

1

A Perspective on
Interpersonal Attraction

TED L. HUSTON

College of Human Development
The Pennsylvania State University
University Park, Pennsylvania

I. Introduction and Overview

The affective bases of social relationships provide the key focus of the chapters in this volume. An understanding of the magnetic qualities that attract persons to one another and the cohesive forces that bond them into social units is necessary for the development of sound comprehension of interpersonal relationships. American society can be viewed as made up of several million subgroups, which, at their most elementary level, involve two-person networks. Each grouping has its own history, quality, and direction. Many of these two-person relationships develop and dissolve as the feelings of the interactants toward one another wax and wane. Friendships, romantic attachments, and marriages, for example, are generally sustained by the affective ties between the partners and are often set aside when such ties weaken. Social scientists have been exploring the origin, nature, and consequences of the sentiments involved in such social relationships so that each of us might better understand our own behavior and the behavior of persons with whom we interact. To this end, this volume illustrates a variety of emphases and perspectives regarding the antecedents and social consequences of attraction.

This introductory chapter sets forth the organization of the volume and presents a brief history of attraction theory and research. Conceptual, measurement, and methodological problems of attraction research are highlighted, and directions that attraction research might fruitfully pursue are indicated. The discussion of the research problems and the suggestions regarding future directions are built upon the chapters making up the volume. The reader, therefore, may find it profitable to read this chapter either as an introduction or an afterword.

A. The Goals and Organization of this Volume

This volume should enrich the attraction literature in several ways. First, its contents provide a much-needed broadened framework for understanding attraction processes. Theorists conceptualizing attraction sometimes note, in passing, the developmental, subcultural, and cultural limitations of their formulations; and researchers often insert a caveat in their reports indicating similar limitations in regard to their findings. Few theorists or researchers, however, have proceeded far with the task of adequately conceptualizing or testing the generalizability of their work beyond its initial data base, which usually involves white, middle-class, college students. Sound theories of attraction, whether they be of the broad, comprehensive type or the "mini-theory" variety, must consider the degree to which their formulations are applicable across different populations. To stimulate thinking along these lines, therefore, a series of chapters (Part II) devoted to developmental, sociological, and cross-cultural considerations in attraction immediately follow this introductory chapter.

A second goal is to bring together in a single volume several major theoretical frameworks for the study of attraction. Part III presents broad conceptual frameworks, whereas Part IV sets forth formulations focusing on relatively circumscribed sets of antecedents of attraction. It is noteworthy that each chapter in these sections assumes the hedonistic character of human behavior and builds a paradigm linking affection for others to the others' potential or actual reward value to the subject. Collectively, the chapters provide a number of contrasting approaches to understanding the nature of social rewards and offer leads to the possible solution of some of the knottier problems of reward theory (see Section VI).

The chapters, in addition, preview two other trends in attraction research that will undoubtedly gain momentum during the 1970s. The first trend is an increasing interest in studying attraction within the context of long-term relationships (see Chapters 2—6, 10, and 16); the other is a growing concern with providing conceptual and empirical links between formerly isolated theoretical frameworks. The latter trend, evident in many chapters, is given particular prominence in the contributions by Lickona (Chapter 2). Levinger (Chapter 5), Altman (Chapter 6), Clore and Byrne (Chapter 7), Tedeschi (Chapter 9), McCall (Chapter 10), Lerner (Chapter 14), and Rubin (Chapter 16).

The third, and final, objective of this volume is to present outlines for the development of a social psychology of romantic attraction, a heretofore neglected aspect of interpersonal attraction. Part V contains two chapters dealing specifically with the manner in which love-based relationships are formed. Several other chapters (Chapters 2—6, 9, and 10) offer discussions of broad relevance to an understanding of both liking and loving and, thus, add breadth and perspective to the material presented in Part V. Until recently, no sophisticated scientific work on the social psychology of romantic attraction existed. Several forces—including things such as the "personal" nature of love, a taboo against the invasion of privacy in regard to emotionally laden feelings, and some complicated methodological problems— seem to have dissuaded investigators from attempting to employ scientific procedures to study love. Research concerned with love, especially the "passionate" variety, was also hindered, according to Walster (1971), because psychologists and funding agencies alike were reluctant to acknowledge the subject as a legitimate area of scientific inquiry. Philosophers, novelists, and poets for centuries have expounded on the nature of love, though; and sociologists provide us with some intriguing data regarding who is likely to marry whom (see Kerckhoff, Chapter 3), as well as specifying the conditions under which sexual intimacy is likely to occur (for recent reviews see Ehrmann, 1964; Cannon & Long, 1971). The recent development of measures of love, coupled with the commitment of social psychologists to the position that a scientific understanding of love is both desirable and possible, promise that progress in this area will now move forward rapidly.

B. Historical Background

The chapters in this volume draw upon half a century of theory and research. Although a few studies of attraction were conducted during the first third of the 1900s, it was not until Moreno (1934) developed the sociometric method that serious attention was paid to the topic. Moreno's sociometry requires that each person in a group designate some subsample with which he or she prefers to associate. By examining the choices of the group, researchers can ascertain which members were chosen most frequently (that is, the popular ones) and which were chosen least frequently (in other words, the unpopular or rejected ones). A spate of studies conducted from the mid-1930s through the early 1950s concentrated on the kinds of personal and social characteristics related to popularity in groups (see Lindzey & Byrne, 1969, for a review of this material). Sociometric procedures more recently have been employed to test theoretical propositions. Davis (1970; Davis & Leinhardt, 1970), for example, has shown that groups divide and crystallize into subgroups that show high internal solidarity and that become hierarchically ordered in terms of status.

The 1950s saw the emergence of several conceptual paradigms that provided further impetus to the exploration of attraction. These included Winch's theory of complementary needs (1958), two theories offered by Festinger—social comparison theory (Festinger, 1954) and cognitive dissonance theory (Festinger, 1957; Festinger & Aronson, 1960)—and Heider's (1958) balance theory. Winch's work focused attention on the role of personality "match" in mate selection and stimulated interest in the age-old question of whether "opposites attract" or "birds of a feather flock together."

Festinger's social comparison theory led to research focusing on the conditions under which persons desire to be with similar, as opposed to dissimilar, others (see Wheeler, Chapter 13, for a discussion of these data), whereas his dissonance theory led, among other things, to research to determine how individuals evaluate others whom they have harmed or aided (see Berscheid & Walster, 1969). It has been learned, for instance, that when subsequent information indicates that an original evaluation was incorrect, persons will adhere to the original evaluation more so if they were publicly, rather than privately, committed to the evaluation (Walster & Prestholdt, 1966).

Heider's balance theory resulted in inquiries directed toward ascertaining the degree to which relations tend toward "symmetry." Do individuals, for example, gravitate toward others who like them? Do persons with similar values more often become friends than persons with dissimilar values? Newcomb (1961), for instance, conducted a longitudinal study of attraction among residents in a student housing project and found, in general, support for the symmetry predictions. Balance theory has also led to research testing the proposition that persons with low self-esteem like persons who dislike them more than they like persons who like them. [See Mettee and Aronson (Chapter 11 of this volume) and Jones (1973) for discussions of this hypothesis.]

A number of "reward" and "exchange" theories of attraction were advanced in the early 1960s. The fundamental thesis of such theories is that people like others who reward them. Reward theory, as set forth by Byrne and his colleagues (see Byrne, 1971) and by Lott and Lott (1968, 1972), has generated a substantial amount of research concentrating on propositions about learning processes. Byrne and his co-workers utilize a classical conditioning paradigm, while the Lotts employ the formulation identified with Hull and Spence (the Yale–Iowa viewpoint).[1] Researchers using the reward formulation have focused on single encounters. The exchange theorists (Altman, Chapter 6 of this volume; Blau, 1964; Homans, 1961;

---

[1]See Lott and Lott (Chapter 8 of this volume) for a discussion of the classical conditioning and the Hull–Spence approaches to learning interpersonal attitudes.

Levinger & Snoek, 1972; Murstein, 1971; Thibaut & Kelley, 1959), in contrast, have tended to examine relationships over a period of time and to emphasize the mutual dependency of the persons involved on the continuing rewards each person provides the other.

Several research programs initiated in the 1960s can be classified as social interactional in nature. They attempt to ascertain how variations in the situational context or the characteristics of the interaction affect the liking of the participants for one another. Folk sayings, circumscribed or minitheories, and the observations and experiences of the researcher are commonly employed as the bases of research predictions. A number of recent studies fall within the social interactional framework (see Aronson, 1970; Jones, 1964; McCall & Simmons, 1966; Pepitone, 1964; Walster, 1971), and many chapters in this volume adopt a social interactional approach to attraction (see Chapters 10, 11, 14, and 15).

II. Problems with Conceptualizations of Attraction

"Attraction refers to any direct orientation (on the part of one person toward another) which may be described in terms of *sign* [+ or −] and *intensity* [italics added; Newcomb, 1961, p. 6]." Newcomb's definition has been employed by most researchers studying attraction. Several conceptually distinguishable sentiments (for example, gratitude, respect, like, and the various forms of love) fall within the purview of the definition, though attraction research has concentrated primarily on liking and its antecedents.

Newcomb appreciated that his definition blurred potentially important distinctions among sentiments, but few theorists or researchers have attempted to develop more differentiated conceptualizations. Until such formulations become available, the following criticism of Marlowe and Gergen (1969) will continue to be on target:

> Social attraction seems to have been relegated to that felicitous state made up of "common understanding" and generalized inexplicitness. Few psychologists would accept such a definition across the wide and unmanageable range of human experience implied [by such a formulation]. The differences among such phenomena as the comradeship felt by members of a team, the respect held for a powerful leader, sexual attraction for a person of the opposite sex, a mother's devotion for a child, and the gratitude of a person relieved of distress far outweigh the similarities [p. 622].

Investigators studying attraction usually view their task as one of ascertaining the antecedents of a positive orientation on the part of one person toward another. Typically, a researcher selects a variable or variables (say, attitudinal similarity, physical attractiveness) and relates the variable(s) to an attraction response, usually liking. Attraction is most often measured by means of an evaluative scale on which the subject indicates the degree to which he has positive or negative feelings toward the other person. Attraction researchers, by employing some variation or elaboration of this approach, have generated a substantial amount of research. Only limited efforts to refine conceptual issues have been made, however. When conceptualizations are offered, they often lack operational integrity. Five major problem areas confront the scholar who wishes to build a theory of attraction-based relationships from available data.

A. Quality and Intensity of Attraction

Operationalizations of attraction tend to focus on the *intensity* of an individual's positive attraction toward another, with little or no regard to qualitative differences among sentiments. Since both the antecedents and social consequences of different sentiments probably differ to some extent from one another (see Berscheid and Walster, Chapter 15 of this volume; Byrne, 1971; Driscoll, Davis, & Lipetz, 1972; Homans, 1971; in this volume, Mettee & Aronson, Chapter 11; also Rubin, Chapter 16), the development of measures capable of distinguishing among them is an important task confronting attraction research. Recent efforts have focused on differentiating liking from romantic love (Rubin, Chapter 16), liking from passionate love (Berscheid & Walster, Chapter 15), and conjugal from romantic love (Driscoll *et al.*, 1972). These efforts to distinguish among liking and qualities of love is complemented by recent work aimed at differentiating liking from respect (see Bales, 1958; Kiesler & Goldberg, 1968; Mettee, Hrelec, & Wilkins, 1971; Simons, Berkowitz, & Moyer, 1970). Rubin (Chapter 16) stands alone in systematically distinguishing between sentiments through his attempts to measure liking and loving.

B. The Patterning of Positive Sentiments

The covariation of positive sentiments (for example, like, respect, and love) has yet to be determined. The behavior of an individual toward a person he or she likes, but does not love, for instance, is undoubtedly quite different in significant respects from the behavior exhibited toward a person who is both liked and loved. The intensity of sentiments and their covariation probably changes as a function of factors such as the role definition of the relationship (mother—daughter, husband—wife, clerk—customer), the extent of the individuals' involvement with one another (first acquaintance versus long-term relationship), and the developmental levels of the persons (young children, adults).

C. Developmental Considerations and Attraction

The interface between psychological development and attraction phenomena is poorly articulated (Lickona, in Chapter 2 of this volume, describes this). Age, for instance, may have a great deal to do with affectively based relationships in at least three ways. First, the cognitive-developmental level of individuals is probably linked to the character and integration of their interpersonal sentiments, thus affecting their social relationships. Egocentric children, as Lickona points out, probably like one another somewhat differently than do their developmentally more mature counterparts. Second, the antecedents of attraction undoubtedly vary with age and the level of cognitive development. Third, individuals at various stages in the life cycle likely experience the "same" sentiments quite differently. Love may mean one thing to the child, another to the newly wed, and something quite different to the middle-aged couple. Consider the following observation from Cuber and Harroff's (1970) study of styles of marital interaction among middle-aged couples:

> Oh, I know he's fat, grouchy, and not romantic any more. Yet the small part of the time he's here is fuller than the rest. I'd miss him if he stayed away altogether. I suppose that's what love *is* by the fifties [p. 104].

Whether this woman, quoted in Cuber and Harroff (1970), has characterized love as it is typically found among married couples in their fifties is arguable. Perhaps she feels trapped, and her expression of love is more a function of circumstances than affection. Individuals who have unsatisfactory relationships may define words such as liking and loving in less glowing terms than those who have satisfactory relationships. It is also possible that couples at varying stages in the life cycle are tied to one another by different patternings of sentiments. Love may be necessary for some relationships in their early phases of development, whereas liking may suffice at later stages.

D. *Attraction and the Form of the Relationship*

Attraction generally has been studied outside the context of ongoing relationships. Since the antecedents, nature, and social consequences of attraction vary in some respects as a function of the *role definition* (see Kerckhoff, Chapter 3; Orlinsky, 1972) and the *extent of the involvement* (see Levinger, Chapter 5 of this volume; Levinger & Snoek, 1972; Murstein, 1970, 1971) of the interactants, theorists wishing to extrapolate from laboratory-based data to "real-life" relationships must proceed with caution.

Kerckhoff (Chapter 3) and McCall (Chapter 10) argue that attraction cannot be understood without taking account of both the attributes of the other and the role which the other occupies in relation to the person. Male aggressiveness, for example, may be viewed by some women as "masculine" and desirable, and by other women as "brutal" and deplorable. Female aggressiveness may arouse fears of emasculation in some men and result in hostility toward women, but may appear attractive to other men. These qualities may also take on different meanings for different kinds of male–female relationships; in a mixed-sex volleyball game, female aggressiveness may be prized; in marriage it may be derogated by some men, with the reverse true for other men. The perceived appropriateness of attributes for various social roles would affect the attractiveness of persons playing the roles.

Levinger (Chapter 5; Levinger & Snoek, 1972) has distinguished between levels of relationships in terms of the degree of the involvement of the persons with one another and has suggested that the antecedents and consequences of attraction vary for the different levels. According to Levinger, attraction in the early stages of a relationship is largely based on the *expected* rewards and costs of a relationship as estimated from the image projected by the other person. Image includes factors such as physical appearance (body build, facial attractiveness, clothing, grooming, etc.), demeanor, and attitudes toward a limited number of topics. At later stages of interdependency, however, *actual* rewards and costs are seen by Levinger to take on greater importance in determining attraction. Further explication of the nature of these rewards and costs, and understanding how they operate in long-term relationships (see Altman, Chapter 6), are necessary for developing a balanced view of attraction-related phenomena.

E. Cross-Cultural Considerations in Attraction

Since most conceptualizations of attraction, as Rosenblatt (Chapter 4) points out, are based on data gathered from experiments using an unrepresentative sample of Americans, it is difficult to assay their generalizability. The nature and patterning of sentiments aroused in various social situations differ from culture to culture. Sexual attraction for individuals of the same sex, for example, is negatively sanctioned in the United States and occurs less frequently here than in cultures where it is not looked upon with such disfavor (Ford & Beach, 1951; Lewinsohn, 1958). Rosenblatt (Chapter 4) indicates that substantial cross-cultural variation exists with regard to the antecedents of attraction and with regard to the relevance of the personal feelings of prospective spouses as these feelings influence decisions to marry and bear upon success in marriage.

The question of subcultural variations in the degree to which particular attributes are regarded as attractive has also been accorded only limited attention. Kerckhoff (Chapter 3) suggests, for example, that subcultural differences in conceptions of social roles affect the desirability of the attributes people possess. Conceptions of proper roles, Kerckhoff notes, vary from social class to social class and, therefore, the expectations regarding appropriate role behavior also vary.

In such terms, attraction clearly is a complex construct. The Roman poet, Gaius Catullus, writing about 60 B.C. regarding his ambivalent feelings toward his lover, captured some of this complexity:

> Ah, then I love you, not with a passion wild,
> But as a father loves a trusted child.
> I know you better now, and here confess
> I love you more, though I esteem you less.
> 'How can that be?' You say. Yours ways, my dear
> Make love more ardent but less kind, I fear.

> [quoted in Hunt, 1959, p. 59]

Attraction researchers must come to scientific grips with the kind of ambivalence and complexity noted by Catullus. To do so, they need to devote more attention to establishing adequate conceptualizations and operational measures of attraction. Kaplan (1972) has recently presented a modification of the semantic differential technique, which allows researchers to distinguish between ambivalence and indifference. Further developments in methodology, however, are needed to improve the cumulative quality of research. Research should not focus exclusively on measurement and methodological problems, but, ideally, should concentrate on linking various sentiments to their antecedents and examining the importance of such factors as the developmental level of the interactants, the role definition of the relationship, the extent of the involvement of the interactants, and the socio-cultural context. In addition, research should continue to explicate the behavioral consequences of attraction.

III. Attraction as a Multifaceted Attitude

There are two basic ways of examining attraction as a multifaceted attitude. First, attraction can be viewed as a constellation of sentiments which comprise the evaluative orientation of one person toward another. (The rationale behind this approach was described in Sections II.A and II.B.) Second, attraction-based attitudes can be seen as including the following three elements: (*a*) an *evaluative* component, which refers to the quality and strength of one's sentiments toward another person; (*b*) a *cognitive* component, which refers to the belief or beliefs one has about another person, as well as the cognitive processes by which these beliefs are developed; and (*c*) a *behavioral* component, which refers to one's tendency to approach or avoid another person, as well as to the manner in which these behavioral tendencies are manifested. The composite of feelings, beliefs, and behavioral dispositions provide a comprehensive description of the attitude toward that person.

The linkages among evaluations, cognitions, and behavioral orientations are complex. The three components influence one another reciprocally. Not only do the personal characteristics ascribed to a person (beliefs) influence evaluations, and not only do evaluations influence behavior, but the reverse patterns are also true. A person who works hard to develop a relationship, because of his investment, may begin to like the other person more. This enhanced liking may lead, in turn, to selective perception, distortion of memory, or behaviors designed to elicit responses from others confirming the validity of the original evaluation (see Lott & Lott, 1972, and Warr & Knapper, 1968, for reviews of the effect of attraction on perception).

Three competing viewpoints concerning the origin of interpersonal *evaluations* have been proffered by theorists and researchers. Evaluations can be based on a rather dispassionate analysis of the characteristics of another person ("he's intelligent, friendly, and good-looking, therefore I like him"), on the interpretation of physiological and psychological arousal ("I feel tense and excited when I'm around her, I must love her"), or may result from one's behavior toward the other person ("I keep doing him favors, I must like him").

Anderson and his colleagues (Anderson, 1971; Kaplan & Anderson, in press a, b; Kaplan & Olczak, 1970) have suggested that evaluations derive from a consideration of the traits of the person judged. Tedeschi (Chapter 9) acknowledges the affective-arousal basis of evaluation, but emphasizes that attraction is founded on "the expectancy that the other person will altruistically provide benefits or favors across a number of situations and over time." Presumably, any personal characteristic ascribed to another person believed to be related to this expectancy will lead to attraction. Byrne and his colleagues (Byrne, Clore, Griffitt, & Mitchell, in press a, b; in this volume, Clore and Byrne, Chapter 7), in contrast, have emphasized the affective bases of evaluation, but propose that evaluations typically involve both affect and cognition. Berscheid and Walster (Chapter 15) base their theory of love on the assumption that when persons are physiologically aroused, they seek to interpret their arousal; sometimes, the most plausible interpretation is "love" for the person presumed to be the cause of the arousal. Several consistency theory formulations (see Abelson, Aronson, McGuire, Newcomb, Rosenberg, & Tannenbaum, 1968; Zajonc, 1968) predict that persons who behave positively, rather than negatively, toward another individual will consequently like the individual to a greater extent.

The source of the beliefs that constitute the *cognitive* component of interpersonal attitudes may be communications from a third party (that is, reputational material), observations of the individual in his or her interactions with others, or face-to-face interactions with the individual. In the first instance, the source and the information are evaluated for their credibility. In the latter two instances, characteristics are inferred from the individual's behavior. A person who has a similar smile for everyone, for example, may be perceived as friendly; a person who gives a big smile to one individual and lesser smiles to others may be seen as particularly attracted to the person who receives the big smile and, thus, is defined somewhat differently from the first person. Models describing how such inferences are made have been provided by Heider (1958), Jones and Davis (1965), and Kelley (1967).[2]

The availability of information and the weight attached to information about a person depends on many factors, including the length, depth, and breadth of the association, the role definition of the relationship, and the cognitive-developmental level of the interactants. The role definition of the father—daughter relationship, for instance, may bring out different behaviors and awarenesses than those brought forth by the mother—daughter relationship. Fathers and mothers, in addition, are likely to place different weights (in terms of importance) on the various traits they ascribe to the daughter.

---

[2]See Jones, Kanouse, Kelley, Nisbett, Valins, and Weiner (1972) for elaborations and extensions of these models.

Individuals differing in personal characteristics (for example, attitudes and values, self-esteem, moods, personality, and physical appearance), cognitive-developmental level, stage in the life cycle, motivation, sociocultural background, and cognitive structure undoubtedly weight and evaluate (in terms of being attracted to, or repelled by) the same information about other persons quite differently. Research, however, has concentrated on linking differences in personal characteristics of evaluators to their evaluations of others and has given little attention to the other factors.

Each element of information regarding another person ought to be able to be weighted and integrated into a composite view of the individual being judged (Anderson, 1971). Since the situational context may activate motives that change the relative weight attached to the various attributes, overall impressions of another person may change even though no new information is availed. Ability in mathematics, for example, may be heavily weighted when selecting a study partner for a course in experimental psychology, but of minimal importance in choosing a beer-drinking buddy. In the latter case, we might deem humor, compatibility of attitudes, and joviality as very important and attach minimal importance to math ability, at least until we find that the other person consistently underestimates his share of the bill!

The link between *behavior* and evaluative orientation is complex and has been a perennial battleground on which cognitive and behavioral theorists have debated the relative merits of the two approaches to understanding social-interactional phenomena. A brief discussion of factors predicting the degree to which behavior follows from attraction illustrates the complexity of the link between the two dimensions. First, whether attraction toward another is behaviorally manifested depends on the attractiveness of the person under consideration relative to alternative choices—more simply, whether you approach someone may depend as much on who else is available as it does on whether you are attracted to the person you approach (Thibaut & Kelley, 1959). The relative attractiveness of people may also vary from one situation to another depending on the motives aroused in the individual (see, Section VI.B; Lott and Lott, Chapter 8; McCall, Chapter 10). Second, when an individual is unsure whether or not a behavioral approach will meet with acceptance, he or she may hesitate to make the approach (see Huston, 1973). Third, individuals learn that certain behaviors are appropriate manifestations of particular sentiments. Kissing, for instance, is generally viewed as an appropriate expression of love, but not of respect. In contrast, deferential acts are probably more consistently linked to respect than to love. Fourth, behavioral expressions of attraction are influenced by their appropriateness to the nature of the relationship. Attraction expressed in the form of sexual intimacy, for example, is generally regarded by Americans as inappropriate in parent–child relations, but appropriate to some heterosexual relations between adults. Fifth, certain behavioral manifestations of attraction are positively and negatively sanctioned in different cultural contexts. Husbands, for instance, offer access to their wives to visiting males in several societies (Ford & Beach, 1951). Sixth, there are differences among individuals in ways of expressing attraction. People vary in the degree to which they like physical intimacy, enjoy disclosing personal feelings to others, and value gregariousness. Preferences and aversions of the interactants undoubtedly affect how well specific behaviors can be predicted from knowledge of attraction. Finally, since behaviors occur in interrelated patterns, exclusive focus on one behavior may result in unreliable conclusions about the relationship between attraction and behavior in general (see Altman, Chapter 6).

IV. The Measurement of Attraction

In contrast to the relatively meager efforts by scholars to conceptualize attraction, researchers have provided numerous measures of the phenomenon. The measures include verbal indices, such as semantic differential ratings, scales, and sociometric choices. Nonverbal behaviors such as eye contact, the distance one stands or sits from another, and body position and body lean have also been employed as indicators of attraction. Since several reviews of attraction measures are available (see Byrne & Griffitt, 1973; Berscheid & Walster, 1969; Lindzey & Byrne, 1969), we will briefly consider the rationale behind their development and usage, indicate some problems, and suggest possible solutions to these difficulties.

Two assumptions underlie most measures of attraction. The first is that the operations employed to measure attraction define it. Thus, the closer one makes one's mark to the positive end of a liking scale, the greater one's liking by definition. Second, the indicant of attraction is assumed to be a response that derives meaning to the extent that it can be linked to other variables and it needs no further justification. Byrne (1969) described the rationale behind the development of the Interpersonal Judgment Scale (IJS), which he and many others use to measure attraction:

> Though a question is sometimes raised concerning the 'validity' of the attraction measure, the question is not an appropriate one. The response to the IJS is not conceptualized as either an imperfect substitute for everyday life attraction or as an inadequate index of the subject's real though unobserved feelings of attraction. Rather, this attraction response constitutes the dependent variable which our research is designed to explicate.... It may nevertheless be said that any relationship or lack of relationship between the attraction measure and other variables is of interest. The concern here is not with validating the measure in a psychometric sense but with establishing its generality as a construct [p. 67].

The integration of attraction data gathered by researchers, according to the view toward measurement offered by Byrne (1969), depends on the comparability of measures. Although some efforts have been made to assess such comparability, more work needs to be done. Attraction responses, to the extent that they represent evaluations of others on a good—bad dimension, should show at least a moderately positive correlation.

The need for new measures and approaches to attraction becomes apparent, however, if one desires to study the commonalities and differences among the various sentiments. Attraction must be regarded as a multifaceted construct composed of several interrelated subcomponents (that is, sentiments) in order for sophisticated measurement procedures to emerge. This view is in sharp contrast to that heretofore employed (with the possible exception of Rubin, Chapter 16 in this volume) in that it places a premium on grounding measures in a conceptual context and in establishing the reliability and validity of measures. Such an approach would allow for determination of the antecedents of global evaluations and the precursors of the various sentiments. Measures that confound, or do not distinguish among, sentiments do not promise to provide a knowledge base maximizing the integrative possibilities of attraction research.

V. Social Relationships and Attraction

The first part of this section contrasted and compared approaches to studying attraction, briefly described research efforts using the approaches, and directed the reader to representative studies. The second part deals with the assumptions researchers make regarding the developmental nature of social relationships.

A. *Research Approaches to Attraction*

Studies of attraction can generally be analyzed in terms of three significant facets: (*a*) the degree of relationship between the people involved (see Levinger, Chapter 5; Levinger & Snoek, 1972); (*b*) whether measurement of the dependent variable is made on one occasion or on two or more occasions; and (*c*) whether the study is concerned with antecedents of attraction, consequences of attraction, or correlates of attraction. The following discussion is organized around the first two of the three facets, while the third is incorporated within the discussion. The first facets can be visualized in a 2 × 2 matrix with two levels of relationship (strangers versus established pairs) and two types of designs (single occasion of measurement versus longitudinal). This matrix generates four combinations: (*a*) strangers: single occasion of measurement; (*b*) strangers: longitudinal measurement; (*c*) established pairs: single occasion of measurement; and (*d*) established pairs: longitudinal measurement.

1. STRANGERS: SINGLE OCCASION OF MEASUREMENT

Studies in this category, employing subjects who have never met prior to the experiment, provide well over 80% of the research findings about attraction. Research explicating antecedents of attraction has proceeded along several lines. Sometimes the subject never meets the individual, but only receives information about him or her. Byrne and his colleagues (Byrne, 1971; in this volume, Clore and Byrne, Chapter 7 and Griffitt, Chapter 12), for instance, have conducted scores of studies in which subjects were exposed to attitude questionnaires, biographical data sheets, photographs of people, and other kinds of information and then asked to make ratings on a measure of interpersonal attraction of the people to whom the information was attributed. Researchers using this approach, sometimes referred to as the "simulated stranger technique," often vary characteristics of the subject population (for instance, personality, attitudes, and age), as well as the information provided about the other individual.

Some studies have had subjects observe or listen to people interact with one another and then have had them rate one or more of the interactants on a scale of attraction. Aronson, Willerman, and Floyd (1966), for instance, had subjects listen to a tape recording of an individual supposedly being tested to determine whether he would be chosen to appear on a television quiz show. The aspiring contestant performed either in a superior or in an average manner on the test and either did or did not commit a clumsy social blunder (spill coffee on the tester). The findings indicated that the attractiveness of the superior performing individual was enhanced by the blunder, whereas the blunder detracted from the attractiveness of the average performing individual.

Another variation in research method has involved gathering measures of attraction after subjects have engaged in limited interaction with one another or after they have interacted with a confederate trained to behave toward them in a specific manner. Some of the "computer dating" studies (Brislin & Lewis, 1968; Byrne, Ervin, & Lamberth, 1970; Tesser & Brodie, 1971; Touhey, 1972) exemplify the former approach. Touhey (1972), in one such study, matched dates in terms of similarity in religious traditionalism and sexual permissiveness and found, among other things, that for women, similarity in religious traditionalism was more strongly related to attraction after a first date than similarity in attitude toward sexual permissiveness, whereas the reverse was true for men.

Studies concerned with the consequences of attraction which employ subjects unknown to each other prior to the experiment first manipulate attraction and then relate the level of attraction to changes in the perception of the person or to changes in behavior directed toward him or her. Several experiments have induced differing levels of attraction by varying the degree of attitudinal similarity between the subject and another individual. Studies manipulating attraction via attitudinal similarity have investigated things such as the relationship between liking and the amount of money an individual is willing to loan another person (Golightly, Huffman, & Byrne, 1972); seating distance (Byrne, Baskett, & Hodges, 1971; Tesch, Huston, & Indenbaum, 1973); the decisions of subjects acting as jurors about the guilt or innocence of a defendant and the length of the sentence accorded guilty defendants (Griffitt & Jackson, 1971); and the amount of imitation of successful and unsuccessful models (Baron, 1970).

Attraction has also been studied by attributing to another individual judgments of a positive or negative character about the subjects and also by having a confederate behave in a friendly or in an unpleasant manner toward subjects. Wright (1966), for instance, sent subjects notes—some of which were flattering, others demeaning—as a manipulation of attraction and then measured the degree to which the alleged note senders were able to influence the subjects. Sampson and Insko (1964) measured the degree to which subjects were influenced by persons who had previously interacted with them in either a pleasant or in a nasty manner.

Several chapters (Chapters 7–9 and 11–15) rely heavily on data gathered in ways similar to those described above. The use of subjects in controlled laboratory settings who have had no prior interaction with one another is the approach by means of which competing explanations of the antecedents and consequences of attraction traditionally have been tested.

2. STRANGERS: LONGITUDINAL MEASUREMENT

Studies concerned with continuing and developing kinds of relationships in which the partners were near strangers at the beginning of the study are rare. It is difficult, of course, to identify beforehand which interpersonal contacts have a reasonable chance of eventuating into relationships or to control the interpersonal network in which people live. Newcomb (1961) overcame these difficulties in a study conducted in a rooming house near the University of Michigan campus. He recruited male freshmen—none of whom knew one another prior to the study—to live in a rooming house and provided them with room and board in return for data. The roomers responded several times during the academic year to a series of questionnaires and attitude scales, ranked one another in terms of attractiveness, and made estimates of each other's attitudes. Levinger (1972), as well as Duck and Spencer (1972), provide additional examples of longitudinal research similar in design to Newcomb's (1961) study.

Altman and his colleagues (Altman, Chapter 6; Altman & Taylor, 1973) have studied relationships from their inception forward using depth and breadth of participants' self-disclosure as an index of relationship development. Relationships over short time periods, such as from the beginning to the end of a single conversation, have been studied within this framework (Taylor, Altman, & Sorrentino, 1969), as well as relationships over longer periods, such as in studies where pairs of strangers are isolated together in a small room for a 10-day period (Altman & Haythorn, 1965, 1967a, b).

Some of the "computer dating" studies have traced the success of such matching over time. Walster, Aronson, Abrahams, and Rottmann (1966) correlated several variables with the attractiveness of "computer arranged" partners to one another after they had been together for a couple of hours on a first date and then 4–6 months later determined whether there had been any subsequent attempts by the partners to date one another. A more recent study (Sindberg, Roberts, & McClain, 1972) compared computer matched dates who subsequently married with those couples who did not marry, with regard to similarity in social background, attitudes and interests, and personality characteristics.

3. *ESTABLISHED PAIRS: SINGLE OCCASION OF MEASUREMENT*

Sociologists and psychologists for several decades have explored various facets of role-defined relationships, such as friendships, and dating, courtship, and marriage relationships. Studies using nonlongitudinal designs have tended either: (*a*) to compare the similarity—dissimilarity of the social background, values, and personality of partners in established relationships to the degree of similarity and dissimilarity either expected by chance or found in pairs of people who are relatively less well acquainted or are unacquainted; or (*b*) to ascertain correlates of attraction, satisfaction, adjustment, or success within relationships. The former efforts have documented the relationship of similarity of social background to marital choice (see Kerckhoff, Chapter 3), investigated the relationship of attitudinal and value similarity to marriage and friendship, and contributed to the morass of conflicting data concerning similarity and complementarity of needs as these relate to the choice of friends and mates.

Efforts concentrating on correlates of satisfaction, adjustment, and happiness in marriage have problematic meaning for the attraction researcher. Bridges between measures of attitudes held by marriage partners and social—psychological measures of attraction have not yet been built, nor have the reliability and validity of the measures been established (Hicks & Platt, 1970). Also, terms used in such work often lack conceptual and operational clarity. Hicks and Platt (1970) have pointed this out, using "marital satisfaction" as an example: "Satisfaction in marriage is usually measured by a composite instrument which taps such areas as amount of conflict, degree of agreement, shared activities, self-rating on happiness, [and the] perceived permanence of the marriage ... [p. 60]." Thus, marital satisfaction measures do not distinguish marital attraction as an evaluative orientation from potential antecedents of such attraction, and they lump together areas of relationship functioning which are not necessarily highly correlated with one another. Moreover, the measures are heavily value laden in that relationships with little conflict, high attitudinal agreement, and so on, are labeled as more satisfying to the partners than relationships lacking such characteristics—even though such may not be the case. Problems such as these have led Lively (1969) to suggest that marital happiness, marital adjustment, marital satisfaction, and marital success have acquired so many confounding connotations that "there seems to be justification for advocating their elimination from the field [p. 113]."

Three recent studies that employ social—psychological measures of attraction illustrate the value of nonlongitudinal data gathered with established pairs. The first study, conducted by Driscoll *et al.* (1972), found that trust was more highly correlated with love among married couples than among courting couples. Rubin (1970; also Chapter 16 in this volume), in one of these studies, found that dating couples who love one another a great deal gazed into each other's eyes more than couples who were less in love. Brenner (1971) found caring about one another to be correlated with the degree to which dating partners remembered each other's performance on a memory task conducted in a group setting.

4. ESTABLISHED PAIRS: LONGITUDINAL MEASUREMENT

Studies in this category have focused primarily on dating couples considering the prospect of marriage, though a few investigations have examined marital satisfaction over time (see Hicks & Platt, 1970, for a review). The usual procedure is to gather information (for example, their degree of attitudinal similarity, need complementarity, perceptions of one another) about couples at one point in time and then to relate these characteristics to indices of relationship development gathered 6–24 months later. Indices have included self-reports of progress toward marriage (Kerckhoff & Davis, 1962; Levinger, Senn, & Jorgensen, 1970; Murstein, 1967, 1972; in this volume, Rubin, Chapter 16), whether the couple stayed together or parted during the interim period (Brenner, 1971; Lewis, 1973), and the degree to which the affective bond between the couple had strengthened or weakened over time (Driscoll *et al.*, 1972).

B. *Developmental Approaches to Social Relationships*

In recent years, several models of how relationships develop have been proposed. Some—such as Levinger's (Chapter 5) and Altman's (Chapter 6)—are intended to apply to a variety of social relationships. Most of the models, however, are designed to explicate the process by which people sort out partners as potential mates (see Kerckhoff & Davis, 1962; Lewis, 1972; Murstein, 1970; Reiss, 1960). Models that either explicitly or implicitly tie relationship development to the strength of affective bonds between couples, however, are more speculative than definitive because the study of attraction in the context of social relationships and the link between attraction and interaction have not been given systematic attention (Levinger & Snoek, 1972).

Consider, for instance, Reiss's (1960) theory of the development of love, which suggests such relationships proceed through four stages: (*a*) a feeling of rapport between the couple; (*b*) self-revelation; (*c*) the development of interdependent habits (that is, mutual dependency); and (*d*) the satisfaction of each person's personality needs. While Reiss presented an interesting discussion of sociocultural factors seeming to affect each stage of the relationship, he failed to adduce supporting evidence for the developmental sequence he described, or to link the stage of the relationship either theoretically or empirically to the strength and character of the love bond. Moreover, Reiss failed to consider factors which qualify or modify the supposed developmental process. It would be interesting to know, for example, the conditions under which self-revelation does or does not lead to the development of interdependent habits. Other stage-developmental frameworks suffer from similar problems.

Understanding how relationships develop might best be advanced by approaches that relate attraction to actual interaction sequences (or summaries thereof) and to indices of relationship development (for example, sharing, use of time, commitment). Several chapters in this volume present frameworks from which investigators might proceed to develop the necessary knowledge base (Altman, Chapter 6; Levinger, Chapter 5; McCall, Chapter 10; Rubin, Chapter 16). Rubin (Chapter 16), with his longitudinal study of dating couples, provides a prototypical example of how relationship-centered research can combine sophisticated theory with sound measurement and methodological procedures.

VI. The Reward Hypothesis

A. Exchange Theory

Attraction researchers often align themselves with the philosophical position that human behavior is hedonistically determined. Exchange theory (see Altman, Chapter 6 in this volume; Blau, 1964; Carson, 1969; Gergen, 1969; Homans, 1961; Levinger, Chapter 5 in this volume; Murstein, 1970; Thibaut & Kelley, 1959) posits that social transactions are regulated by the interactants' desire to derive maximum pleasure and minimum pain from others. More formally, exchange theory suggests that individuals are most attracted to persons who provide the highest ratio of rewards to costs.

The exchange framework can prove most valuable when investigators can pinpoint in advance of a person—other transaction which events are likely to be rewarding and which are likely to be costly, and thereby increase their predictive ability (in this volume see Lott and Lott, Chapter 8; Murstein, 1970). Exchange theory requires a strong foundation of information regarding the rewards and costs of various dimensions of social transactions to predict the course of interaction.

Attraction research generally has failed to approach the reward—cost consequences of social interaction systematically. Instead, research usually begins with an assumption about the rewards and costs of two or more situations; then, if the situations induce differences in attraction, they are assumed to differ in reward value. Thus, we know, for example, that propinquity, cooperativeness, the possession of culturally valued attributes (for example, physical beauty), similarity in personality, social background, and attitudes all lead to attraction and, hence, are presumed to be rewarding. Little research has been directed toward determining the conditions under which most of these and other factors are rewarding, however. When contradictory results accrue—as has been true with regard to need complementarity, for instance—theorists and researchers are forced to examine unintended differences between studies to reconcile the discrepancies. Research utilizing Byrne's (1971) paradigm, as well as work by Mettee and Aronson (Chapter 11), exemplifies the knowledge that can be gained by means of systematic investigation of variations in the reward quality of social stimuli and interpersonal events.

Information that rewards outweigh costs, in itself, does not allow a clear prediction of attraction. Suppose one party to an interaction is making a large profit, while another is making a small profit. Both parties should be attractive to one another—providing their profits equal or exceed those they are used to getting (see Thibaut & Kelley, 1959). But without knowledge of how these particular individuals deal with gain asymmetry, an outcome prediction cannot be made with confidence. To determine whether the parties "deserve" differing rewards and would, therefore, be satisfied with what is happening, questions of "justice" become relevant. Exchange theorists suggest that persons believe the amount of profit they deserve increases with the amount and cost of their investment and the presumed value of their resources in the social market place. If the person receiving only a small profit has but a small investment in the relationship, while the individual reaping a large reward has invested a great deal, for example, then the outcomes for both might be expected to be satisfactory.

Justice prevails in social exchange when the results are distributed "fairly" among the partakers. Several writers (see Adams, 1963; Homans, 1961; Lerner, Chapter 14; Sampson, 1971) have referred to this form of justice as "equity," and attraction researchers generally have assumed that social exchanges employ such a standard of justice. Lerner (Chapter 14), however, suggests that other forms of justice may prevail. He describes three such forms—parity, Marxist, and legal—and suggests that the definition of justice applied to a relationship may depend in part on the degree of attraction. Lovers, for instance, may divide their gains according to a Marxist rationale—that is, in terms of need regardless of relative investments—rather than according to an equity rationale.

An equity theorist might argue that Lerner's typology represents varied conceptualizations of reward, rather than different forms of justice. An individual who makes great sacrifices for another may derive substantial pleasure from enhancing the other's well-being and, thus, find commensurate reward in the relationship. From the perspective of the investor, the exchange is "equitable." Whether there are several forms of justice, or one form with several conceptualizations of reward, is arguable. An interesting empirical question is whether different forms and intensities of attraction, or persons engaged in different types of relationships (husband–wife, parent–child), evidence different patterns of allocating group assets. At this point, as Lerner's review indicates, the data is more promising than clear. Utilization of Rubin's (Chapter 16) scales of liking and love in conjunction with an experimental setting which allows for various ways of allocating group assets might provide important data on this issue. Lickona (Chapter 2) describes several cognitive-developmental dimensions which may aid prediction regarding how people judge rewards and various rationales for distributing such rewards among group members.

B. *Rewards and Motivation*

Lott and Lott (Chapter 8), in their review of the role of rewards in the development of attraction, point out that the motivational state and the history of the interaction between the person and his or her environment must be taken into account if adequate predictions are to be made. Knowledge of the needs, the wants, and the desires of the individual are necessary to predict how he or she will view others who are likely to mediate these needs, wants, and desires. Any discriminant feature of the interpersonal environment associated with pleasurable or unpleasurable affect (for example a freckled face, a relaxed posture, or long hair) can have positive or negative reward value. The array of factors linked to attraction is probably many times greater than the number of persons who have ever lived. The task of attraction researchers is not that of attempting to explicate all the factors related to attraction in the fashion of cataloguers, but rather that of identifying factors which have some generalizability across persons, social situations, and relationships and of relating these factors to motivations and developmental histories.

Four approaches to the question of who is likely to be rewarding to whom can be identified. These approaches, which are not mutually exclusive, represent frames of reference from which investigators can proceed to make predictions about the antecedents of attraction. Integration of data from the four approaches is necessary for a scientifically sound theory of the role of rewards in attraction to emerge.

1. DETERMINING THE GENERALIZABILITY OF A REINFORCER

The experimenter, on the basis of theory, through his knowledge of the culture or subculture, or from analysis of previous research, can identify a stimulus property of persons (for instance, physical attractiveness, likableness) or a social interactional event (for example, the receipt of approval or attention) as reinforcing to most people (see Lott and Lott, Chapter 8). Once such a reinforcer has been identified, the examination of the limits of its generalizability across subject populations and interpersonal contexts, as well as its motivational bases, become the major foci of research efforts.

This process is illustrated by research on the relationship between physical attractiveness and liking. Investigations leave little doubt that physically attractive persons are viewed by college students after minimal social contact with more favor than are their less physically attractive peers (see Berscheid & Walster, in press, for a review). Within the subject population examined, then, physical attractiveness appears to have wide generalizability as a reinforcer. The obvious problem, however, is that the college population does not typify the American population as a whole. Some evidence is available showing that children as young as nursery school age prefer physically attractive playmates (Dion, Berscheid, & Walster, 1972), though among middle-aged and older persons, little is known about the relationship between physical attractiveness and liking. In addition, scant attention has been paid to ascertaining qualities regarded as physically attractive by different people and in different settings. Moreover, research has not investigated whether the valuing of physical attractiveness changes over time and after extensive interaction. Clues to the answers to these questions may evolve from a determination of the motivational underpinnings of the reward value of physical attractiveness.

In circumstances where physical beauty and attraction are closely linked, we can test hypotheses trying to explain why this is so. Physically attractive persons may be appreciated much for the same reason, perhaps, as is good art. A second possibility focuses on social standing. Status may accrue to persons who can form liaisons with physically attractive companions (see Sigall & Landy, 1973). This view is represented in the idea that an executive's success in the business world may depend as much on the beauty and grace of his wife as on his talent. A third possibility, also related to status enhancement, is that successfully attracting a good-looking companion may raise one's own self-esteem. A fourth factor, supported by substantial research (see Berscheid & Walster, in press) is that physically attractive persons are stereotyped in a more positive fashion than are other people. There is, thus, more to physical attractiveness than "meets the eye," with physical attractiveness providing the basis for inferring positive judgments regarding the more "internal" qualities of persons. Factors such as these may dispose persons to behave more favorably toward good-looking and handsome individuals. A self-fulfilling prophecy (see Merton, 1957; Berscheid & Walster, in press) can be set in motion and produce in physically attractive persons the very qualities attributed to them so that, as with many stereotypes, the ascriptions become somewhat accurate generalizations.

Understanding the degree to which each of these factors underlies the appealing quality of physical attractiveness may aid the determination of the social contexts in which it is likely to be a salient quality and related to liking. Should physical attractiveness stereotypes lead to unrealistic expectations about the probable character and quality of interaction, for example, the strong relationship between physical attractiveness and liking found in minimal social interaction studies would be attenuated in the context of long-term relationships.

2. TRAIT AND STATE DIFFERENCES IN MOTIVATITION AND PERSONALITY

Differences in motivation and personality, whether they are stable differences between persons (*traits*) or differences within the same person at varying points in time (*states*), have been employed to predict interpersonal attraction. Research typically proceeds as follows: The investigator (*a*) identifies a particular motive (say, need for approval or achievement) or a personality characteristic (self-esteem, internal—external control, repression—sensitization), (*b*) either measures individual differences in the degree to which persons possess the quality or manipulates the motivational state, and then (*c*) determines the degree of attraction expressed toward a person with whom the subject has interacted or about whom he has been given information. Some investigators, stimulated by Winch's (1958) work on need complementarity, have utilized a different procedure which involves comparing the personality profiles of persons of varying degrees of relatedness (for instance, spouses with friends or with randomly matched pairs of persons).

3. SITUATIONAL FACTORS

Situational factors affect the attractiveness of a stimulus quality or social event in a number of ways. First, the saliency of such factors changes as a function of the motivational state of the person and the interpersonal context. Gewirtz and Baer (1958a,b) have shown, for instance, that the reinforcing quality of approval is greater when individuals have been deprived of approval as compared to when they have been abundantly praised (see Eisenberger, 1970, for a review of related studies). Physical attractiveness, in contrast to something such as moral valuing, is probably more salient in initial interactions than in later interactions. Saliency also varies as a function of the motives and values activated by the situational context; or, in other words, what is happening makes a difference in how people come to feel about things and other people. A male professor selecting candidates for graduate school presumably would be less influenced by a picture of a pretty girl attached to an application than would another individual selecting a beauty contest winner—unless, perhaps, the professor were single and searching.

Second, the meaning attached to an interpersonal event can change as a function of its context. Mettee and Aronson (Chapter 11), for instance, review evidence showing that the response to approval changes as a function of the perceived accuracy of the basis of approval and the degree to which the expression seems genuine. Someone who says he likes you with the obvious desire of getting something from you, for example, is less likely to gain your favor than someone who says the same thing with no apparent ulterior motive. The knowledge that you and another person hold similar, rather than dissimilar, attitudes also generally results in heightened attraction (see Byrne, 1971; Griffitt, Chapter 12 in this volume). When the other person is believed to be mentally unstable, however, the reverse outcome prevails—the dissimilar other is liked more so than the similar one (Novak & Lerner, 1968; Byrne & Lamberth, 1971). Byrne and Lamberth (1971) have pointed out that it is not attitude similarity per se that is reinforcing but, rather, it is the meaning attached to such similarity that determines its reinforcing quality.

4. MOTIVE PATTERNS AND REWARDS

Taxonomies of interpersonal needs and measures capable of ascertaining stable differences among persons, as well as determining variations within the same person in the strength and patterning of needs, would aid in more sophisticated analyses of interpersonal attraction. Instruments capable of measuring affective states subsequent to social interaction would also be useful for allowing investigators to link social outcomes to affect changes and motivations and, thereby, strengthen the foundation of reward theory. Eventually, research might be able to link the needs of one person to the resources of others and allow for a more precise specification of the reward bases of social interaction. Levinger (Chapter 5), utilizing the schema developed by Foa and his colleagues (Foa, 1971; Turner, Foa, & Foa, 1971), provides a programmatic sketch of how researchers might proceed with a taxonomic approach.

Linking the various approaches outlined in the preceding discussion would offer a knowledge base that could help move the reward hypothesis from the point of providing a post hoc integrative framework for interpreting attraction research to the position of providing a basis for predicting the conditions under which certain stimuli or social events are likely to be rewarding to individuals or groups of persons.

VII. Concluding Comments

This chapter has sought to offer a conceptual background for reviewing literature dealing with attraction processes and for understanding the multiple perspectives presented by the contributors to the volume.

Interest in attraction research has shown a substantial increase over the past decade. Research efforts, as well as theoretical and conceptual frameworks, have been expanding at a rapid pace. In circumstances such as these, it is important that workers in the field pause at suitable intervals to assess their progress. Such an assessment allows for an integrated review of the knowledge base and for an analysis of the conceptual and methodological strengths and weaknesses of various approaches. It also affords an opportunity to direct inquiry to the most fruitful avenues of exploration and, thereby, to maximize the scientific and practical value of forthcoming information.

References

Abelson, R., Aronson, E., McGuire, W., Newcomb, T., Rosenberg, M., & Tannenbaum, P. *Theories of cognitive consistency: A sourcebook.* Chicago, Illinois: Rand McNally, 1968.

Adams, J. S. Toward an understanding of inequity. *Journal of Abnormal and Social Psychology,* 1963, **67**, 422–436.

Altman, I., & Haythorn, W. Interpersonal exchange in isolation. *Sociometry,* 1965, **28**, 411–426.

Altman, I., & Haythorn, W. The ecology of isolated groups. *Behavioral Science,* 1967, **12**, 169–182. (a)

Altman, I., & Haythorn, W. The effects of social and group composition on performance. *Human Relations,* 1967, **20**, 313–340. (b)

Altman, I., & Taylor, D. *Social penetration processes: The development of interpersonal relationships.* New York: Holt, 1973.

Anderson, N. H. Integration theory and attitude change. *Psychological Review,* 1971, **78**, 171–206.

Aronson, E. Some antecedents of interpersonal attraction. In W. J. Arnold & D. Levine (Eds.), *Nebraska symposium on motivation, 1969.* Lincoln, Nebraska: University of Nebraska Press, 1970.

Aronson, E., Willerman, B., & Floyd, J. The effect of a pratfall on increasing interpersonal attractiveness. *Psychonomic Science,* 1966, **4**, 227–228.

Bales, R. Task roles and social roles in problem-solving groups. In E. Maccoby, T. Newcomb, & E. Hartley (Eds.), *Readings in social psychology.* (3rd ed.) New York: Holt, 1958.

Baron, R. A. Attraction toward the model and the model's competencies as determinants of adult imitative behavior. *Journal of Personality and Social Psychology,* 1970, **14**, 345–351.

Berscheid, E., & Walster, E. *Interpersonal attraction.* Reading, Massachusetts: Addison-Wesley, 1969.

Berscheid, E., & Walster, E. Physical attractiveness. In L. Berkowitz (Ed.), *Advances in experimental social psychology.* Vol. 7. New York: Academic Press, in press.

Blau, P. *Exchange and power in social life.* New York: Wiley, 1964.

Brenner, M. Caring, love, and selective memory. *Proceedings of the American Psychological Association*, 1971, 275–276.

Brislin, R. W., & Lewis, S. A. Dating and physical attractiveness. *Psychological Reports*, 1968, **22**, 976.

Byrne, D. Attitudes and attraction. In L. Berkowitz (Ed.), *Advances in experimental social psychology*. Vol. 4. New York: Academic Press, 1969.

Byrne, D. *The attraction paradigm*. New York: Academic Press, 1971.

Byrne, D., Baskett, G., & Hodges, L. Behavioral indicators of interpersonal attraction. *Journal of Applied Social Psychology*, 1971, **1**, 137–149.

Byrne, D., Clore, G., Griffitt, W., Lamberth, J., & Mitchell, H. E. When research paradigms converge: Confrontation or integration? *Journal of Personality and Social Psychology*, in press.   (a)

Byrne, D., Clore, G., Griffitt, W., Lamberth, J., & Mitchell, H. E. One more time. *Journal of Personality and Social Psychology*, in press.   (b)

Byrne, D., Ervin, C., & Lamberth, J. Continuity between the experimental study of attraction and real-life computer dating. *Journal of Personality and Social Psychology*, 1970, **16**, 157–165.

Byrne, D., & Griffitt, W. Interpersonal attraction. In P. Mussen & M. Rosenzweig (Eds.), *Annual review of psychology*. Vol. 24. Palo Alto, California: Annual Reviews, 1973.

Byrne, D., & Lamberth, J. Cognitive and reinforcement theories as complementary approaches to the study of attraction. In B. Murstein (Ed.), *Theories of attraction and love*. New York: Springer Publ., 1971.

Cannon, K., & Long, R. Premartial sexual behavior in the sixties. *Journal of Marriage and the Family*, 1971, **33**, 36–49.

Carson, R. C. *Interaction concepts of personality*. Chicago, Illinois: Aldine, 1969.

Cuber, J., & Harroff, P. *Sex and the significant Americans*. Baltimore, Maryland: Penguin, 1970.

Davis, J. Clustering and hierarchy in interpersonal relations: Testing two graph theoretical models on 742 sociomatrices. *American Sociological Review*, 1970, **35**, 843–851.

Davis, J., & Leinhart, S. The structure of positive relations in small groups. In J. Berger (Ed.), *Sociological theories in progress*. Boston, Massachusetts: Houghton-Mifflin, 1970.

Dion, K., Berscheid, E., & Walster, E. What is beautiful is good. *Journal of Personality and Social Psychology*, 1972, **24**, 285–290.

Driscoll, R., Davis, K., & Lipetz, M. Parental interference and romantic love: The Romeo and Juliet effect. *Journal of Personality and Social Psychology*, 1972, **24**, 1–10.

Duck, S. W., & Spencer, C. Personal constructs and friendship formation. *Journal of Personality and Social Psychology*, 1972, **23**, 40–45.

Ehrmann, W. Marital and nonmarital sexual behavior. In H. Christensen (Ed.), *Handbook of marriage and the family*. Chicago, Illinois: Rand McNally, 1964.

Eisenberger, R. Is there a deprivation-satiation function for social approval? *Psychological Bulletin*, 1970, **74**, 255–275.

Festinger, L. A theory of social comparison processes. *Human Relations*, 1954, **7**, 117–140.

Festinger, L. *A theory of cognitive dissonance*. Stanford, California: Stanford University Press, 1957.

Festinger, L., & Aronson, E. The arousal and reduction of dissonance in social contexts. In D. Cartwright & A. Zander (Eds.), *Group dynamics: Research and theory*. New York: Harper, 1960.

Foa, U. Interpersonal and economic resources. *Science*, 1971, **171**, 345–351.

Ford, C., & Beach, F. *Patterns of sexual behavior*. New York: Harper, 1951.

Gergen, K. J. *The psychology of behavior exchange*. Reading, Massachusetts: Addison-Wesley, 1969.

Gewirtz, J. L., & Baer, D. M. The effect of brief social deprivation on behaviors for a social reinforcer. *Journal of Abnormal and Social Psychology*, 1958, **56**, 49–56.   (a)

Gewirtz, J. L., & Baer, D. M. Deprivation and satiation of social reinforcers as drive conditions. *Journal of Abnormal and Social Psychology*, 1958, **57**, 165–172.   (b)

Golightly, C., Hoffman, E., & Byrne, D. Liking and loaning. *Journal of Applied Psychology*, 1972, **56**, 521–523.

Griffitt, W., & Jackson, T. Simulated jury decisions: The influence of jury-defendant attitude similarity–dissimilarity. Unpublished manuscript, Kansas State University, 1971.

Heider, F. *The psychology of interpersonal relations*. New York: Wiley, 1958.

Hicks, M., & Platt, M. Marital happiness and stability: A review of research in the sixties. *Journal of Marriage and the Family*, 1970, **32**, 553–573.

Homans, G. *Social behavior: Its elementary forms.* New York: Harcourt, 1961.

Homans, G. Attraction and power. In B. I. Murstein (Ed.), *Theories of attraction and love.* New York: Springer Publ., 1971.

Hunt, M. *The natural history of love.* New York: Knopf, 1959.

Huston, T. L. Ambiguity of acceptance, social desirability, and dating choice. *Journal of Experimental Social Psychology,* 1973, **9**, 32—42.

Jones, E. *Ingratiation: A social psychological analysis.* New York: Appleton, 1964.

Jones, E., & Davis, K. From acts to dispositions: The attribution process in person perception. In L. Berkowitz (Ed.), *Advances in experimental social psychology.* Vol. 2. New York: Academic Press, 1965.

Jones, E., Kanouse, H., Kelley, H., Nisbett, R., Valins, S., & Weiner, B. (Eds.), *Attribution: Perceiving the causes of behavior.* New York: General Learning Press, 1972.

Jones, S. Self and interpersonal evaluations: Esteem Theories versus consistency theories. *Psychological Bulletin,* 1973, **79**, 361—372.

Kaplan, K. On the ambivalence-indifference problem in attitude theory and measurement: A suggested modification of the semantic differential technique. *Psychological Bulletin,* 1972, **77**, 361—372.

Kaplan, M., & Anderson, N. Comparison of information integration and reinforcement models of interpersonal attraction. *Journal of Personality and Social Psychology,* in press.   (a)

Kaplan, M., & Anderson, N. Comment on "When research paradigms converge: Confrontation or integration? *Journal of Personality and Social Psychology,* in press.   (b)

Kaplan, M., & Olczak, P. Attitude similarity and direct reinforcement as determinants of attraction. *Journal of Experimental Research in Personality,* 1970, **4**, 186—189.

Kelley, H. Attribution theory in social psychology. In D. Levine (Ed.), *Nebraska symposium on motivation.* 1967, Lincoln, Nebraska: University of Nebraska Press, 1967.

Kerckhoff, A., & Davis, K. Value consensus and need complementarity in mate selection. *American Sociological Review,* 1962, **27**, 295—303.

Kiesler, C., & Goldberg, G. N. Multidimensional approach to the experimental study of interpersonal attraction: Effect of a blunder on the attractiveness of a competent other. *Psychological Reports,* 1968, **22**, 693—705.

Levinger, G. Little sand box and big quarry: Comment on Byrne's paradigmatic spade for research on interpersonal attraction. *Representative Research in Social Psychology,* 1972, **3**, 3—19.

Levinger, G., Senn, D., & Jorgensen, B. Progress toward permanence in courtship: A test of the Kerckhoff—Davis hypothesis. *Sociometry,* 1970, **33**, 427—443.

Levinger, G., & Snoek, J. D. *Attraction in relationship: A new look at interpersonal attraction.* New York: General Learning Press, 1972.

Lewinsohn, R. *A history of sexual customs.* New York: Harper, 1958.

Lewis, R. A. A developmental framework for the analysis of premarital dyadic formation. *Family Process,* 1972, **11**, 17—48.

Lewis, R. A. A longitudinal test of a developmental framework for premarital dyadic formation. *Journal of Marriage and the Family,* 1973, **35**, 16—25.

Lindzey, G., & Byrne, D. Measurement of social choice and interpersonal attractiveness. In G. Lindzey & E. Aronson (Eds.), *The handbook of social psychology* (2nd ed.). Vol. 2. Reading, Massachusetts: Addison Wesley, 1969.

Lively, E. Toward a concept clarification: The case of marital interaction. *Journal of Marriage and the Family,* 1969, **31**, 108—114.

Lott, A., & Lott, B. A learning theory approach to interpersonal attitudes. In A. G. Greenwald, T. C. Brock, & T. M. Ostrom (Eds.), *Psychological foundations of attitudes.* New York: Academic Press, 1968.

Lott, A., & Lott, B. The power of liking: Consequences of interpersonal attitudes derived from a liberalized view of secondary reinforcement. In L. Berkowitz (Ed.), *Advances in experimental social psychology.* Vol. 6. New York: Academic Press, 1972.

Marlowe, D., & Gergen, K. Personality and social interaction. In G. Lindzey & E. Aronson (Eds.), *The handbook of social psychology.* (2nd ed.) Vol. 3. Reading, Massachusetts: Addison-Wesley, 1969.

McCall, G. J., & Simmons, J. *Identities and interactions.* New York: Free Press, 1966.

Merton, R. *Social theory and social structure.* New York: Free Press, 1957.

Mettee, D., Hrelec, E., & Wilkins, P. Humor as an interpersonal asset and liability. *Journal of Social Psychology*, 1971, **85**, 51–64.

Moreno, J. L. *Who shall survive?* Washington, D.C.: Nervous and Mental Diseases Monograph, No. 58, 1934.

Murstein, B. The relationship of mental health on marital choice and courtship progress. *Journal of Marriage and the Family*, 1967, **29**, 447–451.

Murstein B. Stimulus-value-role: A theory of marital choice. *Journal of Marriage and the Family*, 1970, **32**, 465–481.

Murstein, B. (Ed.), *Theories of attraction and love*. New York: Springer Publ., 1971.

Murstein, B. Person perception and progress among premarital couples. *Journal of Marriage and the Family*, 1972, **34**, 621–626.

Newcomb, T. *The acquaintance process*. New York: Holt, 1961.

Novak, D., & Lerner, M. Rejection as a consequence of perceived similarity. *Journal of Personality and Social Psychology*, 1968, **9**, 147–152.

Orlinsky, D. Love relationships in the life cycle: A developmental interpersonal perspective. In H. A. Otto (Ed.), *Love today: A new exploration*. New York: Association Press, 1972.

Pepitone, A. *Attraction and hostility*. New York: Atherton Press, 1964.

Reiss, I. Toward a sociology of the heterosexual love relationship. *Marriage & Family Living*, 1960, **22**, 139–145.

Rubin, Z. Measurement of romantic love. *Journal of Personality and Social Psychology*, 1970, **16**, 265–273.

Sampson, E. *Social psychology and contemporary society*. New York: Wiley, 1971.

Sampson, E., & Insko, C. Cognitive consistency and performance in the autokinetic situation. *Journal of Abnormal and Social Psychology*, 1964, **68**, 192–194.

Sigall, H., & Landy, D. Radiating beauty: Effects of having a physically attractive partner on person perception. *Journal of Personality and Social Psychology*, 1973, **28**, 218–224.

Simons, H., Berkowitz, N., & Moyer, R. Similarity, credibility, and attitude change: A review and a theory. *Psychological Bulletin*, 1970, **73**, 1–16.

Sindberg, R. M., Roberts, A. F., & McClain, P. Mate selection factors in computer matched marriage. *Journal of Marriage and the Family*, 1972, **34**, 611–620.

Taylor, D., Altman, I., & Sorrentino, R. Interpersonal exchange as a function of rewards and costs and situational factors: Expectancy confirmation–disconfirmation. *Journal of Experimental Social Psychology*, 1969, **5**, 324–339.

Tesch, F., Huston, T., & Indenbaum, E. Attitude similarity, attraction and physical proximity in a dynamic space. *Journal of Applied Social Psychology*, 1973, **3**, 63–72.

Tesser, A., & Brodie, M. A note on the evaluation of a "computer date." *Psychonomic Science*, 1971, **23**, 300.

Thibaut, J., & Kelley, H. *The social psychology of groups*. New York: Wiley, 1959.

Touhey, J. C. Comparison of two dimensions of attitude similarity on heterosexual attraction. *Journal of Personality and Social Psychology*, 1972, **23**, 8–10.

Turner, J., Foa, E., & Foa, U. Interpersonal reinforcers: Classification, interrelationship, and some differential qualities. *Journal of Personality and Social Psychology*, 1971, **19**, 168–180.

Walster, E. Passionate love. In B. Murstein (Ed.), *Theories of attraction and love*. New York: Springer Publ., 1971.

Walster, E., Aronson, V., Abrahams, D., & Rottmann, L. Importance of physical attractiveness in dating behavior. *Journal of Personality and Social Psychology*, 1966, **4**, 508–516.

Walster, E., & Prestholdt, P. The effect of misjudging another: Overcompensation or dissonance reduction? *Journal of Experimental Social Psychology*, 1966, **2**, 85–97.

Warr, P., & Knapper, C. *The perception of people and events*. New York: Wiley, 1968.

Winch, R. *Mate-selection: A study of complementary needs*. New York: Harper, 1958.

Wright, P. H. Attitude change under direct and indirect interpersonal influence. *Human Relations*, 1966, **19**, 199–211.

Zajonc, R. Cognitive theories in social psychology. In G. Lindzey & E. Aronson (Eds.), *The handbook of social psychology*. Vol. 1. Reading, Massachusetts: Addison-Wesley, 1968.

PART II

The Contexts of Attraction

2

A Cognitive-Developmental Approach to Interpersonal Attraction

THOMAS LICKONA

Center for Early Childhood Education
State University of New York at Cortland
Cortland, New York

I. Introduction

Interpersonal attraction, like many phenomena studied by social psychology, is rarely considered from a developmental perspective. This chapter is an effort to demonstrate the usefulness of viewing attraction as being related in fundamental

31

ways, both in childhood and in adulthood, to the development of cognitive stages.

A clear illustration of cognitive-stage development is provided by changes in the child's conception of identity. The following is a conversation between two young children, Johnny, 4½, and Jimmy, 4:

> JOHNNY: *I'm going to be an airplane builder when I grow up.*
> JIMMY: *When I grow up, I'll be a Mommy.*
> JOHNNY: *No, you can't be a Mommy. You have to be a Daddy.*
> JIMMY: *No, I'm going to be a Mommy.*
> JOHNNY: *No, you're not a girl, you can't be a Mommy.*
> JIMMY: *Yes, I can.*
>
> [Kohlberg, 1966]

Jimmy is where most children are before age 5 in their thinking about gender identity; Johnny is precocious. Four year-olds typically say that a pictured girl could be a boy if she wanted, if she played boy games, or if she had a boy's haircut or clothes. By age 6, most children are fairly certain that a girl is a girl to stay, no matter how she looks or what she does (Kohlberg, 1966).

There are numerous other examples of inconstancy in the young child's thinking about identity. Jimmy, quoted above, also said that airplanes "really get small" (as opposed to just looking small) when they fly up into the sky, and that "the people inside shrink" (Kohlberg, 1966). Piaget (1947) has shown that children below the age of 6—7 do not "conserve" the quantitative characteristics of physical objects. They think that a change in the shape of something means a change in its amount or weight and that a change in the spatial configuration of elements means a change in their length or number. Before 6 years of age, most children say that a live cat turns into a dog when the cat is covered (before their eyes) with a dog mask, or they are no longer sure what it is (DeVries, 1966). At around 6 years of age, children are sure of their ground: a cat's a cat. From a cognitive-developmental viewpoint, this emerging awareness of the permanence of identity is part of a broader cognitive change between the ages of 3 and 7: the general stabilizing of object constancies in the child's conception of the world.

The pervasiveness of the child's view of identity illustrates a basic tenet in the theory of cognitive-developmental stages: *a stage is a unified pattern of thought*, an organizing or structural tendency that shapes responses to questions and tasks that are quite varied in content. The qualitative difference between thinking that boys can become girls and cats can become dogs and thinking that neither boys nor cats can change illustrates a second basic point about cognitive stages: *they represent differences in kind or character of thinking at varying developmental levels*, not merely differences in degree. The fact that all children show a lack of constancy in their conception of identity before they show constancy makes a third point: *the modes of thought represented by stages form an invariant sequence in development*, with some individuals moving faster or farther through a given sequence of stages, depending upon factors such as experience, but all following the same basic order.

The child's concept of his gender identity serves as a stable organizer of his attitudes toward sex role and behavior, Kohlberg (1966) maintains, only when he is categorically certain that gender does not change. This statement implies two additional points about cognitive-developmental theory: (a) It views a given level of cognitive-stage development as a prerequisite for a given level of psychological functioning; and (b) it views the cognitive-structural level of a person's thought as having important behavioral consequences. Stated differently, the cornerstone cognitive-developmental assumption is that social development and social responses are cognitively based, and that the cognitive base changes significantly as a result of development. "There are no affects divorced form cognitive structure," no attitudes that exist as pure intensities (Kohlberg, 1969, p. 372). Liking and loving, like all other complex psychological phenomena, have their roots in the organization of thought.

Developmental psychologists have no monopoly on the idea that the study of social behavior needs a developmental perspective. Levinger and Snoek (1972), in a richly insightful social—psychological essay on levels of interpersonal relationships, conclude with the recognition that:

> A person's needs may change with time and increasing psychological maturity, and thus his readiness for one or another type of intimate relationship. We have hardly begun to understand ... what kinds of relationships the individual is predisposed to form at various ages, or how his developmentally determined needs will interact with the kind and intensity of attraction he feels [pp. 18–19].*

Levinger and Snoek lament that most studies of attraction have focused on feelings people have toward strangers; they contend that the time has come to study "attraction-in-relationship." If social psychology were to take this new direction, it would forge a strong link with a developmental approach to attraction. A developmental perspective, while relevant to the issue of initial attraction and attachment, is most germane to the consideration of interpersonal functioning within ongoing relationships.

A cognitive-developmental conception of attraction would not assume that all individuals have the same capacity to form or to maintain interpersonal relationships. Individual differences in attraction—whether defined as attitudes or behaviors—would be viewed as stemming from differences along some basic cognitive-developmental dimension, such as role-taking capacity, moral reasoning, understanding of psychological causality, or general ego organization. The following discussion relates what developmental psychology has learned about these dimensions to some basic concerns in the study of attraction.

---

*Levinger, George, and Snoek, J. Diedrick, *Attraction in relationship. A new look at interpersonal attraction.* (Morristown, N.J.: General Learning Press.) © 1972 General Learning Corporation.

II. The Cognitive-Developmental Conception of Social Motivation

Social psychologists studying attraction have sought to answer the question: Why does A like B? Or, rephrasing the question: Who will A like, B, C, or D? The general formulation of the answers to this sort of question depends, of course, on how one answers the larger question. Why do people like people at all? Why do they take an interest in, and get attached to, other persons?

The cognitive-developmental answer differs from that of drive theories or external reinforcement theories. The developmental notion is that social interaction and relationships are inherently interesting and reinforcing. The desire for a social bond involving shared activity, communication, and reciprocity with another social self is the "motive" for attachment. It is the same motive to engage the environment in interesting and effective ways that causes a child to explore a new toy or master a new skill in the absence of external praise or payoff. This notion of social motives is White's effectance motivation (1959) applied to the social domain. It denies that "drives" such as sex, aggression, and anxiety are the primary source of human social attachment. If they were, Kohlberg reasons, human attachments would be as unstable and as promiscuously arousable as are drives. Human males can be attached to one female, and simultaneously sexually aroused by another; the two attractions, however, are fundamentally different. "Sexual lust is anchored by a social attachment of sharing which makes it love; without such sharing, it is not a cause of attachment [Kohlberg, 1969, p. 461]."

At the core of human attachment is reciprocity—shared behavior—and reciprocity is its own reward. Kinsey and his colleagues (Kinsey, Pomeroy, Martin, and Gebhard, 1953) dryly gave reciprocity its due in sex: "In a socio-sexual relationship, the sexual partners may respond to each other and to the responses made by each other. For this reason, most persons find socio-sexual relationships more satisfactory than solitary sexual activities [p. 649]." Kohlberg (1969) has pointed out that even simple social play and games are essentially reciprocal: I do this, then you do that, then I do this. The centrality of reciprocity in the development of attachment behavior is suggested by the Harlows' (1962) finding that female monkeys deprived of childhood social interaction subsequently treat their own infants as if they were disturbing physical objects. White (1963) hypothesized that the autistic child's withdrawal to an impersonal world of objects may be caused in part by a feeling of being unable to elicit a predictable reciprocal response from the human environment, in particular, the mother.

Recent analyses of attachment in infancy (see Bowlby, 1969) have conceptualized attachment in terms of the reciprocal interplay between child and parent. The strong appeal of reciprocated behavior is also evident in Dixon's account (1957) of the 8-month-old's fascination with his mirror "twin," who "imitates" everything that he does. I can recall how my own infant son at this age would repeat hand movements again and again to get his mirror companion to reproduce his actions. Even more interesting to the infant, Dixon reports, is the behavior of his real twin and their simple reciprocal play, in which they alternate imitating each other.

The popular definition of a friend as "someone who likes you" reflects the insight that reciprocity is at the heart of human attraction. There are structural developmental changes in the child's understanding and applications of reciprocity (evidenced by changes in his moral reasoning about rights and obligations), but the importance of reciprocated behavior in interpersonal relationships appears to be a developmental constant, observable in the earliest years. Kohlberg (1969) has argued that it is this kind of reciprocal social experience—imitation, sharing, communication, and play—rather than the physical clinging to a mother that tells the child in his second year of life that other people are quite different from physical objects. People become interesting and attractive to the infant not only because they do interesting things, but also because the child can make these interesting things his own by imitation or reciprocal interaction.

If reciprocity is a central dynamic in human attraction, with meaning for everything from making conversation to making love, then the study of attraction at all age levels should examine how reciprocal responsiveness affects both the development and maintenance of relationships. To what extent does one person's behavior react to and incorporate the behavior of the other? The research needs an open-ended concept of active reciprocity—generating new operational definitions that go beyond whether someone accepts an offer of a social engagement. Naturalistic observation of pairs of persons who vary widely in sheer amount of reciprocal interchange might be a way of beginning to gather material for developing a scale of reciprocal responsiveness. As a personal characteristic, reciprocal responsiveness may well prove to be a more powerful determinant of attractiveness than many of the personal attributes studied in the attraction literature.

III. Developmental Changes in Attachment in Early Childhood

The idea that change in attachment behavior is generated by cognitive-structural change finds support in studies of infancy. Cognitive-developmental theory would postulate, for example, that a child cannot develop a specific attachment to a particular person until he develops a cognitive representation that fits that person but no other. Since time is needed to develop such a "schema," infants predictably do not show "stranger anxiety" until 6–9 months of age. Likewise, the infant must understand that the mother exists permanently in time and space before he can miss her and desire her return. Thus separation distress, like stranger anxiety, appears at 6–9 months, the age at which the infant first shows some awareness of the permanence of physical objects (Decarie, 1965; Schaffer & Emerson, 1964). Not surprisingly, infants relatively advanced on a scale of physical-object conception are also advanced on a scale of social relations (Decarie, 1965).

The Piagetian development of the concept of the mother as a permanent, causally independent, but familiar, object is complete by 2 years of age. The next major cognitive milestone with significance for attachment is the development of a new conception of the parent (or older sibling) "as having a mind, intelligence or will different from and superior to the child's own, but one which he can share through processes of learning, conformity, and winning affection [Kohlberg, 1969, p. 464]." This process, at the base of imitation and identification, is complete by age 6—7 and involves the following cognitive developments, according to Kohlberg (1969):

1. the ability to make comparative judgments of self and others;
2. the differentiation of the child's own perspective from that of others (role-taking development);
3. the development of conceptions of shared ascribed social identities (for example, sex-role development);
4. the development of conceptions of shared rules (moral development).

The remainder of this chapter is in large part an elaboration of these cognitive developments as they relate to attraction in human relationships.

A. A Cognitive-Developmental View of Similarity as a Basis for Attachment: Sex-Role Development as a Case in Point

Human attachments, even during infancy, are attachments to another similar self, another center of consciousness and activity like oneself (Kohlberg, 1969). Like reciprocal social interaction, perceived similarity between oneself and another appears to be reinforcing in itself, rather than because of association with some external consequence. Byrne and Griffitt (1966) have speculated that we like others who have similar attitudes because attitude agreement validates our own view of the world.

As children become cognitively more sensitive to similarity, its importance in attraction increases. This is evident in sex-role development, particularly in the growth of the boy's orientation to the father during the years 4—8. The boy's identification with the father is of special interest, Kohlberg (1969) has pointed out, because it is the first strong attachment that cannot be explained as largely the product of physical caretaking.

The cognitive-developmental explanation of the boy's attachment to the father calls attention to the effect of increasing awareness of similarity on the boy's thinking about his sex. By age 3, the child knows his gender (although not yet its permanence) quite well. By 3—4 years old, a boy prefers "boy things" to "girl things" simply because he likes himself and whatever is similar to himself. At this time, he typically begins to like boys better than girls as playmates for the same reason. The boy tends to retain a stronger attachment to the mother, however, until he develops the broader, more difficult similarity category of "we males" to include adults like the father, as well as other boys. The ability to form this category does not emerge until age 5—6, when children manifest the cognitive capacity to group different objects (for example, various toy animals) on the basis of similar attributes (for example, "these all have long tails"), rather than associatively ("these play together"). At 5–6 years, children also begin to group together human figures of diverse ages but all of the same sex, showing the same ability to abstract a dimension of similarity (Kohlberg, 1966).

The link between social bonds and the development of conceptual categories based on similarity is indicated by another portion of the Kohlberg study (1966). Children were shown animal pictures in sets of four, two animals being the same color. They were asked, "Which animals like each other?" Over 70% of children 5 years and more chose, for example, both red animals, whereas 4-year-olds did not choose same-color animals beyond the level of chance. Those boys who scored high on this similarity test also scored high on a doll preference test of father identification. (Sample item: "Now the boy [doll] has to go to bed. Who does he want to go up with him to say goodnight, the father or the mother?") The major cognitive-developmental point here is that the child's definition and experience of social bonds changes as he becomes cognitively more attuned to similarity. Before the emergence of similarity concepts, the child's feelings of "likeness" may be based more on proximity, familiarity, and dependency than upon similarity in role, status, or attributes.

The boy's preference for activities that the culture defines as masculine increases as his sex-role identity stabilizes—"I really am and always will be a boy [Kohlberg, 1969, p. 431]." The more firmly he labels himself a boy, the more he seeks and values whatever is similar to himself. His sex identity determines what is socially reinforcing, rather than the other way around ("I am a boy, therefore I like boy things"). With an increasing preference for boy activities comes an increasing need for the father as a model for these activities. By age 5, the boy preferentially imitates his father (Kohlberg, 1969). This imitation leads to dependency on the father as a model and consequently emotional attachment to him, the final stage in the sex-role identification process. By age 6, boys show a clear preference for orienting social dependency to the male in an experimental situation (Ammons & Ammons, 1949). An equally strong preference for their own sex is found among girls of this age (Kohlberg, 1966). To recapitulate: the boy's attachment to the father is a consequence of modeling, and modeling is a consequence of the development of cognitions of similarity and sex role.

B. Developmental Changes in Perceived Similarity

Perceived similarity plays a well-documented role not only in developing sex-based preferences in children, but also in facilitating empathy and sharing in adolescent and adult friendships (Hess, 1972). In this sense, similarity, like reciprocity, operates as a developmental constant in attraction. There are developmental shifts, however, in the selection of the attributes on which similarity judgments are based. Younger children (3–5 years old) tend to define competence in terms of being big and strong, or owning lots of things. By the earlier school years, as a result of an emerged cognitive capacity to differentiate the physical from the psychological (to know, for example, that a dream is not real), children shift to defining competence psychologically, in terms of being smart, knowing things, doing things right, and being good (Kohlberg, 1969). This is when children begin to distinguish between the "good guys" and the "bad guys." What is salient, then, as a dimension for making similarity judgments changes as a result of development.

In Maccoby's review (1969) of the literature on stimulus selection, she stated that the basic developmental change is improvement in the ability to discriminate a stimulus in a noisy background. If this is so, then children may also grow in their ability to discern interpersonal similarity against a background of dissimilarities. By this reasoning, the older child should be more capable than the younger child of perceiving similarities among differences between himself and other persons. This increasing sensitivity to similarity may result in a greater range of possible friendship matches. A child may like one child because they share a particular interest, a second child because they are similar in another way, etc. In adulthood, similarity perception is acute enough to draw together ostensibly very different types of individuals. How often is a detached observer of a new romantic match heard to say, "I can't imagine what she sees in him," or, "Opposites must attract." What may from the outside look like need complementarity or an utterly inscrutable combination may be only the product of the couple's power to perceive similarity too obscured by a "noisy background" of differences to catch the casual eye.

If people do develop the ability to form attachments based on important similarities defined against a background of differences, then adult attraction would not necessarily depend on high overall similarity between two individuals. It may be possible, in fact, to have too much of a good thing—too much similarity. Variety, no doubt, is part of the spice of attraction, and the notion of an optimal level of *dissimilarity* ought to be introduced into future discussions of similarity's role in friendship and love.[1]

IV.   Cognitive-Structural Levels of Moral Development and Interpersonal Attraction

A.   *Moral Levels as a Context for Relationships*

The social psychological study of valuing, which is acknowledged to be a central dimension in interpersonal attraction, has generally failed to incorporate what is known about the cognitive-structural development of moral valuing. Sex research, to take one example, "has been concerned with the content of sexual attitudes and behavior rather than with the structure or process of reasoning about the morality

---

[1]See Mancuso's (1970) *Readings For a Cognitive Theory of Personality* for an excellent collection and analysis of writings on the motivational value of optimally novel stimuli.

of sexual relationships [Gilligan, Kohlberg, Lerner, & Belenky, 1971, p. 141]." The cognitive-developmental position is that the structural level of moral reasoning, which changes with age and experience, is at the base of thought and action in all interpersonal functioning.

Since 1958, Kohlberg and his associates have studied how children, adolescents, and adults reason about moral dilemmas such as the following:

> In Europe, a woman was near death from cancer. One drug might save her, a form of radium that a druggist in the same town had recently discovered. The druggist was charging $2,000, ten times what the drug cost him to make. The sick woman's husband, Heinz, went to everyone he knew to borrow the money, but he could only get together about half of what [the drug], cost. He told the druggist that his wife was dying and asked him to sell it cheaper or let him pay later. But the druggist said, "No." The husband got desperate and broke into the man's store to steal the drug for his wife. Should the husband have done that? Why? [Kohlberg, 1969, p. 379].*

On the basis of both cross-cultural and longitudinal research, Kohlberg (1971) has defined six structural stages in moral reasoning, which he maintains constitute an invariant sequence in development. Evidence for the universality of the stages sequence comes from studies conducted in Taiwan, Great Britain, Mexico, Turkey, and the United States. These studies have included middle-and lower-class urban boys, and preliterate or semi-literate villagers (in Turkey, Mexico, and Taiwan). The six moral stages are illustrated in Table 1, which presents levels of motives for engaging in moral action, with examples of reasoning about the drug-stealing dilemma.

In assigning an overall stage to a subject's protocol (the product of extended interviewing), Kohlberg scores the person's reasoning on moral issues such as law, conscience, authority, civil rights, contracts and reciprocal exchange, life, truth, punishment, personal-affectional roles and relations, and sexual love. A consideration of the last two issues, affectional relations and sexual love, will make clear the connection between morality and attraction.

Gilligan *et al.* (1971) presented 50 high school juniors ranging in background from lower to upper middle-class with six of the Kohlberg moral dilemmas, three of which concerned moral issues in sexual relationships. Here is one of the dilemma situations:

> A high school girl's parents are away for the weekend and she's alone in the house. Unexpectedly, on Friday evening, her boyfriend comes over. They spend the evening together in the house and after a while they start necking and petting (1) Is this right or wrong? Why? Are there any circumstances that would make it right (wrong)? (2) What if they had sexual intercourse? Is that right or wrong? Why? (3) Does the way they feel about each other make a difference in the rightness or wrongness of having sexual intercourse? Why? What if they are in love? What does love mean and what is its relation to sex? [Gilligan *et al.*, 1971, p. 151].

---

*Lawrence H. Kohlberg, "Stage and sequence: The cognitive-developmental approach to socialization," in David A. Goslin (Ed.), *Handbook of socialization theory and research*, © 1969 by Rand McNally and Company, Chicago, p. 379. Reprinted by permission of Rand McNally Publishing Company.

TABLE 1

Motives for Engaging in Moral Action[a]

Stage 1. Action is motivated by avoidance of punishment and "conscience" is irrational fear of punishment.

> Pro: If you let your wife die, you will get in trouble. You'll be blamed for not spending the money to save her and there'll be an investigation of you and the druggist for your wife's death.

> Con: You shouldn't steal the drug because you'll be caught and sent to jail if you do. If you do get away, your conscience would bother you thinking how the police would catch up with you at any minute.

Stage 2. Action motivated by desire for reward or benefit. Possible guilt reactions are ignored and punishment viewed in a pragmatic manner. (Differentiates own fear, pleasure, or pain from punishment-consequences.)

> Pro: If you do happen to get caught you could give the drug back and you wouldn't get much of a sentence. It wouldn't bother you much to serve a little jail term, if you have your wife when you get out.

> Con: He may not get much of a jail term if he steals the drug, but his wife will probably die before he gets out so it won't do him much good. If his wife dies, he shouldn't blame himself, it wasn't his fault she has cancer.

Stage 3. Action motivated by anticipation of disapproval of others, actual or imagined-hypothetical (e.g., guilt). (Differentiation of disapproval from punishment, fear, and pain.)

> Pro: No one will think you're bad if you steal the drug but your family will think you're an inhuman husband if you don't. If you let your wife die, you'll never be able to look anybody in the face again.

> Con: It isn't just the druggist who will think you're a criminal, everyone else will too. After you steal it, you'll feel bad thinking how you've brought dishonor on your family and yourself; you won't be able to face anyone again.

Stage 4. Action motivated by anticipation of dishonor, i.e., institutionalized blame for failure of duty, and by guilt over concrete harm done to others. (Differentiates formal dishonor from informal disapproval. Differentiates guilt for bad consequences from disapproval.)

> Pro: If you have any sense of honor, you won't let your wife die because you're afraid to do the only thing that will save her. You'll always feel guilty that you caused her death if you don't do your duty to her.

> Con: You're desperate and you may not know you're doing wrong when you steal the drug. But you'll know you did wrong after you're punished and sent to jail. You'll always feel guilty for your dishonesty and lawbreaking.

Stage 5. Concern about maintaining respect of equals and of the community (assuming their respect is based on reason rather than emotions). Concern about own self-respect, i.e., to avoid judging self as irrational, inconsistent, nonpurposive. (Discriminates between institutionalized blame and community disrespect or self-disrespect.)

> Pro: You'd lose other peoples respect, not gain it, if you don't steal. If you let your wife die, it would be out of fear, not out of reasoning it out. So you'd just lose self-respect and probably the respect of others too.

(continued)

Table 1 (*continued*)

Con: You would lose your standing and respect in the community and violate the law. You'd lose respect for yourself if you're carried away by emotion and forget the long-range point of view.

Stage 6. Concern about self-condemnation for violating one's own principles. (Differentiates between community respect and self-respect. Differentiates between self-respect for general achieving rationality and self-respect for maintaining moral principles.)

Pro: If you don't steal the drug and let your wife die, you'd always condemn yourself for it afterward. You wouldn't be blamed and you would have lived up to the outside rule of the law but you wouldn't have lived up to your own standards of conscience.

Con: If you stole the drug, you wouldn't be blamed by other people but you'd condemn yourself because you wouldn't have lived up to your own conscience and standards of honesty.

[a] Source: Rest, 1968.

Instrumental Relativist, or Stage 2, thinking on this type of dilemma, the lowest level found in the study, is simply hedonistic with no notion of relational responsibility or shared expectations. Love equals sexual pleasure; sex is fun. "There's nothing wrong [with intercourse] because I think people can do whatever they want." There is no reference to consent or to avoidance of hurting others. A Stage 2 argument *against* intercourse in this situation has the same structural qualities: "It would be wrong if they had intercourse without thinking about pregnancy— a child can cause a lot of trouble to high school kids." Morality is defined as doing your own thing and avoiding unpleasant consequences.

At Stage 3, the Interpersonal Concordance orientation, the individual is concerned with being a good person, someone of whom others would approve because he sees sex as an expression of love. Definitions of right and wrong fit conventional stereotypes, the goal being to maintain social approval. "It's O.K. as long as you do it as an act of love rather than as an act of sex—if you do it with an emotional tie." Love is no longer just sexual attraction; it means having special feelings of attachment. "It's someone you like to be with no matter what you do." One can use sex to express love. "Sex is part of showing you care. It should be for a special relationship." This kind of conventional thinking can, of course, just as easily be expressed as disapproval of premarital sex: "You can get away with it, but you're not, like, clean anymore."

At Stage 4, the Law and Order stage, the dominant issue is responsibility, defined either as obligation to the rules of society or one's religion, or as willingness to accept the consequences of the sexual relationship that the story depicts. "If they really knew what they were getting into, it might be O.K." On the other side, "It would be wrong in our society—how will they fit in?" At Stage 4, feelings are not seen as affecting the rightness or wrongness of sex. Love is viewed as tied to marriage, which makes sex legitimate within an approved social institution. The authors of the study reported that Stage 4 subjects tend to be against premarital sex in the hypothetical story situation.

Stage 5, Social Contract Orientation, the highest level scored in this study, defines the rightness or wrongness of sexual intercourse in terms of mutual and contractual obligations between the two persons. Love influences the nature of the relationship, but not the morality of the sexual behavior itself; sexual morality is defined by honesty and trust. "Sex is O.K. if they are honest with each other, if they know each other's motives." The contract between the two persons must be understood by both as the basis for trust. In short, "sexual relations are governed by the basic principles of mutual consent, integrity, and trust which govern other relationships between human beings [Gilligan *et al.*, 1971, p. 159]."

Even more sharply illustrative of stages of reasoning about sexual intercourse are responses to a dilemma about a married couple:

> A boy or girl fall in love in high school and get married right after graduation. They have never had sexual relations before marriage. After they are married, the girl finds she doesn't like having sexual intercourse; it just makes her feel bad and she decides not to have intercourse with her husband. Was it right for the wife to do that? Would it be right for the husband to threaten separation? Seek a divorce? Have sexual relations with another girl that he meets? [Gilligan *et al.*, 1971, p. 152].

At Stage 2, marriage is viewed as an economic exchange of satisfactions: "She should give him sex; he has to earn the living." If the husband cannot get sexual satisfaction from his wife, he should seek it somewhere else. At Stage 3, the focus is on feelings and stereotypes of the good wife and good husband: "If she loves him, she should want to [have sex]; she's hurting him." Or, in favor of extramarital sex: "Maybe it will save their marriage and make them happier in the long run." At Stage 4, the married persons must honor their vows or else break them legally. The husband has a "right in marriage" to sexual relations with his wife. Finally, Stage 5 sees marriage as a contract centering around trust and loyalty. A couple can set up their marriage contract any way they like as long as it is open and mutually agreed upon. Adultery is judged wrong if it violates a trust rather than a fixed vow.

There is recent evidence to indicate that sexual moral reasoning is not idle musing about abstract issues, but is strongly related to attitudes and behavior in sexual relationships. In a study of 76 unmarried college couples (D'Augelli, 1972), partners with the same attitudes toward virginity and nonvirginity were likely to have the same moral reasoning orientation. If there were moral differences, the male dominated; when he was law and order oriented, the couple most likely did not have intercourse regardless of the female's orientation. When the woman was law and order oriented, however, she was likely to have had intercourse if her male partner was either at the personal concordance or the social contract level in his moral thinking.[2] D'Augelli and Cross (in press) found that among unmarried col-

---

[2]This is not to imply that nonvirginity necessarily follows, either theoretically or empirically, from the personal concordance or social-contract orientations—any more than virginity is a necessary consequence of Stage 4 law and order morality. Just as people engage in a particular behavior pattern (for

lege women, "liberated nonvirgins" use social contract reasoning, emphasizing reciprocal communication, trust, and common consent. With their partners, they stress agreement on the role of sex within a mutually defined relationship. "Confused nonvirgins," by contrast, tend more often to use instrumental relativist reasoning, emphasizing what can be gained from the partner. These women tend to seek affection and warmth through sexual encounters, and to have unsatisfactory, ambiguous, and short-lived relationships. A third study of unmarried college students on eight different campuses (Jurich, 1972) found a person's moral stage to be a very good predictor of his or her choice of a standard of premarital sexual behavior. Taken together, these studies suggest that interpersonal sexual behavior is consistent with the way an individual reasons about moral issues in relationships.

Moral reasoning about sexual relationships belongs to a larger cognitive-moral context, which Kohlberg (1972) calls the "affectional system". He singles out Stage 3 as a major landmark in the development of this moral system. From an early age, the child has engaged in exchanges of affection, but not until Stage 3 do these exchanges become a *system* regulated by the norm of mutuality. This mutuality requires simultaneous and reciprocal role-taking, which Selman (in press) found to be a cognitive prerequisite for Stage 3 moral reasoning. Selman constructed a guessing game requiring a child to think to himself, "The other kid probably thinks I'll try to fool him, so I won't do what he thinks I'll do." Children who could *not* think this way showed no higher than Stage 2 moral reasoning on a test of understanding the Golden Rule. These subjects said that if a boy just came up and hit you on the street. "The Golden Rule would tell you to hit him back—do unto others as they do unto you." Children who were able to pass the guessing game role-taking task understood the Golden Rule as requiring someone to take two roles at once. Here is one Stage 3 boy's response: "Like if you were rich, you might dream like that you were poor and how it felt, and then the dream would go back in your own head and you would remember and you would help make the laws that way [Kohlberg, 1971, p. 197]."

This kind of imaginative reciprocity becomes the core of the affectional system, replacing the concrete reciprocity of exchange, which characterizes Stage 2. Attitudes loom larger in interpersonal relationships with the advent of this new cognitive capacity: "The value of shared attitudes arises from the consciousness of being shared [Kohlberg, 1972, p. 30]," the awareness of two individuals that they hold an attitude in common. With co-consciousness and mutual role-taking, typically well-developed by the age of 10—11, attraction-in-relationship should be significantly more dependent upon shared attitudes than it would be before the development of reciprocal consciousness. Personal attachments should also be strengthened by the Stage 3 need for esteem in the eyes of the other, a need based on a consciousness of the other person's wishes and feelings (Kohlberg, 1969).

---

example, not paying a portion of their income tax) for reasons that reflect different moral stages, so one can within limits derive different behavior patterns from the same moral stage. A behavior is moral at a particular level if it springs from a decision based on the reasoning of that level.

The new Stage 3 sensitivity to sharing and esteem is part of a general discovery of the intrinsic value of social relationships. This discovery at Stage 3 is clear from Blatt's study (unpublished, cited in Kohlberg, 1969) showing that children's conceptions of friendship go through stages parallel to Kohlberg's moral judgment stages. It is not until Stage 3 morality begins to emerge at 7–8 years that the child thinks he likes his parent or friend even though at the moment they may be frustrating him. Not until the Stage 3 advance beyond a what's-in-it-for-me orientation does the child express the desire to do something for someone he likes and the desire to be liked for himself as distinct from getting rewards.

Consistent with the Stage 3 child's increased valuing of social relationships is Rosenhan's finding (1969) on altruism: it increases dramatically at about 7 years of age. Doing "nice things" for others, being liked in return, and feeling good about one's nice behavior becomes a powerful reinforcer for the child at Stage 3. The nature of what is reinforcing is altered again when the individual advances to Stage 4, which adds loyalty to affection and defines dyadic interpersonal obligations in terms of the values of a larger social–moral system. Behavior that satisfied one's sense of duty and place within that system would be reinforcing to the Stage 4 person. Old reinforcers (for example, social approval) still operate, but under new conditions. It would not be reinforcing, for example, to have someone's approval for an action that violated one's sense of honor or duty. Reinforcement changes once again at Stage 5, where self-respect and the respect of others are the reward for moral behavior that is rational and consistent with freely made social contracts. At the highest level, Stage 6, a person would gain satisfaction primarily from having lived up to his self-chosen moral principles, a fidelity to conscience that transcends the institutional or interpersonal context. All of this is to suggest that for some decisions—perhaps some of those most central to our interpersonal lives—the nature of reinforcement is defined by the developmental level from which the decision derives. Since most people operate at several different developmental levels, they would be capable of experiencing different levels of reinforcement. Thus, a developmental approach sheds some light on the question that plagues every reinforcement-based theory: What is a reinforcer?

B. Moral Level as a Determinant of Initial Attraction and Stability of Attraction-in-Relationship

Moral stages, in addition to providing a cognitive context for affectional relations, have a potential impact on attraction both in the early and later stages of a relationship. Experimental research (Turiel, 1966; Rest, Turiel, & Kohlberg, 1969) has demonstrated that individuals faced with a moral conflict tend to reject reasoning below their own level and prefer reasoning one level above theirs. Similar tendencies may operate in forming relationships, at least in those cases where moral values are a salient feature of the initial interaction. It seems improbable that a Stage 5 or 6 person would be strongly drawn to a Stage 3 moral conformist, or a conventional "nice guy" Stage 3 attracted to a blatantly self-seeking Stage 2. To reverse directions, a hedonistic Stage 2 (and there are adults still at this level) seems unlikely to be attracted to a solid citizen Stage 4, or a Stage 4 to a Stage 6, who places moral principles above the law.

Clearly, there could be exceptions to this rule of moral congruence (if indeed it is one). A Stage 3 person, for whom conventional notions of good behavior are central, might be attracted to a principled Stage 5 or 6 individual, whose general behavior would most likely conform to Stage 3 conventional standards (deviating perhaps when such standards conflicted with his moral principles). The higher-level individual might reciprocate the attraction for any number of reasons (physical attractiveness, status, etc.), especially if he or she defines the other person in a fixed interpersonal role, rather than as a full moral equal. But there should be a stronger interest in moral compatibility as one ascends the moral ladder. At the principled stages, there is a greater consciousness of "morality" as an abstract issue and presumably a greater tendency to view the world and others in moral terms.

This line of conjecture, however, requires qualification. People are not pure moral stage types; they typically show a mix of levels, one level being dominant. Secondly, persons who are at structurally different stages of thinking may nonetheless share much in the way of attitudes as a basis for attraction (both may be members of the same political party, but for quite different reasons). Finally, people do not wear their moralities on their sleeves. Extended interaction or unusual situations are ordinarily necessary to make morals salient or central to interpersonal evaluation. Research on people's beliefs about relationship development supports this supposition. Subjects rated easily visible characteristics like height or physical attractiveness as more important at first contact than later in a relationship (Levinger, 1964). At advanced stages in a relationship, characteristics such as considerateness or a need to give love were rated as most critical in determining attachment. Cognitive level of moral reasoning may take even longer than most "deeper characteristics" to surface, since it is a structural characteristic—the *way* a person reasons rather than *what* he thinks. Or as Kohlberg and Gilligan (1971) put it, "Cognitive-developmental stages do not tell us what's on the person's mind, but only how he thinks about what is on his mind [p. 1076]."

Lapse of time tends to reveal interpersonal moral differences. A friend of mine lamented that a recent visit from an old college buddy convinced him that the basis for the close friendship was there no longer. My friend, presently very much a social activist, said his old chum was more concerned about accumulating middle-class symbols of success than he was about social issues. Another friend says that she parted paths with her first serious boyfriend when she became convinced that he "had no character." Harder evidence that morality affects the duration of attraction comes from Newcomb's finding (1961) that value positions are more stable than attraction to friends. College students readily shift their friendship preferences in favor of individuals with whom they are more closely in value agreement.

Deepening interpersonal involvement also brings morality to the foreground.

As people become more intimate, their relationship touches more directly and frequently on issues of rights and obligations, such as those highlighted in the Gilligan sexual dilemmas. Conflicts will occur that need to be resolved. Such conflicts will be harder to resolve when a gap in the quality of moral reasoning yawns between the partners. A husband seeking to impose a conventional role definition on a wife with a more equalitarian notion of relationships is headed for trouble. (A recently divorced, postconventional female, who clearly knew Kohlberg's theory, was heard to say that the problem with her marriage was simply that she had a Stage 4 husband.)

On the basis of moral factors alone (which in reality interact with a host of other factors), one would expect to find greater stability of attraction at higher moral levels. The higher one goes on the moral scale, the greater the capacity for role-taking, one of those critical "maintenance" activities needed to work through interpersonal conflict and to enhance positive feelings (Levinger & Snoek, 1972). Feffer's research (1970) has shown that communication depends on role-taking, measured by an individual's ability to make up a story and retell it from the viewpoint of each of the characters in a way that coordinates each successive viewpoint with the previous ones. College students who performed well on Feffer's role-taking task were able to communicate words in a password game more quickly and with fewer clues than were dyads of persons scoring lower on the role-taking exercise.

At higher moral levels, one would also anticipate more acts of altruism born of consideration for the other person's needs, acts that would increase mutual affection. At principled levels, there should be more flexibility, greater ability to deal with needs and conflicts through mutual agreements, as well as more honesty and openness about personal behavior as it relates to contractual understandings. This is not to imply that high morality assures happiness in relationships; love, as the song says, is a many-splendored thing. Relationships can surely go bad at Stages 5 and 6, but there exists at these levels a view of human relations that has much potential for interpersonal equilibrium and growth.

C. Moral Stages and Levels of Social Relationships

The notion of parallelism between individual moral levels and levels of relationships can be examined in the context of the three-level theory of relationships proposed by Levinger (Chapter 5; Levinger & Snoek, 1972).

1. *Awareness* (Level 1): A likes or dislikes B on the basis of an impression formed without joint interaction. Moral level would enter into this impression only insofar as the evaluated person's moral thinking is important and salient to the judging person, as it might be in the case of a political leader.

2. *Surface Contact* (Level 2): Liking depends on satisfaction, defined on the basis of self-centered criteria or rewards and costs of role interactions. Each person behaves in accordance with the appropriate social role. There is little or no genuine concern for the other and little knowledge of how the other person experiences the

relationship. Levinger's relationship Level 2 is most comparable to Kohlberg's moral Stage 2. Both are self-centered and devoid of real mutuality.

3. *Mutuality* (Level 3): A values B as a unique person in his own right; both A and B assume responsibility for the other's feelings and outcomes in the relationship. Joint views and pride in "we-ness" emerge, along with mutually understood and modifiable contracts. Trust, self-disclosure, empathy, and altruism are the defining characteristics. Levinger's Level 3 appears quite similar to Kohlberg's highest moral levels, Stages 5 and 6.

Three critical qualifications of Levinger's schema would flow from a cognitive-developmental perspective.

1. Missing is a relationship roughly parallel to Kohlberg's conventional moral level, where thinking about relationships is role stereotyped, but nevertheless includes empathy, role-taking, and concern for the welfare of others (as illustrated by Stage 3 reasoning on the sexual dilemmas). The fact that most individuals operate at Stage 3 or 4 (Kohlberg & Turiel, 1971) suggests that most interpersonal relationships also function at a conventional level.

2. The Levinger schema appears to assume that most persons are capable of progressing from surface contact to mutuality, given the right "facilitative conditions." The cognitive-developmental position would be that the mutuality characteristic of Levinger's third level is accessible only to persons who have moved beyond role-bound conventional morality. Kohlberg's research indicates that only 25% of the population reaches postconventional principled morality (Kohlberg, 1971).

3. Levinger's Level 2, defined to exclude any moral elements of role-taking or fairness, is not a stage of relationship through which all persons would have to pass on their way to mutuality. Levinger is probably right that almost all human interaction begins with rather stereotyped role-oriented interchange. Most persons, however, function at a moral level that includes some empathy and concern for the other person. In view of this, one cannot define Levinger's initial role-oriented level of relationship as being as barren of reciprocal morality as he portrays it.

This critique does not attempt to do justice to Levinger's careful presentation of his relationships theory. The intention is only to underscore the point that a social–psychological analysis of interpersonal relationships needs to be anchored in a cognitive-developmental framework.

V. The Development of Formal Logical Operations

A. *Consequences of Formal Operations for Affective Development and Attraction*

The major cognitive-developmental advance in early childhood is the transition at 5–7 years of age from preoperational thinking to concrete operational thinking (Kohlberg, 1969). Concrete operational thinking involves the capacity to reason logically about classes, relations, and quantities when dealing with concrete objects. The concrete operational child can seriate relations, conceptualize a large class and its subclass at the same time, and conserve properties such as number, class membership, length, and amount in the face of apparent change.

The next major revolution in thinking is the achievement of the final stage in Piaget's theory of intellectual development: formal operations, or "operations on operations" (Inhelder & Piaget, 1958). The adolescent at the formal operational level can conceptualize his own thought; he can take his own ideas as objects and reason about them. Elkind (1968) has found that only at 11–12 years do children spontaneously introduce concepts of belief, intelligence, and faith into definitions of their religious denomination. The ability to think about thought enables the formal operational individual to construct a range of possibilities, to be aware that what is observed is only a subset of the logically possible. Provided with four differently colored pieces of plastic, for example, the adolescent at the formal logical level can systematically generate all the possible combinations; the concrete operational child cannot (Elkind, 1968).

What are the affective consequences of formal operational thought? One is that the adolescent, capable of conceptualizing alternatives, compares how things are with how they might be. "Not unlike the child, who always finds another child's toys more appealing than his own, the adolescent finds possible situations enviable and his own situation unbearable [Elkind, 1968, p. 152]." Dissatisfaction with his parents, for example, may cause him to search for personal identity and purpose through peer friendship, where there appears to be greater freedom to construct a relationship of his own making. In general, the adolescent's attraction to particular relationships begins to be a function of what Thibaut and Kelley (1959) would call his "comparison level alternatives."

Another consequence of formal operational thought is that affect for the first time is felt for ideas and ideals, rather than simply for particular persons or events (Inhelder & Piaget, 1958). "The adolescent is in love with Sally because he is in love with love, whereas the juvenile is simply stricken with Sally [Kohlberg, 1958, p. 60]." Elkind (1968) has suggested that the adolescent "crush" arises from the desire to idealize someone in order to make the person fit an idealized human relationship. The result of this attempt at idealization, which may soon bang up against reality, is that romances in early adolescence are often shallow and short-lived.

Formal reflective thought also opens the door for the emergence of a subjective self, with a more complex view of reality (Kohlberg & Gilligan, 1971). External reality becomes only one of several possibilities of subjective experience. The external is no longer the real, and the internal or subjective no longer the "unreal." Kohlberg asked a 15-year-old girl, "What is the most real thing to you?" and she answered unhesitatingly, "Myself."

Part of this new "inner reality" is the intensified emotionality, sexual or otherwise, characteristic of adolescents and experienced more as "states of the self," rather than as the direct result of external events (Ellinwood, 1969). This experience of emotion as a subjective state fosters a tolerance of ambivalence absent in younger children. A person who makes one angry sometimes and happy at other times does not have to be accepted as good or rejected as bad. One can feel positively and negatively about the same person simultaneously. This new capacity for ambivalence, combined with increased role-taking powers, should strengthen stability in affective relationships. In line with this prediction, seventh- and eighth-grade children studied over $1\frac{1}{2}$ years showed a high degree of consistency of friendship preferences (Singer, 1951). By contrast, friendships among 400 sixth-grade children were found to be highly unstable, with a quarrel commonly cited as the reason for the changed relationship (Austin & Thompson, 1948). One theory (Mussen, Conger, & Kagan, 1969) attributes this instability of relationships at the younger ages to rapidly fluctuating interests, which begin to stabilize during adolescence. A cognitive-developmental viewpoint would see another stabilizing process at work: cognitive-structural changes in the experience of emotion and the self. The quarrel that breaks up a childhood friendship can be absorbed in adolescence.

Along with quarreling, a lack of proximity ("I don't see much of him anymore") was found to be a frequent cause of friendship changes among sixth-grade children (Austin & Thompson, 1948). The decreasing importance of proximity as a sustaining factor in adolescent friendship can be attributed to the formal operational ability to reflect on one's feelings about a friend and one's relationship with him. Attraction no longer needs continuous interaction to maintain it. Childhood and college friends, military service buddies, or friends from a previous residence may still be considered good friends even though seldom seen (Hess, 1972). The literature on social isolation offers a clue to this phenomenon. While isolation increases the responsiveness of preschool and grade-school children to social reinforcement, the deprivation of social contact has no such effect on adolescents (Walters & Parke, 1964). The adolescent can spend his time in thought; he provides his own reinforcement. A friendship can be interiorized.

At the same time that formal operational thought makes the adolescent more subjective, more aware of himself, it also heightens his awareness of the thinking of others. Elkind (1968) has written that while the young child is egocentric in that he cannot take another person's view, the young adolescent becomes ensnared in a new kind of egocentrism, the belief that everyone is as conscious of him as he is of himself. He therefore feels "on stage" in social relations and "is constantly performing for an audience which is, in part at least, of his own making [Elkind, 1968, p. 153]." This egocentric preoccupation with social attention and approval, Elkind theorized, makes the adolescent particularly dependent upon the peer group. Hence the rise of the "clique" and the "crowd" during this period (Dunphy, 1963).

It follows from these observations that an adolescent friendship will be successful to the extent that it helps the friends to deal with their own and others' feelings. Friendship can be a "therapeutic" experience in which two persons express their feelings and find evidence that others have the same doubts, hopes, and anxieties (Mussen et al., 1969). Given the intensity of this need for information and reassurance during early adolescence, there should be a strong correlation between the degree of attraction in a relationship and the degree of its participants' self-disclosure.

B. Sensitive Periods in Cognitive Development and Implications for Attraction

A major finding from the research on formal operational thinking (defined as the ability to construct possibilities systematically and test hypotheses) is that many people never achieve it. In a study of 265 lower and upper middle-class parents and their children, these were the percentages of persons at various ages showing clear formal operational reasoning on a task requiring the isolation of variables that determine the speed of a pendulum's movement (Kohlberg & Gilligan, 1971): 10—15 years: 45% formal operational; 16—20 years: 53% 21—30 years: 65%; 45—50 years: 57%.

These cross-sectional data suggest (longitudinal data are needed for proof) that most persons who attain formal logical reasoning on the pendulum task develop it in early adolescence. Another 8% appear to develop it from 16 to 20 years old, and another 12% from 21 to 30 years of age, after which there is no increase (extrapolating again from the cross-sectional to the longitudinal). These data will vary from task to task. Assuming, however, that the pendulum problem results are a rough approximation of a general developmental timetable, one can say that early adolescence has considerable importance in the development of the mature reflective thought that underlies self-analysis, flexibility, and mutuality in the interpersonal realm. An 18-year-old who is still functioning below the level of full formal operations is less likely ever to achieve that level than a 13-year-old who is preformal operational.[3] In this sense, early adolescence could be considered a sensitive period in cognitive-structural development and therefore an important period in the development of the capacity for mature friendship and love.

Adolescence also appears to be a crucial period for moral development. Movement to Kohlberg's postconventional moral stages requires first of all the attainment of formal operational thought. Formal thinking is a prerequisite for the Stage 5 perception of relativism in values, the "awareness that any society's definition of right and wrong ... is only one among many, both in fact and theory [Kohlberg & Gilligan, 1971, p. 1072]." This perception generates a democratic social-contract orientation toward reconciling different value positions, and later in some persons a differentiation between arbitrary social conventions and universally valid moral principles of justice, equality, and respect for persons. Kohlberg's longitudinal research (Kohlberg & Turiel, 1971) reveals that the sensitive transitional period

---

[3]One should qualify this line of reasoning by noting that some individuals may develop relatively rapidly, then fixate, while some slower developers catch up and move on to higher levels. The very high correlations, however, between moral maturity in early adolescence and moral maturity in adulthood (Kohlberg & Turiel, 1971) suggest that a similar pattern holds for the development of logical thinking.

for the development of postconventional moral thought is late adolescence—ages 15—19—the years just following the sensitive period for the transition to formal logical thought. His results suggest that individuals who do not use at least 20% principled moral reasoning by the end of high school are unlikely to develop principled thinking in adulthood; they tend to get "locked into" a lower-stage way of viewing the world. If one grants that principled morality has significant consequences for interpersonal functioning, then late adolescence can be seen as a second important period in the development of attraction. This line of reasoning has clear interventionist implications. Kohlberg and Turiel (1971) state that moral educational influences during adolescence, particularly structured opportunities for role-taking in conflict situations, can have lifelong positive effects on moral development. The same may be said for growth in one's capacity to love.

VI. The Development of Inference and Understanding of Social—Psychological Causality

Levinger and Snoek (1972) have observed that the ability to interpret cues is necessary to decide how much another person has enjoyed an interchange. People rarely discuss with their partner how they feel about an interaction. Once an inference has been made about how someone feels, there is a second task: understanding why. Thus, the ability to infer psychological states and the ability to understand psychological causality are two central cognitive underpinnings of any social relationship. A cognitive-developmental approach to attraction consequently is concerned with developmental changes in children's ability to infer feelings and thoughts and to understand causally related sequences of behavior in interpersonal relationships.

Piaget's (1959) concept of egocentrism, the unawareness that one's own viewpoint may be different from those of others, is directly relevant to the issue of inference. Piaget notes that until the age of 7 or 8 "egocentric factors of verbal expression . . . and of understanding itself . . . are too important to allow any general understanding between children [p. 125]." In a study by Burns and Cavey (1957), 3—5-year-olds, unlike older children, judged drawings in terms of what they themselves would feel in the situation, rather than in terms of the cues presented. Gates (1923) and Walton (1936) found that children's ability to identify emotions portrayed by an actress in a photograph increased with age. Lerner's (1937) study of social perspective-taking showed that younger children projected their own viewpoint onto all the characters in a story situation. Ausubel (1955) has demonstrated that with age children improve in their ability to predict their own or their classmates' sociometric ratings.

The study of children's perceptions of causality has concentrated on the impersonal, rather than the personal, world. Reed (1971) summarized the research as showing three main levels in the development of children's explanations of physical events. At Level 1 (ages 4—7 +), children tend to confuse physical events with their own actions or thoughts (clouds move "because they are following people"). At this level, children also causally link events related only by accident ("thunder makes it rain"), and they often do not make causal connections at all in giving mechanical explanations or in narrating stories (Piaget, 1959). At Level 2 (ages 7—8 to 11—12), children explain events in terms of the concrete contingencies they observe, distinguishing between their own actions and events that are external to them. They try to formulate general rules of explanation, which may be erroneous ("big things sink and little things float"). They have trouble in going beyond immediate concrete data to develop mediating concepts and in isolating the causal variable when more than two or three contingencies are involved. At Level 3 (ages 11—12), explanations are of the formal operational type. Possibilities are systematically considered, with an interest in testing them as hypotheses. There is also an ability to vary one factor while holding others constant. At all three levels, it appears likely that the same mental processes that determine the child's interpretations of physical events also determine his understanding of social phenomena.

Flapan (1968) has extended the study of inference and thinking about causality directly into the realm of social interaction. She showed 6-, 9-, and 12-year-old children dramatic film excerpts that portrayed a variety of feelings, motivations, family relationships, and social situations. One excerpt, for example, depicted a girl practicing on her new skates. A boy demands a turn with her skates, but the girl refuses. When the boy calls her a pig, she angrily pushes him down. Later, back at the house, after the boy denies the name-calling, the girl's father harshly orders her to give the boy the skates or else to go to bed without supper. She chooses the latter. Angered, the father now says that she has to give the boy the skates as a present. Crushed, the girl goes to her room. The father shows some guilt and sadness, repeatedly looking up from his newspaper. Nevertheless, he refuses to grant his daughter's request for a good-night kiss when she calls down from her room. The father tries to return to reading his paper, but soon gives up.

Children in the study were asked to pretend that the experimenter had not seen the film and to tell her what happened. Following this, each child was asked a series of questions about how a character in the film felt and why he said or did what he did. For example: How do you think the girl felt when she took off her skates and said she was going to bed without any supper? Why do you think the father kept looking up instead of reading the newspaper? Why do you think the girl asked to kiss her father good night? How do you think the father felt when the girl asked to kiss him?

The developmental trends that Flapan (1968) found are presented in considerable detail in her fine monograph, *Children's Understanding of Social Interaction*. In brief, the trends were as follows:

1. With age there was an increase in the number of children who gave causal explanations, and who either interpreted feelings or inferred thoughts and inten-

tions that were not obviously expressed in the film. The accounts of 6-year-olds, the youngest subjects, were largely literal descriptions of what happened.

2. There was a shift with age in the kinds of explanations given: from physical-situational (age 6) to psychological, the latter explanations focusing on a person's feelings, or motives, or his perception of a co-actor's feelings or motives (ages 9 and 12).

3. There was also a developmental shift in the kinds of inferences and interpretations made: inferences about thoughts and intentions came first; then inferences about an actor's feelings; then inferences about one actor's perceptions of a co-actor's psychological state (comparable to Feffer's third stage of coordinating viewpoints and to Kohlberg's Stage 3 role-taking).

4. Six-year-olds described the characters more often as just reacting with feelings, while older children described them as more actively thinking and having goals in mind.

5. The most conspicuous developmental increases occurred between 6 and 9 years of age, suggesting that this period is the most important transitional phase in the development of inferential and explanatory thinking about interpersonal events.

As an example of the contrast between the thinking of the youngest and the oldest children in the study, here are portions of two re-tellings of the episode about the little girl and the skates, the first by a 6-year-old:

> At the beginning her daddy was sitting in the chair in the living room looking at the paper, and the little girl got out of her bed and said, "Pa, will you kiss me good night?" And the daddy said, "Go to bed," and the little girl went to bed crying. And he tore up the paper and he threw it on the floor [Flapan, 1968, p. 31].*

An account of a 12-year-old, in addition to reporting events, infers the father's thoughts, conflicts, and intentions:

> The father was reading the newspaper, but he was thinking about something else. He couldn't really read it. And the little girl was looking down and asked her father if he didn't want to kiss her good night. The father wanted to say good night, but then he thought she did something bad, so he said, "No. Go back to bed." And the girl was crying and did go back to bed. And the father tried to read the newspaper again, but he couldn't read it ... He wanted to go up to her and say it wasn't so bad, but he decided he better not [Flapan, 1968, p. 32].*

With increasing powers of inference and understanding of social causation should come higher levels of empathy, sympathy, communication, and ability to solve interpersonal conflicts. These factors obviously play an important role in maintaining reciprocal positive feeling in any social relationship and in restoring positive relations after negative interaction occurs. Flapan's finding that older

*Reprinted by permission of the publisher from Dorothy Flapan, *Children's understanding of social interaction*. (New York: Teachers College press, copyright 1968 by Teachers College, Columbia University), pp. 31 and 32.

children conceptualize another's behavior in terms of that person's inferred goals suggests that developmentally mature children are capable of long-range accommodation to the needs and interests of another. This capacity affords the possibility of a greater interlocking of goals as a foundation for friendship. The child's increasing awareness of the meaning and causes of behavior also has implications for initial attraction. First impressions should be more accurate with increasing age, less determined by superficial events, and freer from distortions due to cues that the observer cannot relate to the fabric of unseen causes.

The understanding of intentions and social causation are also determinants of attribution of responsibility for interpersonal actions, which is related to attraction. Attraction will increase among members of a group following reduction in threatened punishment only if group members perceive each other as responsible for the reduction (Pepitone & Kleiner, 1957). Pepitone and Sherberg (1957) also found a clear relation between attraction and perceived intentionality. Subjects liked a well-meaning person who insulted another person for that person's own good significantly more than they liked an individual making the same insulting remarks for selfish reasons. Children younger than 7 years, however, even if they are made aware of intentions, will typically count consequences more than motives in evaluating a person's moral responsibility (Lickona, in press).

Although Flapan's procedures did not find a marked shift in social understanding from 9 to 12 years of age, other cognitive-developmental research indicates qualitative differences in causal thinking between children and adolescents. Reed's (1971) description of Level 3 thinking pinpoints two major differences: problem-solving becomes systematic hypothesis-testing, and a capacity appears for constructing mediating principles to explain observed events. An example of the shift from concrete to formal operations in causal thinking comes from the work of Peel (1967). He asked children ages 8−15 to make inferences about stories such as the following: "A fighter pilot flying over the Alps collided with an aerial cable-way, and cut a main cable causing some cars to fall to the glacier below. Several people were killed." A concrete operational child said about this story, "I think the pilot was not very good at flying." A formal operational child responded: "He was either not informed of the mountain railway on his route or he was too low; also his flying compass may have been affected by something before or after take-off [quoted in Kohlberg & Gilligan, 1971, p. 1061]." The concrete operational child, treating his hypothesis as fact, assumes that if there was an accident, the pilot must have been a bad pilot. The formal operational child, aware that a hypothesis is only that, constructs several possible explanations.

Elkind (1968) has noted the same difference between children and adolescents in their approach to a concept-formation task. Adolescents can be heard to verbalize, "No, that's not right. Let's try . . ." Elementary school children, by contrast, tend to formulate a particular strategy and stick to it despite repeated failures.

The ability to think hypothetically, to distinguish assumption from fact, to get at the cause of an event by checking out several possibilities, rather than accepting the first idea that comes into one's head—this is the highest achievement of formal operational thought. It is the antithesis of the mentality that says, "The whole trouble with him is ..." or, "If only we could (change one thing), our problems would be solved." The same formal operational capacity that permits a person to isolate a cause allows him to deal with multiple causation and interactions of variables. Along with reciprocal role-taking, formal hypothetical thinking also enables an individual to analyze his own potential roles in bringing about an interpersonal problem, or in solving one. A good deal of hard formal operational "maintenance work" is undoubtedly needed to keep any close relationship alive and well.

VII. Levels of Ego Development as a Framework for the Study of Attraction

The understanding of psychological causality has been incorporated by Loevinger and Wessler (1970) into a larger theory of levels of ego development. They define the "ego" as a unified personal system that includes impulse control and character, interpersonal style, conscious preoccupations, self-concept, and cognitive style—all involved in "the search for coherent meanings in experience [p. 8]." Although the ego levels are not presented as meeting the formal criteria of cognitive-structural stages (for example, universality, irreversibility, and generality), they constitute a useful developmental framework for examining an individual's world view as it relates to interpersonal attraction. The Loevinger approach also has the methodological advantage of using a straightforward sentence-completion test for which there is a published manual (Loevinger, Wessler, & Redmore, 1970).

Level 1 in the Loevinger sequence involves the transition during the first years of life from presocial functioning to symbiotic interaction .At the second, or Impulsive, level, character is defined in terms of opportunistic hedonism. Psychological causation is understood only in concrete terms ("Men are lucky because—*they are cute*"). There is low capacity for solving interpersonal problems ("If I can't get what I want—*I run away*").*

At the Self-Protective Level, a substage of the Impulsive Level, interpersonal style is wary and manipulative, reflecting greater orientation to the motives of others ("Being with other people—*I will watch myself*"). The self-protective person is "concerned with controlling and being controlled, with snaring, with domination, and with competition. Life is a zero-sum game. What you win, I lose [Loevinger & Wessler, 1970, p. 4]."

Conformity defines the third level, which is achieved by most children in the early years of school. There is a strong concern about physical appearance and sex-role stereotypes ("A woman should always—*be friendly and nice*"). Inner psychological life is described only in vague affective terms (for example, happy, sad, sorry), and neither conflict nor individual differences among people are acknowledged. There is no sharp separation between the way things or people are and the way they ought to be. "People at the conformist stage," Loevinger and Wessler (1970) write: "constitute either a majority or a large minority of any social group [p. 5]."

---

*All quotes illustrative of ego levels taken from Loevinger, Jane, and Wessler, Ruth, *Measuring Ego Development*. © 1970 by Jossey-Bass, San Francisco, Chapter 4, pp. 54—109.

The fourth ego level, Conscientious, appears to be a clear concomitant of formal operational thought. There is a distinction between *is* and *ought*, a heightened consciousness of self and inner feelings, and a new perception of multiple possibilities. The person at this level has a sense of controlling his or her own fate ("A woman's body—*is what she makes it*"; "Men are lucky because—*they have great control over their own destinies*"). This feeling of self-determination tends to spill over into a feeling of controlling others. There is a clear conception of companionship, duty, and mutual emotional support. Interaction is conceptualized in terms of communication and role-taking ("When people are helpless—*they need to be offered help in a manner they are able to accept*"). Finally, notions of psychological causality involve subtle inference ("When people are helpless—*they may be too disturbed to be rational in the situation*").

At Stage 5, the Autonomous Level, the individual moves beyond the "excessive striving" of the Conscientious stage to a "deepened respect for people and their need to find their own way and even make their own mistakes [p. 6]." There is greater tolerance of ambiguity and conflict as part of the human condition, and a still more complex understanding of social–psychological causality, including a grasp of the circularity of social interaction ("If my mother—*were different, I would be different, too. If she were more interested, I'd care more*"). Sex, like all other phases of human interaction, is seen in a context of mutuality ("Usually she felt that sex—*should be enjoyed by both, or you might as well not expect a very happy marriage*").

The final, or Integrated, stage, according to Loevinger, is reached by no more than 1% of adults. It is a level of transcending conflict and reconciling polarities; of combining respect for another's autonomy, search for self-fulfillment, the values of justice and idealism, and reconciliation to one's destiny ("A woman should always —*as should a man, treat other individuals with respect and work toward the betterment of the whole of people, not just of herself*").

The Loevinger ego levels clearly have rich implications for the issue of interpersonal attraction. As with Kohlberg's moral stages, one would expect persons to choose friends or romantic partners at the same, or adjacent, ego levels, rather than persons far removed in the developmental sequence. Second, one would expect at least a crude isomorphism or parallelism between individual levels of ego development and levels of social relationships. Third, there should be at the more mature ego stages a higher degree of interpersonal equilibrium, and greater stability and growth of mutual affection as a result of the deeper interpersonal sensitivity present at these stages. Fourth, one could predict that transitions in relationships, say, from Conformist to Conscientious, or Conscientious to Autonomous, would require the growth of both partners. Advance to a new level by only one partner would have the potential of creating a gap in the experience of the relationship that could threaten attraction. Finally, and most fundamentally, attraction cannot be treated as a phenomenon that is constant either in its antecedents or consequences across such qualitatively different levels of personal being. Clearly there will be radical differences in the dynamics of liking and loving between people who view relationships as a zero-sum game and people who view relationships as an opportunity to develop each other's autonomous selves.

VIII. Conclusion

This discussion falls short of developing the full potential of the cognitive-developmental approach to interpersonal attraction. Interpersonal functioning over the entire life span can be viewed from a cognitive-developmental perspective. Does cognitive-structural regression ever occur, and if it does, what are the behavioral consequences? Piaget and Inhelder (1962) have reported evidence that cognitive abilities among senile persons disintegrate in reverse order of their formation in childhood. Looft (1972) has argued that increasing ridigity and social disengagement in old age are manifestations of a return to the egocentric attachment to a single approach or point of view. Kohlberg and Gilligan's (1971) data suggest a slippage in formal operations in some persons as old age approaches. Will such cognitive regressions cause regression in social relations and a deterioration of attraction, or will long-established patterns of affective behavior hold sway?

The interaction between developmental stage and situational factors in determining a person's behavior constitutes a second major area where groundbreaking is needed. The interaction issue offers the clearest case for an integration of the cognitive-developmental and social—psychological approaches. What conditions maximize the cognitive-stage component of behavior and what conditions minimize it? Given the fact that people have a number of developmental levels available to them, what circumstances facilitate functioning at the person's highest level? One can also reverse perspective and ask how behavior affects development. What kinds of interpersonal behavior patterns bring about the individual developmental growth of the partners and their advancement to higher levels of mutual affection?

The first research priority for a cognitive-developmental approach would be to substantiate more directly the relationship between attraction and developmental variables such as perception of similarity, role-taking, moral reasoning, logical thinking, understanding of causality, and organization of ego. Much important work remains to be done. What is offered here is the rough blueprint for a developmental approach to a social phenomenon, and the suggestion that interpersonal attraction could become a crossroads for developmental and social psychology.

References

Ammons, R., & Ammons, H. Parent preference in young children's doll-play interviews. *Journal of Abnormal and Social Psychology,* 1949, **44**, 490—505.

Austin, M. C., & Thompson, G. C. Children's friendship: A study of the bases on which children select and reject their best friends. *Journal of Educational Psychology,* 1948, **39**, 101—116.

Ausubel, D. P. Socioempathy as a function of sociometric status in an adolescent group. *Human Relations,* 1955, **8**, 75—84.

Bowlby, J. *Attachment and loss.* Vol. 1. New York: Basic Books, 1969.

Burns, N., & Cavey, L. Age differences in empathic ability among children. *Canadian Journal of Psychology,* 1957, **11**, 227—30.

Byrne, D., & Griffit, W. A development investigation of the law of attraction. *Journal of Personality and Social Psychology*, 1966, **4**, 699—702.

D'Augelli, J. The relationship of moral reasoning, sex-guilt, and interpersonal interaction to couples' premarital sexual experience. Unpublished doctoral dissertation, University of Connecticut, 1972.

D'Augelli, J., & Cross, H. J. The relationship of sex-guilt and moral reasoning to premarital sex in college women. *Journal of Consulting and Clinical Psychology*, in press.

Decarie, T. *Intelligence and affectivity in early childhood*. New York: International Universities Press, 1965.

DeVries, R. The development of constancy of object identity. Unpublished doctoral dissertation, University of Chicago, 1966.

Dixon, J. C. Development of self-recognition. *Journal of Genetic Psychology*, 1957, **91**, 251—256.

Dunphy, D. C. The social structure of urban adolescent peer groups. *Sociometry*, 1963, **26**, 230—246.

Elkind, D. Cognitive development in adolescence. In J. F. Adams (Ed.), *Understanding adolescence*. Boston, Massachusetts: Allyn & Bacon, 1968. Pp. 128—158.

Ellinwood, C. Structural development in the expression of emotion by children. Unpublished doctoral dissertation, University of Chicago, 1969.

Fetfer, M. Developmental analysis of interpersonal behavior. *Psychological Review*, 1970, **77**, 197—214.

Flapan, D. *Children's understanding of social interaction*. New York: Columbia University Teachers College Press, 1968.

Gates, G. S. An experimental study of the growth of social perception. *Journal of Educational Psychology*, 1923, **14**, 449—461.

Gilligan, C., Kohlberg, L., Lerner, E., & Belenky, M. Moral reasoning about sexual dilemmas: the development of an interview and scoring system. In *Technical Report of the Commission on obscenity and pornography*, Vol. 1. (No. 5256-0010). Washington, D. C.: Superintendent of Documents, U. S. Government Printing Office, 1971.

Harlow, H., & Harlow, M. Social deprivation in monkeys. *Scientific American*, 1962, **207**, 136—146.

Hess, B. Friendship. In M. W. Riley, M. Johnson, & A. Foner (Eds.), *Aging and society*. Vol. 3. New York: Russel Sage, 1972. Pp. 357—393.

Inhelder, B., & Piaget, J. *The growth of logical thinking from childhood through adolescence*. New York: Basic Books, 1958.

Jurich, A. P. The formation of premarital sexual standards. Unpublished doctoral dissertation, Pennsylvania State University, 1972.

Kinsey, A., Pomeroy, W. B., Martin, C. E., & Gebhard, P. H. *Sexual behavior in the human female*. Philadelphia, Pennsylvania: Sanders, 1953.

Kohlberg, L. The development of modes of moral thinking and choice in the years ten to sixteen. Unpublished doctoral dissertation, University of Chicago, 1958.

Kohlberg, L. A cognitive-developmental analysis of children's sex-role concepts and attitudes. In Eleanor Maccoby (Ed.), *The development of sex differences*. Stanford, California: Stanford University Press, 1966. Pp. 82—173.

Kohlberg, L. Stage and sequence: The cognitive-developmental approach to socialization. In D. A. Goslin (Ed.), *Handbook of socialization theory and research*. Chicago, Illinois: Rand McNally, 1969. Pp. 347—380.

Kohlberg, L. From is to ought: How to commit the naturalistic fallacy and get away with it in the study of moral development. In T. Mischel (Ed.), *Cognitive development and epistemology*. New York: Academic Press, 1971. Pp. 151—284.

Kohlberg, L. Moral issue scoring guide. Unpublished manuscript, Harvard University, 1972.

Kohlberg, L., & Gilligan, C. The adolescent as a philosopher: The discovery of the self in a post conventional world. *Daedalus*, 1971, **100**, 1051—1086.

Kohlberg, L., & Turiel, E. Moral development and moral education. In G. S. Lesser (Ed.), *Psychology and educational practice*. Glenview, Illinois: Scott Foresman, 1971. Pp. 410—465.

Lerner, E. The problem of perspective in moral reasoning. *American Journal of Sociology*, 1937, **43**, 249—269.

Levinger, G. Stage effects on complementarity in the sequence of relationship formation. Unpublished paper, Western Reserve University, 1964.

Levinger, G., & Snoek, J. D. *Attraction in relationship: A new look at interpersonal attraction*. New York: General Learning Press, 1972.

Lickona, T. Research on Piaget's theory of moral development. In T. Lickona (Ed.), *Man and morality: A handbook of moral development and behavior*. New York: Holt, in press.

Loevinger, J., & Wessler, R. *Measuring ego development (measuring ego development 1): Construction and use of a sentence completion test*. San Francisco, California: Jossey-Bass, 1970.

Loevinger, J., Wessler, R., & Redmore, C. *Measuring ego development 2: Scoring manual for women and girls*. San Francisco, California: Jossey-Bass, 1970.

Looft, W. R. Egocentrism and social interaction across the life span. *Psychological Bulletin*, 1972, **78**, 73–92.

Maccoby, E. The development of stimulus selection. In J. P. Hill (Ed.), *Minnesota symposia on child psychology*. Minneapolis, Minnesota: University of Minnesota Press, 1969. Pp. 68–96.

Mancuso, J. (Ed.), *Readings for a cognitive theory of personality*. New York: Holt, 1970.

Mussen, P. H., Conger, J. J., & Kagan, J. *Child development and personality*. (3rd ed.) New York: Harper, 1969.

Newcomb, T. *The acquaintance process*. New York: Holt, 1961.

Peel, E. A. *The psychological basis of education*. (2nd ed.) London: Oliver & Boyd, 1967.

Pepitone, A., & Kleiner, R. The effects of threat and frustration on group cohesiveness. *Journal of Abnormal and Social Psychology*, 1957, **54**, 192–199.

Pepitone, A., & Sherberg, J. Intentionality, responsibility, and interpersonal attraction. *Journal of Personality*, 1957, **25**, 757–766.

Piaget, J. *The psychology of intelligence*. London: Routledge, Kegan Paul, 1947.

Piaget, J. *The language and thought of the child*. (3rd ed.) New York: Humanities Press, 1959.

Piaget, J., & Inhelder, B. *Le development des quantities physiques chez l'enfant*. Pairs: Delachaux & Niestle, 1962.

Reed, J. L. Children's explanations. In G. Lesser (Ed.), *Psychology and educational practice*. Glenview, Illinois: Scott Foresman, 1971. Pp. 191–216.

Rest, J. Developmental hierarchy in preference and comprehension of moral judgment. Unpublished doctoral dissertation, University of Chicago, 1968.

Rest, J., Turiel, E., & Kohlberg, L. Relations between level of moral judgment and preference and comprehension of the moral judgment of others. *Journal of Personality*, 1969, **37**, 225–252.

Rosenhan, D. Determinants of altruism: observations for a theory of altruistic development. Unpublished paper, Stanford University, 1969.

Schaffer, H. R., & Emerson, P. E. The development of social attachment in infancy. *Monograph of the society for research in child development*, 1964, **29** (Serial No. 94), 1–77.

Selman, R. The importance of reciprocal role-taking for the development of conventional moral thought. In L. Kohlberg & E. Turiel (Eds.), *Recent research in moral development*. New York: Holt, in press.

Singer, A., Jr. Certain aspects of personality and their relation to certain group modes, and constancy of friendship choices. *Journal of Educational Research*, 1951, **45**, 33–42.

Thibaut, J. W., & Kelley, H. H. *The social psychology of groups*. New York: Wiley, 1959.

Turiel, E. An experimental test of the sequentiality of developmental stages in the child's moral judgment. *Journal of Personality and Social Psychology*, 1966, **3**, 611–618.

Walters, R. H., & Parke, R. D. Social motivation, dependency and susceptibility to social influence. In L. Berkowitz (Ed.), *Advances in experimental social psychology*. Vol. 1. New York: Academic Press, 1964.

Walton, W. E. Empathic responses in children. *Psychological Monographs*, 1936, **48**, 40–67.

White, R. Motivation reconsidered: The concept of competence. *Psychological Review*, 1959, **66**, 297–333.

White, R. Ego and reality in psychoanalytic theory. *Psychological Issues*. Vol. 3. New York: International Universities Press, 1963.

3

The Social Context
of Interpersonal Attraction

ALAN C. KERCKHOFF

Department of Sociology
Duke University
Durham, North Carolina

I. Introduction

In this chapter I am concerned, first of all, with attraction between prospective spouses, rather than interpersonal attraction of all kinds. Second, I concentrate on the significance of the matrix of social relations within which the particular dyad experiences such attraction, rather than the dynamics of the dyadic relationship itself. In this regard, my purpose is to emphasize the social context within which interpersonal attraction occurs and thereby provide an added dimension of meaning to the observed patterns of attraction.

A number of years ago, Winch (1958) introduced the concept "field of eligible spouse-candidates" into the literature on mate selection. By "field of eligible spouse-candidates," he referred to individuals in any population who are viewed as a possible spouse for any given person. The field of eligibles is defined by a set of categories of persons who are seen as both appropriate and probable candidates for marriage. Winch emphasized that people in our society both preferred to marry persons in these categories and actually tended to marry such persons. These categories are, for the most part, defined in terms of endogamous marriage patterns—the tendency to prefer to marry someone in one's own racial group, religious denomination, social class, general age category, and so on. Winch's purpose in that discussion was to acknowledge that there were broad social definitions of a field of eligibles so that he could then go on to stress the importance of criteria of selection within that field.

In one respect, my purpose here is the direct opposite of Winch's. Given the strong emphasis in the mate selection literature over the past two decades on interpersonal (and even individual) factors in the selection process, I wish to reaffirm the significance of the social context of selection. In doing so, I want to go well beyond a discussion of endogamy and the field of eligibles as Winch used these terms. Although I begin this discussion with these notions, they represent only the point of departure for a more basic examination of the social context of attraction. In an earlier statement (Kerckhoff, 1964), I suggested that it is necessary to explore carefully the degree to which the field of eligibles is a "field of availables" or a "field of desirables." By this I meant that we need to determine the degree to which observed patterns of selection are a function of the distribution of kinds of people in our society or are a function of preferences. It would not be unimportant, of course, if "likes attract only because they are the only ones around," but, certainly, one's interpretation of the outcome would be quite different in that case than it would be if "likes seek each other out." I want to look at both distributional and normative bases of selection.

My general purpose, therefore, is to interpret a body of literature bearing on the relevance of the social context for the interpersonal attraction between prospective spouses by using the homogamy[1] findings as a point of departure. I wish to consider two rather distinct ways in which the social context has relevance. One way is through the enunciation, inculcation, and enforcement of social norms for the selection process—the social definition of a field of desirables. The second is through the structuring of social interaction so that only certain kinds of people are likely to interact in ways that permit them to define each other as spouse candidates—the delimitation of the field of availables.

In the course of the discussion, several other issues are emphasized. First, I want to stress that *interpersonal attraction* must be understood within the context of a definition of the relationship involved; the attraction is an attraction to engage in a particular kind of interaction. Thus, the characteristics deemed attractive will tend to vary according to the kind of relationship involved. Second, to the extent that normative definitions of the particular relationship and of the kind of person most appropriate to it are social products, different social groups may have different

---

[1]The terms homogamy and endogamy are not always clearly differentiated. In this chapter, however, I use them in quite distinct ways. Homogamy refers to the observed tendency for spouses to have similar social characteristics; endogamy refers to the normative definition within a social group specifying a preference for such similarity. Thus, homogamy refers to what happens, while endogamy refers to a definition of the desirable outcome.

definitions. Similarly, an individual's position in (or in relation to) any such group will influence the significance of the group's norms for his behavior. Finally, I want to point out how the failure to take such matters into account has led to some serious distortions in the interpretation of the mate selection evidence and would, presumably, lead to similar distortions in other areas of interpersonal attraction research.

Much of the discussion revolves around the evidence of homogamy in this country. This is done to provide an example of the effect of the larger social system on the patterns of interpersonal attraction, although, as the later discussion emphasizes, it is certainly not the only effect of the larger social system. Because of the centrality of homogamy in this discussion, it is important at the outset to record the fact that marriages in this society have tended for some time to occur very largely within homogeneous segments of the population. The vast majority of husbands and wives (especially in first marriages) are very close to the same age, with the husband tending to be somewhat older (Hollingshead, 1951; Bowerman, 1956). Even more clear-cut is the tendency to marry only within one's racial group. Only a very small proportion of American marriages involve spouses of different races (Burma, 1963; Schmitt, 1971). Also, although there has been some increase in interfaith marriages over the past 40 years, marriage within one's own religious group, at least within the categories of Protestant, Catholic, and Jew, is still much more common than interfaith marriages (Glick, 1960; Bumpass, 1970). Finally, there is considerable evidence that most marriages involve individuals who are similar in socioeconomic status (Sundal & McCormick, 1951; Dinitz, Banks, & Pasamanick, 1960). In fact, homogamy with respect to education and social origin has been remarkably stable throughout the twentieth century (Warren, 1966).

The point of the present discussion, however, is not to document such homogamy[2] but to examine the reasons for it. The interest here is in the social factors that influence the selection process. The data that demonstrate the homogamous patterns are used as an example of socially significant outcomes of the selection process which call for further explanation. The major purpose of this discussion is to suggest a form of explanation that will help both in understanding data on homogamy and in understanding other patterns in the selection process. In the course of the discussion, I review a good deal of the literature on mate selection, but I conclude the chapter by emphasizing its failings more than its strengths. I want primarily to stress that if one adopts the basic premise of this discussion (that the larger social system influences the dynamics of interpersonal attraction), one must be critical of the theories of mate selection that have been proposed; and by implica-

---

[2]Some readers may object to the applicability of the statistics in these and other reports referred to later in the chapter because of the rapid changes in our society over the past decade or two. It may be argued that homogamy is not nearly as common today as it was in the 1950s and 1960s. This may well be the case (although I doubt if as much change has occurred as might be assumed). But even if it is, the thrust of the present argument remains. The point is that social and cultural factors in the larger society influence selection. If changes in these factors lead to changes in the pattern of selection, it would be further evidence of the significance of the larger social context of selection.

tion, at least, I suggest that one must be skeptical of most other theories of interpersonal attraction, as well.

II. The Field of Desirables

The American rendition of the mate selection process is one in which the two individuals somehow "find" each other, fall in love, and mutually decide to marry. Although few actually believe that "there is one and only one in the world for me," the emphasis is on the freedom of the individual to choose his own marriage partner from among a wide range of candidates. It is, thus, not surprising that the strong homogamy patterns observed in the United States have been interpreted as an indication of a *preference* for a spouse who is like oneself. Such an endogamous preference is easily explainable psychologically because it brings together two individuals who have a greater sense of commonality and who more easily empathize with each other. At the social level, the endogamous principle is understandable in that such pairings more fully maintain social and cultural patterns of both the couple and those persons who associate with them; the flow of social intercourse is thereby eased for everyone. The preference for homogamy can therefore be seen as characteristic of both persons who are choosing mates and persons with whom they associate. The sociological literature, in this way, treats the fact of homogamy as evidence of endogamy, that is, as evidence of a *norm* shared by the members of a group. The implication is both that such a norm is internalized by the participants in the selection process so that they *want* to make homogamous choices and that the norm is *enforced* by others through the use of effective sanctions.

What evidence is there that such a normative interpretation is justified, beyond the homogamous pattern itself? Perhaps the most convincing evidence comes from deviant cases, involving persons who violate the tendency to make homogamous unions. Such deviant cases have repeatedly been found to involve persons who are in one respect or another outside the social context within which such normative influence usually occurs. For instance, Heiss (1960) found that individuals who entered interreligious marriages tended to come from families in which religion was a very weak influence or they had seriously strained relations with their parents. Similarly, Freeman (1955) was impressed with the fact that even in Hawaii, where social relations among ethnic and racial groups are generally quite amicable, marriages were very generally homogamous with respect to ethnic and racial identity.[3] Freeman (1955) made an intensive investigation of couples who either had married or were dating exclusively outside their own group, and found that such persons were seriously alienated from members of their own group, and

[3]A recent study (Schmitt, 1971) has shown that, although interracial marriage rates in Hawaii have increased since the time of Freeman's (1955) study, the modal pattern is still racial homogamy.

that "a self-perpetuating cycle was built up in which deviation intensified rejection and rejection enhanced deviation [p. 372]." The literature on interracial marriages and interracial dating has clearly demonstrated the significance of external pressures toward homogamy. Golden (1953, 1954) has described the subtle (and not so subtle) ways in which friends and relatives pressure individuals who are dating interracially to move back to the normatively approved pattern.

The pressures toward homogamy are not all external, however. There also seems to be a strong preference for homogamy on the part of the participants. It is true that individuals who are less under the direct influence of such norm enforcers as parents are more likely to deviate from the norm. College students living at home more fully abide by the endogamy norm than do those living away from home; the same difference is found between persons who met their mate or fiance while living at home and those who met their mate or fiance away from home (Leslie & Richardson. 1956; Coombs, 1962). Yet, even those who are relatively free from immediate conformity pressures are very likely to abide by the endogamy norm. Furthermore, the participants are often abiding by the endogamy principle even when they seem to be violating it. Studies of homogamy by socioeconomic characteristics generally show that couples are more homogamous according to their achieved status level than they are according to their status of origin (Sundal & McCormick, 1951; Kerckhoff, 1964). That is, if a young person experiences social mobility in relation to his family origin, his marriage partner is more likely to be similar to his adult status than to his childhood status.

Thus, the similarity between spouses on social characteristics seems to flow from a normative definition that such similarity is desirable.[4] This normative definition is not only enforced from outside the couple but also generally tends to be accepted by the participants in the selection process. Yet, one may still question whether this is the whole explanation. Two major sources of doubt have been suggested. The first is based on the observation that most people live rather circumscribed lives so far as their encounters with varying kinds of people are concerned; they thus may not really have an equal opportunity to meet, fall in love with, and marry people who are different from themselves. The second is based on the finding, reported above, that when people move from one social context to another their homogamous tendencies seem to change; thus, they either did not have such a tendency in the first place, or the tendency is subject to alteration. The first of these possible explanations makes one doubt the reality of the endogamy norm; the second makes one wonder whether the norm is as simple and stable as it might appear to be. Although these ideas are closely related to each other, I discuss them separately in the following sections.

---

[4]Indirect evidence suggests that there is a general desire for similarity between oneself and one's chosen mate, so that one tends to see the chosen one as even more similar to oneself than he really is (Trost, 1967).

III. The Field of Availables

The premarital residential propinquity of spouses has been recognized for several decades. It has been found in a variety of cities and over a long period of time that persons who marry very often have premarital addresses that are very close to each other. There is little basis for surprise over such a pattern, but it does raise the question of the relationship between this finding and the finding of homogamy. It can be argued, for instance, that the general pattern of homogamy simply reflects the fact that in our society people of similar social characteristics live in contiguous areas, that they therefore interact with each other more, and that they are thus more likely to be able to identify prospective spouses within the socially homogeneous neighborhood than outside it.[5] On the other hand, the residential propinquity finding can be seen as resulting from the greater ease with which one can practice endogamy in one's own neighborhood than outside it.

The available evidence does not justify the argument that it is *either* propinquity *or* normative emphasis which leads to homogamy. It is equally difficult to determine *how much* of the observed homogamy can be attributed to each of these two factors. Most discussions of the matter simply take a leap of theoretical faith and conclude that the mate selection process is undoubtedly influenced by both (Katz & Hill, 1958); under the circumstances this seems the most reasonable conclusion. Certainly it is true that in the great majority of cases, persons seeking a prospective mate do not and cannot explore beyond a rather limited portion of the hypothetically available area, and that limited portion is very likely to be rather homogeneous with respect to the basic social characteristics of race, religion, social class, and so on. It is equally true that when a rather wide range of kinds of persons are available, there is some tendency for the level of homogamy to drop, even though it does continue to be the modal pattern. So, although the norm is hardly rigidly effective, it seems to be operative; and even though homogeneity of social surrounding seems to be an important factor in maintaining the norm, it does not seem to be the only factor.[6]

There are bits and pieces of evidence relating to the interplay of the normative and the propinquity principles, although they do not provide a basis for systematic assessment of their relative significance. Burchinal (1960) found that, holding socioeconomic status constant, university students expressed more support for endogamy than did high school students. Given the greater freedom from direct parental

---

[5]There is considerable evidence of residential segregation by social status, and ethnic and racial identity (see Duncan & Duncan, 1960; Lieberson, 1963; Taeuber & Taeuber, 1965).

[6]In an intriguing interpretation of the propinquity finding in general and their own in particular, Catton and Smirich (1964) suggest. "In keeping with a prevalent assumption, sociologists are in the habit of explaining this homogamy as the result of norms. The propinquity studies, however, may indicate that the norms arise from the fact of homogamy rather than vice versa [p. 523]." However, neither Catton and Smircich, nor anyone else, so far as I know, has provided the necessary data to support the idea.

supervision and influence experienced by university students and the more liberal view of religion usually reported for more highly educated people, such a finding suggests that expressions of support for the endogamy norm may increase as the reality of marriage approaches, even when the social setting is relatively permissive. Some of my own data, though based on a very limited college sample, suggest that college women may become somewhat less endogamous in orientation when they first go to college than in their later college years and that they are very likely eventually to choose a spouse in their own religious group. At the same time, women who have been either geographically or socially mobile during their adolescence are somewhat less likely to have fiances who are of the same religion than those women who have not been mobile (Kerckhoff, 1964).

Studies based on larger and more diverse samples provide a somewhat different basis for interpretation. There is evidence, for instance, that the rate of intermarriage of members of a minority group with persons outside their own group varies according to the relative size of the minority group. For instance, Burchinal and Chancellor (1962c) investigated the rate of intermarriage of Catholics in Iowa and found a correlation of .66 between the proportion of Catholics in the county and the proportion of Catholic marriages that were homogamous with respect to religion.

Coming at the matter in a somewhat different way, Dinitz *et al.* (1960), using marriage data for Columbus, Ohio, compared the socioeconomic level of the tracts from which the spouses came. They found an increasing tendency, during the 25 years covered by the study, for marriages to occur between two people who lived relatively far apart. At the same time, there was a tendency for individuals who lived rather far apart to come from socioeconomically comparable areas. Thus, although propinquity as a factor in spouse selection declined, there was not a parallel decline in homogamy.

Finally, although the data came from Oslo, Norway, it may be relevant to report the findings of Ramsøy (1966). She found evidence of both propinquity and homogamy (of occupational level), but the two patterns were independent of each other. That is, people who lived close to each other were no more likely to be homogamous than were those living far apart.

It seems apparent from these findings that one cannot wholly explain the observed patterns of homogamy by either propinquity or normative commitment. There seems to be a clear preference for homogamous marriages, but deviations from homogamy occur, and they are more likely to occur where homogamous prospective spouses are relatively scarce. Usually, making a homogamous match is rather easy, but where it becomes more difficult, deviations increase. From the perspective of this discussion, therefore, it seems reasonable to conclude that both the distributional and the normative aspects of the social system are relevant to an explanation of the observed patterns of homogamy. Two other matters need to be considered, however, before we can use such findings as a basis for a theory of mate selection. One is the fact that the adherence to social norms actually varies from one part of the population to the next. The other is the fact that different groups have different norms. The following two sections deal with these matters.

IV. Normative Adherence

The normative emphasis on endogamy and the observed patterns of homogamy and propinquity described in the preceding section are demonstrably present in our society. These are *modal* patterns, with all of the studies referred to showing considerable deviation. This deviation varies according to the dimension involved, racial endogamy being most fully adhered to; but in all cases deviations occur. As suggested earlier, the distribution of these deviations is itself indicative of the ways in which external social influences of the mate selection process operate.

One of the most consistent findings is that degree of homogamy varies by the age of the spouses. Several studies have found that the older the partners, the more likely they will deviate from the homogamous pattern. This has been found to be true of interracial marriages in Los Angeles (Burma, 1963). Interreligious marriages in Iowa also occur more frequently among couples who are 30 or more years old, although very young couples (16 and under) also tend to deviate more often from the religious homogamy pattern (Burchinal & Chancellor, 1962b). Finally, there tends to be greater age difference between spouses as the age at marriage increases (Bowerman, 1956).

Deviations from homogamy also seem to occur more often in couples who are of a relatively lower socioeconomic status. Schmitt (1971) reported a consistent tendency over two decades for interracial marriages in Hawaii to be more common the lower the occupation of the groom. Burchinal and Chancellor (1962a) found a higher incidence of interreligious marriages in Iowa when the groom was of low status. Heiss (1960) found the same thing with an urban sample. Glick (1957, pp. 127–128) reported an inverse relation between the husband–wife age gap and the husband's level of education.

The matter of social status of the two individuals is complicated, however, by the fact that homogamy with respect to status has different implications for men and women. Since the social status of the newly formed couple depends more on the status of the man than on that of the woman, it is easier for men to "marry down" than it is for women. Earlier analyses of homogamy by social status have actually reported more cases in which the husband, rather than the wife, has the higher status (Sundal & McCormick, 1951). It has been suggested, however, that the norm of status endogamy is more strongly held in the upper strata than in the lower (Centers, 1949), and some recent evidence suggests that this is so. Rubin (1968) reported that, although there is little *general* tendency for American men or women to marry either up or down, there does seem to be a tendency in the white collar, professional, and managerial status levels for more men than women to marry down.[7] In other words, when deviations from homogamy occur in these high status levels, they more frequently involve the "safe" form in which the woman's status is obscured by that of her husband. Deviations in blue collar status levels are more frequently in the opposite direction.

These findings suggest that persons for whom divergence from the endogamy norms is most threatening actually adhere to them the most. Mate selection is a process that usually occurs in early adulthood, and adherence to endogamy norms is found much more clearly there than in older age groups (and sometimes more so than in the very young age groups). Also, persons who would have the most to lose through violation of the norm (higher socioeconomic status people) appear less likely to violate it. Degree of conformity to the norm, therefore, may well be a function of the location of the individuals in the social system in which the norm is relevant.

V. Normative Definition

In addition to varying degrees of normative relevance, commitment, and adherence, it is evident that different segments of the population espouse and adhere to different norms for the same relationship. Although the kinds of endogamy norms I have already discussed are very prominent in all segments of the population, definitions of other desirable qualities of a spouse seem to vary considerably. Part of this variation seems to be a function of different definitions of what it means to be a boy or girl and a man or woman. For instance, different levels of male dominance and of overt sexuality seem to be expected. Such differences are apparent between blacks and whites (Broderick, 1965), and social class differences, irrespective of race, are well documented (Bell, 1966, Chapter 5).

It is also clear that such different definitions of sex roles tie in with different patterns of dating and courtship. Lowrie (1961) has noted two broad patterns. One pattern, which is more characteristic of native whites with high levels of education and relatively high socioeconomic status, involves early dating and a tendency to "play the field" both before and after occasional experiences of going steady. The other, more characteristic of ethnic minority group youngsters with low levels of education and from relatively low social-status families, involves a later beginning of dating with a more immediate pairing off.

Even within populations that are relatively homogeneous in race and class, there are differences between the norms in different locales. The several studies

---

[7]A recent study by Elder (1969) presents evidence suggesting that women who possess culturally valued attributes are more likely to ascend socially through marriage than are women who lack such attributes. Elder found that physically attractive women and women with high educational attainments tended to "marry up" more often than did their less attractive and less well-educated counterparts.

of "rating and dating" on college campuses suggest that both the criteria of rating and the degree of significance of such prestige hierarchies vary from one campus to the next.[8] The differences do not seem to reflect different pools of individuals at these colleges so much as they do different campus "cultures," which act as a source of influence on the individuals involved (Reiss, 1965).

These kinds of variations by race, class, and locale suggest that the male—female, and ultimately the husband—wife, relationship itself is defined differently by various segments of our society. Put in terms used earlier in the chapter, this means that the characteristics deemed desirable—those that lead to interpersonal attraction—vary depending on the definition of the relationship one anticipates having with the other person. Such definitions are part of the cultural context within which mate selection occurs. It is not simply a matter of the "compatibility" of the personal characteristics of the two individuals.

The further question is how that "fit" between the two personalities functions within a relationship having a particular normative definition. The "fit" of a passive—receptive male and an active—dominant female is hardly functional in a relationship that calls for male dominance. The couple's personal characteristics must therefore be understood within a normative context, as well as within an interpersonal context. It makes at least as much sense, therefore, to seek an explanation of mate selection within the framework of role theory, by identifying patterns of role compatibility, as to seek it within the framework of interpersonal dynamics.[9]

This is not to argue for a depersonalization of our view of the mate selection process, nor is it a call for a rejection of personality-based explanations of mate selection. It is, rather, a suggestion that interpersonal attraction patterns cannot be understood in a vacuum; they must be viewed in the context of the role relationship being entered into by the two parties. Most of the mate selection literature suffers from an implicit bias that ignores the larger social context and the role definitions of husband and wife. These issues are discussed further in the final section of this chapter.

VI. Social Structure, Role Definition, and Interpersonal Attraction

The discussion thus far has been designed to provide a basis for several important propositions. The first suggests that there are dominant, society-wide definitions of what constitutes a desirable spouse. I have used the literature on endogamy in mate

---

[8]The contrasts between the original analysis of Waller (1937) and the later studies by W. M. Smith (1952), Blood (1955), and Rogers and Havens (1960) cannot be wholly attributed to changes over time since the three later studies also vary among themselves.

[9]This general position has been taken by a number of students of the mate selection process. [See Burr (1971), Dyer, (1962), Mangus (1957), and Murstein (1967).]

selection to demonstrate this, although one might want to argue that other, more personal characteristics (for example, willingness to "give and take") are equally widely accepted. Second, these society-wide definitions are most relevant to (and are most fully adhered to) by those who are following a "normal" mate selection process. Persons alienated from the usual pattern of social ties (for example, from parents), persons who are marrying "too late" or "too early," persons who have less to lose by violating the norms, are less likely to adhere to the norms—and evidently they are less likely to be expected to do so. Third, the structure of social relations in the larger society is such that there is a less than chance probability of one's meeting individuals who are different from oneself in terms of characteristics such as race, religion, and socioeconomic status. I have used the literature on residential propinquity to support this proposition, although I argue later in this section that there is much more segregation of homogeneous pools of prospective spouses involved than that found in residential segregation. Finally, beyond these society-wide definitions of a desirable mate, there are varying definitions of the male—female and the marriage relationship in different segments of the society, and these promote different views of what is desirable in a spouse and they thus lead to different kinds of pairing.

There is not a very adequate literature on the last of these points, but there is certainly sufficient knowledge to justify the statement that definitions of the husband—wife relationship vary. Without attempting to specify all of the reasons for such a statement, I will use a basic differentiation suggested by Bernard (1964) to guide the discussion. Bernard concluded from her review of the literature on husband—wife relations that two general patterns can be distinguished. The first of these, she has called a "parallel" pattern:

> If the man is a good provider, not excessive in his sexual demands, sober most of the time, and good to the children, this is about all a woman can reasonably ask. Similarly, if the woman is a good housekeeper and cook, not too nagging, a willing sex partner, and a good mother, this is all a man can really expect. Each lives his or her own life primarily in a male or female world. There are sometimes even strong mystic barriers between the sexes in such a pattern, and neither violates the boundaries of the other's world....Companionship in the sense of exchange of ideas or opinions or the enhancement of personality by verbal play or conversation is not considered a basic component in this pattern [p. 687].*

In contrast to this, the "interactional" pattern is one that:

> ...demands a great deal more involvement in the relationship on the part of the participants... Emphasis is placed on personality interaction. The role qualifications specified in the parallel pattern are taken for granted; they may even be added to. But whatever they are, they constitute only a minimum; far more is demanded. Companionship, expressions of love, recognition of personality (as distinguished from mere role performance) are among the other and characterizing specifications of this pattern [p. 688].*

*Jessie Bernard. "The Adjustments of Married Mates," in Harold T. Christensen (Ed.), *Handbook of marriage and the family*, © 1964 by Rand McNally and Company, Chicago, pp. 687 and 688. Reprinted by permission of Rand McNally Publishing Company.

Although Bernard's (1964) use of the term "role" is different from mine,[10] the significant point is that these are very different definitions of the "same" relationship found within a single society. In the terms I have been using, the roles of husband and wife are not defined in a completely consistent fashion throughout the society. Thus, any two persons responding to the same set of prospective spouse candidates may view them quite differently, depending on their definitions of the spouses' roles. With such varying definitions of the "same" roles current within the society, any attempt to generate a theory of interpersonal attraction that ignores the normative framework within which the attraction occurs is doomed to failure.

The great bulk of the writing on mate selection has indeed overlooked the varied nature of the normative context and has sought to construct a theory that considers only the society-wide norms (such as those associated with endogamy) in conjunction with the personal characteristics of the partners. In effect, it has thus dealt with only the macro and the micro levels of analysis and has glossed over the critical subsocietal group structures within which mate selection occurs.

The relative success that has been experienced by the research and theory-building in this area can actually mislead us. I wish to suggest that this success is a function of the fact that almost all of our knowledge at the micro level of interpersonal attraction between prospective spouses is based on college samples. Although we are almost wholly ignorant of the dynamics of mate selection within the wider society, what we do know supports the contention that the middle-class, college-educated mate selection process is quite different from that engaged in by other members of the society.

The mate selection literature suggests not only that people tend to follow the endogamy norms, but also that they tend to marry spouses with whom they share basic values. There is, in addition, some evidence that spouses (or intended spouses) are more likely to have certain personality combinations rather than others. The general thrust of this literature is to provide an image of the marital relationship in the United States as much more like Bernard's (1964) interactional pattern than like her parallel pattern. As Bernard points out, the interactional pattern is more common in middle-class couples than in those from the working or lower class. This suggests that the description of mate selection that is most often set forth by the literature is a description of middle-class patterns.

Numerous other sources of information are consistent with this suggestion. General discussions of the value orientations of the persons at various social class levels indicate that higher status people value psychological development, interpersonal response, self-direction, and self-fulfillment more than those at lower status levels (Hyman, 1953; Kohn, 1969). Studies of values associated with dating and courtship have provided evidence that as young people move through the system of higher education, original male—female value differences diminish and

---

[10]I would prefer to refer to both these "patterns" as normative definitions of what spouses should do and thus view them as different role definitions. The requirement of greater concern for personality in the interactional pattern is equally a definition of a role as is the definition of the parallel pattern.

much more individualized bases of preference become salient (Hill, 1945; Smith & Monane, 1953; Blood, 1956). Value consensus, one of the presumed bases of mate selection according to the usual interpretation of the research that has been done, seems clearly to be a middle and upper middle-class phenomenon, rather than a general characteristic of American couples (Dentler & Hutchinson, 1961; Kerckhoff, 1972). Similarly, we find, consistent with the Bernard (1964) typology, that higher status couples are more sensitive to the interpersonal aspects of their relationship, and it is easier to discern a differentiated interpersonal structure among higher status couples (Kerckhoff & Bean, 1970).

Our dependence on college samples may have resulted in more than a middle-class bias, however. There is some suggestion (Hobart, 1960) that the college setting itself is conducive to a different set of attitudes toward marital roles than is the "outside world." Young people who move from college to a more total involvement in the world of work and adult responsibilities seem to change their views of marriage. This change involves both the level of romanticism and their opinions about marital roles. Such findings make it even more necessary to study mate selection outside the college setting before generating general theories based on college samples alone.

Social class differences and contrasts between college and work settings also provide added meaning to the residential propinquity data, and make it possible at least to speculate about the relevance of the ecology of mate selection and the importance of the social forces that influence the ecological patterns involved. Since there is a total lack of literature on these matters, I must be content with speculation, but I hope that such speculation will provide an impetus to carry out additional middle-range research.

I will use the logic of the research on residential propinquity to discuss other structural bases of mate selection. The basic logic is that, in order to fall in love and get married, two people must not only meet, but must also interact for a period of time in situations in which they are defined as legitimate spouse candidates for each other. Any characteristic of the social system that segregates unmarried males and females into more delimited noninteracting subpopulations or that differentiates among them according to criteria of prestige is likely to have the same kind of effect on patterns of mate selection that residential propinquity has. It will increase the probability that persons who interact more and persons who are defined as of equal prestige will choose each other as marriage partners.

It will help if one can think of the total population of potential spouse candidates as a flow of persons who move through a network of social and spatial channels. The basic structure of that network is established by the residential distribution of families with adolescent children. Beyond that, however, there are other factors influencing the flow. The most obvious of these is the school system. Whoever determines school district boundary lines (or busing patterns) contributes in highly significant ways to the definition of the students' fields of eligibles. Although there are other mechanisms through which school-age youngsters meet (clubs, churches, hangouts and so on), the great majority of initial boy—girl relationships seem to be established in school. Even within the school, there are significant degrees of segregation and differentiation. Whether it is in stratified "streams" of greater and lesser academic demand or in different substantive programs (college preparatory, technical, and so on), the effect is the same: students tend to spend a much greater amount of time with their own stream or program mates than with students in other streams or programs.[11] There also tends to evolve an intergroup separatism that is reinforced by negative definitions each has of the other. Invidious terms of reference ("dummies," "stuck-up," "grease monkeys," etc.) are used to denigrate the out-group and to encourage in-group cohesion. The structural limitations are thus normatively reinforced. Under such conditions, boy—girl relationships are almost certain to be restricted to within the separate groups.

Such a sorting process does not end with the public school system. As young people leave school, they follow various paths into other institutional settings. Some, of course, are already married or about to be, the effects of residential propinquity and the school system's structure probably having been the major factors in delimiting their choice. Most, however, move on to higher education or the world of work before getting married.

Whichever direction they go, sorting continues to occur. Personnel directors and admissions officers act as gatekeepers limiting access to these settings. In that way they also act as marriage brokers.[12] Furthermore, the organizations into which these young people move also affect their marriage prospects through various internal structures such as coeducational dormitories, required courses, and spatial separation of factory and office functions. The individuals in such subunits as work groups, dormitories, fraternities, and so on tend to have more continued and intense association with each other than with outsiders. There is likely to develop a degree of group identity and cohesion in such subunits, as well as invidious intergroup definitions.

The literature on dating and rating patterns on college campuses has suggested that group affiliations are important in that setting, but as far as I know, no one has investigated dating patterns within a factory or a large corporate office complex. It seems likely, however, that the structure of the work situation will not only limit the possibility of meaningful contacts to a subset of persons potentially eligible, but it may also serve to define persons in some other subunits as less desirable.

Such sorting of young people both reflects and reinforces differences in values and norms in the larger society. It reflects these to the extent that those individuals

---

[11]Of course, this segregation is much greater in some cases than in others, placing students in different buildings rather than just different classrooms in the same building. In both cases though, the effect is probably the same.

[12]In fact, it has been claimed by at least one student of mate selection (Bell, 1962) that most female college students view their college experience as largely a pathway to marriage, rather than as an educational experience as such. To that extent, one needs to view the choice of a college as a student's decision to delimit her field of availables, and the admissions process determines if her preferred delimitation will actually occur.

who do the sorting (both the participants themselves and the gatekeepers) do so on the basis of criteria of appropriateness for the kinds of experiences found in the several settings. Youngsters who have not been academically adept in high school neither want, nor are permitted, to attend college. Those who object to orderliness and cleanliness neither want, nor are permitted, to work in an insurance office. The official activities in such settings reflect not only a particular task orientation, but also a whole set of values and definitions of the proper way for people to interact. One doesn't expect interpersonal relations of any kind to be quite the same in the factory and in the front office, and that applies to male–female relations, as well as to other relationships. It is not necessary to solve the chicken and egg problem of whether such differences are due to the selection process or to the dynamics of the setting itself to recognize that social relations between men and women vary widely in different settings. What is viewed as attractive in the opposite sex thus also varies, and the patterns of mate selection occurring in such settings cannot be expected to be the same. Both selection and experience in the setting operate to establish highly varied fields of available spouses for different groups of young men and women.

VII. Conclusion

The basic point of this discussion is that if one is going to understand the process of mate selection one needs to take into account more than the personal characteristics of the two people involved. The larger social setting is significant both because of its delimitation of contacts with prospective spouse-candidates and because of its varied definitions of what is desirable in a spouse. Although some society-wide definitions of a proper pairing are found (and may rightly be viewed as rules of endogamy), there is also considerable subsocietal differentiation in the sorting process and in the criteria of selection. "Attraction" in mate selection is the appeal of the other as a partner in a particular *kind* of social relationship, and the definition of this relationship is not uniform throughout the society. Thus, the criteria of selection cannot be the same, and different characteristics will be predictive of attraction between prospective spouse candidates in different parts of the society.

The great majority of studies of mate selection are based on very limited samples and thus reflect the process in only a very special segment of the population. Value consensus, personality fit, and so on may well be important in mate selection where the expected marital pattern is interactional. But there is no reason to believe that these same factors should affect the choice of a spouse in the same way when the expected marital pattern is parallel. Similarly, it is clearly the case that different subpopulations experience different kinds and degrees of restriction on their fields of availables. Residential propinquity does not help much to explain the selection process among college students, although it is highly significant in the case of urban blacks living in the ghetto (Kerckhoff, 1956). Thus, these two parts of what passes for a "theory of mate selection" actually seem most relevant to rather different portions of the population. What is needed is a more informed understanding of the flow of people through social structures and of the varied definitions of the marital relationship in different subpopulations. Without that understanding, the patterns of interpersonal attraction leading to marriage cannot adequately be explained.

Although this chapter is limited to a discussion of such wider social factors in the process of mate selection, I would also suggest that a similar approach is appropriate to an analysis of interpersonal attraction of any kind. I suspect that it could be shown more generally that the kind of relationship (and the particular definition of that relationship) is a highly significant variable in the attraction process. What determines whether a woman is viewed as attractive by a man will depend on whether he is considering marrying her, buying her sexual favors, working with her (or for her), asking her for help on a math problem, or whatever. The sociometric literature has acknowledged such differences ("With whom would you like to serve on a committee?" "With whom would you like to be friends?"), but such differentiation has seldom been carried over to the interpersonal attraction literature. Equally important for an understanding of interpersonal attraction in any situation is the fact that the particular relationship involved may be defined in quite different ways by different groups. And finally, since attraction can occur only between persons who know each other, it is essential to consider which factors limit contact and which limit the degree to which a person is defined as available even if contacted.

References

Bell, R. R. Some factors related to coed marital aspirations. *Family Life Coordinator*, 1962, **11**, 91—94.

Bell, R. R. *Premarital sex in a changing society*. Englewood Cliffs, New Jersey: Prentice-Hall, 1966.

Bernard, J. The adjustments of married mates. In H. T. Christensen (Ed.), *Handbook of marriage and the family*. Chicago, Illinois: Rand McNally, 1964. Pp. 675—739.

Blood, R. O. A retest of Waller's rating complex. *Marriage and Family Living*, 1955, **17**, 41—47 .

Blood, R. O. Uniformities and diversities in campus dating preferences. *Marriage and Family Living*, 1956, **18**, 37—45.

Bowerman, C. E. Age relationships at marriage, by marital status and age at marriage. *Marriage and Family Living*, 1956, **18**, 231—233.

Broderick, C. B. Social heterosexual development among urban Negroes and whites. *Journal of Marriage and the Family*, 1965, **27**, 200—203.

Bumpass, L. The trend of interfaith marriage in the United States. *Social Biology*, 1970, **3**, 253—259.

Burchinal, L. G. Membership groups and attitudes toward cross-religious dating and marriage. *Marriage and Family Living*, 1960, **22**, 248—253.

Burchinal, L. G., & Chancellor, L. E. Ages at marriage, occupations of grooms and interreligious marriage rates. *Social Forces*, 1962, **40**, 348—354.   (a)

Burchinal, L. G., & Chancellor, L. E. Factors related to interreligious marriages in Iowa, 1953—1957. *Iowa Agriculture and Home Economics Experiment Station Research Bulletin*, No. 510, 1962.   (b)

Burchinal, L. G., & Chancellor, L. E. Proportions of Catholics, urbanism and mixed-Catholic marriage rates among Iowa counties. *Social Problems*, 1962, **9**, 359—365.   (c)

Burma, J. H. Interethnic marriage in Los Angeles, 1948—1959. *Social Forces*, 1963, **42**, 156—165.

Burr, W. R. An expansion and test of a role theory of marital satisfaction. *Journal of Marriage and the Family*, 1971, **33**, 368—372.

Catton, W. R., & Smircich, R. J. A comparison of mathematical models for the effect of resident propinquity on mate selection. *American Sociological Review*, 1964, **29**, 522—529.

Centers, R. Marital selection and occupational strata. *American Journal of Sociology*, 1949, **54**, 530—535.

Coombs, R. H. Reinforcement of values in the parental home as a factor in mate selection. *Marriage and Family Living*, 1962, **24**, 155—157.

Dentler, R. A., & Hutchinson, J. G. Socio-economic versus family membership status as sources of family attitude consensus. *Child Development*, 1961, **32**, 249—254.

Dinitz, S., Banks, F., & Pasamanick, B. Mate selection and social class: changes during the past quarter century. *Marriage and Family Living*, 1960, **22**, 348—351.

Duncan, O. D., & Duncan, B. Residential distribution and occupational stratification. *American Journal of Sociology*, 1960, **60**, 493—503.

Dyer, W. G. Analyzing marital adjustment using role theory. *Journal of Marriage and the Family*, 1962, **24**, 371—375.

Elder, G. E. Appearance and education in marriage mobility. *American Sociological Review*, 1969, **34**, 519—533.

Freeman, L. Homogamy in interethnic mate selection. *Sociology and Social Research*, 1955, **39**, 369—377.

Glick, P. C. *American families*. New York: Wiley, 1957.

Glick, P. C. Intermarriage and fertility patterns among persons in major religious groups. *Eugenics Quarterly*, 1960, **7**, 31—38.

Golden, J. Characteristics of the Negro-white intermarried in Philadelphia. *American Sociological Review*, 1953, **18**, 177—183.

Golden, J. Patterns of Negro—white intermarriage. *American Sociological Review*, 1954, **19**, 144—147.

Heiss, J. S. Premarital characteristics of the religiously intermarried in an urban area. *American Sociological Review*, 1960, **25**, 47—55.

Hill, R. Campus norms in mate selection. *Journal of Home Economics*, 1945, **37**, 554—558.

Hobart, C. W. Attitude changes during courtship and marriage. *Marriage and Family Living*, 1960, **22**, 352—359.

Hollingshead, A. B. Age relationships and marriage. *American Sociological Review*, 1951, **16**, 492—499.

Hyman, H. The value systems of different classes: A social psychological contribution to the analysis of stratification. In R. Bendix & S. M. Lipset (Eds.), *Class, status and power*. Glencoe, Illinois: Free Press, 1953. Pp. 426—442.

Katz, A. M., & Hill, R. Residential propinquity and marital selection: A review of theory, method and fact. *Marriage and Family Living*, 1958, **20**, 27—35.

Kerckhoff, A. C. Notes and comments on the meaning of residential propinquity as a factor in mate selection. *Social Forces*, 1956, **34**, 207—213.

Kerckhoff, A. C. Patterns of homogamy and the field of eligibles. *Social Forces*, 1964, **42**, 289—297.

Kerckhoff, A. C. Status-related value patterns among married couples. *Journal of Marriage and the Family*, 1972, **34**, 105—110.

Kerckhoff, A. C. & Bean, F. Social status and interpersonal patterns among married couples. *Social Forces*, 1970, **49**, 264—271.

Kohn, M. L. *Class and conformity: A study in values*. Homewood, Illinois: Dorsey, 1969.

Leslie, G. R., & Richardson, A. H. Family versus campus influences in relation to mate selection. *Social Problems*, 1956, **4**, 117—121.

Lieberson, S. *Ethnic patterns in American cities*. New York: Free Press, 1963.

Lowrie, S. H. Early and late dating: Some conditions associated with them. *Marriage and Family Living*. 1961, **23**, 284—291.

Mangus, A. R. Role theory and marriage counseling. *Social Forces*, 1957, **35**, 200—209.

Murstein, B. I. Empirical tests of role, complementary need, and homogamy theories of marital choice. *Journal of Marriage and the Family*, 1967, **29**, 689—696.

Ramsøy, N. R. Assortative mating and the structure of cities. *American Sociological Review*, 1966, **31**, 773–786.

Reiss, I. L. Social class and campus dating. *Social Problems*, 1965, **13**, 193–205.

Rogers, E. M., & Havens, A. E. Prestige rating and mate selection on a college campus. *Marriage and Family Living*, 1960, **22**, 55–59.

Rubin, Z. Do American women marry up? *American Sociological Review*, 1968, **33**, 750–760.

Schmitt, R. C. Recent trends in Hawaiian interracial marriage rates by occupation. *Journal of Marriage and the Family*, 1971, **33**, 373–374.

Smith, E., & Monane, J. H. G. Courtship values in a youth sample. *American Sociological Review*, 1953, **18**, 635–640.

Smith, W. M., Jr. Rating and dating: A restudy. *Marriage and Family Living*, 1952, **14**, 312–317.

Sundal, A. P., & McCormick, T. C. Age at marriage and mate selection, Madison, Wisconsin, 1937–1943. *American Sociological Review*, 1951, **16**, 37–48.

Taeuber, K., and Taeuber, A. *Negroes in cities*. Chicago, Illinois: Aldine, 1965.

Trost, J. Some data on mate-selection: Homogamy and perceived homogamy. *Journal of Marriage and the Family*, 1967, **29**, 739–755.

Waller, W. The rating and dating complex. *American Sociological Review*, 1937, **2**, 727–734.

Warren, B. L. A multiple variable approach to the assortative mating phenomenon. *Eugenics Quarterly*, 1966, **13**, 285–290.

Winch, R. F. *Mate-selection: A study of complementary needs*. New York: Harper, 1958.

4

Cross-Cultural Perspective on Attraction

PAUL C. ROSENBLATT

Department of Family Social Science
University of Minnesota
St. Paul, Minnesota

I. Introduction

Cross-cultural research illuminates many different areas in the study of interpersonal attraction. Ideally, cross-cultural research of relevance would be cited in each chapter of this volume, and there would be little need for a separate cross-cultural chapter. But cross-cultural research is not well integrated into the mainstream of attraction research. This weak integration is unfortunate, because for many of us the goal of the social sciences is to illuminate and explain panhuman phenomena. The curse of *the* cross-cultural chapter in a volume devoted to a multifocused topic such as attraction is that it must either be multifocused and noncohesive or it must be monofocused and exclude much material of value. This chapter represents a choice of the former route—multiple foci and weak cohesion.

The social psychology and sociology of interpersonal attraction commonly taught in the United States may be merely an ethnographic description of one nonrepresentative human culture, the United States white middle class, ages 17–23, who have never been married. Even the great interest of Americans in attraction may be deviant from most cultures. A cross-cultural perspective on attraction can give us a better sense of what has been happening to us in this culture, a better sense of what is basically human, and a feeling for the ethnographic element in many of the research findings and theories dealing with attraction in the United States. Knowledge of our own society alone might leave us blind to many aspects of interpersonal attraction.

This chapter deals with attraction in relatively homogeneous, non-Euro-American cultures (for example, those of Navajo Indians, Burmese peasants, Eskimos of the Northwest Territory of Canada). Cultures are not the same as countries. Countries are usually too complex to characterize neatly. Where it is possible, the chapter deals with studies comparing many cultures, rather than comparisons of two cultures, or case studies of individual cultures. There are myriad explanations of a difference between two cultures, and inference about humanity is even more indeterminate from a single case (Campbell, 1961). However, where case studies are intriguing and large-sample cross-cultural studies are absent, cases are cited. Cases can be of heuristic value, though of much less epistemological strength than large-sample comparative studies.

Research techniques of the sort discussed elsewhere in this volume have rarely been applied in societies very different from our own. In Europe, Japan, Australia, Israel, and various nodes of urban civilization, questionnaire and laboratory techniques have been used. But in most areas of the world, questionnaire and laboratory techniques are rarely used, and even where they are used, the research priority of attraction processes is very low. Hence, most of the data on interpersonal attraction in non-Western and nonurban societies come from ethnographic accounts, written largely by professional anthropologists, literate natives, missionaries, and colonial officials.

Most of these accounts appear in works focused on phenomena other than attraction. Moreover, the aspects of attraction that are described often differ from what is dealt with elsewhere in this book—in particular, deemphasizing psychological processes. Most of these ethnographic studies are based on an epistemology that substitutes redundancy of informal measurement, consistency among many informal measures, and global intuition for the precision typical of sociological and social psychological research. Although the power of quantification, precision, and control is enormous, ethnographic research methods have strengths lacking in the standard research approaches to interpersonal attraction. Ethnographic research may pick up details of processes, penetrate deeply into potentially embarrassing areas, more sharply separate verbal report from other behavior, respond more flexibly to individual differences in respondent thinking and behaving, and identify more clearly social context influences on the course of a relationship. The usefulness of such an approach in dealing with attraction in American culture may be great.

Marriage in some form seems universal in human cultures (Murdock, 1949, Chapter 1), a fact that may say something about the value of legitimate paternity, of relationship stability, or of the linkage of groups through a sexual relationship. There are much more cross-cultural data on marriage than on other types of relationships where attraction could be relevant. Consequently, this chapter focuses on phenomena relevant to marriage. Moreover, by emphasizing *attraction* in male–female relations relevant to marriage, we will be ignoring most of a vast anthropological literature on political, economic, and other nonpsychological factors in relation to marriage.

II. Attraction and Freedom of Choice of Spouse

For many peoples in the world, first marriage preceded by strong attraction is undesirable and uncommon, especially for young women. Across cultures there seems to be a reciprocal relation between the domination of family authorities in mate selection and the extent to which attraction operates in mate selection. In support of this, Rosenblatt and Cozby (1972) found in a study of 59 societies that there were strong correlations between freedom of choice of spouse in first marriages and (*a*) impractical grounds of choice of spouse, (*b*) importance of sex as a source of attraction premaritally, and (*c*) the operation of feelings of love and affection premaritally. Although it is possible to make up a story about human beings that would plausibly tell how attraction is important no matter what degree of freedom of choice people have in marrying, attraction at first marriage is in fact much more important in societies such as our own, with substantial freedom of choice.

Attraction is actively suppressed in societies with minimal freedom of choice. By discouraging attraction, the economic, political, and other interests served by marriage-arranging are enhanced. In suppressing attraction, family authorities segregate the sexes, socialize children to accept the arrangement system, restrict and punish premarital sex severely, and, in some societies, arrange marriages relatively early in the sexual career of their dependents (Goode, 1959). It is interesting to think of these restrictive customs as representing a folk belief that interaction produces attraction, a belief that receives general support in behavioral science research (Lott & Lott, 1965). There may be other insights into attraction processes to be found in the folk assumptions underlying customs restricting or encouraging attraction processes.

Attraction processes may be actively promoted through socializing children to accept and value attraction and by providing opportunities for attraction to operate. However, the encouragement of attraction does not seem nearly as difficult as its discouragement. By allowing or encouraging attraction where freedom is not minimal, many things of worth may be accomplished. First, attraction contributes to commitment. For people in societies with large amounts of freedom of choice of spouse, there are alternatives to choose from, including perhaps the alternative of not marrying or not marrying now. With a choice to be made, a decision must be well justified (see Greenfield, 1965). Attraction can provide some or all of this justification.

Attraction can serve many other functions. Rainwater (1971) has observed that in four "cultures of poverty," young women use falling in love as a means of escaping the parental home and entering the available respectable role, that of married woman. Perhaps it is no accident that love occurs, rather than mere choice of leaving home to marry someone. Love provides a great deal more momentum toward breaking whatever ties hold a person back (see Parsons, 1943), and toward overcoming whatever ambivalence a person may have in thinking about the possible unpleasant aspects of marriage.

Love has also been found to be more important as a basis of marriage where economic dependence between spouses is weak. The cross-cultural documentation comes from a study of marital residence and a study of the degree of balance in food-getting activities between men and women. In the marital residence study (Rosenblatt, 1967), it was found that in societies where young couples live with kin, romantic love is more important as a basis of marriage. One interpretation of that finding is that love or some other tie is needed in such a society to compensate for the economic support the kinsmen provide; in other words, coresident kinsmen provide so much labor and other services that something like romantic love is needed to bind couples together.

In the other cross-cultural study in this area, Coppinger and Rosenblatt (1968) reported that romantic love is more important the more imbalanced are the typical levels of food production of men and women in a society. Where food is disproportionately obtained from the activities of one sex, couples are held together less by mutual economic dependence. In order to maintain relationships some other bond is needed. Romantic love seems to be that bond in these societies. Assuming that further study confirms that love is used as a functional substitute for other bonds, we may guess about American society that the average level of love is high in part because for most Americans there is little economic reason for marrying. Furthermore, we would expect that individual differences in the importance of romantic love in the United States would be related to the existence of other bonds holding a couple together, including their mutual economic dependence, pressures from relatives, and ties to children.

An additional interpretation of the marital residence study is that love becomes customary where it is needed to protect marriages from kin intrusion. Applying this to the United States would suggest that perhaps here, too, love is more important where kin are more intrusive through visiting and telephoning and through making demands that intrude in the relationship. However, love is not a simple cure-all. Cozby and Rosenblatt (1971) and Gluckman (1955, Chapter 3) have pointed out that love can create tensions with kin through threatening the relationship between parents and their married offspring. Parents, for example, may be jealous of the love involvement of a married child. An adaptation to this problem is the use of residential privacy. Cozby and Rosenblatt (1971) have provided documentation for this in that the importance of romantic love is related to privacy of sleeping quarters. Private sleeping quarters hide love involvement from kinsmen, who might otherwise become jealous or threatened.

Attraction undoubtedly serves many other functions, such as providing entertainment, providing the rewards of an escalating exchange relationship, legitimating sexuality where sexuality not based on attraction is disapproved, and providing psychic compensations for deficiencies one sees in oneself. But all these are individual level functions, which are difficult to document with the kinds of ethnographic data available.

III. Cultural Context of Attraction

A. *Attraction within the Rules*

Cross-culturally, heterosexual attraction operates within rules. Some of these rules define categories of persons as acceptable or not acceptable targets for attraction—whom one may marry, who would be preferable to marry, whom one should not marry, and whom one would be better off not marrying. (Chapter 3 in this volume focuses on these rules as they operate in American society.) From society to society, different people fall into these categories, and often the nonmarriageable category is very broad. Even illegal, nonmarital relations typically fall within these boundaries dealing with kinship, ethnicity, and so on. It seems that rule-violating attraction can be inhibited by most people and that kin relationship, ethnicity, and other elements in the rules become factors in reacting to the attractiveness of another (just as physical appearance and personality are). This is easy to see in the area of group endogamy. One's own ethnic and class pattern in dress, speech, social interaction, and the like can easily be learned as the attractive pattern, deviant and different patterns as unattractive or repulsive (Rosenblatt, 1964). It is harder to see in the area of incest rules, but, for whatever it's worth, incest and incestuous feelings of attraction are reported relatively infrequently in the published ethnographic literature.

Both the form of normatively approved behavior and the form of deviance are culturally patterned. Most Americans think only in terms of a few of the myriad alternative possibilities for establishing and functioning within marital and nonmarital sexual relationships. When we are aware of other ways in which attraction could and does operate, these are not nearly so tolerated by us. For example, few Americans would consider an extramarital sexual relationship with someone under the age of 10 or over the age of 90, and few would consider a permanent, intense affair carried out by mail or only during the Christmas holidays of each year. When people step out of bounds they ordinarily step into the boundaries for stepping out of bounds. Nonetheless, the channeling of deviance may break down when the channels are too rigid. Premarital sex with someone in the nonmarriageable category may be more likely, but not more acceptable, if the only individuals available are in that category. Rape may become more common, but not more accepted, where premarital sex is rigidly prohibited and men must marry late (Levine, 1959, discussing a single case, the Gusii of Kenya).

B. Culturally Defined Opportunity Situations

Opportunities for meeting someone who could be attractive are minimized in societies where freedom of choice of spouse is minimal, but opportunities are allowed and often culturally defined where there is substantial freedom of choice. As part of the cultural context of attraction, there are common situations in which people who are going to be attracted to others meet. For Americans, the list would include parties, blind dates, classes, youth groups, singles clubs, recreational gathering places, and so on. In the cross-cultural data, one of the interesting findings is that where freedom of choice of spouse is present, dances are frequently present as a meeting place (Rosenblatt & Cozby, 1972; see Bernot & Blancard, 1953, dealing with a French community).

Why dances and dancing might be important is a matter for speculation. Here are some guesses. Dances may make the familiar more attractive—with people dressing up and showing off agility. The excitement of activity, rhythm, and the anticipation of possible liaisons, as Berscheid and Walster might argue from their reasoning in Chapter 15, and as Rosenblatt and Cozby (1972) have argued, may be mistaken for sexual or romantic excitement. Additionally, dancing may, through a related mechanism, enhance attraction through spread of affect from the elation of the dance. [See Gouaux (1971) for an experimental demonstration of such a spread of affect when the affect comes from a film.]

The usefulness of having dances or market places or parties that are understood by people as opportunity situations seems obvious, though unsupported by data. Relationship-building can be established much faster and with much less anxiety in a situation defined as a relationship-building one, and attendance becomes a means of communicating interest in a relationship.

IV. Interaction in the Building of Attraction

Interaction probably is the most important basis of attraction, but it is not adequately dealt with in the cross-cultural literature. The give and take of subtle and not so subtle rewards and punishments, the way a thing is said or done, how anger is expressed, jockeying for power, how disagreements are negotiated, what is done with hurts, the fate of dependence needs, are among processes that receive poor coverage in the ethnographic literature. There are, however, aspects of interaction about which cross-cultural research says something of value.

A. *Antagonism, Flirting, and Love Magic*

There appear to be some cross-cultural uniformities in flirting behavior. Expressions of antagonism between men and women occur commonly during flirtation and courtship where there is freedom of choice (Rosenblatt & Cozby, 1972). Joking and teasing are an element of such antagonism (Christensen, 1963; Cozby & Rosenblatt, 1972; Sykes, 1966). Such expressions may stem from conflicts, frustrations, and ambiguous definitions of the situation associated with the establishment of a relationship. In addition to being symptomatic of tension, such antagonistic behavior may be of value in attracting attention or in creating arousal states that may contribute to feelings of attraction (Cozby & Rosenblatt, 1972; Rosenblatt & Cozby, 1972).

Early returns on the ethological (behavioral biology) study of facial expressions in flirting also show cross-cultural similarities (Eibl-Eibesfeldt, 1970, pp. 416–20). These involve a pattern of smiling, eyebrow raising, and turning away that seems to represent conflict between approach and withdrawal. It is plausible that flirting behavior is based in part on the same mechanism of ambivalence, apprehension, intrapersonal conflict, and frustration cross-culturally and that it has a similar topography cross-culturally as a consequence. Yet even in our own culture, flirting has not been well studied. In recent research, however, Cozby and Rosenblatt (1972) obtained some questionnaire documentation for the role of teasing, joking, and interpersonal antagonism in flirting in the United States.

Love magic, which at first thought would seem to represent exotic superstition, is ordinarily used to communicate attraction and interest to the object of one's affection (Rosenblatt, 1971). Cross culturally, the use of love magic is associated with anxiety about sex (Minturn, Grosse, & Haider, 1969; Shirley & Romney, 1962; Rosenblatt, 1971). It seems plausible that indirect communication would be used by the most anxious. In some societies, anxious courters use go-betweens. In the United States, flirting seems to serve functions analogous to love magic.

Love magic, go-betweens, and flirting all can deal with anxiety by allowing for an alternative to self-blame if one is rejected, by reducing direct confrontation with the source of anxiety, and by having the potential to be effective. They can also have a positive impact because they communicate liking. There is ample evidence in the attraction literature (see Lott & Lott, 1965) that liking another person tends to increase the liking the other has for one. The indirection may also provide an element of mystery or intrigue that is attractive in itself or that augments attraction by producing emotions that can be mistaken for feelings of attraction. Furthermore, feeling that one is doing something that may work can increase self-confidence in ways that make one more attractive.

B. Use of Sexual Intercourse in Building Attraction

Premarital sex is restricted in societies where family authorities have an interest in influencing mate selection (Goode, 1959). Where there is a social class difference in patterns of such control, poor people seem to control premarital sex less [for example, central Italy (Silverman, 1967); French Canada (Miner, 1939, p. 209); Seychelles (Benedict, 1967); southern Spain (Pitt-Rivers, 1954, p. 109); Rotuma (Howard & Howard, 1964); Polynesia, in general (Danielsson, 1967, p. 835); China, Nuer, and Dobu (Goode, 1959)]. This makes sense if we assume that rich people have more to lose than poor people by a bad marriage. Rich people also may have more resources with which to control premarital sexual activities (Goode, 1959).

Rosenblatt, Fugita, and McDowell (1969) have suggested that in societies where betrothal is customary, whether sexual intercourse with the fiance is more freely permitted or more restricted during betrothal than before is related to wealth, power, and commitment considerations. The wealth and power considerations have to do largely with bridewealth, dowry, and alliances. Where marriage has large financial and alliance implications, sex is more restricted during betrothal than before. In contrast, where marriage has little or no financial or alliance implication, sex is more freely permitted. The explanation offered is that sexual intercourse builds commitment for some couples, but it also risks a break-up. Where stakes are high, it is too risky to allow sexual interaction that might lead to disenchantment. Commitment of the couple being married in these situations may be built on the excitement, enthusiasm, and involvement of people with interests being served by the marriage. Where financial and alliance implications of a marriage are less, as is the case in American society, there is more need for commitment to be built by the couple on an individual basis, and sexual interaction that could develop such commitment is often more freely permitted than before the betrothal.

Another kind of evidence from the cross-cultural literature of the role of sexual intercourse in building attraction comes from data on the difficult to marry. Although there is no formal, well-controlled study of the topic, there are a number of instances where women who are in danger of becoming old maids are allowed more freedom in premarital sex. [Examples come from rural Guatamala (Wagley, 1949, p. 36); the Ilocanos of the Phillipines (Nydegger & Nydegger, 1963, p. 741); the Rotumans of Polynesia (Howard & Howard, 1964, p. 275).] Conceivably, this could mean that older married females are harder to control, but it may be more important that sex increases their marriageability.

Although sexual intercourse seems to be useful in building attraction, it may reduce attraction in some instances. It may, for example, reduce attraction where premarital shared sex is seen as predictive of marital disloyalty (Davenport, 1965, p. 177; Rainwater, 1970, p. 56 and Chapter 11), or where it creates shared guilt that one would rather not be reminded of, or where the responsibility and involvement of a closer relationship is frightening (Rainwater, 1970, Chapter 11), or in cases in which it reveals previously unknown, undesirable factors (Rainwater, 1970, p. 305).

V. Personal Characteristics and Attraction

A. *Physical Characteristics*

Ford and Beach (1951, pp. 85—90) have asserted that physical appearance is important throughout the species in the establishment of sexual partnerships. They point out, however, that standards of physical attractiveness vary widely from culture to culture. If any standards seem to predominate, they are health and feminine plumpness. Plumpness may seem an implausible standard for us, living in a society of diet-conscious women. But in a world where food is often scarce and nutritional and digestive-tract illnesses often epidemic, plumpness is an indication of wealth and health.

Ford and Beach (1951, p. 86) have also reported that feminine beauty standards receive much more explicit consideration than male handsomeness in the societies they studied. For them, it implies that male skills and prowess matter more than physical appearance. I would be inclined to hypothesize, however, that the sex difference in interest in physical attractiveness stems either from the preponderance of male ethnographers or from sex differences in power, decision-making and self-determination. I suspect that feminine beauty is more important where women have little control over whom they marry and little power in the family, and that feminine attractiveness is not noticeably more important than male attractiveness where women have as much say as men about whom they marry and about what goes on in their families.

Cleanliness is also mentioned by Ford and Beach (1951, p. 89) as a commonly desirable trait cross-culturally. My impression is that bathing and cleanliness reach a peak during the courtship period, when people are trying hardest to present themselves as attractive to the opposite sex. This may be true in the United States, as well, and the subject might make an interesting research topic.

Much more research can be done in the area of physical attractiveness. For example, we lack systematic cross-cultural research on the trade-offs between beauty or other impractical characteristics and practical factors such as economic or political gain, though it seems clear enough that those trade-offs occur in the United States (Elder, 1969). Physical appearance, however, may not account for much of the variance in attraction cross culturally. In fact, where marriage alternatives or relationship alternatives are severely limited by local demography and incest regulations or by norms of marriage arrangement, strongly dominating standards of beauty may be maladaptive, disrupting the only possible relationships in some cases, or the most useful relationships in others. In the previously cited paper by Rosenblatt and Cozby (1972), impractical grounds in choice of spouse (largely beauty) correlated .70 (p < .01) with freedom of choice of spouse, which suggests that beauty is important only where people must choose spouses on their own and perhaps where decisions are difficult and not easily justified on more practical grounds.

B. Competence

I believe that the attraction literature underrepresents the importance of competence in attraction—competence economically, in interaction, in rituals, in sex, and in other ways. Although divorce grounds may be poor indicators of the source of marital difficulties, divorce in many societies can be on grounds of economic incompetence, of sexual incompetence, or some other kind of incompetence (Murdock, 1950). It also seems true that economic or domestic competence is a more importance criterion in mate selection where a person is marrying into an extended family, that is, into a group of people with whom she or he will have to cooperate (Rosenblatt & Cozby, 1972; Goode, 1963, p. 376; Stephens, 1963, pp. 197–200). Hence, economic and domestic competence may be less important in the United States than in societies with extended families; there is less pressure from kin for such rationality. It remains unclear what competencies human beings commonly desire in an opposite-sex partner for themselves, or for a dependent, or how they go about assessing such competencies. Perhaps persons are more often presumed to possess economic and domestic competence in societies where adult-level roles are well practiced premaritally. Furthermore, trial marriage and bride-service requirements can be seen in part as competence tests, and these may occur where there tends to be a broader range of variation in economic and domestic competence.

C. Similarity

From a cross-cultural perspective, it is so common that people marry people who speak their language, share their basic beliefs, and practice their customs, that it is hardly an open question whether similarity produces relationships; but this outcome may represent no subtle psychological process. People can relate only to the people they meet, and most people can relate only to people with whom they can communicate. However, there seems to be a substantial amount of social-class and ethnic-group endogamy where people have some choice of spouses. But that may not represent the similarity—attraction mechanisms so thoroughly studied by Donn Byrne and others. Instead, the crucial factors may be (*a*) the learning of ingroup aesthetics and (*b*) the concerns of family members. Rich people may not want poor allies, and neither rich nor poor may want to get into an imbalanced exchange relationship. Economic exchange characterizes relationships between families united by marriage in a number of cultures, and in many of these cultures an imbalanced exchange relationship can prove punishing for both families.

D. Familiarity

Familiarity may be vitally relevant to attraction cross-culturally, but it is hard to say whether it is or how it operates. In many societies, people marry people they know quite well, but in all, they avoid marrying some of the most familiar people, some of their closest kinsmen. Some might argue that maybe they would so marry if they could, if incest were not prohibited. Lindzey (1967, p. 1055) for example, argues that the commonality of the incest taboo indicates that there are widespread impulses to incestuous behavior. However, I question the commonality of the taboo. From many societies we have no report of such a taboo, though in most it seems clear that incestuous behavior is uncommon. Lindzey (1967, p. 1052) has further maintained that prohibition of incest stems from fear of genetic abnormalities, but his data on what people perceive to be the products of incest are not so clearly interpretable. For example, he cites Segner and Collins (1967) on the high rate of deformity of offspring of incestuous unions (in one-third of folk tales involving incest), but in native phenomenology those deformed persons may be considered especially powerful individuals, whose strength stems from the deformity and is to be envied and emulated. Nonetheless, Lindzey's major arguments seem sound; that incest is genetically risky, that incest taboos may get established when people realize this possibility and that incest motivations may be common and strong.

In a set of papers that deserves the attention of persons interested in attraction, Wolf (1966, 1968, 1970) cites quantitative data from Taiwan indicating that child marriages in which a young girl lives in the family of her husband-to-be and grows up with him are less stable in terms of divorce, adultery, and the propensity of husband to visit prostitutes, and are less productive of children. But the women in such "minor" marriages are lower status (coming from poor families and being forced into Cinderella drudgery at an early age), and this may be what makes them less attractive to their husbands. Kirkpatrick (1972) has suggested that the hostility of the women in these marriages, resentful of their childhood treatment as drudges, may be responsible for the marital problems. Alternatively, it may be that couples in such "minor" marriages lack the commitment that stems from the element of personal choice present in "major" marriages. Also, it may be that the semantic equation of "minor" spouse-to-be with opposite sex sibling, peculiar to the language of the Taiwanese group studied, is responsible for the difficult situation.

Conceivably, the area of familiarity is one of the areas for future development of cross-cultural research on attraction. Four research foci seem particularly enticing to me: (a) The behavior of polygynists with old and new wives; (b) Customs to avoid or minimize familiarity effects (for instance, the Muria taboo on marriage with the person who was one's sex partner in the dormitory for unmarried persons—Elwin, 1968, p. 194); (c) Familiarity effects in the choice of extramarital, premarital, or marital partner; and (d) The effect of familiarity on marital relations in societies with low freedom of choice of spouse. To my knowledge, none of these topics has been treated in a systematic cross-cultural study.

VI. Ceremonies and Ritual in Commitment Building

Rituals and ceremonies seem to commit people, and they are common, though not universal, in marital relations. In a random sample of well-described societies, they were judged as occurring in 38 of 44 cases (Rosenblatt & Unangst, in press). In marriage ceremonies not only do the man and woman become committed to each other, but various family members may become committed to something. Most commonly, these family members must lose control over an offspring, accept an in-marrier, accept an alliance with another family, or participate in a series of financial, or work, transactions. Everybody may become committed to somebody's residence change. The commitment process includes publicity and elements of voluntariness, both of which may be present even where ceremonies are absent. Often the couple being married must engage in effortful activity. The activity may consist of elaborate preparation, sexual intercourse in front of witnesses, prolonged boredom, having hairs plucked, not smiling or speaking during ceremonies, fasting, learning a difficult sequence of words or acts, a long-term labor such as brideservice, trials of strength and suffering, hazing, teasing, or other public embarrassment. Sharing these effortful experiences may help to unite bride and groom.

Virginity tests, part of marriage ceremonies in some societies, may be presumed to serve in part to enforce restrictions on premarital sex by providing the threat of sanctions for norm violators. In addition, either virginity tests or virginity may serve a commitment function. Without any previous sexual relations, a woman may feel more attached to her new husband, and the man may feel more loyal to his new wife; this would, of course, be especially so in a society that defined the situation this way. Furthermore, where virginity is important, once a woman has committed herself to lose her virginity, she has committed herself in a clear and presumably irrevocable way. Thus, premarital sexual abstinence may be of service to commitment.

Commitment may also stem from magical, religious, astrological, or divinatory activity. If horoscopes, or the entrails or scapulas of sacrificed animals, say that a marriage will be a good one, people may be committed in ways that will lead them to do things to help to make the marriage a good one. Sagada Igorot (Eggan & Scott, 1965) marriages, for example, are supported by surviving an alert scrutiny of the environment for bad signs during certain ceremonies and certain inter-ceremonial periods. [Similar search for omens occurs among the neighboring Ifugao (Barton, 1969, p. 15).] A marriage that survives these periods of scrutiny (for what may be relatively improbable natural occurrences) can be expected to be one that people will be more committed to. However, in some societies these "superstitious" techniques may, either because of covert bribery of the practitioner or because of practitioner perceptiveness, be devices to break off an undesirable match. Blaming the "objective" indicators would minimize intergroup and intra-group hostilities over the termination of marriage plans.

Ceremonies often provide important commitment elements in societies where freedom of choice of spouse is slight. However, commitment is achieved in a roundabout way in such societies. In such societies, a person's own initial commitment may be unimportant because he is in a coercion situation, which requires little decision justification. Furthermore, the relationship with a spouse typically is less important in societies with low freedom of choice, while relationships with kinsmen and same-sex peers and elders are more important (Stephens, 1963, Chapter 4). Nonetheless, it is hard to imagine that a relationship could survive without commitment by the spouses. It is doubtful that a sexual relationship can persist or can survive the decline and eventual death of the family authorities who coerced it if commitment building and maintaining processes have not been operating.

Token public commitment seems common for persons being married in societies with little freedom of choice. The persons being married commit themselves "voluntarily" to marrying, or to marrying each other. This may be accomplished through a ceremonial act that may be somewhat coerced, but even in these cases there often seems some freedom to back down; enough freedom, in any event, to produce some commitment. Thus, in the study by Rosenblatt and Cozby (1972) only 5 of 34 societies were rated as having *no* freedom on one of the measures of freedom of choice of spouse; and only 2 of 44 societies were rated as having *no* freedom on the other measures. Complete lack of freedom of choice seems rare, and its rarity may well stem from the need for at least token commitment. It would be instructive to investigate those societies in which there seems to be complete lack of freedom of choice. Possibly, most of them are poorly described societies, without adequate description of the subtleties of producing marital commitment.

Perhaps the most significant commitment process in all societies, including our own, occurs in the natural course of living together. The development of habitual patterns that are related to the behavior of one's spouse makes leaving the relationship difficult.

VII. Long-Term Development of a Relationship

A. Adjustment Devices

Premarital sexual liaisons and trial marriage are often seen in the scholarly literature as adjustment devices (see Westermarck, 1921, Chapter 4; Rainwater, 1970, p. 57, for a urban ghetto in the United States; Kanin & Howard, 1958). The role of premarital sex in compatability testing might be seen more clearly if there were systematic research on the regulation of premarital sex in societies where it appears to be freely allowed. It may be that the freedom is only apparent and that most often premarital sex is encouraged only with people who appear to be eligible and potentially interested marriage partners. This seems to be the case, for example, among the Nuer (Evans-Pritchard, 1951, pp. 53–54).

In Section II of this chapter, love and residential privacy were discussed as cultural inventions for promoting adjustment in marital relations. Avoidance of coresident in-laws is another common adjustment mechanism, and it, like love, is associated with privacy (Cozby & Rosenblatt, 1971). The privacy seems to protect the couple from the tensions and inconvenience of in-law avoidance.

Honeymoons occur here and there cross culturally, but seem more often a device for protecting a young woman from the full brunt of married work and mother-in-law supervision than a device for promoting sexual adjustment. These honeymoons may include having a period of lightened or no work, extensive early visiting to the family one has left, or being accompanied to one's new community by a friend or relative.

Much more can be found out about adjustment devices than is now available from cross-cultural research. However, it seems reasonable to assume that the principle cross-cultural adjustment device is the extensive delineation of response patterns contained in well-known, shared conceptions of roles. People come into marriage knowing an enormous amount about the roles of married persons. As long as a couple's role expectations match, their relationship will go relatively smoothly.

B. Seven-Year Itch, Adultery, and Children

One can infer from the cross-cultural literature that single-minded monogamy is not a common human disposition. Polygyny is allowed in far more societies than not, though its incidence may not be high in most places due to demographic (Ford & Beach, 1951, pp. 107–108) or economic factors or Westernization. Polyandry is very rare cross-culturally (Ford & Beach, 1951, p. 109), though this may say more about sex differences in power than about differences in the nature of male and female sexuality.

Extramarital sex in a number of places is allowed at some times with some people (Ford & Beach, 1951, pp. 113–118). However, adultery is not a simple thing to analyze. It may be a functional alternative to other means of dealing with childlessness (Rosenblatt & Hillabrant, 1972). It may be a device for building or maintaining alliances between men who are hunting or trading partners, and it may serve religious and ceremonial purposes. Possibly, however, the religious and ceremonial purposes are excuses for the sexual activity. Adultery may provide an outlet for hostility, as it seems to on Romonum, Truk, in the Pacific (Swartz, 1958), but Trukese aggression in adultery may represent the same dynamics as aggression in flirting.

Children are of more economic value in most other societies than they are in the United States, and in many places parents derive more economic benefit from grown children than in this country. The pressures to have children are often greater than they are here, and fertile spouses seem the most desirable spouses in almost every society in which fertility receives ethnographic discussion (Newton, 1967, p. 191; Westermarck, 1921, pp. 132–135, 144, 160–161).

It seems reasonable to expect that in many societies a childless marriage is less rewarding. It may provide less payoff in terms of such things as economics, alliances, security, status, affection, and entertainment. Hence, if alternative sources of children—adoption, fosterage, taking an additional spouse or a tolerated spouse-surrogate, or adultery—are unavailable or are too costly, marital breakup may be a desirable response. Of course, marital breakup is not without costs. Families may lose brideprice or dowry and fixed costs of marriage-building; alliances may be disrupted. There may be, in addition, psychic costs, obvious enough in American society, though difficult to assess from published descriptions of other societies.

In a society like ours, where children are of limited economic value, marriage stability due to children may be less than in many other societies (see Monahan, 1955; opinions given by a substantial proportion of respondents in Kiefert & Dixon, 1968). What stability there is in American society may be due in part to attachments of affection and loyalty to children and in part to the voluntariness of conception and subsequent strong commitment that is possible for couples who use birth control. Furthermore, in the United States, there seems to be a folk belief, unverified by social science research, that parental divorce damages children. This belief thus may be a deterrent to divorce.

The attachment to children in American society may represent a cross-culturally deviant romanticizing of children and parenthood. This romanticizing may serve as a substitute for the broad range of functions children serve in other societies.

VIII. Conclusion

Looking at attraction from a cross-cultural perspective, we can see that first of all attraction has a cultural context. Attraction processes may be encouraged, tolerated, or suppressed. Where attraction processes occur, they ordinarily operate in the service of varying needs, including societal needs, and they ordinarily operate only within defined channels. Some elements of heterosexual attraction seem to be panhuman. These include ambivalent feelings and indirect communication early in interaction, choice-making, and a tendency for sex, whether bottled up or given free rein, to influence commitment. In addition, it is clear that many exogenous factors influence commitment to a spouse or potential spouse.

The cross-cultural literature on attraction reminds us that many times knowledge follows data availability. Some questions are easier to work on cross culturally, others are easier to work on in the United States, using laboratory or questionnaire methodology. For persons approaching attraction from these different perspectives, there is frustration with persons working from the other perspective for not tackling the "important questions." However, for those who can modify their thinking to work from the alien perspective, there is likely to be a gain in insight into the phenomena they want to view clearly.

References

Barton, R. F. Ifugao Law. *University of California Publications in American Archaeology and Ethnology*, 1919, **15**. (Republished: Berkeley, California: University of California Press, 1969.)

Benedict, B. The equality of the sexes in the Seychelles. In M. Freedman (Ed.), *Social organization: Essays presented to Raymond Firth.* Chicago, Illinois Aldine, 1967. Pp. 43–64.

Bernot, L., & Blanchard, R. *Nouville.* Paris: Institut d'ethnologie, 1953.

Campbell, D. T. The mutual methodological relevance of anthropology and psychology. In F. L. K. Hsu (Ed.), *Psychological anthropology.* Homewood, Illinois: Dorsey, 1961. Pp. 333–352.

Christensen, J. B. Utani: Joking, sexual license and social obligations among the Luguru. *American Anthropologist*, 1963, **65**, 1314–1327.

Coppinger, R. M., & Rosenblatt, P. C. Romantic love and subsistence dependence of spouses. *Southwestern Journal of Anthropology*, 1968, **24**, 310–319.

Cozby, P. C., & Rosenblatt, P. C. Privacy, love, and in-law avoidance. *Proceedings of the American Psychological Association*, 1971, **6**, 277–278.

Cozby, P. C. & Rosenblatt, P. C. Flirting. *Sexual Behavior*, 1972, **2**(10), 10–16.

Danielsson, B. Sex life in Polynesia. In A. Ellis & A. Abarbanel (Eds.), *Encyclopedia of sexual behavior.* (2nd ed.) New York: Hawthorne, 1967. Pp. 832–840.

Davenport, W. Sexual patterns and their regulation in a society of the southwest Pacific. In F. A. Beach (Ed.), *Sex and behavior,* New York: Wiley, 1965, Pp. 164–203.

Eggan, F., & Scott, W. H. Ritual life of the Igorots of Sagada: Courtship and marriage. *Ethnology*, 1965, **4**, 77–111.

Eibl-Eibesfeldt, I. *Ethology: The biology of behavior* (translated by Erich Klinghammer). New York: Holt, 1970.

Elder, G. H., Jr. Appearance and education in marriage mobility. *American Sociological Review*, 1969, **34**, 519–533.

Elwin, V. *The kingdom of the young.* London and New York: Oxford University Press, 1968.

Evans-Pritchard, E. E. *Kinship and marriage among the Nuer.* London and New York: Oxford University Press, 1951.

Ford, C. S., & Beach, F. A. *Patterns of sexual behavior.* New York: Harper, 1951.

Gluckman, M. *Custom and conflict in Africa.* London: Blackwell, 1955.

Goode, W. J. The theoretical importance of love. *American Sociological Review*, 1959, **24**, 38–47.

Goode, W. J. *World revolution and family patterns.* New York: Free Press, 1963.

Gouaux, C. Induced affective states and interpersonal attraction. *Journal of Personality and Social Psychology*, 1971, **20**, 37–43.

Greenfield, S. M. Love and marriage in modern America: A functional analysis. *Sociological Quarterly*, 1965, **6**, 361–377.

Howard, A., & Howard, I. Pre-marital sex and social control among the Rotumans. *American Anthropologist*, 1964, **66**, 266–283.

Kanin, E. J., & Howard, D. H. Postmarital consequences of premarital sex adjustments, *American Sociological Review*, 1958, **23**, 556–562.

Kiefert, R. H., & Dixon, G. I. J. A preliminary study of the childless couple. *Rocky Mountain Social Journal*, 1968, **5**, 119–128.

Kirkpatrick, J. Some unexamined aspects of childhood association and sexual attraction in the Chinese minor marriage. *American Anthropologist*, 1972, **74**, 783–784.

Levine, R. A. Gusii sex offenses: A study in social control. *American Anthropologist*, 1959, **61**, 965–990.

Lindzey, G. Some remarks concerning incest, the incest taboo, and psychoanalytic theory. *American Psychologist*, 1967, **22**, 1051–1059.

Lott, A. J., & Lott, B. E. Group cohesiveness as interpersonal attraction: A review of relationships with antecedent and consequent variables. *Psychological Bulletin*, 1965, **64**, 259–309.

Miner, H. *St. Denis: A French-Canadian parish.* Chicago, Illinois: University of Chicago Press, 1939.

Minturn, L., Grosse, M., & Haider, S. Cultural patterning of sexual beliefs and behavior. *Ethnology*, 1969 **8**, 301–318.

Monahan, T.P. Is childlessness related to family stability? *American Sociological Review*, 1955, **20**, 446–456.

Murdock, G. P. *Social structure*. New York: MacMillan, 1949.

Murdock, G. P. Family stability in non-European cultures. *The Annals of the American Academy of Political and Social Science*, 1950, **22**, 195–201.

Newton, N. Pregnancy, childbirth, and outcome: A review of patterns of culture and future research needs. In S. A. Richardson & A. F. Guttmacher (Eds.), *Childbearing: Its social and psychological aspects*. Baltimore, Maryland: Williams & Wilkins, 1967. Pp. 147–228, 233–244.

Nydegger, W. F., & Nydegger, C. Tarong: An Ilocos barrio in the Philippines. In B. B. Whiting (Ed.), *Six cultures: Studies of child rearing*. New York: Wiley, 1963. Pp. 693–867.

Parsons, T. The kinship system of the contemporary United States. *American Anthropologist*, 1943, **45**, 22–38.

Pitt-Rivers, J. A. *The people of the Sierra*. London: Weidenfeld & Nicholson, 1954.

Rainwater, L. *Behind ghetto walls*. Chicago, Illinois: Aldine, 1970.

Rainwater, L. Marital sexuality in four "cultures of poverty." In D. S. Marshall & R. C. Suggs (Eds.), *Human sexual behavior*. New York: Basic Books, 1971. Pp. 187–205.

Rosenblatt, P. C. Origins and effects of group ethnocentrism and nationalism. *Journal of Conflict Resolution*, 1964, **8**, 131–146.

Rosenblatt, P. C. Marital residence and the functions of romantic love. *Ethnology*, 1967, **6**, 471–480.

Rosenblatt, P. C. Communication in the practice of love magic. *Social Forces*, 1971, **49**, 482–487.

Rosenblatt, P. C., & Cozby, P. C. Courtship patterns associated with freedom of choice of spouse. *Journal of Marriage and the Family*, 1972, **34**, 689–695.

Rosenblatt, P. C., Fugita, S. S., & McDowell, K. V. Wealth transfer and restrictions on sexual relations during betrothal. *Ethnology*, 1969, **8**, 319–328.

Rosenblatt, P. C., & Hillabrant, W. J. Divorce for childlessness and the regulation of adultery. *Journal of Sex Research*, 1972, **8**, 117–127.

Rosenblatt, P. C., & Unangst, D. Marriage ceremonies. *Journal of Comparative Family Studies*, in press.

Segner, L., & Collins, A. Cross-cultural study of incest myths. Unpublished manuscript, University of Texas, 1967. Cited by G. Lindzey, Some remarks concerning incest, the incest taboo, and psychoanalytic theory, *American Psychologist*, 1967, **22**, 1051–1059.

Shirley, R. W., & Romney, A. K. Love magic and socialization anxiety: A cross-cultural study. *American Anthropologist*, 1962, **64**, 1028–1031.

Silverman, S. F. The life crisis as a clue to social functions. *Anthropological Quarterly*, 1967, **40**, 127–138.

Stephens, W. N. *The family in cross-cultural prespective*. New York: Holt, 1963.

Swartz, M. J. Sexuality and aggression on Romunum, Truk. *American Anthropologist*, 1958, **68**, 188–193.

Sykes, A. J. M. Joking relationships in an industrial setting. *American Anthropologist*, 1966, **68**, 188–193.

Wagley, C. The social and religious life of a Guatemalan village. *Memoirs of the American Anthropological Association*, 1949, No. 71.

Westermarck, E. *The history of human marriage*. Vol. 1. (5th ed.) New York: MacMillan, 1921.

Wolf, A. P. Childhood association, sexual attraction, and the incest taboo: A Chinese case. *American Anthropologist*, 1966, **68**, 883–898.

Wolf, A. P. Adopt a daughter-in-law, marry a sister: A Chinese solution to the problem of the incest taboo. *American Anthropologist*, 1968, **70**, 864–874.

Wolf, A. P. Childhood association and sexual attraction: A further test of the Westermarck hypothesis. *American Anthropologist*, 1970, **72**, 503–515.

PART III

Conceptual Frameworks

5

A Three-Level Approach to Attraction: Toward an Understanding of Pair Relatedness

GEORGE LEVINGER

Department of Psychology
University of Massachusetts
Amherst, Massachusetts

> The good life is one inspired by love and guided
> by knowledge. . . . Although both love and know-
> ledge are necessary, love is in a sense more funda-
> mental, since it will lead intelligent people to seek
> knowledge, in order to find out how to benefit those
> whom they love.
>
> BERTRAND RUSSELL (1957, p. 56)*

I. Introduction

Russell's (1957) concept of love moves on a continuum between two contrasting poles: "... on one side, pure delight in contemplation; on the other, pure benevolence [p. 57]." One end of the continuum describes love for inanimate objects, as for a landscape or a sonata. Russell suggested that this type of feeling is stronger in young children than in adults, and among people "apt to view objects in a utilitarian spirit." He further noted that " ... it also plays a large part in our feelings toward human beings, some of whom have charm and some the reverse, when considered simply as objects of aesthetic contemplation [p. 57]."

The other end of Russell's continuum refers to desire for another's welfare, to one's active sympathy. It represents altruism in its fullest sense. Russell (1957) wrote that " ... love at its fullest is an indissoluble combination of the two elements, delight and well-wishing [p. 58]." And he intended his definition to apply to all varieties of loving, including "parental love" and "sex love at its best."

Research on interpersonal attraction has tended to confine itself near the pole of Russell's continuum that considers the target of attraction as an object of contemplation, rather than as another human being who stands in vibrant reciprocity. Modestly perhaps, social psychologists have avoided the investigation of such love, focusing instead on one person's evaluative feelings toward another. There has been little attention to the interpersonal context that affects the meaning of attraction, or how we may conceive of depth in interpersonal relationships. My own recent thinking, however, has been concerned with this contextual issue, and this chapter deals with the problem of trying to understand the dyadic context within which people show their attraction.

Attraction refers in this discussion to the positivity of one person's attitudes toward another (see Levinger & Snoek, 1972, p. 3). Such attitudes may be measured by a variety of procedures. In considering the *context* of attraction attitudes, I am concerned here mainly with the *depth* of the person–other relation and focus on the distinction between the shallow "relation" and the deep "relationship." This distinction corresponds to one recently proposed by Kurth (1970, p. 136) with respect to friendship. She conceives of "friendly relation" as an uncommitted pleasant association deriving from the partners' role-governed interaction; in contrast, she sees "friendship" as an intimate personal relationship involving each individual as a total person. By analogy, *relation* here refers to any degree of person–other interchange, no matter how limited; *relationship* will imply mutual interdependence, marked by some degree of mutual personal involvement.

The chapter first distinguishes among three different "levels" of interpersonal relatedness. These levels, which vary from surface to depth, qualify the meaning, and the determinants and consequences of person–other attraction. My description of each level is illustrated with an example of social–psychological research conducted at that level. In addition, the chapter considers ways of developing indices of pair relatedness. It concludes by examining some implications for "reinforcement" explanations of interpersonal attraction.

II. Levels of Human Relatedness

In your lifetime, you will come into contact with only a small fraction of the world's several billion people. The rest you will never meet. That condition of "no contact" constitutes the zero point for any individual's existing social relations.

Beyond that point, three levels of relations may develop between two persons: (*a*) a unilateral awareness, where one person has some attitude toward the other, without any sense of reciprocation or interaction; (*b*) a bilateral surface contact, where interaction either is fleeting, or is governed primarily by the participants' social roles; or (*c*) a mutual relationship, where two persons respond to each other to some degree as unique individuals. At the third level, the two individuals have some past joint experience and future anticipation.

Figure 1 (adapted from Levinger & Snoek, 1972) depicts these three levels graphically. Note that Level 3 is conceived as a continuum. Its base line is a Level 2 surface contact; its ultimate realization is the total interpenetration of two human beings, as defined by their joint attitudes, joint behavior, and joint property.

The levels of relationship shown in Figure 1 may be considered as a series of potential stages in the development of interpersonal relationships. Let us now examine each of the three general levels of relatedness.

A. Unilateral Awareness (Level 1)

As I write this, I glance outside my window into the dusk and see a stranger walking past. He is silhouetted in the light of a street lamp. His image is that of a college student, a bit on the stocky side, carrying a stack of books. He walks slowly and deliberately up the path, his eyes fixed on the ground ahead of him. I see him as a representative of other students on campus; beyond that impression, I experience little sense of knowing him.

The largest portion of our relations with others consists of such momentary impressions of which the perceived other is not aware. And in social psychology, the bulk of research on person perception or impression formation pertains to subject—target encounters, where limited information is provided about another as a perceptual object. It is not assumed that the subject will ever meet the other whom he evaluates. The subject's view is one of *unilateral awareness* and has little significance for either creating or maintaining a longer association.

At this level of unilateral awareness (Level 1), the other is likely to be seen entirely in terms of his or her external characteristics:

> ... The psychological processes here closely resemble a person's appraisal of other non-human aspects of his environment. The Other tends to be viewed as a combination of attributes, which evoke positive or negative reactions according to how much they either further one's goals or confirm one's own values [Levinger & Snoek, 1972, p. 6].*

---

*Levinger, George, and Snoek, J. Diedrick. *Attraction in relationship: A new look at interpersonal attraction.* (Morristown, N.J.: General Learning Press.) © 1972 General Learning Corporation.

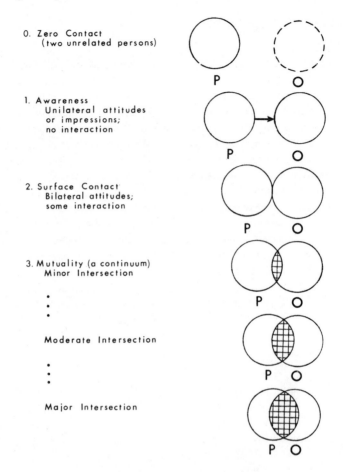

0. Zero Contact
   (two unrelated persons)

1. Awareness
   Unilateral attitudes
   or impressions;
   no interaction

2. Surface Contact
   Bilateral attitudes;
   some interaction

3. Mutuality (a continuum)
   Minor Intersection
   .
   .
   .

   Moderate Intersection
   .
   .
   .

   Major Intersection

Figure 1 Levels of pair relatedness.

ATTRACTION TO A STRANGER: AN ILLUSTRATION

Much attraction research has dealt with the person's perception of a stranger. In the tradition of research on impression formation (see Anderson, 1965; Asch, 1946; Kelley, 1950; Tagiuri, 1969; Woodworth, 1938), the following experimental format has become popular:

A subject comes to the laboratory, having weeks earlier completed a questionnaire about his attitudes toward a variety of interesting items. He is told that the study is investigating" ... the extent to which one person can form valid judgments about another person just by knowing a few of his attitudes [Byrne, 1971, p. 51]." The subject then receives a completed form, containing another subject's responses to the same items he had earlier responded to himself; the subject tries to indicate his best judgment of the other's personal characteristics, including how much he thinks he would like the other.

In this study, one subject receives information about a stranger whose responses to the questionnaire form are identical to his own; another subject in the same experiment finds drastic dissimilarity in the stranger's completed questionnaire. The results are that the first stranger is rated high in attractiveness; the second stranger is rated rather low.

This is a typical finding from experiments conducted during the past decade by Byrne and his collaborators (Byrne, 1971). The finding that attraction to another varies directly with his or her perceived similarity has been extended widely to comparisons among subjects who differ in age, in nationality, or in mental diagnosis; and among stimulus persons who differ in characteristics such as race, status, sex, or physical attractiveness. To explain the effects of similarity on attraction Byrne and others have posited principles linked to reinforcement theory (see Chapters 7 and 12 in this volume). In the terminology of our present framework, the methodological format of their research spotlights one person's unilateral awareness of a noninteracting social object.

B. Surface Contact (Level 2)

A person's reciprocal contacts range from surface into depth, from the trivial meeting to the profound attachment. A surface contact can occur in two ways, either as a transitory first meeting or as a segmental role relation. Transitory meetings take place in cafeterias, at bus stops, at large parties. They also occur in the typical dyadic experiment of the social psychologist. One person meets another and receives limited information about him, while also providing limited information to the other about himself. Within this context, impressions are formed about the other individual and about the self—other relation.

A segmental role relation involves a person's interaction with people whom he meets repeatedly, but with whom he exchanges little more than a token "hello." The bus driver, the building custodian, the colleague in the office down the hall— these are people a teacher may see often, but with whom he or she usually has minimal contact. Each day I show the bus driver my identification card and he glances at it, we nod to each other, and I pass by him. Other surface relations go further. But the actors' words and actions remain governed primarily by their socially defined roles. Interaction at this surface level transmits little information about the unique individuals who enact the roles.

To the extent that actors in surface contact play their roles uniquely, they may transmit information that helps others decide whether or not to go forward in the relationship. If, for example, I were to discover that my bus driver is an avid chess player, the two of us might some day break out of our usual roles and enter into a mutually involving encounter over a chess board. Surface interaction is useful for learning whether the other is a person whom one would like to get to know better, to share more with, or to build a mutual relationship with (see Thibaut & Kelley, 1959, Chapter 5).

SURFACE CONTACTS: A RESEARCH EXAMPLE

The situations social psychologists create for studying pairs experimentally usually involve surface contacts. Two strangers meet, their responses are monitored over a short time period; then conclusions are drawn. Though investigators thus are enabled to devise tightly controlled experiments, the format limits the generality of their conclusions. A variable that is particularly important for affecting attraction in surface meetings will not necessarily have the same impact in deeper relationships.

With respect to the effect of similarity on attraction, for instance, it is easy to manipulate information about a stranger's similarity in a first meeting. But it is quite difficult to study the effects of such similarity in existing relationships. It is simple to illustrate that another's similarity exerts a substantial influence on one's liking for him in a short-term laboratory dyad, but very difficult to demonstrate within a long-term dating or roommate relationship (Levinger, 1972).

As an example of research at Level 2, consider the field study done some years ago at the University of Minnesota (Walster, Aronson, Abrahams, & Rottmann, 1966):

> Incoming freshman girls and boys were invited to take part in a computer dance during Welcome Week. When they registered for the dance, participants in the study were given a variety of psychological tests, their physical attractiveness was rated, and a variety of other measures were obtained. Altogether, 327 couples came to the dance—having been matched merely so that no girl was taller than her male partner. During an intermission, the dates rated their feelings toward each other. What measures or indices would distinguish between those partners who felt strongly attracted versus those who were weakly attracted to their matched date? What test scores would differentiate between compatible and incompatible couples?
>
> Contrary to the investigators' expectations, none of the psychological measures differentiated significantly. Of all the measures obtained before the dance, the only important determinant of liking for the partner was the partner's *physical attractiveness*. This determined how much one liked one's date, how much one wanted to date him or her again, and whether or not the male decided to ask the female to go out again. (However, it did *not* predict the actual frequency of further dates together.)

If these computer dates are considered to be examples of "surface contacts," then it is not surprising that the other's physical appearance was the only variable that exerted a significant effect. The pairs typically met at the dance itself and were together for hardly more than 2 hours on a noisy dance floor. Dates, therefore, had little opportunity to react to more than superficial characteristics.

Berscheid and Walster (1972) have reviewed various additional studies showing that good looks elicit favorable attitudes and behavior in a wide variety of interpersonal settings. It remains unclear, however, under what conditions initial impressions of a "beautiful person" are outweighed by subsequent interaction with him or her; or how an "ugly" person may gradually or suddenly become attractive for reasons other than a change in physical appearance. Consider this striking autobiographical excerpt from Nikos Kazantzakis:

> When I was five years old, I was taken to some woman, vaguely a teacher, to learn how to draw *i*'s and kouloúria on the slate. . . . She was a simple peasant type, short and fattish, a little humpbacked, with a wart on the right side of her chin. . . . At first, I wanted nothing to do with her. I liked neither her breath nor her hump. But then, though I don't know how, she began to be transformed little by little before my eyes: The wart disappeared, her back straightened, her flabby body grew slim and beautiful, and finally after a few weeks, she became a slender angel wearing a snow-white tunic and holding an immense bronze trumpet. . . . Angel and Madame Teacher had become one [Kazantzakis, 1965, p. 42].*

This excerpt illustrates how a small boy's valuation of his teacher eventually went beyond her outer appearance, how his feelings were captured by what he saw as her inner worth. His changing feelings are an example of the development of a deeper interpersonal relationship.

C. Mutuality (Level 3)

Some pairs move from role-directed surface contact toward sharing a more personal relationship. The development of a Level 3 pairing implies the expansion of person–other (P–O) interdependence beyond that of a transient encounter, or one based on externally structured roles. The P–O relationship is mutual to the extent that the partners possess shared knowledge of each other, assume responsibility for furthering each other's outcomes, and share private norms for regulating their association. The bond between P's and O's lives—suggested graphically by the size of the P–O intersections in Figure 1—represents the investment of the partners' joint efforts and joint experiences.

Various characteristics of dyadic relationships at Level 3 have been detailed elsewhere (Levinger & Snoek, 1972, pp. 8–11). But two processes must be emphasized here: the first process pertains to interpersonal discovery and disclosure, the second to the investment that the partners have put into their common bond.

---

*© 1965 by Simon and Schuster, reprinted by permission of the publisher.

MUTUAL DISCLOSURE

Strangers tend to communicate about peripheral matters; their discussion is confined to topics such as the weather, their social backgrounds, and to their relatively public attitudes. If a relationship develops further, though, participants will disclose increasingly more about their unique selves and will share emotionally significant attitudes or feelings. Self–other attraction thus has been found to be associated significantly with degree of self-disclosure (Jourard, 1959; Taylor, 1968). And, while routine "friendly relations" are not usually conducive to intimate revelation, "close friendship" seems to require the exchange of intimate information (Kurth, 1970, p. 140).

Another aspect of mutual discovery involves the partners' "shared awareness" (Friedell, 1969). At Level 3, two persons not only know much about one another, but each one further knows what the other knows about him. Still further, each knows that the other knows that he knows it; and so on. In the intimate dyad, then, there is a spiral of shared assumptions.

MUTUAL INVESTMENT

Disclosure is only one important process in the development and maintenance of pair mutuality. A second process refers to behavior coordination and emotional investment (see Thibaut & Kelley, 1959; Levinger, Senn, & Jorgensen, 1970). As two persons get to know each other, they learn how to accommodate to each others' responses and preferences. And, as a relationship unfolds, each partner takes increasing pleasure from the other's satisfaction. The deeper the relationship, the larger is its cargo of joint experiences and shared feelings. As the intersection between two people's lives grows, the distinction between "I" and "you" lessens and merges into a larger "we." An ultimate merging would be characterized by the following quote from the ninth-century Mohammedan mystic. Sari-al-Sakadi: "... perfect love exists between two people only when each addresses the other with the words, 'O myself!' [as quoted in Kazantzakis, 1965, p. 370]."

DETERMINANTS OF ATTRACTION TO A "STEADY PARTNER": RESEARCH AT LEVEL 3

Compared to the many experimental studies at Levels 1 and 2, there are few studies of the determinants of attraction or change in attraction in long-term relationships. There are several reasons for this paucity of research. For one thing, it is not possible to create Level 3 relationships artificially in the way that it is possible to synthesize superficial relations. Furthermore, deep relationships are complex, and it is more difficult to disentangle the causal variables. A brief examination of two field studies will illustrate the complexity of research at Level 3:

Both studies employed the same method. Large samples of college dating couples were approached in the fall of the school year (Time$_1$) and asked to participate in research on "seriously attached couples." In each couple, both partners filled out lengthy questionnaires concerning their personal backgrounds, values, and personality characteristics; they also rated the current relationship with their "steady." Six or seven months later (Time$_2$) the participants responded once more, this time answering questions about possible changes in their relationship during the intervening half year. The central aim was to uncover Time$_1$ differences between couples who "progressed" toward a closer relationship and those who did not "progress" during the succeeding interval.

The first study, done at Duke University by Kerckhoff and Davis (1962), found that high Time$_1$ value agreement facilitated progress primarily among couples with a relatively "short" relationship (one shorter than 18 months). In contrast, complementarity of personal needs facilitated progress mainly by those couples who had been going together for a "long" time.

The second study, done with college couples at state universities in Massachusetts and Colorado, by Levinger *et al.* (1970), failed to replicate the Kerckhoff and Davis findings on the respective contributions of value consensus and need complementarity. In this study, the strongest predictors of relationship progress were the partners' Time$_1$ involvement in their pairing, their own prediction of future progress, and the amount of their past joint activity.

On the basis of their 1962 study, Kerckhoff and Davis proposed a theory of "filtering factors" to explain the determinants of progress in dating relationships. It suggested that

> ... early in a relationship, similarity in backgrounds and interests encourages partners to come to know each other; somewhat later, similarity in attitudes or values becomes salient to the development of a couple's bond; still later, deeper aspects of "need" fit are the most salient determinants of further progress [paraphrased in Levinger *et al.*, 1970, p. 428].

Varying versions of a filter theory have been suggested by other writers. Despite our own failure to replicate Kerckhoff and Davis 1962 findings, I remain impressed by their suggestion that a filter theory will account for changes in the determinants of attraction in pairs who progressively increase their closeness. Nevertheless, our failure to repeat the earlier results underscores problems of conducting generalizable research in this area. The differences between the 1962 and the 1970 findings can be attributed to a variety of causes: historical drift in dating patterns, changes in personal needs or values, differences in geographical or cultural locale, or unidentifiable errors in one or both of the two studies (Levinger *et al.*, 1970, pp. 436—38). In any case, it is obviously difficult to conduct longitudinal studies *in natura*—to choose the strategic variables, to find adequate measures, and to obtain appropriate samples.

Compounding such difficulties is the inadequacy of current definitions of stages or levels of relationship. For example, Kerckhoff and Davis (1962) divided their total sample into two groups of ostensibly differing bond strengths on the basis of how long the partners had been going together. Yet sheer chronological length of a relationship is only a meager index of its depth; in the Levinger *et al.* study, *length* of relationship was not found to be significantly correlated with a couple's degree of involvement. (Below, I discuss other approaches toward defining the depth dimension of dyadic relations.)

A "THIRD DIMENSION" OF PAIR RELATEDNESS

Can we consider the history of a pair's interaction as the third dimension of its relatedness? Can we conceive of the number and variety of its actual and potential joint behavior repertoires as one aspect of the relationship's depth? Viewed this way, contacts that have neither a past nor a future would be considered one- or two-dimensional.

In a unilateral P–O contact (Level 1), P sees only his own possible actions—for example, approach or avoidance—with regard to the passive O whom he evaluates. In a minimal surface contact at Level 2, both actors' behavior repertoires are relevant. If a relationship expands into Level 3, the number and the importance of the dyadic outcome matrices increase. Figure 2 graphically displays the contrast between a single two-actor outcome matrix and the infinitely expansible collection of matrices available to a deeper dyadic relationship.

The matrix at the left of Figure 2 contains only one set of behavior options for each of the two partners. It exemplifies the matrices used by exchange theorists (see, for example, Thibaut & Kelley, 1959) and by game theorists (for example, Rapoport,

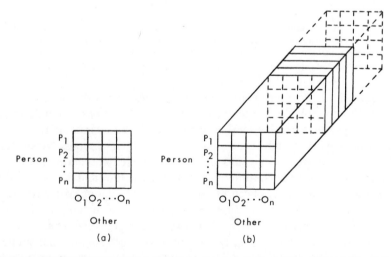

Figure 2. Dyadic outcome matrices shown in two and in three dimensions: (a) Level 2: surface contact (two dimensional); (b) Level 3: deep relationship (three dimensional).

1966). The collection of matrices shown at the right of Figure 2 describes the multiple possibilities that exist in real-world pair relationships, where the inter- actors can relate to each other in situations other than their current one. While a first contact may indeed contain only a single matrix of dyadic outcomes, the continuation of an interrelation entails the increase of the actual and the potential store of dyadic situations. And two pairs whose relationship has equal depth may differ considerably in the distribution of their behavior contingencies.

DYADIC BEHAVIOR CONTINGENCIES OF COUPLES VARYING IN DEGREE OF INTERPERSONAL INVOLVEMENT: PILOT STUDY

A 1972 pilot study by Mack illustrates the potential variety of pair behavior, engaged in by some couples, but not by others. Mack's purpose was to ascertain what behaviors are believed to be associated with different degrees of intimacy in heterosexual couples. To this end, 84 undergraduates at the University of Massachu- setts were asked how likely it is that couples at four different degrees of involvement would engage in each of 52 different joint activities. Mack's four categories of pair involvement were described as follows: (*a*) "casually acquainted"; (*b*) "good friends, but not in love"; (*c*) "couples who are 'romantically attracted' without being fully committed"; and (*d*) "couples who are 'very much in love,' and are entirely com- mitted to continue the relationship."

For each of these four categories of involvement, each judge rated how likely it was that a couple at that depth would engage in each of 13 possible couple be- haviors (see the examples of such behaviors in Table 1). Judges were instructed as follows:

> Estimate how likely it is that such couples will engage in each of the listed behaviors. In other words, considering 100 such couples, how many of them (from 0 through 100) would you expect to do any particular behavior to- gether? We are interested in what you believe to be true, not what you think is socially correct or proper.

Table 1 presents findings for a few of the 52 behaviors rated by Mack's subjects. Some behaviors, such as "smile at each other," were believed likely to be performed by almost all reasonably well-met pairs, and the ratings did not discriminate among different degrees of relatedness. At the opposite extreme, behaviors such as "refuse to date other persons" were believed to indicate a degree of exclusivity appropriate for only the deepest category of pair bonds.

Behaviors shown in Table 1 showed other sorts of discriminability. Holding each other's hands, for example, was seen as unlikely among the casually acquainted and less than typical among mere good friends, but it was perceived as highly and almost equally probable among couples in the two deepest categories. Parallel pat- terns were found for behaviors such as giving back rubs, preparing meals together, and trying to be alone with the other person. In contrast, activities such as staying

TABLE 1

Perceived Probabilities That Each Activity Is in Repertoire of Male–Female College Couples Varying in Interpersonal Involvement

	Type of couple			
Activity	Casually acquainted	Good friends, not in love	Romantically attracted	Much in love, fully committed
Communication:				
smile at each other	89[a]	98	95	98
stay up late and talk	52	78	79	79
confide in each other	26	69	76	94
Physical contact:				
stand close to one another	51	79	90	93
hold hands	18	44	82	93
give "back rubs"	12	36	76	86
Joint actions:				
study together	55	65	74	82
watch TV together	57	82	79	89
go to parties together	29	61	84	93
prepare meals together	21	47	70	85
go camping together	13	43	54	74
live together	10	33	61	88
have sexual intercourse	3	28	61	79
Shared ownership:				
collect items together	36	51	61	75
exchange clothing	20	43	53	75
Exclusive commitment:				
try to be alone with other	13	25	76	85
refuse to date other persons	3	7	29	90

[a]Mean percentage of couples at each degree of involvement estimated "to engage in each of the listed behaviors." (The raters were 84 college students.)

up late to talk together, or confiding in the other, discriminated mainly between the casually acquainted and couples in the later three categories of intimacy.

Mack's study offers a method for ascertaining how various behaviors are perceived to differentiate among varying degrees of relatedness. The results shown in Table 1, however, pertain only to a particular population of judges (that is, University of Massachusetts undergraduates) rating the relations among heterosexual pairs of their peers. Mack's results do not necessarily apply to judges or to judged couples from a different culture or of different ages. For instance, while in United States college circles today it is generally expected that pairs of 19-year-olds who are in love will hold hands, the presence or absence of the same behavior is not necessarily an indicator of whether or not a pair of 49-year-olds is strongly or weakly attached. The meaning of behaviors must always be considered with reference to the situation in which they occur: where, with whom, and why.

A second limitation of Mack's findings is that they merely reflect impressions or stereotypes. They do not describe the actual behavior of differentially related pairs. The following section is concerned with the mapping of actual behavior differences among real couples who vary in relatedness.

III. Behavioral Indices of Relatedness

In this section, I explore the variety of possible indicators of pair involvement. I first consider some examples of relevant empirical research, and then look more systematically at the range of indices available to future investigators.

A. *Illustrations*

SELECTIVE PERCEPTUAL DISTORTION

The typical subject in the perceptual illusion room designed by Adelbert Ames at Princeton University distorts the size of other persons whom he observes moving around the room. This effect is particularly pronounced when the subject has never seen the other person before. When spouses observe their own partner, however, they show a significantly smaller perceptual distortion than when they are looking at strangers (Wittreich, 1952).

MUTUAL EYE GAZING

A pair of subjects—one male, the other female—arrive in the psychological laboratory. Seated across from each other at a table, they discuss a human relations case. Observers in adjoining rooms monitor the couple's eye-gazing behavior. It is found that strongly-in-love pairs focus more upon one another's eyes simultaneously than do weakly-in-love couples (Rubin, 1970).

"PEAK" AND "SCALLOP" EFFECTS

Imagine that a group of subjects sits around a large table, and that subjects around the table follow each other in pronouncing strange words or syllables. Later, when the individual participant is asked to recall the responses of each one who spoke, he is found to have good recall of his own responses ("peak" effect), but to have relatively poor recall of the responses by those nearby subjects who responded 9 sec either before or after he took his own turn ("scallop" effect).

In a memory experiment with dating couples based on this finding, sets of 12 couples participated in the same verbal memory test. Members of each couple were seated directly across the table from each other in the circle of 24 subjects. The dating partners were found to have almost as high a peak and scallop effect for their mate as for themselves. The size of the effect was associated significantly with subjects' degree of involvement in their pairing; strongly involved partners appeared to experience almost as much stage fright for their mate as for themselves. Another, less novel, finding of this study was that pair involvement was strongly correlated with the pairs' mutual touching behavior before and after the memory task (Brenner, 1971).

PAINTING AS A PAIR

Two people are given a large piece of paper and each receives a brush and two colors of acrylic paint. The paper is empty, except for a fold line down the middle. Some pairs paint two separate pictures, respecting each other's territory on the opposite side of the sheet. Other pairs paint a single picture with one unified theme, considering the entire sheet to be pair territory. Some pairs share their paint colors, others do not. Some couples stand very close and/or show much physical touching, others do not. Which of these indices is associated with the partners' self-report of emotional involvement?

In a recent exploratory study of this question, touch and proximity were clearly associated with pair involvement, paint sharing was less so. In this study, contrary to expectation, joint painting was not associated with emotional togetherness; strangers were almost equally likely to paint a unified picture as were intimate couples (DeLamarter & Levinger, 1973).

In each of the preceding experiments, researchers attempted to ascertain empirically the differences between established and ad hoc pairings. In these illustrative studies, certain indices distinguished very clearly—such as touching behavior in the studies of Brenner (1971) and DeLamarter and Levinger (1973). Other indices showed only a barely significant association with depth of relation—such as perceptual distortion (Wittreich, 1952), mutual looking (Rubin, 1970), or using one another's paint colors (DeLamarter & Levinger, 1973).

B. A Framework for Constructing Indices

There are few other published examples of work where investigators constructed measures of pair relatedness. If an investigator wants to study attraction at different levels of involvement, though, it seems necessary to devise an array of indices that describe the strength of a pair bond—the breadth and depth of the interlocking of two persons. The following discussion is a small step in that direction.

If the mutual bonds depicted in Figure 1 were physical bonds, their strength might be tested by attempting to force them asunder and ascertaining the resistance to such force. Interpersonal psychological bonds are also subject to forces that weaken or dissolve them, but respect for the dignity of ongoing relationships prohibits subjecting interpersonal bonds to such experimental stressors. One must look for other sorts of indices of bonding. In devising such indices, it seems sensible to employ principles pertaining to the perception of social units in general.

Campbell (1958) has proposed that collections of human beings are perceived to be "entities" to the extent that their members exhibit proximity, appear similar to one another, and share a common fate. To Campbell's suggestions, one can add other Gestalt theory criteria of a "good figure": for instance, the extent to which the elements of an aggregate reside within a common boundary, and whether their relation is patterned symmetrically and predictably.

The perception of an interpersonal bond, either by outsiders or by the partners themselves, is important for confirming degree of relatedness. If outside observers *believe* that two persons constitute a couple, such observers behave differently toward the couple than if they perceive two separate individuals. If others believe that a certain girl is "attached" to a particular boy, she becomes less likely to receive competing offers of companionship. Recognition of a pairing by outsiders and insiders, then, provides stability both for the outsiders and for the couple itself. Although there are significant exceptions, I would hypothesize that the very perception of a pair's interdependence generally acts to reinforce its continued existence.

TOWARD A FRAMEWORK FOR DEVISING INDICES

In suggesting various indices of relatedness, we can distinguish among *objects* of such indices and among *sources* of indices. The object of a pair index may be the behavior or attitude of either the individual member or of the pair as a unit. The source of a pair index is an observer, whose own relation to the member or pair will vary.

A source may observe the pair from afar or from nearby, but his own relation to pair members will affect the kind of information he can receive. If he were related to the members at Level 1, he would observe them only at a distance; as he might if he were a stranger sitting across the aisle from them in a bus. At Level 2, he would interact with the pair members more directly; as he would, for instance, in the role of a survey interviewer or laboratory experimenter. If he knew the pair members intimately (at Level 3), his observation would proceed, of course, from the vantage point of someone such as a close friend or kin. The observer's relation to the pair members, then, governs the cues available to him.[1]

[1]Scientists agree that the very observation of natural phenomena exerts indeterminable effects on subsequent events. An example of how my own Level 2 relation to one dating couple may have affected that pair is contained in a thank-you note I received from the couple a year after their participation in our research study. The couple wrote that they had gotten married during the following summer; they said they had not realized how well suited they were for each other until they filled out the research questionnaire.

Table 2 lists a variety of indices that we are currently considering in our own research on pair relationships. The list is offered tentatively; few of these measures have actually been tried in empirical work.

OBSERVATION AT LEVEL 1

The indices listed in the top half of Table 2 all refer to "behavioral data." From these overt actions, the observer can make inferences about P—O relatedness.

Assume for instance, that an observer sees one individual gazing at another. Depending on its context, such a gaze may have a variety of meanings. Unreciprocated looking may signify mere curiosity, or interest. In some instances, the target of such a stare may interpret it as a threat that elicits a flight reaction (see Ellsworth, Carlsmith, & Henson, 1972). Yet, though unilateral gazing is little more than a preparatory act, mutually responsive gazing seems to provide consummatory satisfaction, particularly for strongly attached pairs.

Patterns of individual approach and pair proximity can also provide information about relatedness; proximity is both a determinant and a consequence of attraction. So, proximity determines the probability of P—O interaction and, therefore, liking

TABLE 2

Possible Indices of Pair Relatedness

	Object of Index[a]	
Source of data	Individual actor(s)	Pair as actor
Observation at Level 1 (behavioral data)	Gazing at the other	Mutual gazing
	Approach behavior	Pair proximity
	Offering (or asking for) space	Shared space
	Reaching toward other	Mutual touch
	Doing something for other	Doing it together
	Helping or asking help	Mutual helping
	Lending or borrowing	Shared possession
Observation at Level 2 (self-report data)	Knowledge about other	Shared knowledge
	Liking for other	Reciprocated liking
	Love for other	Reciprocated love
	Commitment to relationship	Mutual commitment
	Pronoun usage (*I—you* versus *we*)*	Agreement on various items*
	Perceptual distortion*	Past joint activity*
	Memory distortion*	Future joint goals*

[a]Where two unstarred indices are listed on the same line, the first refers to behavior that can be performed by one person regardless of the other's action; the second index refers to the pair members' *joint* behavior. The starred indices bear no such connection to each other.

(see Festinger, Schachter, & Back, 1950; Homans, 1950). Proximity is also a result of P—O attraction (Byrne, 1971; Sommer, 1969).

Similarly, each of the remaining unilateral or bilateral behaviors listed in Table 2 either has been used, or can be used, to indicate pair relatedness. Approach behavior implies one person's interest in another (though not necessarily positive interest), and it permits the development of a relation; sharing each other's space, however, confirms a marked degree of pair interdependence. Reaching out toward another may be interpreted as a desire to communicate positivity and warmth; mutual touching can be the partners' confirmation of mutual need. Offering or asking for help are signs of showing care for the other, although either an offer or a request may be rejected; mutual helping verifies that both partners care for each other. Borrowing another's property is an admission of at least some degree of colleagueship, as is the willingness to lend one's property's; while shared ownership means that "mine" and "yours" have been merged into "ours." Revealing one's self to the other indicates willingness to be open; reciprocal disclosure not only retains interpersonal symmetry, but also furthers the development and maintenance of a pair bond.

OBSERVATION AT LEVEL 2

Many indications of interpersonal closeness are derived not from what people are observed to *do*, but from what they *say* to the investigator. If we want to ascertain someone's "knowledge of the other," we can discover it only through his report of what he thinks he knows. Similarly, "shared knowledge" (Friedell, 1969) is indicated by matching what two persons say about each other. The same is true for superficial degrees of self-other liking, whether singular or reciprocated; and for deep degrees of love or emotional commitment.

The bottom three lines of Table 2 represent indices that have no direct individual—pair counterparts. The three last indices in the left column refer to an individual's cognitive processes, which are affected by the relation between self and other. For example, the pronouns *I* or *we* are pronounced by only one individual, although P's tendency to use *we* depends on P's relation to O. Perceptual distortions, such as those observed at Princeton University (Wittreich, 1952), are committed by only one perceiver. Memory distortions, such as Brenner's (1971) peak and scallop effects, are observed in the individual pair member, though they can be duplicated in the other.

In contrast, other cognitive indices of pair relatedness necessarily are based on *two* persons' responses; these are indices that derive from the correlation or coordination of both members' behavior. Indices of pair agreement or consensus are one such example; they can be derived only from the responses of two persons. Other examples are measures of two people's joint pair activity or experience, and indices of two people's joint goal interdependence (Levinger *et al.*, 1970).

IV. The Context of Interpersonal Reinforcement

We have considered one serious problem in research on interpersonal attraction—the problem of indexing degrees of pair relatedness in peer relations that may develop gradually and voluntarily, as distinct from pair relations defined by kinship or other societal ascriptions. At Level 3, we have focused on heterosexual relationships, although same-sex pairs can also reach deep levels of intimacy. Another problem for students of attraction is the difficulty of specifying the nature of the rewards or reinforcements that affect interpersonal attraction. This problem is discussed in the next two sections.

A. What Is Reinforcing?

The principle of reinforcement applied to interpersonal attraction suggests that persons will like those others who reward them and dislike those who punish them (see Berscheid & Walster, 1969; Byrne, 1971; Newcomb, 1961). Reinforcers act either directly or indirectly, and lead to either instrumental or consummatory rewards (see Levinger & Snoek, 1972, p. 3). Variables that are susceptible to a "reinforcement" interpretation include: (*a*) conditions that facilitate the formation or maintenance of a P—O relation, such as P—O proximity or familiarity; (*b*) psychological characteristics of O that promise probably P—O harmony, such as O's similarity to P in background, attitude, or value; or (*c*) O's actual response to P, such as his disclosure of compatible feelings, his supportiveness, or his expressed liking for P. Each of these factors may be experienced by P as positive or rewarding.

Nevertheless, it hardly serves to subsume such antecedents under the general label of "reinforcers" unless this approach provides answers to the following basic question: *What* constitutes reward, *when*, and between *whom*? At present, we do not possess systematic knowledge about when actions or attributes of a reinforcing agent will be perceived as rewarding, or when P will react with distaste or indifference. It remains to specify those contexts that determine how O's characteristics affect P's feelings toward O and toward the P—O bond.

A filter theory, such as that suggested by Kerckhoff and Davis (1962) and others, offers a promising approach to the problem of the effects of the level of relationship on the reinforcement process. It is likely that initial determinants of P—O attraction decrease in importance as the relationship develops. Unfortunately filter theories remain largely unsupported by solid data, a condition that allows me to speak only programmatically rather than empirically.

A GENERAL PRINCIPLE

Several statements are derivable from the general principle that *nothing is reinforcing to P unless P perceives the condition*. That is, unless P knows of the existence of some attribute of either O or the P—O relation, it cannot affect P's attraction.

Thus, as P comes to know O better, a wider range of O's attributes and behaviors become reinforcing. According to our levels framework, getting to know O better exposes P to previously unknown attributes of O. And, as previously unperceived determinants enter P's valuation (or devaluation) of O, the relative weight of determinants perceived earlier should decrease.

At the surface of P—O interaction (at Levels 1 or 2), P perceives only O's external characteristics—unless he accepts information about O from third parties (such as a psychological experimenter?). At that level, then, superficial information about O should have the primary reinforcement value. Such information would include O's visible attributes—for example, face and figure, height, and skin color. There may also be cues about O's tendency toward P—O coorientation, including O's background, attitudes, or organizational memberships.

If interaction proceeds beyond the surface, P receives additional cues about O. By this stage, P knows not only about O's promise as an interactor, but also about his fulfilment of promises. Thus, P is now likely to have first-hand information about O's demonstrated abilities, as well as his cooperativeness, friendliness, and O's satisfaction with P—O outcomes. Each of these qualities or feelings can now enter into the relationship and can have reinforcement value.

B. Resource Theory

Concern with identifying "what" is reinforcing under which circumstances has been expressed by a number of investigators. Murstein (1971) for example, has asked attraction researchers to spell out more clearly the conditions under which specified behaviors will serve as rewards or as costs. Weinstein, DeVaughan, and Wiley (1969), after finding themselves unable to predict the outcome of interpersonal exchanges, concluded that current exchange theory is not sufficiently specific for appraising the relative merit of alternative resources. Levinger (1972) has pointed out that the strength of reinforcement theory is simultaneously its weakness; that which explains everything explains nothing. The "laws" of reinforcement and of exchange must be moved toward greater specificity and their elements differentiated.

In attempting to move toward a more sophisticated theory of interpersonal reinforcement, the recent work of Foa (see Foa, 1971; Turner, Foa, & Foa, 1971) and his collaborators would appear particularly useful. Following a series of studies of "resource exchange," these authors proposed a new classification scheme for resources, distinguishing among six broad categories of interpersonal resources. The classes are labeled *money, goods, information, services, status,* and *love.* They cover the major qualities that one person appears to offer to, or receive from, another.

Foa has arranged these six types of resources into a two-dimensional circular order, which distinguishes among such resources in terms of their "particularism" and their "concreteness." *Particularism* refers to "the extent to which the value of a resource is influenced by the particular person who delivers it" [Turner *et al.*, 1971, p. 170]." Love is considered the most particularistic resource, and money the least particularistic, or the least personal, resource. The resources of services and status are considered less particularistic than love, but more particularistic than either goods or information.

Concreteness of a resource refers to its form of expression, ranging from concrete to symbolic. The resources of goods or services, which involve the exchange of tangible products or activities, are regarded as the most concrete. In contrast, status and information, which require verbal or paralinguistic communication, are considered the most symbolic. Love and money are said to occupy an intermediate position in Foa's scheme.

Foa's studies have been more concerned with establishing the theoretical structure of his six resource classes than with specifying empirically who gives what to whom, when, and with what consequences. He has found that the receipt of an interpersonal resource is contingent upon the nature of the resource that was offered; a person is most likely to return a resource in the same class as the one originally given him. A receiver is least likely to reciprocate with resources of the "money" category, and most likely to reciprocate with "love" (Turner *et al.,* 1971).

Foa's studies are relevant to the theme of this chapter. His scheme suggests a linkage between general classes of reinforcers and the present emphasis on levels of pair relatedness. Taken together, the two approaches would imply, for example, that the gift of a highly particularistic resource has the greatest reward value in a strongly personal relationship with the giver; it tends not to be appreciated in an impersonal relationship. Conversely, a deeply personal relationship may be damaged by an offer of an impersonal resource, such as money, in exchange for an extremely personal one, such as love.

A joke about a husband who, after sexual intercourse, absentmindedly leaves a $10 bill on his wife's pillow attests to the inappropriateness of the exchange of money for an act that presumably is love. Would his gift of a $1000 bill have greater reinforcement value? While it might be easier to interpret the larger amount as symbolic of appreciation or benevolence, if it were purely a material repayment for services rendered, it too would probably be regarded as unsatisfying. The growth of love demands personal reciprocation. Love, it appears, is begotten only by love.

V. Summary

This chapter is concerned with the dyadic contexts that affect interpersonal attraction. It outlines a three-level framework for distinguishing among varying depths of pair relations. The description of each level is illustrated by attraction research conducted at that level. It is also suggested that relationships at the deepest level may be conceived in terms of a "third dimension," referring to the diversity of exchanges possible in a developed dyad.

After considering the differences among levels of relatedness conceptually, a new problem becomes focal: How are we to distinguish operationally among degrees of relatedness? The chapter examines various individual and pair behaviors that may constitute evidence of pair relatedness. Examples of indices are presented; it is concluded that a mature treatment of the problem must await additional empirical work.

The last section of the chapter deals with the issue of how to define what will be rewarding or reinforcing in a dyadic relationship. It is suggested that the deeper a relationship between a person and another, the more particularistic are those resources of the other that are likely to exert effective reinforcement. Foa's (1971) recent classification of interpersonal resources seems to offer a useful approach for improving the theoretical perspective on this problem.

This chapter began with a quote from Bertrand Russell, suggesting that love is fundamental to the good life. Russell proposed various definitions of love, ranging on a continuum from contemplative association of a passive other to vibrant interactive involvement—from, shall we say, the beginning to the end of love. Attraction researchers may choose between further mapping the delimited area near the first pole of Russell's continuum and trying to define the uncharted terrain of love "at its fullest." My treatment here has explored a few of the problems confronting those who would choose the latter alternative.

Acknowledgments

Work on which this chapter was based was supported by research grants from the National Institute of Child Health and Human Development and from the National Science Foundation. Much of this chapter was written in the quiet atmosphere of the Institute for Social Research in Oslo, Norway.

For their perceptive comments on an earlier version of this chapter, I am indebted to Ann Levinger, Alice Eagly, Ted Huston, and Ivan Steiner.

Discussions with Sheryl DeLamarter and Richard Mack were helpful in formulating some of the ideas discussed in Section III of the chapter.

References

Anderson, N. H. Adding versus averaging as a stimulus combination rule in impression formation. *Journal of Experimental Psychology*, 1965, **70**, 394–400.

Asch, S. E. Forming impressions of personality, *Journal of Abnormal and Social Psychology*, 1946, **41**, 258–290.

Berscheid, E., & Walster, E. *Interpersonal attraction*. Reading, Massachusetts: Addison-Wesley, 1969.

Berscheid, E., & Walster, E. Beauty and the best. *Psychology Today*, 1972, **5**, 42–46, 74.

Brenner, M. Caring, love, and selective memory. *Proceedings of the Annual Convention of the American Psychological Association*, 1971, **6**, 275–276.

Byrne, D. *The attraction paradigm*. New York: Academic Press, 1971.

Campbell, D. T. Common fate, similarity, and other indices of the status of aggregates of persons as social entities. *Behavioral Science*, 1958, **3**, 14–25.

DeLamarter, S. K., & Levinger, G. Painting in pairs: Exploring measures of pair relatedness. Unpublished technical report, 1973.

Ellsworth, P. C., Carlsmith, J. M., & Henson ~~A. The stare as a stimulus to flight in human subjects.~~ *Journal of Personality and Social Psychology,* ~~1972, 3, 302.~~

Festinger, L., Schachter, S., & Back, K. *Social pressures in informal groups.* New York: ~~Harper, 1950.~~

Foa, U. G. Interpersonal and economic resources. *Science,* 1971, **171,** 345—351.

Friedell, M. F. On the structure of shared awareness. *Behavioral Science,* 1969, **14,** 28—39.

Homans, G. C. *The human group.* New York: Harcourt, 1950.

Jourard, S. M. Self-disclosure and other-cathexis. *Journal of Abnormal and Social Psychology,* 1959, **59,** 428—431.

Kazantzakis, N. *Report to Greco.* New York: Simon & Schuster, 1965.

Kelley, H. H. The warm-cold variable in first impressions of persons. *Journal of Personality,* 1950, **18,** 431—439.

Kerckhoff, A. C., & Davis, K. E. Value consensus and need complementarity in mate selection. *American Sociological Review,* 1962, **27,** 295—303.

Kurth, S. B. Friendship and friendly relations. In G. J. McCall, M. M. McCall, N. K. Denzin, G. D. Suttles, & S. B. Kurth (Eds.), *Social relationships.* Chicago, Illinois: Aldine, 1970.

Levinger, G. Little sand box and big quarry: Comments on Byrne's paradigmatic spade for research on interpersonal attraction. *Representative Research in Social Psychology,* 1972, **3,** 3—19.

Levinger, G., Senn, D. J., & Jorgensen, B. W. Progress toward permanence in courtship: A test of the Kerckhoff—Davis hypotheses. *Sociometry,* 1970, **33,** 427—443.

Levinger, G., & Snoek, J. D. *Attraction in relationship: A new look at interpersonal attraction.* New York: General Learning Press, 1972.

Murstein, B. I. Critique of models of dyadic attraction. In B. I. Murstein (Ed.), *Theories of attraction and love.* New York: Springer Publ., 1971.

Newcomb, T. M. *The acquaintance process.* New York: Holt, 1961.

Rapoport, A. *Two-person game theory.* Ann Arbor, Michigan: University of Michigan Press, 1966.

Rubin. Z. Measurement of romantic love. *Journal of Personality and Social Psychology,* 1970, **16,** 265—273.

Russell, B. What I believe. In *Why I am not a Christian.* New York: Simon & Schuster, 1957.

Sommer, R. *Personal space.* Englewood Cliffs, New Jersey: Prentice-Hall, 1969.

Taguiri, R. Person perception. In G. Lindzey & E. Aronson (Eds.), *Handbook of social psychology.* Vol. 3. Reading, Massachusetts: Addison-Wesley, 1969.

Taylor, D. A. The development of interpersonal relationships: Social penetration processes. *Journal of Social Psychology,* 1968, **75,** 79—90.

Thibaut, J. W., & Kelley, H. H. *The social psychology of groups.* New York: Wiley, 1959.

Turner, J. L., Foa, E. B., & Foa, U. G. Interpersonal reinforcers: Classification, interrelationship, and some differential properties. *Journal of Personality and Social Psychology,* 1971, **19,** 168—180.

Walster, E., Aronson, V., Abrahams, D., & Rottmann, L. Importance of physical attractiveness in dating behavior. *Journal of Personality and Social Psychology,* 1966, **4,** 508—516.

Weinstein, E. A., DeVaughan, W. L., & Wiley, M. G. Obligation and the flow of deference in exchange. *Sociometry,* 1969, **32,** 1—12.

Wittreich, W. J. The Honi Phenomenon: A case of selective perceptual distortion. *Journal of Abnormal and Social Psychology,* 1952, **47,** 705—712.

Woodworth, R. S. *Experimental psychology.* New York: Holt, 1938.

The Communic... ...
of Interpersonal Attitudes:
An Ecological Approach

IRWIN ALTMAN

Department of Psychology
University of Utah
Salt Lake City, Utah

I. Introduction

Indicators of interpersonal attraction at verbal, paraverbal, nonverbal, and environmental levels of behavior are described in this chapter, and a theoretical model that integrates these behavioral indicators is offered herein. A basic theme is that these levels of behavior fit together as a coherent system and that knowledge of their functioning is important to understanding attraction phenomena.

Traditionally, social—psychological research has centered on antecedent or independent variables, rather than on dependent or behavioral variables. That is, research has emphasized manipulation and control of antecedent factors that affect social behavior, but has devoted relatively less attention to complex, multilevel measures of dependent variables. Obviously, there has been concern with behavioral measures, but the typical approach is to select a single or limited number of measurable responses that fit within the constraints of the independent variable structure of a study. Much research begins with independent variable statements, proceeds to development of methodology for manipulating variables, and ends with selection of a single response measure.

There are several implications of this traditional approach. For example, if a single, successful dependent measure is established (that is, if it yields differences among independent variable conditions), then a whole line of research often ensues that continues to use this and few other behavioral measures. Energy is often then expended in testing the generality of indepedent variable conditions, while the generality of dependent measures is often overlooked. One potential consequence is noncomparability of research findings, since different investigators may employ different behavioral measures, or, if a response measure is successful, it may be widely adopted and used to construct a conceptual model that, in its extreme, may be top heavy on the independent variable side and relatively light on the dependent variable side. Finally, relative lack of emphasis on dependent variables can lead to incomplete knowledge about interrelationships among response measures and about "patterns" of behavior. These issues have been highlighted by Campbell and Stanley (1963) and Campbell and Fiske (1959) in discussions of multitrait, multimethod approaches to research, where they call for multiple methods applied to the same phenomenon, and multiple forms of measurement of the same and similar response classes. Webb, Sechrest, Campbell, and Schwartz (1966) were also concerned with this issue, and argued for nonreactive, *multiple* behavioral measures, especially at several levels of functioning. In summary, there has been a recent movement to expand research strategies from *multiindependent variable—singular dependent variable approaches* to include greater emphasis on the impact of independent variables on *multiple and simultaneous behavioral events*.

What would a response, or dependent, variable approach involve? One approach is found in applied research in community, industrial, and military settings, where the goal is to solve a problem, develop a procedure, or design a system. A first step is to focus on criterion variables or behaviors to be produced. Attention is directed to antecedent variables only as they may affect specific behaviors. Thus, the logic of solution involves initial emphasis on *behavioral end products*, for example, a desired performance level or system output, and later concern with independent variables.

Another approach to dependent variable oriented research is reflected in our work on a formal, taxonomic system of small-group variables (McGrath & Altman, 1966). A multidimensional system emphasized behavioral aspects of empirical relationships, with behaviors described in terms of their *object* (member, group, or environment); *Judgmental nature* of data (descriptive versus evaluative); *mode* or dynamic—static quality of behaviors; *source* of data (member, group, or instrument); and *viewpoint* from which the data were collected (subjective versus objective). This system was applied to 250 small-group studies, with a resulting "common language" for describing variables in the field. While useful, the system was primarily descriptive, did not lead to theoretical concepts, and was, essentially, a descriptive taxonomy of behaviors.

In a next stage, we blended dependent and independent variable approaches. In studies of socially isolated groups, we developed measures of various facets of group functioning such as stress and emotional symptomatology (Haythorn, Altman, & Myers, 1966; Taylor, Wheeler, & Altman, 1968); performance (Altman & Haythorn, 1967b; Altman, Taylor, & Wheeler, 1971; Haythorn & Altman, 1967); social interaction (Altman & Haythorn, 1967a; Altman *et al.*, 1971); use of the environment (Altman & Haythorn, 1967a; Altman *et al.*, 1971); personality (Cole, Machir, Altman, & Haythorn, 1967; Taylor, Altman, Wheeler, & Kushner, 1969); and self-disclosure (Altman & Haythorn, 1965). This work emphasized two themes: (*a*) a multilevel dependent variable strategy in which self-reports, performance, use of space, and social activities were studied; (*b*) a longitudinal approach, with tracking of behavior over a 10-day period.

Both themes fit together nicely in the data. For example, unsuccessful and successful groups showed different patterns of behavior over time. Early in isolation, successful group members addressed themselves to establishment of a functional unit and showed higher territorial and synchronous behavior, worked and relaxed as a team, and exhibited an effective, orderly, and paced routine of life. Unsuccessful groups showed a disorganized approach to group formation. While valuable, this multilevel longitudinal approach has several problems. It is expensive and requires extensive manpower, training, and complicated logistics. Furthermore, it demands that the investigator become expert in many areas of measurement—self-report instruments, performance and task measures, observational techniques. Finally, because such studies are massive, the consequences of failure are much greater than those of a typical smaller study.

Next, we attempted to build a "model" of interpersonal behavior specific to the area of interpersonal exchange, which (*a*) incorporated various levels of interpersonal information, (*b*) included a temporal component, and (*c*) attended to relevant independent variables (Altman & Lett, 1970). Several classes of independent variables were used as inputs: physical–physiological and personal characteristics of social actors, interpersonal variables, and properties of the environment. The model hypothesizes that these antecedent factors generated a subjective *situation definition* or set of expectancies, which became translated into overt behaviors at verbal, nonverbal, and environmental levels. The model also included an evaluation and assessment process and feedback loops back to situational expectations and behaviors.

From the initial behavioral taxonomy to the empirical studies on isolated groups, the Altman and Lett (1970) model struggled toward (*a*) a statement of relevant interpersonal behaviors, (*b*) an integration of behaviors into patterns at several levels, and (*c*) an emphasis on social interaction as a temporal process. But this approach, primarily a dependent variable framework, presented only a general strategy, not substantive hypotheses about interpersonal functioning. It did not spell out how behaviors interrelated, only that they did so. It did not indicate specific nonverbal, verbal, or environmental behaviors to study, only that such behaviors need to be considered. In short, the model was a heuristic device and, like most heavily oriented dependent variable approches, tended to be somewhat abstract.

In summary, the traditional independent variable approach typically develops specific, delimited measures of behavior and ties them to a range of antecedent conditions. This approach produces little information about interrelationships among classes of dependent measures. Since there have been few bridges between behavior domains, a somewhat fragmented view of interpersonal relationships has developed. Strict behavior-oriented approaches, which might overcome such difficulties, however, are abstract and do not often lead to integrating theoretical concepts.

II. An Ecological Orientation to Interpersonal Relationships

Understanding interpersonal attraction ideally requires emphasis on *both* antecedent and dependent variables. The remainder of this chapter sets forth a theoretical analysis of interpersonal attraction, including behavioral indicators of attraction. The ideas can be characterized as "ecological," and they are guided by several assumptions implicit in the preceding discussion:

1. *Social processes, including interpersonal attraction, occur at several behavioral levels*: Interpersonal exchange is multichannel, with communication occurring at several levels of behavior. People not only use verbal means to communicate, but they also employ nonverbal and environmentally oriented behaviors. An ecological orientation calls for inclusion of as many of these behaviors as possible in a program of study.

2. *Interpersonal attraction behaviors function as a system*: Various channels of behavior operate as a holistic, integrated set that substitute and complement one another. Therefore, the ideal is to study *patterns* of behavior, rather than single behaviors.

3. *Behavioral processes are dynamic and change over time*: This theme calls for the longitudinal analysis of social process, with interpersonal attraction viewed as a set of time-linked events.

4. *Understanding interpersonal attraction is ideally pursued through a theoretical framework*: To a great extent, the three preceding themes are methodological and dependent variable oriented. Taken to its extreme, a dependent variable approach is empty and abstract, and a theory or conceptual framework is essential to research on interpersonal attraction.

The remainder of this chapter attempts to implement these propositions through the vehicle of a theoretical framework of interpersonal attraction termed "social penetration" theory.

III. A Conceptual Framework of Interpersonal Attraction

The theoretical framework focuses on *social penetration processes*, or what people do, say, think, and feel as they form, nurture, and disengage from relationships (see Altman & Taylor, 1973, for a full statement of the theory). The term "social penetration" refers to overt behaviors and internal, subjective processes, which precede, accompany, and follow interpersonal exchange. Overt behaviors include: verbal behaviors involving information exchange; nonverbal behaviors involving use of the body; and environmentally oriented behaviors such as use of space and objects. Subjective, internal processes include expectations, attribution processes, and evaluative judgments about the other person.

The theory is also directed toward understanding the impact of certain antecedent variables on the growth of interpersonal relationships: (*a*) *personal characteristics of participants*, including biographical, personality, and social characteristics, (*b*) *outcomes of exchange* or interpersonal reward/cost factors, and (*c*) *situational factors* or properties of situations and environments.

One major theme of the theory is that social penetration processes proceed systematically, with interpersonal exchange progressing gradually from superficial, nonintimate areas to increasingly intimate, deeper layers of the personalities of the actors. A second theme is that the rate and level of penetration is a function of interpersonal reward/cost outcomes, distinguished as *immediate* rewards and costs, and *forecast*, or projected, rewards and costs. Mutual exploration will proceed to more intimate areas if actual and projected outcomes are favorable. Thus, some basic hypotheses are: (*a*) the developmental history of an interpersonal relationship is mediated by personal, interpersonal reward—cost, and situational factors; (*b*) relationships show systematic growth from superficial layers of personality to central, intimate ones; (*c*) the developmental history of a social bond is gradual and systematic; and (*d*) interaction occurs at many levels of functioning—verbal, environmental, subjective.

A. A Conception of Personality

Because the framework hypothesizes gradual overlapping of personalities, some assumptions about personality structure are necessary. A relatively simple "onion skin" model was adopted, which views personality as a series of successive layers varying in accessibility to others, and as a systematic organization of "items" within and across layers, analogous to Rokeach's beliefs (Rokeach, 1960, 1968) and Lewin's regions (Lewin, 1935, 1964a, b) (see Figure 1). One dimension of personality is *breadth category*, which refers to broad areas of personality, for example, sex, family. Within each category are specific items; for example, sex might include attitudes about premarital sex, sexual experiences, fears about sex. The number or frequency of items in each broad area is termed *breadth frequency*. According to the model, personality also has a series of layers differing along a *depth* or central—peripheral dimension (Lewin, 1964a, b; Rokeach, 1960, 1968). As one progresses

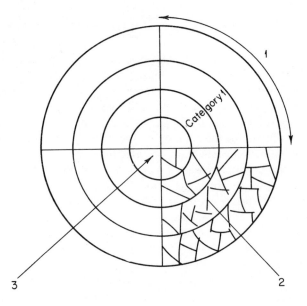

Figure 1 Dimensions of personality: (1) category breadth dimension (areas of personality); (2) breadth frequency dimension (items within categories); (3) depth dimension (peripheral—central).

toward central layers, it is assumed that there are increasingly more integrative characteristics that influence peripheral layers, and that are very fundamental, less accessible to others, and more unique to an individual. In addition to the writings of Rokeach and Lewin, the concept of *depth* of personality also appears in psychoanalytic thinking (Fromm, 1956), clinical theory (Rogers, 1958a, b), and in social—psychological writings (Newcomb, 1959, 1961).

Figure 2 describes four possible social relationships based on depth and breadth frequency dimensions. In Quadrant 1, only superficial layers of personality have

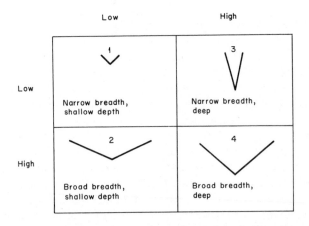

Figure 2 Social relationship profiles based on breadth and depth dimensions of personality.

been made accessible to another person (depth low) and there has not been much expanded exposure (breadth frequency low). This is the prototype of a very casual, shallow, and superficial relationship. Quadrant 2 also involves low accessibility to intimate areas of personality (low depth), but considerable openness at superficial layers (breadth high); for example, a casual relationship where parties know much superficial information about one another, but have had very little intimate exchange. Quadrant 3 could be a "summer romance," "quickie marriage," or an encounter group, where people move very quickly to central, core areas of one another's personalities, but exhibit little expansion, or breadth, of exchange. Quadrant 4 is a broad-gauged relationship, where considerable information exchange has occurred (breadth frequency high), and in intimate areas (depth high). Thus, from a few concepts of personality it is possible to derive prototype social relationships relevant to the attraction process.

The theoretical system also views personality in another, complementary way. The first model focused on Lewin's central—peripheral concept of personality (that is, more influential properties in central areas), whereas here we emphasize Lewin's *inner—outer dimension*, or "distance" from the psychological environment. Personality is conceived of as a series of *behavioral levels*, with innermost layers including needs, values, and feelings that contribute to a self-perception and subjective definition of the situation (Altman & Lett, 1970; Altman, 1973; Goffman, 1959). Behavioral events, then, occur at the "boundary of the skin," where a social image is created through relatively stable, nonverbal behaviors; for example, postures and other props such as clothing. The person also uses the physical environment at this level—interpersonal distance and environmental structuring—by use of objects and areas such as furniture, lighting, seating arrangements. The last layer includes ongoing or shifting verbal behavior, nonverbal behavior, and use of the environment.

B. The Course of Development of Interpersonal Relationships: Changes in Depth and Breadth

Depth of social penetration is hypothesized to increase over time, figuratively represented by the movement of a pin toward the center of the onion skin model of personality. Thus, as relationships develop they gradually move toward more intimate areas of exchange. With respect to *breadth category*, more and more broad areas of personality are made mutually accessible as a relationship grows, that is, pins are inserted into different parts of the onion skin. Finally, both parties engage in greater amounts of behavioral exchange (*breadth frequency*) at all levels of intimacy and in all areas of personality. However, increases in breadth occur first at superficial layers and later at intimate levels, yielding a wedge, or pie-shaped, profile, broad in outer layers and narrow in central areas. Movement on the breadth frequency dimensions is analogous to cutting a gradually increasing wedge in an onion.

C. The Role of Interpersonal Rewards and Costs

Thibaut and Kelley (1959) refer to rewards as pleasures, satisfactions, and gratifications, and to costs as unsatisfactory outcomes. Homans (1950, 1956, 1961) adopts a similar definition; Schutz (1958) focuses on compatibility or mutual satisfaction; Newcomb (1956, 1959, 1961) describes interpersonal rewards in terms of respect, trust, and liking. All these approaches are appropriate to our framework. Following initial contact, persons *evaluate immediate rewards and costs* from the exchange and make *forecasts*, or projections, to potential rewards from future exchange. If evaluations and forecasts are favorable, the relationship should continue to grow; if they are negative, the bond should terminate or proceed slowly. The model also assumes that evaluations and forecasts flow into a "central memory"—a cumulative reservoir of reward/cost experiences, where new outcomes are integrated and compared with prior ones, thereby placing a specific exchange in context. The cycle of reward/cost evaluations, forecasts, and interaction occurs throughout subsequent interactions. To the extent that newly obtained rewards outweigh costs, outcomes confirm forecasts, and the cumulative level of positive outcomes in central memory outweighs cumulative costs, the relationship should continue at the same and at more intimate levels of exchange. Based on these general ideas, a few specific aspects of the social penetration process can now be stated.

1. *Interaction proceeds from superficial to intimate levels of exchange*: Were forward development based solely on *immediate* rewards and costs, interaction might continue only at the same level of intimacy, where outcomes were known. However, *forecasting* rewards and costs propels the relationship to new and potentially more satisfying interactions in intimate areas.

2. *Interactions also continue at the same level of intimacy of exchange*: Developing relationships continuously widen (breadth) and deepen (depth). Thus, they proceed to more intimate levels of exchange and also expand at prior levels, yielding a blend of interaction in new, unexplored areas and in established domains.

3. *Ease of interaction within an area is affected by reward—cost experiences*: interactions should occur readily in any part of an area of personality previously exposed. Thus, a husband and wife often move easily from mundane to intimate subject matters once areas have been opened up. However, increased permeability is probably greater for positive experiences; negative areas may become impermeable and sealed off, with an "agreement to disagree."

4. *Interaction moves forward gradually and systematically*: Growth is hypothesized to be gradual and orderly, because reward/cost outcomes are more certain for adjacent areas of intimacy than for distant ones. Thus, people should move slowly from peripheral to intimate areas. Furthermore, the magnitude of rewards and costs is hypothesized to increase in central areas, producing uncertainty about outcomes. It is expected, therefore, that most people adopt a conservative approach, moving

into areas where outcomes are more predictable. Norms of personal privacy, decorum, and courtship may be cultural mechanisms for pacing and regulating interpersonal exchange. Without such braking mechanisms, social relationships might be unpredictable and volatile.

5. *The rate of development of relationships varies over time and with reward–cost characteristics*: Social penetration processes should show a faster rate of growth during early stages and a slowdown during later stages, because central layers of personality have stronger psychological barriers. Naturally, the pattern of rewards and costs also affects the rate of progress; for instance, if rewards barely outweigh costs, then a slower growth is anticipated than if rewards far outweighed the costs.

A fair amount of research and theory support these ideas. With respect to developmental processes, Lewin (1936) described differences in cultures in terms of superficiality–intimacy of social relationships and also described marital partners as gradually moving from outer to inner regions of their personalities over time. The sociological writings of Simmel (1950) analyzed friendship in terms of a central–peripheral dimension, and the psychoanalytic writings of Fromm (1956) and others have described personality in terms of layers, and suggested close relationships involve overlap of central core properties. The therapy approach of Rogers (1958a, b) pointed to eight stages of successful therapy, with early ones involving resistance to communication and final stages involving richer experiencing of the self and others by means of enhanced communication. Thus, concepts of depth and breadth, movement from the periphery to the core of personality, and associated ideas are prevalent in social–psychological, sociological, psychoanalytic, and clinical writings.

Thibaut and Kelley's (1959) and Homans's (1950, 1956, 1961) reward–cost analyses of social relationships are also compatible with the ideas expressed here. Newcomb's (1959, 1961) analysis of the acquaintance process not only contributed to our notions about the development of interpersonal relationships from superficial to intimate areas, but presumed interpersonal rewards to be intrinsic to growth. Recently, Levinger and Snoek (1972) proposed a three-level framework of social relationships analogous to the depth continuum: simple awareness of the other person, bilateral surface contact, and mutuality. Furthermore, their model incorporates rewards and costs in the form of perceptions of favorable attributes at the first level, outcomes of exchange at the second level, and satisfaction based on unique emotional involvement, interdependencies, and mutualities at the third level. Jourard (1971a, b) has also been concerned with levels of intimacy of interaction and interpersonal rewards and costs. He describes self-disclosure as a mutual unfolding of people to one another and as highly dependent upon favorable outcomes such as liking and reciprocity.

Substantiation also comes from our own research. A longitudinal study of college roommates (Taylor, 1968) demonstrated (*a*) more exchange in superficial versus intimate areas, (*b*) gradual development of social penetration processes over time, with initial exchange primarily at superficial levels, and only gradually increasing exchange in intimate areas, and (c) a negatively accelerated penetration process, with rapid disclosure early in the relationship and a slower rate later on. A second study (Altman & Haythorn, 1965) examined self-disclosure in groups socially isolated for 10 days. Again, there was greater disclosure in nonintimate versus intimate areas, with development of disclosure over time occurring in a systematic fashion. Similar results were obtained in a study by Frankfurt (1965), who content-analyzed written communications. Studies by Colson (1968), Taylor, Altman, and Sorrentino (1969), and Page (1968) confirmed these findings in studies of overt verbal exchange.

Some of this work also investigated the impact of rewards and costs. Frankfurt (1965) simulated developmental stages of interpersonal relationships by means of a series of progressive interaction scenarios, which depicted either a high com-patibility—high reward situation or a low reward relationship with a hypothetical other person. Subjects indicated, in open-ended fashion, what they would be willing to talk about with the other person. Content analysis showed that subjects in high reward conditions disclosed more about themselves, but primarily in intimate top-ical areas. In superficial areas, disclosure was similar for compatible and incom-patible conditions. These results were confirmed and extended by Taylor *et al.* in a study wherein subjects talked over an intercom with a confederate in one of four reward—cost conditions: (a) continuous positive (the confederate was positive throughout a lengthy discussion); (b) later positive (the confederate began by dis-approving and then switched to a positive role); (c) continuous negative (the confederate was consistently disagreeable); and (d) later negative (at first the confederate responded favorably and then became negative). High reward condi-tions resulted in more disclosure than high cost conditions. Later positive con-ditions almost reached the level of disclosure of continuous positive conditions, but never quite did so, suggesting the importance of the cumulative reservoir of rewards and costs. The results also indicated that reward—cost effects on disclosure were greater in intimate areas.

Most empirical work on the social penetration process has emphasized verbal exchange. In accord with the multilevel behavioral approach proposed earlier, research should also weave together different facets of behavior relevant to the at-traction process. The following section considers potential indicators of social penetration at verbal, nonverbal, and environmental levels of behavior.

IV. Behavioral Indicators of Social Penetration

Although verbal, nonverbal, and environmental levels of behavior operate as an integrated set, sometimes substitutively, sometimes complementary, and sometimes mutually amplifying, each is considered separately in this section.

A. Verbal and Paraverbal Behaviors

Work in this area has examined either *substantive* or *structural* aspects of verbal behavior. Systems to categorize *substance* have been developed in the small-group field and in clinical psychology, where the goal was to code content or substance of interaction into categories, such as problem-solving statements, giving opinions, exhibiting dominance, showing friendliness. Another approach oriented toward *Structural* or *formal* properties of verbal output examined paraverbal, paralinguistic, or linguistic features of speech.

1. SUBSTANTIVE ASPECTS OF VERBAL BEHAVIOR

There have not been any broad-gauged analyses of substantive indicators of attraction, although specific measures might be derived from behavioral classification systems or from specific studies of the social penetration process. Much early work relied on questionnaires (Jourard, 1971a, b; Taylor & Altman, 1966a, b), or self-reports of content disclosed to various other persons. Sometimes questionnaire items were scaled for topical intimacy, allowing for measurement of disclosure at different levels of depth. In a few cases, questionnaire items have been adapted for use in experimental studies of face-to-face interaction (Jourard, 1971b; Taylor *et al.*, 1969; Worthy, Gary, & Kahn, 1969).

Beyond questionnaires or face-to-face techniques, there has not been development of general systems for categorizing verbal content directly relevant to the social penetration process. But good possibilities exist for content oriented approaches. During the 1950s a variety of behavior observation systems were developed to code interactions of members of small groups in therapy, discussion, and problem-solving settings. Some of these systems, reviewed by Heyns and Lippitt (1954) and by Weick (1968) could be adapted to analyses of the social penetration process. Some systems have categories relevant to social—emotional exchange, such as giving and receiving affection, supportive and nonsupportive statements, positive and negative verbalizations, hostile and friendly communications. Perhaps because of the open-endedness of substantive approaches and because of the resources necessary to code reliably features of verbal output, relatively more attention has been given to structural aspects of verbalization.

2. STRUCTURAL ASPECTS OF VERBAL BEHAVIOR

There are several reviews of work in this area (Argyle & Kendon, 1967; Duncan, 1969; Mahl & Schulze, 1964; Matarazzo, Wiens, Matarazzo, & Saslow, 1968; Mehrabian, 1971). Mahl and Schulze (1964) proposed a general classification of extralinguistic vocal behavior in terms of (*a*) *language styles*, for example, verb/adjective ratios, parts of speech, verb tense; (*b*) *vocabulary selection and diversity*, for example, types of speech/tokens or number of outputs; (*c*) *pronunciation and dialect*;

(d) *voice dynamics*, for example, quality, rhythm, continuity or pauses, and intrusions; (e) *speech rates*; (f) *temporal phenomena*, for example, speech duration and latency; (g) *verbal output*; (h) *voice quality*, for example, pitch, rate, and loudness; (i) *vocalizations*, for example, characterizers such as yawning and crying.

While there are many studies of structural facets of verbal behavior, only a small proportion have been directed to attraction phenomena. For example, in a study described earlier, Taylor *et al.* (1969) examined the impact of reward/cost factors on the penetration process. Structural measures of disclosure included average speech duration, breadth frequency or number of items talked about, and depth or average intimacy scale value of selected items. In other studies described earlier, Taylor (1968) and Altman and Haythorn (1965) used self-disclosure questionnaires to study the growth of social bonds. Breadth frequency of exchange was based on number of items revealed to others, subdivided according to intimacy level of items.

There have been other studies of paraverbal characteristics that bear on attraction processes. For example, Chapple (1940), Lennard and Bernstein (1960), and Jaffee (1962) found increased similarity between speech lengths of patients and psychotherapists as therapy progressed; that is, paraverbal behavior became more synchronized and mutually attuned over time. Kendon (1967) reported similar behavioral synchrony between husbands and wives. A series of studies also reported synchrony of speech duration and frequency between interviewers and interviewees and between astronauts and ground controllers, suggesting that such structural measures reflect key properties of social relationship (Matarazzo, Hess, & Saslow, 1962; Matarazzo, Holman, & Weins, 1967; Matarazzo, & Weins, 1967; Matarazzo, Weins, Saslow, Dunham, & Voas, 1964; Matarazzo *et al.*, 1968).

Another approach directly relevant to the attraction process distinguishes between *immediacy* and *nonimmediacy* in communications, using a series of verbal and nonverbal dimensions (Mehrabian, 1965, 1967a, b, 1968a, b, c, 1971; Mehrabian & Weiner, 1966; Weiner & Mehrabian, 1968). Immediacy behaviors involve increased sensory stimulation and contact between people, with verbal immediacy reflected in more intense and direct personal references, assumption of direct personal responsibility for feelings, and the use of active, as opposed to passive, speech forms. In several studies, Mehrabian (1967a, b) and Mehrabian and Weiner (1966) found more immediacy in communications about liked people than about disliked people, as well as greater attribution of positive qualities to a communicator who used more immediate forms of expression.

In summary, there are several productive avenues to verbal and paraverbal indicators of attraction. While a base exists for the analysis of substantive features of verbal behavior in small-group observation systems, relatively little direct application has been made to attraction processes. The vast field of structural analysis is also available, and there have been some attempts to use specific measures on attraction-related phenomena. However, aside from the work of Mehrabian and his associates, most of these applications have not been cast within a general strategy of the attraction process.

B. Nonverbal Behaviors

Research on nonverbal communication has increased rapidly in the past several years, although a general theoretical approach has not yet evolved. Hall (1966), Ekman and Friesen (1969), Ekman, Ellsworth, and Friesen (1971), and Argyle and Kendon (1967) have proposed general classifications of nonverbal behavior, aspects of which relate to the social penetration framework.

Hall (1966) related nonverbal behaviors, for example, kinesthetic, postural, physical distance and orientation, thermal, olfactory, and visual cues, to various physical interpersonal distances. At closer distances between interacting people, the head, pelvis, eyes, and trunk can be brought into actual contact, there is exchange of heat and body odors, and ability to see microshifts in eye movements and facial musculature. With increased distance, nonverbal communication plays a less finely tuned, though important, role.

Ekman and Friesen (1969) proposed a classification of nonverbal behaviors based on *origin* (how they became part of behavioral repertoires), *usage*, and *interpersonal significance, or coding*. Five classes of nonverbal behavior were described: (1) emblems, (2) illustrators, (3) affect displays, (4) regulators, and (5) adaptive behaviors. *Emblems* often are substitutes for words, for example, fist-shaking as a hostile communication, sign language of the deaf. *Illustrators* complement verbal statements, for example, sketching a path or direction of thought, pointing to objects. *Affect displays* convey emotions, and *regulators* (head nods, patterns of eye contact, postural shifts) manage and pace interaction. *Adaptors* are remnants of earlier behaviors unique to a person, such as covering the eyes, face, or mouth. Recent work (Ekman, in press; Ekman & Friesen, 1971) has identified some pancultural facial expressions of emotion, for instance, surprise, disgust, happiness. Although this approach does not bear directly on social penetration processes, it has some implications for attraction phenomena. First, with growth of a relationship, there should be enhanced efficiency in communicating and interpreting nonverbal cues. Friends, lovers, husbands, and wives often communicate rapidly with a flick of the eyebrow, a subtle gesture, or a particular glance conveying unique meaning. Second, there should be more use of alternate modes of communication, with emblems and their verbal counterparts becoming more interchangeable, illustrators and their words coming together better, affect displays more readily communicated, and regulators and adaptors more easily understood. Third, with growth, there should be richer and more unique nonverbal displays, with various behaviors having a distinct meaning only to the dyad.

From another perspective, Argyle and Kendon (1967) have described social interaction as a series of performances distinguished in terms of *standing features* and *dynamic features*. Standing features are behaviors that change relatively infrequently during an interaction (physical distance, body orientation, and postures) and set the structure within which dynamic events occur, including movements of the body, changes in facial expression, and eye contact.

Eye contact, for example, has been a heavily researched area. Argyle and Dean

(1965) proposed several interpersonal functions of eye contact, such as seeking information, signaling open channels, and providing feedback. They posited an equilibrium level of eye contact involving approach and avoidance forces and demonstrated that eye contact and interpersonal distance form an integrated behavioral set, such that the closer the distance, the less eye contact, and vice versa (see also Goldberg, Kiesler, & Collins, 1969). In work bearing on social penetration processes, Exline found reduced eye contact when intimate information was disclosed to a stranger (Exline, Gray, & Schuette, 1965), greater trust in a speaker who looked at his audience (Exline & Eldridge, 1967), and more eye contact in cooperative situations by individuals high in need affiliation (Exline, 1963). Argyle, Lalljee, and Cook (1968) also reported feelings of discomfort, low speech synchrony, and more interruptions and pauses when visual contact was low.

Another approach to nonverbal behavior stems from a psychiatric and anthropological tradition (Scheflen, 1964, 1965, 1968; Birdwhistell, 1963, 1970). Scheflen views nonverbal behavior as an integrated set of events, organized in a hierarchical arrangement from discrete molecular units to holistic, integrated patterns. At a molecular level, *points* include specific behaviors such as flexing or extending arms, shifting eye positions, and changing head positions. A sequence of points involving more of the body and gross postural orientations comprises a *position*. *Presentations* encompass the totality of positions, can endure for minutes or hours, and are terminated by a change in location. This approach, which is non quantitative, emphasizes interrelationships among aspects of nonverbal behavior. In a similar, but more detailed, vein, Birdwhistell (1963, 1970) offered a system for describing nonverbal positions and movements.

Mehrabian (Mehrabian, 1968a, b, 1969; Mehrabian & Ferris, 1967; Mehrabian & Williams, 1969) conducted a number of studies which identified various nonverbal behavior *patterns* relevant to attraction phenomena and suggested a systematic relationship to interpersonal attraction of distance, eye contact, body orientation, and body accessibility (openness of arms and legs). The more favorable a relationship, the closer the distance between people, the greater their eye contact, the more smiling they exhibited, and the greater their forward body lean. Mehrabian (1968a, b) also suggested a nonmonotonic relationship of eye contact and attraction, with maximum eye contact for moderately liked persons and less eye contact for extremely liked or disliked persons. However, Rubin (1970), in a process analysis of partner interaction, demonstrated experimentally that people strongly in love (as measured by a questionnaire) exhibited considerably more mutual gazing than those less strongly attracted to one another.

Mehrabian (1968a, b) also found body accessibility to be related to favorable attraction, but the results were mixed, with positive evidence for females and none for males or mixed dyads. He also concluded that body orientation and general tension are indicators of relaxation. Either very little or a great deal of relaxation is exhibited toward disliked persons, with moderate relaxation shown toward liked persons. Moderate relaxation often involves a forward and slight sideways lean, a curved back and, for women, an open-arm position. Arm and leg asymmetry contribute to a general syndrome of relaxation and are more prevalent in positive relationships.

Mehrabian (1970) summarized much of this work in a study that identified three pervasive dimensions of nonverbal behavior: *evaluation, potency,* and *responsiveness.* In positive attraction situations, there is generally an increase in positive evaluation as indicated by a closer distance, more forward lean, more eye contact, and more direct orientation. There also seems to be an increase in potency, reflected in postural relaxation. Finally, increased responsiveness in positive social relationships is indicated by greater facial expression and active speech.

At a strictly empirical level, Rosenfeld (1965, 1966a, b, 1967) identified specific behaviors associated with compatibility and incompatibility. Subjects instructed to seek approval of another person approached close, were talkative, smiled, and made positive gestures, including head nods and postural shifts.

It is evident that there are a number of nonverbal behaviors associated with interpersonal attraction. In addition, some work indicates that specific behaviors are organized into complex patterns within the nonverbal area and with other modalities. For investigators interested in interpersonal attraction, the task is twofold: (a) to weave nonverbal behaviors into ongoing studies, and (b) to identify complex behavior patterns associated with social penetration processes, not only within the nonverbal area, but also in regard to verbal and environmentally oriented behaviors.

C. Environmental Behaviors

The physical environment can be viewed from two perspectives—as a determinant of behavior and as a manifestation of behavior (Altman, 1972). Aside from the work of Barker (Barker, 1963, 1968; Barker & Wright, 1955), little research was conducted on the environment until the late 1950s, when a considerable output began to appear (see reviews by Argyle & Kendon, 1967; Altman & Lett, 1970; Craik, 1970; Proshansky, Ittelson, & Rivlin, 1970; Sommer, 1967).

This research has traditionally emphasized the environment as an independent variable; many studies have found that physical proximity is associated with heightened sociometric attraction, friendship, and liking, in housing developments (Deutsch & Collins, 1951: Festinger, Schachter, & Back, 1950), in small groups (Blake, Rhead, Wedge & Mouton, 1965), and in classrooms (Byrne, 1961; Byrne & Buehler, 1955). But the environment can also be viewed from a behavioral perspective, since people actively use the environment in a fashion similar to their use of words and nonverbal behaviors. A fundamental environmental behavior involves personal space or interpersonal distance from another person. Hall (1959, 1966) proposed a system of interpersonal distance or *proxemics,* with four distance zones linked to different degrees of interpersonal intimacy. An *intimate* zone, ranging from actual body contact to about 18 inches distance, is usually appropriate to intimate relationships in private situations, and permits extensive communication involving olfaction, heat, sound, smell, and close physical contact. A second zone, *personal* distance, spans the area 1.5—4.0 feet and also permits considerable exchange of visual, olfactory, auditory, and kinesthetic cues. The next zone, *social* distance, covers 4—12 feet and occurs in impersonal, work, or casual relationships. A *public* zone occurs beyond 12 feet and is appropriate to formal meetings in interactions with high-status persons.

Distance zones represent different levels of intimacy of exchange and should reflect, in a tangible and measurable way, properties of interpersonal attraction. A number of studies have shown that people place themselves, are placed by others, or are seen as being physically closer to friends than acquaintance and liked, rather than disliked, persons (see Lett, Clark, & Altman, 1969; Patterson, 1968, for a review of interpersonal distance literature). Though distance reflects use of the physical environment, it actually is a *medium* within which different patterns of nonverbal and verbal attraction-related behaviors are embedded.

Research also indicates that attraction processes involve active behavioral use of environmental *objects and areas* (Altman & Taylor, 1973; Sommer, 1967, 1969). People sitting in corner-to-corner table positions, for example, interacted more than those in other arrangements (Sommer, 1959); those working cooperatively sat side-by-side or corner-to-corner, whereas those anticipating a competitive relationship sat across from one another (Norum, 1966; Sommer, 1965). Conversely, people who wished to avoid interaction in a library chose end positions to actively discourage others from sitting at a table (Sommer, 1966). Sommer and Becker (1969) replicated these results and also reported use of markers to defend spaces and to regulate interaction with others. Thus, several studies provide indirect evidence for systematic use of environmental features in relation to the attraction process.

In the ecological model described earlier (Altman & Lett, 1970), a distinction was made between public and private objects, space and areas. Movement along a type of environmental depth continuum might be hypothesized to occur when personal objects or areas are made mutually accessible by members of a dyad. Thus, unique-to-the-dyad use of objects and areas may be an important indicator of the intimacy of a relationship. Exchange or giving of objects to strengthen interpersonal bonds is evident in anthropological and historical studies. Gift giving, dowries, and similar social practices reflect use of environmental areas and objects as symbols of the solidification of an interpersonal bond. Unfortunately, little research has been done on environmentally oriented behaviors in relation to interpersonal attraction, although a few studies we conducted illustrated how the physical environment is actively used in the management of interpersonal relationships.

In one study noted earlier, we (Altman & Haythorn, 1967a, b) investigated social activities and territorial behavior of dyads socially isolated for 10 days. Compatible and incompatible pairs were formed according to need dominance, need achievement, need affiliation, and dogmatism. Pairs incompatible on need dominance and need achievement exhibited more stress (Haythorn *et al.*, 1966) and less effective performance (Haythorn & Altman, 1967; Altman & Haythorn, 1967b) than compatible dyads. In addition, groups incompatible on need dominance (both men were high on need to control others) became quite territorial over days. The men used chairs, areas of the room, and beds in an exclusive, nonoverlapping way, and competitively interacted a great deal. Compatible dyads, where one man was high on dominance and the other was low, showed high territoriality during early days of isolation. However, territoriality lessened over days, with more use of one another's space and objects as time progressed. Data from the study described next was coupled with these results to form the hypothesis that lack of organization of the environment reflects lack of group formation. Subjects who initially established mutual physical boundaries and then gradually reduced them seemed to have more effective interpersonal bonds.

The second social isolation study also involved an analysis of use of space and establishment of territories, disclosure, performance, and stress (Altman *et al.*, 1971; Taylor *et al.*, 1968, 1969). Members of unsuccessful or abort groups (persons who left the situation on their own prior to the end of the isolation period) did not seem to organize effectively. This was particularly evident during the first days, where abort group members spent less time together, learned little about one another as individuals, and did not seem to work out a viable pattern of functioning. They also exhibited lower territorial behavior for beds, chairs, and sides of the table during the first couple of days, in isolation. As days progressed, aborters' territorial behavior rose markedly, parhaps reflecting an attempt to cope with the situation.

On the other hand, successful groups (as did the compatible groups of the earlier study) showed high initial territorial behavior, which then dropped over time. Successful group members also seemed to synchronize their environmental behavior, at least in terms of patterns of bed usage. Within dyad correlations of amount of time in bed and number of times on—of bed indicated that members of unsuccessful groups had little similarity in their bed behavior—correlations were zero or minus. Successful group members, on the other hand, showed high correlations in use of beds, suggesting that they attuned themselves to one another. It was concluded from these and other data that successful and compatible groups showed a process of group formation early in isolation, which was also reflected in the way they used the physical environment.

In laboratory studies of the social penetration process, Taylor *et al.* (1969) and Page (1968) have also found relationships between interpersonal attraction and use of the environment. In the Taylor *et al.* (1969) study, described earlier, subjects interacted with a confederate for 3 hours under varying conditions of compatibility. The more favorable the relationship, the more verbally open were the subjects. Following this part of the experiment, subjects evaluated several architectural floor plans of a two-compartment undersea capsule. (They were navy sailors who were told that they were being considered for an undersea two-man team to live and work together for an extended period.) Those who had had compatible exchanges more often chose to live in a *single* area with the other man, whereas those in incompatible situations chose a *live-apart* arrangement, indicating that structuring the general physical environment was responsive to feelings of attraction. Similar results were obtained by Page (1968) in a study of college students and dormitory room designs.

The range of possible behaviors involving active use of the environment is diverse—from simple measures of interpersonal distance to complex indicators of use of areas and objects. Notions of willingness to share, giving and receiving objects and areas, movement in and out of distance zones, openness and accessibility to mutual environments, are concepts capable of translation into operational definitions of environmentally related aspects of the attraction process. The way is open for imaginative indicators of attraction reflected in use of the physical environment. Illustrative examples presented in this section indicate that such behaviors can be developed and may be sensitive indicators of the interpersonal attraction process. However, extensive application of environmental indicators of attraction may require movement out of laboratory situations or more detailed attention to manipulable characteristics within laboratory settings. Instead of laboratory research emphasizing control and constancy, we also might create environments that are movable and manipulable, thereby permitting them to be extensions of behavior. Finally, use of the environment should not be viewed as a separate behavioral measure of the social penetration process, but as part and parcel of a multilevel set of dynamic behavioral events.

V. Summary

This chapter proposes a general theoretical approach to interpersonal attraction organized around an "ecological" orientation that emphasizes study of: (a) multilevel behavioral indicators of attraction (for example, verbal, nonverbal, and environmentally oriented behaviors); (b) *patterns* of such attraction behaviors, rather than behaviors one at a time; (c) dynamic, longitudinal, temporally occurring changes in social processes.

The approach discussed in this chapter, termed *social penetration* theory, viewed the growth of an interpersonal relationship from acquaintanceship to close friendship as a systematic and gradual process, which moves over time from peripheral and superficial levels of exchange to intimate, personal areas. Such movement is hypothesized to vary as a function of interpersonal reward—cost, personality, and situational factors. Various properties of the social penetration process were outlined, with particular emphasis on the role of interpersonal rewards and costs. Finally, the chapter reviewed possible behavioral indicators of attraction, such as (a) substantive and structural aspects of verbal behaviors, (b) nonverbal behavior involving use of the body, and (c) environmentally oriented behaviors such as interpersonal distance and use of areas and objects in the environment.

References

Altman, I. An ecological approach to the functioning of social groups. In J. E. Rasmussen (Ed) *Individual and group behavior in isolation and confinement.* Chicago, Illinois: Aldine Press, 1973 Pp. 241—269.

Altman, I., & Haythorn, W. W. Interpersonal exchange in isolation. *Sociometry*, 1965, **23**, 411–426.

Altman, I., & Haythorn, W. W. The ecology of isolated groups. *Behavioral Science*, 1967, **12**, 169–182. (a)

Altman, I., & Haythorn, W. W. The effects of social isolation and group composition on performance. *Human Relations*, 1967, **20**, 313–340. (b)

Altman, I., & Lett, E. E. The ecology of interpersonal relationships: A classification system and conceptual model. In J. E. McGrath (Ed.), *Social and psychological factors in stress*. New York: Holt, 1970.

Altman, I., & Taylor, D. A. *Social penetration: The development of interpersonal relationships*. New York: Holt, 1973.

Altman, I., Taylor, D. A., & Wheeler, L. Ecological aspects of group behavior in social isolation. *Journal of Applied Social Psychology*, 1971, **1**, 76–100.

Argyle, M., & Dean, J. Eye-contact, distance and affiliation. *Sociometry*, 1965, **28**, 289–304.

Argyle, M., & Kendon, A. The experimental analysis of social performance. In L. Berkowitz (Ed.), *Advances in experimental social psychology*. Vol. 3. New York: Academic Press, 1967.

Argyle, M., Lalljee, M., & Cook, M. The effects of visibility on interaction in a dyad. *Human Relations*, 1968, **21**, 3–17.

Barker, R. G. (Ed.) *The stream of behavior*. New York: Appleton, 1963.

Barker, R. G. *Ecological psychology*. Stanford, California: Stanford University Press, 1968.

Barker, R. G., & Wright, H. T. *Midwest and its children*. New York: Harper, 1955.

Birdwhistell, R. L. The kinesic level in the investigation of emotions. In P. H. Knapp (Ed.), *Expression of the emotions in man*. New York: International Universities Press, 1963.

Birdwhistell, R. L. *Kinesics and context*. Philadelphia, Pennsylvania: University of Pennsylvania Press, 1970.

Blake, R. R., Rhead, C. C., Wedge, B., & Mouton, J. S. Housing architecture and social interaction. *Sociometry*, 1956, **19**, 133–139.

Byrne, D. The influence of propinquity and opportunities for interaction on classroom relationships. *Human Relations*, 1961, **14**, 63–69.

Byrne, D., & Buehler, J. A. A note on the influence of propinquity upon acquaintanceships. *Journal of Abnormal and Social Psychology*, 1955, **51**, 147–148.

Campbell, D. T., & Fiske, D. Convergent and discriminant validation by the multitrait-multimethod matrix. *Psychological Bulletin*, 1959, **56**, 81–105.

Campbell, D. T., & Stanley, J. *Experimental and quasi-experimental designs for research*. Chicago, Illinois: Rand McNally, 1963.

Chapple, E. D. Measuring human relations: An introduction to the study of interaction of individuals. *Genetic Psychological Monograph*, 1940, **22**, 3–147.

Cole, J., Machir, D., Altman, I., Haythorn, W. W., & Wagner, C. M. Perceptual changes in social isolation. *Journal of Clinical Psychology*, 1967, **23**, 330–333.

Colson, W. N. Self-disclosure as a function of social approval. Unpublished M.A. thesis. Howard University, Washington, D. C., 1968.

Craik, K. H. Environmental psychology. In K. H. Craik, B. Kleinmetz, R. L. Rosnow, J. A. Cheyne, & R. H. Walters (Eds.), *New Directions in Psychology*. Vol. 4. New York: Holt, 1970.

Deutsch, M., & Collins, M. B. *Interracial housing: A psychological evaluation of a social experiment*. Minneapolis, Minnesota: University of Minnesota Press, 1951.

Duncan, S. Jr. Nonverbal communication. *Psychological Bulletin*, 1969, **72**, 118–137.

Ekman, P. Universals and cultural differences in facial expressions of emotion. In J. Cole (Ed.), *Nebraska Symposium on Motivation, 1972*. Lincoln, Nebraska: University of Nebraska Press, in press.

Ekman, P., Ellsworth, P. & Friesen, W. V. *The face and emotion: Guidelines for research and integration of findings*. Oxford: Pergamon, 1971.

Ekman, P., & Friesen, W. V. The repertoire of nonverbal behavior: Categories, origins, usage and codings. *Semiotica*, 1969, **1**, 49–97.

Ekman, P., & Friesen, W. V. Constants across cultures in the face and emotion. *Journal of Personality and Social Psychology*, 1971, 124–129.

Exline, R. Explorations in the process of person perception: Visual interaction in relation to competition, sex and need for affiliation. *Journal of Personality*, 1963, **31**, 1–20.

Exline, R., & Eldridge, C. Effects of two patterns of a speaker's visual behavior upon the perception of the authenticity of his verbal message. Paper presented at Eastern Psychological Association, Boston, Massachusetts, 1967.

Exline, R., Gray, D., & Schuette, D. Visual behavior in a dyad as affected by interview content and sex of respondent. *Journal of Personality and Social Psychology*, 1965, **1**, 201–209.

Festinger, L., Schachter, S., & Back, K. *Social pressures in informal groups: A study of human factors in housing.* New York: Harper, 1950.

Frankfurt, L. P. The role of some individual and interpersonal factors in the acquaintance process. Unpublished doctoral dissertation. The American University, Washington, D. C., 1965.

Fromm, E. *The art of loving.* New York: Harper, 1956.

Goffman, E. *The presentation of self in everyday life.* Garden City, New York: Doubleday, 1959.

Goldberg, G. N., Kiesler, C. A., & Collins, B. E. Visual behavior and face-to-face distance during interaction. *Sociometry*, 1969, **32**, 43–53.

Hall, E. T. *The silent language.* Garden City, New York: Doubleday, 1959.

Hall, E. T. *The hidden dimension.* Garden City, New York: Doubleday, 1966.

Haythorn, W. W., & Altman, I. Personality factors in isolated environments. In M. H. Appley & R. Trumbull (Eds.) *Psychological stress: Issues in research.* New York: Appleton, 1967. Pp. 363–386.

Haythorn, W. W., Altman, I., & Myers, T. Emotional symptomatology and stress in isolated pairs of men. *Journal of experimental Research in Personality*, 1966, **1**, 290–305.

Heyns, R. W., & Lippitt, R. Systematic observational techniques. In G. Lindzey (Ed.), *Handbook of Social Psychology.* Vol. 1. Reading, Massachusetts: Addison-Wesley, 1954. Pp. 370–405.

Homans, G. C. *The human group.* New York: Harcourt, 1950.

Homans, G. C. Social behavior as exchange. *American Journal of Sociology*, 1956, **63**, 597–606.

Homans, G. C. *Social behavior: Its elementary forms.* New York: Harcourt, 1961.

Jaffee, L. D., & Polansky, N. A. Verbal inaccessibility in young adolescents showing delinquent trends. *Journal of Health and Human Behavior*, 1962, **3**, 105–111.

Jourard, S. M. *Self disclosure.* New York: Wiley, 1971.   (a)

Jourard, S. M. *The transparent self.* Princeton, New Jersey: Van Nostrand Reinhold, 1971 (rev. ed.). (b)

Kendon, A. Some functions of gaze direction in social interaction. *Acta Psychologica*, 1967, **26**, 22–63.

Lennard, H. L., & Bernstein, A. *The anatomy of psychotherapy.* New York: Columbia University Press, 1960.

Lett, E. E., Clark, W., & Altman, I. A propositional inventory of research on interpersonal distance. Technical Report No. 1. Naval Medical Research Institute, Bethesda, Maryland, 1969.

Levinger, G., & Snoek, J. D. *Attraction in relationship: A new look at interpersonal attraction.* New York: General Learning Press, 1972.

Lewin, K. *A dynamic theory of personality.* New York: McGraw-Hill, 1935.

Lewin, K. Some social psychological differences between the United States and Germany. *Character and Personality*, 1936, **4**, 265–293.

Lewin, K. *Field theory and social science.* New York: Harper, 1964.   (a)

Lewin, K. Regression, retrogression, and development. In K. Lewin (Ed.), *Field theory and social science.* New York: Harper, 1964. Pp. 87–129.   (b)

Mahl, G. F., & Schulze, G. Psychological research in the extralinguistic area. In T. A. Sebeok, A. S. Hayes, & M. C. Bateson (Eds.), *Approaches to semiotics.* The Hague, Netherlands: Mouton, 1964.

Matarazzo, J. D., Hess, H. F., & Saslow, G. Frequency and duration characteristics of speech and silence behavior during interviews. *Journal of Clinical Psychology*, 1962, **18**, 416–426.

Matarazzo, J. D., Holman, D. C., & Wiens, A. N. A simple measure of interviewer and interviewee speech durations. *Journal of Psychology*, 1967, **66**, 7–14.

Matarazzo, J. D., & Wiens, A. N. Interview influence on durations of interviewee silence. *Journal of Experimental Research in Personality*, 1967, **2**, 56—69.

Matarazzo, J. D., Wiens, A. N., Matarazzo, R. G., & Saslow, G. Speech and silence behavior in clinical psychotherapy and its laboratory correlates. In J. Shlein (Ed.), *Research in Psychotherapy*. Vol. 3. Washington, D.C.: American Psychological Association, 1968.

Matarazzo, J. D., Wiens, A. N., Saslow, G., Dunham, R. M., & Voas, R. B. Speech duration of astronaut and ground communicator. *Science*, 1964, **143**, 148—150.

McGrath, J. E., & Altman, I. *Small group research: Snythesis and critique of the field.* New York: Holt, 1966.

Mehrabian, A. Communication length as an index of communicator attitude. *Psychological Reports*, 1965, **17**, 519—522.

Mehrabian, A. Attitudes inferred from neutral verbal communications. *Journal of Consulting Psychology*, 1967, **31**, 414—417.   (a)

Mehrabian, A. Orientation behaviors and nonverbal attitude communication. *Journal of Communications*, 1967, **17**, 324—332.   (b)

Mehrabian, A. Inference of attitudes from the posture orientation and distance of a communicator. *Journal of Consulting and Clinical Psychology*, 1968, **32**, 296—308.   (a)

Mehrabian, A. Relationships of attitude to seated posture, orientation and distance. *Journal of Personality and Social Psychology*, 1968, **10**, 26—30.   (b)

Mehrabian, A. The effect of context on judgments of speaker attitude. *Journal of Personality*, 1968, **36**, 21—32.   (c)

Mehrabian, A. Significance of posture and position in the communication of attitude and status relationships. *Psychological Bulletin*, 1969, **71**, 359—373.

Mehrabian, A. A semantic space for nonverbal behavior. *Journal of Consulting and Clinical Psychology*, 1970, **35**, 248—257.

Mehrabian, A. *Silent messages.* Belmont, California: Wadsworth, 1971.

Mehrabian, A., & Ferris, S. R. Inference of attitude from nonverbal communications in two channels. *Journal of Consulting Psychology*, 1967, **31**, 248—252.

Mehrabian, A., & Wiener, M. Non-immediacy between communicator and object of communication in a verbal message. *Journal of Consulting Psychology*, 1966, **30**, 420—425.

Mehrabian, A., & Williams, M. Nonverbal concomitants of perceived and intended persuasiveness. *Journal of Personality and Social Psychology*, 1969, **13**, 37—58.

Newcomb, T. M. The Prediction of interpersonal attraction. *American Psychologist*, 1956, **11**, 575—586.

Newcomb, T. M. Individual systems of orientation. In S. Koch (Ed.), *Psychology: A study of a science.* Vol. 3. *Formulation of the person and the social context.* New York: McGraw-Hill, 1959. Pp. 384—422.

Newcomb, T. M. *The acquaintance process.* New York: Holt, 1961.

Norum, G. A. Perceived interpersonal relationships and spatial arrangements. Unpublished master's thesis, University of California, Davis, 1966.

Page, J. Social penetration processes. The effects of interpersonal reward and cost factors on the stability of dyadic relationships. Unpublished doctoral dissertation, The American University, Washington, D.C., 1968.

Patterson, M. Spatial factors in social interactions. *Human Relations*, 1968, **21**, 351—361.

Proshansky, H., Ittelson, W., & Rivlin, L. (Eds.) *Environmental psychology.* New York: Holt, 1970.

Rogers, C. R. The characteristics of a helping relationship. *Personnel and Guidance Journal*, 1958, **37**, 6—15.   (a)

Rogers, C. R. A process conception of psychotherapy. *American Psychologist*, 1958, **13**, 142—149.   (b)

Rokeach, M. *The open and closed mind.* New York: Basic Books, 1960.

Rokeach, M. *Beliefs, attitudes and values: A theory of organization and change.* San Francisco, California: Jossey-Bass, 1968.

Rosenfeld, H. M. Effects of an approval-seeking induction on interpersonal proximity. *Psychological Reports*, 1965, **17**, 120—122.

Rosenfeld, H. M. Approval-seeking and approval-inducing functions of verbal and nonverbal responses in the dyad. *Journal of Personality and Social Psychology*, 1966, **4**, 597—605.   (a)

Rosenfeld, H. M. Instrumental affiliative functions of facial and gestural expressions. *Journal of Personality and Social Psychology*, 1966, **4**, 65—72.   (b)

Rosenfeld, H. M. Nonverbal receiprocation of approval: An experimental analysis. *Journal of Experimental Social Psychology*, 1967, **3**, 102—111.

Rubin, Z. Measurement of Romantic love. *Journal of Personality and Social Psychology*, 1970, **16**, 265—274.

Scheflen, A. E. The significance of posture in communication systems. *Psychiatry*, 1964, **27**, 316—331.

Scheflen, A. E. Quasi-courtship behavior in psychotherapy. *Psychiatry*, 1965, **28**, 245—257.

Scheflen, A. E. Human communication: Behavioral programs and their integration and interaction. *Behavioral Science*, 1968, **13**(1), 44—55.

Schutz, W. C. *FIRO: A three dimensional theory of interpersonal behavior*. New York: Holt, 1958.

Simmel, G. *The sociology of Georg Simmel* (translated by K. H. Wolff). New York: Free Press of Glencoe, 1950.

Sommer, R. Studies in personal space. *Sociometry*, 1959, **22**, 247—260.

Sommer, R. Further studies of small group ecology. *Sociometry*, 1965, **28**, 337—348.

Sommer, R. The ecology of privacy. *The Library Quarterly*, 1966, **36**, 234—248.

Sommer, R. Small group ecology. *Psychological Bulletin*, 1967, **67**, 145—152.

Sommer, R. *Personal space: The behavioral basis of design*. Englewood Cliffs, New Jersey: Prentice-Hall, 1969.

Sommer, R., & Becker, F. D. Territorial defense and the good neighbor. *Journal of Personality and Social Psychology*, 1959, **11**, 85—92.

Taylor, D. A. Some aspects of the development of interpersonal relationships. Social penetration processes. *Journal of Social Psychology*, 1968, **75**, 79—90.

Taylor, D. A., & Altman, I. Intimacy-scaled stimuli for use in research on interpersonal exchange. (Tech. Reports No. 9 MF022.01.03-1002.) Naval Medical Research Institute, Bethesda, Maryland, May, 1966.   (a)

Taylor, D. A., & Altman, I. Intimacy scaled stimuli for use in studies of interpersonal relations. *Psychological Reports*, 1966, **19**, 729—730.   (b)

Taylor, D. A., Altman, I., & Sorrentino, R. Interpersonal exchange as a function of rewards and costs and situational factors: Expectancy confirmation-disconfirmation. *Journal of Experimental Social Psychology*, 1969, **5**, 324—339.

Taylor, D. A., Altman, I., Wheeler, L., & Kushner, E. N. Personality factors related to response to social isolation and confinement. *Journal of Consulting and Clinical Psychology*, 1969, **33**, 411—419.

Taylor, D. A., Wheeler, L., & Altman, I. Stress reactions in socially isolated groups. *Journal of Personality and Social Psychology*, 1968, **9**, 369—376.

Thibaut, J. W., & Kelley, H. H. *The social psychology of groups*. New York: Wiley, 1959.

Webb, E. J., Campbell, D. T., Schwartz, R. D., & Sechrest, L. *Unobtrusive measures: Non-reactive research in the social sciences*. Chicago, Illinois: Rand McNally, 1966.

Weick, K. E. Systematic observational methods. In G. Lindzey & E. Aranson (Eds.), *Handbook of social psychology*. Vol. 2. Cambridge, Massachusetts: Addison-Wesley, 1968. pp. 357—452.

Wiener, M., & Mehrabian, A. *Language within language: Immediacy, a channel in verbal communication*. New York: Appleton, 1968.

Worthy, M., Gary, A. L., & Kahn, G. M. Self-disclosure as an exchange process. *Journal of Personality and Social Psychology*, 1969, **13**, 59—64.

7

A Reinforcement-Affect Model
of Attraction

GERALD L. CLORE

Department of Psychology
University of Illinois
Champaign, Illinois

and

DONN BYRNE

Department of Psychology
Purdue University
Lafayette, Indiana

I. A Description of the Model

The reinforcement-affect model is a conception of interpersonal attraction that stresses the role of affect and conditioning in the development of liking between people. Although a complete statement of the model has been published only recently (Byrne & Clore, 1970), the general theoretical conception is basic to a decade of attraction research (Byrne, 1971a). We discuss the reinforcement approach at several different levels of abstraction, ranging from statements about the general world view from which it stems to descriptions of specific experiments, but we delay a full delineation of these levels until a later section of this chapter.

A. Evaluation and Reinforcement as Basic Processes

The reinforcement-affect model of attraction proposes an association between two processes that may be seen as basic to the evolution of the species. Speculatively, it is suggested that making interpersonal evaluations and responding appropriately to reinforcement are each behavioral characteristics that have considerable survival value and, therefore, that they constitute important problem areas for psychological research.

1. INTERPERSONAL EVALUATIONS

We know from the classic studies of trait language that most of the 18,000 English adjectives we use to describe each other are strongly evaluative; in varying degrees, most of them are either insulting or complimentary (Allport & Odbert, 1936; Cattell, 1957). In addition, upon analysis, the connotative meaning of the rest of the words in the language proves to be primarily evaluative, as well (Osgood, Suci, & Tannenbaum, 1957). Cross-cultural research using factor analyses of responses to words from various languages invariably shows that the first factor of meaning is that of evaluation (Triandis & Osgood, 1958).

Man's language system, then, shows him to be extraordinarily concerned with evaluating the people and things he encounters. According to Osgood (1969), the meaning structure of human language reflects innate emotional responses of considerable evolutionary significance. When one is confronted by a novel stimulus, the first order of business is to determine whether it is good or bad (*evaluation*). After that, one needs to know whether it is strong or weak (*potency*) and whether its approach is fast or slow (*activity*). Since man is without specialized adaptive mechanisms (for example, hard scales or a shell, protective coloration, or poisonous venom), his ability to represent symbolically the good versus bad aspects of the other creatures he encounters is clearly of survival benefit (Osgood, 1969). Civilized man continues to respond evaluatively to novelty, even in safe surroundings. For example, when people are first exposed to a painting or some other art object, their initial response is generally, "I like it," or "I don't like it." Other people are almost invariably described along dimensions of favorability—unfavorability. Osgood's observations suggest that man's pervasive tendency to make evaluations, especially interpersonal evaluations, is a legacy from his evolutionary past.

2. REINFORCEMENT AND AFFECT

The theoretical approach we have adopted to explain interpersonal evaluations asserts that attraction is based on the positive affect accompanying reinforcement. The material below suggests that the link between reinforcement and affect is also a product of the struggle for survival.

The biological role of pleasurable sensations, or positive affect, in animals is apparent in the taste modality (Le Magnen, 1967). Substances are tasted in the mouth before they are ingested, and taste is apparently an important cue in making the decision to ingest. As it happens, sweet tastes are correlated with substances that promote survival, while bitter and sour tastes more frequently occur in substances deleterious to survival. Since the life or death of a species hinges on what it eats, natural selection has presumably culled out those species that found pleasure in the taste of bitter substances (Tapp, 1969).

The notion that affect might explain some of the effects of reinforcement has a long history. Herbert Spencer (1870), a friend of Darwin's, made the argument first, and his discussion of reinforcement predated Thorndike's (1911) by 40 years. Spencer maintained that during the course of evolution, natural selection produced a relationship between feelings of pleasure and actions that promote survival and between feelings of pain and injurious actions (Wilcoxon, 1969). Spencer formulated a theory of learning that has a modern ring to it; this was the first systematic attempt to give a plausible explanation of the process whereby an organism chooses one course of action, rather than another. The important point for our purposes is that Spencer, like others of the period, stressed the pleasure—pain dimensions of reinforcement and saw the response of a species to reinforcement as the behavioral key to its survival. Several recent theorists have also stressed the importance of affect in reinforcement. For example, Young (1966) and Pfaffman (1969) have both offered explanation of reinforcement based on the hedonic value or pleasantness of stimuli.

B. *The Reinforcement-Affect Model*

In one way or another, the idea that interpersonal evaluation depends on reinforcement has been proposed by numerous observers. Until recently, however, no one has specified exactly *how* reinforcement and punishment might influence the development of attraction. We have suggested that the process is similar to that of classical conditioning (Byrne & Clore, 1970; Clore, 1966). With regard to interpersonal attraction, our conditioning model makes several basic assertions: (*a*) a variety of social communications and other interpersonal events can be classed as either reinforcing or punishing; (*b*) reinforcing events elicit positive affect, while punishing events generate negative affect; (*c*) stimuli associated with positive or negative affect develop the capacity to evoke that affect; and (*d*) stimuli that evoke positive affect are liked, while stimuli that evoke negative affect are disliked. Thus, one likes others who reward him because they are associated with one's own good feelings.

Figure 1 shows these elements cast into the framework of classical conditioning. The basic idea in the Byrne—Clore (1970) paper was related to similar theorizing by Albert and Bernice Lott and elaborated into a general model of evaluative responses toward tasks, people, objects, and other discriminable stimuli.

When we refer to a reinforcement or a classical conditioning model, we explicitly intend to appeal to the body of literature on reinforcement and classical conditioning as a source of hypotheses about attraction. As with any other analogy, the classical conditioning metaphor suggests the similarity, or points of contact, between two domains of experience. In the poetic metaphor, "the road was a ribbon

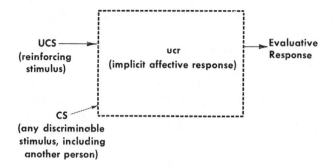

Figure 1   Evaluative responses as a function of conditioning of implicit affective responses to discriminable stimuli through association with reinforcing stimuli. (After Byrne & Clore, 1970, p. 107.)

of moonlight," one intends to say that the road had some (but certainly not all) of the qualities of a ribbon. When a model is used as an aid in scientific description, the intention is the same. We suggest that the process whereby attraction develops between people has some, but not all, of the properties of classical conditioning. Specifically, we maintain that people's positive and negative feelings spread from one stimulus to another by association.

The assertion that people like others because they associate them with their own affective responses in no way suggests that man is not a cognitively active, conscious, and amazingly complex creature. While we maintain that real-life instances of attraction and dislike follow the process just described, it is also true that many everyday situations and most laboratory settings involve higher-order associations. Many of the associations made in the process of attraction development are between words, thoughts, images, or collections, rather than between buzzers, electric shocks, or visceral responses. It is clear that one must frequently engage in all kinds of cognitive processing in order to glean every last reinforcement from what people say and do. Thus, the reinforcement-affect model, with its assumption that attraction is essentially associated affect, does not necessarily dictate, a decorticate model of man. There is no inherent incompatibility between the notion of man as cognitively active and the idea that he responds positively to reinforcement.

C. Some Evidence for Four Hypotheses from the Model

1. STIMULI ASSOCIATED WITH REINFORCEMENTS (PUNISHMENTS) ARE LIKED (DISLIKED): HYPOTHESIS I

Perhaps the most straightforward assertion of the reinforcement model is simply that reinforcement influences attraction. More specifically, the conditioning aspect of the model predicts that neutral stimulus associated with reinforcement will be evaluated positively. In support of this hypothesis, it has been found that subjects liked their partner in an experiment more when they received reinforcement (extra credit for their research participation) in his presence, than when they did not (Griffitt, 1968). In a more elaborate project, subjects received high or low creativity ratings in response to stories they told to a series of TAT pictures (Griffitt & Guay, 1969). Later they evaluated the experimenter, the apparatus, the experiment, the pictures, and other persons; although these stimuli were the same for all subjects, the evaluation of the stimuli depended on whether the subjects had encountered them in association with reinforcement (high creativity ratings) or punishment (low creativity ratings). Griffitt's studies make it clear that even when they are not the source of the reinforcement, stimuli associated with reinforcement tend to be liked regardless of whether they are human or inanimate. Similar results have been found by Baskett (1971), Golightly (1965), and by Lott and Lott (1960). Hughes (1969) has suggested that this spread of affect will occur as long as the subject is unable to identify confidently the specific cause of his affect.

Of course, the idea that people will like things associated with reinforcement is not new. An extensive literature documents the effect for the attractiveness of such diverse stimuli as puzzles (Gewirtz, 1959), colors (McGinley, 1970), toys (Hunt, 1955), nonsense syllables (Knott, 1971), sociopolitical slogans (Razran, 1940), tasks (Locke, 1965), and proper nouns (Staats & Staats, 1958). Although one investigator has suggested that these effects may have been due merely to the subtle demands of the experimental situations (Page, 1969), a more recent experiment eliminated such demand characteristics and still produced both positive and negative affective conditioning by pairing words with the offset and onset of shock (Zanna, Kiesler, & Pilkonis, 1970).

2. STIMULI THAT INFLUENCE ATTRACTION ARE REINFORCING: HYPOTHESIS II

Many of the basic investigations in the study of attraction have involved manipulations of attitude similarity. The effect of such similarities on attraction has been interpreted as a special case of a more general relationship between reinforcement and attraction, an assertion that requires evidence that attitude similarity can act like traditional reinforcers. Impressive support for that hypothesis comes from a study by Lombardo, Weiss, and Buchanan (1972), who conducted an ingenious experiment in which subjects held a conversation via an intercom connecting two rooms. On each of 12 trials, a topic was announced over the intercom, and the subject was confronted with a lighted sign saying "throw switch if you wish to comment." Unknown to the subject, the purpose of this study was to see how quickly he would throw the switch as a consequence of agreement or disagreement on the part of the other subject. After each topic was announced, the subject threw the switch, commented on the issue for about 20 sec, and then heard agreeing or disagreeing comments from the other subject (a confederate). As usual, agreements led to attraction, and disagreements to dislike; but more important, strong conditioning effects were obtained. In two different experiments, the Disagree subjects responded relatively slowly, while the Agree subjects showed increasingly rapid responding across the 12 trials. This effect represents unambiguous evidence that attitudinal similarity is reinforcing. The evidence is especially noteworthy because the procedure used eliminates explanations based on demand characteristics or on the subjects' interpretation of their behavior as correct or incorrect.

In addition, earlier studies using a different methodology have provided evidence that evaluation-relevant stimuli can alter the probability of the occurrence of any response with which they are associated (Byrne, Griffitt, & Clore, 1968; Byrne, Young, & Griffitt, 1966; Clore 1966; Golightly & Byrne, 1964; Reitz, Douey, & Mason, 1968; Reitz & McDougall, 1969; Smith, 1970; Smith & Jeffery, 1970). Thus, the reinforcement value of attraction-producing stimuli has been demonstrated in a variety of ways.

3. STIMULI ASSOCIATED WITH POSITIVE (NEGATIVE) AFFECT ARE LIKED (DISLIKED): HYPOTHESIS III

We have seen that reinforcements influence attraction and that stimuli that influence attraction are reinforcing. Reinforcement is less central to the model, however, than the affective response it produces. As can be seen in Figure 1, the core of the model is the idea that attraction toward a person depends on the affect associated with him, and reinforcement is simply one source of that affect.

In a test of the model, Griffitt and Veitch (1971) experimentally generated affect in an unusual manner. The subjects performed a variety of tasks in a 7 by 9 ft chamber in which both temperature and population density were varied. The effective temperature (representing a combination of temperature and humidity) was either hot (93.5°F) or comfortable (73.4°F), and the room was either crowded (12–15 people) or not crowded (3–5 people). The results show that both variables had a significant influence on self-reported affect and on attraction toward agreeing and disagreeing others. Thus, when communications from a stranger were associated with the subject's own discomfort, the stranger was liked significantly less than under comfortable conditions. In other research on this problem, Griffitt (1970) had previously reported significant temperature effects, and Gouaux (1971) and Schwartz (1966) have successfully used films to manipulate the affective state of the subject and hence his attraction toward associated others.

4. STIMULI THAT INFLUENCE ATTRACTION ELICIT AFFECTIVE RESPONSES: HYPOTHESIS IV

To complete the various links among reinforcement, affect, and attraction, evidence is required that indicates that the stimuli that influence attraction also elicit affect. One line of research involves obtaining self-reports of feelings in response to similar and dissimilar attitudes. Subjects generally report positive affective responses to agreement and negative responses to disagreement (Byrne & Clore, 1970).

Another approach to the affect question has been to record physiological responses to attitudinal stimuli (Clore & Gormly, 1969; Gormly, 1971). Skin conductance was recorded during face-to-face interactions between a subject and a confederate. Similar strangers were found to be more attractive than dissimilar ones, and dissimilarity was significantly more arousing physiologically than similarity. In a subsequent analysis of Clore and Gormly's data, strong relationships were found between attraction toward the agreer and arousal ($r = .54$) and between dislike toward the disagreer and arousal ($r = .38$). Consistent with the traditional interpretation of skin conductance as an index of sympathetic, or emotional, responce, it appears that intensity of interpersonal evaluation is associated with intensity of affective response.

We have emphasized four classes of studies relevant to the model that test its most basic hypotheses. The experiments concerned with reinforcement demonstrate that persons and objects associated with reinforcement or punishment will be differentially liked and that stimuli such as attitudes that influence attraction also are effective as reinforcers in a learning task. In an analogous way, the experiments concerned with affect indicate that persons and objects associated with positive or negative affect will be differentially liked and that stimuli that influence attraction also can be shown to elicit affect.

D. Affect and Information

The reader may feel that his own reactions to people are more cognitive and less visceral in nature than the model suggests. It may seem that one likes others not on the basis of one's own emotional reactions to them (affect), but because of the admirable qualities one knows them to possess (information). These two influences are frequently intertwined and difficult to differentiate, but within psychology each has its own relatively independent research tradition. Investigators who study "interpersonal attraction" have generally emphasized the affective elements, while those who study "impression formation" have usually emphasized information factors.

Recently, several writers noted the overlap of interest between studies of impression formation and studies of interpersonal attraction (Griffitt, Byrne, & Bond, 1971; Kaplan, 1971a). However, we had no sooner discovered the common ground between the areas than we were confronted by apparent differences between them as well (Kaplan & Anderson, in press a, b). When presented with two different theoretical statements, one may have an initial impulse to attempt to decide which is right and which is wrong. However, with two research programs as extensive as those of attraction (Byrne, 1971a) and impression formation (Anderson, 1971), it is unreasonable to expect that one approach will be discovered to be true and the other false (Byrne, Clore, Griffitt, Lamberth, & Mitchell, in press a, b). Rather, it seems probable that the kind of research and theorizing done will be dependent on the kind of stimulus situations studies.

Figure 2 suggests that there are two different evaluative components of the stimuli used in research on attraction and impression formation. In the figure,

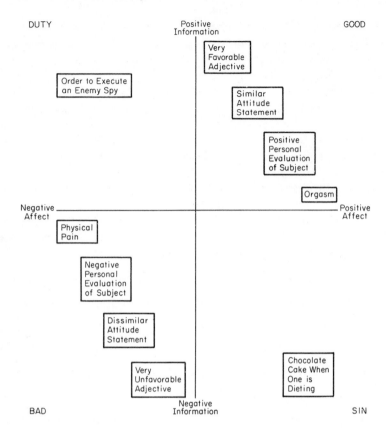

Figure 2 A schematic representation of the informational and affective components of evaluative stimuli. In the Good–Bad quadrants are some of the stimuli that have been used in attraction and impression-formation research.

positive and negative *informational* stimuli fall along the vertical axis. Use of highly evaluative adjectives such as "intelligent" or "stupid" to describe an unknown third person would exemplify the extreme poles of this informational dimension. The horizontal axis defines positive and negative *affective* stimuli. Examples of the extremes of this dimension would be the experience of orgasm at one end and that of physical pain at the other.

The distinction between affect and ideas constitutes a time-honored concern in psychology. The following statement by Titchener (1897) is a fair summary of the current problem:

> Practically, it is not hard to draw the distinction between feeling and affectively toned idea; the two are sufficiently well-marked in actual experience. In scientific analysis, however, they differ only in the amount of their affective constituent; and as we have no

means of measuring this amount at all accurately, psychology can distinguish them only by the general statement that the feeling is more affection than it is idea, the affectively toned idea more idea than it is affection [p. 215].

1. CONCEPTUAL EFFECTS OF THE INFORMATION—AFFECT DISTINCTION

Research on interpersonal evaluation uses stimuli falling in the *Good* and *Bad* quadrants in Figure 2. Investigations of impression formation have remained close to the vertical (information) axis, using adjectival descriptions of other persons as stimuli (Anderson, 1971; Edwards & Ostrom, 1971; Kaplan, 1971b; Singh & Byrne, 1971). Some studies of attraction have been close to the horizontal (affect) axis, using manipulations of physical comfort (Griffitt, 1970) and mood (Gouaux, 1971), but most work in attraction has involved stimuli somewhere in the middle of the two quadrants (for example, attitude statements) that are partly informational and partly affective. Presumably, the more the stimuli provide the subject with information about *himself*, the stronger the affective component.

Earlier, we made the point that survival and feeling good are generally related. Thus, the two activities most important for the continuation of the species, sex and eating, are at the same time two of the most pleasurable of activities. The species that finds pleasure in the things that promote its survival is clearly due a long (and happy) life. But the correlation between goodness and pleasure is by no means perfect. For example, when one continues to eat even though he is dangerously (or unattractively) overweight, we call it gluttony, which is considered sinfully self-indulgent. In Figure 2 we have used *Sin* in the lower right quadrant as a designation for something affectively positive, but informationally negative. Conversely, some things are necessary or good in the sense of promoting survival, but unpleasant. Every society generates a variety of essential but unpleasant requirements that people perform dutifully. In the upper left quadrant of the figure we have used *Duty* as a designation for things that are affectively negative, but informationally positive. Research in these latter two quadrants has not been central to either the attraction or impression formation literature. Examples of the kind of research that has been done, however, would include, in the Duty quadrant, work on altruism, obedience, and delay of gratification (see Latané & Darley, 1970; Milgram, 1963; Mischel, 1966), and, in the Sin quadrant, investigations of guilt, conscience development, and socialization anxiety (see Mosher, 1965; Sears, Maccoby, & Levin, 1957; Whiting & Child, 1953).

In view of the distinction between the affective and informational components of evaluative stimuli, the development of two distinct theories and research strategies seems inevitable. Thus, with descriptive adjectives of other persons as the primary stimuli, one would not be led toward an affective theory, and hence would not devise studies with affective manipulations to test the theory. Similarly, with attitude statements and personal evaluations of the subject as primary stimuli, one would not be likely to develop a purely cognitive, information-processing formulation. Nevertheless, it seems probable that both orientations may prove useful and that, in the words of George Kelly (1955), each has its own "range and focus of convenience." The following behavior modification research on sexual attraction illustrates Kelly's point.

According to Bandura (1969), a number of investigators have been successful in creating sexual attraction toward previously unarousing stimuli by pairing the stimuli with masturbatory pleasure. For example, Davison (1968) was able to replace sadistic masturbatory fantasies with normal ones by having his client masturbate to *Playboy* nudes, and Rachman (1966) has created a shoe fetish in the laboratory by such means. The effects in these and other such studies seem more likely to fall within the range of convenience of an affective conditioning approach than within one based on information processing. Giving the subjects positive information, even positive information about how sexually satisfying a particular stimulus would be to him, would clearly be less effective than having the stimulus paired with actual arousal.

Of course, sexual arousal represents a relatively pure form of affective stimulation, but as indicated in Figure 2, other interpersonal events have important affective components also. It should be noted that the informational and effective components of these stimuli are not conceptualized as oppositional factors. Rather, the affective components are generally dependent on information processing for their emergence, and information can change the meaning and, hence, the affective quality of a stimulus. A positive personal evaluation from someone who wants one to hire him (ingratiation) is not the same, for example, as a positive evaluation from a person whom one is asking for a job. Mueller (1969) has demonstrated this point by providing subjects with information that reversed the meaning of the positive and negative evaluations they received from another person.

2. PREDICTION AND THE INFORMATION–AFFECT DISTINCTION

Apart from the heuristic function served by the reinforcement-affect model, quantitative predictions of attraction in our research have been generated by the law of attraction. As revised by Byrne and Rhamey (1965), the law states that

$$Y = m \left[\frac{\Sigma(\text{PR} \times M)}{\Sigma(\text{PR} \times M) + \Sigma(\text{NR} \times M')} \right] + k$$

(where Y is the attraction, M and M' are magnitudes, and m and k are the slope and Y intercept, respectively), or that attraction toward a person is a positive linear function of the sum of the weighted positive reinforcements (Number × Magnitude) associated with him, divided by the total number of weighted positive and negative reinforcements associated with him.

In actual practice, any positive stimulus element has been treated as a reinforcement and any negative element as a negative reinforcement (that is, punishment). In the past we have been able to treat all kinds of stimuli simply with respect to their positive—negative components, while ignoring any distinction between their information—affect components. Thus, descriptive adjectives (Griffitt *et al.*, 1971; Singh & Byrne, 1971) can be handled in the same manner as temperature or mood variations (Griffitt, 1970; Gouaux, 1971).

It has been demonstrated repeatedly that accurate predictions can be made by considering many different kinds of events as positive or negative stimulus elements of varying weight. Even though the consolidation of the affect—information dimensions has been useful, we are likely to find that predictive accuracy, as well as conceptual clarity, could be improved by separating them. For example, in the linear prediction equation, the values of the slope (m) and Y-intercept (k) have been found to vary across certain types of experiments. It is tempting to suggest that this variation is a function of the affective qualities of the stimuli used. Some data are consistent with that logic. For example, the slope was small (2.98) in McDonald's (1962) study involving feedback on a specific task; it was somewhat larger (5.44) in Byrne and Nelson's (1965) study involving attitude similarity; and larger still (10.17) in Byrne and Rhamey's (1965) study involving both attitudes and personal evaluations of the subject.

Similar variations have been found within given experiments. The slope of the similarity—attraction function has been found, for example, to be directly related to the affective involvement of the subjects as measured by skin conductance (Clore & Gormly, 1969), and the same relationship was found with respect to self-reports of the subject's involvement (Byrne & Clore, 1967). In addition, the Y-intercept in the Griffitt *et al.* (1971) data was affected by subject involvement. Similar effects have been shown in the various studies using affective manipulations (see Gouaux, 1969). This array of data suggests that the strength of the affective components of evaluative stimuli may influence the slope and Y intercept of the familiar linear attraction function: a precise specification of the influence, if any, will have to wait for investigators to ask the question in a more systematic fashion.

The separation of informational and affective stimulus components will necessitate changes in the formal representation of the attraction function, presumably yielding greater conceptual clarity and more precise empirical predictions.

II. A Multilevel Conceptualization of Theory Construction and Theory Testing

One sign of the viability of a conceptual schema is that it attracts others who strive to support it or to demolish it. Because the reinforcement model is the target of both kinds of activity, it would seem useful to state as specifically as possible what it is that is being admired or attacked and to clarify as much as possible how and in what way confirmation or disconfirmation may be relevant.

A. An Opinion-Laden Parable

Scientific activity in psychology may be described as an attempt to penetrate a murky forest of confusion, unpredictability, and uncontrolled events in order to reach a probably distant goal where it will be possible to understand, predict, and control behavior. On the far side of the woods lies that Emerald City in which conceptual omniscience, accurate prediction, and beneficient application will bring everlasting joy and contentment. If that is overstating the situation, at least we might agree that an increase in behavioral knowledge is likely to make things better than they are; it is difficult to imagine such knowledge making things worse.

In any event, our problem is not to find the yellow brick road, but to build it. And it must be admitted that none of us has any sure way of knowing where to start, what building elements to use, or what is precisely the best way to proceed with our work. Much of the labor is begun in seemingly random fashion with a path started here and a tree hacked down there, and not much seems to come of it. Real progress begins when a group such as Paradigm Builders A works together in a concerted and planful fashion to clear the way and construct an integrated configuration of bricks, bridges, and even an occasional lamp post to illuminate the shadows. It is obvious that this group could be starting in the wrong place, or using the wrong building blocks, or generally going about the task in quite the wrong way. No critic can be certain that such is the case, and the workers cannot be certain that their approach will ultimately be justified. It seems obvious, however, that any concerted effort may eventually penetrate the forest and reach the goal, whereas unconcerted random activity is much less likely to do so. The first moral of our story is that paradigm research is preferable to preparadigm research (Kuhn, 1970).

A familiar problem that arises is what one might do when he comes upon Paradigm Builders A and perceives what they are up to. In our view there are three reasonable alternatives, plus a fourth, which is most often a waste of time. First, one can join Group A and help with the construction by adding to what is being done, trying to extend and to expand the work, and otherwise trying to improve its quality. These activities may range from an uncritical acceptance of that which Group A is doing to proposals for major changes and improvements in conceptions or methodology. In either instance, there is a basic acceptance of the value of A's previous efforts and an attempt to promote its continuation. Second, one can know in one's heart that Group A is inexorably headed toward the dismal swamp and therefore decide to cast one's lot with Paradigm Builders B. Though it seems obvious that there may be several alternate roads to the same goal and that there is no way to determine if one will prove to have any advantages over another, some workers apparently feel that any deviation from their chosen path is evidence of intellectual or character weakness. Third, one can decide that everyone in sight is misguided and conclude that the only sensible step is to start all over again in a new place and in a new way with one's own Group C. Such creativity is not improved by a preceding denunciation of all existing work, nor is there any necessity for the innovation to be denigrated by those whose work is implicitly being rejected.

Concrete examples of three independent paradigms in the area of attraction research would be the reinforcement theorists, the cognitive-consistency theorists, and the interactional theorists.

The fourth alternative is for one to expend his efforts attacking an existing paradigm with logical arguments, contrary anecdotes, or supposedly invalidating data. In spite of the historical respectability of this fourth choice, it appears wasteful because work is seldom abandoned on the basis of an attacker's arguments, anecdotes, or data and because the attacker could much better spend his time taking one of the other alternative courses. It's better to light a single candle than to curse the bricklayers, to coin a phrase. The most useful roads to knowledge will be apparent to all observers when they succeed, and the useless roads will be similarly apparent to all when they are abandoned. The existence of abandoned roads to knowledge is characteristic of all fields of science, and such roads are frequently described in texts as historical curiosities. Unless there is an expansionistic growth of ideas, applicability to new problems, and/or demonstrations of practical utility, old investigators lose interest and new investigators are not attracted to the work. When a given approach reaches a cul-de-sac, there is a gradual decline in activity. Research areas tend to die from ineffectiveness and boredom, rather than from the searing brilliance of critiques.

It is easy to be misunderstood when one casts doubts on the utility of criticism. To suggest that attacks are futile does not imply that one must adopt a servile obeisance to existing paradigms. If one sees deficiencies, problems, weaknesses or whatever, one can attempt to modify, or redirect, or improve a paradigm as suggested in our first alternative. The difference between attack and modification may seem to be a subtle one, but it is the difference between "Stop what you are doing, you damn fool" and "Let's try a variation on what you are doing because it might work better." The former usually elicits defensiveness and counterattack, while the latter can lead to an expansion and enhancement of a paradigm. One possible utility of an attack is to spur the defenders to creative defensive efforts. It may be that scientific creativity is greatest in the heat of battle, but we prefer to believe otherwise. A second possibility is that attacks are not designed to convince those who are attacked, but are actually directed toward the uncommitted bystanders in an effort to persuade them to join the attacker in his own work. If so, some of our findings in the field of attraction suggest that negative and dogmatic attacks may elicit a negative evaluation of the attacking individual (Hodges & Byrne, 1972a, b). The second moral of our story is that construction is preferable to destruction.

Because the implications of neither moral are universally accepted and because it is heretical to suggest that theoretical attacks waste time, our parable will undoubtedly be roundly ignored, as is the fate of parables.

B. *Six Levels of a Theoretical Superstructure*

Returning to the problem at hand, we will attempt to describe the current state of the reinforcement model in terms of a series of levels which are conceptualized as a continuum. The continuum is multidimensional and can be described as ranging from abstract to concrete, from general to specific, from theoretical to empirical, from deductive to inductive, and probably along several other dimensions as well. A summary diagram of the levels is shown in Table 1.

It is important to identify these levels because (*a*) the meaning of confirmation and disconfirmation differs from level to level and (*b*) the meaningfulness of confirmation or disconfirmation at a given level for work at another level is an inverse function of the distance between them.[1] We will describe a conceptual progression from each end of the continuum and then indicate how the two are linked together.

1. LEVEL I: EMPIRICAL FACTORIAL RESEARCH

The lowest level is represented by findings that *X* has an effect on *Y*. It is not being argued that there really are basic facts unaffected by theory or methodology, but only that variables can be identified and operationalized and their relationship determined without explicit reference to, or dependence on, a formal theory.

In our attraction research, an example of such an empirical relationship was the finding that similar attitudes elicit a more positive attraction response than do dissimilar attitudes (Byrne, 1961); an extension provided more conclusive evidence that a stimulus continuum of similarity—dissimilarity affects a response continuum of attraction (Byrne, 1962). The stimuli were described at the time as specific instances of positive and negative reinforcement, but these labels represented a statement of faith, rather than a supportable interpretation. The same relationships could be, and have been, described by quite different theoretical labels and even atheoretically as a simple extension of common observation (see Aronson & Worchel, 1966; Murstein, 1971; Newcomb, 1971; Winslow, 1937).

At Level I, confirmation and disconfirmation have relatively straightforward and limited meanings, unrelated to theoretical issues. If such findings were not successfully replicated, the original findings could represent chance variations, which have no meaning. The attempted replication also might have failed because of intentional or unintentional alterations in the stimulus, the response, the situational context, or in the subject population. In the latter instances, the original findings might be seen as being relatively unimportant since their generalization is severely limited. In the present paradigm, it was considered important to establish the generalizability of the empirical relationships with respect to variations in the stimulus (Byrne & Clore, 1966), the response (Byrne, Bond & Diamond, 1969), the situational context (Byrne, Ervin, & Lamberth, 1970), and the subject population (Byrne, Gouaux, Griffitt, Lamberth, Murakawa, Prasad, Prasad, & Ramirez, 1971; Byrne, Griffitt, Hudgins, & Reeves, 1969).

If Level I were decimated by repeated nonreplications, or delimited by highly restrictive boundary conditions, the original findings would be dismissed as error variance or trivia. Successful replications and generality tests at Level I allow one

---

[1]The influence of Level VI on Level I (most likely as an unconscious process) could be represented by restructuring the figure as a circle, thus bringing together the two extremes.

TABLE 1

A Schematic Representation of the Six Levels of Theoretical and Empirical Formulations Constituting the Attraction Paradigm

Level	Description	Representative references	Meaning of repeated disconfirmations
VI	Basic metatheoretical assumptions and values	Selections ranging from Epicurean philosophers through Hume and Bentham to the neobehaviorists	Irrelevant and impossible
V	Formal statement of a general and inclusive theoretical model	Byrne and Clore (1970)	Not really possible, but a non useful model can fade into obscurity
IV	Derived hypotheses and their empirical tests	Clore and Gormly (1969) Golightly and Byrne (1964) Griffitt (1970) Griffitt and Guay (1969)	Hypothesis is probably incorrect
III	Linkage of empirical and theoretical work	Clore (1966) Gouaux (1971) Lamberth and Craig (1970) McDonald (1962)	Unity of total theoretical structure becomes questionable
II	Low-level empirical laws	Byrne and Nelson (1965) Byrne and Rhamey (1965) Clore and Baldridge (1968)	Descriptive formulation must be modified or discrepant data must be reinterpreted to fit existing formulation
I	Empirical factorial research	Byrne (1961, 1962)	Original findings not replicable or of limited generalizability

to state with an increasing degree of confidence that X does in fact have an effect on Y over a relatively broad array of conditions. That being the case, the stage is set to move to Level II.

2. *LEVEL II: LOW-LEVEL EMPIRICAL LAWS*

It is an obvious advantage in science to be able to represent a functional relationship between or among variables in precise mathematical terms. The symbolic representation of the effect of X upon Y permits a much more inclusive and predictively specific kind of statement. The first such functional relationship in the present paradigm was established after proportion of similar attitudes was identified as the effective stimulus variable in the attitude-attraction studies. When data from more than 700 subjects were plotted showing attraction as a function of that stimulus, it was found that the relationship was a linear one and that it could best be described by the empirically derived formula, $Y = 5.44X + 6.62$, in which Y represents attraction as measured by the Interpersonal Judgment Scale and X represents proportion of similar attitudes (Byrne & Nelson, 1965). Note that the shape of the function and the constants designating the slope and the Y intercept are determined by the data as obtained with a specific set of operations and are not dictated by any general theoretical conceptualization.

It is possible to omit a more general theory from one's statement of the empirical relationship and to have more than one set of theoretical labels applied to the operational variables that are involved in the relationship. For example, the elements in Byrne and Nelson's equation need not be labeled "positive and negative reinforcements," but could be identified in integration theory terms as "favorable and unfavorable information," or even descriptively as "agreeing and disagreeing attitudes." The empirical relationship between proportion of similar attitudes and attraction is not dependent on one's chosen theoretical labels.

Though such a formula represents an increase in generality and abstraction compared to work at Level I, it is advantageous to take a further step and to assign theoretically relevant labels to the X and Y variables. While other observers might be inclined to accept the empircal formula and simultaneously to reject our labels, the function of such labels should at least be understood. At this level of conceptualization, theoretical interpretations are in part arbitrary. The data do not "support" the theoretical base, nor do the theoretical statements provide new information about the variables. The surplus meaning of the theoretical terms can be of importance, however, because they indicate the underlying orientation of the theorist, and they provide strong suggestive guides for future research. In the present instance, the law of attraction was formulated, not as a matter of attitude similarity, but more generally as the relationship between positive and negative reinforcers and attraction. The formula could thus be expressed as

$$Y = m \left[\frac{\sum \mathrm{PR}}{(\sum \mathrm{PR} + \sum \mathrm{NR})} \right] + k,$$

or that attraction toward an individual is a positive linear function of the proportion of positive reinforcements associated with him.

At Level II, disconfirmation of an empirically derived formula can occur in various ways. If the original formulation is based on a large body of data and the disconfirmation is based on a small sample, the lack of fit may be attributable to chance variations. Such discrepancies become a matter of concern only when the deviations are repeatedly and consistently found. Then, it becomes necessary either to modify the descriptive formulation to fit the obtained data or to reinterpret the data to fit the existing formulation.

Both types of response have proven useful in our attraction research. The formula underwent change, for example, when stimuli of different magnitudes of effect were simultaneously associated with a single stranger. Here, it was necessary to conceptualize stimuli as differing in weight in order to maintain the basic function as a simple linear relationship (Byrne & Rhamey, 1965). At that point, the formula was changed to reflect the changed empirical information by including the weighting coefficients as described earlier in the chapter. The new formula can be seen as a more general and more precise version of that originally proposed by Byrne and

Nelson. In other instances, the formula has been retained by reconceptualizing the stimuli of a given experiment in terms of positive and negative reinforcements of various weights. Thus, when Novak and Lerner (1968) seemingly disconfirmed the formula's utility by identifying the stranger not simply as a peer, but as a peer with emotional problems, their findings could be incorporated into the existing structure by assuming that knowledge of the stranger's emotional disturbance acted as a combined positive–negative unit, which contributed to the total proportion of weighted positive reinforcements (Byrne & Lamberth, 1971). As indicated earlier, that assumption has permitted us to conceptualize a variety of manipulations simply as positive and negative stimuli; hence, they can be incorporated in a single formulation. Thus, physical attractiveness (Byrne, London, & Reeves, 1968), race and racial prejudice (Byrne & Ervin, 1969), trivial and important attitudes (Byrne, London, & Griffitt, 1968; Glore & Baldridge, 1968), personal evaluations (Clore & Baldridge, 1970), and the stranger's competence (Palmer, 1969) are not treated as an array of different and discrete variables that influence attraction, but as manifestations of the *same* stimulus dimension—positive and negative informational and affective stimuli of varying weights. Analogously, when apples and bananas and pears are classified as fruit, a higher level of abstraction and generality is attained.

Presumably, future "disconfirmations" will lead to further modifications of the existing formulation, not because the present statement is "wrong," but because a modified formulation fits the total body of data more closely (Byrne, Clore, & Griffitt, 1967). The only way an empirically derived formulation can be "incorrect" is if the data on which it is based are faulty or if the formulators use faulty arithmetic. Furthermore, the theoretical labels are not "correct" or "incorrect," but their relative utility can be demonstrated in subsequent research.

At this point, the model can most clearly be described by moving to the other end of the theoretical dimension.

3. LEVEL VI: BASIC METATHEORETICAL ASSUMPTION AND VALUES

Here we have the most general and most difficult aspects to verbalize of any theoretical model: the underlying assumptions and values that determine the theorist's world view and that determine what kinds of variables and what kinds of explanations make sense to him. These elements are almost certain to be only partly conscious and only partly supported by internally consistent logic. They are probably based on a multitude of experiences ranging from the way the theorist was toilet trained to the facts, values, and myths absorbed from his subculture. Speculations about the evolutionary significance of affective and evaluative responses represent one of the kinds of activity typical of Level VI.

With respect to the present attraction paradigm, elements that may be identified include an adherence to the hedonist tradition that man behaves so as to maximize pleasure and minimize pain, a belief in determinism, an affinity for the stimulus–response language system as a way to describe behavior, and undoubtedly much else besides. Thus, the idea that attraction is a function of affect-eliciting reinforcing stimuli was adopted as an appealing and sensible explanation before there were supportive data and even before there was a clear formulation on how these constructs might be interrelated. With or without supporting data, the idea that attraction is based on homeostatic cognitive forces (such as the resolution of dissonant cognitions) was intrinsically unappealing. At this highest level of generality and lowest level of specificity, we are dealing with what Holton (1964) described as the thematic imagination in science.

It should be obvious, but it clearly is not, that confirmation or disconfirmation at this level is impossible. No amount of rhetoric or logical argument or anecdote or data can confirm or disconfirm one's world view. Supportive communications tend to be much more pleasant than those which are nonsupportive, but they do not actually serve to validate one's convictions. Confirmation or validation in this context refers to either an incontestable logical entailment or an unarguable empirical verification. One can, of course, provide reasons to support any view and can even obtain consensual validation when others agree that one's reasons are convincing. Our suggestion (which is itself a possible topic of debate) is that an individual's position with respect to Level VI questions is not based on the reasons he provides, or on logic, or on empirical data. Level VI views are nevertheless held with considerable passion, and one is well advised to accept this as a truism. When cognitive theorists and reinforcement theorists, for example, attempt to undermine the conceptual foundations of their antagonists, they might be encouraged to seek a more constructive outlet for their energies.[2] A related activity that *can* be constructive and informative, however, is the initiation of discussions and comparisons of contrasting Level VI assumptions and their differential implications as conceptualizations of man. Once again, a distinction is made between an attempt to elucidate one's own beliefs, or those of others, and an attempt to invalidate or destroy a competing system. As Goodman Ace noted in his column in the *Saturday Review*, he has great respect for opinions which are contrary to his own; he just doesn't like them. We would all do well to attempt to understand and to respect the views of others at Level VI, at the same time admitting and accepting our dislike of such views.

4. LEVEL V: FORMAL STATEMENT OF A GENERAL AND INCLUSIVE THEORETICAL MODEL

At a step more specific than in Level VI, it is possible to verbalize the basic constructs and their presumed interrelationships with respect to a given phenomenon.

As indicated previously, Byrne and Clore (1970) first elaborated the general outlines of the present reinforcement-affect model in terms of classical conditioning. Is that classical conditioning model correct or incorrect? The question

---

[2]As a somewhat irrelevant side issue, it is interesting to note that examples exist of sudden and dramatic conversions with respect to religious convictions and political beliefs. If similar examples exist of scientific conversions, it would be of considerable value to identify their antecedents.

cannot definitely be answered, because at this level confirmation and discon-firmation are still not possible. One can interpret a vast number of findings using such a model, and one can devise demonstrations consonant with the model (Byrne & Clore, 1970; Sachs & Byrne, 1970). If such a model is useful, it generates research, results in increasingly general and precise predictions, and promotes the possibility of pragmatic applications. If the model is not useful, it will gradually fade into obscurity (Kuhn, 1970). Old models never die; they just gradually turn yellow in archival journals.

5. *LEVEL IV: DERIVED HYPOTHESES AND THEIR EMPIRICAL TESTS*

If a model is to be useful, it must be stated in such a way that it is possible to derive testable hypotheses. Such hypotheses permit us to move back toward the empirical end of the continuum, and they provide evidence that the model possesses relational fertility. Work at Level IV is represented by the four hypotheses derived from the reinforcement-affect model and the experimental tests of them described in Section IC.

The basic idea of theory testing via confirmation or disconfirmation of hypotheses is best demonstrated in work at Level IV. The idea can be described easily enough. Hypotheses are derived from the general theory, and experiments are carried out that lead one to accept or reject each hypothesis. Confirmed hypotheses lend strength to the theory, and disconfirmed hypotheses lead to an alteration of the theory, or perhaps to its abandonment. As it happens, however, this is not quite the way things work. First, the derivation of hypotheses from the kind of theory discussed here is not an automatic and logical mathematical step, but more gene-rally an intuitive and, at times, creative venture. For this reason, there can be genuine differences of opinion as to whether a given hypothesis is or is not appro-priately derived from the theory. The relationship between the theoretical propo-sitions of Level V and the data of Level IV is one of the more puzzling aspects of science. That there is an interdependence is obvious, but the interpolative role of the scientist is a vital part of the connection. Second, an experiment may fail for numerous reasons that have nothing to do with the veridicality of the hypothesis. In most psychological experiments with human subjects, there are unknown ele-ments in the independent variables, the situational context, and the response measure. Anything from prior knowledge of the experiment among the subjects to the mistakes of an assistant can lead to disaster. For these reasons, the greatest confidence in hypotheses is generated when many experimenters agree on the deri-vation and independently confirm it in a variety of experimental settings. In a similar way, disconfirmation tends to be most meaningful when many experi-menters who agree on the derivation repeatedly fail to confirm the prediction.

6. *LEVEL III: LINKAGE OF EMPIRICAL AND THEORETICAL WORK*

A vital part of the total conceptual scheme lies in this central level, which ex-tends the empirical meaning of the theory and which generates theoretical meaning for the empirical statements.

Such linkage is illustrated when the theoretical deductions at Level IV are integrated with the empirical relationships at Level II. At Level IV, the model predicts that reinforcements influence attraction (Hypothesis I, discussed in Section IC). At Level II, we have frequently found that the proportion of similar attitudes is linearly related to attraction. Thus, an example of work at Level III would be to link reinforcement and linearity, that is, to find a linear relationship between attraction and proportion of positive reinforcements. Precisely such a link was provided by the Byrne and Nelson (1965) reanalysis of McDonald's (1962) data and by the Byrne (1971a) reanalysis of the data of Kaplan and Olczak (1970).

Other Level III research stems from Hypothesis II. Since, according to that hypothesis, stimuli that determine evaluative responses are found to have reinforcing properties, it follows that stimuli that differentially affect attraction should differentially affect performance in a learning task. More specifically, differential weighting coefficients derived in attraction research would be expected to function as differential magnitudes of reinforcement in learning research. The interpretation of weighing coefficients as reward magnitude has received consistent support (Clore, 1966; Lamberth & Craig, 1970; Lamberth & Gay, 1969).

The same Level III logic, that phenomena in attraction research should have some counterpart in studies of learning, has generated other experiments. For example, Gormly, Gormly, and Johnson (1971) have looked for effects with attitudes that would be analogous to number of trials in learning studies. Another example is the additional evidence obtained in a learning experiment by Lombardo, Weiss, and Buchanan (1972) for Stapert and Clore's (1969) hypothesis (from an attraction study) that disagreement is drive arousing.

Some Level III work also stems from Hypotheses III. Since stimuli that elicit affective responses are found to influence evaluative responses, it follows that affect manipulations could be treated simply as positive and negative stimulus information and hence incorporated in the linear function. Gouaux (1971) was able to show not only the effects of movie-induced affect on attraction, but also that states of elation and depression could be assigned specific weighting coefficients (+ 9 and − 9) and neatly incorporated into Byrne and Rhamey's formula. The utility of these weighting coefficients was then successfully cross-validated using Griffitt's (1970) data in which affect was manipulated by means of variations in temperature and humidity.

Finally, there is also linkage research with respect to Hypothesis IV. If stimuli that influence attraction elicit affective responses, it should be demonstrable that affective responses vary as a positive linear function of proportion of positive reinforcements. Singh (1973) has not only documented the linear relationship, but has shown that manipulations that affect the slope and Y intercept of the affective response show parallel effects on the attraction response.

It is our belief that Level III provides the most important arena for theory testing and the point at which confirmation and disconfirmation are most relevant. That is, linkage research provides the evidence necessary to verify the theoretical interpretations of data at Levels I and II and the evidence necessary to verify the relevance of the theoretical formulations at Levels IV and V to those empirical descriptions. Again, a given experiment could fail for a number of reasons, but repeated failures to obtain linkage would raise serious questions about the cohesiveness of the total theoretical structure. Analogously, repeated successes at this level serve to tie the paradigm's structure into a consistent and unified whole.

C. A Brief Look at Specific Criticisms

Critics of the reinforcement model tend to run into difficulty because of understandable confusions about the meaning of theoretical levels. It is hoped that the present exposition will help in this regard. Surprisingly, it seems to be Levels I and II which generate the greatest concern among those who hope to find fault with the paradigm.

Perhaps the most common criticism is that something is wrong with the theory because Level I and II data are based on laboratory research, rather than on "real-life" encounters (see Aronson & Worchel, 1966; Levinger, 1972, Murstein, 1971; Taylor, 1970; Wright, 1971). This general assertion is frequently encountered, but it is neither factually correct nor relevant to theory construction. A search for generalizability and applicability has been an integral and successful part of the paradigm almost from its inception. This issue has been discussed in some detail elsewhere (Byrne, 1971a, b; Byrne & Blaylock, 1963; Byrne, Ervin, & Lamberth, 1970; Byrne & Griffitt, 1966). Questions of the generalizability or applicability of laboratory findings represent legitimate, though atheoretical, concerns.

A second type of criticism revolves around the law of attraction. In an attempt to point out the theoretical and empirical implications of Level II findings, Byrne and Nelson (1965, p. 662) proposed a tentative law of attraction: attraction is a positive linear function of proportion of positive reinforcements. That seemingly innocuous proposal elicits two quite different responses. First, the reinforcement statement is ignored totally, as when Taylor (1970) criticizes "... Byrne's reference to the similarity-attraction relationship as 'the law of attraction' [p. 107]." In all honesty, the law is not based on similarity but on reinforcement, and there is no similarity theory but rather a reinforcement theory. Similarity per se does not necessarily hold any special theoretical status, and similarity is not expected to be a powerful determinant of attraction under any and all conditions. This particular straw man seems, however, to be endowed with vitality and good health (Murstein, 1971). Second, the reinforcement statement may be perceived accurately, but it can serve as a red flag for those who are made intellectually uncomfortable by the Level VI assumptions, which are implied by the terminology of learning theorists (Murstein, 1971; Wright, 1971). In a similar vein, the reinforcement notion is somehow seen to be invalidated because attitudinal stimuli arouse expectancies (Aronson & Worchel, 1966; Ettinger, Nowicki, & Nelson, 1970) even though the concept of expectancies fits easily within the reinforcement framework (Griffitt, 1969). Critics of the reinforcement notion tend with surprising consistency to ignore the supporting research at Levels III and IV.

The third criticism raised by work at Level II is of much greater merit than the two previous types of criticism, but is still clouded by a confusion concerning levels. Anderson (1971) and, in greater detail, Kaplan and Anderson (in press a, b) assert that data from Anderson's impression-formation paradigm are directly applicable to the present formulation at Level II and that the data indicate necessary altera-tions in our empirically derived statement. While the suggestion of the possible congruencies of the attraction and impression-formation literature are valuable and lead to the necessary connecting research (Griffitt, Byrne, & Bond, 1971; Rosenblood, 1970; Singh & Byrne, 1971), and while the call for changes in the empirical law could turn out to be partially or even totally correct, the criticism goes one step further. Kaplan and Anderson (in press a, b) propose that possible adjustments of Level II formulas have implications for all other levels of the model. When criticisms are directed toward the lower levels with the intention of dis-crediting metatheoretical issues, we get nowhere. The difference between the spe-cific mathematical function that currently describes the data and the overall rein-forcement model is, of course, a necessary distinction (Byrne *et al.*, in press a, b).

In summary, from our perspective, work at Level II invites various lines of critical attack which largely ignore the remaining levels and which vary in accuracy and theoretical relevance. From an avowedly biased perspective, it appears that the reinforcement model has received extensive positive support and only ques-tionable negative criticism. This last statement suggests yet another reason why construction is preferable to destruction; the former tends to be incorporated with enthusiasm, while the latter is rejected, ridiculed, vilified, and generally made sport of. Negative affect is aroused, and work on the yellow brick road is neglected.

It is easier to describe and to integrate past research than to prognosticate regarding the direction of future research. Three general research paths flow directly from present efforts. First, various types of applicability are being sought at Levels II through IV with work on decision-making processes (Golightly, Huffman, & Byrne, 1972; Mitchell & Byrne, 1973); compatibility in dating and marriage (Byrne, Ervin, & Lamberth, 1970); affective determinants of behavior (DeNinno, 1972; Griffitt & Veitch, 1971); task performance (Nelson & Meadow, 1971); and in the search for ways to maximize interpersonal tolerance (Clore & Jeffery, 1972; Hodges & Byrne, 1972). Second, theoretical refinements and improvements are being sought at Levels II through V with work on the relation-ship between cognitive and affective components of the evaluative process (Moss, Byrne, Baskett, & Sachs, 1971; Singh & Byrne, 1971); work on the motivational construct underlying response to attitude statements (Good & Good, 1971; Palmer, 1969); and attempts to specify the conditions under which a set-size effect may be obtained (Singh, 1971). Third, the expansion of the total paradigm is faciliated by work that seeks connecting theoretical and empirical links with other paradigms. Work on the reinforcement model has been shown to be directly relevant to work on impression formation (Rosenblood, 1970), game theory (Schlenker & Tedeschi, in press), aggression (Sachs, 1972), sexual responsiveness (Byrne, Fisher, &

Lamberth, 1972), Hull—Spence drive theory (Lombardo, Libkuman, & Weiss, 1970), and Capaldi's sequential learning theory (Lamberth, 1971). It seems safe to predict that while all three of these avenues of research will be actively pursued, future research will also develop in new and, at times exciting, directions. There is much roadwork to be done.

Acknowledgments

Preparation of this Chapter was facilitated by Research Grant MH 14510–04 to Gerald Clore from the National Institute of Mental Health, United States Public Health Service, and GS-2752 to Donn Byrne from the National Science Foundation.

We wish to express our appreciation to Frances Cherry, William Griffitt, Ted Huston, Martin Kaplan, George Levinger, Herman Mitchell, Rick Pomazal, Joseph Rychlak, Calvin Schrag, Ramadhar Singh, and Linda Winslow for their comments and suggestions in response to an earlier draft of this chapter. Thanks are due Gene Byron Miles for his contribution to our understanding of the function of models in science.

References

Allport, G. W., & Odbert, H. S. Trait-names: A psycho-lexical study. *Psychological Monographs*, 1936, **47** (Whole No. 211).

Anderson, N. H. Integration theory and attitude change. *Psychological- Review*, 1971, **78**, 171–206.

Aronson, E., & Worchel, P. Similarity versus liking as determinants of interpersonal attractiveness. *Psychonomic Science*, 1966, **5**, 157–158.

Bandura, A. *Principles of behavior modification*. New York: Holt, 1969.

Baskett, G. D. Evaluation of experiments as a function of attitude similarity—dissimilarity. Unpublished manuscript, Georgia Institute of Technology, 1971.

Byrne, D. Interpersonal attraction and attitude similarity. *Journal of Abnormal and Social Psychology*, 1961, **62**, 713–715.

Byrne, D. Response to attitude similarity—dissimilarity as a function of affiliation need. *Journal of Personality*, 1962, **30**, 164–177.

Byrne, D. *The attraction paradigm*. New York: Academic Press, 1971. (a)

Byrne, D. Can Wright be wrong? Let me count the ways. *Representative Research in Social Psychology*, 1971, **2**, 12–18. (b)

Byrne, D., & Blaylock, B. Similarity and assumed similarity of attitudes between husbands and wives. *Journal of Abnormal and Social Psychology*, 1963, **67**, 636–640.

Byrne, D., Bond, M. H., & Diamond, M. J. Response to political candidates as a function of attitude similarity-dissimilarity. *Human Relations*, 1969, **22**, 251–262.

Byrne, D., & Clore, G. L. Predicting interpersonal attraction toward strangers presented in three different stimulus modes. *Psychonomic Science*, 1966, **4**, 239–240.

Byrne, D., & Clore, G. L. Effectance arousal and attraction. *Journal of Personality and Social Psychology*, 1967, **6**, No. 4(Whole No. 638).

Byrne, D., & Clore, G. L. A reinforcement model of evaluative responses. *Personality: An International Journal*, 1970, **1**, 103–128.

Byrne, D., Clore, G. L., & Griffitt, W. Response discrepancy versus attitude similarity-dissimilarity as determinants of attraction. *Psychonomic Science*, 1967, **7**, 397–398.

Byrne, D., Clore, G. L., Griffitt, W., Lamberth, J., & Mitchell, H. E. When research paradigms converge: Confrontation or integration? *Journal of Personality and Social Psychology*, in press. (a)

Byrne, D., Clore, G. L., Griffitt, W., Lamberth, J., & Mitchell, H. E. One more time. *Journal of Personality and Social Psychology*, in press. (b)

Byrne, D., & Ervin, C. R. Attraction toward a Negro stranger as a function of prejudice, attitude similarity, and the stranger's evaluation of the subject. *Human Relations*, 1969, **22**, 397—404.

Byrne, D., Ervin, C. R., & Lamberth, J. Continuity between the experimental study of attraction and real-life computer dating. *Journal of Personality and Social Psychology*, 1970, **16**, 157—165.

Byrne, D., Fisher, J. D., & Lamberth, J. Evaluations of erotica: Facts or feelings? Paper presented at the meeting of the Midwestern Psychological Association, Cleveland, Ohio, May, 1972.

Byrne, D., Gouaux, C., Griffitt, W., Lamberth, J., Murakawa, N., Prasad, M. B., Prasad, A., Ramirez, M., III. The ubiquitous relationship: Attitude similarity and attraction. A cross-cultural study. *Human Relations*, 1971, **24**, 201—207.

Byrne, D., & Griffitt, W. Similarity versus liking: A clarification. *Psychonomic Science*, 1966, **6**, 295—296.

Byrne, D., Griffitt, W., & Clore, G. L. Attitudinal reinforcement effects as a function of stimulus homogeneity-heterogeneity. *Journal of Verbal Learning and Verbal Behavior*, 1968, **7**, 962—964.

Byrne, D., Griffitt, W., Hudgins, W., & Reeves, K. Attitude similarity—dissimilarity and attraction: Generality beyond the college sophomore. *Journal of Social Psychology*, 1969, **79**, 155—161.

Byrne, D., & Lamberth, J. Cognitive and reinforcement theories as complementary approaches to the study of attraction. In B. I. Murstein (Ed.), *Theories of attraction and love*. New York: Springer Publ., 1971. Pp. 59—84.

Byrne, D., London, O., & Griffitt, W. The effect of topic importance and attitude similarity-dissimilarity on attraction in an intrastranger design. *Psychonomic Science*, 1968, **11**, 303—304.

Byrne, D., London, O., & Reeves, K. The effects of physical attractiveness, sex, and attitude similarity on interpersonal attraction. *Journal of Personality*, 1968, **36**, 259—271.

Byrne, D., & Nelson, D. Attraction as a linear function of proportion of positive reinforcements. *Journal of Personality and Social Psychology*, 1965, **1**, 659—663.

Byrne, D., & Rhamey, R. Magnitude of positive and negative reinforcements as a determinant of attraction. *Journal of Personality and Social Psychology*, 1965, **2**, 884—889.

Byrne, D., Young, R. K., & Griffitt, W. The reinforcement properties of attitude statements. *Journal of Experimental Research in Personality*, 1966, **1**, 266—276.

Cattell, R. B. *Personality and motivation: Structure and measurement*. Yonkers-on-Hudson: World Book, 1957.

Clore, G. L. Discrimination learning as a function of awareness and magnitude of attitudinal reinforcement. Unpublished doctoral dissertation, University of Texas, 1966.

Clore, G. L., & Baldridge, B. Interpersonal attraction: The role of agreement and topic interest. *Journal of Personality and Social Psychology*, 1968, **9**, 340—346.

Clore, G. L., & Baldridge, B. The behavior of item weights in attitude-attraction research. *Journal of Experimental Social Psychology*, 1970, **6**, 177—186.

Clore, G. L., & Gormly, J. B. Attraction and physiological arousal in response to agreements and disagreements. Paper presented at the meeting of the Psychonomic Society, St. Louis, November, 1969.

Clore, G. L., & Jeffrey, K. M. Emotional role playing, attitude change, and attraction toward a disabled person. *Journal of Personality and Social Psychology*, 1972, **23**, 105—111.

Davison, G. C. Elimination of a sadistic fantasy by a client-controlled counterconditioning technique: A case study. *Journal of Abnormal Psychology*, 1968, **73**, 84—90.

DeNinno, J. A. Humor as a variable in interpersonal attraction. Unpublished master's thesis, Purdue University, 1972.

Edwards, J. D., & Ostrom, T. M. Cognitive structure of neutral attitudes. *Journal of Experimental Social Psychology*, 1971, **7**, 36—47.

Ettiger, R. F., Nowicki, S., Jr., & Nelson, D. Interpersonal attraction and the approval motive. *Journal of Experimental Research in Personality*, 1970, **4**, 95—99.

Gewirtz, H. B. Generalization of children's preferences as a function of reinforcement and task similarity. *Journal of Abnormal and Social Psychology*, 1969, **58**, 111—118.

Golightly, C. The reinforcement properties of attitude similarity—dissimilarity. Unpublished doctoral dissertation, University of Texas, 1965.

Golightly, C., & Byrne, D. Attitude statements as positive and negative reinforcements. *Science* 1964, **146,** 798—799.

Golightly, C., Huffman, D. M., & Byrne, D. Liking and loaning. *Journal of Applied Psychology*, 1972, **56,** 521—523.

Good, L. R., & Good, K. C. An objective measure of the vindication motive. *Psychological Reports*, 1971, **29,** 983—986.

Gormly, J. Sociobehavioral and physiological responses to interpersonal disagreement. *Journal of Experimental Research in Personality*, 1971, **5,** 216—222.

Gormly, J., Gormly, A., & Johnson, C. Interpersonal attraction: Competence motivation and reinforcement theory. *Journal of Personality and Social Psychology*, 1971, **19,** 375—380.

Gouaux, C. Interpersonal attraction as a function of induced affect and social dependence. Unpublished master's thesis, University of Texas, 1969.

Gouaux, C. Induced affective states and interpersonal attraction. *Journal of Personality and Social Psychology*, 1971, **20,** 37—43.

Griffitt, W. Attraction toward a stranger as a function of direct and associated reinforcement. *Psychonomic Science*, 1968, **11,** 147—148.

Griffitt, W. Attitude evoked anticipatory responses and attraction. *Psychonomic Science*, 1969, **14,** 153—155.

Griffitt, W. Environmental effects on interpersonal affective behavior: Ambient effective temperature and attraction. *Journal of Personality and Social Psychology*, 1970, **15,** 240—244.

Griffitt, W., Byrne, D., & Bond, M. H. Proportion of positive adjectives and personal relevance of adjectival descriptions. *Journal of Experimental Social Psychology*, 1971, **7,** 111—121.

Griffitt, W., & Guay, P. "Object" evaluation and conditioned affect. *Journal of Experimental Research in Personality*, 1969, **4,** 1—8.

Griffitt, W., & Veitch, R. Hot and crowded: Influences of population density and temperature on interpersonal affective behavior. *Journal of Personality and Social Psychology*, 1971, **17,** 92—98.

Hodges, L. A., & Byrne, D. Verbal dogmatism as a potentiator of intolerance. *Journal of Personality and Social Psychology*, 1972, **21,** 312—317.   (a)

Hodges, L. A., & Byrne, D. Evaluative responses produced by positive vs. negative wording of another's statements. Paper presented at the meeting of the Midwestern Psychological Association, Cleveland, May, 1972.   (b)

Holton, G. The thematic imagination in science. In H. Woolf (Ed.), *Science as a cultural force*. Baltimore, Maryland: Johns Hopkins Press, 1964.

Hughes, R. L. "Object" evaluation: a reinterpretation of affect conditioning in the reinforcement model of attraction. Unpublished master's thesis, University of Texas, 1969.

Hunt, D. E. Changes in goal-object perference as a function of expectancy for social reinforcement. *Journal of Abnormal and Social Psychology*, 1955, **50,** 372—377.

Kaplan, M. F. Attitude similarity and attraction: Toward a theoretical reconciliation. Paper presented at the meeting of the Midwestern Psychological Association, Detroit, May, 1971.   (a)

Kaplan, M. F. Context effects in impression formation: The weighted average versus the meaning-change formulation. *Journal of Personality and Social Psychology*, 1971, **19,** 92—99   (b)

Kaplan, M. F., & Anderson, N. H. Comparison of information integration and reinforcement models for interpersonal attraction. *Journal of Personality and Social Psychology*, in press.   (a)

Kaplan, M. F., & Anderson, N. H. Comment on "When research paradigms converge: Confrontation or integration?" *Journal of Personality and Social Psychology*, in press.   (b)

Kaplan, M. F., & Olczak, P. V. Attitude similarity and direct reinforcement as determinants of attraction. *Journal of Experimental Research in Personality*, 1970, **4,** 186—189.

Kelly, G. A. *The psychology of personal constructs*. New York: Norton, 1955.

Knott, P. D. Effects of frustration and magnitude of reward on selective attention, size estimation, and verbal evaluation. *Journal of Personality*, 1971, **39,** 378—390.

Kuhn. T. S. *The structure of scientific revolutions*. (2nd ed.) Chicago, Illinois: University of Chicago Press, 1970.

Lamberth, J. Sequential variables as determinants of human performance with attitudinal reinforcements. *Psychonomic Science*, 1971, **22**, 350—352.

Lamberth, J., & Craig, L. Differential magnitude of reward and magnitude shifts using attitudinal stimuli. *Journal of Experimental Research in Personality*, 1970, **4**, 281—285.

Lamberth, J., & Gay, R. A. Differential reward magnitude using a performance task and attitudinal stimuli. Paper presented at the meeting of the Western Psychological Association, Vancouver, June, 1969.

Latané, B., & Darley, J. M. *The unresponsive bystander: Why doesn't he help?* New York: Appleton, 1970.

Le Magnen, J. Habits and food intake. In C. F. Code (Ed.), *Handbook of physiology*. Sect. 6. Alimentary canal. Vol. I. *Control of food and water intake*. Washington, D.C.: American Physiological Society, 1967. Pp. 11—30.

Levinger, G. Little sand box and big quarry: Comment on Byrne's paradigmatic spade for research on interpersonal attraction. *Representative Research in Social Psychology*, 1972, **3**, 3—19.

Locke, E. A. The relationship of task success to task liking and satisfaction. *Journal of Applied Psychology*, 1965, **49**, 379—385.

Lombardo, J. P., Libkuman, T. M., & Weiss, R. F. The energizing effects of disagreement-induced drive. Unpublished manuscript, University of Oklahoma, 1970.

Lombardo, J. P., Weiss, R. F., & Buchanan, W. Reinforcing and attracting functions of yielding. *Journal of Personality and Social Psychology*, 1972, **21**, 359—368.

Lott, B. E., & Lott, A. J. The formation of positive attitudes toward group members. *Journal of Abnormal and Social Psychology*, 1960, **61**, 297—300.

McDonald, R. D. The effect of reward-punishment and affiliation need on interpersonal attraction. Unpublished doctoral dissertation, University of Texas, 1962.

McGinley, W. H. The development of a conditioned reinforcer through direct and vicarious reinforcement. *Journal of Experimental Social Psychology*, 1970, **6**, 364—377.

Milgram, S. Behavioral study of obedience. *Journal of Abnormal and Social Psychology*, 1963, **67**, 371—378.

Mischel, W. Theory and research on the antecedents of self-imposed delay of reward. In B. A. Maher (Ed.), *Progress in experimental personality research*. Vol. 3. New York: Academic Press, 1966. Pp. 85—132.

Mitchell, H. E., & Byrne, D. The defendant's dilemma: Effects of jurors' attitudes and authoritarianism. *Journal of Personality and Social Psychology*, 1973, **25**, 123—129.

Mosher, D. L. Interaction of fear and guilt in inhibiting unacceptable behavior. *Journal of Consulting Psychology*, 1965, **29**, 161—167.

Moss, M. K., Byrne, D., Baskett, G. D., & Sachs, D. H. Informational versus affective determinants of interpersonal attraction. Unpublished manuscript, Purdue University, 1971.

Mueller, L. M. Interpersonal attraction as a function of inferred similarity—dissimilarity: A reversal effect. Unpublished doctoral dissertation, University of Texas, 1969.

Murstein, B. I. Critique of models of dyadic attraction. In B. I. Murstein (Ed.), *Theories of attraction and love*. New York: Springer, Publ., 1971. Pp. 1—30.

Nelson, D., & Meadow, B. L. Attitude similarity, interpersonal attraction, actual success, and the evaluative perception of that success. Paper presented at the meeting of the American Psychological Association, Washington, D.C., September, 1971.

Newcomb, T. M. Dyadic balance as a source of clues about interpersonal attraction. In B. I. Murstein (Ed.), *Theories of attraction and love*. New York: Springer Publ., 1971. Pp. 31—45.

Novak, D. W., & Lerner, M. J. Rejection as a consequence of perceived similarity. *Journal of Personality and Social Psychology*, 1968, **9**, 147—152.

Osgood, C. E. On the whys and wherefores of E, P, and A. *Journal of Personality and Social Psychology*, 1969, **12**, 194—199.

Osgood, C. E., Suci, G. J., & Tannenbaum, P. H. *The measurement of meaning*. Urbana, Illinois: University of Illinois Press, 1957.

Page, M. Social psychology of a classical conditioning of attitudes experiment. *Journal of Personality and Social Psychology*, 1969, **11**, 177—186.

Palmer, J. Vindication, evaluation, and the effect of the stranger's competence on the attitude similarity-attraction function. Unpublished doctoral dissertation, University of Texas, 1969.

Pfaffman, C. Taste preference and reinforcement. In J. Tapp (Ed.), *Reinforcement and behavior.* New York: Academic Press, 1969. Pp. 215–241.

Rachman, S. Sexual fetishism: An experimental analogue. *Psychological Record,* 1966, **16,** 293–296.

Razran, G. H. S. Conditioned response changes in rating and appraising socio-political slogans. *Psychological Bulletin,* 1940, **37,** 481. (Abstract)

Reitz, W. E., Douey, J., & Mason, G. Role of homogeneity and centrality of attitude domain on reinforcing properties of attitude statements. *Journal of Experimental Research in Personality,* 1968, **3,** 120–125.

Reitz, W. E., & McDougall, L. Interest items as positive and negative reinforcements: Effects of social desirability and extremity of endorsement. *Psychonomic Science,* 1969, **17,** 97–98.

Rosenblood, L. Information saliency: An explanation of the set size effect in impression formation and similarity–attraction research. Unpublished doctoral dissertation, Ohio State University, 1970.

Sachs, D. H. Attraction and aggression: A study in paradigm linking. Unpublished doctoral dissertation, Purdue University, 1972.

Sachs, D. H., & Byrne, D. Differential conditioning of evaluative responses to neutral stimuli through association with attitude statements. *Journal of Experimental Research in Personality,* 1970, **4,** 181–185.

Schlenker, B. R., & Tedeschi, J. T. Interpersonal attraction and the exercise of coercive and reward power. *Human Relations,* 1972, **25,** 427–439.

Schwartz, M. S. Effectance motivation and interpersonal attraction: Individual differences and personality correlates. Unpublished doctoral dissertation, University of Texas, 1966.

Sears, R. R., Maccoby, E. E., & Levin, H. *Patterns of child rearing.* New York: Harper 1957.

Singh, R. The effect of set size and proportion of positive descriptions on evaluative response and certainty of its accuracy. Unpublished manuscript, Purdue University, 1971.

Singh, R. Affective implications of the weighting coefficient in attraction research. Unpublished doctoral dissertation, Purdue University, 1973.

Singh, R., & Byrne, D. Cognitive certainty and affective neutrality as a function of stimulus homogeneity–heterogeneity. *Psychonomic Science,* 1971, **25,** 207–208.

Smith, R. E. Social anxiety as a moderator variable in the attitude similarity–attraction relationship. Paper presented at the meeting of the Western Psychological Association, Los Angeles, April, 1970.

Smith, R. E., & Jeffery, R. W. Social-evaluative anxiety and the reinforcement properties of agreeing and disagreeing attitude statements. *Journal of Experimental Research in Personality,* 1970, **4,** 276–280.

Spencer, H. *The principles of psycholoty.* Vol. I. (2nd. ed.) New York: Appleton, 1870.

Staats, A. W., & Staats, C. K. Attitudes established by classical conditioning. *Journal of Abnormal and Social Psychology,* 1958, **57,** 37–40.

Stapert, J. C., & Clore, G. L. Attraction and disagreement-produced arousal. *Journal of Personality and Social Psychology,* 1969, **13,** 64–69.

Tapp, J. T. Current status and future directions. In J. Tapp (Ed.), *Reinforcement and behavior.* New York: Academic Press, 1969. Pp. 387–416.

Taylor, H. F. *Balance in small groups.* Princeton, New Jersey: Van Nostrand-Reinhold, 1970.

Titchener, E. B. *An outline of psychology.* New York: MacMillan, 1897.

Triandis, H. C., & Osgood, C. E. A comparative factorial analysis of semantic structures of monolingual Greek and American college students. *Journal of Abnormal and Social Psychology,* 1958, **57,** 187–196.

Whiting, J. W. M., & Child, I. L. *Child training and personality: A cross-cultural study.* New Haven, Connecticut: Yale University Press, 1953.

Wilcoxon, H. C. Historical introduction to the problem of reinforcement. In J. Tapp (Ed.), *Reinforcement and behavior.* New York: Academic Press, 1969. Pp. 1–46.

Winslow, C. N. A study of the extent of agreement between friends' opinions and their ability to estimate the opinions of each other. *Journal of Social Psychology*, 1937, **8**, 433—442.

Wright, P. H. Byrne's paradigmatic approach to the study of attraction: Misgivings and alternatives. *Representative Research in Social Psychology*, 1971, **2**, 66—70.

Young, P. T. Hedonic organization and regulation of behavior. *Psychological Review*, 1966, **73**, 59—86.

Zanna, M. P., Kiesler, C. A., & Pilkonis, P. A. Positive and negative attitudinal affect established by classical conditioning. *Journal of Personality and Social Psychology*, 1970, **14**, 321—328.

8

The Role of Reward
in the Formation
of Positive Interpersonal Attitudes

ALBERT J. LOTT *and* BERNICE E. LOTT

Department of Psychology
University of Rhode Island
Kingston, Rhode Island

I. Introduction

In this chapter we examine how rewards contribute to the process of learning to like another person. Most discussions of the determinants of interpersonal attraction tend to organize the antecedents of liking in terms of "the rewards others provide [Levinger & Snoek, 1972]," or contain some statement such as "individuals like those who reward them [Walster, 1971]," or "we like people most whose overall behavior is most rewarding [Aronson, 1969]." Although we do not question the validity of this suggested relationship between one's liking for a person and his or her instrumental value as an agent of satisfaction, our view is that this is merely the most obvious aspect of a far more general proposition. It is with the general proposition that we are concerned.

The basic hypothesis that underlies all of our work on the antecedents of interpersonal attraction is that liking for a person will result under those conditions in which an individual experiences *reward in the presence of that person*, regardless of the relationship between the other person and the rewarding event or state of affairs. Under what varying sets of circumstances can the condition of reward in the presence of another person be met? (*a*) The other person, because of the nature or quality of his or her characteristics (for example, beauty, kindliness) may be able to provide pleasure to an individual by merely being in the same place at the same time. (*b*) The person may be able to directly provide positive consequences by such overt behaviors as a smile of approval, an expression of agreement, or some positive evaluation. (*c*) The person may be instrumental in mediating certain positive ends; for example, the person may be powerful or competent enough to assure success on a task, acquisition of desired goods, or escape from danger. (*d*) There remain, however, situations in which neither the person nor any variables directly related to the person can be said to provide reward, but in which the person will nonetheless acquire attractiveness because of a consistent association with entirely independent reinforcing, or satisfying, states of affairs. It is through the relaxing evening before the fire, the excitement of a discussion, or the fun of a great party that the person who was always there will be liked even though he or she was not directly responsible for any of these pleasures.

In the first of a series of papers concerned with the formation of positive interpersonal attitudes (Lott & Lott, 1960), we suggested that attraction, or liking, might be parsimoniously conceptualized as a positive attitude, and that this attitude could then be related to the implicit anticipatory response concept ($r_g - s_g$) within Hullian learning theory, as had been previously urged by Doob (1947). Two sets of necessary assumptions were made. The first set is relevant to persons: (*a*) that persons-as-objects can function as discriminable stimuli; and (*b*) that persons-as-actors learn to make responses to such stimuli. The second set of assumptions concerns the effects of the experience of reinforcement, or reward, on our responses to stimuli present at the time and includes the following: (*a*) an individual who experiences reward will react to it with some observable or covert goal response; (*b*) this response (like any other) will become conditioned to all discriminable stimuli present at the time of reinforcement; and (*c*) a person present at the time of reinforcement (like any other discriminable stimulus) will be able to evoke the goal response, or its fractional and anticipatory component, which is an expectative response or a positive attitude. From these assumptions came the general proposition that a sufficient condition for the acquisition of a positive attitude toward previously neutral (but discriminable) persons is the experience of reinforcement in their presence.

By means of a series of investigations concerned with the antecedents of liking, and in a theoretical exposition (Lott & Lott, 1968), the concept of interpersonal attraction, defined as an anticipatory response, was placed within a large nomological net with other S–R concepts that are already linked theoretically and empirically. From this large framework, hypotheses specific to the investigation of social behavior can be derived, and this has been our primary objective. The conditions that are associated with the evocation and differential strength of anticipatory responses should be, in general, the same variables that can be shown to influence the acquisition of liking for one individual by another. Thus, we have obtained evidence in support of a positive relationship between the development of attraction toward a person and receipt of reward (either direct or vicarious) in his or her presence (Lott & Lott, 1960; Lott, Lott, & Matthews, 1969); frequency of reward (James & Lott, 1964); delay of reward (Lott, Aponte, Lott, & McGinley, 1969); and incentive quality and variations in the drive state of rewarded individuals (Lott, Bright, Weinstein, & Lott, 1970).

Since stimuli that evoke fractional anticipatory goal responses are stimuli that are then classifiable as *secondary reinforcers* (Hull, 1952; Lott & Lott, 1968), it follows that not only will the general conditions under which nonperson stimuli acquire their secondary reinforcing characteristics be descriptive of conditions under which persons acquire attractiveness, but also that liked persons will be able to function as positive secondary reinforcers in influencing behavior. Since the antecedents of liking, derived from general behavior principles, are the same as those which predict the establishment of secondary reinforcers (that is, stimuli that can evoke anticipatory responses), the consequences of liking must also be predictable. As positive secondary reinforcing stimuli, people we like should have consequences for perception and memory, stemming from their heightened salience and distinctiveness; consequences for performance, stemming from their incentive or drive-arousing quality; and consequences for learning, because they can function as rewards. If the presence of a liked person is made contingent upon some behavior, that behavior should be strengthened. The derivation of these consequences of liking from learning theory principles is the subject of a recent paper (Lott & Lott, 1972), which also considers empirical support for the predictions and their applicability to some contemporary social issues.

II. The Meaning of Reward

Our focus here is on the determinants of liking, not its effects, and prime consideration is given to an analysis of the concept of reward, the pivotal variable. Though often manipulated and referred to, the ultimate value of this concept in understanding complex social behavior is frequently questioned. It is obviously difficult to specify beforehand what will constitute a reward for human beings for whom the same event or objective stimulus can vary in meaning as a result of differences in past experiences, in present motives, and in the context of the situation. To be agreed with, for example, may clearly be rewarding for one individual, while "disagreement which leads to improvement may carry its own rewards" for another person (Aronson, 1969). This is nothing more than a recognition of the ancient wisdom that "one man's (or woman's!) nectar is another's poison."

It has long been recognized, although often lost sight of, that effective reinforcement must be relevant to the motivational state and/or preceding experiences of the organism being reinforced. When considering the nature of reward for a human being (or any other animal), one must know what that human being needs or wants, what he or she considers valuable, desirable, or positive, and to what conditions the human being has been previously exposed. Fowler (1971), at the recent Pittsburgh conference on learning devoted exclusively to the nature of reinforcement, presented evidence in support of viewing the concept as an incentive-motivational phenomenon, as a " 'hoped for' or 'feared' anticipation of events that are either preferred or averted relative to the setting condition under which the animal is operating [p. 177]." A positive reinforcement is thus seen as a preferred outcome, governed by "both long-term and momentary" factors. Glaser (1971), summarizing the conference, concluded: "The diverse ways in which response contingencies can have their effects, e.g., informational and incentive functions or attention and arousal functions, make it apparent that the situation in which behavior occurs must be characterized before the mechanism of reinforcement can be specified. [p. 13]."

The fact that reinforcement is relative does not preclude the possibility that we can make reasonable and valid assumptions about the rewarding nature of certain classes of events based on our knowledge of the culture in which particular individuals have been socialized. A head nod or verbal um—hum may be aversive and annoying to some individuals, but it is likely to be a desirable outcome for most. More often than not, we will be correct in assuming that approval, success, and attention, for example, will function as rewards for most Americans.

Specifying in advance what conditions will be interpreted as rewarding is no different, in principle, for the social psychologist than for any other psychologist. And although this may appear to be a difficult requirement, it is of fundamental importance. It is precisely this objective which is self-consciously voiced by Frazier in describing his utopian *Walden II* (Skinner, 1948): "By a careful cultural design we control not the final behavior, but the *inclination* to behave—the motives, the desires, the wishes [p. 262]." Once motivation is determined there is little question about the nature of the events that will be positively reinforcing. (It is not necessary to share Skinner's social objectives in order to recognize the sagacity of his analysis.)

Questions relevant to the meaning of reward are found in explicit or implicit form in much current research on attraction. In considering some of these questions in this chapter, we examine recent investigations that we believe illustrate specific issues relevant to the problem of how rewards function in the learning of liking. Our intent is to examine the *sources of reward* typically available to an individual in another person's presence.

III. Sources of Reward

A. *Direct Reward Provided by Another Person*

There are numerous empirical demonstrations that the likability of a person will increase after he or she performs some act that benefits another individual. Thus, for example, subjects rated cooperative players in a game higher on a liking scale than competitive players (Kleinke & Pohlen, 1971). And subjects who received shocks from opponents indicated greater attraction afterwards to subjects who were relatively nonaggressive than to those who set high shock levels (Hendrick & Taylor, 1971). It also comes as no surprise (but is reassuring, nevertheless) to find that subjects will report liking a confederate more if he has helped them perform a boring task than if he has not helped them, and they will like the confederate who has helped them voluntarily more than one who has helped them because he was so instructed (Nemeth, 1970). In the latter case, one receives not only aid, which is usually desirable in and of itself, but also a feeling that one is the focus of another's concern.

Direct reward from another person in the studies just cited, appears to have affected most subjects in the same general way. The needs elicited within most of the subjects can be assumed to have been similar, and to have been satisfied by the other person's behavior. In other cases, however, we find that different individuals are differently affected by the same potential reward. Thus, for example, being asked for a date by a man did not produce the same degree of liking for him by college women in an experiment conducted by Walster (1965). Immediately after being asked for the date by a male confederate the subjects were presented, by the experimenter, with different feedback from a pseudopersonality test. Those women whose self-esteem was lowered by negative test results subsequently indicated a greater liking for the male confederate than did the women whose self-esteem was raised by positive feedback. These findings fit a drive-reduction interpretation of reinforcement. Liking for the male was greater on the part of those subjects who needed the ego boost of the forthcoming date. The date offer had been made just prior to the self-esteem manipulation, but the date itself was an anticipated potentially positive experience. The liking measure intervened between the self-esteem manipulation and the expectation of a pleasurable event. Reward in this example has two aspects: first, the date offer and, second, the anticipation of the forthcoming experience.

Similarly, a study by Kiesler (1966) shows how different situations (rather than differences in individual motivation) can affect the meaning, or significance, of the same potentially reinforcing behavior. High school students, working in pairs with nonfriends, were instructed either to cooperate or to compete in a word game. The partner, who always won most of the money, then shared or did not share the money with the subject. Liking was found to increase more for partners who behaved "appropriately," (that is, who shared under cooperative instructions and who didn't share under competitive ones) than for partners who behaved "inappropriately." Thus, although it might ordinarily be assumed that the act of sharing what one has will be viewed positively by the recipient, this is not always the case. Altruistic behavior can be interpreted as inappropriate, and, under certain other conditions, as belittling, or patronizing, insincere, or manipulative (see Schopler, 1970). To predict which of these alternative reactions an individual will make requires knowledge of what the individual expects and wants in a particular situation.

A further example of the relatively of reward can be found in a report by Sigall

(1970). Under conditions of high involvement in a task in which subjects were required to organize a persuasive speech (as opposed to low involvement in which subjects simply read a prepared speech), listeners who changed their opinions from strong disagreement to mild disagreement (a 5-point change on a 30-point scale) were better liked than listeners who changed from agreement to a bit stronger agreement (a one-point change). Therefore, subjects who worked to affect some change in the opinion of their audience were gratified by a larger change, despite the fact that the audience still mildly disagreed. In another condition, subjects not only succeeded in effecting a five-point change, but also in moving the opinion of the listeners from disagreement to agreement. These listeners, as we would expect, were liked best of all.

1. POSITIVE EVALUATIONS

A number of investigations make use of one person's judgments about another as a means of manipulating reward. The culturally based expectation is that most people will seek, or be gratified by, the positive appraisal of others. And we do, indeed, find that persons who provide us with such positive evaluations are, in general, better liked than those who evaluate us poorly (see Byrne & Rhamey, 1965; Landy & Aronson, 1968; Shrauger & Jones, 1968). The attractiveness of a black stranger can be increased even for prejudiced white subjects under these kinds of conditions. Byrne and Ervin (1969) found that white subjects with strong antiblack bias were more attracted to a black stranger who evaluated them positively, on a variety of personality characteristics, than to one who evaluated them negatively. The level of liking for the positive black evaluator was, of course, less for prejudiced white subjects than for subjects low in prejudice. We can assume that for the less prejudiced, being told they were considered moral, well-adjusted, and intelligent was gratifying whether the evaluator was white or black, while for the highly prejudiced subjects the value of such an appraisal, though still positive, was diminished when it was provided by a stranger who was black.

The same phenomenon may be operating when one receives a positive evaluation that is believed to be inaccurate. Such evaluations are not unequivocally positive, and we know that they are generally less effective in heightening the attractiveness of the evaluator than appraisals that are *both* complimentary and accurate (Hewitt, 1969; Lowe & Goldstein, 1970).

Relevant to the question of what other factors affect the way in which we receive evaluations of ourselves from others are two studies, one almost a replication of the other, that provide contradictory results. Deutsch and Solomon (1959) found that persons with high self-opinions, as manipulated by task success, liked other persons who shared this positive opinion of themselves better than persons who did not; but that subjects who were led to believe that they had done poorly did not prefer positive to negative evaluators. Skolnick (1971) largely reproduced the conditions of this experiment and found that *all* subjects, regardless of prior task success, favored the positive evaluators and, furthermore, that subjects who believed they had done poorly on the task liked the positive notewriters even more than subjects who believed they had done well. Skolnick's analysis of the reasons for obtaining findings different from those of Deutsch and Solomon focused on the different meanings that the positive feedback may have had in the two experiments to the individuals who believed that they had failed. Subjects in the Deutsch and Solomon study were telephone operators and might have known one another. They were perhaps less ego-involved in the task set for them, and more suspicious and unbelieving. Skolnick's subjects, on the other hand, are described by him as highly involved college students, strangers to one another, and more likely to have accepted the notes they received at face value.

Data reported by Dutton and Arrowood (1971) further illustrate that the meaning of reward can vary with the conditions of its receipt and with individual goals and that these variations must be taken into account in understanding changes in the likability of persons providing the reward. Female subjects presented arguments on a contemporary issue and were then evaluated on their performance. When a subject presented her one position, her liking for the evaluator depended primarily on his agreement with her views, but when she argued for a position opposite to her own, her liking for the evaluator depended primarily on whether his evaluation of her performance agreed with her own.

2. GAIN–LOSS SEQUENCES

Attention has been directed recently to the important question of the effect on likability of a person who provides positive appraisal (or agreement) after initial negative appraisal (or disagreement). Two lines of investigation can be distinguished: one in which the same evaluator provides all the feedback; and a second in which feedback comes from different sources.

Illustrative of the latter are studies by Worchel and Schuster (1966) and Stapert and Clore (1969). Both investigations found that attraction to an agreeing person is greater following disagreement by others than following agreement. Disagreement was assumed to be arousing and consequent agreement was interpreted as drive reducing. Thus, the effectiveness of agreement is seen to be a positive function of the individual's drive state.

Aronson and Linder (1965) obtained similar results when subjects overheard themselves being evaluated by the same person, another student, on successive occasions. The evaluator who changed from negative to positive appraisals was significantly better liked than the evaluator who maintained a positive view throughout.

Mettee (1971b) has suggested that when individuals are being judged on different tasks, an evaluator who is consistently positive is not believable. In addition, Mettee (1971a) has found that when judgments are made by the same person on different and independent aspects of a subject's performance, positive judgments that are made first are more effective in increasing the evaluator's attractiveness than such judgments made later. Perhaps, as Mettee noted, it is primarily when later judgments can be interpreted as replacing prior judgments (as is true in the other studies cited above), that later, positive appraisals have greater significance.

B. The Characteristics of Another Person as a Source of Reward

Interpersonal attitudes are influenced not only by what another person does for us directly, such as providing us with attention, help, or praise, but also by the nature of the characteristics that person possesses and our evaluation of these characteristics along some "good—bad" continuum. A simple illustration of this phenomenon is the fact that persons who are judged to be physically attractive are better liked by individuals of both sexes at the outset, than are physically unattractive persons; this phenomenon is especially true of men's reactions to women (Byrne, London, & Reeves, 1968; Strobe, Insko, Thompson, & Layton, 1971; Walster, Aronson, Abrahams, & Rottmann, 1966).

Frequently what we think about a person takes the form of a series of descriptive adjectives, supplied either by some third party or by ourselves following actual observation of the person. In either case, it can be assumed that the traits in others which we consider to be "good" will function as rewards for us because anticipated interaction with persons possessing such traits is likely to result in satisfying outcomes. Conversely, interaction with persons who possess "bad" traits is more likely to lead to interpersonal consequences of an aversive nature. Sometimes what we learn about another person is simply the degree to which he or she is similar to us in terms of certain characteristics. Under ordinary circumstances, mere similarity of personality traits seems to be rewarding for the same reason that "good" traits are; similarity, too, increases the likelihood that interaction with the similar person will produce satisfying consequences. [Later in this chapter we deal with similarity in *attitudes*. We believe such similarity constitutes a different source of reward, that of validating one's interpretation of events (Byrne, 1969) and, therefore, enabling one to operate more effectively within the social environment (Byrne & Clore, 1967).]

1. DESCRIPTIVE ADJECTIVES

An early, classic demonstration of the impact of personal characteristics on likability was provided by Razran (1938), who found a drop in the liking for girls after it was learned that they were Jewish, as compared with other girls who were identified by other ethnic labels. It would be belaboring the obvious to provide further empirical demonstrations of this phenomenon, namely the influence of one's religion, ethnicity, occupation, color, and other statuses on one's attractiveness to other persons. The ubiquitous tendency to order personal characteristics in terms of some generalized scale of "social desirability" is nicely illustrated by the fact that even the first names of children have been found to have a predictable relationship to their sociometric position within school groups (McDavid & Harari, 1966; Schoenfeld, 1942), depending upon the "desirability" of the name, as judged by persons who had no knowledge of the children themselves.

It is less surprising and more reasonable to discover that, in general, certain personality characteristics are preferred to others. Strangers described as dominant, or as extroverted, for example, are significantly better liked than strangers described as submissive, or as introverted (Hendrick & Brown, 1971; Palmer & Byrne, 1970); and trait adjectives such as sincere, honest, understanding, and loyal are rated high in "favorableness," while traits such as cruel, mean, phony, and liar are rated lowest (Anderson, 1968).

Lott, Lott, Reed, and Crow (1970) had two independent samples of college student subjects from two different areas of the United States describe actual acquaintances whom they liked very much, disliked, and felt neutrally about, by choosing appropriate words from Anderson's (1968) list of most meaningful personality-trait adjectives. The most discriminating words, (that is, those used predominantly and frequently to describe persons of one interpersonal-attraction category) were as follows: for liked persons—energetic, considerate, happy, intelligent, and truthful; for disliked persons—complaining, insincere, narrow-minded, quarrelsome, and self-centered. That interaction with persons described by the first five words should produce more favorable and satisfying outcomes than interaction with persons described by the last five is self-evident.

It is interesting, however, that although the agreement between the two samples (one from Kentucky and the other from California) was strong with respect to the ascription of the above traits to differentially liked persons, differences existed that we believe are attributable to distinctive cultural values. Kentucky students (but *not* students in California) said that persons they liked very much were, among other things, courteous, punctual, sentimental, sociable, and well mannered, while California students (but *not* Kentuckians) said their best-liked friends were confident, easy going, independent, and serious. We see these differences in the positive value of certain personal characteristics as being veridical reflections of dominant differences in the Kentucky and California student scenes. Similarly, specific trait preferences will also be found to vary among individuals depending upon the characteristics of their own personalities (see Posavac, 1971).

The effect of receiving heterogeneous, or conflicting, information about a person on the impression one forms of that person has been the subject of considerable investigation. When both favorable and unfavorable information is provided in varying sequences, a number of problems emerge, similar to those encountered in studies of changes in the evaluations that one individual receives from another. The problems are well illustrated by results reported recently by Levin and Schmidt (1969). These investigators showed to each subject a set of six, sequentially presented, personality-trait adjectives (three of high value and three of low value, in all possible orders) and asked, after each adjective, whether the subject liked or disliked the person being described. Not only were recency effects obtained, but there was also a tendency for high-value adjectives to have lesser weight than low-value adjectives, and for a given adjective to be weighted less when it was affectively inconsistent with adjectives presented earlier in the set.

One investigator has reported that variance in the favorableness of an individuals's reported characteristics is itself a negatively valued attribute, producing unfavorable impressions, probably because such variance is associated with instability and unpredictability (Levy, 1967). Of the models that attempt to deal with such impression-formation data, Anderson's "integration theory" (1971), which takes an averaging, rather than an additive, approach, is probably the most ambitious. Anderson has suggested that each piece of information we receive about a person (or *any* object or event) has both a scale value (that is, some position along an attitude dimension) and a weight (that is, degree of importance), both of which will vary for different individuals. Weight of any information is determined primarily by factors such as the status, reliability, and expertise of its source, as well as by primacy and recency factors. Anderson conceptualizes the impression-formation process as involving attitude change through "the integration of information into evaluative judgments that have social relevance," but he prefers to view his theory in "cognitive, information-processing" terms, rather than in terms of reinforcement. Such a distinction may be unnecessary. Since the evaluative dimension is introduced to describe variations in the value of the information we receive about a person (and Anderson's "scale value" is just such a dimension), it follows that the information will have positive, neutral, or negative qualities for its recipient and, therefore, affect the recipient's behavior (attitudes and judgments) in a predictable manner.

2. OBSERVATIONS OF BEHAVIOR

Sometimes we learn about a person's characteristics by observing how the person behaves in a situation in which we take no active part; we may simply overhear or oversee what the person says or does in relation to other people or things. In such cases we may apply to the persons we observe certain personality-trait descriptions which then enter into the evaluative responses we make to them. In one study (Landy & Aronson, 1968), confederates were observed making judgments of photographs and paintings. The more discriminating (apparently "discerning") judges were subsequently liked better by subjects, regardless of whether the confederates previously had praised or had criticized them. Hendrick, Bixenstine, and Hawkins (1971) found that subjects who observed actors discussing the war in Vietnam on videotape subsequently liked actors who displayed a high level of expressive behavior better than those who were less expressive. This was true under conditions where subjects were exposed to both audio and visual information, as well as to only the video portion of the tape. Similarly, subjects who observed confederates interacting with other subjects (Holstein, Goldstein, & Bem, 1971) liked confederates who displayed positive expressive behavior more than those who did not; and subjects who overheard a discussion liked a participant most when he refrained from engaging in justifiable aggression against another participant (Wheeler & Smith, 1967).

Two studies by Aronson (Aronson, Willerman, & Floyd, 1966; Helmreich, Aronson, & Le Fen, 1970) and his associates on the effects of observing another person blunder seem relevant here. A clumsy mishap appears to enhance the attractiveness of the erring person more under some conditions, for instance, when the blunder is committed by a "superior" as opposed to a "mediocre" person (Aronson, Willerman & Floyd, 1966); and for certain kinds of observers, for example, subjects of average self-esteem as opposed to subjects on the extreme ends of this dimension (Helmreich, Aronson, & Le Fen, 1970). Although in both studies the superior, or more competent, person was significantly better liked whether he made a blunder or not, the mishap seemed to serve to bring him closer to the level of the average person, to make him "more human," and thus to increase his attractiveness for individuals who view this state of affairs as desirable. (We are reminded here of Senator Hruska's plea that President Nixon appoint to the Supreme Court a mediocre justice so as to better represent the large numbers of mediocre people in the United States!)

We suggest that it is from the imagined or projected interaction with a person that the nature of his or her characteristics derive their potentially reinforcing or punishing properties. What is important is not simply the information about a person, but what that information leads us to expect or to suppose will happen if and when we should be confronted with the actual presence of the person. This interpretation is supported by findings of Kiesler, Kiesler, and Pallak (1967). Subjects observed an experimenter and two confederates, one of whom behaved and dressed "appropriately" and the other "inappropriately." Only when future interaction was explicitly anticipated did appropriateness positively relate to liking.

3. SIMILARITY OF PERSONAL TRAITS

To know that another person is like ourselves in social and personality characteristics provides an especially good basis for assuming positive outcomes from interaction. This is illustrated in such diverse ways as the following: attraction to a stranger is found to be significantly affected by the similarity of his economic status (Byrne, Clore, & Worchel, 1966); there is a tendency to select as friends individuals who are closer to one's own height (Berkowitz, 1969); and members of East African tribes manifest more positive attitudes (lesser social distance) toward groups they perceive as more similar to themselves (Brewer, 1968). Griffitt and his associates have found consistent relationships between attraction to a stranger and personality similarity with respect to self-descriptions (Griffitt, 1966), self-concept and ideal self-statements (Griffitt, 1969), and scores on the Repression—Sensitization Scale (Byrne, Griffitt, & Stephanic, 1967).

The strength of the positive incentive quality of similarity in personality characteristics is demonstrated in a study by Miller and Zimbardo (1966) in which high school boys, made fearful of a forthcoming "blood chemistry experiment," chose to await the new situation with other persons, rather than alone, and preferred persons who were similar to themselves in personality over others who were simply also fearful, but not similar in personality.

It may be that similarity in personal characteristics signifies to us similarity in experiences or background. That shared experiences can lead to increased liking for a person has been shown in a recent investigation by Clore and Jeffery (1971). Subjects who traveled around in a wheel chair for an hour playing the role of a disabled individual subsequently differed from control subjects in manifesting, on a number of measures, more positive attitudes toward both a specific disabled person and such persons in general.

There are, of course, circumstances under which a person who is similiar to one-self is less preferred (or more ambivalently regarded) than one who is different, as, for example, when the similar person is said to be emotionally disturbed (Novak & Lerner, 1968). Although similar mental patients were rated higher on a liking measure than dissimilar ones, subjects tended to indicate less willingness to interact with the former. Less ambiguous findings have been reported by Taylor and Mettee (1971), who found that while similar confederates are liked more than dissimilar ones when both behave pleasantly, the reverse is true when both behave obnoxiously.

C. Another Person's Attitude Similarity as Evidence for One's Own Competence

Byrne (1969, 1971), in an extensive research program with various associates, has provided systematic evidence of a positive linear relationship between attraction to a stranger and the proportion of attitudes held in common with that stranger. It is Byrne's view that similarity leads to liking because it provides an individual with independent evidence of the correctness of his interpretation of social reality, a kind of validation of his point of view, which should enable him to deal more confidently and effectively with his environment. Thus, similarity is said to reinforce one's "need for competence" (Byrne & Clore, 1967). We suggest that this is primarily the case when another person is similar to ourselves in attitudes, beliefs, or opinions. It is these aspects of a person which indicate ways of structuring the environment and which, therefore, by their similarity to our own, provide evidence that our dominant reactions are valid. Personality traits, status, or physical characteristics, on the other hand, are relatively unambiguous and not generally classifiable as reflections of how we view the world; they are aspects of ourselves which we accept as real even though we may evaluate some of them negatively. Thus, similarity can be seen as providing two kinds of potential reinforcement: in one case, to know that other persons are like ourselves usually encourages us to expect more positive outcomes from interaction with them; in the case of similarity of attitudes, there is additionally the reassurance we get that our views are shared, thereby increasing the probability of our effectance or competence.

The findings of Byrne, Nelson, and Reeves (1966) provide data that support the preceding analysis. Some subjects believed they were similar or dissimilar to a stranger with respect to a number of unverifiable opinions; for other subjects, the opinions were verifiable in the future; while for a third group, the opinions related to verifiable fact. The need for social validation can be assumed to have been the strongest for the first group of subjects, and it is within this group that opinion similarity had the greatest effect on liking. Batchelor and Tesser (1971) varied not the verifiability of opinions, but the reasons why other persons were said to hold particular attitudes that were similar to those of the subjects. Similar, other persons whose attitudes were said to be expressive of their values were liked more, while similar persons whose attitudes were said to be ego defensive were liked less. If the reinforcing effect of attitude similarity stems from its satisfaction of competence (or validation) needs, then it is to be expected that when support for one's own views is obtained from a negative source, as in this case from a source whose views are of dubious validity, then this support will not reduce these needs as much as when it comes from a positive source.

In another relevant investigation, Reagor and Clore (1970) had subjects take a vocabulary test under conditions where cues to the correctness of their responses were minimized by the difficulty of the items. Subjects could obtain evidence of their own competence only by comparing their responses with those of another person. Strangers who had spelled 83% of the words in the same way as the subject were liked better than strangers who had spelled the words differently. Senn (1971), too, has found that subjects performing similarly and successfully on a reaction-time task were more attracted to each other than similarly performing, but unsuccessful, subjects and than dissimilarly performing ones. Thus, not only similar attitudes, but similar behaviors, which relate to one's abilities and one's competence, will be reinforcing.

D. The Receipt of Reward in Another Person's Presence

Our own research has been designed to demonstrate the effectiveness of reward in increasing the attractiveness of noninstrumental, previously neutral persons, who are simply associated with such reward. Thus, we have shown that children will come to prefer members of their own play groups over other peers after they have successfully achieved the goals of a game within their own group, but not when they have been unsuccessful (Lott & Lott, 1960). Similarly, children in a classroom situation who were systematically rewarded by a teacher who recognized, positively responded to, and maintained eye contact with them, increased their liking for classmates significantly more than did other children who had either been ignored by the teacher or responded to critically (Lott & Lott, 1968). Such differential experience by the children for a period of time as short as 30 min succeeded in producing changes in the liking of classmates who were present, but had no instrumental connection with either the positive or negative treatment provided by the teacher.

We prefer naturalistic situations such as those described above, but other investigators have utilized simple classical conditioning procedures in more controlled laboratory situations to produce the same effect—the conditioning of attitudinal responses to neutral persons through association with positively valued stimuli. Early (1968) had children learn to associate first names of other children with highly valued adjectives (for instance, neat) or with words of low value and found significant changes in the behavior of subjects toward children whose names had been used as conditioned stimuli. Similarly, Sachs and Byrne (1970) found that subjects evaluated more positively peers whose pictures had been presented in association with similar attitudes than they did peers whose pictures were associated with dissimilar attitudes.

In another study of children, we found that those who assisted another child in a series of Bingo games, but who themselves won nothing, reacted like the winners and developed more positive attitudes toward the other children present than did losers and their assistants (Lott, Lott, & Matthews, 1969). Evidence was also obtained in this investigation that it was not the mere fact of winning or losing, either directly or vicariously, that was important, but how a child felt about it. Since it is the affective reaction to a potentially rewarding stimulus that is important, and not the more delivery or availability of the stimulus itself, the development of reliable techniques to assess goal reactions would be of great value. The rewarding properties (desirability) of a stimulus could then be validated independently of measures of the dependent variable in a particular study. Such independent assessments of individual reactions to potential rewards are only sometimes made.

A sizable number of investigations have accumulated to support the relationship between an individual's experience of reward (as assumed by the investigator) and his or her subsequent positive attitude toward neutral persons present at the time. Sometimes the situation is ambiguous in that the persons present can be viewed as partially responsible for one's good or bad fortune, as in studies by Sinha (1968) and Streufert and Streufert (1969). In the latter study, for example, individuals in dyads credited with success in decision-making became more favorable in their attitudes toward one another than did individuals in unsuccessful dyads. Our major interest is in what occurs under circumstances where there is clearly no likelihood of attributing responsibility for one's success or gratification to another person who is present. This phenomenon can be dramatically illustrated by data from a study with Dutch teenagers (Rabbie & Horowitz, 1969), who, after coming together as strangers, were formed into pairs of four-person groups. In one condition, flipping a coin decided which group would obtain a prize of four radios. As is predictable from our proposition, ratings of own-group members were significantly more positive on the part of these winners than were ratings of out-group members. Similarly, Griffitt (1968) found that subjects who received five class-credit bonus points for participating in a study in which an anonymous stranger was evaluated, liked the stranger more than did subjects receiving only the minimum of one credit. This source of reinforcement, though clearly effective, could not readily be attributable directly to the stranger. Subsequently, Griffitt and Guay (1969) found that evaluations of a confederate who was responsible for judging subjects' "creativity" and a confederate who was simply present were positively related to the proportion of positive appraisals, with no difference between the two confederates.

A recent report by Senn (1971) noted that among pairs of subjects, one of whom was successful and the other unsuccessful on reaction-time tasks, the successful ones did not like their partners any more than the failing ones. This finding is atypical; however, since each subject could neither see nor hear the other person, but was simply made aware of his or her performance by a panel light, the partners in Senn's investigation cannot really be said to have been in one another's presence.

Environmental conditions under which we are called upon to evaluate or respond affectively to another person were manipulated by Griffitt, who found in one study (1970) that subjects responded to an anonymous, bogus-stranger, after inspecting his responses to an attitude questionnaire, significantly more positively when temperature and humidity were "normal" (that is, effective temperature = 67.5°F) than when temperature and humidity conditions produced an effective temperature of 90.6°F. What is of particular importance, we believe, is that across all experimental conditions, attraction to the stranger was positively correlated with positiveness of the subjects' "feelings" in the situation (on a good—bad continuum). In a later study (Griffitt & Veitch, 1971), more negative attitudes toward a stranger were found to be expressed by individuals who were both "hot" and "crowded" (that is, in a situation of high population density).

When we "feel good" in a situation in which other persons are present, this affective reaction will be conditioned to those other persons, who then will evoke a component of this feeling in the form of a positive attitudinal response. In the studies cited thus far, positive affective reactions were induced by events experienced in the presence of others, but there is also evidence that indicates we can bring to a situation positive feelings that were aroused just prior to it, and that these feelings, too, will increase our liking for persons present in the subsequent and new situation. Isen (1970), for example, found that subjects who had been successful on a task later behaved more generously and helpfully toward a stranger than did subjects who had failed; and he attributed these findings to the presence of a "warm glow of success." That this "warm glow" can come from sources other than success, but again function similarly in influencing interpersonal attraction, is evident from a report by Gouaux (1971), who used a film to induce "elation" or "depression" in women students. Afterward, the students were tested for attraction to a stranger whose attitudinal similarity to themselves was varied. Both the similarity variable and the prior affective state of elation or depression were found to be independently related to liking for the stranger.

These findings suggest the possibility that individuals who differ in such things as mood, overall optimism, and "good feeling," enter a new situation already predisposed to regard the persons who will be present differentially. Some recent studies of men's reactions to photographs of women under conditions of false heart-rate feedback (Valins 1966, 1967; Barefoot & Straub, 1971) indicate strongly that simply being told, or being led to believe, that one "feels good" is also a positive state of affairs and similarly leads to increased attraction toward stimuli present at the time.

Mention might be made, at this point, of some recent findings relevant to the investigation of Zajonc's now famous "mere exposure" hypothesis (1968). Zajonc suggested that attitudes toward a novel stimulus become increasingly positive as a simple function of continued exposure to, or experience with, that stimulus "if no other events—negative in their consequences for the organism—accompany these encounters . . . ." It seems to be the case, however, that the absence of negative associations is not sufficient; instead it is the exposure with positive associations that appears to be responsible for the liking effect (Burgess & Sales, 1971). In an experiment utilizing person stimuli, Perlman and Oskamp (1971) presented, with varying frequencies, pictures of black and white persons in positive, neutral, or negative contexts to a sample of white college students. The exposure—favorability relationship was found to be strongest for pictures presented in positive contexts (for example, person-as-physician), weak for those in neutral contexts (person-in-yearbook), and slightly reversed for pictures in negative contexts (person-as-prisoner). These findings conform to our proposition and support Amir's (1969) conclusion relative to the effects of contact between ethnic groups, namely that it is not contact per se, but the conditions under which the contact takes place, which affects intergroup attitudes.

VARIATIONS IN THE CONDITIONS OF REWARD

An advantage of reviewing interpersonal attraction within the framework of general learning theory is that specific predictions relevant to the development of positive attitudes toward persons can be derived from theory-related variables. For example, one variable that should affect the strength of association between a previously neutral stimulus and an anticipatory goal response is the length of time between the ending of the reward-producing response and the actual receipt of the reward (Hull, 1952). To test the specific hypothesis that attraction to a person will be greater when that person is associated with immediate, as compared with delayed, reward, we had first-grade children perform a simple task in the alternate presence of two adult assistants (Lott, Aponte, Lott, & McGinley, 1969). One assistant ("Mr. I") was consistently associated with immediate reward contingent upon the child's task completion in each of 14 trials, while the other assistant ("Mr. D") was associated with a 10-sec delay in reward for the same number of trials. For control subjects, both assistants, Misters I and D, were paired with an equal number of immediate and delayed reinforcements. In every case, rewards in the form of cranberry beans were delivered to a child automatically and *not* by the assistants who simply gave "ready," "start," and "stop" signals and maintained relatively impassive facial expressions. Each subject accumulated beans in order to obtain a toy that had been chosen previously. On three dependent measures of attraction, reliable differences were found between experimental and control subjects in their relative liking of the two assistants. In addition, children in the experimental groups said (verbally) that they liked Mr. I better than they liked Mr. D, rated Mr. I higher on a liking scale, and judged him on a semantic differential scale to have been happier, cleaner, kinder, and better than Mr. D. To control for personality differences, each assistant functioned for half the subjects as Mr. I, and for the other half of the subjects as Mr. D.

Liking should also be influenced by other variables that are known to affect the learning of responses in general and the strength of anticipatory responses in particular. In two subsequent studies (Lott, Bright, Weinstein, & Lott, 1970) we investigated the role of drive and incentive in the development of positive attitudes toward persons. In one experiment the quality or desirability of the rewarding stimuli was manipulated. First-grade children played a series of games in which photographs of strangers were systematically associated with highly desirable or undesirable food snacks, as previously determined for each subject. Those children run under contrast conditions (that is, who received both high- and low-valued incentives in association with different photographs), gave higher ratings to the person associated with the highly valued snack, whereas children who received the same food snacks (either high or low preference) in association with two different photographs rated both persons relatively equally.

The second study, concerned with drive, utilized college students differing in need for academic recognition, as measured by *Liverant's Goal Preference Inventory* (Liverant, 1958). The level of relevant drive in individuals who were rewarded was found to relate positively to the attractiveness of reward-associated stimulus persons, as predicted. On three different measures, students high in the need for academic recognition showed significantly greater liking for a person who was present when they made high scores on a portion of an "intelligence" test than for a person who was present when they did poorly on another portion of the test; low-drive subjects, on the other hand, did not show a reliable difference in their liking for these two persons. Independent evidence that the high- and low-drive subjects did in fact differ motivationally came from their responses to a question asking them to rate their degree of interest in the tests. Those subjects with high need-for-academic-recognition scores indicated significantly greater interest than subjects with low scores.

Whether an event or a stimulus is a reward is thus seen to depend upon whether or not it satisfies a present need. Only those individuals in this investigation for whom academic status was important, and for whom high test scores were thereby a source of pleasure, were differentially affected by high and low attainment. Similarly, what is rewarding depends upon special qualities of the stimulus, which are sometimes idiosyncratically valued, with corn chips being a more mouth-watering snack for some of the children in our investigation, peanuts for others, and so on. And, to be maximally rewarding, the same desirable event or object should be obtainable sooner rather than later, that is, without significant delay.

IV. Interpersonal Attraction and the Reward Hypothesis

Two approaches, other than our own, which make explicit use of the concept of reinforcement and S—R learning principles in analyzing the development of evaluative responses (attitudes) to person stimuli are those of Byrne (Byrne & Clore, 1970; also see Clore and Byrne, Chapter 7 in this volume) and of Staats (1968). Byrne, beginning with empirical demonstrations that persons will be positively attracted to strangers having similar attitudes in direct proportion to the extent of that similarity, attempted to account for this relationship by use of a classical conditioning model. Attitude similarity was interpreted as an unconditioned stimulus that evokes an implicit affective response. This response is automatically evoked because attitude similarity is "reinforcing," and therefore positively valued, by virtue of being able to satisfy a need for effectance. Consequently, a discriminable stimulus such as one of Byrne's "bogus-strangers" can serve as a conditioned stimulus and through association with the UCS (similar attitude statements) come to evoke the same positive affect. Although Byrne's model was formulated to account for specific empirical findings regarding the role of attitude similarity in interpersonal attraction, he has since come to recognize its more general potential. In Clore and Byrne's contribution to this volume, for example (Chapter 7), they object to being criticized for referring to the similarity—attraction relationship as "the law of attraction" and assert that "there is no similarity theory but rather a reinforcement theory." This position clearly coincides with our own (Lott & Lott, 1960, 1968).

Staats (1968) prefers Skinnerian terminology, but also views the attitude-acquisition process as the result of a classical conditioning procedure, which typically takes place within the context of an operant reward situation. He defines attitudes as emotional or affective responses toward stimuli; and stimuli that come to elicit such responses are called attitudinal stimuli. When a neutral stimulus is paired with an unconditioned stimulus that elicits a positive emotional response, this response will be classically conditioned to the neutral stimulus. Although developed with respect to attitudes in general, this analysis is clearly applicable to attitudes toward persons. We agree with Greenwald (1968) that: "By appropriate translation between the two systems [Staats's and the Lotts'], it may be expected that different theoretical predictions would not be generated. Significant differences . . . are to be found principally in the types of research problems suggested by their respective formulations [p. 372]."

We think that our position can best be distinguished from others that view attitude acquisition as a learning phenomenon primarily by the fact that we have from the beginning proposed and demonstrated that the receipt of reward in a person's presence is a primary antecedent for the development of positive attitudes toward that person, with reward interpreted in drive-reduction terms. We have also sought explicitly to utilize the principles associated with the Yale—Iowa viewpoint (of Hull, Spence, Mowrer, and others) to generate and test an interrelated set of hypotheses relevant to both the acquisition and consequences of attraction toward persons. Thus, we have found it heuristically useful to identify a positive interpersonal attitude, or liking, as an anticipatory goal response ($r_g - s_g$) and a liked person as a secondary reinforcer (Lott & Lott, 1968, 1972).

It seems to us that while only a small number of investigators unabashedly make systematic use of reinforcement-related principles to generate testable hypotheses regarding interpersonal attraction, a great many investigators actually manipulate conditions of reward in their investigations and utilize the concept of reward to explain their empirical results. The reward hypothesis thus appears to be alive and well in the literature, if not always give its due recognition, perhaps illustrating the wisdom of an old Yiddish proverb: "The truth never dies—it just leads a miserable existence!"

References

Amir, Y. Contact hypothesis in ethnic relations. *Psychological Bulletin*, 1969, **5**, 319—342.

Anderson, N. H. Likableness ratings of 555 personality trait words. *Journal of Personality and Social Psychology*, 1968, **9**, 272—279.

Anderson, N. H. Integration theory and attitude change. *Psychological Review*, 1971, **78**, 171—206.

Aronson, E. Some antecedents of interpersonal attraction. In W. J. Arnold & D. Levine (Eds.), *Nebraska Symposium on Motivation*. Lincoln, Nebraska: University of Nebraska Press, 1969.

Aronson, E., & Linder, D. Gain and loss of esteem as determinants of interpersonal attractiveness. *Journal of Experimental Social Psychology*, 1965, **1**, 156—171.

Aronson, E., Willerman, B., & Floyd, J. The effect of a pratfall on increasing interpersonal attractiveness. *Psychonomic Science*, 1966, **4**, 227—228.

Barefoot, J. C., & Straub, R. B. Opportunity for information search and the effect of false heart-rate feedback. *Journal of Personality and Social Psychology*, 1971, **17**, 154—157.

Batchelor, T. R., & Tesser, A. Attitude base as a moderator of the attitude similarity-attraction relationship. *Journal of Personality and Social Psychology*, 1971, **19**, 229—236.

Berkowitz, W. R. Perceived height, personality, and friendship choice. *Psychological Reports*, 1969, **24**, 373—374.

Brewer, M. B. Determinants of social distance among East African tribal groups. *Journal of Personality and Social Psychology*, 1968, **10**, 279—289.

Burgess, T. D. G. II, & Sales, S. M. Attitudinal effects of "mere exposure": A reevaluation. *Journal of Experimental Social Psychology*, 1971, **7**, 461—462.

Byrne, D. Attitudes and attraction. In L. Berkowitz (Ed.), *Advances in Experimental Social Psychology*. Vol. 4. New York: Academic Press, 1969.

Byrne, D. *The attraction paradigm*. New York: Academic Press, 1971.

Byrne, D., & Clore, G. L. Effectance arousal and attraction. *Journal of Personality and Social Psychology*, 1967, **6**, No. 4(Whole No. 638).

Byrne, D., & Clore, G. L. A reinforcement model of evaluative responses. *Personality: An International Journal*, 1970, **1**, 103—128.

Byrne, D., Clore, G. L., & Worchel, P. Effect of economic similarity—dissimilarity on interpersonal attraction. *Journal of Personality and Social Psychology*, 1966, **4**, 220—224.

Byrne, D., & Ervin, C. R. Attraction toward a Negro stranger as a function of prejudice, attitude similarity and the stranger's evaluation of the subject. *Human Relations*, 1969, **22**, 397—404.

Byrne, D., Griffitt, W., & Stephanic, K. D. Attraction and similarity of personality characteristics. *Journal of Personality and Social Psychology*, 1967, **5**, 82—90.

Byrne, D., London, O., & Reeves, K. The effects of physical attractiveness, sex and attitude similarity on interpersonal attraction. *Journal of Personality*, 1968, **36**, 259—271.

Byrne, D., Nelson, D., & Reeves, K. Effects of consensual validation and invalidation on attraction as a function of verifiability. *Journal of Experimental Social Psychology*, 1966, **2**, 98—107.

Byrne, D., & Rhamey, R. Magnitude of positive and negative reinforcements as a determinant of attraction. *Journal of Personality and Social Psychology*, 1965, **2**, 884—889.

Clore, G. L., & Jeffrey, K. M. Emotional role playing, attitude change and attraction toward a disabled person. Unpublished manuscript, University of Illinois, 1971.

Deutsch, M., & Solomon, L. Reactions to evaluations of others as influenced by self-evaluations. *Sociometry*, 1959, **2**, 93–112.

Doob, L. W. The behavior of attitudes. *Psychological Review*, 1947, **54**, 135–156.

Dutton, D. G., & Arrowood, A. J. Situational factors in evaluation congruency and interpersonal attraction. *Journal of Personality and Social Psychology*, 1971, **18**, 222–229.

Early, C. J. Attitude learning in children. *Journal of Educational Psychology*, 1968, **59**, 176–180.

Fowler, H. Implications of sensory reinforcement. In R. Glaser (Ed.), *The nature of reinforcement*. New York: Academic Press, 1971.

Glaser, R. Introduction. In R. Glaser (Ed.), *The nature of reinforcement*. New York: Academic Press, 1971.

Gouaux, C. Induced affective states and interpersonal attraction. *Journal of Personality and Social Psychology*, 1971, **20**, 37–43.

Greenwald, A. G. On defining attitude and attitude theory. In A. G. Greenwald, T. C. Brock, & T. M. Ostrom (Eds.), *Psychological foundations of attitudes*. New York: Academic Press, 1968.

Griffitt, W., & Veitch, R. Hot and crowded: Influences of population density and temperature on interpersonal affective behavior. *Journal of Personality and Social Psychology*, 1971, **17**, 92–98.

Griffitt, W. B. Interpersonal attraction as a function of self-concept and personality similarity-dissimilarity. *Journal of Personality and Social Psychology*, 1966, **4**, 581–584.

Griffitt, W. B. Attraction toward a stranger as a function of direct and associated reinforcement. *Psychonomic Science*, 1968, **11**, 147–148.

Griffitt, W. B. Personality similarity and self-concept as determinants of interpersonal attraction. *Journal of Social Psychology*, 1969, **78**, 137–146.

Griffitt, W. B. Environmental effects on interpersonal affective behavior: Ambient effective temperature and attraction. *Journal of Personality and Social Psychology*, 1970, **15**, 240–244.

Griffitt, W. B., & Guay, P. "Object" evaluation and conditioned affect. *Journal of Experimental Research in Personality*, 1969, **4**, 1–8.

Helmreich, R., Aronson, E., & Le Fen, J. To err is humanizing—sometimes: Effects of self-esteem, competence, and a pratfall on interpersonal attraction. *Journal of Personality and Social Psychology*, 1960, **16**, 259–264.

Hendrick, C., Bixenstine, V. E., & Hawkins, G. Race versus belief similarity as determinants of attraction: A search for a fair test. *Journal of Personality and Social Psychology*, 1971, **17**, 250–258.

Hendrick, C., & Brown, S. R. Introversion, extraversion, and interpersonal attraction. *Journal of Personality and Social Psychology*, 1971, **20**, 31–36.

Hendrick, C., & Taylor, S. P. Effects of belief similarity and aggression on attraction and counter-aggression. *Journal of Personality and Social Psychology*, 1971, **17**, 342–349.

Hewitt, J. Interpersonal attraction as a function of the accuracy of personal evaluations. *Psychonomic Science*, 1969, **17**, 95–96.

Holstein, C. M., Goldstein, J. W., & Bem, D. J. The importance of expressive behavior, involvement, sex, and need-approval in reducing liking. *Journal of Experimental Social Psychology*, 1971, **7**, 534–544.

Hull, C. L. *A behavior system*. New Haven, Connecticut: Yale University Press, 1952.

Isen, A. M. Success, failure, attention, and reaction to others: The warm glow of success. *Journal of Personality and Social Psychology*, 1970, **15**, 294–301.

James, G., & Lott, A. J. Reward frequency and the formation of positive attitudes toward group members. *Journal of Social Psychology*, 1964, **62**, 111–115.

Kiesler, C. A., Kiesler, S. B., & Pallak, M. S. The effect of commitment to future interaction on reactions to norm violations. *Journal of Personality*, 1967, **35**, 585–599.

Kiesler, S. B. The effect of perceived role requirements on reactions to favor-doing. *Journal of Experimental Social Psychology*, 1966, **2**, 298–310.

Kleinke, C. L., & Pohlen, P. D. Affective and emotional responses as a function of other person's gaze and cooperativeness in a two-person game. *Journal of Personality and Social Psychology*. 1971, **17**, 308–313.

Landy, D., & Aronson, E. Liking for an evaluator as a function of his discernment. *Journal of Personality and Social Psychology*, 1968, **9**, 133—141.

Levin, I. P., & Schmidt, C. T. Sequential effects in impression formation with binary intermittent responding. *Journal of Experimental Psychology*, 1969, **79**, 283—287.

Levinger, G., & Snoek, J. D. *Attraction in relationship: A new look at interpersonal attraction.* New York: General Learning Press, 1972.

Levy, L. H. The effects of variance on personality impression formation, *Journal of Personality*, 1967, **35**, 179—193.

Liverant, S. The use of Rotter's social learning theory in developing a personality inventory. *Psychological Monographs*, 1958, **72**, No. 2.

Lott, A. J., Aponte, J. F., Lott, B. E., & McGinley, W. H. The effect of delayed reward on the development of positive attitudes toward persons. *Journal of Experimental Social Psychology*, 1969, **5**, 101—113.

Lott, A. J., Bright, M. A., Weinstein, P., & Lott, B. E. Liking for persons as a function of incentive and drive during acquisition. *Journal of Personality and Social Psychology*, 1970, **14**, 66—77.

Lott, A. J., & Lott, B. E. A learning theory approach to interpersonal attitudes. In A. G. Greenwald, T. C. Brock, & T. M. Ostrom (Eds.), *Psychological foundations of attitudes.* New York: Academic Press, 1968.

Lott, A. J., & Lott, B. E. The power of liking: Consequences of interpersonal attitudes derived from a liberalized view of secondary reinforcement. In L. Berkowitz (Ed.), *Advances in experimental social psychology*, Vol. 6. New York: Academic Press, 1972.

Lott, A. J., Lott, B. E., & Matthews, G. Interpersonal attraction among children as a function of vicarious reward. *Journal of Educational Psychology*, 1969, **60**, 274—282.

Lott, A. J., Lott, B. E., Reed, T. & Crow, T. Personality-trait descriptions of differentially liked persons. *Journal of Personality and Social Psychology*, 1970, **16**, 284—290.

Lott, B. E., & Lott, A. J. The formation of positive attitudes toward group members. *Journal of Abnormal and Social Psychology*, 1960, **61**, 297—300.

Lowe, C. A., & Goldstein, J. W. Reciprocal liking and attributions of ability: Mediating effects of perceived intent and personal involvement. *Journal of Personality and Social Psychology*, 1970, **16**, 291—297.

McDavid, J. W., & Harari, H. Stereotyping of names and popularity in grade-school children. *Child Development*, 1966, **37**, 453—459.

Mettee, D. R. Changes in liking as a function of the magnitude and affect of sequential evaluations. *Journal of Experimental Social Psychology*, 1971, **7**, 157—172.   (a)

Mettee, D. R. The true discerner as a potent source of positive affect. *Journal of Experimental Social Psychology*, 1971, **7**, 292—303.   (b)

Miller, N., & Zimbardo, P. Motive for fear-induced affiliation: Emotional comparison or interpersonal similarity? *Journal of Personality*, 1966, **34**, 481—503.

Nemeth, C. Effects of free versus constrained behavior on attraction between people. *Journal of Personality and Social Psychology*, 1970, **15**, 302—311.

Novak, D. W., & Lerner, M. J. Rejection as a consequence of perceived similarity. *Journal of Personality and Social Psychology*, 1968, **9**, 147—152.

Palmer, J., & Byrne, D. Attraction toward dominant and submissive strangers; similarity versus complementarity. *Journal of Experimental Research in Personality*, 1970, **4**, 108—115.

Perlman, D., & Oskamp, S. The effects of picture content and exposure frequency on evaluations of Negroes and whites. *Journal of Experimental Social Psychology*, 1971, **7**, 503—514.

Posavac, E. J. Dimensions of trait preference and personality type. *Journal of Personality and Social Psychology*, 1971, **19**, 274—281.

Rabbie, J. M., & Horwitz, M. Arousal of ingroup—outgroup bias by a chance win or loss. *Journal of Personality and Social Psychology*, 1969, **13**, 269—277.

Razran, G. Conditioning away social bias. *Psychological Bulletin*, 1938, **35**, 693.

Reagor, P. A., & Clore, G. L. Attraction, test anxiety, and similarity-dissimilarity of test performance. *Psychonomic Science*, 1970, **18**, 219—220.

Sachs, D. H., & Byrne, D. Differential condition of evaluative responses to neutral stimuli through association with attitude statements. *Journal of Experimental Research in Personality*, 1970, **4**, 181—185.

Schopler, J. An attribution analysis of some determinants of reciprocating a benefit. In J. Macaulay & L. Berkowitz (Eds.), *Altruism and helping behavior*. New York: Academic Press, 1970.

Schoenfeld, N. An experimental study of some problems relating to stereotypes. *Archives of Psychology*, 1942, **38**, 270.

Senn, D. J. Attraction as a function of similarity–dissimilarity in task performance. *Journal of Personality and Social Psychology*, 1971, **18**, 120–123.

Shrauger, J. S. & Jones, S. C. Social validation and interpersonal evaluations. *Journal of Experimental Social Psychology*, 1968, **4**, 315–323.

Sigall, H. Effects of competence and consensual validation on a communicator's liking for the audience. *Journal of Personality and Social Psychology*, 1970, **16**, 251–258.

Sinha, J. B. The n-Ach/n-cooperation under limited/unlimited resource conditions. *Journal of Experimental Social Psychology*, 1968, **4**, 233–246.

Skinner, B. F. *Walden Two*. New York: MacMillan, 1948 (Paper Edition, 1962.)

Skolnick, P. Reactions to personal evaluations: A failure to replicate. *Journal of Personality and Social Psychology*, 1971, **18**, 62–67.

Staats, A. W. Social behaviorism and human motivation: Principles of the attitude-reinforcer-discriminative system. In A. G. Greenwald, T. C. Brock, & T. M. Ostrom (Eds.), *Psychological foundations of attitudes*. New York: Academic Press, 1968.

Stapert, J. C., & Clore, C. L. Attraction and disagreement produced arousal. *Journal of Personality and Social Psychology*, 1969, **13**, 64–69.

Streufert, S., & Streufert, S. C. Effects of conceptual structure, failure, and success on attribution of causality and interpersonal attitudes. *Journal of Personality and Social Psychology*, 1969, **11**, 138–147.

Stroebe, W., Insko, C., Thompson, V. D., & Layton, B. D. Effects of physical attractiveness, attitude similarity, and sex on various aspects of interpersonal attraction. *Journal of Personality and Social Psychology*, 1971, **18**, 79–91.

Taylor, S. E., & Mettee, D. R. When similarity breeds contempt. *Journal of Personality and Social Psychology*, 1971, **20**, 75–81.

Valins, S. Cognitive effects of false heart-rate feedback. *Journal of Personality and Social Psychology*, 1966, **4**, 400–408.

Valins, S. Emotionality and information concerning internal reactions. *Journal of Personality and Social Psychology*, 1967, **6**, 458–463.

Walster, E. The effect of self-esteem on romantic liking. *Journal of Experimental Social Psychology*, 1965, **1**, 184–197.

Walster, E. Passionate love. In B. I. Murstein (Ed.), *Theories of attraction and love*. New York: Springer, Publ., 1971.

Walster, E., Aronson, V., Abrahams, D., & Rottmann, L. Importance of physical attractiveness in dating behavior. *Journal of Personality and Social Psychology*, 1966, **4**, 508–516.

Wheeler, L., & Smith, S. Censure of the model in the contagion of aggression. *Journal of Personality and Social Psychology*, 1967, **6**, 93–98.

Worchel, P., & Schuster, S. D. Attraction as a function of the drive state. *Journal of Experimental Research in Personality*, 1966, **1**, 277–281.

Zajonc, R. B. Attitudinal effects of mere exposure. *Journal of Personality and Social Psychology*, 1968, **9**, 1–27.

9

Attributions, Liking, and Power

JAMES T. TEDESCHI

Department of Psychology
State University of
New York at Albany
Albany, New York

I. Introduction

Theories of interpersonal attraction designate the basic phenomenon of interest an "organismic variable," that is, a hypothetical construct. It is the nature of hypothetical constructs that they can be only indirectly assessed. For this reason, the concept of attraction is being continually redefined as the antecedent and consequent events organized by the concept are more carefully delineated. The term "attraction" presently is so ambiguous the Marlowe and Gergen (1969) have suggested that it is useful primarily as a generic orienting construct which focuses research on particular kinds of problems. As a result, data from such research is not coherently explained by existing theories of attraction. This chapter offers a reconceptualization of attraction generated from a set of anomolous research findings, but which is, nevertheless, consistent with other data. In it I argue that only by uncovering the implications of attraction for interpersonal power can available evidence be coherently organized.

Research on the antecedents of attraction indicates that similarity (along a number of different dimensions, including attitudes, values, and socioeconomic level), likableness, need complementarity, propinquity, and reward mediation are all associated with the willingness of subjects to phenomenologically report liking for another (Berscheid & Walster, 1969; cf. Bramel, 1969; Byrne, 1971; Lindzey & Byrne, 1968). The consequences of liking were reviewed by Tedeschi, Schlenker, and Bonoma (1973). Liking arouses the expectancy for cooperation in interactions, induces actual cooperation in mixed-motive situations, renders a target individual more susceptible to persuasive communications, induces conformity to group judgments and demands, mediates more imitation of a model, increases the effectiveness of social reinforcers, and reduces the probability that another will use coercion or mediate harm. A number of alternative concepts of attraction could probably organize these data, but, as is often the case, the more interesting findings are those where the expectations of all the theories are disconfirmed. Let us examine these anomolous findings.

II. Some Unexplained Findings

A. Reciprocity and Liking

The positive reciprocity norm states that one should help those who help him, and the negative reciprocity norm states that one should harm those who harm him (Gouldner, 1960). Both norms have been shown to regulate behaviors of subjects in the laboratory (see Epstein & Taylor, 1967; Frisch & Greenberg, 1968; Goranson & Berkowitz, 1966; Helm, Bonoma, & Tedeschi, 1972; Pruitt, 1968; Wilke & Lanzetta, 1970). There is also evidence that receiving favors does generate a feeling of obligation and a desire to reciprocate (Goranson & Berkowitz, 1966). If liking elicits expectation of a cooperative and rewarding relationship and induces trust, it would be reasonable to expect that liking would affect the magnitude or strength of reciprocity behaviors. Heider (1958) proposed that "one might assume that with a positive sentiment, positive retribution will arise more easily than with a negative sentiment, and vice versa [p. 267]."

Four recent studies have failed to find a relationship between attraction and reciprocity behaviors. Stapleton, Nacci, and Tedeschi (1972) used a very simple research setting in which subjects were given a fixed number of points tradable for extra time toward fulfilling an introductory psychology course requirement for research participation. The points were given to subjects either one, five, or nine times out of ten opportunities by a liked or disliked confederate. The results showed no effect of liking on reciprocity behavior; subjects reciprocated approximately according to what they received, no matter whan their personal feelings for the confederate.

Nemeth (1970) paired each subject with a confederate and gave each member of the pair independent problems to solve. The first one to finish his problem (*a*) was required to help the other person, (*b*) could voluntarily help the other person, or (*c*) was not allowed to help the other person. The experiment was contrived so that the confederate always finished first. After completion of this initial phase of the study, subjects were asked to rate the attractiveness of the confederate. When the experiment was allegedly terminated, the confederate asked the subject to help him to collect data for a survey. More subjects volunteered their help when the confederate had given them help in the voluntary condition of the experiment than when the confederate had given help under compulsory conditions or when the confederate was not allowed to provide help. There was no correlation of liking for the confederate with the willingness of subjects of volunteer help on the survey.

Regan (1971) manipulated liking by allowing subjects to overhear a confederate talking on the telephone; the confederate was either very pleasant or very insulting to his alleged telephone partner. The conditions of the experiment included: (*a*) the confederate left the room, returned with two cokes, and told the subject that he had been allowed a couple of minutes to buy a coke and he had also brought one back for the subject; (*b*) the experimenter brought cokes for both the confederate and the subject; or (*c*) no favor was provided the subject by either the confederate or the experimenter. When the experiment had allegedly terminated, the confederate asked the subject to help him collect data for a survey. The results showed that when the subject was given a favor (by either the confederate or the experimenter) and an obligation could be perceived, reciprocity occurred; attraction did not affect compliance. However, when the subject was not obligated because he had received no favors during the experiment, attraction did mediate compliance — the more liking, the more compliance.

Hendrick and Taylor (1971) induced liking or disliking for a confederate by manipulating perceived similarity or dissimilarity of their attitudes. Subjects then participated with the confederate in a reaction-time experiment. Each participant could set the shock level intensity that would be received by the other person if the latter had the slower reaction time to a light signal. Each person was provided with feedback concerning the other's shock intensity settings. The confederate could be programmed to increase his settings gradually, sharply, or not at all. It was found that subjects reciprocated shock intensity settings, but that attraction had no effect on their behavior.

The clear conclusion from these studies is that attraction does not affect reciprocity behavior. Liking, however, apparently does mediate favor-doing when the actor is not indebted to the recipient. In addition to the foregoing findings, a set of investigations of reward power has produced unexpected results. Let us examine these additional anomolous findings in some detail.

B. Attraction and Reward Power

Lott and Lott (1968) have proposed that learning to like another person is "essentially learning to anticipate reward when that person is present [p. 68]."

If this expectancy is the basis of attraction, it would be reasonable to predict that a source would choose to influence a liked target with reward rather than coercive power, because he could expect positive reactions to promises (that is, rewarding behavior) from the liked target. Similarly, a target of promises should be disposed to believe that a liked source will keep his word to provide the promised rewards; thus, the target should respond positively to the source's requests. These hypotheses have been tested.

Schlenker and Tedeschi (1972) carried out an experiment based on the hypothesis that a person would choose to use reward, rather than coercive power, to influence a liked target. They induced relative differences in liking for a confederate by an attitude similarity–dissimilarity technique (see Byrne, 1961). Subjects were provided with a power advantage over the confederate in a modified Prisoner's Dilemma game, which differed across conditions of the experiment: (a) a message was available that promised the confederate-target a side payoff for the latter's cooperative response; (b) a message was available that threatened that the confederate-target would be fined if he did not make the cooperative response; or (c) both promise and threat messages were available for the subject's use. Liking did not affect the frequency with which the two types of messages were sent; in all conditions subjects used threats more frequently than promises. Attraction did affect the manner with which promises were used. Subjects who liked the confederate were more cooperative themselves when they used promises, while subjects who were not attracted to the confederate more often used promises as ploys for exploitative purposes. Unexpectedly, subjects who disliked the confederate provided the promised side payoff proportionately more often than did subjects who liked the confederate.

When subjects were targets of promises in the context of a mixed-motive game, attraction had no effect on the amount of compliance they gave to a confederate source's contingent promises (Lindskold & Tedeschi, 1971; Schlenker, Bonoma, Tedeschi, Lindskold, & Horai, 1971). In both studies, however, subjects cooperated more often on nonmessage trials of the game when they liked the confederate than when they did not. The latter finding is consistent with the results of a number of experiments that show that subjects who like one another are more cooperative in mixed-motive interactions than are subjects who dislike one another (see Tedeschi *et al.*, 1973). The question here is why liking mediates cooperation when no communications occur between the two parties, but does not do so when explicit contingent promises are communicated.

One further study merits attention because it shows effects of subject and situational variables on cooperative or competitive behavior when subjects are permitted to communicate with one another, but not when they must resolve conflicts without communicative opportunities. We have just seen that liking produces effects in mixed-motive situations only when specific promises are not exchanged. Schlenker, Helm, and Tedeschi (1973) defined trust as the reliance on a communication of a stranger in a risky situation. They divided subjects into high- and low-trust groups on the basis of scores obtained from Rotter's (1967) paper-and-pencil measure of interpersonal trust. Subjects were then given the role of targets of a series of noncontingent promises from a confederate. The promise in each case stated that the confederate would unilaterally cooperate on the next play of the mixed-motive game. The confederate either always kept his promise or never did. High-trust subjects cooperated more frequently on the promise-relevant trials, thereby indicating their reliance upon the promise as a basis for choosing game strategies. The credibility of the promise, a situational basis for the development of trust, also directly mediated cooperation by subjects on message-relevant trials. Neither the trust of subjects nor the credibility of promises had any effect on the degree of cooperativeness displayed by subjects on nonmessage trials. Thus, trust had exactly the opposite effect of interpersonal attraction on responses of subjects in a mixed-motive game. Yet, in the trust study, the higher the credibility of the confederate's promises, the more subjects liked him, and the highly trusting subjects liked the confederate more than did the distrustful subjects.

It is difficult to see how any existing theory of attraction could explain the pattern of results found across the experiments reported here. Liking does not mediate reciprocity behavior, not does disliking interfere with the repayment of obligations. These findings may be considered somewhat optimistic, since they imply that even enemies can deal with one another on the basis of a quid pro quo. Liking apparently does mediate favor-doing *as long as the benefactor does not perceive himself obligated because of indebtedness to provide help.* Liking does mediate cooperation in a risky situation as long as no explicit offers of reward are proferred to the individual for his cooperation. Attraction has no effect on the source's choice of reward or coercive power for use against a target, nor does attraction play any part in the responses of targets to the promises of a source. It is clear that trust and attraction are related to one another and that each produces separate effects in mixed-motive situations. Attraction mediates cooperative behavior in dyadic interactions when no rewards are offered by explicit communications, and trust mediates cooperative responses only when promises of reward are explicitly communicated. The conception of attraction to be proposed in the following section, which is consistent with the cited pattern of data and with the other antecedents and consequents that have been associated with attraction, freely borrows from the important work of Blau (1964), Heider (1958), Jones and Davis (1965), and Kelley (1967).

III. The Nature of Attraction

Attraction may be defined as an attitude, possessing cognitive, affective, and dispositional properties. The cognitive component involves a ubiquitous expectancy that liking or disliking elicits. The affective component concerns the variety and intensity of emotions that are aroused and labeled in response to the other person. The dispositional component of attraction refers to the readiness of the perceiver to act in certain characteristic ways with respect to the other person. Each of these three components has effects on the others, but whether they combine to affect the intensity, kind, or strength of attraction is an empirical question. In the present formulation, the cognitive component is considered the central factor determining the strength and type of attraction and is the primary basis for the action of the perceiver.

A. Cognitive Component of Attraction

The cognition aroused by liking relationships, and consistent with all the evidence reviewed, is: the expectancy that the other person will altruistically[1] provide benefits or favors of various types and values across a number of situations and over time. The greater the range of utilities, the greater the variety of situations, the longer the time, and the more confidence the person has in the expectancy, the stronger the attraction. Negative attraction, or disliking, refers to the expectancy that another person would mediate harm without provocation. The strength of negative attraction is a function of the amount of harm involved, the number of situations in which the other person could be expected to mediate the harm, the length of the projected future for which the expectations would be relevant, and the confidence the person has in his expectancy. It is clear that a person could both like and dislike a single other person, since he can have expectations of altruistic behaviors for some situations and expectations of unprovoked harmful actions for other situations.

Of course liking for another individual is learned over time and is based on perceptual and attributional processes. When an actor benefits a person, the person must ascertain whether the beneficial act was intentional or unintentional. This judgment can be made by assessing the knowledge and the ability of the actor. If the actor has knowledge of the effects of his action and the ability to carry out actions to bring about those effects, then the person will probably perceive the action as intentional (Heider, 1958). If the beneficial action is to be perceived as altruistic, the person must not be able to ascertain any selfish motive for the action other than the actor's wish to benefit the person. This attribution is more likely to be made when:

1. The recipient views the outcomes as personally beneficial or hedonically relevant (Jones & Davis, 1965).

2. The recipient perceives the behavior to be directed toward him in particular, rather than to anyone or everyone. Jones and Davis (1965) have referred to this attributional factor as "personalism." Kelley (1967) also has pointed out that the

---

[1]The usual meaning of altruism carries with it the implication that behavior is impersonal and directed toward a number of other people. Here I use the word in the sense of *personal* altruism. There is no implication that the behaviors in question are actually altruistic; rather, the emphasis is on the fact that behaviors are *perceived* as altruistic.

distinctiveness of actions is important for attributions. If an actor provides favors promiscuously, then the favor that is done for the person is less discriminating, less personal, and hence may be perceived as more socially than personally altruistic.

3. The action produces no discernible benefits to the actor and in fact brings him costs. The more it costs the actor to provide benefits, the more altruistic he should be perceived.

4. The frequency with which the actor provides benefits or favors when opportunities present themselves over time.

5. The favor-doing or beneficial behaviors are invariant with regard to the person's own behaviors. The attribution of altruism will be stronger when the actor provides benevolent behaviors invariantly, regardless of whether the person acts selfishly, indifferently, lovingly, angrily, or whatever. The implication is that non-contingent rewards may be perceived as more altruistic than contingent rewards. An actor may, of course, altruistically make rewards contingent on some behavior of the person. As long as the recipient cannot perceive any selfish gains achieved by the actor's benevolent actions, it is possible to believe that the contingency criterion is applied for the recipient's own best interests, at least as perceived by the person.

6. A comparison indicates that the actor provides more favors and benefits than does the average individual with whom the person interacts. This social comparison processs is associated with distinctiveness.

7. The social consensus of others may lay to rest suspicions about the intentions of the actor, reaffirm the recipient's attributions of altruism, or help to interpret an actor's intentions when they are not unambiguously interpretable.

Common-sense observation indicates that persons can form deep attachments that are not reciprocated; instances of unrequited love sometimes occur. Such examples can be handled by the present conception of attraction if an expected value (or some other decision model) interpretation of the expectancy involved is accepted. If the probability (that is, confidence) and value (that is, worth of benefits or favors) aspects of the cognition are multiplicative, then the product of a great value and a small probability could still yield a rather substantial expected value. Similarly, friendship can exist between persons if the probability of the expectancy is very high and the values at stake not so great. In the case of unrequited love, the person might also perceive his possible alternative relationships as quite poor. Given the combination of a small probability and great value for his expectancy of altruistic behavior from the other and no good alternative relationship, the person loves in the hope of being loved.

The expectancy under consideration here may be fit within the social learning theory of Rotter (1954). A person may develop a generalized expectancy that strangers will act altruistically toward him or he may develop the generalized expectancy that strangers will mediate unprovoked harm. It is possible that the person would have both types of generalized expectancies and, as a consequence, would find himself torn between approaching and avoiding strangers. [The obvious connection to Horney's (1945) theory that some persons move toward others, while some move away, can be seen.] The notion of diffuse attraction as consisting of a generalized expectancy may have been indicated at a more empirical level by the studies of Kelley and Stahelski (1968a, b, c). Persons were identified as *cooperators* if they expected others to cooperate with them and indicated their own preference as cooperative. *Competitors* expected others to compete with them and indicated their own intentions to behave competitively. The studies showed that in a mixed-motive situation, cooperators adjusted to the behavior of their opponent by cooperating if the latter cooperated and competing if the latter competed. Competitors were inflexible in their behavior and competed no matter what their opponent did. The interpretation here is that the differences found were a function of diffuse attraction. The expectancy that a stranger will altruistically provide benefits or that a stranger will administer unprovoked harm is learned by the person through generalizing his experiences and using them as a basis for predicting the future. When the person has information about the actor, however, the specific expectancies associated with the actor render irrelevant any diffuse attraction.

The definition of attraction as an expectancy that an actor will altruistically provide benefits of various types and values over situations and time makes it possible to differentiate types of attraction. Presumably, the favors, benefits, or rewards, and the situations in which they would be rendered, could be classified in a manner that could discriminate among mother—son, brother—sister, man—woman, man—man, and other forms of love, While it would be suitable to expect a lover to provide sexual gratification, for example, it would not be appropriate to expect such behavior from a mother.

The cognitive component of specific attraction as defined above is consistent with Heider's (1958) statement that "different situations give rise to different actions and feelings that in some way are appropriate to the sentiment [of liking] . . . the sentiment is the connecting link between the variety of situations on the one hand and the events that transpire on the other [p. 175]." The sentiment of liking gives meaning to impressions of others because it allows prediction about the others' probable future behaviors in certain situations.

B. Affective Component of Attraction

Schachter (1964) has stated that:

> an emotional state may be considered a function of a state of physiological arousal and of a cognition appropriate to this state of arousal. The cognition, in a sense, exerts a steering function. Cognitions arising from the immediate situation as interpreted by past experiences provide the framework within which one understands and labels his feelings. It is the cognition which determines whether the state of physiological arousal will be labeled 'anger,' 'joy,' or whatever [pp. 50–51].

Walster (1971) has employed Schachter's framework as a basis for a theory of passionate love. A series of studies has established that subjects can be caused to attribute emotions to such things as drugs, the environment, or another person (Mintz & Mills, 1971; see also Nisbett & Valins, 1971; Schachter & Singer, 1962; Schachter & Wheeler, 1962). For example, Valins (1966) provided male subjects with false heart-rate feedback while they rated the attractiveness of pictures of seminude females taken from *Playboy* magazine. He found that pictures were rated as more attractive when the false heart beat had been quicker during the time the subject had examined the picture.

Although there is considerable evidence that arousal varies in intensity, there is no evidence to indicate any qualitative differences in emotion at the physiological level of analysis (Schachter, 1964). If this is so, then all emotions have the same physiological base. The number and types of emotions that a person experiences may be culturally determined, like his language. Just as an Eskimo has many different names for snow, and a pygmy very few, if any, so there may be large differences in emotional vocabulary across cultures. The identification of emotions is learned during the socialization process. When physiologically aroused, the person labels his emotions according to the cues available. The person not only learns to identify his arousal to situational cues by cognitive labels, but the reverse is also learned—that is, which stimulus conditions and cognitive labels should produce physiological arousal. Thus, in one time or culture, viewing a lady's ankle may be quite arousing, while at another time, or in another culture, nothing less than a glimpse of a thigh will produce arousal. Persons are not born with ideas of physical beauty, nor are they genetically disposed to be aroused by pictures of semi-nude female or males in magazines or on television commercials. It is likely that both the condition of the arousal and the labeling of it are learned. Indeed, a cue may first elicit the label, which, in turn, may bring about arousal. Thus, emotions often have a cognitive basis (Zimbardo, 1969).

Rewarding and punishing experiences may always produce arousal states. If arousal states occur while another person is present, either as a mediator of reinforcements, or merely as a bystander, the arousal may be associated with that other person. This principle has been stated by Clore and Byrne (see Chapter 7 of this volume): "stimuli associated with positive (negative) affect are liked (disliked)." In their contribution to this volume, Lott and Lott state that "the basic hypothesis that underlies all of our work on the antecedents of interpersonal attraction is that liking for a person will result under those conditions in which an individual experiences *reward in the presence of that person* regardless of the relationship between the other person and rewarding event or state of affairs [italics in the original]." Both sets of theorists find empirical support for this secondary reinforcement effect. Both the principle and the data could be accepted within the present formulation. However, once the "warm glow of success" or arousal state (identified positively or negatively) dissipates, the attraction aroused should also dissipate. Attraction requires a basis in cognition, and temporary arousal states cannot lay a firm foundation for a liking relationship.

Learning the conditions and language of emotions is a very subtle and difficult task. Those who have failed to learn the socially approved emotional language well and who misidentify their emotions (in the sense of the norms of appropriateness) may feel unhappy or experience concern about their mental health. Arousal in the presence of a parent may be misidentified, for example, and given a label more appropriate to a lover, bringing distress to the person who "experiences" it. Arousal identified in terms of attraction may lead to many different emotions, ranging from the exquisitely pleasurable to the sadly poignant. The cognitive component of attraction gives organization and meaning to the many different emotions that may be "experienced" with respect to another individual.

Eye contact, spatial distance, orientation in space, rate of speech, tone of speech, and other social cues are manipulated by persons and responded to by others on the basis of their experience with such emotional cues. These cues may elicit arousal, which may be labeled in a manner that bring forth cognitive associations. The aroused expectancy may then determine the behavior of the person in the situation

C. Dispositional Component of Attraction

Liking is characterized by the readiness of the individual to do favors or to provide benefits for another without concern for specific or immediate reciprocity Liking provides the basis for what Blau (1964) has described as "social exchange." The crucial distinction between economic and social exchange is that the latter entails unspecified obligations. "Social exchange, whether it is in ceremonial form or not, involves favors that create diffuse future obligations, not precisely specified ones, and the nature of the return cannot be bargained about but must be left to the discretion of the one who makes it [p. 93]." Ludwig von Mises (1949) referred to this feature of social relations as autistic exchange: "Making one-sided present without the aim of being rewarded by any conduct on the part of the receiver or of a third person is autistic exchange . . . if presents are given in order to influence some people's conduct, they are no longer one-sided, but a variety of interpersonal exchange between the donor and the man whose conduct they are designed to influence [p. 196]." Jones (1964) has referred to the deliberate attempt to create debt for purposes of facilitating influence as favorable self-presentation, an ingratiation strategy.

A series of studies supports the hypothesis that persons will behave more benevolently toward someone they like than toward someone they dislike. For example Sawyer (1966) found that friends behaved more altruistically toward friends than antagonists or strangers. Golightly, Huffman, and Byrne (1972) found that graduate students majoring in business were more likely to lend money to similar than to dissimilar, strangers. Staub and Sherk (1970) found that fourth-grade children shared their crayons for a longer period of time with liked, then with disliked, partners. Thus, liking does appear to be related to the readiness of the person to do favors, or provide benefits, for others.

The individual makes attributions about the causes of his own conduct. If he can find no environmental reason for his behavior, he will attribute his actions to his own volition (Bem, 1967). Thus, the dissonance-like effect recognized by Aristotle derives from self-attribution. "Benefactors seem to love those whom they benefit more than those who have received benefits love those who have conferred them [cited in Blau, 1964, p. 78]." In other words, a person who bestows benefits upon others is likely to perceive his own actions as altruistic and freely undertaken and, as a consequence, to infer that he must like the person benefited. A recent experiment reported by Schopler and Compere (1972) confirmed Blau's hypothesis. By drawing from attribution theory (Kelley, 1967), it can be deduced that the more a person benefits another across time, situations, and modalities, and as discriminated from other persons, the stronger will be the actor's self-attribution that he likes the benefited person. The cyclical relationship between actor and self-attribution should be obvious. The more benefits provided, the more the actor should infer self-liking for the other person, and the more often benefits will be given. As Heider (1958) suggested, "'p likes o' induces 'p benefits o' [p. 213]." Also, Bramel (1969) has stated that one should give those he likes what he thinks they want and those he dislikes what he believes they don't want.

The strength of the readiness to benefit another will be adjusted by the person to the strength of the cognitive component of attraction, and a balance will be maintained between the two components. If a liked other disappoints the person by not providing benefits when they are expected, the person will adjust the strength or range of his expectancy, and an adjustment of the dispositional component of attraction will also occur. Sometimes, the person will attempt to escalate the intensity of liking by engaging in a series of altruistic actions and presenting himself for possible reciprocity. When such escalation strategies fail, the individual adjusts his disposition accordingly (except in cases of unrequited love). In general, a balance will be maintained between the steering cognition and the person's action dispositions, Evidence indicates that group members in a variety of settings believe that their liking for others will be closely reciprocated (Blumberg, 1967; Newcomb, 1961; Tagiuri, Blake, & Bruner, 1953).

D. Summary

Attraction is an attitude composed of cognitive, affective, and dispositional components. The cognitive component involves an expectancy that another person will altruistically provide benefits of various types and values, across situations and time. The expectancy and the values involved are multiplicatively related in determining the strength of attraction. The affective component of attraction is comprised of physiological arousal, cues in the environment, and labels culled from the language of emotions learned from socialization experiences. The cognitive component of attraction helps to organize different emotions with respect to a single other person. Affective labels may arouse the cognitive or dispositional factors related to attraction, and the cognitive and dispositional components, when aroused, may elicit an affective response. Finally, the dispositional component of attraction comprises the general readiness to provide benefits of various types and values for another person across situations and over time. The strength of the dispositional properties of attraction will generally be balanced with respect to the cognitive component of attraction.

IV. Attraction as a Power Resource

If liking elicits the expectation of a rewarding interaction and disposes the individual to act cooperatively or benevolently toward another, then it should be clear that there are implications of attraction for the processes of interpersonal power. More fundamentally, however, the present view is that attraction is primarily a power resource. In the language of learning theory, a person values attraction because of the rewards that a positive liking relationship brings to him. The consideration of attraction as a power resource is equivalent to asking why people like to be liked. Of course, there are many reasons. For one thing, a person likes to be liked because he expects that the other person will provide him with benefits. A person also likes to be liked because under such conditions others are less apt to harm him. No direct tests of this proposition has been carried out, although there is evidence that persons are reluctant to harm liked others. Krauss (1966) induced either positive or negative attraction between persons using attitude similarity—dissimilarity manipulations before they participated in a trucking game. Subjects were then told that their judgments of the other person's attitudes were either valid or invalid. Subsequently, subjects were allowed to use gates to block their opponent's access to the shorter and most profitable of two available routes to get their trucks to the appropriate destinations. The object of the trucking game is to maximize profits. Time is money, since the greater the time consumed in delivering the commodity, the greater the costs, and the less the profits. When subjects believed their judgments of the other person were valid, they used threatening and punishing gates more often against the disliked, than against the liked, other person. A plausible basis for such behaviors would be the norm that benevolent friends should never (without provocation) deliberately harm or injure the other person.

A person may also like to be liked because the intentions that are attributed to him may mitigate responsibility for harm-doing. This was nicely demonstrated in an experiment by Shaver (1970). Subjects were provided with a scenario in which a car was parked on a hill and a witness testified that the hand brake was firmly set. Nevertheless, the car rolled down the hill, crashed into a store window, slightly injured a small girl, and caused a merchant to be hospitalized for a year. The driver had no insurance and subsequent police investigation indicated that the brake cable was badly rusted. Subjects were asked to assume that the defendant's personal characteristics were either "very much like your own," or "not at all like your own." Since similarity is a consistent antecedent of attraction (Byrne, 1971), it may be assumed that attraction differences were created. When subjects perceived the defendant to be like themselves, less responsibility was attributed to him, and the subjects were more lenient in assigning penalties to him. Similar findings have been reported by Griffitt and Jackson (1970) and Landy and Aronson (1969). Apparently, kind and benevolent persons are not held responsible for harmful actions, which may be rationalized as accidental (that is, unintentional).

A source of persuasive communications is more likely to be perceived as having the intent to be impartial and truthful (that is, trustworthy) if he is liked, and when altruistic or benevolent intentions can be attributed to him by the target. Evidence shows that a target has suspicions about the intentions and the objectivity or accuracy of a disliked source of influence (see Bramel, 1969; Hovland, Janis, & Kelley, 1953; Mills, 1966; Mills & Jellison, 1968). When the source makes it clear that his self-interest is involved, liking for him may not affect the trust that the target places in his communication. Generally, if a source is liked, he will be more influential than if he is not liked. A person will like to be liked, therefore, because he will gain more compliance to his persuasive communications.

Most generally, a person likes to be liked because he can count on others for help when help is needed (a friend in need is a friend, indeed). The stronger the attraction between persons, the more willing each should be to provide favors, help, or benefits whenever the other requests or needs them A good friend is a social insurance policy that accrues cash value that can be borrowed any time without collateral and for an unstated interest rate or premium payments. The timing and the nature of the repayment is up to the borrower. But, if the borrower waits too long or repays too little, he will forfeit future credit.

Each of these functions of attraction as a power resource has been identified (albeit by different labels) in a factor analytic study of expectations associated with friendship. Canfield and La Gaipa (1970) conducted 150 open-ended interviews with college students, and obtained 1800 friendship statements. After redundancies were removed, 152 items were submitted to 30 judges who rated the items as most essential or least essential for 5 levels of friendship: best friends, close friends, good friends, social acquaintances, and casual acquaintances. Finally, 80 Likert-type items were isolated and given to over 1000 high school and college students, who were asked to determine which items were most important for each level of friendship. Across ratings and people, eight major factors were identified:

1. *Genuineness,* or the expectation that a friend will be open, honest, and straightforward. This factor indicates that liking induces trust.

2. *Intimacy potential,* or the emotional accessibility of a friend. This factor implies that attributions are easier to make with friends. Friends let down "face."

3. *Acceptance,* or unconditional positive regard. This factor seems consistent with the attribution of altruism.

4. *Utility potential,* or the willingness to endure high costs as the intensity of the relationship increases. This factor refers to the dispositional aspects of attraction and allows a clear attribution that actions are altruistic.

5. *Ego-reinforcement,* or the expectation that a friend will provide social reinforcements in the form of sympathy or empathy.

6. *Admiration,* or esteem.

7. *Similarity.*

8. *Ritualistic social exchange,* such as is involved in exchanging birthday and Christmas gifts.

With respect to the last factor, it is interesting to note that society presents a set of norms about how friends should treat one another and provides a set of rituals that are appropriate to various types of liking relationships.

Attraction as a complex and subtle relationship between persons must be delicately calibrated in terms of benefits given and received consistent with an implicit norm of reciprocity. Yet, some insist on simplifying the attraction relationship to an emotional response. Simons, Berkowitz, and Moyer (1970) cautioned that a distinction must be made between cognitive bases for a receiver's image of a source of influence, such as expertise or status, and affective bases, such as likability and friendliness. They note that failure to make this distinction has led to confounded operationalizations of attraction. For example, Byrne's (1969) much used Interpersonal Judgment Scale asks subjects whether they think they will like their experimental partner and how much they would like to work with the other person in the future. Byrne and Rhamey (1965) found that the two items are strongly and positively correlated (+.85). The ratings of subjects on these two items are therefore summed to obtain an overal attraction score.

Simon and his co-workers have suggested that it is quite possible that a subject would choose to work with someone he dislikes, but who has skills relevant to problem solution and subsequent reinforcements. In such a case, expertise and not attraction is the basis of choice. In many situations, the two items used by Byrne should be positively correlated, but in other situations, the relationship may be negative. The criticism by Simons and his colleagues is well founded; however, it does not lead to their conclusion that attraction is purely an affective reaction. A friend who is failing a course would not be much help in studying for an exam however altruistic and cooperative he is, while the top student in the class may be difficult to work with but more helpful, as well. The choice of working with a friend or a nonfriend may be a function of expectancies, rather than affect.

Simons and his co-workers have noted that a number of theorists have viewed attraction as a base of power (see French & Raven, 1959; Lasswell & Kaplan, 1950). A theorist who views attraction from a power perspective must be careful to discriminate between the various bases of power. The essential elements of an influence relationship are a source, a message, and a target. Many characteristics of the source may be important for his success in influencing the target. In a review of factor analytic studies of small-group behavior and of influence settings, Tedeschi *et al.* (1973) concluded that a few source characteristics can account for most of the variance in interpersonal influence interactions. These are expertise, prestige, status, trustworthiness, and attraction.

Expertise refers to the special abilities, experience, or education of the person. *Prestige* is quite similar to Heider's (1958) definition of power and is the product of capability and intentions. Capability refers to the material or physical resources of the person, while intentions are concerned with his willingness to expend his resources for purposes of influence. Either lack of capability or lack of "will" can lead to the perception that the person is weak. *Status* derives from a person's role position and implies the need for deference from those lower in the hierarchy; status depends upon the legitimization of the role structure. *Trustworthiness* is the target's perception that the source intends to communicate a valid message (Hovland, Janis, & Kelly, 1953). The orientations of a target to a source who has the characteristics of expertise, prestige, status, and trustworthiness are respect, fear or awe, deference, and trust, respectively.

Each of these source characteristics can be identified denotatively (at least partially), except for attraction. A person may be chastised for not showing sufficient respect for another on the grounds that the source possesses diplomas, degrees, or certificates. A person may be chided for not having sufficient fear or awe of a powerful or wealthy person, or for not showing proper deference to a person who holds a role position high in authority. Social consensus may affirm the trustworthiness of a source. However, one cannot point to anything objective about another person that should necessarily be connected with liking for him. Arguments about intentions are difficult to resolve objectively. The fact that attraction is more subjective than the other source characteristics important for interpersonal realtionships was recognized by Blau (1964):

> "Associations that are intrinsically rewarding, however, are unique in the sense that they cannot be compared except in the purely subjective terms of the gratifications they provide. Since there are no independent standards, an individual's subjective judgment that an association is intrinsically rewarding for him cannot be considered wrong in any meaningful sense; it is right by fiat [p. 36]."

The factor analytic studies of source characteristics which serve as bases of interpersonal power are more successful in telling us what attraction is not than what it is. Although attraction should not be confused with expertise, there is evidence that experts are generally liked (Blau, 1964). Similarly, liking should be distinguished from status and prestige; yet, there is evidence that higher status persons are more liked than lower status persons (Masling, Greer, & Gilmore, 1955; Petersen, Komorita, & Quay, 1964); and a source who displays positive intentions and the capability of rewarding the person (that is, high prestige) is liked (Pepitone & Kleiner, 1957). It is clear the conceptions of attraction must carefully differentiate liking from other bases of power. Also, the correlations between liking and expertise, status, and prestige need to be explained.

V. Interpretations of the Evidence

We are now in a position to understand the anomolous findings with respect to attraction, reciprocity, and the use of, and responses to, promises. In the reciprocity studies, the subject was first a recipient of benefits and then, *after indebtedness had been created,* was given the power to reciprocate benefits. Heider (1958) argued that "p will not feel grateful for a benefit and will not feel obligated when he accepts it, if he thinks that it was owed to him by o, that o ought to benefit him, that it was o's duty to benefit him [p. 264]." If attraction is fundamentally a power-based resource, it will serve as a basis of "altruistic" behavior only when the actor can gain credit from, or create indebtedness in, the recipient. Attraction does not affect reciprocity because by definition such behavior is the payment of a debt, and mediation of benefits or favors cannot be perceived as altruistically given under such circumstances. To let liking affect behavior when no credit can be gained could be costly, since the investment is not apt to produce a profit. When the person is under no specific obligation and has the opportunity to benefit someone he likes, the benefits should be mediated by attraction (Regan, 1971).

When a person uses contingent promises, he makes the basis of the exchange quite explicit, as in economic exchanges, and hence renders attraction irrelevant to both his own behavior and that of the target. In mixed-motive games without communications, unilateral gestures of conciliation and benevolence may be displayed and perceived, and hence credit can be gained. Liking, therefore, influences the amount of cooperative behavior that persons emit in mixed-motive games. When the subject in a mixed-motive game is the target of a noncontingent promise of cooperation, he cannot avoid the implication that he also *ought* to cooperate. If the target does not cooperate, he will exploit the promisor if the latter keeps his word. The target can communicate distrust and dislike by refusing to cooperate, but he cannot emit behavior that will lead the promisor to a strong attribution of altruism. Receiving a gift may not indicate friendship, but refusing to accept a gift is a refusal of friendship (Mauss, 1967).

Status, expertise, and prestige are correlated with liking because it is more probable that the beneficial act of a powerful person will be seen as intentional and altruistic (Thibaut & Riecken, 1955). Heider (1958) has suggested that a powerful person can be perceived as possessing relatively more stable benevolent or malevolent traits than a less powerful person. Also, those who possess power can mediate the kinds of rewards a person wants. Trust mediates liking because reliable communications are helpful to the person and enable him to gain rewards and/or to avoid punishments. Actors who provide helpful information without appearing to gain anything for themselves induce attraction. Trust, defined as reliance on another's communications in a risky situation, should not be confused with the cognitive component of attraction, which is the expectancy of altruistic benefits from the other person. The obligating of another person by acting benevolently is not an act of trust, but an act indicating attraction. Liking induces trust whenever attraction appears relevant to the source's communications. Attraction is relevant to communication when the source is perceived as trying to altruistically help the target. If an explicit interest of the source is involved in the communication, attraction should not elicit the perception that the source is trustworthy.

The view that attraction is the anticipation of rewards (Lott & Lott, 1968; Newcomb, Turner, & Converse, 1965) does not separate attraction from other characteristics of the person, such as his status, expertise, and prestige, and cannot account for the anomolous results in the reciprocity and promise studies, and does not discriminate between accidental and intentional rewards. Experiments have shown that rewarded persons will more positively evaluate others who were merely present at the time of reinforcement (see Lott & Lott, 1960, 1968); that positively labeled arousal states produced in one condition can mediate attraction and helping behavior toward a formerly neutral person (Gouaux, 1971; Isen, 1970); and that negatively identified arousal states can mediate disattraction (Griffitt & Veitch, 1971). As has been previously argued, however, these transitory effects of arousal would probably no longer have effects after the arousal dissipates—unless a cognitive basis of attraction exists. This latter notion may explain why several studies have not yielded data in support of a secondary reinforcement principle of interpersonal attraction. Pepitone and Kleiner (1957) have shown that the rewards or punishments mediated by another must be perceived by the recipient as purposefully given if attraction between them is to be induced. Thus, over a number of studies it has been found that accidental rewards yield no credit to the bestower and accidental punishments mitigate the responsibility of a harm-doer. Also, actual rewards may not mediate liking if the person who provides help does so for his own gain (Jones, 1964). The mere expectation of rewards would not imply attraction, since rewards may be obtained by coercion or by clever manipulative tactics.

The antecedents of attraction must be understood in terms of their contribution to the power of the person. The evidence is convincing that similarity between persons is associated with attraction (see Byrne, 1969, 1971). Persons who share similar values will find that each possesses significant reinforcers for the other and that they are less apt to find themselves immersed in conflicts with one another. Perhaps an even more important consideration is that people with similar attitudes assign greater plausibility to each other's persuasive communications. Waly and Cook (1965) and Selltiz and Cook (1966) found that persons consider an argument with which they agree to be a more plausible or effective argument than one with which they disagree. Brigham and Cook (1970) asked liberals and right-wing conservatives to rate whether arguments were favorable or unfavorable toward interracial marriage, minority rights, and speed of desegration. Subjects were asked to rate the arguments on a scale from very effective to very ineffective. The more a subject favored a particular argument, the more effective he rated it. The implication is that people who share values can present arguments to one another more effectively than can people who initially disagree with one another with regard to basic values.

Direct evidence for this conjecture was found by Manis (1960, 1961), Berkowitz and Goranson (1964), and Kelman and Eagly (1965). Subjects were induced either to like or dislike a person, who then expressed an opinion that disagreed strongly with each subject's own opinion. Subjects perceived the liked person's opinions as closer to their own and perceived the disliked person's opinions as more different from what they really were. Levinger and Breedlove (1966) showed that highly satisfied marriage partners assumed greater agreement with their mates than did dissatisfied partners. Hence, not only will similar others be more liked, but people who are liked will be perceived as more similar. These considerations led Simons and his co-workers to propose that "attitude change toward the position advocated by the source depends on the extent to which interpersonal similarities or dissimilarities are perceived as having instrumental value for the receiver [p. 12]." Similarity breeds attraction, at least in part, because it gives both parties to the relationship persuasive power over the other.

Similarity, likableness, and complementarity of needs may all be antecedents of attraction because they reflect probable success in exercising influence and avoiding conflicts. Similarity may provide a priori credibility to persuasive communications; likability may predispose others to take a benevolent orientation towards the person; and complementarity of needs should allow for exchanges in which what is given costs little and what is received is worth a great deal.

Byrne (1969) has argued that comparison processes and reinforcement of effectance motivation are at the base of the similarity—attraction relationship. Certainly, the evidence is consistent with such a view. Worchel and McCormick (1963) found that subjects liked an agreeing person more when they were uncertain, rather than certain, about their own points of view. Gerard and Greenbaum (1962) found a similar result—when subjects' confidence in their own judgments was shaken, they liked a confederate who supported them better than when they had more confidence in their own judgments and the confederate supported them. Worchel and Schuster (1966) led each subject to believe that he was a member of a five-man group working on a human relations problem. The fourth person either disagreed with the first three and agreed with the subject, or the fourth person agreed with the first three and also the subject. The person was liked more when he disagreed with the rest of the group, but agreed with the subject.

A power-oriented view of attraction would interpret the results of these studies quite differently from Byrne (1969). A person generates a reputation for himself as a communicator of threats, promises, statements of fact, and persuasive messages. The higher his credibility, the more effective he is apt to be as a source of influence and power. Agreement or consensual validation for a person's views, particularly when his communications are most in doubt, affirms or restores his credibility. Thus, agreement with one's views is tantamount to providing a gratuitous increment of power, which is an act that should affect liking.

Friendship obviously brings many benefits to a person, and hence it could be expected that an individual will spend much time and effort to induce others to like him. Many behaviors that on the surface may appear to have little meaning or significance can be understood as efforts to acquire the power of attraction. Gossip, small talk, chit chat, recounting of past experiences, self-disclosure, humor, and many everyday courtesies have the function of communicating benevolence, credibility, similarity of attitudes, values, and interests.

The power relevance of attraction must be muted phenomenologically or else attraction would not occur. If the person were always aware of the function that his activities had for inducing attraction, for example, he would be practicing ingratiation. During socialization, the person must learn to disattend to the planned aspects of behaviors intended to reap attraction and to the implicit reciprocity basis of attraction. If perceived altruisim is at the basis of attraction, the instrumentality of the beneficial actions for the actor must remain disguised to the recipient. Most psychologists view human behavior as rather strictly determined and as hedonistically guided. If these assumptions are accepted, then no behavior could actually be altruistic. To perceive a behavior as altruistic requires that the perceiver be ignorant of the selfish motives such actions fulfill. That attraction is not simply a matter of altruism is demonstrated when failure to reciprocate disrupts a friendship.

VI. Some Final Thoughts

Detailed consideration of the many further implications of the concept of attraction presented here cannot be carried out in this limited space. Yet, I cannot resist underscoring the similarity between the present conception of attraction and that presented in Fromm's (1956) *Art of Loving*. However Machiavellian the present concept of attraction may seem, it apparently captures some of the humanistic nuances delineated by Fromm. The saving grace for the person in the present conception is that he is usually not aware phenomenologically of his own *real* purposes in providing favors, help, or benefits to a friend or loved one.

Fromm defined love as primarily giving, not receiving. He stressed the altruistic and dispositional aspects of attraction. The nature of true love is contrasted to the behavior of the marketing character: "The marketing character is willing to give, but only in exchange for receiving; giving without receiving for him is being cheated [p. 22]." The marketing character is apparently unable to time bind, or to deal with others on subtle terms of exchange.

From the point of view of this chapter, the difference between true love and the false love of the marketing character is a matter of timing, illusion, and appearances. Illusions and appearances are important and become part of reality. Just as in a play by Pirandello, it becomes difficult to separate reality from appearances. The person should believe that he is willing to give without selfish intent, but implicitly his behavior depends upon expected reciprocity at some later, unstated time, and in a form to be decided upon by the other person. As Aristotle (cited in Blau, 1964) said: "most men wish what is noble, but choose what is profitable; and while it is noble to render a service not with an eye to receiving one in return, it is profitable to receive one. One ought, therefore, if one can, to return the equivalent of services received, and to do so willingly [p. 88]."

Fromm stated that love implies care, an active concern for the life and growth of the other person. Care and concern imply responsibility. To be responsible means that the person is able and ready to respond when needed. Furthermore, love implies respect. Respect is defined as the absence of exploitation. Care, responsibility, and respect are implied by the formulation of attraction I have presented, particulary by the affective and dispositional components. The central place that attraction plays in interpersonal relations is based on the ultimate helplessness of all men: "Inasmuch as we are all human, we are all in need of help. Today I, tomorrow you [Fromm, 1956, p. 48]." Thus, Fromm acknowledged that love is not completely altruistic, but rather is based on the fact that we depend upon others for reinforcements, and that attraction is one basis for eliciting positive behaviors from others. Finally, Fromm indicated that there is a conscious cognitive aspect to love: "To love somebody is not just a strong feeling—it is a decision, it is a judgment, it is a promise [p. 56]."

Acknowledgments

The author acknowledges his debt to Lauren Ayers, Robert Becker, Thomas Bonoma, Daniel Ceranski, Robert McKinstry, Peter Nacci, Chris Parker, Barry R. Schlenker, Richard Stapleton, and Peg Tedeschi for their helpful comments on the ideas expressed in this paper. The work was supported by Grant No. GS-27059 from the National Science Foundation.

References

Bem, D. J. Self-perception: An alternative interpretation of cognitive dissonance phenomena. *Psychological Review*, **74**, 183–200.

Berkowitz, L., & Goranson, R. E. Motivational and judgmental determinants of social perception. *Journal of Abnormal and Social Psychology*, 1964, **69**, 296–302.

Berscheid, E., & Walster, E. H. *Interpersonal attraction*. Reading, Massachusetts: Addison-Wesley, 1969.

Blau, P. M. *Exchange and power in social life*. New York: Wiley, 1964.

Blumerg, H. H. Liking and the perception of liking: Changes over time. Doctoral dissertation, Johns Hopkins University, No. 67–13, 788. Ann Arbor, Michigan: University Microfilms, 1967.

Bramel, D. Interpersonal attraction, hostility, and perception. In J. Mills (Ed.), *Experimental social psychology*. New York: Macmillan, 1969. Pp. 1–120.

Brigham, J. C., & Cook, S. W. The influence of attitude on judgments of plausibility: A replication and extension. *Educational and Psychological Measurement*, 1970, **30**, 283–292.

Byrne, D. Interpersonal attraction and attitude similarity. *Journal of Abnormal and Social Psychology*, 1961, **62**, 713–715.

Byrne, D. Attitudes and attraction. In L. Berkowitz (Ed.), *Advances in experimental social psychology*. Vol. 4. New York: Academic Press, 1969. Pp. 35–89.

Byrne, D. *The attraction paradigm*. New York: Academic Press, 1971.

Byrne, D., & Rhamey, R. Magnitude of positive and negative reinforcements as a determinant of attraction. *Journal of Personality and Social Psychology*, 1965, **2**, 884–889.

Canfield, F. E., & LaGaipa, J. J. Friendship expectations at different stages in the development of friendship. Paper read at the annual meeting of the Southeastern Psychological Association, Louisville, April, 1970.

Epstein, S., & Taylor, S. P. Instigation to aggression as a function of degree of defeat and perceived aggressive intent of the opponent. *Journal of Personality*, 1967, **35**, 265–289.

French, J. R. P., Jr., & Raven, B. The bases of social power. In D. Cartwright (Ed.), *Studies in social power.* Ann Arbor, Michigan: Institute for Social Research, 1959. Pp. 150—167.

Frisch, D. M., & Greenberg, M. S. Reciprocity and intentionality in the giving of help. *Proceedings of the 76th annual convention of the Amercian Psychological Association,* 1968, 383—384.

Fromm, E. *The art of loving.* New York: Harper, 1956.

Gerard, H. B., & Greenbaum, C. W. Attitudes toward an agent of uncertainty reduction. *Journal of Personality,* 1962, **30**, 485—495.

Golightly, C., Huffman, D. M., & Byrne, D. Liking and loaning. *Journal of Applied Psychology,* 1972, **56**, 521—523.

Goranson, R. E., & Berkowitz, L. Reciprocity and responsibility reactions to prior help. *Journal of Personality and Social Psychology,* 1966, **3**, 227—232.

Gouaux, C. Induced affective states and interpersonal attraction. *Journal of Personality and Social Psychology* 1971, **20**, 37—43.

Gouldner, A. The norm of reciprocity. *American Sociological Review,* 1960, **25**, 161—178.

Griffitt, W., & Jackson, T. Simulated jury decisions: The influence of jury-defendant attitude similarity—dissimilarity. Unpublished manuscript, 1970.

Griffitt, W. & Veitch, R. Hot and crowded: influences of population density and temperature on interpersonal affective behavior. *Journal of Personality and Social Psychology,* 1971, **17**, 92—98.

Heider, F. *The psychology of interpersonal relations.* New York: Wiley., 1958.

Helm, B., Bonoma, T. V., & Tedeschi, J. T. Reciprocity for harm done. *Journal of Social Psychology,* 1972, **87**, 89—98.

Hendrick, C., & Taylor, S. P. Effects of belief similarity and aggression on attraction and counteraggression. *Journal of Personality and Social Psychology,* 1971, **17**, 342—349.

Horney, K. *Our inner conflicts.* New York: Norton, 1945.

Hovland, C. I., Janis, I. L., & Kelley, H. H. *Communication and persuasion.* New Haven, Connecticut: Yale University Press, 1953.

Isen, A. M. Success, failure, attention, and reaction to others: The warm glow of success. *Journal of Personality and Social Psychology,* 1970, **15**, 294—301.

Jones, E. E. *Ingratiation.* New York: Appleton, 1964.

Jones, E. E., & Davis, K. E. From acts to dispositions. In L. Berkowitz (Ed.), *Advances in experimental social psychology.* Vol. 2. New York: Academic Press, 1965, Pp. 219—266.

Kelley, H. H. Attribution theory in social psychology. In D. Levine (Ed.), *Nebraska Symposium on Motivation.* Lincoln, Nebraska: University of Nebraska Press, 1967. Pp. 192—238.

Kelley, H. H., & Stahelski, A. J. Social interaction as a basis of cooperators' and competitors' beliefs about each other. *Journal of Personality and Social Psychology,* 1970, **16**, 66—91.   (a)

Kelley, H. H., & Stahelski, A. J. Errors in perception of intentions in a mixed-motive game. *Journal of Experimental Social Psychology,* 1970, **6**, 379—400.   (b)

Kelley, H. H., & Stahelski, A. J. The inference of intention from moves in the Prisoner's Dilemma game. *Journal of Experimental Social Psychology,* 1970, **6**, 401—419.   (c)

Kelman, H. C., & Eagly, A. H. Attitude toward the communication content and attitude change. *Journal of Personality and Social Psychology,* 1965, **1**, 63—78.

Krauss, R. M. Structural and attitudinal factors in interpersonal bargaining. *Journal of Experimental Social Psychology,* 1966, **2**, 42—55.

Landy, D., & Aronson, E. The influence of the character of the criminal and his victim on the decisions of simulated jurors. *Journal of Experimental Social Psychology,* 1969, **5**, 141—152.

Lasswell, H. D., & Kaplan, A. *Power and society.* New Haven, Connecticut: Yale University Press, 1950.

Levinger, G., & Breedlove, J. Interpersonal attraction and agreement: A study of marriage partners. *Journal of Personality and Social Psychology,* 1966, **3**, 367—372.

Lindskold, S., & Tedeschi, J. T Reward power and attraction in interpersonal conflict. *Psychonomic Science,* 1971, **22**, 211—213.

Lindzey, G., & Byrne, D. Measurement of social choice and interpersonal attractiveness. In G. Lindzey & E. Aronson (Eds.), *Handbook of social psychology.* Vol. 2. (2nd ed.) Reading, Massachusetts: Addison-Wesley, 1968. Pp. 452—525.

Lott, A. J., & Lott, B. E. The formation of position attitudes toward group members. *Journal of Abnormal and Social Psychology*, 1960, **61**, 297—300.

Lott, A. J., & Lott, B. E. A learning theory approach to interpersonal attitudes. In A. G. Greenwald, T. C. Brock, & T. M. Ostrom (Eds.), *Psychological foundations of attitudes*. New York: Academic Press, 1968. Pp. 67—88.

Manis, M. The interpretation of opinion statements as a function of recipient attitude. *Journal of Abnormal and Social Psychology*, 1960, **60**, 340—344.

Manis, M. The interpretation of opinion statements as a function of recipient attitude and source prestige. *Journal of Abnormal and Social Psychology*, 1961, **63**, 82—86.

Marlowe, D., & Gergen, K. J. Personality and social interaction. In G. Lindzey & E. Aronson (Eds.), *Handbook of social psychology*. Vol. 3. (2nd ed.) Reading, Massachusetts: Addison-Wesley, 1968. Pp. 590—665.

Masling, J., Greer, F. L., & Gilmore, R. Status, authoritarianism, and sociometric choice. *Journal of Social Psychology*, 1955, **41**, 297—310.

Mauss, M. *The gift*. New York: Norton, 1967.

Mills, J. Opinion change as a function of the communicator's desire to influence and liking for the audience. *Journal of Experimental Social Psychology*, 1966, **2**, 152—159.

Mills, J., & Jellison, J. M. Effect on opinion change of how desirable the communication is to the audience the communicator addressed. *Journal of Personality and Social Psychology*, 1968, **9**, 153—156.

Mintz, P. M. & Mills, J. Effects of arousal and information about its source upon attitude change. *Journal of Experimental Social Psychology*, 1971, **7**, 561—570.

Nemeth, C. Effects of free versus constrained behavior on attraction between people. *Journal of Personality and Social Psychology*, 1970, **15**, 302—311.

Newcomb, T. M. *The acquaintance process*, New York: Holt, 1961.

Newcomb, T. M., Turner, R. H., & Converse, P. E. *Social psychology*. New York: Holt, 1965.

Nisbett, R. E., & Valins, S. *Perceiving the causes of one's own behavior*. New York: General Learning Press, 1971. Pp. 1—16.

Pepitone, A., & Kleiner, R. The effects of threat and frustration on group cohesiveness. *Journal of Abnormal and Social Psychology*, 1957, **59**, 192—199.

Petersen, R. J., Komorita, S. S., & Quay, H. C. Determinants of sociometric choices. *Journal of Social Psychology*, 1964, **62**, 65—75.

Pruitt, D. G. Reciprocity and credit building in a laboratory dyad. *Journal of Personality and Social Psychology*, 1968, **8**, 143—147.

Regan, D. T. Effects of a favor and liking on compliance. *Journal of Experimental Social Psychology*, 1971, **7**, 627—639.

Rotter, J. B. *Social learning and clinical psychology*. Englewood Cliffs, New Jersey. Prentice-Hall, 1954.

Rotter, J. B. A new scale for the measurement of interpersonal trust. *Journal of Personality*, 1967, **35**, 651—665.

Sawyer, J. The altruism scale: A measure of cooperative, individualistic, and competitive interpersonal orientation. *American Journal of Sociology*, 1966, **71**, 407—416.

Schachter, S. The interaction of cognitive and physiological determinants of emotional state. In L. Berkowitz (Ed.), *Advances in experimental social psychology*. Vol. 1. New York: Academic Press, 1964. Pp. 49—80.

Schachter, S., & Singer, J. E. Cognitive, social and physiological determinants of emotional state. *Psychological Review*, 1962, **69**, 379—399.

Schachter, S., & Wheeler, L. Epinephrine, chlorpromazine, and amusement. *Journal of Abnormal and Social Psychology*, 1962, **65**, 121—128.

Schlenker, B. R., Bonoma, T. V., Tedeschi, J. T., Lindskold, S., & Horai, J. The effects of referent and reward power upon social conflict. *Psychonomic Science*, 1971, **24**, 268—270.

Schlenker, B. R., Helm, B., & Tedeschi, J. T. The effects of personality and situational variables on behavioral trust. *Journal of Personality and Social Psychology*, 1973, **25**, 419—427.

Schlenker, B. R., & Tedeschi, J. T. Interpersonal attraction and the use of reward and coercive power. *Human Relations*, 1972, **25**, 427–439.

Schopler, J. & Compere, J. S. The effects of being kind or harsh to another on liking for him. Unpublished manuscript, 1972.

Selltiz, C., & Cook, S. W. Racial attitude as a determinant of judgments of plausibility. *Journal of Social Psychology*, 1966, **70**, 139–147.

Shaver, K. G. Defensive attribution: Effects of severity and relevance on the responsiblity assigned for an accident. *Journal of Personality and Social Psychology*, 1970, **14**, 101–113.

Simons, H. W., Berkowitz, N. N., & Moyer, R. J. Similarity, credibility, and attitude change: A review and a theory. *Psychological Bulletin*, 1970, **73**, 1–16.

Stapleton, R. E., Nacci, P., & Tedeschi, J. T. Interpersonal attraction and the reciprocation of benefits. Unpublished manuscript, State University of New York at Albany, 1972.

Staub, E., & Sherk, I. Need for approval, children's sharing behavior, and reciprocity in sharing. *Child Development*, 1970, **41**, 243–252.

Taguiri, R., Blake, R. R., & Bruner, J. S. Some determinants of the perception of positive and negative feelings in others. *Journal of Abnormal and Social Psychology*, 1953, **48**, 585–592.

Tedeschi, J. T., Schlenker, B. R., & Bonoma, T. V. *Interpersonal conflict, social power, and experimental games.* Chicago, Illinois: Aldine, 1973.

Thibaut, J. W., & Riecken, H. W. Some determinants and consequences of the perception of social causality. *Journal of Personality*, 1955, **24**, 113–133.

Valins, S. Cognitive effects of false heart-rate feedback. *Journal of Personality and Social Psychology*, 1966, **4**, 400–408.

von Mises, L. *Human action.* New Haven, Connecticut: Yale University Press, 1949.

Waly, P., & Cook, S. W. The effect of attitude on judgments of plausibility. *Journal of Personality and Social Psychology*, 1965, **2**, 745–749.

Walster, E. H. Passionate love. In B. I. Murstein (Ed.), *Theories of attraction and love.* New York: Springer Publ., 1971. Pp. 85–99.

Wilke, H., & Lanzetta, J. T. The obligation to help: The effects of amount of prior help on subsequent helping behavior. *Journal of Experimental Social Psychology*, 1970, **6**, 488–493.

Worchel, P., & McCormick, B. L. Self-concept and dissonance reduction. *Journal of Personality*, 1963, **31**, 588–599.

Worchel, P., & Schuster, S. D. Attraction as a function of the drive state. *Journal of Experimental Research in Personality*, 1966, **1**, 277–281.

Zimbardo, P. G. *The cognitive control of motivation.* Glenview, Illinois: Scott, Foresman, 1969.

10

A Symbolic Interactionist Approach to Attraction

GEORGE J. McCALL

Department of Sociology and Anthropology
University of Missouri—St. Louis
St. Louis, Missouri

I. Reconceptualizing Interpersonal Attraction

The theoretical perspective of symbolic interactionism, though deeply rooted in nineteenth-century American psychology, has until recently been the exclusive province of sociologists. Though sociologists have long been concerned with sociometric structures and patterns of association, the phrase "interpersonal attraction" has been largely confined to the vocabulary of psychologists. Interpersonal attraction has been used to refer to a wide range of phenomena, including general need for affiliation, marital satisfaction, and even attitudes toward experimentally fictitious personality profiles (Berscheid & Walster, 1969; Lindzey & Byrne, 1968). For a symbolic interactionist to discuss interpersonal attraction, therefore, he must begin with an attempt to pin down and delimit the meaning of the term, while relating it to distinctions important within the symbolic interaction framework.

In that framework, interpersonal attraction might initially be construed as ego's desiring interaction with alter. The emphasis (or contrastive focus) should be taken as falling on the prepositional object (Dretske, 1972). A desire to *interact* with any alter does not entail a desire to interact with a specific *alter*. Trapped in a long line at the supermarket, I may strongly desire to be able to execute my interaction with the checkout girl. But this situation must be distinguished from another in which two checkout lanes are free of customers, but I prefer to enter the lane run by a pretty young girl, rather than the lane run by a dumpy old lady. I shall assume here (Distinction 1) that the second situation indicates interpersonal attraction, whereas the first situation does not.

Where I desire to interact with *alter*, this desire may take either of two forms. I may desire to have an interactive *encounter* with alter, or I may desire to have an interactive *relationship* with alter (M. M. McCall, 1970). That is, I may simply be interested in sharing a single interactive episode with him, or I may be interested in having recurrent, somewhat regularized interaction with him. This sort of differentiation is often observed in connection with sexual desires, for example. Again, I shall assume here (Distinction 2) that the second situation is more characteristic of interpersonal attraction than is the first.

In other writings (G. J. McCall, 1970) I have distinguished two types of interactive relationships. In one type, each person perceives himself and the other to be the members of a particular role relationship (for instance, clerk—customer) and feels constrained to interact with the other in a manner befitting their common membership in this collectivity. Where such a role relationship is the primary constraint on the interaction, we can speak of a *formal* relationship between two persons. In the second type, the common collectivity of which the two persons are members may be an acquaintanceship—merely mutual recognition. The form their interaction takes is constrained by what one person knows of the other and by what one thinks or hopes the other knows of him. Where such knowledge, rather than a role relationship, is the primary constraint on the form of interaction, we can speak of a *personal* relationship between two persons. Although virtually all concrete social relationships are blends of formal and personal relationships, I assume (Distinction 3) that desire for a *personal*, rather than formal, relationship with alter more properly characterizes interpersonal attraction.

I have previously (G. J. McCall, 1970; McCall & Simmons, 1966) suggested several factors that commonly dispose a person toward such recurrent, regularized interaction with another person. These factors (or interpersonal bonds) include:

1. *ascription*, the linkage among persons owing simply to their occupancy of social positions that happen to be interrelated;

2. *commitment*, the fact of having privately and publicly pledged oneself to honoring an exchange agreement with alter;

3. *investment*, the fact of having expended scarce personal resources, such as money, time, and life chances, in the enterprise of establishing interaction with alter;

4. *reward dependability*, the personal knowledge that alter is a dependable source of various social rewards; and

5. *attachment*, the incorporation of alter—and especially alter's actions and reactions—into the contents of one's various conceptions of self.

For each social position a person occupies, aspires to occupy, or has imagined himself occupying (for example, husband, first violin, third baseman), he sustains a *role identity*, an imaginative view of himself as an occupant of that position. A wealth of concrete detail is included in these imaginations of self, ranging from fantasied heroic accomplishments to how one fancies he should hold his head to express exactly the proper attitude in an important encounter.

The reactions of other people to one's hypothetical performances occupy an important place in these daydreams. Not all people who figure in one's imaginary performances (as objects, accomplices, or audiences) are known persons, but perhaps the majority are (Singer, 1966). In this way, specific persons are built into the contents of one's role identities and become crucial to the legitimation and enactment of these identities. Such attachments to specific persons can be either positive in content (liking, love) or negative (rivalry, enmity), depending upon whether these persons are perceived primarily as sources of social rewards or as sources of social costs. (Chambliss, 1965).

Although the five foregoing factors tend to blend together, I propose (Distinction 4) that disposition toward recurrent interaction with alter, based upon the factor of *attachment*, is most clearly characteristic of interpersonal attraction. In any case, this is certainly the conclusion of Waller (1938) and Bolton (1961) in their analyses of romantic love, the epitome of interpersonal attraction.

In light of the above four distinctions, then, I shall construe interpersonal attraction of ego toward alter as *ego's desiring a personal interactive relationship with alter based on ego's positive attachment to alter.*

II. The Problem of Interpersonal Attraction

A central focus of the study of interpersonal attraction concerns the question: What is it about alter that leads ego to form such an attachment to alter? For symbolic interactionists, what ego finds attractive about alter is some property (or properties) of alter's "character."

"Character" is employed here in essentially the same sense as in the language of the theater and in the dramaturgical perspective in sociology (Goffman, 1959; Lyman & Scott, 1970; Park, 1927). A *character* is a person with a distinctive organization of personal characteristics, such as appearance, mannerisms, habits, traits, motives, and social positions. A *role*, on the other hand, is the plausible line of action truly expressive of the personality of a character. If the actor's appearance and performance (all of his actions that can be construed as pertinent to the immediate scene) are congruent with his role, the audience attributes to him the corresponding character. The audience is taken in by the act and is absorbed in the emergent dramatic reality (Simmel, 1968). If, however, the actor's appearance and performance are *not* congruent with that role, the audience regards him as being "out of character."[1]

The success or failure of a performance, of course, is not entirely in the hands of the actor himself. The props, supporting cast, and even the audience itself can make or break an actor's performance. Audiences, as well as actors, differ widely in their ability to see plausible characters and roles in what are merely parts and in their ability to transmute them into a dramatic reality. The same performance may strike one audience as overdrawn and unconvincing, yet completely capture a different audience (Cantril, Gaudet, & Hertzog, 1940).

A person's character may differ widely in differing social scenes, since it is not an attribute of its possessor, but rather a product of the whole scene of his action. As Simmel (in Wolff, 1950) noted:

> If A and B have different conceptions of M, this by no means necessarily implies incompleteness or deception. Rather, in view of the relation in which A stands to M, A's nature and the total circumstances being what they are, A's picture of M is true for him in the same manner in which, for B, a different picture is true. It would be quite erroneous to say that, above these two pictures, there is the objectively correct knowledge about M, and that A's and B's images are legitimated to the extent to which they coincide with this objective knowledge. Rather, the ideal truth which the picture of M in the conception of A approaches— to be sure, only asymptotically—is something different, even as an ideal, from that of B. It contains as an integrating, form-giving precondition the psychological peculiarity of A and the particular relation into which A and M are brought by their specific [natures] and destinies [p. 309].*

It is not that an individual has a definite and basic character or personality which he selectively and differentially reveals to various others. Rather, in relation to different others, his "whole scene of action" varies, so that these different scenes generate different characters for him. The important consequence of this for present purposes is that individuals confront each other, not as definite personalities, but as characters, as "dramatic effects arising diffusely from a scene that is presented" (Goffman, 1959, p. 253). What ego knows of alter is the character generated for alter by the scene of his action. Therefore, if ego is attracted to alter, what he finds attractive must be alter's interactively determined character.

Why ego is attracted to alter thus breaks down into two separate questions:

First, what is it about ego, alter, and the structure of the interpersonal situation that leads alter to display the character that he does?

---

[1] To minimize possible confusions on this point, let me emphasize that I am using the term "role" here in the dramaturgical sense just described. I am not using it in the more ordinary, sociological sense of "social role"—as a set of expected behaviors customarily associated with a given social position. Were I so employing the term, attribution theory (Jones & Davis, 1965) might suggest a contrary conclusion—that audiences would discern the actor's character *only* through deviant, or incongruous, departures from his (social) role.

*From *The Sociology of George Simmel*, edited by K. Wolff. Copyright 1950 by the Free Press.

Second, what is it about ego that leads him to develop a positive attachment to alter's character?

III. Determinants of Alter's Character

The central concept in my elaboration of symbolic interactionism (McCall & Simmons, 1966) is that of role identity, already treated somewhat in my discussion of attachment. There I spoke of a role identity as a person's imaginative view of himself, the way he likes to think of himself as an occupant of a particular social position. At this point we can now more technically regard a role identity as the character and role that an individual imaginatively devises for himself as an occupant of that position.

Role identities are not simply idle musings and entertaining daydreams; they exert important influences on daily life. In the first place, they probably serve as the primary source of plans of action. The imagined performances that constitute such a large portion of the content of any role identity are proving grounds and rehearsal halls for actual performances. The imagined reactions of various others to these hypothetical performances constitute important criteria for evaluating plans for overt action (Singer, 1966).

The contents of a person's role identities also provide him with criteria for monitoring and appraising his actual performances. Overt actions that are inconsistent with his imaginations of himself as an occupant of a particular social position are regarded as embarrassing, threatening, and disconcerting (Gross & Stone, 1964); if possible, they will be discontinued and superseded by actions more in keeping with his view of self. The lengths to which persons will go in order to avoid embarrassment and to maintain face have been amply demonstrated (Modigliani, 1968; Brown & Garland, 1971; Goffman, 1955).

Finally, role identities are important influences on our interpretations of situations, events, and other people since they provide us with plans of action and the systems of object classification these plans entail (Mead, 1938). Our role identities particularly affect our interpretations of the identity and meaning of both ourselves and other *persons* (Secord, Backman, & Eachus, 1964).

A person's set of role identities is organized in a complex fashion. The most distinctive aspect of this organization is the hierarchical arrangement of the role identities in terms of their individual prominence in a person's thinking about himself. The contents of the more prominent identities afford persisting priorities and dispositions that lend continuity of direction to the person's life. This hierarchy of prominence, sometimes called the "ideal self," is not the sole personal determinant of conduct, however, for if it were, only the most prominent role identities would ever be performed.

Situational factors can cause less prominent role identities to become temporarily salient. One such factor is the person's current level of need or desire for the various kinds of rewards associated with enactment of a given role identity. Such rewards will be more systematically considered in Section IV, but warrant some exemplification here. Performing the role identity of violin virtuoso might, for example, generate such rewards as lucrative concert fees, societal prestige, association with famous and powerful people, fulfillment of long-standing ambitions, and the pleasures of skillful rhythmic movements. The rewards associated with the performance of the role identities of butterfly collector, gardener, or mother are likely to be significantly different from these. Whatever the case, a role identity whose enactment would probably gain the person more of those rewards most valued at the moment is more likely to be acted upon. Desires for the various types of rewards fluctuate, of course, as a function of recent history through satiation, deprivation, mood shifts, and the like.

A related factor affecting the differential salience of role identities in a given situation is the perceived opportunity to obtain various kinds and amounts of social reward, albeit at certain costs. The situation—and especially the other persons in it—is appraised in terms of potential profit to the actor (that is, in terms of various reward/cost ratios). Identities whose enactment appear most profitable in the present situation will likely be acted upon.

The resulting hierarchy of role identities in terms of salience represents their relative order of priority as possible sources of performance in the situation (Stryker, 1965). The salience hierarchy may usefully be referred to as the "situational self" (as distinguished from the "ideal self," or prominence hierarchy). The individual seeks to incorporate into his actual performance those identities that are high in the order of salience and is less concerned with incorporating those that are low in the order.

That subset of his role identities which the person strives to incorporate into his performance in a given encounter constitutes the character he seeks to assume in that encounter. His performance before the other persons present is devised with the aim of acting in a manner consistent with, and expressive of, that character or subset of role identities, in order to legitimate them.

A person's character and role are not entirely at his own discretion, to be chosen on the basis of his salience hierarchy alone. Rather, these matters are considerably influenced by the audience, which may refuse to support a given role, or to confer the corresponding character. Character and role are *social objects* determined jointly through the interaction of performer and audience. Each party has certain preferences concerning characters and roles, but the resulting social objects typically represent compromises between performer and audience, compromises achieved through *bargaining* in terms of the various social rewards that may serve as inducements.

Such bargaining takes place through the medium of several cognitive and expressive processes. The first cognitive process is that of *imputing a role to alter* (or, more conventionally, role-taking). Ego attempts to infer alter's preferred character on the basis of his appearance and, more important, his behaviors. Ego seeks to discover not alter's qualities as a person, but rather the role he is performing before ego and, thereby, alter's operative identities (Turner, 1962). In role-taking proper, ego is not trying to see through the behaviors to alter's "true self" (prominence hierarchy), but is trying to discover the contours of the *role* alter is currently projecting and the *character* (salient subset of identities) that underlies it.

Second, once ego discovers what he takes to be alter's current role, he modifies his own line of action on the basis of perceived implications of alter's role and character for ego's own active and latent plans of action. He *devises* (or improvises) *his own role* (and, thereby, his own character) in terms of how he can best make use of alter's role and character (Thibaut & Kelley, 1959). The interactive role that ego discerns in alter's behavior is appraised in terms of the opportunity structure this role presents for ego.

While ego is thus engaged in imputing a role and character to alter and improvising his own character and role in strategic response, alter is busily doing the same with respect to ego. If ego and alter are to achieve any kind of rudimentary accommodation, the improvised role of each must at least be roughly in line with the role imputed to him. This outcome can be attained only through strategic communication with the other party (Goffman, 1969).

Such communication takes place through various expressive processes. The first of the expressive processes is the selective *presentation of self*, the tactics of which have been very thoroughly explored by Goffman (1959). By carefully controlling his expressive behaviors, ego can convey to alter an image of the character he desires to assume in the situation. If this control is exercised skillfully, if ego's performance thoroughly sustains his role and character, alter will have little ground for denying ego's identity claims. By conducting himself as if he were a certain kind of person, ego exerts leverage on alter to act toward him as if he indeed were that kind of person. Alter's actions thus support ego's performance and his claims, and ego's presented self tends to become a self-fulfilling image.

The second expressive process, that of *altercasting*, resembles presentation of self in its form, but differs in its point of application (Weinstein & Deutschberger, 1963). Not only does ego's performance express an image of who *he* is, but it also simultaneously expresses an image of whom he takes *alter* to be. This image, too, has a tendency to become self-fulfilling, for ego acts toward alter as if he were indeed the sort of person ego takes him to be, and he may continue to do so regardless of alter's own performance.

Yet neither presentation of self nor altercasting necessarily or automatically brings the role and character that ego has devised for himself into line with those imputed to him by alter. The two processes serve only to express to alter the results of ego's cognition. Alter may not even interpret these expressive messages correctly, for there is many a slip 'twixt expressions sent and impressions received. Whether or not accurately read, the expressed roles for self and alter may not be acceptable to alter in terms of his own hierarchy of role identities.

In the latter event, ego's expressive processes do not yet serve to establish an interpersonal accommodation, but only to suggest to alter the direction in which ego would like to modify the roles of each party. Alter, in turn, will employ these processes to indicate to ego the somewhat different direction in which he would like to modify their respective roles. If neither party is willing to yield, they will be talking past each other, acting profitlessly on incompatible bases.

Most often, however, the two parties will negotiate a compromise, each acceding somewhat (though seldom in equal degree) to the other's demands. The negotiation settles which, how many, and how much of his salient role identities each person will be allowed to incorporate into his performance. Weinstein and Deutschberger (1964) have pointed out that there are not one but two bargains to be struck in this connection, one with oneself and one with alter.

In present terms, ego must, first of all, somehow reconcile the role he improvises for himself (in response to the role imputed to alter) with the demands of his own salience hierarchy. Second, he must also reconcile his improvised role toward alter with the demands of *alter's* salience hierarchy. The content of one or more of alter's salient role identities may dictate that ego act toward him in an altogether different fashion than indicated by ego's own improvised and expressed role.

Although the moves of each party are thus motivated by the reward—cost considerations underlying their salience hierarchies, these moves take the form of insinuations about identities. The negotiation is fundamentally a process of bargaining over the terms of exchange of social rewards, yet it does not assume the outward appearance of a crude naming of prices. Rather, the negotiation takes the form of a subtle (often tacit) debate over who each person is. Each move is expressed through a change (or a refusal to change) in the presentation of self or in alter-casting.

Just such a process of negotiation of role and character is portrayed in John Barth's (1967) novel *The End of the Road*. The young hero has just made a pick-up at the beach and is over hastily seducing the lady, who protests:

> 'Don't you understand how you make me feel? Today is my last day at Ocean City. For two whole weeks not a soul has spoken to me or even looked at me, except some horrible old men. Not a *soul*! Most women look awful at my age, but I don't look awful: I just don't look like a child. There's a lot more to me, damn it! And then on the last day you come along and pick me up, bored as you can be with the whole thing, and treat me like a whore!'
>
> Well, she was correct.
>
> 'I'm a cad,' I agreed readily, and rose to leave. There was a little more to this matter than Miss Rankin was willing to see, but in the main she had a pretty clear view of things. Her mistake, in the long run, was articulating her protest. The game was spoiled now, of course: I had assigned to Miss Rankin a role of Forty-Year Old Pickup, a delicate enough character for her to bring off successfully in my current mood; I had no interest whatever in the quite complex (and no doubt interesting, from another point of view) human being she might be apart from that role. What she should have done, it seems to me, assuming she was after the same thing I was after, was assign me a role gratifying to her own vanity—say, The Fresh But Unintelligent Young Man Whose Body One Uses for One's Pleasure Without Otherwise Taking Him Seriously—and then we could have pursued our business with no wounds inflicted on either side. As it was, my present feeling, though a good deal stronger, was essentially the same feeling one has when a filling-station attendant or a cabdriver launches into his life-story: as a rule, and especially when one is in a hurry or is grouchy, one wishes the man to be nothing more difficult than the Obliging Filling-Station Attendant or the Adroit Cabdriver. These are the essences you have assigned them, at least temporarily,

for your own purposes, as a taleteller makes a man The Handsome Young Poet or The Jealous Old Husband; and while you know very well that no historical human being was ever *just* an Obliging Filling-Station Attendant or a Handsome Young Poet, you are nevertheless prepared to ignore your man's charming complexities—*must* ignore them, in fact, if you are to get on with the plot, or get things done on schedule .... Enough now to say that we are all casting directors a great deal of the time, if not always, and he is wise who realizes that his role-assigning is at best an arbitrary distortion of the actors' personalities; but he is even wiser who sees in addition that his arbitrariness is probably inevitable, and at any rate is apparently necessary if one would reach the ends he desires [pp. 24–26].*

The novel goes on to show the eventual and rather unequal compromise that is negotiated through crying, cursing, recriminations, and attempts to leave. What the novel provides in exemplary detail concerning the negotiation of character is empirically substantiated by studies of delinquent youth (Werthman & Piliavin, 1967), pool hustlers (Polsky, 1967), systematic check forgers (Lemert, 1967), and confidence men (Maurer, 1940).

Since ego's desires are often important in determining the character alter assumes, it is not surprising that ego frequently finds certain features of alter's character attractive. But such a result does not entail that ego will become positively *attached* to alter's character. The determinants of ego's attachment involve further matters, to which I now turn.

IV. Determinants of Ego's Attachment to Alter's Character

Ego relates to and evaluates alter primarily as representing an opportunity structure for obtaining the many varieties of rewards to which ego is oriented. If ego believes that alter represents an opportunity *superior to alternative opportunities* for obtaining some important type of reward, he will be differentially—and more favorably—disposed to interact with the alter.

If persons X and Y both represent an opportunity to obtain a given quantity of a certain reward, and if the costs incurred in obtaining it from X are expected to be smaller than in obtaining the reward from Y, then X represents a superior opportunity; the expected price is lower. But superiority of opportunity may also be a function of the expected quantity of reward. If ego believes that X can provide a greater quantity or amount of the reward than can Y, X is the superior opportunity. Finally, if ego believes that X can provide quantities of the reward more reliably or more frequently than can Y, then X is the superior opportunity. Actually, then, superiority of opportunity is some joint function of expected *quantity* and expected *reliability* of supply, as well as of expected *price*.

---

*From *The End of the Road.* Copyright © 1958, 1967 by John Barth. Reprinted by permission of Doubleday & Company, Inc.

A person who represents for ego the superior opportunity for obtaining some important type of reward will become built into ego's relevant role identities. He will tend to come to mind whenever ego considers a plan of action to obtain that particular type of reward. Since various types of reward and various plans of action are differentially associated with ego's several role identities, alter becomes incorporated into the contents of one or more of these identities. Ego develops *positive attachment* to alter. And since all that ego knows of alter (even as an opportunity structure) is alter's interactively determined character, we should properly say that ego develops positive attachment to alter's *character*.

These considerations suggest, then, that to account for ego's positive attachment to the character of some alter, we should look into ego's desires for various rewards and to his perceptions of available potential sources of supply of these rewards.

One broad category of rewards is that of *intrinsic rewards*, pleasures intrinsic to the performing of some activity. For example, ego may find the act of whitewater canoeing intrinsically gratifying. If Joe is the only person ego knows who can steer him through rapids, (that is, afford ego the intrinsic rewards of whitewater canoeing), then whenever ego experiences a desire to shoot rapids, he will think of Joe. Joe will be *built into* ego's role identity of whitewater canoeist; that is, ego has a positive *attachment* to Joe. But should ego come to believe that (*a*) Bill would be willing to steer him through more exciting rapids than Joe would, or (*b*) Bill would be willing to take ego rapid-shooting more frequently than Joe would, or (*c*) shooting rapids with Bill would be less costly than with Joe, then we can expect that Joe will be more or less displaced from this role identity of ego's in favor of an attachment to Bill (more properly, to Bill's character).

Similarly with *extrinsic rewards*, those which are not intrinsic to performance of some activity, but are contingent consequences, or by-products, of it. For example, ego may only somewhat enjoy the act of fishing, but be ecstatic over the flavor of Arctic char, unavailable to him commercially. If Joe is the only person ego knows who could fly him to the Arctic to obtain this delicacy (that is, afford ego this extrinsic reward associated with Arctic fishing), then whenever ego experiences a desire for Arctic char he will think of Joe. Joe will be built into ego's role identity of fisherman. But again, should ego come to perceive Bill as an opportunity to obtain char in greater quantity, or more reliably, or more cheaply, then ego's attachment to Joe will be more or less replaced by a positive attachment to Bill (Bill's character).

But the category of rewards most involved in forming attachments is that of *role support*, the expressed confirmation or legitimation accorded to a performer by his audience(s) for his claims concerning his role identity. This support is not simply support of his claim to occupancy of the social position in question, nor of his claim to the conventional rights and duties associated with that position. Neither is role support to be equated simply with prestige, status, esteem, or social approval of his conduct in that position. Rather, it is a set of reactions and performances by others, the expressive implications of which tend to confirm the person's detailed and imaginative view of himself in the position. Role support involves the implied confirmation of the specific contents of a person's idealized and singular imaginations of self.

Any alter who represents a superior opportunity for obtaining this type of reward is particularly likely to become the object of positive attachment (Chambliss, 1965), since the contents of role identities importantly incorporate specific persons and their reactions. Furthermore, once alter becomes incorporated into the contents of ego's role identity, alter can perforce provide ego with distinctively significant role support and thus represents a superior opportunity. In this manner, a cycle of progressively deepening attachment is initiated.

As with other types of rewards, quantity of role support available through alter importantly affects positive attachment and its displacement. For example, the swain who fancies himself a poet may well be smitten by the first sensitive young thing who takes his verse seriously; that is, he forms a positive attachment to her. But should there come along a young girl who is herself an acknowledged poet and who can, therefore, confer greater legitimation upon his poetic status, his previous attachment will probably be displaced toward her. And again, factors of reliability (frequency) and of cost of such reward function as previously described to affect superiority of opportunity and, thereby, positive attachment.

These illustrations may serve to make positive attachment seem even more precarious than it in fact is. Various contraints—such as the costs and difficulties of interpersonal exploration and the demands of existing relationships (Kurth, 1970; Thibaut & Kelley, 1959)—generally deter people from undertaking very searching comparisons of alternative opportunities. Furthermore, the costs incurred in displacement of positive attachments are themselves quite substantial (Thibaut & Kelley, 1959). The result is that at most points in the life cycle, people are relatively unreceptive to the cultivation of new attachments (Kurth, 1970).

Thus far in my examination of superior opportunity, I have focused primarily on factors of (potential) supply of social rewards. I will turn now to factors of demand for these goods.

Had Jill met Jane on a morning when she was feeling fresh and energetic, she might have asked whether Jane played tennis. Meeting Jane this afternoon when she is tired and depressed, Jill does not even think to inquire. Desire for a given type of reward—such as the intrinsic gratifications of playing tennis—is not an individual constant. Satiation, fatigue, deprivation, and changes in situation can sharply affect level of desire. *The degree to which* (or the likelihood with which) *alter will be perceived as affording an opportunity to obtain a certain type of reward is in good part a function of the degree to which ego currently desires that reward.* Hence, so is the degree (or likelihood) of positive attachment to alter also a function of desire for the given type of reward.

Desire is subject not only to short-run fluctuations due to situational factors, but also to long-run changes due to developmental or maturational factors. The desire to play Cowboys and Indians greatly declines between childhood and adulthood, so that by age 20 this desire is not likely to serve as a basis for forming attachments, no matter how important it may have been at age 5. Similarly, historical or cultural shifts may serve to bring about long-run changes in desire for a certain type of reward, as when the craze for hula-hooping or playing canasta abated. Still more interesting is the possibility that alter himself may teach, persuade, or coerce ego to value some new commodity—may create in ego some additional type of desire—or to cease to value some previously valued reward. Just as alter can affect ego's existing set of alternative opportunities, so he can sometimes widen or narrow ego's existing set of desires.

Such, then, is the gist of my answer to the symbolic interactionist question of what it is about ego that leads him to develop positive attachment to alter's character. I have proposed here that ego's range and levels of desire for various social rewards, coupled with ego's perceived opportunity structure for obtaining those rewards, determine any attachment to alter's character.

Assessment of the explanatory value of this approach is rather difficult at this time. Obviously, no empirical studies have been undertaken expressly to test this newly minted formulation, and few of the conventional studies of interpersonal attraction can be reinterpreted to bear directly upon it, since these studies have not been directed toward positive attachment in the sense I have set forth here. Nonetheless, I have confidence in the plausibility and potential fruitfulness of this framework because the results of a number of somewhat relevant empirical researches, such as investigations of marriage formation (Bolton, 1959; Burgess & Wallin, 1953) and of marriage dissolution (Waller, 1938; Goode, 1956; Dickinson & Beam, 1931). These studies have attempted to examine something close to what I have been calling positive attachment and have found the phenomenon to be quite salient in the inner dynamics of this important type of interpersonal attraction. Although these early studies did not examine the *determinants* of attachment which I have suggested here, they did successfully demonstrate the relevance and practicability of investigating positive attachment as the dependent variable in empirical studies of prototypic forms of interpersonal attraction.

V. Conclusions

In this chapter I have tried to sketch out how the traditional psychological questions concerning interpersonal attraction come to be altered and revised within the framework of symbolic interactionism. Like other approaches to social psychology, symbolic interactionism is not a unitary and consensual perspective, but encompasses a family of related developments. The version employed here is rather narrowly my own. Reliance on this version principally affects details of the treatment in Sections II and IV; the main features of the analysis, however, would probably be assented to by a majority of symbolic interactions identified with the discipline of sociology.

Four critical differences from the traditional psychological approach emerge, which I should like to underline.

1. The conceptualization of the phenomenon of interpersonal attraction is tightened (or narrowed) considerably. By bringing this phenomenon under the

rubric of emergent social organization, the symbolic interactionist account trims off various attitudinal conceptions of interpersonal attraction. As MacIver (1937) put it, interests—not attitudes—explain the emergence of social organizations. I have felt free to speculate here on the central role of social rewards, costs, and perceived profit opportunities in explaining the developmental contingencies of personal relationships based on positive attachment. I have not felt obliged to explain, for example, subjects' attitudes toward experimentally fictitious personality profiles.

2. The symbolic interactionist reworking of attraction effectively adds a dimension to the traditional approach. It does so by requiring us to ask why it is that alter displays various features in the first place. The standard interpersonal attraction literature tends to take alter's features (though not necessarily ego's perception of them) as a given.

3. This perspective forces us to respond most vigorously to a warning note not infrequently sounded in the traditional literature on interpersonal attraction (see Berscheid & Walster, 1969). Namely, that the question of why A likes B cannot be answered simply by examining various features of B, but that we must also examine what it is about A that leads him to find features of B attractive. The symbolic interactionist perspective places this latter question on front and center stage.

4. I should like to distinguish explicitly between the explanatory approach of this perspective and that of various broadly reinforcement-centered viewpoints (Murstein, 1971; Berscheid & Walster, 1969; Byrne, 1971; Lott & Lott, 1968), since both approaches make important reference to the role of rewards. The approach I have been explicating here does not turn on the reinforcing effects of rewards received. Rather, it turns on the energizing and directive effects of *anticipation* of *incremental profits*. It suggests that even if A has a long history of receiving great rewards from B *and* has every reason to anticipate their continuance in the future, A's *attachment* to B will be displayed should A come to perceive a superior *opportunity* to receive those rewards, even though none may yet actually have been received from that alternative source. The contrast to which I am pointing is rather like that between the reinforcement approach and the expected utility approach in decision theory (Edwards, Lindman & Phillips, 1965; Ofshe & Ofshe, 1970). Many standard types of study of interpersonal attraction might benefit considerably from substitution of broadly "expected utility"-centered approaches for the more conventional reinforcement-centered approaches.

References

Barth, J. *The end of the road.* (rev. ed.) Garden City, New York: Doubleday, 1967.

Berscheid, E., & Walster, E. H. *Interpersonal attraction.* Reading, Massachusetts: Addison-Wesley, 1969.

Bolton, C. D. The development process in love relationships. Unpublished doctoral dissertation, University of Chicago, 1959.

Bolton, C. D. Mate selection as the development of a relationship. *Marriage and Family Living*, 1961, **23**, 234—240.

Brown, B., & Garland, H. The effects of incompetency, audience acquaintanceship, and anticipated evaluative feedback on face-saving behavior. *Journal of Experimental Social Psychology*, 1971, **7**, 490—502.

Burgess, E. W., & Wallin, P. *Engagement and marriage*. Philadelphia, Pennsylvania: Lippincott, 1953.

Byrne, D. *The attraction paradigm*. New York: Academic Press, 1971.

Cantril, H., Gaudet, H., & Hertzog, H. *The invasion from Mars*. Princeton, New Jersey: Princeton University Press, 1940.

Chambliss, W. The selection of friends. *Social Forces*, 1965, **43**, 370—379.

Dickinson, R. L., & Beam, L. *A thousand marriages*. Baltimore, Maryland: Williams & Wilkins, 1931.

Dretske, F. I. Contrastive statements. *Philosophical Review*, 1972, **81**, 411—437.

Edwards, W., Lindman, H., & Phillips, L. D. Emerging technologies for making decisions. In T. M. Newcomb (Ed.), *New directions in psychology*. Vol. 2. New York: Holt, 1965. Pp. 259—325.

Goffman, E. On Face-work: An analysis of ritual elements in social interaction. *Psychiatry*, 1955, **18**, 213—231.

Goffman, E. *The presentation of self in everyday life*. Garden City, New York: Doubleday, 1959.

Goffman, E. *Strategic interaction*. Philadelphia, Pennsylvania: University of Pennsylvania Press, 1969.

Goode, W. J. *After divorce*. New York: Free Press, 1956.

Gross, E., & Stone, G. Embarrassment and the analysis of role requirements. *American Journal of Sociology*, 1964, **70**, 1—15.

Jones, E. E., & Davis K. E. From acts to dispositions: The attribution process in person perception. In L. Berkowitz (Ed.), *Advances in experimental social psychology*. Vol. 2. New York: Academic Press, 1965. Pp. 219—266.

Kurth, S. B. Friendships and friendly relations. In G. J. McCall (Ed.), *Social relationships*. Chicago, Illinois: Aldine, 1970. Pp. 136—170.

Lemert, E. M. Role enactment, self, and identity in the systematic check forger. In E. M. Lerert, *Human deviance, social problems, and social control*. Englewood Cliffs, New Jersey: Prentice-Hall, 1967. Pp. 119—134.

Lindzey, G., & Byrne, D. Measurement of social choice and interpersonal attractiveness. In G. Lindzey & E. Aronson (Eds.), *The handbook of social psychology*. Vol. 2. (2nd ed.) Reading, Massachusetts: Addison-Wesley, 1968. Pp. 452—525.

Lott, A., & Lott, B. A learning theory approach to interpersonal attitudes. In. A G. Greenwald, T. C. Brock, & T. M. Ostrom (Eds.), *Psychological foundations of attitudes*. New York: Academic Press, 1968.

Lyman, S., & Scott, M. Stage fright and the problem of identity. In S. Lyman & M. Scott (Eds.), *A sociology of the absurd*. New York: Appleton, 1970. Pp. 159—188.

MacIver, R. M. *Society*. New York: Farrar & Rinehart, 1937.

Maurer, D. W. *The big con*. Indianapolis, Indiana: Bobbs-Merrill, 1940.

McCall, G. J. The social organization of relationships. In G. J. McCall (Ed.), *Social relationships*. Chicago, Illinois: Aldine, 1970. Pp. 3—34.

McCall, G. J., & Simmons, J. L. *Identities and interactions*. New York: Free Press, 1966.

McCall, M. M. Boundary rules in relationships and encounters. In G. J. McCall (Ed.), *Social relationships*. Chicago, Illinois: Aldine, 1970. Pp. 35—61.

Mead, G. H. *The philosophy of the act*. Chicago, Illinois: University of Chicago Press, 1938.

Modigliani, A. Embarassment and embarassability. *Sociometry*, 1968, **31**, 313—326.

Murstein, B. I. (Ed.), *Theories of attraction and love*. New York: Springer Publ., 1971.

Ofshe, L., & Ofshe, R. *Utility and choice in social interaction*. Englewood Cliffs, New Jersey: Prentice-Hall, 1970.

Park, R. E. Human nature and collective behavior. *American Journal of Sociology*, 1927, **32**, 733—741.

Polsky, N. *Hustlers, beats, and others*. Chicago, Illinois: Aldine, 1967.

Secord, P. F., Backman, C. W., & Eachus, H. T. Effects of imbalance in the self concept on the perception of persons. *Journal of Abnormal and Social Psychology*, 1964, **68**, 442—446.

Simmel, G. The dramatic actor and reality. In K. P. Etzkorn (Ed.), *George Simmel: The conflict in modern culture and other essays*. New York: Teachers College Press, 1968, Pp. 91—97.

Singer, J. F. *Daydreaming*. New York: Random House, 1966.

Stryker, S. Identity salience and role performance: The relevance of symbolic interaction theory for family research. Paper presented at the meeting of the American Sociological Association, Chicago, Illinois, August, 1965.

Thibaut, J. W., & Kelley, H. H. *The social psychology of groups*. New York: Wiley, 1959.

Turner, R. H. Role-taking: Process versus conformity. In A. M. Rose (Ed.), *Human behavior and social processes*. Boston, Massachusetts: Houghton Mifflin, 1962. Pp. 20—40.

Waller, W. *The family*. New York: Dryden, 1938.

Weinstein, E. A., & Deutschberger, P. Some dimensions of altercasting. *Sociometry*, 1963, **26**, 454—466.

Weinstein, E. A., & Deutschberger, P. Tasks, bargains, and identities in social interaction. *Social Forces*, 1964, 451—456.

Werthman, C., & Piliavin, I. Gang members and the police. In D. Bordua (Ed.), *The police*. New York: Wiley, 1967. Pp. 56—98.

Wolff, K. (Ed.) *The sociology of George Simmel*. New York: Free Press, 1950.

PART IV

Antecedents of Attraction: Affective Feedback, Attitudes, and Situational Factors

11

Affective Reactions
to Appraisal from Others

DAVID R. METTEE[1]

Department of Psychology
University of Denver
Denver, Colorado

and

ELLIOT ARONSON

Department of Psychology
University of Texas
Austin, Texas

[1]This chapter was started while Mettee was at Yale University.

I. Introduction

In considering the effects that personal evaluations have upon attraction, we will strive to assume the perspective of the man in the street who has a working formula for assessing the meaning of such evaluations. Specifically, the formula thought to determine the common man's attraction response derive from four considerations: (*a*) the *valence* (positive or negative) of the evaluation; (*b*) the *magnitude* of the evaluation; (*c*) the *validity* of the evaluation (that is, the degree of congruence of the evaluation with situationally operative "reality standards"); and (*d*) the *authenticity*, or genuineness, of the evaluation (that is, the degree to which it reflects the evaluator's internally held appraisal).

A. The Scope and Definition of the Antecedent

Personal evaluations refer to evaluations which reflect the *other's personal subjective appraisal* and/or internal disposition toward the recipient's: (*a*) behavior—performance, (*b*) attributes—traits—characteristics and/or (*c*) his personage as a whole. Hence, the "personal" of personal evaluations refers to both the evaluator and the recipient—the evaluation reflects the evaluator's personal subjective appraisal of some personal aspect of the recipient.

The scope of the phenomenon is contained in the definition. In this chapter we examine and interpret findings regarding an other's explicit or implicit personal evaluation. Explicit refers to the evaluation content of verbal communications, whereas implicit refers to nonverbal evaluative communications conveyed via means such as smiles, scowls, frowns, stares, and gestures, as well as by other more gross approach—avoidance behavior. We are not concerned with situations in which an other is an indirect or comparative source of evaluative feedback for the person (for example, an other outperforms the person in competition).

B. The Dichotomous Nature of the Antecedent

Personal evaluations can be either positive or negative in valence. It is customary to think of positive and negative evaluations as forming the endpoints of a single evaluative dimension, and for the most part we adhere to this convention. However, there are substantive reasons for conceiving of positive and negative evaluations as forming an affective dichotomy with each being a separate dimension having neutral as a base-line end point (see Mettee, 1971a; Richey, McClelland, & Shimkunas, 1967; Kanouse & Hanson, 1973). Data examined in this chapter indicate that positive and negative evaluations are more than just affective opposites, or mirror images. Rather, they possess different affective–informational properties. Hence, at times we treat positive and negative personal evaluations as separate dimensions. When we do make a distinction between positive and negative dimensions, we consider them in tandem with each other. This should serve to illustrate more vividly their fundamental asymmetry, as well as their points of correspondence.

C. Attraction as a Dependent Variable

The primary measure of interest in this chapter is like–dislike. Attraction, however, is a more general term and refers to a wider range of phenomena, which do not always correlate highly with like–dislike. Attraction responses as indicated by self-reports, for instance, seem to form two conceptually independent dimensions: liking and respect (see Mettee, Hrelec, & Wilkins, 1971; Bales, 1958; Goldberg & Mettee, 1968; Kiesler & Goldberg, 1968). Moreover, behavioral attraction responses (approach–avoidance reactions), such as desire to associate with, affilation responses, and desire for future interaction, often do not correspond with subjective like–dislike reactions toward an other (see Hardyck, 1968). In fact, in some of the more interesting instances, behavioral approach tendencies and liking are negatively related; for example, strong dislike may impel vigorous approach responses (symbolic attack) designed to reduce the negative effect of the disliked object (see Snoeck, 1962). Given these considerations, we do not treat attraction as a monolithic dependent measure, but do specify what dimension of attraction is involved.

D. Conceptual Paradigm and Parameters

The paradigm we are studying takes the following form: A recipient becomes aware of an other's personal evaluation, which we characterize in terms of four basic parameters—valence, degree or strength of valence, evaluation validity, and evaluation authenticity. Then, following receipt of the evaluation, the recipient's attraction toward the evaluator is determined. In some cases, the recipient's perception of the four basic parameters of the evaluation is also determined.

II. Personal Evaluations Taken at Face Value

Our analysis of personal evaluation–attraction phenomena at times uses a hypothetical, representative human being, Joe Subject (or Joan Subject, as the case may be), as a prototypic host of the factors that, as we argue, operate within persons to determine their responses to others' evaluations of them. We analyze Joe's conceptual processing as observers having access to the process at a high level of awareness, but no assumption is made that persons are fully aware of the psychological processes and products that determine attraction responses to the evaluating other.

Imagine Joe is talking with a girl at lunch when suddenly she tells him he's a very interesting, articulate, and charming person. What is Joe to make of this statement? Is he to accept it at face value, or must he qualify it in some manner? Is the girl after something? Did she really mean it, or was it simply social convention? Let's see how Joe's reacting to this comment:

> "So, she thinks I'm all right. I've never seen her before and I'll probably never see her again and since I thought I was relatively pleasant and convivial during lunch, I bet she genuinely meant what she said and really feels that way about me. She had nothing to gain from saying it and it was more than the usual pleasantries one expects when eating across from a stranger, so her comment sure makes me feel good—it seems I can be naturally charming. You know I kinda like that girl and wouldn't mind seeing her again. I might even drop by here to eat again when I get the chance; maybe I'll run into her."

This hypothetical encounter illustrates that an immediate, unrestrained reaction to personal evaluations from others may be the exception, rather than the rule, due to all the screening and assessment the evaluation may undergo before it is accepted at face value. We are not contending that individuals consciously engage in this screening procedure, but rather we are suggesting that at some level and over varying time periods, the functional equivalent of this screening procedure occurs. It is, of course, an assumption on our part that personal evaluations are perceived as suspect until proven otherwise, rather than vice versa. We shall discover, however, that when *positive* personal evaluations are suspect (that is, their validity and authenticity are called into question), attraction is severely reduced.

We now follow Joe Subject through actual interpersonal encounters created in studies of attraction. In this manner, we determine what the data have to say about Joe's reaction in interpersonal situations; whether he accepts evaluations at face value, the weight he gives evaluation qualifiers—revealed by the screening process—and the nature of the interaction of the qualifier with the perceived valence, strength, validity, and authenticity of the evaluations.

A. Face-Value Reactions to Performance

In a study by Skolnick (1971), Joe Subject was placed in a situation with seven strangers in which the participants were supposed to form impressions of one another on the basis of limited information. Joe was told that he would take two performance tests and that *following* this, the people would be divided into two teams and compete on the same performance test for a $10 prize.

Joe completed the two performance tests and discovered that he had gotten either the highest score in the whole group (success) or the lowest (failure). In another case he was not told his score. Then, the group was split into two teams. To do this, Joe was asked to write a note to the person whose score was marked on his (Joe's) card and someone else would write a similar note to Joe. The note was to include Joe's feelings about the person's performance and whether or not Joe wanted the person on his team. Joe was reminded that the notes were to be used as a basis for forming an impression of the note sender. Joe then wrote his note and waited to receive a note. While Joe was waiting, the experimenter intercepted everyone's note and substituted one of two prearranged notes. One note said, "You are the person I most prefer to have on my team" (positive evaluation) and the other read, "You are the person I least prefer to have on my team" (negative evaluation). After receiving the note, Joe was asked to indicate his impression of the note writer.

The results showed that Joe believed the feedback he received about his performance. In addition, Joe's reaction to the note sender was a straightforward function of whether the note was positive or negative. The positive note writer received the highest rating and the negative note sender received the lowest. This result held even in the case where Joe failed and was told he was the most preferred *potential* teammate. In fact, when Joe failed, he reacted *more* favorably to the positive note sender than when he succeeded. The positive note apparently meant more to Joe when he failed (perhaps he had been fearful that no one would want him as a teammate) and this, in turn, favorably affected his rating of the note sender.

The question here is: Can we accept these face-value results at face value? When Joe failed, he might have been suspicious of the validity and genuineness of the feedback from the positive note sender. Why did Joe accept such a message at face value, especially given that later in the chapter we see that under very similar circumstances this same kind of feedback is suspected? First, note that Joe's failing performance had not been praised; he was merely selected as the note sender's most preferred teammate, which did not contradict the objective feedback, precluding invalidity. Praise would have reeked with insincerity and clearly been invalid. Second, with respect to authenticity, Joe may have reasoned that despite his failing performance, the other person thought he would either be a good "team man," or, perhaps would work hard to redress his previous failure. The above reasoning is plausible because Joe's failing performance had not been detrimental to the note sender in that Joe and the note sender were not teammates at the time of the failing performance. If, however, Joe had clearly caused the note sender's team to lose, then such reasoning on Joe's part would have been less plausible. In the less clear-cut cases it seems that when positive feedback is screened for authenticity, the process may be biased somewhat toward producing an "acceptance" verdict since such a verdict has obvious positive repercussions for the person, at least in a short-term sense.

Positive feedback poses a dilemma to the recipient. Because it can be used readily for many purposes besides conveying a veridical evaluation (for example, ingratiation), it is open to suspicion with regard to objective meaning. At the same time, however, the person should *want* to believe that positive feedback is true. Hence, the screening process carried out may be a joint function of these two opposing forces, with the former blunting and the latter sharpening the evaluative impact of positive feedback. Of course, the opposite dilemma is posed by negative feedback. Here there is less to suspect in terms of ulterior motives (for instance, negative duplicity is not a likely ingratiation tactic), but there is also a far greater desire to legitimize suspicions since defining negative evaluations as invalid and/or inauthentic has positive repercussions for the recipient.

The Skolnick (1971) experiment is not the only one that has obtained face-value reactions to evaluations of performance. In one part of a study by Shrauger and Jones (1968), Joe Subject had to make inferences about a person on the basis of minimal information under conditions where Joe was eventually to find out whether his inferences were correct or incorrect. *Before* he knew whether his answers were right or wrong (precluding invalidity), one of Joe's peers stated that he thought Joe was right on 14 of 16 answers—a positive evaluation. Another peer stated he thought 10 of Joe's 16 answers were wrong—a negative evaluation. These responses were transmitted to Joe by signals, not face to face.

Following this task, all persons in the experiment were asked to rate each other on 15 trait adjectives. Joe rated his positive evaluator significantly more favorably than his negative evaluator. In this case, Joe's screening process apparently reached a quick verdict that the evaluations were authentic. A probable reason for this is that the other person's ability to make inferences about other people was also being tested. In short, Joe was placed in a situation in which it was in the evaluator's self-interest to give an honest and accurate assessment of Joe's performance, and hence there was good reason to believe the evaluations (see Jones, 1966).

B. Face-Value Reactions to Evaluations of Personal Attributes

In an experiment by Aronson and Worchel (1966), Joe Subject was introduced to a confederate of the experimenter who had been instructed to act toward Joe in a particular manner. He and his partner in turn were asked to give their reasons for their answers to a seven-item attitude questionnaire. In the course of doing this, it was discovered that they either agreed or disagreed on five of the seven items. Joe and his partner then made a few written comments about the experiment and then made "decisions" about the other on the basis of the information provided by their discussion and the exchange of their written statements. Joe received either a positive or a negative evaluation of how interesting and informed Joe seemed to be. The evaluations included a line that stated that the evaluator and Joe had either agreed or disagreed about most things depending upon what had transpired during their conversation.

Following this feedback, Joe was told the decision task concerned how much Joe liked his partner and whether he would want to work with him. The results showed that Joe was strongly attracted (that is, liking and desire to work with combined) to the positive evaluator and found the negative evaluator quite unattractive. Moreover, the positive evaluator was liked about equally well whether he was similar or dissimilar, and the negative evaluator was not liked even if he was similar.

From the perspective of Joe's screening process, one particular aspect of this situation appears critical. In most attraction studies, an other is not required to supply reasons for his reactions. But in this case, the confederate was preprogrammed to give good reasons for his answers to the attitude items so that Joe would not think he was a "dummy." Under such conditions, Joe might have had the following thoughts:

> "Say, this guy really found me to be interesting/uninteresting. And since he seems to be the kind of person who is careful about his judgments and has good reasons for them, I'm sure he really means what he said and that there were some concrete things I did or said that interested/bored him."

Thus, the screening process yielded as "accept at face value" verdict, and Joe reacted accordingly.

Pepitone and Wilpinski (1960) conducted another study that found a face-value response to another's evaluations. Joe Subject was asked to reveal his position on some rather personal and, at the time, controversial topics—premarital sex and drinking among minors. Joe stated his views, and then two individuals either agreed or disagreed with him over the course of the discussion. During a break between the discussion and filling out some ratings, the disagreers were downright nasty to Joe. The two disagreers talked among themselves, pointedly excluding Joe from their conversation, and in some cases gave him "dirty" looks.

Not surprisingly, the results showed that Joe liked the nice, agreeing others significantly more than the rejecting, curt, disagreeing others. Several factors existed in this situation which may have induced Joe's evaluative screening process to accept the negative information at face value. First, negative feedback is more distinctive than positive feedback (Hamilton & Zanna, 1972), and, hence, may be intrinsically more credible and believable (Kanouse & Hanson, 1973). Dissimulation of face-to-face negative feedback is probably infrequent because its utility for the dissimulator is somewhat limited. Second, the coalition of the two others in the disagree condition provided "social consensus" for the negative judgment and lent social validity to the evaluation. Third, the feedback was preceded by a substantial discussion in which Joe saw evidence that the others had reasons to back up their opinions. Thus, it is no wonder that their behavior affected Joe strongly and that he disliked them. Further evidence of the perceived validity and potency of the two others' behavior was found in Joe's evaluation of himself. He thought less of himself and his opinions in the rejection, than in the no rejection, condition.

C. Face-Value Reactions to Evaluations of the Whole Person

We turn now to the classic study conducted by Backman and Secord (1959) demonstrating the "face value" finding that we like others who like us more than others who do not like us. Here, Joe again found himself part of a group of strangers, supposedly brought together for the purpose of discussing how to improve instruction in the freshman psychology course. To improve the output of discussion groups, it was said that personality factors were being taken into account. A personality test, taken earlier in the semester, was to be used for this purpose, and, in fact, the test results were to be a topic of discussion in the first meeting of Joe's group. During the course of analyzing the test results, Joe was told that an effort had been made to detect, on the basis of the personality test, who would like whom in his group. Joe was then given a card with three randomly selected names on it, which supposedly indicated those persons in the group (everyone wore name tags) who would probably like him. Joe was led to believe that due to the press of time, his probable liking preferences were unknown, so he believed that no one was expecting him (Joe) to like them. Following the above feedback, a 15-min session ensued about how to promote discussion in large classes. Then the group was informed that they might be broken down into two-person teams and, therefore, everyone was to indicate a first, second, and third choice as to his most desired team partner.

It was found that probable likers were chosen as the most desired partner significantly more often than would be expected on the basis of chance. These findings, however, occurred only at the conclusion of the first group session; in subsequent sessions, 3 and 6 weeks later, the preference for probable likers was far from significant. This, of course, was to be expected since the group members interacted over this period of time and hence the effects of "probable" liking began to fade as actual affective relationships were established.

A striking feature of this finding is that the dependent measure was not in a strict sense a measure of liking, but rather a measure of desire to have another person as a partner for task-oriented discussions. Thus, Joe may have preferred to have one of the probable likers as his partner, not necessarily because he liked the other person, but because he figured that discussion would go smoothly with someone who *liked him*. There is substantial data available to indicate that choice of a partner for any sort of task-oriented activity is frequently unrelated to how much the chosen person is liked; and in situations where task competence detracts from interpersonal pleasantness, the relationship may be negative (Goldberg & Mettee, 1968; Kiesler & Goldberg, 1968; Bales, 1956, 1958; Mettee *et al.*, 1971). It is also true, however, that choice of a partner is often highly related to liking, and in this particular situation, where the structure of the discussion sessions was informal enough to allow for a lot of nontask interaction, the partner preference measure *may* have been a good index of liking.

A second feature has to do with the materials this situation provided for Joe's screening process. The liking information was received from a source other than the liker, and the liker in Joe's eyes was unaware of this information. It is clear that information of this sort is above suspicion with respect to the "liker's" sincerity, and its validity depends upon the faith Joe has in personality tests.

A study by Jones and Panitch (1971) is conceptually similar in some respects to the Backman and Secord (1959) study. A similar pattern of results was obtained. Joe was placed in a situation with another person whose task was to form an impression of Joe by observing him during an interview. The other person indicated his impression of Joe on a rating form, and then Joe was told that, although the other had been led to believe Joe would not see the ratings, it was necessary for Joe to look at them and make comments on their accuracy. Included among the rating scales were items meant to manipulate Joe's perception of how much the other liked him. In the liking condition, the other marked an 8 or 9 on a nine-point likableness scale and attached a written comment stating "I think he's really the kind of person I get along with." In the dislike condition, the likableness scale was marked at 2 or 3, with an accompanying statement which read, "To be honest he's just not the kind of person I get along with."

After Joe looked over these ratings, he was asked to give his impressions of his partner on a number of scales including how likable he thought his partner was. The results showed that Joe rated the partner who liked him much more likable than the partner who disliked him.

The most important point here with respect to feedback validity and authenticity is that Joe believed the evaluator was under the impression that his ratings of Joe were confidential. This, of course, accords his evaluations the stamp of sincerity and authenticity. Moreover, this supposed confidentiality in conjunction with the fact that the evaluator's task was to form accurate impressions increases the perceived validity of the evaluations. Given that these two factors favor a face-value verdict, it is not surprising that Joe fully accepted the feedback and that he reacted as he did.

Finally, it is important to consider the correspondence between the Backman and Secord study and this study in terms of the manner in which the feedback was delivered to Joe. In both cases, the evaluator was not party to informing Joe of his impressions of Joe; instead, an outsider did the informing without the evaluator's knowledge. This, in effect, partially precludes suspicions concerning evaluator intentions and motives, thereby strengthening the authenticity and validity of the feedback's overt content. A primary determinant of whether a person will accept a global evaluation of himself at face value may be the extent to which the evaluator does not directly inform the person of his evaluation (see also Dittes & Kelley, 1956).

D. Conclusions Regarding Face-Value Reactions

The face-value studies seem to have at least one major factor in common: concrete events occur which actively counter possible suspicions regarding the evaluations' "real" meaning. In the studies reported, the "evaluator" spends a considerable amount of time interacting with the subject, and in each case these interactions are ones in which the other is programmed to project the image of a reasonable, sensible individual. In fact, there were cases in which the other was required to demonstrate that his ideas and opinions were well thought out (see Aronson & Worchel, 1966). In other cases, the evaluator was unaware that his evaluations of the subject were being communicated to the subject.

Thus, all the face-value studies contained tangible events which in all likelihood actively alleviated suspicion. This suggests that in order for evaluations to survive the screening process and be accepted at face value, it is necessary to actively establish that the evaluations are above suspicion; just avoiding actual suspicion-arousing events may not be sufficient. But since we have not yet provided evidence that face-value results will *not* be obtained if an evaluation is only passively impeccable, any conclusions regarding this suggestion must, of course, be postponed until we have examined studies that fail to obtain face-value results.

III. The Evaluation Incongruency Pseudoqualification

A vast body of literature has been devoted to the theoretical and empirical pursuit of social psychology's "love affair" with the consistency principle. This rather simple notion states that once individuals develop a particular view of their world, their fellows, and themselves, they desire subsequent information to match that view. Under the rubric of evaluation congruency, this notion has been applied to interpersonal attraction phenomena, generating the "nonobvious" hypothesis that evaluations from others that are more positive than the person's self-evaluation will be less enthusiastically received than less positive, or even negative, evaluations that are more congruent with the self-evaluation. In short, the consistency notion represents a potential qualification with respect to the effects personal evaluations have upon attraction.

Empirically (see Berscheid & Walster, 1969; Jones, 1973), the self-evaluation incongruency qualification turns out to be pseudo since congruent low praise generally is not preferred to incongruent high praise.[2] The reason, we would contend, is that the notion is theoretically flawed. At the core, the basic assumption is that current evaluations from others should be congruent with the person's self-evaluation derived from past evaluations from others. However, this theoretical notion involves an extension of the more basic consistency premise that a person seeks to act and behave in a manner that is congruent with his self-evaluation. What the person does himself may indeed have to be congruent with his self-evaluation to be deemed desirable and appropriate, but there is no compelling reason why the reactions of others should conform to these same strictures. Thus, the flaw rests in assuming that a premise that applies to selfproduced feedback also applies to evaluative feedback originating from external sources. If another sincere-

---

[2]We will be concerned here only with positive incongruency as a possible qualifier (that is, evaluations that are incongruent by virtue of surpassing the self-evaluation).

ly wants to like us, then he can authentically feel that way about us no matter how many others dislike us or how deeply we dislike ourselves.

Validity refers to the evaluation's accuracy. There is no compelling reason why an evaluation would be judged invalid just because it is incongruent with the recipient's self-evaluation. Another can genuinely think well of the person even though the person hates himself, and this evaluation is in a sense valid by definition (that is, it is a fact, an element of external reality). If there is no objective standard present, or the objective quality of a performance or attribute is ambiguous, and/or social consensus is mixed or absent with respect to that particular performance or attribute, then the validity of the other's evaluation cannot be dispelled even if it does not agree with the person's own evaluation. Evaluation validity should be suspect only when situationally salient external standards of reality are violated. In sum, incongruency with a person's existing self-evaluation does not in itself encroach upon the perceived validity of another's evaluation; it is incongruence with situationally operative reality standards that makes evaluation validity suspect. Moreover, as we document in the following section, the proclaimed evidence supporting the congruency notion proves to be riddled with artifacts in which variables besides incongruency with self-evaluation call the validity of another's evaluations into question, and/or factors are present that inspire doubts about the evaluation's authenticity.

A. Evaluations of Performance

A study invariably referenced as supporting the evaluation incongruency notion is that conducted by Deutsch and Solomon (1959). In Section II we discussed the Skolnick (1971) study, which attempted, but failed, to replicate the Deutsch and Solomon (1959) incongruency results. Accounting for the different results of these two studies illustrates our point that evaluation incongruency is a pseudoqualifier.

Deutsch and Solomon placed Joe on a team with three other persons and told them to compete for a prize with another team of four on a problem-solving task. Each member's score counted toward the team total, which determined the winner. Joe and his teammates performed the task, and then Joe received objective evidence that he had scored the highest or lowest of anyone on either team. Joe then received a note from one of his teammates, who expressed an opinion of Joe's performance and indicated whether or not the note writer wanted Joe on the team again if there was to be another contest. Evaluation incongruency existed in the case where Joe scored high and received a negative evaluation and in the case where Joe scored low and received a positive evaluation. In the former case, it is hardly surprising to find that negative incongruency elicited greater dislike for the evaluator than a congruent positive evaluation. It was also the case, however, that Joe did not like an incongruent positive evaluator as much as a congruent negative evaluator. This finding calls for closer inspection since it appears to support the evaluation incongruency qualifier.

One form of the positive evaluation stated, "I see that you have the lowest score for the team. I really think you did a fine job considering your situation. You were a valuable member of the team and I would very much like to have you on my team again." Joe probably had serious doubts about this evaluator's sincerity. If Joe did not regard this as blatant sugar-coated dissimulation, then he undoubtedly perceived the evaluator to be extremely patronizing. In either case, it is little wonder that Joe disliked this evaluator more than one who told him that, "I see you got the lowest score for the team and I think you did a poor job; considering the circumstances, I am very much opposed to having you on my team." Because there were many good reasons to dislike the positively discrepant evaluator, the self-evaluation incongruency taken by itself may have been only an incidental factor.

Support for this possibility can be found in the Skolnick study. Skolnick failed to replicate Deutsch and Solomon, both in terms of results and procedures. In the Deutsch and Solomon (1959) study, Joe had already performed and contributed a very low score to the team effort. Thus, the positive evaluation received by Joe was from a member of a team whose score had just been jeopardized by Joe's poor performance. Hence, for the teammate to say he was pleased with Joe's performance was patently insincere and patronizing. In the Skolnick (1971) study, however, the teams were not as yet formed. Thus, the preference statement came from a would-be teammate who had not been directly affected by Joe's prior low score. This different circumstance may have caused Joe to perceive the statement, "You are the person I most prefer to have on my team," very differently from in the Deutsch and Solomon study. The other's desire to have Joe on his team could reasonably be seen as authentic, with Joe perhaps thinking that the team task would demand cooperativeness and that the evaluator believed Joe would contribute in this area. Such reasoning on Joe's part was, of course, untenable in the Deutsch and Solomon study since Joe had already proven to be a disaster as a teammate. In short, the ambiguity of the cryptic positive evaluation used by Skolnick and the fact that the evaluation pertained to the subject's future usefulness perhaps made the preference statement appear authentic.

Further support for our argument that self-evaluation incongruency per se is not repellent is found in a study by Howard and Berkowitz (1958). Joe Subject performed a novel task on which he had no experience and no conception of what constituted "good" performance. Joe was observed and evaluated by student judges. In the condition most pertinent to our discussion, Joe was evaluated by four judges, with three of them giving him a moderately positive evaluation (60% ranking) and one according him a highly favorable evaluation (85% ranking). Joe's self-evaluation was determined almost exclusively by the moderate evaluations so that the highly favorable evaluation was incongruent with his self-evaluation and with the moderately favorable social consensus. When asked to express his degree of preference for having each of the judges as a partner on a similar task, Joe showed a greater preference for the moderately positive reality defining majority than for the highly positive evaluator. However, this is clearly a case in which the validity of a highly favorable evaluation may be suspect because it conflicts with *current* social consensus regarding the quality of the performance; incongruency with the self-evaluation was perhaps incidental.

A recent study by Dutton (1972) apparently supports the evaluation incongruency notion, but the subjects may have doubted the validity of the positive incongruent evaluation. The procedure in this study was similar to that used by Skolnick (1971). The feedback validity, however, was probably much more suspect in the Dutton (1972) study. Whereas objective and relative performance feedback occurred once in the Skolnick Study, it occurred repeatedly in the Dutton study. Hence situationally present reality standards were much more firmly established in the Dutton study, and, therefore, suspicions about the validity of incongruent positive feedback should have been more pronounced. That is, high preference for a poor performer as a future team member may not unduly raise validity suspicions when there is only one occurrence of the poor performance (see the Skolnick study). But, when an evaluator has repeatedly observed the person perform poorly (see the Dutton study), then the evaluator's preference statement might indeed raise strong suspicions about feedback validity and/or authenticity.

This reasoning is further supported by the cases in the Dutton study where a positive incongruent evaluator was liked more than a negative congruent evaluator. This result was found in two conditions. In the condition were liking for the positive incongruent evaluator was the strongest, suspicions about the validity of the evaluator's preference statement should have been low since Joe Subject performed poorly only half the time—the other half he was average or above average relative to the rest of his group. Here it is fairly reasonable for Joe to be preferred since the evaluator could realistically be seen as believing that Joe's future performance would be above average. In the other condition, validity suspicions should have been high, but the need for positive feedback was extremely strong and the positive incongruent evaluator was liked only moderately more than the negative congruent evaluator. Here validity suspicions were at least partially overcome by a very intense need (the highest of any condition—the subject was repeatedly inferior on an important ability) to believe the favorable feedback. Consistent with our earlier argument with respect to authenticity, a very strong need to believe may cause subjects to distort or disregard evidence of invalidity and accept positive incongruent feedback in spite of the objective evidence (see Jones, 1964, pp. 49–58). In sum, Dutton's procedures probably raised validity suspicions to a high level and so, of course, the negative congruent evaluator was liked more than the positive incongruent evaluator. However, in a case where validity suspicions were relatively low, positive incongruency evoked much greater liking than negative congruency.

B. Evaluations of Characteristics and Attributes

Harvey and Clapp (1965; an updated Harvey, 1962) and Jacobs, Berscheid, and Walster (1971) have provided evidence supporting our argument that self-evaluation incongruency is a pseudoqualifier. Their studies found that positive incongruent evaluators are perceived to be relatively attractive under conditions where evaluation validity and authenticity are assured.

In the Harvey and Clapp study, Joe Subject received an evaluation from a stranger that showed a small or a large positive discrepancy from Joe's stated self-evaluation (that is, how he expected to be rated). The authenticity of the evaluation was established by leading Joe (who was also giving his impressions of group members) to believe that evaluations of several personal characteristics, such as friendliness and maturity, would not be seen by the persons being evaluated. Hence, when Joe later received a stranger's evaluation of him, Joe believed that that evaluation was one the evaluator had thought would remain confidential. Validity was in a sense intrinsic because the stranger's evaluation (a segment of reality) did not conflict with external points of reference present in the situation, either social or objective, as there were none.

Under these circumstances, we would predict that Joe would react favorably to the positive discrepancies from his expectations. This was in fact the case. More to the point, an evaluator whose positive evaluations were very incongruent with Joe's expectancies was liked just as much as an evaluator whose evaluations came very close to matching Joe's expectancies. Hence, relatively greater positive incongruency did *not* produce relatively less liking. Unfortunately, there was no control group, in which evaluations exactly matched Joe's expectancies.

Data from the study by Jacobs and co-workers (1971) clearly demonstrate that authentic, valid feedback that is highly incongruent in the positive direction will nonetheless elicit a very favorable attraction response. Joe Subject was placed in a situation where his dating skill was evaluated by a female his own age. This evaluation was based on a tape-recorded phone conversation in which Joe was required to deal with a difficult social situation such as to pretend to break a date or to persuade a woman to go out with him. The female evaluator listened to this recording and then taped her evaluation of Joe's dating skills.

Prior to hearing the woman's evaluation, Joe received feedback designed either to lower or to raise his self-evaluation. This feedback was supposedly based on the results of several personality tests Joe had taken earlier and provided a global manipulation of his self-esteem. Just prior to hearing the woman's assessment, Joe's self-evaluation was significantly lower in the reduced than in the raised self-esteem condition.

Considering only the lowered self-esteem situation, it was found that Joe was much more attracted to the female evaluator if she evaluated his dating skills positively (that is, incongruently) than if she evaluated them negatively. Moreover, attraction for an ambiguously or moderately positive evaluator fell midway between the negative and positive evaluator.

Examining the female confederate's evaluations and the circumstances under which they occurred indicates that there was little reason to doubt their authenticity or validity. The evaluator was said to be from a different college from Joe's, would likely never meet Joe, was anonymous, and so seemed to have nothing to gain by faking positive feedback. Moreover, the task was to render competent assessments of dating skills. In terms of validity, what possibly could be a more valid index of male dating skill than a same-age female's opinion of that skill? The female evaluator's response to Joe was perhaps not merely in accord with "reality," but rather defined reality with respect to Joe's dating skill.

C. Evaluations of the Whole Person

A study by Dittes (1959) exemplifies the failure of positive evaluation incongruency to generate negative feelings toward the evaluator. The beauty of this study for our purposes is the clear-cut manner in which both evaluation authenticity and validity were established. In a group discussion situation, four to five others rated the desirability of having Joe and each other as members of the group. Group members were led to believe that the ratings would be seen only by the experimenter. Then, during an intermission session, it was "spontaneously" arranged for Joe to see, in private, how group members had rated him. Here Joe received ratings that had, from his viewpoint, been made under confidential conditions, so that there was good reason to believe their authenticity. Moreover, the validity of these ratings was secured by two factors: essentially equivalent ratings were obtained on three occasions during a 1-hour group discussion, and all group members tended to rate Joe's desirability as a group member either well above average or well below average. The group consensus constituted a social standard of reality with which, of course, each member's evaluation agreed.

The greatest attraction for the group was evidenced when Joe's chronic self-esteem, as measured at the experiment's beginning, was low and he received well above-average acceptance ratings. The least attraction was shown when Joe had low self-esteem and received well *below*-average acceptance ratings. Thus, positive incongruency produced the highest attraction and negative congruency the lowest; a striking disconfirmation of the evaluation incongruence qualifier. Moreover, positive incongruency generated slightly more attraction for the group than did positive congruency.

Research by Walster (1965), in which Joan Subject was globally evaluated, reinforces the conclusions of the Dittes (1959) study. The procedures were similar to those in the study by Jacobs and co-workers, except that the subjects were female, the evaluator was a male, and the "evaluation" was not an explicit one, but instead was rather general and implicitly positive. The male confederate arranged a date with the subject. The authenticity of the "evaluation" was never in doubt as the date request occurred before and independent of the actual experiment itself. Thus, there was every reason for the subject to believe that the date request was genuine; indeed, almost all subjects accepted the date. The request is in itself a "reality," and therefore a valid indicator of part of reality. The male's implicit positive evaluation (that is, "you are an attractive female") is in perfect accord with the reality of the evaluator's behavior. Moreover, there is no evidence present to dispute the evaluator's actions (that is, the self-esteem manipulation did not mention datability).

Results showed that subjects' self-evaluations were successfully manipulated by false personality reports. When asked to indicate how much they liked the positive male confederate, low self-esteem subjects showed significantly higher liking than high self-esteem subjects. Again, the incongruency qualifier is shown to be false.

There are two additional studies that apparently obtained positive incongruency effects, but both seem undermined by artifacts. In a study by Jones and Pines (1968), the nature of the attraction measure casts a shadow on an apparent incongruency effect. In a situation where Joe Subject's concretely established low-task ability was to be made publicly manifest, he began to evaluate the *performance* of a negative evaluator more favorably than the performance of a positive evaluator. The problem here is that the supposed "attraction" response consisted of telling the evaluator that his (the evaluator's) own task performance was correct and hence it was clearly a response that may have been of instrumental value to Joe. With the revelation of Joe's poor talent imminent, it would be especially important to Joe to gain new sympathy and support and hence to win over a current source of nonsupport—the negative evaluator—regardless of how much he liked or disliked him.

A study by Jones and Schneider (1968) directly supports our contention that Joe's positive evaluation of the negative evaluator was more an instrumental response than a veridical indicant of liking. Joe was first induced to adopt a low ability self-appraisal and then, just as in the prior study, he performed, was evaluated, and was asked to assess the correctness of his evaluator's evaluating performance. However, in this study, Joe was also directly asked how much he liked his evaluator as a person. The results showed that with a certain or uncertain low self-appraisal, Joe, who had two evaluators, one negative and the other positive, liked his positive incongruent evaluator more than his negative congruent evaluator. However, when Joe was certain of his low self-appraisal, he assessed his negative evaluator's performance more favorably than he assessed his positive evaluator's performance, the reverse of his liking ratings. This reversal demonstrates the subjects' performance-assessment reactions may not have any connection with their liking reactions.[3]

Under certainty conditions it was made very clear by the self-appraisal manipulation that Joe was no good at the task. Hence, Joe's more favorable reaction to his negative evaluator's *performance* was probably a case of Joe responding in accord with reality constraints. But just because Joe had to admit that the negative evaluator was probably more competent at the task than the positive evaluator, it did not

---

[3]Investigators sometimes do not distinguish between these attraction measures (Dutton, 1972) and mistakenly consider reactions to evaluator performance as indicative of liking, even though opposite results are found with a direct liking measure (see Jones & Schneider, 1968).

mean that he also liked the former more. In fact, when certain of his low self-appraisal, Joe liked the positive, less competent, evaluator significantly more than the negative, more competent, evaluator. The positive evaluator's performance judgments were invalid, but they also revealed him to be a "nice guy." The latter apparently dictated Joe's liking response.

These results strongly suggest that studies in which so-called attraction responses involve an assessment of another's competence probably do not provide us with an accurate portrayal of the evaluated person's personal liking for the evaluating other (see Mettee *et al.*, 1971; Kiesler & Goldberg, 1968; Bales, 1958). Hence, paradigms that use an assessment of the other's performance as an index of attraction are doomed to provide us with less than clear data with respect to liking for evaluating others.

A study by Dutton and Arrowood (1971) also apparently supports the evaluation incongruence notion. But in the only condition in which it is even remotely possible that the evaluations were perceived as valid, an incongruent positive evaluator was liked more than a congruent negative evaluator. Joe Subject was required to argue for a position with which he either agreed or disagreed, and then an evaluator indicated that he either agreed or disagreed with the position argued and whether Joe had made a good or bad argument. The crucial point here is that in the portion of the study that actually dealt with evaluation congruence, incongruent evaluations always violated a situationally established reality standard and thus, by our definition, were invalid. This violation of reality occurred because of a peculiar methodological feature of the study. When the objective assessment said Joe did poorly, the incongruent positive evaluator gave a positive evaluation of the *same* performance. This evaluation, directly opposite to the objective feedback was undoubtedly perceived as invalid and incorrect. In addition, in this study incongruent sets of feedback were mutually exclusive since both referred to the same performance. One set had to be right, and the other wrong, with the objective set taking precedence.

There was one case in which an incongruent positive evaluator was liked more, even though his evaluation was objectively invalid. However, this occurred in a condition where independent evidence may have established the other as being a careful, discriminating evaluator. This, in turn, may have allowed Joe to partially disregard the feedback's objective invalidity.

We have presented evidence indicating that if external reality standards are not violated and personal sincerity is established that incongruent positive evaluations elicit very favorable attraction responses. If external reality standards are situationally salient and are violated by positive incongruency, however, then evaluation validity and the affective impact of the evaluation are attenuated. Furthermore, whenever incongruent positive evaluations appear insincere, the evaluation's affective impact is reduced. The depleted liking produced by such qualifications will be consistent with, but not generated by, evaluation incongruency per se. Such results actually stem from the presence of factors besides positive incongruency, which undermine evaluation validity and authenticity. In the absence of these factors, positive incongruency in itself apparently does not undermine validity and authenticity and, therefore, does not reduce the evaluation's affective potency.[4]

IV. The Internal States Qualifier

In this section, we examine the effects of individual differences in internal states on reactions to evaluative feedback. Internal states refer to dimensions along which individuals characteristically differ from each other (chronic differences), as well as dimensions along which the same individuals vary over time (acute differences).

The evaluation incongruence studies we have just examined can all be subsumed under the internal state qualifier. The internal state was the subject's self-evaluation; however, the prime focus was not upon the internal state itself, but upon the perceived *congruence* between the self-evaluation, regardless of level, and subsequent evaluations received from others. These same studies, however, can be examined in terms of the degree to which the individual's self-evaluation needs enhancement and the extent to which others' evaluations satisfy or frustrate this need. Here the focus *is* on the recipient's internal state or condition, and the question of interest is the influence the subject's *degree of need* has upon his reactions to personal evaluations.

A. Studies Concerned with Internal States

In the study by Dittes (1959), individuals with chronically low self-esteem (LSE) were more affected by a group's acceptance—rejection of them than were individuals with chronically high self-esteem (HSE). The straightforward notion here is that individuals with LSE can ill afford to be rejected and should be exceedingly pleased with acceptance. Conversely, individuals with HSE should find rejection more tolerable since they possess such a strong reserve of positive feedback. Dittes' results, in general, confirmed the degree of need notion, especially in the case of rejection, where LSE subjects disliked the rejecting group significantly more than did HSE subjects. Acceptance had only a directionally greater impact, with LSE's liking the accepting group only slightly more than HSE subjects.

---

[4]It should be noted that Jones (1973) independently has attempted to distinguish between conditions in which positive incongruency will and will not be preferred to negative congruency. He argued that recipients of feedback prefer positive incongruency, whereas observers prefer negative congruency. Although agreeing with the latter point pertaining to observers, the evidence cited above shows that recipients do not always manifest a preference for positive incongruency. Factors external to incongruency undermine evaluation validity and authenticity, and sometimes prompt rejection of positive incongruent feedback. In the absence of such extrinsic factors, positive incongruency will be preferred and accepted by recipients, just as Jones (1973) has contended.

Similarly, Walster and her colleagues have consistently found that differences in self-esteem either make no difference in subjects' subsequent attraction to an evaluator, or that the greater the subjects' need for self-enhancement (that is, LSE subjects), the greater the liking for positive evaluators and disliking for negative evaluators. Walster (1965), for example, induced acute differences in self-esteem and found that LSE females liked a previously affectionate male confederate more than did HSE females. Jacobs *et al.* (1971) also found that LSE subjects reacted more strongly to positive feedback than did HSE subjects, but only if the feedback was conclusive and very clearly positive. If the feedback was positive but less than explicit, then HSE subjects reacted more favorably, indicating that LSE subjects are more hesitant to assume that implicit, tentative positive feedback really says what it appears to say.

The latter finding also serves to suggest an answer to a persistent problem vis-à-vis the internal state qualifier: differential internal states sometimes do and sometimes do not produce differential attraction responses to personal evaluations. One possible reason for this inconsistency with respect to self-esteem differences is that the state of the subject's self-evaluation may have two opposing effects, which on occasion offset each other. The LSE subject needs positive feedback more, but finds it harder to believe. When the feedback's believability is firmly established, the LSE subject will respond more vigorously than the HSE subject; when positive feedback is vague and its believability open to question, the LSE subject will respond less vigorously. Furthermore, in the grayer areas of positive feedback believability, the response of LSE subjects may be mixed, a joint product of greater need and greater skepticism, so that on the whole LSE and HSE subjects respond the same.

Another "offsetting" explanation of the capricious effects of differential self-esteem upon reactions to personal evaluations pertains to the evaluation incongruence pseudoqualifier. The evaluation incongruence and degree of need for self-enhancement notions stand in direct opposition to each other. Therefore, these two conflicting variables may occasionally counteract each other, even though in most instances, self-enhancement needs would probably gain significant prominence. Hence, because of his greater need for positive feedback, a low self-esteem subject would be expected in most cases to like a positive evaluator more than would a high self-esteem subject. But if a valid, authentic evaluation were overwhelmingly positive, such extreme evaluation incongruence might be of some concern to the LSE subject (see Mettee, 1968, pp. 39—45), reducing the liking response dictated by his need for self-enhancement sufficiently to make him no more affectionate toward the positive evaluator than the HSE subject. With respect to negative evaluations, HSE subjects may at times respond as strongly as LSE subjects. Although HSE subjects can afford it more, they are not as used to receiving valid negative feedback and hence may be quite susceptible to it.

Another study that bears examination is that by Jones and Panitch (1967). They found that the greater the strength of an individual's low ability self-appraisal, the greater the intensity of his reactions, both behaviorally and attitudinally, to negative feedback. Here again, the greater the self-enhancement need, the more pronounced the reaction (see also Jones & Pines, 1968).

A final study that supports the degree of need rationale was conducted by Jones (1966). Half the subjects were induced to have a high, and half a low, appraisal of their ability. Joe's task performance was either evaluated positively or negatively by three others, and Joe in turn evaluated their task performance. The three others varied in the extent to which prior evidence showed they were good, average, or poor at the experimental task and hence, by inference, were differentially qualified to judge Joe's performance.

The results supported the degree of need rationale in that when Joe's self-appraisal was low, he responded much more favorably to the positive, than to the negative, evaluator; when Joe's self-appraisal was high, he also favored the positive evaluator, but to a lesser degree. Reactions to the poor or relatively incompetent evaluator are of special interest. With a low self-appraisal, Joe didn't bother to differentiate his evaluators in terms of competence. On the other hand, when possessed of a high self-appraisal, Joe discriminated among his positive evaluators, expressing disfavor toward the incompetent positive evaluator. These results suggest that given a low self-appraisal, Joe was so hungry for positive feedback and so susceptible to negative feedback that source differences were of small concern, and information relevant to the *significance* of the evaluation was apparently ignored.[5] In the case of high self-appraisal, however, Joe could afford to be selective, thus moderating his response to relatively insignificant positive and negative feedback from incompetent evaluators.

Significance should not be confused, however, with the ambiguous feedback used in the study by Jacobs *et al.* Here, LSE subjects were less likely than HSE subjects to assume that ambiguous positive feedback could be taken as definite and conclusive; in the Jones study, however, LSE subjects were less likely to quibble over the significance of definite, authentic, valid positive feedback.[6] This might appear inconsistent, since on one occasion, LSE's are more skeptical than HSE's of positive feedback and on another, they are more prone to embrace it. The occasions, however, are clearly different. In one instance, the feedback may not actually be positive, while in the other instance, the feedback is most certainly positive, but may not mean a great deal. This makes for a consistent pattern as it suggests that LSE subjects are in strong need of *positive* feedback and will take almost anything definitely *positive*, but, since negative feedback is strongly aversive, feedback whose valence is not clearly established will be shunned (see Crowne & Marlowe, 1964; Mettee, Taylor, & Fisher, 1971).

We can now address several other interesting variations in Joe Subject's internal

---

[5]Evaluation significance is thought to be a separate factor from evaluation quality (validity and authenticity) since given evaluations could be established as equally valid and authentic and yet mean more or less to the recipient depending upon his need and the source of the evaluation (see Section V).

[6]Feedback in the Jones (1966) study did not violate external standards pertaining to the performance assessed by the evaluator. Hence, validity suspicions were probably modest.

condition at the time he receives a personal evaluation. Lott, Bright, Weinstein, and Lott (1970) found that college students who measured high in chronic need for academic recognition liked an intelligence tester more when they did well on the test than when they did poorly. On the other hand, students low in need for academic recognition showed the same liking for the tester regardless of test performance. Lott *et al.* have argued that the greater liking shown the tester in the "did well" condition was due to the tester's association per se with the reduction of high drive. That is, task performance in and of itself is regarded as the direct reducer of the *academic recognition* drive and, therefore, the primary source of positive affect; the person present is liked because he is associated with a rewarding state of affairs. However, since the drive in question is academic *recognition* and not academic achievement or competence, and since the tester possessed the subject's test scores and probably knew about (that is, recognized) the subject's performance, we submit that the stimulus person was the direct source of drive reduction and positive affect. In short, satisfaction of recognition needs, by definition, requires a knowing social public, and the tester was such a public in this situation.

Need for social approval (Crowne & Marlowe, 1964) also seems to be related to an individual's liking for others who evaluate him. Mettee (1969, 1973) has proposed that chronic and acute need for social approval and the self-approval derived from it may be primary mediators of an individual's affective reactions to others who evaluate him. It may be that in many of the studies we have examined, the various independent variables have exerted some of their impact on liking via influencing the recipient's level of need approval.

A very recent study is one of the few that has directly examined the relationship between need approval and affective reactions to evaluative feedback. In this study (Holstein, Goldstein, & Bem, 1971) the personal evaluations were nonverbal expressions (Rosenfeld, 1966) and, hence, were implicit, rather than explicit. Subjects, whose chronic need for approval had been measured previously, were faced with an interviewer who in all cases said the same thing. In one situation, however, verbal statements were accompanied by nonverbal expressions of approval and acceptance (smiles, eye contact, nods, etc.), while in another situation, eye contact was avoided, and there was no smiling. It was found that subjects liked the nonverbally accepting interviewer more than the nonverbally neutral interviewer, even though analyses of vocal cues indicated that in both cases the interviewer's verbal responses were identical. When subjects were high, as compared to low, in need approval, there was a more pronounced difference in their liking response to a positive versus neutral nonverbal evaluator. This greater responsiveness to nonverbal evaluative feedback on the part of high need for approval subjects was significant only for females, and even here the effect was relatively weak.

Mettee and Fisher (1969) found that males high as compared to low in chronic approval react differently to evaluators. Joe Subject observed an interviewer, who was soon to interview him, behave positively or negatively toward an interviewee of the same sex and age as Joe. Following this observation and prior to actually being interviewed, Joe rated the likability and pleasantness of the interviewer. High need approval subjects rated the positive interviewer higher and the negative interviewer lower than did low need approval subjects.

The study we have just cited, and a study by Milburn, Bell and Koeske(1970), indicate that chronic high need approval males and females react more sensitively than low need approvals to evaluative feedback, whether positive or negative, and do not distort all feedback in a positive direction. This was not the case for high need approval males in the study by Holstein *et al.* (1971); these subjects were sensitive to positive feedback, but downplayed "neutral" feedback. A possible explanation of the different results lies in the functional utility of the feedback. In the study by Milburn, Bell, and Koeske (1970), feedback indicated whether the subject was correct or incorrect and hence provided knowledge important for adjusting subsequent performance. Similarly, in the Mettee and Fisher (1969) study, the interviewer's behavior functioned to prepare the subject for his upcoming interview. Hence, in cases where evaluative feedback was of potential instrumental value in maximizing positive input in the future, female and male high need approvals showed greater sensitivity than low need approvals to evaluative feedback, irrespective of valence. In contrast, the Holstein *et al.* (1971) situation was one in which evaluative feedback was the end point of the experience. Positive implications under such circumstances can be enhanced via muting negative, and highlighting positive, input without risking future negative repercussions. In ongoing feedback situations, however, muting and distorting negative feedback have potentially harmful repercussions.

B. Significance of Internal States Studies

A problem plaguing the *chronic* internal state qualifier is that measured dispositional differences sometimes make recipients respond to evaluative feedback in one direction (Milburn *et al.*, 1970), sometimes in the opposite direction (Holstein *et al.*, 1971) and sometimes show no relationship at all to the response (Lott *et al.*, 1970). Is it possible that Mischel (1968) is correct in asserting that situational factors have the major impact on behavior and that personality is an elusive figment of the observer's imagination? Or is the answer somewhat less radically defrocking of individual differences? We present two arguments in support of the latter position. The first is an extension of the above rationale regarding the instrumental usefulness of feedback and may apply specifically only to the chronic need approval variable. It may be unclear in many situations whether evaluative feedback has immediate future utility or is a closed chapter in the person's battle with the forces of social approval. Given such ambiguity, some high need approval subjects may sharpen and some may blunt their perception of, and consequent response to, negative feedback. This may result in high and low need approval groups of subjects responding similarly to negative feedback. The ambiguity of the future usefulness notion applies only to negative feedback. Inconsistent results have occurred *only with* respect to such feedback. High need approval subjects have reliably responded with greater enthusiasm than low need approvals to positive feedback.

A second consideration concerns the basic laboratory procedure by which personality and social psychologists obtain their experimental data. An attempt is made to isolate variables and to induce them strongly at high levels of intensity in order to test their effects. Under these controlled circumstances, the relative strength of variables tested in conjunction with internal state differences may not be representative of their strength and intensity in real-life situations. Therefore, it is possible that variables manipulated to *overcome* individual differences often swamp personality differences of considerable magnitude. A devastating negative assessment by a respected evaluator, for example, may have such a powerful effect that chronic need for approval would not affect the response.[7] This does *not* suggest that internal states are meaningless because in the complex stimulus arena of uncontrolled, everyday life, external stimuli may generally be limited to moderate intensity levels—a situation in which internal states could be influential. Personality variables correlate distressingly low with behavior occurring under real-life circumstances (Mischel, 1968). But, here, situational stimuli, although moderate, are also profuse. In the presence of multiple stimuli, the influence of any given personality variable upon responses may become diffused and weakened. The ideal compromise is one in which the stimulus factor in question is isolated at a moderate-intensity level so that the response is neither underdetermined nor overdetermined by that factor. This allows one to assess the "veridical" or probabilistic influence of internal state differences upon reactions to a specific factor.

Leaving this issue aside, we can consider two internal state studies that are anomalies in terms of the personal evaluation–attraction framework. In one, the dependent variable is not attraction, and in the other, the internal state difference is not induced until after receipt of a personal evaluation (but, of course, before measurement of reactions to the evaluator). In the latter study, Landy and Mettee (1969) found that when Joe Subject was insulted and berated by an experimenter, liking ratings were significantly higher (actually, less low) when Joe first had the opportunity to look at humorous cartoons, and laugh, and experience a humorous interlude than when the ratings occurred after a neutral interlude, or immediately after the insulting episode. Here the internal state difference ultimately altered Joe's *reaction* to the negative evaluative event, but could not have influenced his initial *perception* of the event, as the internal state difference was not induced until after the event. This suggests that internal states can qualify reactions to equivalently perceived events.

Shaban and Jecker (1968) manipulated self-esteem, and measured preference for several persons as future evaluators. Joe Subject anticipated being placed in an evaluative situation prior to which he was allowed to express his rank-order

---

[7] It might well be that recovery time from such a severe blow to the ego would be faster for the low need approval person. But no one to our knowledge has studied recovery from the effects of evaluative feedback over time as a function of personality differences, a circumstance which has significant real-life analogs and one in which personality variables might exert a profound influence.

preference for four persons who would evaluate his attractiveness and interaction skills. The evaluators differed in terms of the frequency with which they had previously rendered positive evaluations. Joe Subject, when his esteem was high, evidenced a strong preference for a moderately frequent positive evaluator and a low preference for very frequent and very infrequent positive evaluators. On the other hand, when self-esteem was low, Joe showed a very strong preference for the rare positive evaluator who rarely gave positive evaluations, and a low preference for the other three evaluators. These findings appear to indicate that when self-esteem is high, persons prefer evaluators whose evaluations have real meaning attached to them and desire to avoid evaluators whose evaluations may be meaningless. When self-esteem is low, however, individuals prefer a low-pressure evaluative situation. Hence, they chose the rarely positive evaluator, presumably because his negative evaluations are meaningless in that his standards are so high everyone falls short. If the evaluation happens to be positive, so much the better. Thus, with the rarely positive evaluator, Joe has everything to gain and nothing to lose—the pressure is off.

Studies concerned with internal state qualifiers, in sum, provide us with some insight into the mechanisms involved in the liking process. The finding that low, as compared to high, self-esteem subjects like evaluators more (assuming the evaluations are not suspect), for example, suggests that a recipient's liking for his evaluator is mediated by how the recipient comes to feel about himself as a result of the evaluative feedback. This is hardly a profound insight, but it indicates that the impact of an unmarred evaluation on the evaluator's attractiveness resides not so much in the objective niceness or nastiness of the evaluation, but in the subjective self-feelings generated in the recipient.[8] Apparently, it's not what you say, or even how you say it, but how the other person "takes it" that makes the difference. Self-esteem differences illustrate one of the primary reasons the internal states qualifier is an important one: Any internal state which makes a difference in persons' reactions to personal evaluations, provides us with a magnified view of a probable mediator of attraction.

V. Characteristics of the Evaluator

We have argued that many of the evaluation qualifiers reap their effect upon liking via influencing subject perceptions of the authenticity and/or validity of the evaluation. These two factors combined constitute the often studied factor of credibility, which obviously can be an evaluator characteristic. However, in prior sections, credibility followed from and mediated the effects of other qualifiers and was not introduced as an independent factor in its own right. In this section, we address properties of the evaluator that exist independent of his evaluation.

---

[8] The influence of changes in self-feelings on attraction may depend on the extent to which the evaluator is the perceived cause of the changes in self-feelings.

Moreover, these properties will be ones which are more or less enduring traits or attributes of the evaluator. An evaluator characteristic by definition must be perceived as an enduring trait or attribute; otherwise, it is a property of the situation, the recipient, or the evaluation.

Two studies clearly demonstrate the effect of evaluator characteristics. Jones, Hester, Farina, and Davis (1959) examined Joe Subject's reactions to two negative evaluators; one evaluator was described as very well-adjusted, the other as maladjusted. Joe was observed simultaneously by both evaluators and then received their evaluations. In all cases, one evaluator derogated him and the other was more or less neutral.

The results are somewhat difficult to interpret since attraction was reported as the *difference* between Joe's likability ratings of the derogating and nonderogating evaluator. In any case, it was found that a maladjusted derogator was rated a good deal lower than a well-adjusted nonderogator, while a well-adjusted derogator was rated only somewhat lower than a maladjusted nonderogator. The problem here is that the derogators not only differed in terms of their adjustment, but also in terms of the base line to which they were compared. This problem is eased somewhat by comparing recipient subjects with observer subjects since the confound was the same for both. The major finding was that although recipients were somewhat more rejecting of the maladjusted than the well-adjusted derogator, this difference was even *greater* among observers. This effect rested primarily in the well-adjusted derogator condition, where observers were much more positive than recipients toward the derogator. In short, evaluator characteristics and the evaluation jointly determined likability ratings, but the evaluation and the trait did not combine in the same manner for recipients as for observers. For recipients, a well-adjusted derogator's adjustment apparently did not suffice to offset his derogation, as was the case from the standpoint of observer subjects. This makes sense, in that when a person is on the receiving end, an evaluator's adjustment serves a dual function: it is indeed a desirable stimulus property, but it can also add "zap" to the impact of the derogation.

Clearer results with respect to evaluator properties were obtained by Sigall and Aronson (1969). They varied the physical beauty of a female who negatively or positively evaluated a male subject's responses to a personality test. In one case, the evaluator was highly physically attractive; in the other case, the same female was dressed sloppily, wore a bedraggled wig and no makeup, and generally looked unkempt. It was found that the female evaluator's physical beauty had a pronounced influence on the liking reactions of Joe Subject, especially in the case of positive evaluations. A pretty positive evaluator was liked much more than an ugly positive evaluator, while the negative evaluators, regardless of their beauty, were not liked. This finding supports the notion found in the group dynamics literature (see Siegel & Siegel, 1957) that it is the evaluative reactions of others defined as significant (beauty undoubtedly contributes to male perceptions of female significance) that really count; feedback from less significant sources, even if genuine and valid, has less influence.

In the studies that follow, the evaluator's "characteristic" is attitudinal similarity to the recipient. In one of these studies (Walster & Walster, 1963), Joe Subject believed he was going to be an outside participant in one of five already formed groups that would be discussing "dreaming." The members of the group in some cases were very similar to Joe in a general sense, and in others they were very dissimilar. In addition, Joe highly expected either to be liked by the group, disliked by the group, or he was given no specific expectation of the group's probable response (that is, he entered the group as an unknown stranger). Following this, Joe indicated which group he wanted to be in. Joe expressed a strong desire to associate with persons who were characterized as dissimilar when he was assured that the group would like him. When Joe felt uncertain about the group's acceptance of him (that is, was a stranger to the group), he expressed a slight preference for association with a similar group. Interestingly, when he was assured of being disliked, Joe actually showed a slight preference for the dissimilar group. Hence, when uncertain about a group's reaction we seem to prefer the safer affective company of similar others. But, when a group's affective reaction has been settled, dissimilar others are preferred. When we know we will be liked, others' dissimilarity may enhance the affect, whereas when rejection is assured, perhaps we figure it will not hurt as much at the hands of dissimilar others (see Mettee & Wilkins, 1972).

In an experiment by Jones, Bell, and Aronson (1972), it was found that a beautiful female evaluator, a significant evaluative source, who was both attitudinally *similar* and a disliker of the subject, was liked less than a dissimilar disliker. That is, when a disliking other possessed a significant property (female beauty) and was dissimilar, Joe did not react as negatively as he did when the disliker was similar to him. In addition, a similar beautiful female who liked Joe was liked more than her dissimilar counterpart. Apparently, Joe was more sensitive to the reactions of the similar beautiful female, compared to her dissimilar sister. He liked her more in the case of positive feedback and liked her less in the case of negative feedback. On the other hand, when the female was ugly, her attitudinal characteristics simply combined additively with her like—dislike for Joe in determining Joe's liking response (for example, a dissimilar disliker was least liked). The evaluator's ugliness apparently left Joe so uninvolved in the event that he responded as if he were a mere detached observer, coolly adding up the evaluator's good and bad features. This total result pattern is entirely consistent with a recent series of studies by Mettee and his colleagues (Taylor &Mettee, 1971; Mettee & Wilkins, 1972; Mettee & Riskind, 1974).

In concluding this section we should ask what the significance of this qualifier is for understanding the liking process. The results clearly indicate that where personal evaluations are concerned, who says it may be as important as what is said. Unlike the internal state qualifier, whose effectiveness can be capricious depending on the strength of situational forces, the evaluator characteristics qualifier consistently has discernible effects upon the recipient's affective reaction to an evaluation. Moreover, the apparent potency and consistency of evaluator characteristics establishes it as a major qualifier of the effects personal evaluations have upon liking. This potency also suggests that in addition to screening evaluations in terms of validity and authenticity in order to establish their intrinsic base-line worth as evaluations, the recipient also weighs the evaluation in accordance with source characteristics in order to determine the personal significance and value of the evaluation. Finally, the influence evaluator characteristics have on personal evaluations is telling testimony to the fact that a personal evaluation does not exist in the abstract but derives its meaning from its interpersonal quality; that is, it is a sentiment *held by another person* about the recipient. The evaluation itself is simply overt evidence of the evaluator's internal appraisal, and it is the evalua-tion's authorship by another person which infuses it with vitality and generates interpersonal attraction.

VI. The Perceived Intent of the Evaluator: Ingratiation and Other Ulterior Motives

Will the perceived *purpose* or reason behind an evaluation modify the affective impact of that evaluation? This, in essence, is the question posed by the intent factor, and our primary concern here is to determine how a person will react to an evaluator when there is more to his evaluation than meets the eye. We also deal for the first time with the asymmetry of positive and negative evaluations, finding that ulterior motives and purposes are suspected more frequently in the case of positive, than negative, evaluations.

The latter assertion bears immediate examination. It suggests that in social interaction, persons may perceive positive evaluations to have great instrumental potential and that they are often used in this capacity; while negative evaluations may be viewed as having rather narrow and limited social influence value. There is no logical reason, however, why false negative evaluations could not be used to influence others in ways that would benefit the evaluator. For example, many manipulators of men (for example, Lyndon Johnson, Machiavelli, Mafia bosses) have reportedly used denigration, ridicule, and other negative sanctions as effective instrumental tools. In short, negative evaluations can also be dissimulated in order to evoke dispositions in the recipient (for example, fear) that would mediate beneficial outcomes for the dissimulator (for example, the other's obedience). Nonetheless, the negative mode possesses several detrimental influence properties not shared by the positive mode. For one, negative influence might ordinarily procure benefits along task-oriented dimensions, but would be a liability on subjective—affective dimensions. Men who fear you may do your bidding, but they will also probably come to hate you. Second, even in the purely instrumental-task realm, negative influence probably requires greater surveillance of the recipient than positive influence. If others find us attractive, they may of their own volition mediate beneficial outcomes for us; this seems highly unlikely in the case of nega-tive influence. In sum, it seems probable that if left to their own devices, subjects believe that, in most social contexts, the positive mode is often used to paint a tapestry of deceit and deception, whereas the negative mode is generally thought to reflect a true picture.

The most comprehensive account of the role of ulterior motives in social interaction is Jones (1964) volume on ingratiation. Unfortunately, there is a major problem in dealing with the perceived intent qualifier from within Jones' ingratiation model. The central concerns in his work are the motives, the preferred ingratiation tactics, and the reactions of the ingratiator, whereas our interest is confined to the reaction of the *target* of ingratiation when ingratiation is attempted through enhancement of the other. Our interest is also limited to situations in which the other enhancement tactic is less than successful and is to some extent perceived by the target as dissimulation.

An ingratiation study of direct relevance to our concern was conducted by Dickoff (1961). Joan Subject disclosed personal characteristics and experiences to an interviewer while another female observed her from behind a one-way mirror. The observer was to form an impression of Joan. Later, Joan's task was to estimate the nature of the impression formed by the observer. Joan was told either that the observer was a clinical graduate student who was being trained to make objective observations of people and, hence, her goal was to form an accurate impression of Joan (accuracy condition), or that the observer was doing the observing because she needed Joan as a subject in her own experiment and would request Joan's participation at the end of the current session (ulterior motive condition).

Following this message, Joan estimated the impression she had made on the observer. In the course of doing this, she discovered either that the observer had formed a very positive impression, a neutral impression, or an impression that exactly matched Joan's self-evaluation. This meant that, on the average, the latter impression was moderately positive since Joan had a moderately favorable view of herself.

After receiving this information, Joan indicated her attraction for the observer on an 11-item scale known to discriminate among liked and disliked persons. In the accuracy condition, the more positive the observer's stated impressions, the more Joan liked her, with the neutral observer being rated especially low. In contrast, Joan liked the all-positive observer somewhat less than the self-evaluation matching observer in the ulterior motive condition, with the neutral observer again being rated much lower than the other two. Under ulterior motive circumstances, the all-positive observer's attractiveness suffered, and she was viewed as significantly less attractive than she was in the accuracy condition. These results suggest that an overly positive evaluation can boomerang and evoke a less than favorable reaction if there is reason to suspect the evaluator's motives.

Apparently, subjects in the ulterior motive condition looked upon the all-positive evaluation as a rather blatant attempt to win them over and, as a result, seriously questioned the evaluation's validity and authenticity. These doubts, combined with the negative features of the observer's exploitive—manipulative behavior, adequately account for subjects' diminished liking for the observer. It should also be noted that in the accuracy condition, the observer was liked more when her impression exceeded the subject's self-evaluation than when her observations matched the subject's self-evaluation. This result, of course, also supports our analysis of the evaluation incongruency pseudoqualifier. The evaluations of an accuracy motivated observer should have been regarded as authentic and valid, and, under these circumstances, positive incongruency was preferred to self-evaluation congruency.

An extension and sequel to the Dickoff (1961) study was recently reported by Lowe and Goldstein (1970). Joe Subject was again involved in an impression-formation study in which Joe was told an observer would attempt to form an accurate impression of him on the basis of observing him in an interview. During the interview, Joe was asked a number of personal questions and was observed from behind a one-way mirror. Joe then rated himself on ten self-descriptive adjectives on 11-point scales. The observer's evaluations of Joe were then conveyed to him. Joe was either positively or negatively evaluated relative to his self-report. Joe was then asked, with little or no justification for doing so, to give an initial liking rating of the observer on a four-item liking scale.

The intent variable was introduced following the above events so that in this situation any effects that perceived intent had on reactions to the evaluator had to be retroactive. The Accuracy Intent condition corresponded closely to the Dickoff (1961) setup. Joe was told that the observer had applied for a research position and that the observer's accuracy (matching Joe's self-evaluation) in forming impressions was the criterion for getting the position. Thus, it was obvious that the observer's evaluations of Joe reflected his veridical impression, even though the intent here was also ulterior and exploitive.[9] In the Elicit Approval condition, Joe was told that the observer had evaluated him under conditions where selection for the research position depended upon her ability to elicit a positive, approving reaction from Joe. Here the ulterior purpose of the evaluation was both exploitive and manipulative, and probably involved dissimulation and deceit. In both conditions the evaluations were exploitive (that is, designed to benefit the evaluator), but in the accuracy condition there was no attempt to manipulate the recipient's reactions.

There were several problematic features of the experimental operations. First, the elicit approval manipulation directly contradicted the earlier information

---

[9]We should define and differentiate terms that refer to an evaluation's extrinsic usefulness. Ulterior purpose in the most general sense refers to an evaluation that has instrumental value beyond the mere value of the evaluation. Exploitive purpose occurs when an evaluation is expressed as a means of accruing benefit to the evaluator. When an evaluation is expressed as a means of bringing benefits to the recipient, it is not exploitive. An evaluation that is designed to manipulate the recipient can be either exploitive or nonexploitive depending upon whether the evaluation is designed to benefit the evaluator or the recipient. It should be noted that evaluations having an ulterior purpose are not necessarily nonveridical and duplistic. An accurate and honest evaluation could be utilized for the purposes specified above. These purposes, however, make it less probable that the evaluations actually reflect reality as the evaluator views it.

given Joe that the observer was trying to form an accurate impression, while the accuracy condition was entirely consistent with this earlier information. Second, in the elicit approval condition, but not in the accuracy condition, the observer's selection for the research position was to be based on Joe's ratings, and, therefore, the elicit approval final "liking" data are suspect because we can never be sure that the rating represents Joe's actual disposition toward the evaluator, or Joe's attempt to see that the evaluator did or did not get the research position. Finally, the taking of an initial liking measure clouds the meaning of the final liking ratings (see Thibaut & Ross, 1969). This initial measure may have made it obvious to the subjects on the occasion of the final liking ratings that it was expected they would change in accordance with the intent manipulation.

Keeping in mind these methodological strictures, let us consider the results of this study. The interaction of the intent and evaluation valence variables had a powerful effect on subjects' final liking. The accurate positive observer was liked most and the accurate negative observer, least. Moreover, liking for the two positive observers differed significantly, with the elicit approval positive observer falling far below the accurate positive observer. On the other hand, the accurate negative observer was disliked significantly more than his elicit approval counterpart, who engaged in the bizarre behavior of seeking approval via derogating the subject.

These results are entirely consistent with the Dickoff (1961) findings, showing that when a positive evaluator is in all likelihood dissimulating personal evaluations in order to manipulate the recipient for his own benefit, liking for him drops sharply. This drop in liking for the positive approval-seeking evaluator is probably a joint function of disgust over the exploitive manipulation attempt and disappointment over discovering that the positive evaluations were not worth a "plug nickel."

In total, these findings suggest that the mere knowledge that evaluations were used for exploitive—manipulative purposes does not necessarily spark strong animosity. Rather, it seems that the affective implications for the recipient are crucial. If the perception of a manipulative—exploitive motive renders a negative evaluation inauthentic, thus benefiting the target's affective self-interest, the evaluator is disliked *less* than the honest, nonmanipulative negative evaluator. In the case of positive evaluations, the evaluator's character and the recipient's affective self-interest work in concert so that the accurate nonmanipulative positive evaluator is liked a great deal more than the manipulative—exploitive positive evaluator.

Another study concerned with perceived intent was conducted by Pepitone and Sherberg (1957). In this case, Joe Subject functioned as an observer of an imaginary social interchange. For this reason the data are less than compelling because Joe's reactions to observing one person evaluate another are probably not the same as when Joe is the recipient of the evaluation himself (see Jones *et al.*, 1959; Lowe & Goldstein, 1970; Holstein *et al.*, 1971; Jones, 1973).

Joe was given a written script in which a recipient was first insulted and deprecated by an evaluator and then the evaluator revealed to a third party his reasons for the insulting remark. The insult had to do with the recipient's mental density and slim chances of passing an upcoming exam. In one condition, the reason offered for this insult was to shame the recipient into studying so he could pass the test (that is, a nonexploitive—manipulative motive, or a good intention). In the bad intention condition, the reason was solely to impress the professor who, according to the script, was within earshot when the evaluator told the recipient, "You can't pass if you don't study; I've studied and it pays off." Although the evaluator was not directly manipulating the recipient, he was attempting to manipulate a third party for the evaluator's benefit. Thus, in each case the feedback was negative, had an ulterior purpose, and inauthentic. In the bad intention case, the intent was clearly exploitive but nonmanipulative (that is, the evaluator does not care about changing the recipient's behavior). In the good intention condition, the ulterior motive was a positive one in which the evaluation was designed to alter the recipient's behavior solely for his own benefit; thus, the intent was manipulative but nonexploitive.

The results showed, not surprisingly, that observer subjects rated the good-intention insulting evaluator as more attractive than the bad-intention insulting evaluator. However, even the good intention evaluator was not especially liked, as liking for him was on the dislike side of neutral (see Nemeth, 1970, for comparable data with respect to liking others whose intentions in *helping* the subject are good versus bad).

The selfish nature of the exploitation apparently overwhelmed any tendency for the potency of the insult to be reduced because it was inauthentic, at least in the eyes of observer subjects. In contrast, the highly exploitive—manipulative negative dissumulator in the Lowe and Goldstein (1970) study was accorded a neutral reaction when it was discovered that the negative evaluations were probably untrue. This difference between the two studies could be due to the nature of the deceit and exploitation. Negative dissimulation in the service of creating a positive impression in the target person is probably viewed as much less reprehensible than negative dissimulation in the service of extracting an extrinsic benefit from a third party. Another possibility is that the actual recipients of dissimulated negative evaluations, as compared to observers, respond more in terms of the affective implications for themselves and less in terms of the duplicity displayed by the evaluator. Hence, the Pepitone and Sherberg (1957) observers may have focused on what a crass bastard the exploitive negative evaluator was, while Lowe and Goldstein's recipients responded mainly to the discovery that the bad feedback was not true.

VII. The Gain—Loss Model

The gain—loss model of interpersonal attraction proposed by Aronson (Aronson & Linder, 1965) fits within the context of the more general psychological question having to do with sequential effects in the perception and processing of stimulus input. The rationale underlying the gain–loss model is rooted in man's seemingly innate predilection for responding vigorously to *changes* in his stimulus environment, coupled with his corresponding capacity to habituate to stimulus repetition. A stimulus that in itself is trivial can evoke a powerful response if it is a change from customary routines, while the most arresting and dramatic stimulus may come to be regarded with indifference if it is repeated often enough. Examples of these phenomena are numerous, ranging from the firings of individual neurons in the central nervous system to the reactions of entire societies to massive social injustice. In more phenomenological terms, we can imagine that the veteran peanut vendor at the Grand Canyon looks with indifference upon the cascading spectrum of color that flows down the canyon's chasms in the wake of a setting sun. On the other hand, the glory of an unshrouded sun following a series of dismal, gray, New England winter days is awesome to behold.

The gain–loss model is primarily concerned with the effects upon attraction of different sequential arrangements of evaluations. The underlying affective–conceptual principle is that uniform, or nonvariant, evaluative sequences eventually introduce affective redundancy so that the evaluations lose their affective potency; while sequences that involve switches, or changes, in the nature of the affect being received enhance the potency of the part of the sequence that follows the switch. The basic hypothesis derived from this postulate is that others who switch to a given affective stance toward a person will evoke a stronger reaction than will others who have maintained that same stance all along. For example, an other who switches from disliking to liking a person may be liked more than someone who has liked the person all along.

Imagine a husband and wife who have been pleasantly married for 10 years. For the most part they are kind to each other. This long history of positive exchange, however, may lock the couple into positive affective redundancy—anything positive they say to each other almost necessarily repeats prior evaluations. Under these circumstances we might expect this couple to take each other's positive remarks for granted. In contrast, both the husband and wife might be "turned on" by a compliment from a relative stranger or acquaintance in a coffee shop. The positive evaluation, in fact, might mean more and have more impact coming from a stranger than from the spouse. The spouse's positive comment is more of the same, a normative response that accords with the conventions of their relationship, while the stranger's positive comment is a gain, or an advance, on the affective front.

There is, of course, another side to this issue. When it comes to negative evaluations, the roles of stranger and spouse may be reversed. The history of positive responses that mitigates the potency of the spouse's compliments may sharpen the bite of their criticisms and negative remarks. There is a loss on the affective front since a reliable, dependable bulwark of positive support has waxed negative. Where there was once an almost axiomatic positive refuge, there is now the sledge hammer of almost traitorous, negative affect. In this situation we would expect negative affect to possess great potency. Conversely, negative remarks by strangers or at least old enemies may be accorded relatively less weight and potency as little or nothing has been lost.

The gain–loss model is a more formalized statement, in sequential terms, of this descriptive analysis. In brief, it is thought that a series of uniformly positive evaluations (+ +) may not be as rewarding to the recipient as a series in which the evaluations change from negative to positive (− +); and that a series of uniformly negative evaluations (− −) may not be as punishing as a series in which the evaluations change from positive to negative (+ −). The gain and loss halves of the model are both based on two fundamental postulates of equal importance: (*a*) that an affect change, or switch, will augment the potency of the postswitch evaluations; and (*b*) that affect uniformity engenders redundancy and attenuates the potency of evaluations occurring in the later part of a sequential series. The latter postulate tends to be overlooked, though it is as essential to the gain–loss rationale as the first postulate.

The integrative potential of this model is impressive because it is applicable to a diversity of sequential situations (for example, the greater pulling power of the hard-to-get, resistant female relative to an always available female; the intense hatred shown comrades who defect to the enemy compared to hatred for a long-time enemy; and the accolades accorded the late bloomer versus the long-term consistent achiever). Empirical data are available that fit the model nicely, and, more important, the model has generated a sizable amount of attraction research.

A. Supportive Research

Consistent with the gain half of the model, Stevenson, Keen, and Knights (1963) found that positive rewards dispensed by strangers had a stronger effect on a child's performance than the same positive reward dispensed by the child's parents. If we assume that parents have been a continual source of positive reward in the past, this finding is consistent with the gain notion. Similarly, Floyd (1964) found that positive rewards from peer strangers elicited stronger positive reciprocation from children than the same rewards received from their peer friends. Moreover, when a friend was nonrewarding, the child tended to react to this omission by increasing the rewards being sent to the friend; the rewards sent to a nonrewarding friend exceeded those sent to a nonrewarding stranger. It was as though the bird in the hand was not as important as the one in the bush—until the former began to make escape overtures. From another perspective, we see that as long as the status quo was maintained (friends were being rewarding and strangers were nonrewarding), the children did not reward their peer excessively, but when it seemed that the children were either about to gain or lose a friend, their rewarding output was stepped up. The response shown the rewarding stranger clearly fits the gain paradigm, while the case of the nonrewarding friend bears some explanation. The latter is analogous to a loss situation which should evoke strong animosity, but here the child responded with increased positive behavior. However, the friend's behavior may have represented a threat of *impending* loss, rather than an *accomplished* loss, and so the friend was rewarded to prevent a loss. Moreover, being rewarding meant giving the peer an object. The possibility remains, therefore, that internal liking for the nonrewarding friend dropped, even though overt reward output increased.

In a rather different setting, Gerard and Greenbaum (1962) found that agreement from another, following on the heels of a series of disagreements, elicited a much more pronounced positive reaction than did agreement following a series of prior agreements. This finding was interpreted from a different theoretical perspective from that of the gain—loss model, but the data are nonetheless consistent with the model (see Stapert & Clore, 1969).

These three studies serve to illustrate the wide applicability of the gain—loss paradigm, and Aronson (1969) has elaborated upon this in detail.

The prototypic study of the gain—loss model was conducted by Aronson and Linder (1965). In this study, the conceptual roots of the model were explicated and tested, and an attempt was made to delineate possible mediating mechanisms. Because of its importance, it is described here in some detail.

To pit uniform evaluation sequences against nonuniform sequences in a laboratory setting, Aronson and Linder arranged for a subject to *overhear* a series of discrete evaluations over a relatively short span of time. Joan Subject was told that since she had arrived first she would serve as an assistant in a rather special verbal-learning experiment that was testing learning without awareness. Joan was to interact with another subject (actually a confederate) via earphones and was to reinforce particular parts of speech spoken by the confederate. Joan was then told that the learning task was to be broken up into seven discrete parts since the experimenter wanted to break in periodically to see if the reinforced parts of speech would be used with greater than usual frequency in normal conversation. After each section of the task was completed, the confederate was taken into another room by the experimenter. Joan then secretly—so she thought—observed the conversation between the confederate and the experimenter from behind a one-way mirror for the ostensible purpose of recording the frequency of usage of the reinforced parts of speech. During the course of this "normal" conversation, the confederate, who was supposedly ignorant of Joan's presence, rendered a general, overall evaluation of Joan.

In total, Joan received a general, overall evaluation on seven discrete occasions over the course of the experiment, with the evaluations either being affectively uniform throughout the series or differing markedly from the first to the second half of the series. Specifically, in the gain (or − +) condition, Joan received a very negative evaluation the first three times, a somewhat neutral evaluation on the fourth occasion, and very positive evaluations the last three times. In the uniform positive (or + +) condition, very positive evaluations were received on all seven occasions; in the uniform negative (or − −) condition, the subject overheard a very negative evaluation on each of the seven occasions. In the loss (or + −) condition, the subject was evaluated very positively the first three times, rather neutrally the fourth time, and then received very negative evaluations the last three times. At the conclusion of the seventh evaluation, Joan was interviewed by an accomplice, blind to the subject's sequence condition, and asked to evaluate the confederate. This was supposedly necessary in order to compute a correction factor for assessing the confederate's verbal learning data.

The results supported the gain–loss rationale, although only weakly in the loss case. The − + evaluator was liked significantly more than the + + evaluator, while the + − evaluator was liked less than the − − evaluator ($p < .10$). The loss effect was not significant even though the mean difference was greater than in the gain effect case, thus indicating that subjects responded in a highly variable manner to the loss and uniform negative sequences. This makes considerable sense in that the + − subjects should have been ambivalent, wanting to emphasize the initial evaluation for self-interest reasons, while at the same time being hurt and/or bitter about the final evaluations—perhaps some resolved their ambivalence in favor of the initial evaluations and others responded primarily to the negative shift. In the case of the − − condition, some subjects may have been more reluctant than others to express publicly highly negative sentiments.

Two features of the evaluation sequences constructed by Aronson and Linder (1965) should be kept firmly in mind. First, Joan Subject thought that the evaluator was unaware of Joan's access to the evaluation, which should have established its authenticity, as well as its validity (the evaluator's reaction was the only available social reality). Second, on each evaluation in the series, the confederate was assessing the subject as a total person. Specific attributes were mentioned, but the general tenor of each evaluation was that of a global, overall judgment. This makes the evaluation sequence one that consists of seven separate evaluations of the same evaluative object—the global person. Thus, the − + and + − sequences involved a switch in *affect*, but *not* in evaluative object, while in the + + and − − sequences, the affect and the evaluative object remained constant.

B. Mediators of the Gain–Loss Effect

Aronson and Linder (1965) suggested four possible mediators of the effects a change in affect had on the recipients reaction to the evaluator: (*a*) an evaluation contrast effect; (*b*) an evaluator discernment effect; (*c*) a recipient anxiety effect; and (*d*) a recipient competence effect. In the first, the locus of the proposed mediator is in the evaluation itself, with the second-half evaluations in the change sequences being strengthened due to their contrast with the first-half evaluations. The locus of the second proposed mediator is the evaluator. In the nonuniform sequences, the affect reversal may be taken as concrete evidence of the evaluator's sharp, evaluative eye. The recipient of the evaluation is the locus of the third and fourth proposed mediators. In the case of the anxiety mediator, it is thought that the subject experiences sharp alterations in his anxiety level over the course of the nonuniform evaluation sequences, and that this, relative to the stable anxiety levels induced by uniform sequences, accounts for the gain–loss results. This mediator is more applicable to the gain, than to the loss, half of the model. In a − + sequence, anxiety is first aroused in the subject and then reduced by the same evaluator, so it is plausible that he would be liked more than a + + evaluator who never arouses nor, to any extent, reduces anxiety. However, it seems rather clear that a − − sequence should produce increasing anxiety over time. Certainly, a + − sequence should first give the subject a sense of security and then would introduce a great deal of anxiety. But, by the same token, the − − sequence would first arouse anxiety and then this anxiety would be further compounded by the final evaluations, probably making it as intense as the + − anxiety.

In the case of the competence mediator, the subject is thought to be the self-perceived controller or effector of the evaluations he receives in the second half of the − + and + − sequences. In short, it is possible that upon receiving the initial negatives, the − + subject works hard to make a better impression, and when the switch from − to + occurs, he experiences the satisfaction not only of the positive affect, but of having been able to engineer this affective about-face. It is the extra luster of felt competence which makes the − + sequence more powerful than the + + sequence. Conversely, the + − sequence can be viewed as one in which the subject feels especially miserable because he has "blown" a good thing. Here, felt incompetence makes the + − sequence worse than the completely negative − − sequence, in which there was never any prospect of a personally successful interaction.

There is no way of determining, on the basis of the Aronson–Linder data, which of these four mediators is the most viable. (However, an internal analysis showed tentative support for the anxiety mediator with respect to the gain effect.) Since the original Aronson and Linder study, considerable research has been focused on the problem of differentiating the various mediators. This research has met with complications, including an inability to replicate the original findings even when all proposed mediators should be simultaneously operative. We address this problem as we discuss the evidence for the various mediators.

Available evidence indicates that evaluation contrast per se is not sufficient to produce gain–loss results. In a study by Berkowitz, Butterfield, and Zigler (1965) it was found that − + sequences were not more potent reinforcers than + + sequences when the first half of the sequence was rendered by one evaluator and the second half by another. However, when the same evaluator produced both halves of the sequence, the − + sequence was a significantly more potent reinforcer than the + + sequence. Since the degree of contrast per se between the − + and + + sequences was the same in both the conditions, contrast is not a viable explanation of the gain effect found in the one-experimenter condition. The same basic pattern has been obtained in several studies (Gormly, Gormly, & Johnson, 1971; Tognoli & Kiesner, 1972; Mettee, 1971b; Mettee, Taylor, & Friedman, 1973). Thus, it seems clear that evaluation contrast is not a sufficient condition for producing gain–loss results.

The evidence is somewhat conflicting concerning the discernment mediator, but tends to indicate that discernment is a sufficient but not a necessary condition for gain–loss effects to obtain.

Landy and Aronson (1968) attempted to test the discernment mediator directly by establishing a negative or positive evaluator's discernment in another context. That is, evaluator discernment was established independently of the evaluation sequence directed at the subject. Subjects were exposed to unequivocal evidence that the evaluator was a "discerning" or "nondiscerning" judge of art. The nondiscerning judge was one who tended to give the same ratings to several pieces of art, while the discerning judge differentiated among the art pieces, spreading them out evenly along the judgment scale.

The results only partially supported the rationale that discerning evaluators would be more affectively potent than nondiscerning evaluators. The positive discerner was liked significantly more than the positive nondiscerner, but the negative discerner was also liked more than the negative nondiscerner.

The negative evaluation results are inconsistent with the predictions made from the gain–loss model and suggest an alternative explanation of results, which is more compelling. The total positive qualities of the evaluator may have determined subject liking for the differing evaluators. A positive discerning evaluator was best liked, a negative evaluator who was nondiscerning was liked least, and the two mixed quality evaluators fell in between, with the personal evaluation being the more influential variable. This overall positive qualities notion parsimoniously accounts for these results, whereas, the gain–loss model is disconfirmed by the negative evaluation results.

On the basis of these findings, Landy and Aronson concluded that discernment in all likelihood did not play an extensive mediating role in the production of gain–loss effects. Mettee (1971b), however, has argued that perhaps the discernment mediator had been prematurely put to rest, contending that the Landy–Aronson procedure did not adequately test the discernment notion because their discernment manipulation may not have altered perceived evaluator credibility. Landy and Aronson manipulated discernment by having an art critic display a great deal of judgment differentiation in judging art. This ploy may not have varied perceived evaluator credibility and, hence, would not have manipulated discernment since discerning evaluators are ones who make accurate, perceptive, and, therefore, credible judgments. Differentiating among a set of stimulus objects may or may not demonstrate discernment, depending on whether the objects are in reality different. Since Landy and Aronson's subjects had no basis for knowing how different the art objects actually were, they may have been unable to determine whether or not the critic who gave differentiated ratings was discerning.

Mettee (1971b), in order to test this reasoning, executed a design in which a − + evaluation sequence either enhanced credibility above that of a + + sequence or equated the − + and + + sequences for credibility. In both cases, the − + evaluator displayed greater evaluation differentiation than the + + evaluator. The results showed that a − + evaluator was liked more than a + + evaluator in the enhanced credibility condition, while the + + evaluator was liked more in the equated credibility condition. Since care was taken to equate the anxiety and competence factors, it appears that if evaluation discernment is adequately varied, it is capable of mediating a gain effect. We also find in subsequent studies that discernment is not a necessary mediator, as gain–loss effects occur with discernment equated.

Two studies (Mettee, 1971a; Mettee *et al.*, 1973) are directly relevant to an assessment of the anxiety mediator. In the first, the concern was with changes in liking for the evaluator from the first to the second half of − + and + − sequences comprised of differentially important evaluations. The evaluative object was of relatively minor importance in one-half of the sequence, of relatively major importance in the other half. Contrary to the gain–loss model, + − sequences evoked significantly greater final liking than − + sequences. Here there was a primacy effect (+ − > − +), whereas, the gain–loss rationale predicts a strong recency effect.

A comparative analysis indicated that the evaluative object in the Aronson and Linder study remained the same throughout the sequence, while in the Mettee (1971a) study changes in affect were accompanied by changes in the evaluative object. Thus, in the Aronson and Linder study affect change meant that, since the same object was being evaluated, prior affect was *removed* and *replaced by* later affect of opposite valence. Affect change in Mettee (1971a) meant that the object in the second part of the sequence evoked an affective reaction opposite to that evoked by the object in the first part of the sequence. Thus, the prior affect still existed and still represented the evaluator's feelings about the first evaluative object. Moreover, the first and second parts of the sequence had to be combined into a composite evaluation since both objects were interdependent parts of a larger whole.

These differences in the affective properties of the evaluation sequence might account for the conflicting results, especially in terms of the anxiety mediator.[10] Affect change in which prior affect toward an object is transformed into affect of opposite valence toward the same object seems ideally suited for activating the anxiety mediator. In a − + condition, anxiety attendant to the negative affect should be sharply reduced since the negative affect has been transformed into positive affect. Similarly in a + − sequence, a rosy, pleasant picture is shattered and replaced by an ugly, negative one, which should maximize anxiety reactions. Moreover, when the evaluative object is the same, uniform sequences would be highly redundant. In contrast, affect change in which prior affect refers to one evaluative object and subsequent affect to a different object should not activate the anxiety mediator. Here a − + sequence would not remove or reduce anxiety attendant to the initial negative evaluation since that affect still holds. Similarly, a + − sequence does not turn the initial positive evaluation into negative affect, as the former is still valid. Thus, at the end of sequences in which affect change occurs in tandem with changes in the evaluative object, there should be little difference in the anxiety levels of − + and + − subjects. Furthermore, uniform sequences should be highly positive and highly negative since the evaluations in both halves refer to different objects, and, thus, good and bad information is doubled, rather than just being repeated.

---

[10] In both studies every effort was made to make all the sequences highly credible so that discernment was not a factor. In the Mettee (1971b) study, a − + sequence involving different, but independent, evaluative objects elicited high attraction, but in that case, the affect change also enhanced credibility.

In order to examine the anxiety mediator more thoroughly, Mettee *et al.* (1973) designed a study in which the gain–loss sequences (+ +, − +, + −, and − +) were run twice. In one case, each evaluation pertained to *different* components of a trait termed "datability" and hence had to be combined in some way to arrive at an overall evaluation. In the other case, the evaluations in the first and second halves of the sequence pertained to the *same* components of datability. Here the second-half evaluations supplanted the first-half evaluations, since precisely the same objects were being evaluated, but at a later point in time.

In both evaluation conditions, discernment was equated in all sequences by a procedure that firmly established the evaluators as highly credible. Moreover, an attempt was made to lessen the role of the competence mediator by ascribing the affect change in the + − and − + sequences to the change in evaluative object in the interdependent evaluations condition and to changes in the *evaluator's* perception in the evaluation replacement condition. This should have made the competence factor inoperative since, when evaluative change occurs, the *recipient* should experience competence only if *he* feels his actions precipitated the change.

The interdependent evaluations results strongly contradicted the gain–loss model. The + + evaluator was liked most and significantly more than the − + evaluator, and the − − evaluator was liked least and significantly less than the + − evaluator. It is clear that merely arranging a series of evaluations in the appropriate affect sequences is not sufficient to produce gain–loss effects. In fact, results directly opposite to gain–loss predictions were obtained with first- and second-half evaluations that referred to different and interdependent components of a larger evaluative entity.

The replacement condition results were more compatible with the gain–loss model. Overall, the − + evaluator was liked slightly more than the + + evaluator, while the + − and − − evaluators were equally disliked. While these data did not in themselves confirm gain–loss predictions, they were significantly more in accord with the model than the interdependent evaluations results.

These data were hardly overwhelming, and we wondered if the anxiety mediator had been sufficiently activated by our replacement manipulation. A direct measure of final anxiety showed that some − + replacement subjects were still highly anxious following the sequence, whereas, others were very low in anxiety. More important, an internal analysis showed that subjects with low final anxiety liked the − + replacement evaluator a great deal (significantly more than low anxiety + + subjects), while those high in final anxiety did not like the − + replacement evaluator. Perhaps the latter subjects still felt anxious because the affect replacement was not perceived as permanent. The chances of a switchback to the original negative assessment may have seemed high since the − to + switch was very abrupt.

The loss effect picture was not as clear regarding the possible mediating role of anxiety. All + − subjects were anxious, but no more anxious than the − −

subjects, and an internal analysis of the + − liking scores did not reveal any association between liking and anxiety. Perhaps a + − replacement sequence does not engender greater anxiety than a − − replacement sequence. A repetition of a negative evaluation about the same object may confirm the awful truth, making anxiety intense, rather than introduce redundancy and take the sting out of the negative evaluations. Several repetitions may be necessary before negative evaluations become redundant.

To test the above speculations, Mettee and his co-workers (1973) ran a second study with only the replacement sequences. The replacement property of the sequences was strengthened by having the evaluator append a statement to the end of the evaluation sequence. Following the last evaluation, the evaluator indicated in the − + and + − situations that he had reversed his evaluations in the second half of the sequence because of initial misperception on his part. In the + + and − − situations, the evaluator stated he had exactly repeated his initial evaluations because he had seen things right the first time; the second half of the interview had strongly confirmed his initial evaluations. The appended statements were designed to make the evaluator's final judgments appear stable. In all sequences, it was made clear that the evaluator was convinced that his current evaluations were veridical.

A significant gain effect was found (− + > + +), but again the + − and − − evaluators were equally disliked. Moreover, the − + group was shown to be significantly less anxious than the + + group at the end of the evaluation sequences, even though initial measures of anxiety showed these two groups to have started at the same level. Measures of evaluator credibility and felt competence did not yield any differences between the − + and + + groups.

These gain effect data show three things: (*a*) the replacement property of an evaluation sequence is an important determinant of the gain effect; (*b*) this sequential property can exert its effect solely via the anxiety mediator; and (*c*) the anxiety variable is sufficient in and of itself to mediate a gain effect.

On the loss side, however, the story is ambiguous. The + − and − − replacement sequences produced near-equivalent degrees of dislike. A plausible argument is that anxiety cannot function to mediate a loss effect because anxiety reaches ceiling levels in both the + − and − − replacement sequences. Hence, when other potential mediators are equated, as was the case in the second study by Mettee *et al.* (1973), the + − and − − sequences may not differ in terms of degree of dislike. In the Aronson and Linder (1965) study, however, perceived competence may have varied between the + − and − − sequences in that the affect switch was not clearly attributable to the evaluator's more lucid perceptions. This could account for their directional loss effect. The greater disliking in the + − than the − − sequence may have resulted from feelings of incompetence and inadequacy over having let an apparently positive, pleasant situation degenerate into a disaster. This despair may have been absent in the − − sequence, where there was never any hope of a pleasant outcome. It may be that the competence mediator *must be* operative before + − evaluators will be disliked more than − − evaluators.

In regard to the competence mediator, Sigall (1970) conducted a study to test the viability of the notion that if a person feels responsible for inducing a favorable change in an other's position, he will like that other more than an other who has held the favorable position all along. The design involved getting Joe Subject to attribute the outcome of a persuasive message either to his own skillful arrangement of the message or to the content of the message itself. The outcome was one of three kinds: an other who was initially very dissimilar in attitude moved a considerable distance toward similarity so that he was only moderately dissimilar; an other who was initially moderately dissimilar moved the same distance toward similarity so that who he was now within the same category as the subject, but was not exactly similar; or an other started out advocating almost exactly the same views as the subject and did not change his views.

The persuasive message involved making a videotape recording of a speech in which Joe argued for the attitudinal position he in fact supported. Joe had to construct the speech out of a number of basic components provided by the experimenter. In the subject-responsible condition, Joe was told that the influence of the message was heavily determined by the pattern in which the components were arranged. In the content-responsible condition, Joe was simply given the speech already arranged by the experimenter. A control condition was also run in which Joe constructed the speech himself from the components provided, but Joe was told the particular arrangement did not influence the impact of the message.

The results showed that competence can mediate liking results consistent with the gain—loss paradigm. In the content-responsible condition, the standard similarity result was obtained, with others who ended up at the most dissimilar position being liked least and others who ended up at the most similar position being liked most. In the subject-responsible condition in which Joe induced the favorable change in the other, the similar other was liked significantly less than either of the still dissimilar others who had moved considerably closer to the subject's own position.

This greater liking for others who moved the most can be ascribed with some degree of confidence to differential feelings of competence, since the content-responsible results rule out anxiety reduction as a mediator of liking. If, for example, a very dissimilar other made Joe anxious and some attenuation of his extreme dissimilarity was anxiety-reducing, then this reduction should have been equal in the content- and subject-responsible conditions since the degree of movement toward similarity was the same. Moreover, the effort control group (subject arranges message, but arrangement has no functional consequences) showed that just investing energy in what turned out to be an effective message was not sufficient to generate the effect, as the results here paralleled the content-responsible results. It appears that the subject had to perceive that the mover's change was to some extent contingent upon his input into the message before the mover was highly liked.

Taken as a whole, gain—loss studies indicate that discernment, anxiety arousal and reduction and felt competence, but not contrast, can function as mediators of the *gain* effect. However, none of the three seems to be a necessary condition for the gain effect to obtain. The effect emerges no matter which two of the three sufficient mediators is held constant, as long as one is allowed to vary.

On the loss effect side, the picture is not so clear, partially because the necessary research has yet to be done. It seems likely that the anxiety reduction–arousal process is not sufficient to mediate a loss effect. Discernment appears to be an unlikely mediator of the loss effect because the + − and − − sequences may be unable to affect the discernment–credibility factor differentially. Negative evaluations may be relatively immune to doubts regarding their authenticity because they are nonnormative and not obviously self-serving devices for the evaluator. Hence, it may be difficult for + − sequences to acquire greater credibility than − − sequences, which are intrinsically high in credibility.

The empirical mosaic is virtually vacant with regard to felt competence as a mediator of the loss or gain effect. [Sigall's (1970) study pertained to gains in attitude similarity, rather than to an evaluator's gain in esteem for the person.] Theoretically, however, felt competence would appear to be the most potent mediator of the loss effect. To some extent this is a victory by default since the remaining mediators seem to be theoretically weak with respect to the loss effect. However, felt competence in itself appears compelling as a mediator of the loss effect. A subject who believes that he has behaved so as to engender the wrath of an evaluator who initially viewed him in a positive light might indeed dislike the evaluator more than an evaluator whom the subject turned off from the beginning. This reasoning, of course, still needs to be tested using evaluation sequences in which the recipient is clearly the party responsible for the evaluation's valence.

C. Inconsistencies and Other Gain–Loss Studies

Several other direct and indirect tests of the gain–loss model have been conducted with mixed results. However, a good portion of the mixture can be explained in terms of the nature of the evaluations that comprised the sequences and by shortcomings in the creation of conditions necessary for adequately testing the model. These conditions include establishment of the validity and reliability of the affect reversal, which in the original Aronson and Linder (1965) study was accomplished via making the reversal gradual, and having the evaluations be overheard. Moreover, a general consideration that is sometimes overlooked is that the uniform sequences are as much as part of the gain–loss rationale as the affect reversal sequences. Failure to recognize this has led to the construction of, for example, + + sequences which fail to embody any semblance of affect redundancy.

One of the earlier studies that failed to confirm gain–loss predictions was conducted by Sigall and Aronson (1967). The authors attributed their liking results to the measurement method (questionnaire), but since subsequent studies have obtained gain effects with a questionnaire format, this does not seem to adequately account for their nonsupportive results. More compelling is the fact the evaluations used in the sequence were interdependent and had to be integrated or combined to determine the evaluator's overall opinion of the subject. Evaluations of this sort, of course, have consistently failed to produce gain—loss effects and in fact, have produced contradictory results (see Mettee *et al.*, 1973).

A study by Taylor, Altman, and Sorrentino (1969) also did not obtain decisive gain or loss results. Instead they found that a − + sequence elicited just as much— but no more—liking than a + + sequence, and a + − and − − sequence produced equal disliking. But, the uniform evaluation sessions were in a sense cumulative and interdependent, rather than repetitious and redundant. Given these conditions, the gain—loss model would not predict a gain or loss effect since the uniform sequences would not be expected to lose their potency. The data obtained by Taylor and co-workers are consistent with this explanation since it was not the failure of the − + and + −sequences to elicit high and low final attraction, but the very high and very low final attraction evoked by the uniform positive and negative sequences which prevented gain and loss effects from emerging.[11]

Recently Hewitt (1972) and Tognoli and Keisner (1972) failed to replicate the original Aronson and Linder (1965) results. Both failures are explainable within the context of our interdependent versus replacement feedback distinction. In two conditions, Hewitt (1972) used feedback units which were clearly interdependent and obtained liking results that accorded with the total amount of positive feedback received (that is, a + + evaluator was liked the most and a − − evaluator, the least). In a third condition, Aronson and Linder's original evaluations were used. The results here were inconclusive. The failure to confirm the Aronson and Linder results using Aronson—Linder evaluations may be due to a crucial procedural difference between the two studies. In the Hewitt study, the evaluations were not overheard, but instead were directly communicated by the evaluator to the recipient. This overheard property may be crucial to making the + − and − + affect reversals (that is, the same object being evaluated oppositely at different points in time) plausible, believable, and conclusive. Mettee and co-workers (1973) found that with directly communicated evaluations it was necessary to overtly assure subjects that the − + affect reversal was definite and permanent before a significant gain effect emerged. In the Aronson and Linder study, the overheard aspect of the evaluations may have assured subjects that the *gradual* affect reversal was authentic and above suspicion. In sum, the replacement evaluations in the Hewitt study were not overheard, nor were subjects given any overt assurance with respect to the − + and + − replacement sequences, which may have made them suspect, and attenuated subject reactions to them.

Tognoli and Keisner (1972) attempted to replicate the Aronson and Linder (1965) study with overheard evaluations. However, the evaluation sequences differed

---

[11]A rather simple after-only explanation can also account for − + and + + sequences eliciting equal liking and + − and − − sequences eliciting equal disliking. Subjects could be disregarding all evaluations in the sequence but the most recent one. While possible, it seems unlikely that most "normal" recipients respond to an evaluation series as if all but the most recent evaluation had never occurred.

from the Aronson—Linder sequences in that the affect reversals were abrupt. This could have made the affect reversal suspect. Moreover, Tognoli and Keisner did not report the evaluations they used. Therefore, they may have used interdependent feedback statements, which, if true, would clearly account for their failure to replicate Aronson—Linder. In sum, Aronson and Linder's affect reversals were made intrinsically believable and conclusive by (a) making the evaluation reversal gradual and (b) by having the reversal overheard by the subject, rather than directly communicated to him or her. Hewitt, as well as Tognoli and Keisner, omitted one of these features, which may account for their failure to replicate the original results. Mettee and his colleagues (1973) omitted both of these features and were unable to obtain a gain effect unless the conclusiveness of the affect reversal was overtly assured. When the believability of the − + affect reversal, which was built into the Aronson and Linder reversal, was externally impressed on the subjects of the Mettee *et al.* − + reversal, a significant gain effect was obtained.

D. The State of the Gain—Loss Model

What does one make of all these data? Several major points emerge that provide us with a clearer delineation of the gain—loss model's boundaries and the fundamental psychological mechanisms underlying the model. First, the data indicate that there are clear limits to the model's applicability. Varying the sequential arrangements of evaluative feedback in prescribed ways is not a sufficient condition for setting into motion the psychological processes necessary to produce gain—loss results. It appears, for example, that the model is not applicable to sequences characterized by interdependent feedback units, units which are bound together in some fashion with all other parts of the sequence. This seems to be true because a fundamental, implicit assumption of the model does not hold with sequences having an interrelatedness property. Subsequent portions of sequences apparently must replace or exclude affect information supplied by earlier portions of the sequence in order for gain—loss findings to be obtained.

In sequences possessing the replacement feature, the most recent evaluations undo the past so that in a very real sense past events no longer count, or at least are no longer a veridical representation of present reality. Regardless of the specific mediating process involved, this undoing notion seems to hold the key to the entire spectrum of data that pertains to the gain—loss model. Anxiety is aroused for example, and then reduced by the same evaluator, thus producing a gain effect. Here, subsequent evaluations undo the earlier evaluations. A person makes a bad impression on an evaluator and then is able to induce that same evaluator to have a good impression of him. Here the subject's competence in affecting a change undoes the effects of earlier behavior. Even in the case were discernment is allowed to vary, the undoing analysis holds, except in this case, the undoing may occur primarily in the uniform sequences (at least in the + + sequence). An evaluator keeps being uniformly positive so that his credibility drops, thereby undoing the meaning of his earlier positive evaluations and allowing a − + evaluator, whose credibility is established by the affect change, to become more attractive. In sum, the gain—loss rationale appears to be one which pertains only to sequential feedback in which past and present affect interlock in such a way that the past is vanquished and revoked by the present.

VIII. Conclusions

Two specific points should be made before we venture to state a tentative, general conclusion.

First, we earlier posed the as yet unanswered question: Will Joe Subject's screening process classify an evaluation as suspect until it is concretely established as above suspicion? The evidence examined in this chapter suggests that a broad generalization cannot be made. With respect to negative evaluations, the answer appears to be no. The absence of suspicious events is apparently sufficient to prevent doubts about the built-in authenticity and validity of negative evaluations. In the case of positive evaluations, validity suspicions apparently are *not* aroused as long as actual violations of situationally present reality standards are avoided; the evaluation itself is reality datum and valid by definition unless there is evidence to the contrary. On the other hand, the authenticity of positive evaluations may be regarded as somewhat suspect unless concrete steps are taken to establish their truth. That it is important for subjects to believe that the evaluator is *unknowingly* transmitting his evaluations to the target is a case in point. In the evaluation incongruency section, for example, we found that in instances where positive incongruency was preferred to negative congruency, the evaluator was frequently pictured as believing that his evaluations would never be transmitted to the target person. In instances where positive congruency was not preferred, the evaluator was often pictured as being explicitedly aware that his evaluations would be received by the target person. In sum, it appears that if measures are not taken to bolster authenticity, the potency of positive evaluations may be reduced considerably, even to the point in some cases of inducing less attraction than negative evaluations.

Second, the perceived authenticity and validity of evaluations, as well as their significance, were proposed as important determinants of evaluation potency. It was argued that the influence specific qualifying variables have upon attraction is mediated in part by these three parameters. The first two pertain to the perceived veridicality of the evaluation: Does the evaluation reflect the other's true internal feelings (authenticity); does it accurately reflect external reality (validity)? The third, significance, refers to the meaning or importance of the evaluation to the recipient and is probably a joint function of the evaluation source (who said it) and the recipient's need state (the recipient's evaluative requirement).

More generally, what can we tentatively conclude about the influence personal evaluations have upon attraction? Despite the apparent simplicity of the attraction—personal evaluations relationship, this chapter points out that the surface simplicity of the relationship is more apparent than real. Evidence has been presented showing that positive and negative personal evaluations will induce vastly different degrees of liking–disliking depending upon the presence or absence of systematic qualifiers of evaluation potency. These qualifiers include factors such as perceived intent, evaluator characteristics, the need state of the recipient, and the sequential arrangement of a series of evaluations, as well as more central mediating factors such as the perceived authenticity, validity, and significance of the evaluation. Furthermore, we also argued and cited some evidence showing that negative evaluations do not seem to be as susceptible as positive evaluations to the influence of some of these qualifiers. Similarly, reactions to negative evaluations are often more complex [for example, feelings of strong dislike may be accompanied by an increase in approach tendencies or conciliatory behaviors designed to placate or win over the disliked other (Jones & Schneider, 1968; Mettee & Fisher, 1969)].

References

Aronson, E. Some antecedents of interpersonal attraction. In W. J. Arnold & D. Levine (Eds.), *Nebraska symposium on motivation*, Lincoln, Nebraska: University of Nebraska Press, 1969.

Aronson, E., & Linder, D. Gain and loss of esteem as determinants of interpersonal attractiveness. *Journal of Experimental Social Psychology*, 1965, **1**, 156–172.

Aronson, E., & Worchel, P. Similarity vs. liking as determinants of interpersonal attractiveness. *Psychonomic Science*, 1966, **5**, 157–158.

Backman, C. W., & Secord, P. F. The effect of perceived liking on interpersonal attraction. *Human Relations*, 1959, **12**, 379–384.

Bales, R. F. Task status and likeability as a function of talking and listening in decision-making groups. In L. D. White (Ed.), *Tthe state of the social sciences*. Chicago, Illinois: Rand-McNally, 1956. Pp. 148–161.

Bales, R. F. Task roles and social roles in problem-solving groups. In E. Maccoby, T. M. Newcomb, & E. L. Hartley (Eds.), *Readings in social psychology*. (3rd ed.) New York: Holt, 1958. Pp. 437–447.

Berkowitz, H., Butterfield, E. C., & Zigler, E. The effectiveness of social reinforcers on persistence and learning tasks following positive and negative social interaction. *Journal of Personality and Social Psychology*, 1965, **2**, 706–714.

Berscheid, E., & Walster, E. *Interpersonal attraction*. Reading, Massachusetts: Addison-Wesley, 1969.

Crowne, D. P., & Marlowe, D. *The Approval Motive: Studies in evaluative dependence*. New York: Wiley, 1964.

Deutsch, M. & Solomon, L. Reactions to evaluations by others as influenced by self-evaluation. *Sociometry*, 1959, **22**, 93–112.

Dickoff, H. Reactions to evaluations by another person as a function of self-evaluation and the interaction context. Unpublished doctoral dissertation, Duke University, 1961.

Dittes, J. E. Attractiveness of group as a function of self-esteem and acceptance by group. *Journal of Abnormal and Social Psychology*, 1959, **59**, 77–82.

Dittes, J. E., & Kelley, H. H. Effects of different conditions of acceptance upon conformity to group norms. *Journal of Abnormal and Social Psychology*, 1956, **53**, 100–107.

Dutton, D. G. Effect of feedback parameters on congruency versus positivity effects in reactions to personal evaluations. *Journal of Personality and Social Psychology*, 1972, **24**, 366–371.

Dutton, D. G., & Arrowood, A. J. Situational factors in evaluation congruency and interpersonal attraction. *Journal of Personality and Social Psychology*, 1971, **18**, 222–229.

Floyd, J. M. K. Effects of amount of reward and friendship status of the other on the frequency of sharing in children. Unpublished doctoral dissertation, University of Minnesota, 1964.

Gerard, H. B., & Greenbaum, C. W. Attitudes toward an agent of uncertainty reduction. *Journal of Personality*, 1962, **30**, 485–495.

Goldberg, G. N., & Mettee, D. R. Two dimensions of interpersonal attraction. Unpublished manuscript, Yale University, 1968.

Gormly, J., Gormly, A., & Johnson, C. Interpersonal attraction: Competence motivation and reinforcement theory. *Journal of Personality and Social Psychology*, 1971, **19**, 375–381.

Hamilton, D. L., & Zanna, M. P. Differential weighting of favorable and unfavorable attributes in impressions of personality. *Journal of Experimental Research in Personality*, 1972, **6**, 204–212.

Hardyck, J. A. Predicting responses to negative evaluations. *Journal of Personality and Social Psychology*, 1968, **9**, 128–133.

Harvey, O. J. Personality factors in the resolution of conceptual incongruities. *Sociometry*, 1962, **25**, 336–352.

Harvey, O. J., & Clapp, W. F. Hope, expectancy and reactions to the unexpected. *Journal of Personality and Social Psychology*, 1965, **2**, 45–52.

Hewitt, J. Liking and the proportion of favorable evaluations. *Journal of Personality and Social Psychology*, 1972, 231–235.

Holstein, C. M., Goldstein, J. W., & Bem, D. J. The importance of expressive behavior, involvement, sex and need approval in inducing liking. *Journal of Experimental Social Psychology*, 1971, **7**, 534–544.

Howard, R. C., & Berkowitz, L. Reactions to the evaluators of one's performance. *Journal of Personality*, 1958, **26**, 494–506.

Jacobs, L. Berscheid, E., & Walster, E. Shelf-esteem and attraction. *Journal of Personality and Social Psychology*, 1971, **17**, 84–91.

Jones, E. E. *Ingratiation: A social psychological analysis.* New York: Appleton, 1964.

Jones, E. E. Bell, L., & Aronson, E. The reciprocation of attraction from similar and dissimilar others. In C. C. McClintock (Ed.), *Experimental social psychology.* New York: Holt, 1972.

Jones, E. E., Hester, S. L., Farina, A., & Davis, K. E. Reactions to unfavorable personal evaluations as function of the evaluator's perceived adjustment. *Journal of Abnormal and Social Psychology*, 1959, **59**, 363–370.

Jones, S. C. Some determinants of interpersonal evaluating behavior. *Journal of Personality and Social Psychology*, 1966, **3**, 397–403.

Jones, S. C. Self and interpersonal evaluations: Esteem theories versus consistency theories. *Psychological Bulletin*, 1973, **79**, 185–199.

Jones, S. C., & Panitch, D. The self-fulfilling prophecy and interpersonal attraction. *Journal of Experimental Social Psychology*, 1971, **7**, 356–366.

Jones, S. C., & Pines, H. A. Self-revealing events and interpersonal evaluations. *Journal of Personality and Social Psychology*, 1968, **8**, 277–281.

Jones, S. C., & Schneider, D. J. Certainty of self-appraisal and reactions to evaluations from others. *Sociometry*, 1968, **31**, 395–403.

Kanouse, D. E., & Hanson, L. R., Jr. *Negativity in evaluations.* New York: General learning Press, 1973.

Kiesler, C. A., & Goldberg, G. N. Multi-dimensional approach to the experimental study of interpersonal attraction: Effect of a blunder on the attractiveness of a competent other. *Psychological Reports*, 1968, **22**, 693–705.

Landy, D., & Aronson, E. Liking for an evaluator as a function of his discernment. *Journal of Personality and Social Psychology*, 1968, **9**, 133–141.

Landy, D., & Mattee, D. R. Evaluation of an aggressor as a function of exposure to cartoon humor. *Journal of Personality and Social Psychology*, 1969, **12**, 66–71.

Lott, A. J., Bright, M. A., Weinstein, P., & Lott, B. E. Liking for persons as a function of incentive and drive during acquisition. *Journal of Personality and Social Psychology*, 1970, **14**, 66–76.

Lowe, C. A., & Goldstein, J. W. Reciprocal liking and attributions of ability: Mediating effects of perceived intent and personal involvement. *Journal of Personality and Social Psychology*, 1970, **16**, 291–297.

Mettee, D. R. *Attraction for an evaluator as a function of the importance and sequence of evaluations.* (Doctoral dissertation, University of Texas, Austin) Ann Arbor, Michigan: University Microfilms, 1968. No. 68–10, 868.

Mettee, D. R. The mediation of interpersonal attraction. Grant proposal funded by NSF (GS-2749), 1969.

Mettee, D. R. Changes in liking as a function of the magnitude and affect of sequential evaluations. *Journal of Experimental Social Psychology,* 1971, **7**, 157–172.   (a)

Mettee, D. R. The true discerner as a potent source of positive affect. *Journal of Experimental Social Psychology,* 1971, **7**, 292–303.   (b)

Mettee, D. R. A self-evaluative implications model of attraction for others. Grant proposal submitted to NSF, 1973.

Mettee, D. R., & Fisher, S. Need for approval and expectation of approval as determinants of liking, eye contact and physical proximity. Unpublished manuscript, Yale University, 1969.

Mettee, D. R., Hrelec, E. S., & Wilkins, P. C. Humor as an interpersonal asset and liability. *Journal of Social Psychology,* 1971, **85**, 51–64.

Mettee, D. R., & Riskind, J. Some positive consequences of dissimilarity: Liking for an other who "outclasses" you. *Journal of Experimental Social Psychology,* 1974, in press.

Mettee, D. R., Taylor, S. E., & Fisher, S. The effect of being shunned upon the desire to affiliate. *Psychonomic Science,* 1971, **23**, 429–432.

Mettee, D. R., Taylor, S. E., & Friedman, H. Affect conversion and the gain–loss like effect. *Sociometry,* 1973, **36** (Dec.), 505–519.

Mettee, D. R., & Wilkins, P. C. When similarity "hurts": The effects of perceived ability and a humorous blunder upon interpersonal attractiveness. *Journal of Personality and Social Psychology,* 1972, **22**, 246–258.

Milburn, T. W., Bell, N., & Koeske, G. F. Effect of censure or praise and evaluative dependence on performance in a free-learning task. *Journal of Personality and Social Psychology,* 1970, **15**, 43–47.

Mischel, W. *Personality and assessment.* New York: Wiley, 1968.

Nemeth, C. Effects of free versus constrained behavior on attraction between people. *Journal of Personality and Social Psychology,* 1970, **15**, 302–311.

Pepitone, A., & Sherberg, J. Intentionality, responsibility and interpersonal attraction. *Journal of Personality,* 1957, **25**, 757–766.

Pepitone, A., & Wilpinski, C. Some consequences of experimental rejection. *Journal of Abnormal and Social Psychology,* 1960, **60**, 359–364.

Richey, M. H., McClelland, L., & Shimkunas, A. M. Relative influence of positive and negative information in impression formation and persistence. *Journal of Personality and Social Psychology,* 1967, **6**, 322–326.

Rosenfeld, H. M. Approval-seeking and approval-inducing functions of verbal and nonverbal responses in the dyad. *Journal of Personality and Social Psychology,* 1966, **4**, 597–605.

Shaban, J., & Jecker, J. Risk preference in choosing an evaluator: An extension of Atkinson's achievement model. *Journal of Experimental Social Psychology,* 1968, **4**, 35–45.

Shrauger, J. S., & Jones, S. C. Social validation and interpersonal evaluations. *Journal of Experimental Social Psychology,* 1968, **4**, 315–323.

Siegel, A. E., & Siegel, S. Reference groups, membership groups, and attitude change. *Journal of Abnormal and Social Psychology,* 1957, **55**, 360–364.

Sigall, H. Effects of competence and consensual validation on a communicator's liking for an audience. *Journal of Personality and Social Psychology,* 1970, **16**, 251–258.

Sigall, H., & Aronson, E. Opinion change and the gain–loss model of interpersonal attraction. *Journal of Experimental Social Psychology,* 1967, **3**, 178–188.

Sigall, H., & Aronson, E. Liking for an evaluator as a function of her physical attractiveness and the nature of evaluations. *Journal of Experimental Social Psychology,* 1969, **5**, 93–100.

Skolnick, P. Reactions to personal evaluations: A failure to replicate. *Journal of Personality and Social Psychology,* 1971, **18**, 62–67.

Snoek, J. D. Some effects of rejection upon attraction to a group. *Journal of Abnormal and Social Psychology,* 1962, **64**, 175–182.

Stapert, J. C., & Clore, G. L. Attraction and disagreement-produced arousal. *Journal of Personality and Social Psychology*, 1969, **13**, 64—69.

Stevenson, H. W., Keen, R., & Knights, R. M. Parents and strangers as reinforcing agents for children's performance. *Journal of Abnormal and Social Psychology*, 1963, **67**, 183—186.

Taylor, D. A., Altman, I., & Sorrentino, R. Interpersonal exchange as a function of rewards and costs and situational factors: Expectancy confirmation—disconfirmation. *Journal of Experimental Social Psychology*, 1969, **5**, 324—339.

Taylor, S. E., & Mettee, D. R. When similarity breeds contempt. *Journal of Personality and Social Psychology*, 1971, **20**, 75—81.

Thibaut, J., & Ross, M. Commitment and experience as determinants of assimilation and contrast. *Journal of Personality and Social Psychology*, 1969, **13**, 322—329.

Tognoli, J., & Keisner, R. Gain and loss of esteem as determinants of interpersonal attraction: A replication and extension. *Journal of Personality and Social Psychology*, 1972, **23**, 201—204.

Walster, E. The effect of self-esteem on romantic liking. *Journal of Experimental Social Psychology*, 1965, **1**, 184—197.

Walster, E., & Walster, G. W. Effect of expecting to be liked on choice of associates. *Journal of Abnormal and Social Psychology*, 1963, **67**, 402—404.

12

Attitude Similarity and Attraction

WILLIAM GRIFFITT

Department of Psychology
Kansas State University
Manhattan, Kansas

I. Introduction

It is apparent to the most casual observer that the tone of interpersonal interactions is to some extent linked to the expression of similar and dissimilar viewpoints by the participants. A number of philosophers and novelists, including Aristotle, Spinoza, and Swift (Byrne, 1971) have noted the unpleasantness of interactions that involve the exchange of dissimilar views about topics such as religion, politics, morals, and war. On the other hand, the expression of similar views concerning such topics is observed to be associated with positive interpersonal responses. Formal scientific interest in the similarity–attraction notion did not develop until the latter part of the nineteenth century. The purposes of this chapter are to trace briefly the development of methodology in this area, to summarize some empirical findings, and to describe the major theoretical propositions concerning the relationship between attitude similarity and attraction.

II. Correlational Research on Attitude Similarity and Attraction

A. Spouses and Friends

A great deal of correlational research has been conducted concerning the similarity–attraction proposition. Most frequently, mutual attraction pairs (spouses, friends) have been selected and assessed with respect to attitudes or other characteristics and their degree of similarity has been determined through correlational analyses. The attitudes of husbands and wives have been found to correlate positively on topics dealing with economic, racial, political, and religious matters, birth control, war, and a variety of other issues (Newcomb & Svehla, 1937; Schooley, 1936). The attitudes of friendship pairs have similarly been found to correlate positively across a number of issues including foreign policy, religion, economic policy, and governmental affairs (Winslow, 1937). Thus, when existing attraction pairs of spouses and friends are considered, similarity and attraction are positively related.

B. Sequence of the Similarity–Attraction Relationship

It is not possible on the basis of such correlational studies to conclude that similarity is, in fact, the antecedent of attraction. It is equally possible that friendship leads to attitudinal agreement (Lott & Lott, 1965). The findings of Newcomb (1961), however, provide support for the notion that similarity breeds friendship. Two separate samples of previously unacquainted students were provided rent-free housing at the University of Michigan. In each sample, subsequent attraction among the students was found to be positively related to preacquaintance similarity across a variety of attitudinal issues.

III. Experimental Research on Attitude Similarity and Attraction

A. Paradigm Research

Scientific research concerning any phenomenon is ideally characterized by activities that lead to a cumulative and comparable body of findings allowing increases in the precision, reliability, and scope of available knowledge. Theoretical propositions may be continually modified and reformulated to account for relevant data. The acquisition of a scientific paradigm makes the practice of such "normal science" possible (Kuhn, 1970). A scientific paradigm is characterized by a specific body of research consisting of operations, procedures, measuring devices, empirical laws, and a theoretical superstructure, all of which are accepted by a given group of scientists interested in the same phenomena (Griffitt & Byrne, 1970). A number of potential paradigms for similarity—attraction research may be found in experimental studies.

B. Potential Similarity—Attraction Paradigms

1. SMALL GROUPS

Schachter (1951) investigated the consequence of attitudinal deviation by a member from the remainder of a group. In a group discussion task, experimental confederates behaved in specific ways in order to create a given degree of opinion similarity—dissimilarity between themselves and the group. Following discussion, attraction was assessed through sociometric rank ordering of group members by each subject. Opinion deviates (disagreers) received the lowest rankings. The extent and degree of intermember attraction is generally regarded as an indicant of the *cohesiveness* of a group (Lott & Lott, 1965). In a number of studies, attitudinal similarity among group members has been found to be related positively to group cohesiveness. Similarly, when subjects are led to believe that group cohesiveness is high, attitudinal similarity is generally increased (Lott & Lott, 1965).

2. PSEUDOGROUPS AND PSEUDOINTERACTIONS

In a setting in which "group" members did not actually interact, Berkowitz and Howard (1959) investigated the influence of opinion deviation on acceptance—rejection. Subjects sat in separate cubicles and received fictitious opinion information about each member prepared by the experimenters. Again, opinion deviates were rated more negatively than other group members. *Pseudointeraction* situations in which subjects observe or participate in simulated dyadic interactions have been utilized in a number of studies of similarity and attraction (see Lerner & Becker, 1962; Jones, Stires, Shaver, & Harris, 1968). The latter investigators varied the extent to which agreers and disagreers were dependent on the target of agreement and disagreement. Agreeing persons were evaluated more negatively when dependent on the target for monetary rewards than in the absence of financial dependency. The effects of variations in the social context of agreement—disagreement on attraction may be usefully studied with such procedures.

3. LONG-TERM RELATIONSHIPS

A number of investigators have investigated the relationship between attitudinal similarity and attraction in long-term "real-life" situations (Levinger & Snoek, 1972; Newcomb, 1961). As noted earlier, attitude similarity and attraction are generally positively related when long-term friendships, courtships, and marriages are examined. The strength of the similarity—attraction relationship has been shown by such studies to be complexly related to the type and length of inter-personal relationship (Levinger, 1972).

4. SIMULATED STRANGERS

In a number of studies, the subject's attraction responses to simulated strangers whose attitudes, beliefs, opinions, or values were presented via systematically prepared recordings, movies, or questionnaires have been assessed. In such experiments, subjects are typically pretested with respect to attitudes and then later exposed to the simulated responses of another individual. Following inspection of the individual's responses, attraction toward the stranger is assessed (Byrne, 1971).

Of the three designs first described, only one has been systematically utilized to the extent that it approaches the status of a paradigm for research on the similarity–attraction relationship. An attempt to conduct paradigm research based on extensions of the simulated stranger design is described in the following pages. It should be emphasized that the ultimate value of the selection of any one starting point for paradigm research cannot be determined on an a priori basis. Judgments concerning the potential methodological and theoretical limitations and advantages of any given starting point are, of course, possible. The relative values of such factors as experimental control, precision of measurement, and immediate relevance of procedures to naturally occurring situations clearly are intuitively weighed in paradigm-selection decisions. The utilization of *some* set of standard procedures, however, is necessary if progress in research is desired (Griffitt & Byrne, 1970). The research program described in the following section is one characterized by the use of consistent procedures, operations, and measuring devices, as well as by systematic examination of the specificity and generality of the findings.

In the schema for conducting paradigmatic research on similarity and attraction outlined by Byrne (1971), the first building block is referred to as the *base relationship* between the stimulus (similarity) and the response (attraction). *Analytic research* with respect to the base relationship concerns detailed analyses designed to identify precisely the stimulus and response components involved in the base relationship. On the other hand, research concerned with *stimulus generality* and *response generality* is primarily characterized by efforts to identify the boundary conditions of the base relationship by examining the influence of variations in stimulus and response operations and dimensions. Finally, paradigm research is concerned with building, testing, and reformulation of *theoretical conceptualizations* concerning the empirical findings.

IV. A Similarity–Attraction Research Paradigm

A. Methodology

In the basic procedure (Griffitt & Byrne, 1970), subjects, either individually or in small groups, are told that they are participating in a study of interpersonal judgment in which they will be given certain information about another individual and then asked to make several judgements concerning him. Prior to exposure to the stranger's attitudes, subjects are administered an attitude scale designed to assess their own attitudes on a variety of issues. The information about the stranger provided in the experimental session is, then, the stranger's responses to the same attitude issues. The more important characteristics of the basic materials are now described.

1. THE ATTITUDE SCALE

The attitudes scales utilized have covered 4—56 topics (Byrne, 1971). Individuals are asked to indicate their opinions on subjects such as belief in God, political parties and gardening. Responses are made on six-point verbally labeled scales with three alternatives expressing positive and three alternatives expressing negative attitudes concerning the topic (Byrne, 1971). Two-week test—retest reliablities of the individual items are generally high, in the range .55—.95 (Griffitt & Byrne, 1970).

2. THE ATTRACTION MEASURE

The primary measure of attraction consists of two rating scales asking the subject to indicate how much he would like the stranger and whether he believes he would enjoy or dislike working with him. The two variables are measured on seven-point scales and summed to constitute the measure of attraction, which ranges from 2 (most negative) to 14 (most positive) and has a split-half reliability of .85 (Byrne & Nelson, 1965). When no additional information concerning the strangers is presented, the 1-week test—retest reliability of the attraction measure is .82 (Griffitt & Nelson, 1970). The two items are imbedded in the six-item Interpersonal Judgment Scale (IJS) (Byrne, 1971); the remaining four items calling for judgments of the stranger's intelligence, knowledge of current events, morality, and adjustment.

3. THE SIMULATION METHODS

Two methods have been utilized to simulate the attitudes of the bogus stranger. With the *unique stranger technique*, bogus attitude responses are prepared in advance to agree with the attitudes of the subjects according to a prearranged schedule of proportion of agreements dictated by the experimental design. Using the "constant discrepancy" method, similarity is defined as a response that is on the same side of the neutral point and one scale point discrepant from the subject's response. A dissimilar response is defined as one that is three scale points discrepant from the subject's and on the opposite side of the neutral point. The use of the constant discrepancy method eliminates scale point discrepancy differences among similar items and dissimilar items and insures that the total scalar discrepancy will be the same for each subject within each similarity condition.

With the *standard stranger technique*, each subject receives one of two predetermined patterns of responses from a stranger. The proportion of similar attitudes and discrepancies are determined by comparing the subjects' own responses with those of the standard pattern *after* the subject has participated in the experiment. These procedures are described more fully in Byrne (1971) and Griffitt and Byrne (1970).

B. The Base Relationship

The base relationship in this research paradigm refers to the empirically established relationship between variations in attitude similarity—dissimilarity (manipulated as described here) and attraction as measured by the IJS. While a number of early studies demonstrated that attraction and similarity are positively related in such an experimental situation, the relevant stimulus dimension was unclear.

Byrne and Nelson (1965) varied the *number* of similar and dissimilar attitudes, as well as the *proportion* of similar and dissimilar attitudes, independently, and found the crucial stimulus dimension in regard to attraction to be the *proportion* of similar attitudes. With the stimulus dimension identified, data from a number of previous studies were combined, and attraction responses were found to vary positively and linearly with proportion of similar attitudes. Within this type of experimental situation, then, the base relationship refers to the positive linear relationship between proportion of similar attitudes and attraction. The general formulation of this relationship is represented by Eq. (1):

$$Y = m \left[\frac{\sum S}{\sum (S + D)} \right] + k. \tag{1}$$

In Eq. (1), Y is attraction, S and D are similar and dissimilar attitudes, respectively, and m and k are empirically derived constants (Byrne, 1971).

C. Analytic Research

Detailed analyses of the base relationship described in Eq. (1) have disclosed more precisely the nature of the stimulus dimensions to which subjects respond.

1. TOPIC IMPACT

Intuitively, it would seem that agreement or disagreement concerning trivial attitudinal issues such as "Western movies" would have less impact on attraction than agreement—disagreement concerning "belief in God." Research designed to examine this relatively "obvious" expectation has shown that agreement and disagreement on issues varying in importance and/or interest to subjects influence attraction responses only under specific conditions. If a stranger expresses opinions which vary in importance to the subject, if the similarity level is at an intermediate point between 0.00 and 1.00, and if differential importance is not equally represented in similar and dissimilar items, then topic importance influences responses (Byrne, London, & Griffitt, 1968). Items of high importance are found to exert an influence on attraction responses approximately three times that of low-importance items.

2. RESPONSE DISCREPANCY

In Section III.A.3, the "constant discrepancy" simulation method was described as one which eliminated attitudinal response discrepancies within any given similarity condition. With the "standard stranger technique," however, such discrepancy differences cannot be experimentally controlled. It is possible, then, that the relatively small response discrepancy differences which occur within proportion of similarity conditions influence attraction responses. That is, slight disagreement on specific topics might be expected to elicit less negative attraction responses than greater magnitudes of disagreement on the same topics. Byrne, Clore, and Griffitt (1967) found that attraction in such a situation was influenced *jointly* by proportion of similarity and relatively minute differences in response discrepancy. With differential topic impact and response discrepancy conceptualized as additional stimulus dimensions, the expanded base relationship may be written as in Eq. (2):

$$Y = m_1 \left[\frac{\sum (S \times M)}{\sum (S \times M) + \sum (D \times M)} \right] - m_2 \left[\frac{\sum d}{I} \right] + k. \qquad (2)$$

In Eq. (2), the new elements are M (weights applied to attitudes which differ in impact), d (subject–stranger response discrepancy on an item), and I (total number of items) (Byrne, 1971).

3. STRUCTURAL SIMILARITY AND SEQUENTIAL EFFECTS

Tesser (1971) proposed that attraction responses would be influenced not only by attitude content similarity, but also by structural similarity (the degree to which the stranger's attitudes are interrelated similarly to those of the subject). In an experiment in which both dimensions were varied, attraction was found to be influenced jointly by structural and attitudinal similarity. In a subsequent study (Johnson & Tesser, 1972) attitude similarity was positively related to attraction in a situation that put a premium on attitude uniformity, while structural similarity enhanced attraction in a situation calling for prediction of the stranger's attitudes. A conceptually related finding is one by Kaplan (1972) that similarity and attraction were more strongly associated when the stranger's attitudes were low, rather than when high, in terms of *interrelatedness*.

Byrne, Lamberth, Palmer, and London (1969) examined the influence of variations in the sequence of similar and dissimilar attitudes on attraction. Briefly, recency effects were obtained when attraction responses were assessed following each attitude, but no sequential effects were found when subjects responded only after receiving all of a series of attitudes. Recency was also found when subjects were required only to *think* about how attracted they were to the stranger after the presentation of each new piece of information.

4. SET SIZE

Set-size effects in impression-formation tasks refer to findings that impressions of targets described by only one or two positive traits are less positive than those of targets described by a large number of positive traits (Anderson, 1967). In attitude attraction research, findings that the number of attitude items has no effect on attraction (Byrne & Nelson, 1965) are inconsistent with the set-size notion. Relatively recent findings (Rosenblood, 1970; Posavac & Pasko, 1971), however, suggest that set-size effects may be obtained in a between-subjects design when only a small number of attitudes (one to six) is used, or when set size is made salient in a within-subjects design.

D. Stimulus Generality

Investigations of stimulus generality include a variety of studies examining the influence of variations of the basic stimulus materials on attraction responses. Such research addresses the question of the extent to which the base relationship is dependent upon the particular stimulus presentation utilized in the initial investigations. Stimulus generality research has also focused on determination of the more complex effects of various combinations of multiple stimuli on attraction. Thus, such research seeks systematically to extend the generality of the base relationship from the well-controlled laboratory situation to the more complex stimulus world encountered in real-life situations.

1. MODE OF PRESENTATION

In the initial studies demonstrating the similarity—attraction relationship, subjects were exposed to the simulated attitudes of strangers, which were presented on mimeographed attitude scales. The similarity—attraction relationship has been found to hold, also, when attitudinal information is presented via audio tapes, movies (Byrne & Clore, 1966), videotapes (Griffitt & Jackson, 1973), in face-to-face interactions involving confederates (Byrne & Griffitt, 1966a), or "real" subjects expressing their "true" attitudes (Brewer & Brewer, 1968), and in completely uncontrolled interactions wherein males and females are matched for dates on the basis of similarity—dissimilarity (Byrne, Ervin, & Lamberth, 1970). It should be noted that attraction responses are sometimes more positive when the stranger is physically present in the experimental setting (Byrne, 1971), or if subjects anticipate future contact with the stranger (Darley & Berscheid, 1967).

2. SIMILARITY AND ADDITIONAL ATTITUDINAL INFORMATION

The combined effects of attitude similarity and additional attitudinal stimulus information have been examined in a variety of stimulus generality studies.

a. Attitudinal Commitment. Veitch and Griffitt (1973) hypothesized that attraction would be influenced, not only by the attitudes expressed by a stranger, but also by the degree to which the stranger was committed to such attitudes. Subjects were exposed to a stranger whose attitudes were either highly similar or highly dissimilar to their own and who was either highly committed to his similar attitudes and uncommitted to his dissimilar attitudes, or highly committed to dissimilar attitudes and uncommitted to similar attitudes. Commitment and proportion of similar attitudes interacted in the determination of attraction. Responses were more positive to a similar target who was highly committed to similar, and uncommitted to dissimilar, attitudes than to a similar target who was uncommitted to his similar and committed to his dissimilar attitudes. Furthermore, highly dissimilar targets who were committed to their dissimilar attitudes and uncommitted to their similar attitudes were rated more negatively than dissimilar targets who were uncommitted to dissimilar attitudes, but committed to similar attitudes. In short, attitudes to which the stranger was committed (similar or dissimilar) exerted a stronger effect on attraction than did those to which the stranger was uncommitted.

In a conceptually related study (Blake & Tesser, 1970), it was found that similar targets with stable attitudes and targets with dissimilar, but unstable, attitudes were more attractive than similar targets with relatively unstable attitudes. Thus, the tenacity with which an individual maintains his attitudes appears to influence attraction. Such effects are consistent with notions concerning the reward value of social comparison, consensual validation, or attitude vindication agents. These areas are considered later in this chapter.

b. Attitude Base. Batchelor and Tesser (1971) varied the reasons why targets held attitudes that were similar or dissimilar to those of subjects. The authors defined four different motivational bases for holding attitudes: (*a*) value expressive; (*b*) need for cognition; (*c*) utilitarian; and (*d*) ego defensive. In addition to the usual similarity effect, attraction was influenced by attitude base. Strangers espousing value-expressive attitudes were best liked and those expressing ego-defensive attitudes were least liked. A significant interaction indicated that the similarity—attraction relationship was stronger for value-expressive than ego-defensive attitudes.

Lombardo, Weiss, and Stich (1971) varied the degree to which similar attitudes expressed by targets were based on supporting arguments. Attraction was more positive to a stranger who presented three arguments in support of his attitudes than to one whose attitudes were based on only one argument. It appears that in situations in which the bases for the stranger's attitudes are known, attraction will be a joint function of similarity, motivational base of attitude, and the number of arguments put forward.

c. Attitude Commonality. It was reasoned by Kaplan and Olczak (1971) that subjects who perceived their own attitudes as minority viewpoints (low commonality) would respond more strongly to agreement—disagreement than subjects who perceived that the majority of their peer group supported their attitudes (high commonality). Consistent with the hypothesis, the similarity—attraction relationship was greater when subjects were led to believe that their opinions were minority viewpoints than when they believed their opinions to be shared by the majority.

3. PERSONAL EVALUATIONS OF SUBJECT

Byrne and Rhamey (1965) studied the influence on attraction of attitude similarity and strangers' personal evaluations of subjects. Each subject was exposed to the attitudes of a stranger which agreed with his own on 1.00, 0.67, 0.33, or 0.00 of the topics and to the stranger's positive or negative evaluation of the subject on the six items of the IJS. Proportion of similarity, positiveness of evaluation, and the interaction of similarity and evaluation were found to influence attraction responses. The effect of evaluations was found, however, to be approximately three times that of the effect of attitudes on attraction responses. In two subsequent studies (Aronson & Worchel, 1966; Byrne & Griffitt, 1966a) involving attitudes and face-to-face exchanges of personal evaluations, the effects of similarity and evaluation were again significant, and the three-to-one evaluation attitude effect on attraction was replicated. For reasons discussed later in the chapter, similar attitudes and positive evaluations are considered positive reinforcers, while dissimilar attitudes and negative evaluations are considered negative reinforcers. With a weight of three for evaluations and one for attitudes, it is possible to plot attraction responses as a function of proportion of weighted positive reinforcements. The relationship obtained is a positive linear one (Byrne, 1971). Related work by Jones, Bell, and Aronson (1972) illustrated some of the situational factors which modify the relative impacts of agreement and personal evaluations.

4. OVERT STIMULUS CHARACTERISTICS

In the previously described experiments, subjects were exposed to little, if any, information concerning a stranger, other than his attitudes. The possible influences of overt stranger characteristics such as physical appearance, race, and prestige were controlled through the use of written materials or by having the same confederate play different roles across conditions. The manner in which similarity and overt stimulus characteristics of targets *combine* to influence attraction, however, is of major interest.

a. Stranger Prestige. The prestige or status of the stranger expressing similar or dissimilar attitudes would logically appear to be a potentially important determinant of attraction responses. Byrne, Griffitt, and Golightly (1966) conducted two experiments to test the hypothesis that the similarity—attraction effect would be greater for high-prestige strangers than for low-prestige strangers. In each experiment, three levels of stranger occupational prestige, ranging from high through medium to low were combined with two levels of attitude similarity. In both experiments, similarity and attraction were positively related, but neither prestige, nor the similarity by prestige interaction, influenced attraction. It was suggested that the attitude information enabled subjects to judge the strangers without regard to stereotypes concerning prestige, but that if no attitudinal information were provided, stranger prestige and attraction would be positively related. A subsequent study (Bond, Byrne, & Diamond, 1968) confirmed this expectation.

b. Physical Attractiveness. Byrne, London, and Reeves (1968) exposed subjects to similar or dissimilar attitudes attributed to photographically depicted attractive or unattractive, same-sex or opposite-sex strangers. Regardless of the sex of the subject or stranger, attraction was more positive to similar, than to dissimilar, strangers and to physically attractive, than to unattractive, strangers. In another study (Stroebe, Insko, Thompson, & Layton, 1971), physical attractiveness and similarity were positively related to attraction when opposite-sex strangers were utilized. The similarity effect on the IJS attraction measure was greater for females than for males. Additional findings indicated that the effect of physical attractiveness on the "work partner" IJS item and on ratings of the stranger's desirability as a dating and marriage partner was greater for male, than for female, subjects.

Furthermore, the physical attractiveness effect was greater on the "dating" measure than on the "marriage" and IJS "liking" items for both males and females. It is apparent that the effects of similarity and physical attractiveness on attraction are complex and dependent on a variety of factors, including sex of subject, the dependent variables utilized, and the combination of these two factors.

c. Race of Stranger. The "race versus belief" controversy (Rokeach, Smith, & Evans, 1960; Triandis, 1961) was directly concerned with the combined effects on attraction of attitude similarity and the stranger's race (black versus white). Rokeach *et al.* (1960) proposed that racial prejudice is reducible to prejudice concerning the presumed attitudes of blacks and reported an experiment in which the effects of racial membership were largely outweighed by attitude similarity—dissimilarity in the determination of friendship choices by white subjects. Triandis (1961), on the other hand, utilized a social-distance measure of attraction and concluded that race has a greater effect than attitudes. Inconsistency has characterized the findings of a number of additional studies concerning this issue. Recent investigations (Hendrick, Bixenstein, & Hawkins, 1971) have suggested various reasons why the findings have differed from laboratory to laboratory, the most important of which are variations in stimulus (race and belief) presentations and independent variable (attraction) assessments.

Research within the present paradigm has also considered the effects on attraction of racial characteristics in combination with attitude similarity—dissimilarity. The use of consistent operations and measuring devices has led to a set of comparable findings concerning the issue.

The mechanism by which overt stranger stimulus characteristics influence attraction is presumably related to the nature of the expectancies aroused in subjects by such characteristics (Byrne & Griffitt, 1973). With respect to racial characteristics, subjects would be expected to vary widely concerning the positiveness of the expectancies elicited by such information. White subjects' expectancies concerning the negative consequences of interaction with blacks are positively related to degree of antiblack prejudice (Byrne & Andres, 1964). It is necessary, therefore, to take into account the prejudice level of subjects when studying the effects of race on attraction. Early research within the present paradigm indicated that in the absence of attitude information, subjects high in prejudice were less attracted to a black stranger than to a white stranger and less attracted to a black stranger than were subjects low in prejudice. Moreover, high-prejudice subjects were shown to assume greater dissimilarity of attitudes between themselves and black strangers than between themselves and white strangers. A similar difference was not obtained for low-prejudice subjects (Byrne & Wong, 1962).

Experiments have subsequently been conducted in which the effects of attitude similarity, racial information, racial prejudice, and personal evaluations of subjects were examined. For high-prejudice subjects, similarity and race of stranger were both found to influence attraction, with black strangers receiving lower ratings than white strangers. For low-prejudice subjects, however, the race effects were not found. For both high- and low-prejudice subjects ratings of blacks identified by photographs were more positive than ratings of black strangers without photographic information. The latter effect is apparently one of physical attractiveness, since only attractive black strangers were used in the studies concerned (Byrne, 1971). It is also possible that the photographs served to "humanize" the strangers, leading to more positive attraction responses.

Byrne and Ervin (1969) studied the combined effects of prejudice, similarity, and personal evaluations, utilizing only black strangers. The expected prejudice, similarity, and personal evaluation effects were obtained. On the basis of this and the previous studies, the authors were able to consider the relative contributions of several types of stimulus information to the determination of attraction responses. The attraction data were found to be linearly and positively related to the weighted proportion of positive stimulus information with weights of ± 1 applied to each attitudinal item, ± 3 to each personal evaluation item, $+4$ to the presence of a physically attractive photograph of the stranger, -11 for black racial membership information for high-prejudice subjects, and 0 for the latter information for low-prejudice subjects. It should be clear that the effects of race and belief on attraction are quite complex and dependent on the details of the experimental situation. It should be equally clear, however, that paradigm research is capable of spotlighting such complexity and increasing the precision of predictions when multiple determinants are involved.

d. Emotionally Disturbed Strangers.   Novak and Lerner (1968) proposed that evidence concerning similarity between oneself and a handicapped other would produce unpleasant feelings, while evidence that the individual is dissimilar to oneself would be relatively positive. The authors hypothesized, therefore, that an emotionally disturbed dissimilar stranger would evoke more positive responses than would an emotionally disturbed similar stranger, but that responses to "normal" strangers would be positively related to similarity. The usual similarity—attraction effect was obtained on the IJS attraction measure for normal strangers, as well as a weaker effect for disturbed strangers. Most consistent with the hypothesized effects was the finding that disturbed dissimilar strangers were rated slightly more positively than normal dissimilar strangers. Novak and Lerner (1968), thus, were successful in creating overt stimulus characteristics which partially mitigated the similarity—attraction relationship. Similarly, Taylor and Mettee (1971) found similar but obnoxious strangers to be liked less than dissimilar obnoxious strangers.

Byrne and Lamberth (1971) conceptualized the Novak and Lerner (1968) information concerning emotional disturbance as an additional stimulus dimension, which, with appropriate weights established, would combine with similarity information to influence attraction linearly as a function of weighted positive reinforcements. Through appropriate combinations of weighted stimulus information, the investigators were able both to eliminate and to duplicate the Novak and Lerner (1968) emotional disturbance effect, demonstrating that the determinants of attraction in such complex situations may usefully be conceptualized in terms of combinations of quantified stimulus elements operative in the situation.

5. OTHER TYPES OF SIMILARITY

Attraction should be positively related to similarity along a number of dimensions, in addition to attitudes. Utilizing the simulated stranger techniques described previously, attraction has been found to be positively related to similarity across a variety of personality characteristics, including repression—sensitization (Byrne & Griffitt, 1969); self-concept (Griffitt, 1969); dominance—submissiveness (Hodges & Byrne, 1972); self-esteem (Hendrick & Page, 1970); masculinity—femininity (Haywood, 1965); ability (Reagor & Clore, 1970); and a number of other variables (Byrne, 1971). Paradigm research has found similarity and attraction to be positively related when economic factors, task performance, relatively simple behavioral acts, and erotic arousal to sexual stimuli (Byrne & Griffitt, 1973) are considered.

E. Response Generality

Response generality research examines the extent to which the base relationship may be generalized to different classes of responses. Three general classes of investigations have been conducted. First, the base relationship has been investigated across a variety of populations which differ from the one originally used in establishing the relationship. Second, the influence of relatively stable and/or temporarily created individual differences on the base relationship has been examined. Finally, the relationship of the original response measure to additional measures conceptualized as indicants of attraction has been investigated.

1. POPULATIONS

Attitude similarity and attraction as operationalized within the present paradigm are linearly related when American college students serve as experimental subjects. Any lawful relationship would be severely limited in scope if it were found to hold only for such a restricted range of individuals. College student samples are primarily composed of relatively young and bright individuals who come predominantly from the white middle class. The generality of the similarity—attraction relationship has, however, been investigated in a variety of noncollege populations.

Byrne and Griffitt (1966b) utilized as subjects primary and secondary school children of both sexes enrolled in grades 4—12 and ranging in age from 9 to 20 years. The standard stranger technique, with eight attitude topics, was utilized. As with the college samples, attitude similarity and attraction were positively and linearly related. Gaynor, Lamberth, and McCullers (1972) have subsequently found the relationship to hold down through kindergarten age. Griffitt, Nelson, and Littlepage (1972) studied the other end of the age dimension in an experiment in which the subjects were "senior citizens" and members of a local golden age club. The mean age of the subjects was 76 years, and the "strangers" consisted of both age peers and college students. Regardless of age of stranger, similarity and attraction were positively related. Clearly, the base relationship holds across a wide age range.

Byrne, Griffitt, Hudgins, and Reeves (1969) studied similarity and attraction in a variety of additional, noncollege samples. The base relationship was found to hold when the experimental subjects consisted of hospitalized alcoholics, schizophrenics, and surgical patients, as well as Job Corps trainees. Among individuals who differ from college students in terms of characteristics such as age, educational level, adjustment, and intelligence, then, evidence for response generality was again obtained.

Finally, the base relationship has been found to hold across cultures as well (Byrne, Gouaux, Griffitt, Lamberth, Murakawa, Prasad, Prasad, & Ramirez, 1971). In this experiment, similarity, and attraction were found to be positively related among Chinese, Japanese, Indian, and Mexican students.

2. INDIVIDUAL DIFFERENCES

a. Relatively Stable Individual Differences. The search for relatively stable dimensions of individual differences (personality variables) which reliably influence the similarity—attraction relationship has occupied the efforts of a large number of investigators within the paradigm. The findings may easily be summarized with respect to a number of variables. Individual differences in authoritarianism (Byrne, 1965); dogmatism (Gormly & Clore, 1969); repression—sensitization (Byrne & Griffitt, 1969); cognitive complexity (Baskett, 1968); need for approval (Nowicki, 1971); self-ideal discrepancy (Griffitt, 1969); and self-esteem (Hendrick & Page, 1970) have been found to have little or no *consistent* influence on the basic similarity—attraction relationship (Byrne, 1971; Byrne & Griffitt, 1973). Other variables, including need for affiliation (Byrne, 1962); manifest anxiety (Sachs, 1969); test anxiety (Reagor & Clore, 1970); and social-evaluative anxiety (Smith, 1970) have yielded a mixed bag of effects. In short, no dimension of stable individual differences has been found which exerts reliable and consistent effects on the base relationship. Such findings may be seen as attesting to the "robustness" of the base relationship, the relatively weak influence of personality variables, or to some combination of the two.

   b. Temporarily Created Individual Differences. While stable individual differences seem to exert little influence on the base relationship, it is reasonable to expect that temporarily created, "acute" individual differences may be effective. For a number of reasons (see Chapter 7 of this volume) manipulations of the affective feelings of subjects seem likely to influence the similarity—attraction function. Griffitt (1970) manipulated feelings of comfort—discomfort through variations of ambient temperature and found responses to similar and dissimilar strangers to be more negative under "hot," than under "normal," conditions. In a second study (Griffitt & Veitch, 1971), the temperature effect was replicated, and it was additionally found that attraction was more negative under extremely crowded, than less crowded, conditions. In each case, attraction was negatively related to subjective ratings of discomfort in the experimental situation.

   Gouaux (1971) induced affective feelings of "elation" or "depression" in subjects through exposure to movies prior to the similarity—attraction task. "Depressed" subjects were found to respond more negatively to similar and dissimilar strangers than did "elated" subjects. In the latter studies, the lowered attraction scores of hot, crowded, and depressed subjects were attributed to generalized negative affective feelings created by the experimental manipulations.

   Rather than exert generalized positive or negative effects on attraction responses, sexual arousal was hypothesized by Griffitt, May, and Veitch, (in press) to affect attraction as a joint function of the sex of the subject and the sex of the stranger. Male and female subjects were exposed to either a series of erotic written stimuli or to a series of nonerotic control passages and responded to same- or opposite-sex attitudinally similar or dissimilar stangers. While male and female subjects alike responded more positively to similar, than to dissimilar strangers, regardless of sex, female subjects were also found to respond more positively to male strangers than to female strangers when sexually aroused, as well as more positively to male targets when aroused than when nonaroused. Sexual arousal exerted no influence on males' attraction responses.

3. OTHER RESPONSES

   Conceptually, interpersonal attraction is a construct referring primarily to an individual's affective evaluation of another individual. Within the present base relationship, attraction is operationally defined in terms of the IJS. The search for response generality has involved the determination of the relationship between the IJS attraction response and other frequently utilized indices of attraction. Relevant findings are summarized in this section and are more extensively discussed in Byrne (1971).

   With respect to other verbal measures, IJS attraction responses were significantly related to ratings of social distance (Schwartz, 1966); willingness to expend effort for a stranger (Byrne, 1971); desirability as a date and marriage partner (Stroebe *et al.*, 1971); sexual and physical attractiveness of strangers (Moss, 1969); and ratings of strangers on the affective dimensions of the semantic differential (Griffitt & Guay, 1969). Furthermore, ratings of the stranger's adjustment, knowledge of current events, intelligence, morality, and desirability as a roommate were positively related to IJS attraction (Byrne, 1971). Nonverbal indices of attraction, including standing and seating proximity (Byrne, Baskett, & Hodges, 1971); visual interaction (Efran, 1969); and compliance with requests from similar and dissimilar targets (Baron, 1970) were also systematically related to the base relationship measure of attraction.

Finally, IJS attraction as a function of similarity–dissimilarity has been found to act as a mediator of other behaviors and ratings with respect to strangers. Griffitt and Jackson (1973) found that simulated jury recommendations concerning prison sentences were more severe for defendants who were attitudinally dissimilar to subjects than for similar defendants. Decisions to hire job applicants were positively related to the similarity of the applicants to subjects in yet another study (Griffitt and Jackson, 1970). Additional studies have shown that similar (liked) others receive larger financial loans (Golightly, Huffman, & Byrne, 1972); receive more votes (Byrne, Bond, & Diamond, 1969); and are more often imitated (Baron, 1970) than dissimilar (disliked) others. More detailed consideration of attraction as a mediator of behavior may be found in Byrne and Griffitt (1973) and Lott and Lott (1972).

Research designed to extend the empirical generality of the similarity–attraction base relationship beyond the relatively narrow scope of the initial laboratory investigations has generally been quite successful with respect to both the stimulus and response dimension. The broadened scope of the findings renders it possible to begin to make empirical and conceptual sense of the manner in which similarity influences attraction in nonlaboratory situations.

V. Similarity–Attraction Theories

It should be abundantly clear at this point that attraction and attitude similarity are positively related across a variety of circumstances. The major theoretical propositions concerning the "why" of this relationship may be broadly categorized as (*a*) *cognitive* and (*b*) *reinforcement* theories.

A. Cognitive Theories

Cognitive theories (Heider, 1958; Newcomb, 1968) are characterized by their focus on the relational elements of a closed triadic system comprised of at least two individuals—person and other (P and O)—and an object (X) of communication. The basic unit of such systems is the cognition, which refers to any knowledge, belief, or opinion held by an individual. In the P—O—X triadic system, "balanced" configurations among cognitions occur in two situations: (*a*) P likes, O, and P and O agree concerning their attitudes toward X, and (*b*) P dislikes O, and P and O disagree concerning X. When P likes O, and P and O disagree concerning X, a state of imbalance is said to exist (Newcomb, 1968). Inasmuch as balance is the psychologically preferred state, individuals will strive to maintain cognitions that preserve or attain a balanced configuration. Thus, when P and O agree concerning X, balance is possible (for P) only if P likes O. On the other hand, if P and O disagree concerning X, balance occurs when P dislikes O.

Attraction will thus be positively related to similarity of attitudes concerning X as a by-product of attempts to maintain or to restore cognitive balance. The obtained positive relationship between agreement and attraction is clearly consistent with the balance predictions. In addition, the prediction that when X consists of P's self-concept, positive O/X evaluations should lead P to like O (assuming that P likes himself) has generally been supported (Skolnick, 1971). Cognitive consistency theories also predict that P will respond positively to an O who evaluates him negatively if P's self-concept is negative. The latter prediction has received little empirical support (Skolnick, 1971; see Chapter 11 of this volume).

B. Reinforcement Theories

Reinforcement theories (Byrne, 1971; Byrne & Clore, 1970; Lott & Lott 1972), in contrast to cognitive theories, tend to focus on stimuli and responses as the basic units comprising interpersonal interactions, on the positive and negative properties of relevant stimuli, and on the utility of borrowing concepts from learning theory to apply to the attraction situation (see Chapters 7 and 8 of this volume). Similar and dissimilar attitudes are considered, respectively, as positive and negative reinforcers which elicit positive and negative affective responses in subjects (Lamberth, Gouaux, & Padd, 1971). Stimuli (primarily persons) associated with such affective responses become conditioned stimuli capable of evoking positive and negative affective responses, which mediate liking and disliking (Byrne, 1971). Two kinds of evidence support the proposition that similar and dissimilar attitudes function as positive and negative reinforcers. First, such stimuli are effective reinforcers of instrumental behaviors (Byrne, Young, & Griffitt, 1966); and, second, persons or other objects associated with agreeing or disagreeing attitude statements are evaluated, respectively, positively or negatively (Byrne & Clore, 1970).

The reinforcement properties of similar and dissimilar attitudes are widely assumed to derive from a general motive to be logical, accurate, and correct (effective) in interpreting one's environment. With respect to the physical environment, one may usually determine the effectiveness of one's belief system through direct perceptual evidence (for instance, fire is hot; it is raining). With respect to the social environment, the accuracy, logicalness, and correctiness of beliefs and attitudes concerning issues such as politics, war, and religion may be evaluated only by consensual validation or invalidation through social comparison with others (Festinger, 1954; see, in this volume, Chapter 13). The motive involved is thus satisfied by consensual validation (agreement) and frustrated by consensual invalidation (disagreement) (Byrne, 1971). Similarity, therefore, is positively reinforcing, while dissimilarity is negatively reinforcing.

Byrne and Clore (1967) conducted a series of studies in which attempts to manipulate such a motive (labeled "effectance") were coupled with the similarity—attraction task. It was proposed that the effectance motive could be aroused by exposing subjects to a film composed of confusing and meaningless visual and auditory sequences. Subjects were shown either the experimental film or a non-arousing control film and then responded to attitudinally similar or dissimilar strangers. While it was expected that the similarity—attraction relationship would be strongest in highly confused and aroused subjects (as assessed by a five-item scale), the relationship actually was strongest in moderately aroused subjects. The authors proposed that highly aroused subjects were, in fact, so confused that attention to the attitudinal stimuli was disrupted, resulting in less responsiveness to similarity—dissimilarity. These and similar data (Byrne, 1971) consistently indicated that moderate levels of effectance arousal enhance the influence of similarity on attraction.

It will be recalled that the effect of agreement on attraction has been found to be greater when strangers are "committed," than when "uncommitted," to their attitudes; when their attitudes are very stable, as opposed to unstable; and when strangers provide multiple, rather than single, arguments in support of their attitudes. Similarly, the demonstration of value-expressive attitudes or low-commonality attitudes influences attraction to a greater extent than the expression, respectively, of ego-defensive or high-commonality attitudes. Such findings are consistent with an effectance interpretation in that the strangers who are committed to their attitudes, hold stable attitudes, provide multiple supporting arguments, and hold value-expressive or low-commonality attitudes may be viewed as more powerful validating or invalidating agents than their respective counterparts.

Palmer (1969) proposed that, as opposed to a need to *evaluate* one's attitudes (effectance), the need to defend (vindicate) one's attitudes mediates the similarity—attraction relationship. In his experiment, similarity and attraction were more strongly related for "competent," than for "incompetent," strangers. Palmer interpreted the findings as indicating that competent strangers served as more potent supporters or challengers with respect to one's position than did incompetent strangers. While Palmer (1969) suggested that the construct of effectance be discarded in favor of "need for vindication," the defining operations at present, are insufficiently developed to provide a clear distinction between the two concepts.

An additional formulation (Aronson & Worchel, 1966; Nelson, 1966) suggests that similarity and attraction are related primarily because of the mediation of anticipated liking from the stranger. When similar attitudes are expressed by a stranger, the subject assumes that the stranger will like him. The assumed response of the stranger is presumed to elicit the attraction rating. From this point of view, attitudes serve mainly as cues concerning inferred liking from the stranger on the basis of past experience with similar and dissimilar persons. Why attitudes elicit such responses is, however, not considered by Aronson and Worchel (1966) or Nelson (1966). Similarly, Kaplan and Anderson (1973) regard similar and dissimilar attitudes as "informers" which indicate to subjects that strangers have positive or negative qualities to their personalities. Such a formulation also bypasses questions concerning *why* similar and dissimilar attitudes are cues to positive and negative personality attributes (Byrne, Clore, Griffitt, Lamberth, & Mitchell, 1973).

A great deal of research has been conducted concerning attitude similarity and attraction, of which only a small portion has been described in this chapter. A significant current trend in such research involves various investigators' concern with the potential applicability of findings and the identification of behaviors which are influenced by liking. For example, Lott and Lott (1966) discovered that the mere presence of liked persons served to facilitate the learning of relatively simple verbal material, but interfered with learning when the task was moderately difficult. The potential influence of interpersonal attraction on classroom learning and performance are fully discussed by Lott and Lott (1972). As noted previously, decisions concerning loan granting (Golightly *et al.*, 1972); hiring (Griffitt & Jackson, 1970); and punishments for transgressions (Mitchell & Byrne, 1973) are influenced by the degree to which decision makers like target persons. Smith, Meadow, and Sisk (1970) found that subjects evaluated identical performances on a verbal learning task more positively when the performer was liked than when disliked.

Clearly, a variety of behaviors, including decisions about, and evaluations of, others are influenced by similarity-induced liking and dissimilarity-induced disliking. Rejection, negative evaluation, and intolerance of dissimilar others are well-documented phenomena of the interpersonal attraction literature. With dissimilarity alone negatively influencing important decisions (guilt, employment, etc.) and evaluations concerning others, it becomes important to discover factors which are effective in reducing intolerance for disagreement. Hodges and Byrne (1972) found that disagreeing persons were rejected less when disagreement was expressed in "open-minded" terms than when expressed in dogmatic terms. Future research undoubtedly will reveal a variety of factors which are effective in reducing the impact of disagreement on interpersonal rejection.

The similarity–attraction paradigm outlined in the preceding pages is also proving useful as a methodology for studying the effects of environmental conditions such as temperature (Griffitt, 1970); crowding (Griffitt & Veitch, 1971); and noise (Bull, Burbage, Crandall, Fletcher, Lloyd, Ravneberg, & Rockett, 1972), as well as mood states (Gouaux, 1971), on interpersonal behaviors. Continued progress along such lines may lead to greater understanding some of our most pressing social problems—those involving the affective quality of interpersonal relationships.

Acknowledgments

Preparation of this paper was facilitated by Research Grant 16351–03 from the National Institute of Mental Health. I wish to express my appreciation to Donn Byrne for his comments and suggestions in response to an earlier draft of this chapter.

References

Anderson, N. H. Averaging model analysis of set-size effect in impression formation. *Journal of Experimental Psychology*, 1967, **75**, 158–165.

Aronson, E., & Worchel, P. Similarity versus liking as determinants of interpersonal attractiveness. *Psychonomic Science*, 1966, **5**, 157–158.

Baron, R. A. Attraction toward the model and model's competence as determinants of adult imitative behavior. *Journal of Personality and Social Psychology*, 1970, **14**, 345–351.

Baskett, G. D. Interpersonal attraction as a function of attitude similarity-dissimilarity and cognitive complexity. Unpublished doctoral dissertation, University of Texas, 1968.

Batchelor, T. R., & Tesser, A. Attitude base as a moderator of the attitude similarity-attraction relationship. *Journal of Personality and Social Psychology*, 1971, **19**, 229–236.

Berkowitz, L., & Howard, R. C. Reactions to opinion deviates as affected by affiliation need (*n*) and group member interdependence. *Sociometry*, 1959, **22**, 81–91.

Blake, B. F., & Tesser, A. Interpersonal attraction as a function of the other's reward value to the-person. *Journal of Social Psychology*, 1970, **82**, 67–74.

Bond, M., Byrne, D., & Diamond, M. J. Effect of occupational prestige and attitude similarity on attraction as a function of assumed similarity of attitude. *Psychological Reports*, 1968, **23**, 1167–1172.

Brewer, R. E., & Brewer, M. B. Attraction and accuracy of perception in dyads. *Journal of Personality and Social Psychology*, 1968, **8**, 188–193.

Bull, A. J., Burbage, S. E., Crandall, J. E., Fletcher, C. I., Lloyd, J. T., Ravneberg, R. L., & Rockett, S. L. Effects of noise and intolerance of ambiguity upon attraction for similar and dissimilar others. *Journal of Social Psychology*, 1972, **88**, 151–152.

Byrne, D. Authoritarianism and response to attitude similarity–dissimilarity. *Journal of Social Psychology*, 1965, **66**, 251–256.

Byrne, D. *The attraction paradigm*. New York: Academic Press, 1971.

Byrne, D., & Andres, D. Prejudice and interpersonal expectancies. *Journal of Negro Education*, 1964, **33**, 441–445.

Byrne, D., Baskett, G. D., & Hodges, L. Behavioral indicators of interpersonal attraction. *Journal of Applied Social Psychology*, 1971, **1**, 137–149.

Byrne, D., and Bond, M. H., & Diamond, M. J. Response to political candidates as a function of attitude similarity–dissimilarity. *Human Relations*, 1969, **22**, 251–262.

Byrne, D., & Clore, G. L., Predicting interpersonal attraction toward strangers presented in three different stimulus modes. *Psychonomic Science*, 1966, **4**, 239–240.

Byrne, D., & Clore, G. L., Effectance arousal and attraction. *Journal of Personality and Social Psychology*, 1967, **6**, No. 4(Whole No. 638).

Byrne, D., & Clore, G. L. A reinforcement model of evaluative responses. *Personality: An International Journal*, 1970, **2**, 103–128.

Byrne, D., Clore, G. L., & Griffitt, W. Response discrepancy versus attitude similarity-dissimilarity as determinants of attraction. *Psychonomic Science*, 1967, **7**, 297–298.

Byrne, D., Clore, G. L., Griffitt, W., Lamberth, J., & Mitchell, H. E. When research paradigms converge: Confrontation or integration? *Journal of Personality and Social Psychology*, 1973, **28**, 313–320.

Byrne, D., & Ervin, C. R. Attraction toward a Negro stranger as a function of prejudice, attitude-similarity, and the stranger's evaluation of the subject. *Human Relations,* 1969, **22**, 397–404.

Byrne, D., Ervin, C. R., & Lamberth, J. Continuity between the experimental study of attraction and real-life computer dating. *Journal of Personality and Social Psychology,* 1970, **16**, 157–165.

Byrne, D., Gouaux, C., Griffitt, W., Lamberth, J., Murakawa, N., Prasad, M. B., Prassad, A., & Ramirez, M. The ubiquitous relationship: Attitude similarity and attraction. *Human Relations,* 1971, **9**, 201–207.

Byrne, D., & Griffitt, W. Similarity versus liking: A clarification. *Psychonomic Science,* 1966, **6**, 295–296. (a)

Byrne, D., & Griffitt, W. A developmental investigation of the law of attraction. *Journal of Personality Social Psychology,* 1966, **4**, 699–702. (b)

Byrne, D., & Griffitt, W. Similarity and awareness of similarity of personality characteristic as determinants of attraction. *Journal of Experimental Research in Personality,* 1969, **3**, 179–186.

Byrne, D., & Griffitt, W. Interpersonal attraction. *Annual Review of Psychology,* 1973, **24**, 317–336.

Byrne, D., Griffitt, W., & Golightly, C. Prestige as a factor in determining the effect of attitude similarity—dissimilarity on attraction. *Journal of Personality,* 1966, **34**, 434–444.

Byrne, D., Griffitt, W., Hudgins, W., & Reeves, K. Attitude similarity–dissimilarity and attraction: Generality beyond the college sophomore. *Journal of Social Psychology,* 1969, **79**, 155–161.

Byrne, D., & Lamberth, J. Reinforcement theories and cognitive theories as complementary approaches to the study of attraction. In B. I. Murstein (Ed.), *Theories of love and attraction.* New York: Springer Publ., 1971.

Byrne, D., Lamberth, J., Palmer, J., & London, O. Sequential effects as a function of explicit and implicit interpolated attraction responses. *Journal of Personality and Social Psychology,* 1969 **13**, 70–78.

Byrne, D., London, O., & Griffitt, W. The effect of topic importance and attitude similarity-dissimilarity on attraction in an intrastranger design. *Psychonomic Science,* 1968, **11**, 303–304.

Byrne, D., London, O., & Reeves, K. The effects of physical attractiveness, sex, and attitude similarity on interpersonal attraction. *Journal of Personality,* 1968, **36**, 259–276.

Byrne, D., & Nelson, D. Attraction as a linear function of proportion of positive reinforcements. *Journal of Personality and Social Psychology,* 1965, **1**, 659–663.

Byrne, D., & Rhamey, R. Magnitude of positive and negative reinforcements as a determinant of attraction. *Journal of Personality and Social Psychology,* 1965, **2**, 884–889.

Byrne, D., & Wong, T. J. Racial prejudice, interpersonal attraction, and assumed dissimilarity of attitudes. *Journal of Abnormal and Social Psychology,* 1962, **65**, 246–253.

Byrne, D., Young, R. K., & Griffitt, W. The reinforcement properties of attitude statements. *Journal of Experimental Research in Personality,* 1966, **1**, 266–276.

Darley, J. M., & Berscheid, E. Increased liking as a result of the anticipation of personal contact. *Human Relations,* 1967, **20**, 29–40.

Efran, M. G. Visual interaction and interpersonal attraction. Unpublished doctoral dissertation, University of Texas, 1969.

Festinger, L., A theory of social comparison processes. *Human Relations,* 1954, **7**, 117–140.

Gaynor, C., Lamberth, J., & McCullers, J. C. A developmental study of interpersonal attraction. Unpublished manuscript, University of Oklahoma, 1972.

Golightly, C., Huffman, D. M., & Byrne, D. Liking and loaning. *Journal of Applied Psychology,* 1972, **56**, 521–523.

Gormly, A. V., & Clore, G. L. Attraction, dogmatism, and attitude similarity-dissimilarity. *Journal of Experimental Research in Personality,* 1969, **4**, 9–13.

Gouaux, C. Induced affective states and interpersonal attraction. *Journal of Personality and Social Psychology,* 1971, **20**, 37–43.

Griffitt, W. B. Personality similarity and self-concept as determinants of interpersonal attraction. *Journal of Social Psychology,* 1969, **78**, 137–146.

Griffitt, W. Environmental effects on interpersonal affective behavior: Ambient effective temperature and attraction. *Journal of Personality and Social Psychology,* 1970, **15**, 240–244.

Griffitt, W., & Byrne, D. Procedures in the paradigmatic study of attitude similarity and attraction. *Representative Research in Social Psychology,* 1970, **1**, 33–48.

Griffitt, W., & Guay, P. "Object" evaluation and conditioned affect. *Journal of Experimental Research in Personality*, 1969, **4**, 1–8.

Griffitt, W., & Jackson, T. The influence of information about ability and non-ability on personnel selection decisions. *Psychological Reports*, 1970, **27**, 959–962.

Griffitt, W., & Jackson, T. Simulated jury decisions: The influence of jury-defendent attitude similarity-dissimilarity. *Social Behavior & Personality*, 1973, **1**, 1–7.

Griffitt, W., & Nelson, P. Short term temporal stability of interpersonal attraction. *Psychonomic Science*, 1970, **18**, 119–120.

Griffitt, W., Nelson, J., & Littlepage, G. Old age and response to agreement-disagreement. *Journal of Gerontology*, 1972, **27**, 269–274.

Griffitt, W., & Veitch, R. Hot and crowded: Influences of population density and temperature on interpersonal behavior. *Journal of Personality and Social Psychology*, 1971, **17**, 92–98.

Griffitt, W., May, J., & Veitch, R. Sexual stimulation and interpersonal behavior: Heterosexual evaluative responses, visual behavior, and physical proximity. *Journal of Personality and Social Psychology*, in press.

Haywood, C. H. Heterosexual perception and attraction as a function of personality cues. Unpublished manuscript, University of Texas, 1965.

Heider, F. *The psychology of interpersonal relations*. New York: Wiley, 1958.

Hendrick, C., Bixenstine, V. E., & Hawkins, G. Race versus belief similarity as determinants of attraction: A search for a fair test. *Journal of Personality and Social Psychology*, 1971, **17**, 250–258.

Hendrick, C., & Page, H. A. Self-esteem, attitude similarity, and attraction. *Journal of Personality*, 1970, **38**, 588–601.

Hodges, L. A., & Byrne, D. Verbal dogmatism as a potentiator of intolerance. *Journal of Personality and Social Psychology*, 1972, **21**, 312–317.

Johnson, M. J., & Tesser, A. Some interactive effects of evaluative similarity, structural similarity and type of interpersonal situation on interpersonal attraction. *Journal of Experimental Research in Personality*, 1972, **6**, 154–161.

Jones, E. E., Bell, L., & Aronson, E. The reciprocation of attraction from similar and dissimilar others: A study in person perception and evaluation. In C. C. McClintock (Ed.), *Experimental social pyschology*. New York: Holt, 1972.

Jones, E. E., Stires, L. K., Shaver, K. G., & Harris, V. A. Evaluation of an ingratiator by target persons and bystanders. *Journal of Personality*, 1968, **36**, 349–385.

Kaplan, M. F. Interpersonal attraction as a function of relatedness of similar and dissimilar attitudes. *Journal of Experimental Research in Personality*, 1972, **6**, 17–21.

Kaplan, M. F., & Anderson, N. H. Comparison of information integration and reinforcement models for interpersonal attraction. *Journal of Personality and Social Psychology*, 1973, **28**, 301–312.

Kaplan, M. F., & Olczak, P. V. Attraction toward another as a function of similarity and commonality of attitudes. *Psychological Reports*, 1971, **28**, 515–521.

Kuhn, T. S. *The structure of scientific revolutions*. (2nd ed.) Chicago, Illinois: University of Chicago Press, 1970.

Lamberth, J., Gouaux, C., & Padd, W. The affective eliciting and reducing properties of attraction stimuli. Unpublished manuscript, University of Oklahoma, 1971.

Lerner, M. J., & Becker, S. Interpersonal choice as a function of ascribed similarity and definition of the situation, *Human Relations*, 1962, **15**, 27–34.

Levinger, G. Little sand box and big quarry: Comment on Byrne's paradigmatic spade for research on interpersonal attraction. *Representative Research in Social Psychology*, 1972, **3**, 3–19.

Levinger, G., & Snoek, J. D. *Attraction in relationship: A new look at interpersonal attraction*. New York: General Learning Press, 1972.

Lombardo, J. P., Weiss, R. F., & Stich, M. H. Interpersonal attraction as a function of amount of information supporting the subject's opinions. *Psychonomic Science*, 1971, **24**, 79–80.

Lott, A. J., & Lott, B. E. Group cohesiveness as interpersonal attraction: A review of relationships with antecedent and consequent variables. *Psychological Bulletin*, 1965, **64**, 259–309.

Lott, A. J., & Lott, B. E. Group cohesiveness and individual learning. *Journal of Educational Psychology*, 1966, **57**, 61–73.

Lott, A. J., & Lott, B. E. The power of liking: Consequences of interpersonal attitudes derived from a liberalized view of secondary reinforcement. In L. Berkowitz (Ed.), *Advances in experimental social psychology.* Vol. 6 New York: Academic Press, 1972.

Mitchell, H. E., & Byrne, D. The defendent's dilemma: Effects of jurors' attitudes and authoritarianism on judicial decisions. *Journal of Personality and Social Psychology*, 1973, **25**, 123–129.

Moss, M. K. Social desirability, physical attractiveness, and social choice. Unpublished doctoral dissertation, Kansas State University, 1969.

Nelson, D. Attitude similarity and interpersonal attraction: The approval-cue hypothesis. Paper presented at the Southwestern Psychological Association, Arlington, Texas, May, 1966.

Newcomb, T. M. *The acquaintance process.* New York: Holt, 1961.

Newcomb, T. M. Interpersonal balance. In R. P. Abelson, E. Aronson, W. J. McGuire, T. M. Newcomb, M. J. Rosenberg, & R. H. Tannenbaum (Eds.), *Theories of cognitive consistency: A sourcebook.* Chicago; Illinois: Rand McNally, 1968.

Newcomb, T., & Svehla, G. Intra-family relationships in attitudes. *Sociometry*, 1937, **1**, 180–205.

Novak, D. W., & Lerner, M. J. Rejection as a function of perceived similarity. *Journal of Personality and Social Psychology*, 1968, **9**, 147–152.

Nowicki, S., Jr. Ordinal position, approval motivation and interpersonal attraction. *Journal of Consulting and Clinical Psychology*, 1971, **36**, 265–267.

Palmer, J. A. Vindication, evaluation, and the effect of the stranger's competence on the attitude similarity–attraction function. Unpublished doctoral dissertation, University of Texas, 1969.

Posavac, E. J., & Pasko, S. U. Interpersonal attraction and confidence of attraction ratings as a function of number of attitudes and attitude similarity. *Psychonomic Science*, 1971, **23**, 433–434.

Reagor, P. A., & Clore, G. L. Attraction, test anxiety, and similarity–dissimilarity of test performance. *Psychonomic Science*, 1970, **18**, 219–220.

Rokeach, M., Smith, P. W., & Evans, R. I. Two kinds of prejudice or one? In M. Rokeach (Ed.), *The open and closed mind.* New York: Basic Books, 1960.

Rosenblood, L. Information saliency: An explanation of the set size effect in impression formation and similarity–attraction research. Unpublished doctoral dissertation, Ohio State University, 1970.

Sachs, D. H. The effects of manifest anxiety (drive) and attitude similarity–dissimilarity on attraction. Unpublished Master's thesis, University of Texas, 1969.

Schachter, S. Deviation, rejection and communication. *Journal of Abnormal and Social Psychology*, 1951, **46**, 190–207.

Schooley, M. Personality resemblances among married couples. *Journal of Abnormal and Social Psychology*, 1936, **31**, 340–347.

Schwartz, M. S. Prediction of individual differences in the arousal of the effectance motive and in interpersonal attraction toward a stranger identified with the arousal of the effectance motive. Unpublished doctoral dissertation, University of Texas, 1966.

Skolnick, P. Reactions to personal evaluations: A failure to replicate. *Journal of Personality and Social Psychology*, 1971, **18**, 52–67.

Smith, R. E. Social anxiety as a moderator variable in the attitude similarity-attraction relationship. Presented at the Western Psychological Association, Los Angeles, 1970.

Smith, R. E., Meadow, B. L., & Sisk, T. K. Attitude similarity, interpersonal attraction and evaluative social perception. *Psychonomic Science*, 1970, **18**, 226–227.

Stroebe, W., Insko, C. A., Thompson, V. D., & Layton, B. D. Effects of physical attractiveness, attitude similarity and sex on various aspects of interpersonal attraction. *Journal of Personality and Social Psychology*, 1971, **18**, 79–91.

Taylor, S. E., & Mettee, D. When similarity breeds contempt. *Journal of Personality and Social Psychology*, 1971, **20**, 75–81.

Tesser, A. Evaluative and structural similarity of attitudes as determinants of interpersonal attraction. *Journal of Personality and Social Psychology*, 1971, **18**, 92–96.

Triandis, H. C. A note on Rokeach's theory of prejudice. *Journal of Abnormal and Social Psychology*, 1961, **62**, 184—186.

Veitch, R., & Griffitt, W. Attitude commitment: Its impact on the similarity-attraction relationship. *Bulletin of the Psychonomic Society*, 1973, **1**, 295—297.

Winslow, C. N. A study of the extent of agreement between friends' opinions and their ability to estimate the opinions of each other. *Journal of Social Psychology*, 1937, **8**, 433—442.

13

Social Comparison and Selective Affiliation

LADD WHEELER

Department of Psychology
The University of Rochester
Rochester, New York

I. Introduction

Social comparison theory (Festinger, 1954) states that when objective, nonsocial means of evaluation are not available, a person evaluates his opinions and abilities through comparison with others who have similar opinions and abilities. If one encounters another person with a dissimilar opinion or ability, there is a tendency to change oneself, or to change the other, or to reject the other as a comparison person. The tendency to reject the other is heightened if he is perceived as being different on attributes related to the opinion or ability. For example, a liberal would not compare his opinion on racial equality with the opinion of a member of an anti-black group; nor would most weekend tennis players evaluate their ability through comparison with a varsity star. In the case of opinions, but generally not in the case of abilities, rejection of the other as a comparison person will be accompanied by hostility or derogation.

The overall result of this process of selection and change is to produce social groupings in which there is a high degree of uniformity with respect to the opinions and abilities that are important and relevant to the grouping. People who care about politics will tend to associate with others of similar political views, and tennis players will tend to play against others who are approximately equal in skill. This produces a situation in which everyone feels more or less comfortable and confident. Each participant feels that his ability is adequate and that his opinion is correct.

This is the essence of social comparison theory as stated in 1954, and although there has not been a major restatement, empirical work has broadened the scope of the theory in two ways. First, the theory has been extended to the comparison of emotional states and of aspects of personality. Second, additional motives for comparison have been recognized and investigated. The original theory was limited to what Israel (1956) has called the *informative* aspect of comparison—the need to have an accurate opinion and an accurate appraisal of one's abilities. Israel postulated three other aspects: the wishful, the corroborative, and the normative. The *wishful* aspect refers to comparison with the ideal. The *corroborative* aspect refers to the need to defend a strong belief, and is accomplished by comparison with those so similar that no new information can be obtained, or by comparison with those much worse off than oneself in order to maintain a certain level of self-esteem. The *normative* aspect concerns those situations in which the evaluator observes the behavior of others and models his behavior after others. Israel's classification is not well known and has not generated research; rather, research has drifted in the direction of recognizing autistic motives for comparison—motives unrelated to accurate perception of the world.

Since the last review of the research on social comparison and affiliation (Radloff, 1968), and the last summary of the status of social comparison theory as a whole (Singer, 1966), research has continued to appear steadily, but without any clear pattern or direction. Hopefully, this review will set the stage for a coherent research program.

II. Opinion Comparison and Affiliation

Evidence indicates that, all other things being equal, people are attracted to those who agree with them and tend to reject those who disagree with them (Byrne, 1971). This may or may not have anything to do with social comparison needs. It may simply indicate an avoidance of social disruption, or the liking of a person whom one would expect to reciprocate the liking. What is needed is experimental evidence relating uncertainty about an opinion to needs for affiliation. According to social comparison theory, the greater the uncertainty or unverifiability of an opinion, the greater the need for social evaluation and support. There are several studies supporting this prediction.

Brodbeck (1956) had subjects listen to a persuasive communication arguing for or against the subjects' opinion about wire tapping. She classified subjects from most to least confident as follows: (a) those who heard a communication agreeing with them, (b) those who heard a disagreeing communication, but did not lower their confidence in their original opinion, and (c) those who heard a disagreeing communication and lowered their confidence. Subjects were then asked to choose someone else in the group to discuss the matter with further. As predicted, the less confident the subject, the more likely he was to choose a discussion partner who agreed with him.

Radloff (1961) elicited the opinions of female college students about whether individuals or the government should pay the cost of higher education. He then exposed the coeds to (a) the opinions of the experts, (b) the opinions of other college students, (c) the opinions of high school students, or (d) no information about others' opinions. It was presumed that knowing the opinions of experts would create the greatest certainty and that having no information would produce the least certainty. Following this, each subject indicated the strength of her desire to take part in a discussion group with other female students about financing higher education. The most confident subjects indicated the least desire to participate in such discussions, the least confident subjects indicated the most desire.

Gordon (1966) attempted to contrast affiliation for purposes of comparison, with affiliation for purposes of influencing others. Groups of four subjects were given three case histories, each requiring them to predict the behavior of other people. The subject was given feedback after each of the first two problems showing him to be either correct or incorrect—thereby creating four groups. The subject was then told that the predicted behavior in the third case study had not yet occurred, so that feedback would be limited to differences between subject's prediction and those of the other group members. All conditions were crosscut with feedback of a large discrepancy or a small one. Desire for affiliation was measured by asking subjects if they would be willing to come back for group discussion with the persons in their group.

There was a weak (.10 level) interaction showing that correct individuals wanted to affiliate with an incorrect group (influence); incorrect individuals with a correct group (comparison). There was a strong interaction showing that correct individuals wanted to affiliate when there was a large discrepancy with other group members (influence); incorrect members, when there was a small discrepancy (comparison).

Stapert and Clore (1969) exposed subjects in small groups to the attitudes of bogus strangers. The last stranger to give his attitude always agreed with the subject, but any number from zero to three strangers disagreed before that. Disagreement increased subjects' attraction toward the final stranger, but the number of prior disagreers made no difference.

Byrne, Nelson, and Reeves (1966), in one of the studies on attitude similarity and attraction, found that similarity and attraction were more closely related for nonverifiable issues (beliefs) than for verifiable issues (opinions about facts). Shrauger and Jones (1968) found similar results when groups of three subjects evaluated one another's responses on a social-sensitivity inventory. The subject received general agreement from one peer and disagreement from the other. Furthermore, half the subjects believed the test to be objective and scorable, while the others believed it was subjective and had no correct answers. When the test was believed to be subjective, the disagreeing peer was liked less, and the agreeing peer more, than when the test was believed to be objective. Both these studies show that the more important social comparison is in determining our feeling of accuracy in our opinions, the stronger we desire agreement or similarity.

These few studies clearly demonstrate a direct link between affiliation and the need to evaluate an opinion. They show that uncertainty or unverifiability about an opinion leads to affiliation with, or attraction toward, persons who offer support.

We would ordinarily expect others who are similar in various ways to be more likely to support our opinions. There is some evidence, however, that agreement by dissimilar others may strongly increase our confidence. Goethals and Nelson (1973) exposed subjects to a confederate who agreed with them on either a belief (the relative academic success of two students) or a value (which of the two students they liked more). The confederate was presented as either similar or dissimilar to the subject in terms of his style of judging other people. As predicted, agreement by a similar other increased subjects' confidence on the value issue more than did agreement by the dissimilar other. For the belief issue, on the other hand, agreement by a dissimilar other increased confidence the most.

A belief is a probability statement about reality. Agreement by a dissimilar other is evidence that one's belief is based upon reality, rather than on one's personal biases. A value is, according to Goethals and Nelson, an affective response, and a person's confidence in an affective response should be increased most by a similar other, or what Jones and Gerard (1967) have called a "co-oriented peer."

We normally seek support from similar others because we expect to find support from them and because our normal social interactions tend to be with similar others. It may take a traumatic experience, such as the disconfirmation of an important expectation, before we will actually seek social support from dissimilar others. An example of this is presented in *When Prophesy Fails* (Festinger, Riecken, & Schachter, 1956).

III. Emotional Comparison and Affiliation

Schachter (1959), in his well-known work on anxiety and affiliation, first frightened female college students with the anticipation of electric shock and then allowed them to choose to wait alone or with other subjects for a few minutes prior to the anticipated experience. High-fear subjects (strong shock), more than low-fear subjects (mild shock), chose to wait with other students, but only if the others were also waiting to take part in the same experiment. Schachter interpreted these results as meaning one of two things: (*a*) subjects chose to wait with others in order to reduce their fear; or (*b*) they chose to wait with others in order to compare and to evaluate their level of fear.

Wrightsman (1960) had subjects wait together or alone prior to a stressful experiment and found that, for the group of subjects as a whole, waiting together or alone produced about the same degree of fear reduction. However, groups waiting together, at least those groups with a moderate initial dispersion of fear ratings, became much more homogeneous in fear ratings as a function of the waiting. The comparison group for this conclusion was a statistical combination of subjects waiting alone. Although one cannot logically argue from a result of a behavior to the motivation for the behavior, Wrightsman's experiment is consistent with Schachter's idea that subjects chose to wait together in order to compare their fear with that of others. Comparison should result in homogeneity, with each person using the others as a cue to the appropriate level of fear.

A number of other investigators have attempted to refine the evidence concerning emotional comparison. Gerard and Rabbie (1961) attached electrodes to subjects and gave them false feedback about their physiological responses. Schachter's high- or low-fear instructions were given, and subjects were exposed to meter readings (*a*) showing the strength of their own emotional reactions and those of three other subjects in separate rooms, or (*b*) only their own reactions. A third group received no information. Subjects exposed to low-fear instructions were given a low meter reading, and a high meter reading was given to high-fear subjects. In the condition in which subjects were given information about the emotional reactions of the three other participants, the reactions were about the same as their own. Almost all subjects wanted to wait with other people before receiving the shock, but the investigators had the good sense to measure the strength of this desire. Their measure indicated that subjects who were given information about their own reaction and that of the other subjects had a lesser desire to be with others. Furthermore, subjects exposed to high-fear instructions had a generally greater desire to be with others than subjects in the low-fear condition. These results support Schachter's interpretation, because subjects given information about their own and others' emotional state should have less need to be with others for purposes of comparison.

Gerard (1963), who also gave subjects false physiological feedback by way of meter readings, created uncertainty in some conditions by having a wavy meter needle jump around erratically following high-fear instructions. In the uncertainty condition, there were four situations in regard to the other participants: (*a*) no information (no meter), (*b*) others showing a steady average similar to the average of the subject's erratic reading, (*c*) others showing a steady average greater than the subjects, and (*d*) others showing a steady average less than the subject's. In the certainty condition, subjects were exposed to a steady meter reading of their emotional reaction. There were two information conditions here: (a) no information, and (b) others similar to the subject's.

The results of this experiment were consistent with the social comparison explanation of affiliation under stress. First, the uncertainty condition produced more desire for affiliation than did the certainty condition. Second, within the uncertainty condition, subjects given information that others were similar indicated more desire for affiliation than did subjects who thought the others were dissimilar.

Rabbie (1963) induced uncertainty in yet another way. Using the fear of electric shock paradigm, he told uncertainty subjects that the shocks had been experienced as painful by about one person in four. The certainty subjects were told that the shocks would be painful for everyone. While this manipulation did not produce differences in level of fear, subjects who were not sure whether the shock would be painful were more desirous of being with other subjects. In addition, although subjects were not given any information about their own emotional reactions, they were given meter information that one of the other subjects was very afraid, one moderately afraid, and one only slightly afraid. Subjects tended to choose to wait with the subject closest to their own self-reported levels of fear, except that highly fearful subjects tended to choose moderately fearful partners. This suggests that a desire for fear reduction, as well as a desire for social comparison, plays a role in affiliation under stress.

Social comparison is probably the dominating motive for affiliation under stress. Support for this statement appeared in Schachter's (1959) finding that subjects in the high-anxiety condition wanted to wait with others who were to take part in the same experiment, but not with students merely waiting to see their professors. In an attempt to clarify this result, Zimbardo and Formica (1963) gave subjects the choice between waiting with subjects who were to take part in the experiment or subjects who had already taken part in it. Once again, subjects wanted to wait with others who were going to participate in the experiment. Waiting with others who had been through the experience would have been the logical choice if the subjects had wanted only more information about the experience, or if they had just wanted to reduce their fear. But if they wanted primarily to compare their current emotional state to that of others in the same situation, the results make sense. There are alternative explanations, of course. Those who had gone through the experience may have been actively avoided by the subjects because of (a) not wanting to show fear to those who might not be sympathetic or (b) an expectation that there might be attempts to make them afraid.

Darley and Aronson (1966) attempted in a somewhat different manner to distinguish between fear reduction and social comparison as motives for affiliating under stress. They used Schachter's original instruction to create high-fear and low-fear groups; in addition, they created a high-uncertainty condition by saying that the experiment had just begun and that they had no idea how painful most subjects would find the shocks. After the instructions, the subject was asked to indicate verbally his degree of nervousness on an 11-point scale. Then the other two subjects (confederates) indicated their ratings aloud, one of them choosing a position two points below that of the subject and the other choosing a position one point above the subject. To the extent that fear reduction was a motive for affiliation, the subject should have chosen to wait with the less nervous confederate; to the extent that social comparison was a motive, the subject should have chosen to wait with the more similar, but also more fearful, confederate.

High-fear subjects, as expected, were more interested in waiting with the slightly more fearful confederate. Low-fear subjects showed little preference one way or the other, while subjects in the uncertainty condition preferred the less fearful confederate. It appears that subjects in the uncertainty condition were frightened only very little by the shock instructions, but did not want to chance becoming more frightened by spending time with someone who was frightened. This makes sense, but one difficulty is that in Gerard's (1963) experiment, subjects with a "wavy meter" uncertainty manipulation preferred others who were similar over others who were less fearful. Unfortunately, uncertainty was manipulated differently in the two experiments, and it would be helpful if an analysis could be made of the difference that makes a difference in the two manipulations.

Darley and Aronson (1966) ran an additional high-fear condition in which one confederate reported that she was one point more nervous than the subject, while the other confederate reported exactly the same degree of nervousness as the subject. The results were clearly in accord with social comparison theory: Subjects strongly preferred affiliating with the equally nervous confederate.

The evidence discussed thus far has clearly tended to support a social comparison interpretation of affiliation under stress. However, in all of these studies, subjects were given a choice between waiting alone or waiting with others who were peers. Helmreich and Collins (1967) investigated the possibility, suggested by Janis (1963), that the need for affiliation under stress might be a dependency reaction. In Experiment I of their paper, subjects were given low-, moderate-, or high-fear of shock instructions, with the shock to be delivered while the subjects were attempting to solve some problems. Subjects could choose to work on the problems alone, or in a peer group of three other subjects receiving the same shocks, or in a "leader" group consisting of two other high school students and a graduate student leader. Low- and moderate-fear subjects did not differ in their fear ratings and were thus combined for comparison with high-fear subjects. The results are strangely different from the previously described research. High fear produced a *decrease* in peer-group choice and approximately equivalent increases in alone and leader-group choices. The authors speculated that this could be due to their study having allowed others the choice of a leader group or having used a working-together, as opposed to a waiting-together, situation.

The first study was essentially replicated in Experiment II, and, in additional conditions, subjects were given the same choices (leader, peer, and alone) about waiting prior to the task. The only effect of the manipulations was that high fear produced an increase in choice of leader groups relative to peer groups. This was equally true for the waiting-together and working-together conditions.

If we take these two experiments together and ignore the birth-order data, they show that increasing fear of shock leads to an increased desire for participation in groups, whether working groups or waiting groups, having a designated higher-status leader.

The research discussed in this section can be explained thus: Subjects want some guidance as to how they should feel about an anticipated stressful situation, and their need for guidance is stronger when their own reactions seem to be inconsistent, as in Gerard's wavy meter conditions. Given the choice of waiting alone or with others who are anticipating the same event, they choose others who can supply some information. Given the choice of waiting with others who seem to be responding the same as themselves, or others who seem to be responding differently, they are more inclined to trust similarly responding people as guides for appropriate response. Given a situation in which there is little fear, but in which there might be cause for fear, they will avoid persons who can create fear. Given a situation in which they can obtain information from peers or from older and wiser persons (for example, graduate student leaders), they will trust the older person. And they want comparative, rather than factual, information—witness the lack of interest in waiting with subjects who had already gone through the experiment (Zimbardo & Formica, 1963).

In short, if the situation is so ambiguous that there is the possibility of avoiding fear, choices will be made toward that end. If some degree of fear is obviously unavoidable, choices will be of those individuals who are likely to give the best information about the appropriate level of response.

A. Alone or Together before and during the Fear Manipulation

In Schachter's (1959) original experiments, subjects were in small groups at the time they received their fear instructions. The opportunity to observe the reactions of the other subjects to the instructions may have provided enough information to reduce somewhat the need for affiliation.

To control the amount and type of information about the emotional reactions of others, the subject was alone when he received the fear instructions in experiments by Gerard and Rabbie (1961), Gerard (1963), and Rabbie (1963). If he received information about the others, he received it via meter readings. The results differed from those of Schachter in that most subjects chose to wait with others. The results had to be analyzed in terms of strength of the desire to affiliate, rather than the proportion of subjects choosing to affiliate. It is possible that watching a person react to a stressful stimulus is more informative than receiving scientifically measured information about his emotional response.

Contradictory evidence, however, is provided by Helmreich and Collins (1967). In Experiment I, subjects worked alone on questionnaires for about an hour prior to the fear manipulation, which was also given individually. In Experiment II, subjects worked on questionnaires in groups and were given the fear manipulation in groups. Contrary to what we would expect, subjects in Experiment II showed a much higher desire for affiliation than they did in Experiment I. The investigators suggested that the time spent working on the questionnaires prior to the fear manipulation produced a set of being alone or together. There were, indeed, other differences between Experiments I and II, but none that would seem to produce a strong difference in the desire for affiliation. It is possible that observing others react to the fear instructions reduces the need for affiliation for purposes of comparison, and that being alone prior to receiving the fear instructions creates a set for solitude. In the Helmreich and Collins research, the latter effect may have overwhelmed the former. Another possibility is that weak manipulations, as all the fear manipulations are, cannot be expected to produce totally consistent results.

B. Emotional Arousal Leading to Decreased Affiliation

In a well-known experiment, Sarnoff and Zimbardo (1961) replicated Schachter's (1959) results relating affiliation and fear of electric shock. But in another set of conditions, they demonstrated that oral anxiety, produced by instructions to suck on objects associated with infantile oral behavior, reduced affiliative tendencies. Presumably, subjects did not want to expose their anxiety to others and be embarrassed by it.

There may be a basic difference between fear of an objectively frightening stimulus, such as electric shock, and fear of a stimulus situation reinvoking childhood conflicts. Or it may be that any emotional response that seems to the subject to be too extreme for the circumstances leads to the choice of solitude. Or perhaps the high-anxiety subjects in the Sarnoff and Zimbardo (1961) experiment were similar to the high-uncertainty subjects in the Darley and Aronson (1966) experiment—they did not want to take the chance of being made anxious by other people.

Some relevant evidence on this last point was provided by Gerard and Rabbie (1961). Although high-fear-of-shock subjects generally wanted to wait with other people, the *most* fearful of these subjects chose to wait alone. Also, Sheatsley and Feldman (1964) reported that respondents who were most disturbed by the assassination of John Kennedy were most desirous of being alone in the days following the killing.

A more recent experiment (Buck & Parke, 1972), using looking behavior during the waiting period as the measure of affiliation, attempted an extended replication of the Sarnoff and Zimbardo (1961) finding that embarrassment produces less affiliative behavior than does fear of electric shock. Having created fear by threat of electric shock and embarrassment by the sucking manipulation, they assigned subjects to wait alone, or to wait with a neutral other person, or to wait with a supportive other person. There was no difference in affiliation between embarrassment and fear subjects who waited with a supportive other, but the Sarnoff and Zimbardo results were replicated for subjects who waited with a neutral other. This suggested that lessened affiliation under embarrassment conditions may be due to a lessened expectation of support from others.

Latané and Wheeler (1966) interviewed young naval recruits after recruits had participated in clean-up operations at the site of the wreckage of a commercial airplane. Some of the men were involved only in traffic control around the site, while others searched for and put together pieces of human bodies. Men were independently classified as more or less emotional, using Lykken's Activity Preference Inventory (1957). Highly emotional men who had participated in the body search indicated little desire to talk to others in the week following the crash and had an extremely negative attitude toward airplanes. They also wrote fewer letters home. Nonemotional men, on the other hand, indicated a greater desire to talk and wrote more letters home if they had participated in the body search than if they had not.

Taken together, these studies suggest that it is not so much the type of emotion produced, but rather the intensity, that determines the choice between affiliation or solitude. The relationship may be mediated by (*a*) the desire to avoid embarrassment or a depressive reaction; (*b*) the absence of any need to reduce uncertainty; or (*c*) a desire to avoid having the emotional response further stimulated.

IV. Ability Comparison and Affiliation

According to social comparison theory, uncertainty about the level of an ability should lead to affiliation. Some evidence on this thesis has been provided by Singer and Shockley (1965). Subjects were given a score that represented their ability on a perceptual task. They were then given (*a*) no further information or (*b*) a distribution of the scores of other group members. Thereafter, they were told that there would be a waiting period before continuation of the experiment and were asked to choose between waiting with others and waiting alone. As predicted, subjects without information were most affiliative.

Another prediction from the theory is that persons who are markedly different from others in ability (either superior or inferior) will be less accurate and stable in self-evaluation than persons of average ability who have more similar others available for comparison.

This idea was nicely demonstrated by Radloff (1966b). In Experiment I, subjects were given a series of pretest trials on a variable-speed pursuit rotor. Each subject was told that he was superior, average, or inferior compared to the other three subjects in his group. Subjects were then asked to estimate their performance after each trial. Rank-order correlations over these trials between actual and estimated performance showed that subjects told that they were average were more accurate than other subjects.

Experiment II was a replication of Experiment I, with a single exception: instead of being given information about the abilities of 3 other people, subjects were given information about 200 other people (distributed normally). Thus, superior, average, and inferior subjects occupied the same position on the feedback scale as in Experiment I, but superior (or inferior) subjects saw 17—22 other subjects as being better (or worse) than themselves. In other words, nonaverage subjects were part of a distribution containing even more extreme cases.

The prediction that nonaverage subjects would now be as accurate in evaluating their performance as were average subjects was not supported. Average subjects continued to be markedly more accurate. (Providing a few similar others did not eliminate the inaccuracy of self-evaluation produced by being nonaverage in performance.) One possibility, of course, is that the hypothesis is wrong. Another is that providing performance data on 200 subjects had opposing effects: (*a*) the intended effect of providing nonaverage subjects with some similar comparison persons and (*b*) an unintended effect of making the nonaverage subjects feel more deviant by showing that they were at either the tenth or ninetieth percentile.

In Experiment III, subjects were given their own scores in the same position of the feedback scale as in Experiments I and II, but the 200 other scores they saw were in the shape of a negatively skewed distribution for average and superior subjects; no inferior group was included. This placed superior subjects at about the seventy-fifth percentile and told them that some other subjects were markedly superior to them. (In Experiment I, superior subjects had estimated themselves to be at the sixty-fifth percentile, and in Experiment II, they could see that they were at the ninetieth percentile.)

The results were as predicted. Superior subjects were as accurate in evaluating their performance as were average subjects, and more accurate than superior and inferior subjects in Experiments I and II.

A possible implication of these experiments for affiliation is that people with a nonaverage level of ability, and particularly those with superior ability, should have very strong preferences for affiliation with similar others. An average person, on the other hand, will find adequate comparison others more or less by chance, and should be less motivated to seek particular others for comparison.

Hakmiller (1966b) has investigated the relation between agreement, perceived similarity, and comparison choice. Groups of four subjects were given a paper-and-pencil Abstract Social Reasoning Ability Test (ASRAT; 0—90 scale) and were asked to provide a "base-line" estimate of their own and other subjects' ASRAT scores. In the two series of social judgment tasks which followed, subjects indicated their own decisions and received controlled feedback of the other subjects' "decisions" via a Crutchfield apparatus. In Series I, two experimental conditions were created: one-concurrer (on a majority of the trials one of the others independently concurred with the subject's own decision) and two-concurrer (on a majority of the trials, the two others independently concurred). At the end of this series, subjects again estimated their own and others' ASRAT scores. As expected, subjects in the two-concurrer condition were more likely to increase estimates of their own ASRAT scores, and all subjects perceived themselves to be more similar in ASRAT score to concurrers than to nonconcurrers.

In Series II, the social judgment problems were to be answered with one of five alternative decisions, rather than the agree—disagree decision format of Series I. In addition, subjects were not automatically shown the decision of all other subjects, as before, but had to choose to see the response of only one.

Since subjects in the one-concurrer condition should have a greater need for self-evaluation, they should show more preference for the concurrer than for the nonconcurrers. This effect was clear in the data. Subjects in the two-concurrer condition, on the other hand, showed no systematic preference.

In summary, agreement by two others, as opposed to one other, increased confidence and reduced need for self-evaluation so that the choice of a comparison other was random.

These few studies show that uncertainty about an ability leads to affiliation, preferably with someone who will increase one's confidence in the ability; and that being widely discrepant in ability from available comparison others produces inaccuracy in evaluating one's performance.

V. Personality Comparison and Affiliation

A recent line of work involves giving a subject a personality test, providing him with a bogus score on the test, and then allowing him to choose to see the score of someone various ranks above or below himself in the group in which he has been tested. Within this general framework, a number of things can be varied, such as the desirability and importance of the personality trait, the subject's position within the group, the subject's expectations about his score, and the amount and type of information provided about the other group members' characteristics and scores. The dependent variable is the score the subject chooses to see in order to evaluate his own score.

The major reason for using personality traits is that subjects conceive of personality traits as more or less enduring characteristics, similar to abilities, and that the traits can be described as either desirable or undesirable. Thus, Festinger's (1954) postulated unidirectional drive upward in the comparison of abilities can be investigated as a directional drive upward *or* downward in the comparison of personality traits, giving the postulated drive more generality.

This section first deals with experiments using the same basic experimental paradigm. Subjects are given a paper-and-pencil test measuring either intellectual flexibility, described in glowing terms, or intellectual rigidity, an awful thing. Subjects are tested in groups of nine, and each subject is presumably given one of the identification letters A through I. In reality, each subject is assigned the same identification letter. The tests are quickly scored, and the identification letters are written on a blackboard in rank order from highest score obtained to lowest score obtained. The identification letter assigned to each subject is placed at rank five in the nine-person group. Each subject is given privately the numerical score he presumably obtained on the test, in all cases, 310. The subject is then told that he can choose to see the numerical score obtained by the person at any one rank in the group. Before seeing the chosen score, the subject is allowed a second choice to be seen in addition to the first. His choices are the major dependent variable. Will he choose to compare his to similar scores (those close to him in the rank order) or to dissimilar scores? Will he choose to compare his score with those more desirable than his (higher in the rank order of intellectual flexibility and lower in the rank order of intellectual rigidity) or those less desirable than his?

Two variations of this situation produced quite different results and are discussed separately. The *no-range* variation is exactly as described above—the subject is given no information concerning the numerical values of the highest and lowest scores obtained in the group, or even about what scores are possible. In the *range* variation, all subjects are told that the highest score in the group is 550–600 and that the lowest score between 25 and 75.

A. The No-Range Variation

There are 28 possible first- and second-choice combinations a subject can make (ignoring order), so that the chance percentage of subjects making any two-choice combination is 3.6%.

In 14 different no-range variations that have been run (Wheeler *et al.*, 1969; Gruder, 1971; Gruder, personal communication), only one two-choice combination has regularly exceeded chance expectation of 3.6%. This is the combination of choosing to see the highest and lowest scores in the group. The percentages selecting this option were: 50, 53, 53, 54, 54, 54, 55, 60, 68, 70, 72, 75, 78, 78. In view of the fact that sample sizes were frequently small and that replications were deliberately different in various ways, these data are quite consistent. And in comparison with the chance expectation of 3.6%, they are remarkably strong.

These results make sense as attempts to establish the end anchors of the scale, but in some ways they are surprising. In such an ambiguous situation, one might expect subjects to reject as comparison persons those who are extremely divergent and to concentrate on exploring similarity. But it seems apparent from the data that similarity is of little concern when the boundaries of the scale are unknown.

B. The Range Variation

Both Wheeler *et al.* (1969) and Gruder (1971) ran conditions identical to those described in the preceding section, except that subjects were given range information before they made their choice. They were told that the highest score was between 550 and 600 and that the lowest score was between 25 and 75. This placed the subject's score of 310 at about the arithmetic average and was consistent with his being in the middle of the rank order. In both experiments, the trait was described as intellectual flexibility for half the subjects and as rigidity for the other half.

The two experiments differed somewhat with regard to the percentage choosing the two most similar others. However, because they were replications, I attribute the difference between them to error and combine them. The following statements refer to the combination.

Of the subjects, 22% chose the highest and lowest scores, while 26% chose to see the two most similar scores. Chance expectation for each of these combinations was 3.6%, and no other combination of choices significantly exceeded chance.

These results are surprising if one assumes that subjects are seeking information for purposes of self-evaluation. Knowing within a small range of 50 points the scores of the most extreme people in the group, and knowing within a large range of more than 230 points, the scores of the most similar others, why is there an almost equally strong tendency to choose the extreme others? For purposes of seeking information, it would seem that choice of extreme others would not be very functional. Brehm (personal communication) suggested that choice of the extremes was the only way to avoid meaningful information. In a similar vein, Arrowood and Friend (1969) noted that choice of a similar other could be very disappointing —showing the subject to be much worse than the person better off than he and not much different from the person not as well off. This seems to be a plausible explanation: the self-esteem of some subjects was threatened, and they avoided the possibility of further damaging information. It would be interesting to see if there are personality differences between the two groups. Presumably, subjects choosing similar others were seeking an accurate self-evaluation.

The only experiment directly testing the effect of threat to self-esteem was conducted by Hakmiller (1966b). The trait allegedly being measured by physiological responses to TAT slides was "hostility to one's parents," and it was described as extremely neurotic (high threat) or rather positive (low threat). All subjects had previously taken the MMP1, which was said to be a predictor of the more precise physiological measure. Each subject was given predictive information from the MMP1 that he would score at the fifth rank in a group of six subjects; in other words, the subject was led to expect a fairly low hostility score. After the physiological measurement, the subject was given a true score of either 60 or 80 on a 0—100 scale; in other words, a much higher score than expected. The subject was then allowed to see the physiological score of one other person in the predicted rank order.

The results were that 54% of the high-threat subjects, compared to 22% of the low-threat subjects, chose to see the score of the person predicted to be most hostile. Thus, ego threat led to comparison with extremely divergent others, presumably because this was the safest comparison.

Using a rather different situation, Hakmiller (unpublished mimeo) has replicated this effect, finding that subjects in a threat condition chose to compare with others of distinctly inferior status, while subjects in a nonthreat condition chose to compare with others of superior status.

In both of Hakmiller's experiments, the subject was given unexpectedly negative information about himself and precomparison information that someone else in the group was likely to be even worse off than he. By choosing to see the score of that person, the subject could confirm the fact that he did not have the worst score in the group.

In the experiments described so far in this section, subjects were allowed to see only the numerical scores of other people. In an experiment by Israel (1956), subjects were allowed to choose others with whom they wanted to interact.

Subjects were tested in groups of six for their ability to make logical inferences. The subject was told that his score was 7 on a 0–15 scale, and that the scores of the other group members were 12, 8.67, 7, 5.33, and 2. Subjects were then told that next week they were to engage in a group task involving logical inference, and that they would be paid the same regardless of the group's performance, but that the task required only four people out of the six. Consequently, each subject was asked to rank the other group members according to how much he would like to work with them. The other with a score of 8.67 was most preferred, and the other with a score of 12 was second most preferred. The other with a score of 7, the same as the subject's, received a chance ranking. Israel pointed out that social comparison theory would predict rejection of score 12 and greater acceptance of score 7 because of greater similarity.

In another condition in Israel's experiment, the subject and those with scores of 12 and 2 were of higher social status than the other subjects. Israel predicted from social comparison theory an increase in preference for others of social status similar to the subject. This prediction was not confirmed. In this experiment, at least, similarity on attributes other than the one to be evaluated did not affect comparison choices.

C. *Personality Similarity and Liking*

Jellison and Zeisset (1969) arranged a situation in which the subject shared a personality trait with another person—the trait being either desirable or undesirable, and either common or uncommon in the population. A shared desirable trait produced more attraction when it was uncommon, while a shared undesirable trait resulted in less attraction when uncommon. Presumably, similarity on an uncommon trait is more salient than similarity on a common trait.

Novak and Lerner (1968) created a situation in which the subject found himself to be similar or dissimilar to either a normal individual or a former mental patient. The similar normal person was most liked and approached, while the similar mental patient was most avoided. In a further investigation of this effect, Taylor and Mettee (1971) found that a pleasant similar other was liked more than a pleasant dissimilar other, but that an obnoxious similar other was disliked more than an obnoxious dissimilar other. Taylor and Mettee argued that similarity of personality makes another person more salient for additional comparisons and thereby produces stronger affective responses toward that person, regardless of direction.

It could be maintained that similarity with an obnoxious person produces anxiety that one may also be obnoxious, and that the anxiety is reduced by derogation of the person. In the Taylor and Mettee study, however, subjects who were assured that they did not possess the obnoxious trait nevertheless derogated the similar partner severely.

An alternative explanation (Cooper & Jones, 1969) is that subjects will derogate a similar obnoxious partner solely to disassociate themselves from the partner in the experimenter's eyes. This cannot account for the results of the Taylor and Mettee study, however, because subjects believed that neither their personality scores, nor their relationship to the partner, would be known by the experimenter.

It appears that Taylor and Mettee (1971) are correct in arguing that some personality similarity with another person makes him more salient as a comparison person and more able to elicit positive or negative affective responses. And the Jellison and Zeisset (1969) data shows that similarity on an uncommon trait is more salient than on a common trait.

VI. Individual Differences in Social Comparison

Schachter's (1959) serendipitous finding that first-born children were both more frightened and affiliative under high-fear instructions than later-born children has produced a renaissance in birth-order research. [For a full discussion, see Sampson (1965).] I limit this discussion to emotional comparison because evidence on other dimensions is extremely spotty. Schachter compared first-borns and later-borns who were equally and highly anxious and found that first-borns indicated greater desire for affiliation under stress. Anxiety did not increase the tendency for affiliation among later-borns.

Schachter's basic argument was that one of the motives for affiliation is self-evaluation of an emotional state. His strongest evidence was Wrightsman's (1960) experiment on the effects of affiliation after emotional arousal. Wrightsman frightened subjects with threat of a glucose injection, measured anxiety, assigned subjects to wait 5 min either alone or in groups of four, and then measured anxiety again. Although first-borns were not more anxious than later-borns after the fear instructions, waiting with others reduced their anxiety, but not that of the later-borns. Wrightsman also constructed an index of homogeneity, indicating the extent to which the four group members became more similar in anxiety rating as a function of waiting together. Compared with statistically created groups who waited alone, subjects who waited together showed marked increases in homogeneity—which can be taken as an indication that they were using one another for purposes of comparison and self-evaluation. The burr in the spinach is that there were no birth-order differences. If later-borns have the same tendency to compare their emotions as do first-borns, why do they persistently refuse to affiliate when anxious? This finding weakens the evidence for self-evaluation as a motive for affiliation in Schachter's (1959) work.

Nevertheless, other investigators have reported that first-borns are more affiliative under stress than later-borns (Darley & Aronson, 1966, Gerard & Rabbie, 1961; Zimbardo & Formica, 1963). The difference in preference between first-borns and later-borns in the Darley and Aronson experiment was truly miniscule (0.12 on a 7.00-point scale), but statistically significant. In contrast, the same experimenters reported a mean difference of 2.0 in the uncertainty condition—showing that first-borns want to be alone, supposedly not taking any chances of having their fear increased.

Additional evidence for the birth-order affiliation relationship was obtained by Helmreich and Collins (1967). First, they found no difference in fear ratings (of shock) between first-borns and later-borns (nor did Darley and Aronson). And in Experiment I, they found no difference in affiliative choices. In Experiment II, however, with increasing fear, first-borns increased preference for waiting with peers, rather than alone, while later-borns moved slightly toward a preference for waiting alone. Latané, Eckman, and Joy (1966) had dyads work on a task during which (*a*) both were shocked, (*b*) one was shocked, or (*c*) neither was shocked. The greatest liking for the partner was among first-borns when both were shocked. This was not due to fear or pain reduction because shared-shock subjects found the shock *most* disturbing and unpleasant. The best guess is that first-borns sharing shock with another person like the other because of the satisfaction of self-evaluative needs.

Buck and Parke (1972), using looking behavior during the waiting period as the measure of affiliation, found that first-borns affiliated more with a supportive other than with a neutral other, both under conditions of embarrassment and fear. Later-borns did not. First-born affiliators were higher in self-esteem than were were first-born nonaffiliators. There was no difference for later-borns. The authors suggested that first-borns affiliate under stress for purposes of "esteem-enhancement" and that this would be a particularly strong need for first-borns with high self-esteem.

In summary, first-born children seem to have stronger needs for emotional comparison than do later-borns when the situation is clearly stressful. When there is some doubt about whether the situation will be stressful, as in the Darley and Aronson (1966) uncertainty condition, first-borns may avoid emotional comparison.

Aside from birth order, there have been few reports of individual differences related to comparison needs. Only one study seems relevant to this context. Shapiro and Alexander (1969) used the Schachter paradigm and found no birth-order differences. However, they found a clear relationship, under high fear only, between affiliation and extroversion—introversion as measured by the Myers—Briggs instrument. The interpretation was that both groups of subjects were trying to evaluate their anxiety *in order to* reduce it, but that they had different methods of doing so. The introvert needs to escape distractions and examine his feelings, while the extrovert uses social comparison.

Using Spielberger's A-Trait measure of chronic anxiety, Teichman (1971) found that emotional arousal created by the prospect of self-disclosure or by the sucking manipulation decreased desire for affiliation for high A-Trait subjects, but increased it for low A-Trait subjects. This suggests a curvilinear relationship between arousal and affiliation consistent with the results reported by Latané and Wheeler (1966).

VII. Conclusions

A. *Summary*

Investigators in the area of social comparison have not carried on the systematic limited-variations-on-a-theme research that Byrne and his colleagues call "paradigmatic" (see Chapters 7 and 12 in this volume). Nor are they particularly wedded to Festinger's 1954 theory. The spirit of work on the subject is best characterized as a search for situations that may lead to new insights. Under such conditions, summaries cannot be neat, but matters appear to stand this way in regard to the major concerns of this chapter.

1. *Opinions.*   There is evidence that uncertainty about an opinion leads to affiliation; that individuals doubting the accuracy of their opinion choose to affiliate with others in agreement with them and with others whom they expect to be correct; that prior disagreement increases attraction toward someone who agrees; and that agreement is most closely related to attraction if the issues are nonverifiable and nonobjective. Agreement by a dissimilar other increases confidence more than agreement by a similar other on belief issues: the opposite is true for questions of value.

2. *Emotions.*   In general, the evidence indicates that emotional arousal (usually fear) leads to affiliation with others in the same situation and with others who are responding with the same emotional intensity. This tendency is heightened if the subject's reactions appear to be erratic. Being with others results in a homogenization of emotional intensity within the group.

There is some evidence that older and wiser people are preferable to peers for purposes of emotional comparison.

Under some circumstances, emotional arousal leads to a reduction in affiliation. These circumstances have not been adequately specified, but they may include motives such as embarrassment about one's emotional response, depressive reactions, lack of emotional support, and fear of further emotional stimulation.

3. *Abilities.*   There is evidence that uncertainty about an ability leads to affiliation, particularly with someone of similar ability; and that people of nonaverage ability have difficulty making an accurate judgment of their performance and may, therefore, have unusually strong affiliative preferences.

4. *Personality traits.*   If subjects are uncertain about the possible or actual range of a personality trait, they choose to learn about other subjects at the extremes.

If they know the upper and lower limits of obtained scores, there is a shift toward learning about the most similar scores, but there is still a tendency to choose extreme scores even when they provide very little information. This is probably a defensive choice. There is additional evidence that when subjects receive unexpectedly negative information about themselves, they want to learn about someone who is worse off.

Some personality similarity with another person makes him more salient as a comparison person and more able to elicit positive or negative affective responses.

5. *Individual differences.*   There is some evidence that first-born children have stronger affiliative needs under emotional arousal than do later-borns. First-borns also like those with whom they share stress, and they avoid affiliation when it might stimulate negative emotions. First-borns affiliate more than later borns with both a supportive and a neutral other under both conditions of embarrassment and fear. First-borns who affiliate were found in one study to have a higher level of self-esteem than those who did not affiliate.

Extroverts have been found to be more affiliative under stress than introverts (though not under normal conditions). Finally, individuals low in chronic anxiety affiliated more in a study when they were emotionally aroused due to the anticipation of self-disclosure or the sucking manipulation; the reverse was found for individuals high in chronic anxiety.

B. Afterthoughts

Most of the research discussed in this chapter involved performing certain manipulations upon the subject and then giving him certain alternative choices. In effect, the subject must choose to wait under one condition or the other, to learn the judgment of one person or another, or to see the score of one person or another. We seldom ask ourselves if our manipulations have actually created any need for comparison. Yet the phenomenon of social comparison is most interesting when viewed as an active seeking for information appropriate to one's need state. Experimental situations in which the subject must expend some effort to obtain comparison information seem to be particularly imperative.

A second difficulty with the usual experimental situation is that subjects are generally highly similar to one another on a variety of dimensions. Thus, most research on the effects of similarity—dissimilarity in social comparison is done against a background of pervasive similarity. In some situation, this may create an exaggerated picture of the effects of dissimilarity; in others, an attenuated picture. In the no-range variations conducted by Wheeler *et al.* (1969) and Gruder (1971), subjects chose to compare with extremely dissimilar others. Entirely different results might be obtained from groups such as those composed of people of different ages, sexes, and occupational levels.

Acknowledgments

I thank Karl Hakmiller and Roland Radloff for their comments on an earlier draft of this chapter. In addition, Larry Gruder and Hakmiller supplied unpublished data.

References

Arrowood, A. J., & Friend, R. Other factors determining the choice of a comparison other. *Journal of Experimental social Psychology*, 1969, **5**, 233–239.

Brodbeck, M. The role of small groups in mediating the effects of propaganda. *Journal of Abnormal and Social Psychology*, 1956, **52**, 166–170.

Buck, R. W., and Parke, R. D. Behavioral and physiological response to the presence of a friendly or neutral person in two types of stressful situations. *Journal of Personality and Social Psychology*, 1972, 24, **2**, 143–153.

Byrne, D. *The attraction paradigm*. New York: Academic Press, 1971.

Byrne, D., Nelson, D., & Reeves, K. Effect of consensual validation and invalidation on attraction as a function of verifiability. *Journal of Experimental Social Psychology*, 1966, **2**, 98–107.

Cooper, J., & Jones, E. E. Opinion divergence as a strategy to avoid being miscast. *Journal of Personality and Social Psychology*, 1969, **13**, 23–30.

Darley, J. M., & Aronson, E. Self-evaluation vs. anxiety reduction as determinants of the fear-affiliation relationship. *Journal of Experimental Social Psychology, Supplement 1*, 1966, 66–79.

Festinger, L. A theory of social comparison processes. *Human Relations*, 1954, **7**, 117–140.

Festinger, L., Riecken, H., & Schachter, S. *When prophecy fails*. Minneapolis, Minnesota: University of Minnesota Press, 1956.

Gerard, H. B. Emotional uncertainty and social comparison. *Journal of Abnormal and Social Psychology*, 1963, **66**, 568–573.

Gerard, H. B., & Rabbie, J. M. Fear and social comparison. *Journal of Abnormal and Social Psychology*, 1961, **62**, 586–592.

Goethals, G. R., & Nelson, R. E. Similarity in the influence process: The belief-value distinction. *Journal of Personality and Social Psychology*, 1973, **25**, 117–122.

Gordon, B. F. Influence and social comparison as motives for affiliation. *Journal of Experimental Social Psychology*, 1966, Supplement 1, 55–56.

Gruder, C. L. Determinants of social comparison choices. *Journal of Experimental and Social Psychology*, 1971, **7**, 473–489.

Hakmiller, K. L. Need for self-evaluation, perceived similarity and comparison choice. *Journal of Experimental Social Psychology, Supplement 1*, 1966, 49–54.   (a)

Hakmiller, K. L. Threat as a determinant of downward comparison. *Journal of Experimental Social Psychology, Supplement 1*, 1966, 32–39.   (b)

Hakmiller, K. L. Defensive social comparison and assumed similarity. Unpublished mimeo, University of Connecticut.

Helmreich, R. L. & Collins, B. E. Situational determinants of affiliative preference under stress. *Journal of Personality and Social Psychology*, 1967, **6**, 79–85.

Israel, J. Self-evaluation and rejection in groups: Three experimental studies and a conceptual outline. Stockholm: Almquist & Wiksell, 1956.

Janis, I. L. Group identification under conditions of external danger. *British Journal of Medical Psychology*, 1963, **36**, 227–238.

Jellison, J. M., & Zeisset, P. T. Attraction as a function of the commonality and desirability of a trait shared by others. *Journal of Personality and Social Psychology*, 1969, **11**, 115–120.

Jones, E. E., & Gerard, H. B. *Foundations of social psychology*. New York: Wiley, 1967.

Latané, B., Eckman, J., & Joy, V. Shared stress and interpersonal attraction. *Journal of Experimental Social Psychology*, Supplement 1, 1966, 80—94.

Latané, B., & Wheeler, L. Emotionality and reactions to disaster. *Journal of Experimental Social Psychology*, Supplement 1, 1966, 95—102.

Lykken, D. T. A study of anxiety in the sociopathic personality. *Journal of Abnormal and Social Psychology*, 1957, **55**, 6—10.

Novak, D. W., & Lerner, M. J. Rejection as a consequence of perceived similarity. *Journal of Personality and Social Psychology*, 1968, **9**, 147—152.

Rabbie, J. M. Differential preference for companionship under threat. *Journal of Abnormal and Social Psychology*, 1963, **67**, 643—648.

Radloff, R. Opinion evaluation and affiliation. *Journal of Abnormal and Social Psychology*, 1961, **62**, 578—585.

Radloff, R. Social comparison and ability evaluation. *Journal of Experimental Social Psychology*, Supplement 1, 1966, 6—26.

Radloff, R. Affiliation and social comparison. In E. Borgatta & W. W. Lambert (Eds.), *Handbook of personality theory and research*. Chicago: Rand McNally, 1968.

Sampson, E. E. The study of ordinal position: Antecedents and outcomes. In B. A. Maher (Ed.), *Progress in experimental personality research*. Vol. 2. New York: Academic Press, 1965.

Sarnoff, I., & Zimbardo, P. G. Anxiety, fear and social affiliation. *Journal of Abnormal and Social Psychology*, 1961, **62**, 356—363.

Schachter, S. *The psychology of affiliation*. Stanford; California: Stanford University Press, 1959.

Shapiro, K. J., & Alexander, I. E. Extraversion—introversion, affiliation and anxiety. *Journal of Personality*, 1969, **37**, 387—406.

Sheatsley, P. B., & Feldman, J. J. The assassination of President Kennedy. *Public Opinion Quarterly*, 1964, **28**, 195—215.

Shrauger, J. S., & Jones, S. C. Social Validation and interpersonal evaluations. *Journal of Experimental Social Psychology*, 1968, **4**, 315—323.

Singer, J. E. Social comparison—progress and issues. *Journal of Experimental Social Psychology*, Supplement 1, 1966, 103—110.

Singer, J. E., & Shockley, V. L., Ability and affiliation. *Journal of Personality and Social Psychology*, 1965, **1**, 95—100.

Stapert, J. C., & Clore, G. L. Attraction and disagreement-produced arousal. *Journal of Personality and Social Psychology*, 1969, *13*, **1**, 64—69.

Taylor, S. E., & Mettee, D. R. When similarity breeds contempt. *Journal of Personality and Social Psychology*, 1971, **20**, 175—181.

Teichman, Y. Emotional arousal and affiliation. Unpublished doctoral dissertation, University of Missouri, Columbia, 1971.

Wheeler, L. Shaver, K. G., Jones, R. A., Goethals, G. R., Cooper, J., Robinson, J. E., Gruder, C. L., & Butzine, K. W. Factors determining choice of a comparison other. *Journal of Experimental Social Psychology*, 1969, **5**, 2, 219—232.

Wrightsman, L. S., Jr. Effects of waiting with others on changes in levels of left anxiety. *Journal of Abnormal and Social Psychology*, 1960, **6i**, 216—222.

Zimbardo, P. G., & Formica, R. Emotional comparison and self-esteem as determinants of affiliation. Journal of Personality, *1963*, **31**, 141—162.

14

Social Psychology of Justice and Interpersonal Attraction

MELVIN LERNER

Department of Psychology
University of Waterloo
Waterloo, Ontario, Canada

I. Introduction: Some Theoretical Considerations

Two areas of concern in this chapter are attraction and the social psychology of justice. The concept of justice employed here and the manner in which it fits into the person's psychological processes has been described more completely in an earlier paper (Lerner, 1971a). In brief, the person's concern with justice arises partly from learning and internalizing the societal norms. More important, however, the desire for justice is viewed as an extension of the more basic commitment to deserving one's own outcomes. This commitment to deserving appears to be the natural result of a familiar developmental process.

Typically, each child moves toward acting on the "reality," rather than the "pleasure" principle. The child, through encounters with the environment and his developing cognitive structure, abandons the use of the power he has at hand to satisfy his strongest immediate desires. Instead, he develops a *personal contract* with himself to give up the directly obtainable gratifications and to undertake certain efforts and suffer self-deprivation on the assumption that these behaviors will be followed by more desired outcomes. As he matures, this personal *contract* is extended to larger areas of his life. In other words, through the normal developmental process, people come to structure their lives around "deserving" their desired outcomes, with deserving here defined as meeting the appropriate preconditions for a given outcome. Of course, the "society" into which one is born defines what particular investments or preconditions are appropriate for any given outcome.

The person's concern with justice and the deserving of others arises mainly from the desire to maintain the validity of his personal contract, his ability to deserve his own outcomes. The personal contract, however, is never completely firm and binding. Situations arise in which the person wants to let go and just do what feels good. Such impulses, which he usually attempts to control for his general welfare, are never completely eliminated. At the same time, it is apparent that the validity of his personal contract is based on the nature of his world. Acting in tems of deserving requires faith that the environment is so constructed that if one makes the required investments of effort and self-deprivation, the appropriate outcomes will, in fact, occur. The awareness of someone else in the same "world" *not* getting what he deserves will be a threat to the contract's validity, especially when the observer has to control his own impulses to take and grab or do what feels good at the time. As long as he wishes to continue living by and maintaining his personal contract, the person will care about whether he lives in a just world or not. Of course, he recognizes that not every human lives in his "world." And so, the perception of same or different world will mediate his reaction to the fate of others.

In addition to this factor of generalizing the implications of another person's fate to the viability of one's personal contract, there are more direct reasons for the interest in justice for others. We recognize very early in our lives that there are other people in our world who want to deserve the same outcomes we wish. How are these conflicting interests to be resolved so that each person's trust in his environment is maintained? We also learn that it is sometimes possible to achieve otherwise unattainable outcomes by working with others. How are the fruits of these joint endeavors to be distributed? If we wish to maintain our personal contract, rules based on deserving and justice must be developed to distribute these generally desired resources. Clearly, our ability to deserve our own outcomes depends upon the behavior of others in our world and the outcomes of such behavior.

The socialization process in our society ties considerations of justice and deserving to the self-concept and public esteem of its members. Part of being a "good" person is deserving one's outcomes and treating others justly. A good citizen will not only behave according to rules of justice and deserving, but will also take his share of responsibility in seeing to it that others are treated justly—that justice prevails in the society. Failure to do so can lead to formal or informal public sanctions and self-punishment—loss of self-esteem, guilt, and similar consequences.

It is also important to recognize that in our society various forms of justice—rules for determining how the desired pool of resources are to be deserved—have developed. In some situations, rules of *competition* prevail so that the contestant's performance decides who is deserving. The needs, costs, and investments of the participants are irrelevant. In other situations, particularly where there is a perception of essential "similarity," rules of parity prevail. Each person in the unit deserves the same outcome regardless of differences in investment or needs (Sampson, 1969). Justice often takes the form of *"equity,"* where there is a joint endeavor and where the resources are capable of being distributed. Under this form of justice each person's share is proportional to his investments and costs (Adams, 1963; Homans, 1961). The greater the investments and/or costs, the greater the share. Finally, there is the justice that arises from the recognition of "identity"—seeing others as an extension of one's self—all are members of one family. In this situation *Marxian justice* applies: the resources are distributed to meet the most pressing needs of all the members, without regard to their individual contribution.

The crucial point is that no single formula for defining what is a just outcome for a person will fit the variety of situations in which justice considerations appear. In some cases, investments and costs will be relevant, in others, only the needs of the people involved, and in yet others, performance is the sole criterion.

Considerably less needs to be said here about the notions of attraction and liking. Other contributors to this volume are more qualified to speak directly to this issue. The assumption employed here is that (*a*) direct expressions of positive affect toward another, (*b*) expressions of intention or desire to approach or avoid another, (*c*) ascriptions of evaluative attributes to another person (he is mature, likable, selfish, cold), and (*d*) acts or expressions of desire to benefit or harm another person are all indices of attraction.

Essentially, attraction or liking is an attitude in the traditional sense of a predisposition to act based on an affective, cognitive, and dispositional set toward someone. This attitude can vary along a dimension of positive–negative and can be assessed by tapping any of the components. Persons acquainted with the attitude–behavior literature will appreciate the complexity of social encounters *in vivo* and recognize the risks in making this assumption.

II. Attraction and the Perception of Justice

With these theoretical notions as a background we turn our attention first to the relation between attraction and justice, leaving for later sections the way attraction is tied to the reaction against injustice. Although it is somewhat artificial to separate issues of justice and injustice, the emphasis in the former will be on the way people decide consciously or otherwise what constitutes a just fate for someone. It is only after discussing the relation between this decision process and interpersonal attraction that we can consider profitable what happens when the conditions of justice are not met—there is the perception of an injustice.

In this section, then, we look first at the way the person's beliefs concerning social causality and the kinds of people who populate his word affect whether he sees someone's fate as merited. Most often these beliefs contain criteria for evaluating other people who are good, attractive, bad, unlikable. As we see in the second part of this section, such attitudes can be a determinant of the form of justice which is seen as applicable in a given situation. Finally, we focus on attraction toward a "victim" as a "dependent variable," an outcome, when considerations of justice and deserving have been satisfied.

A. Belief Systems

There are various beliefs prevalent in our society that preclude viewing someone who is deprived or suffering as the victim of an injustice. The remnants of the "psychology of the frontier" and the myth of open mobility, which assume equal and limitless opportunity for all, provide support for the idea of many citizens having "earned" their own way. Thus, some people believe that the stricken or underprivileged caused their own fate and so are not suffering unjustly. MacDonald (1971) has shown that people who hold beliefs in line with the Protestant ethic— success comes through effort and self-deprivation—are prone to condemn persons who live in poverty. Similarly, Lerner and Elkinton (1970) found that within the upper social strata, those who believe that people have great control over their fate were most likely to condemn people who accepted welfare payments. Their view of the world held poverty as a self-inflicted fate.

Also, from the perspective of some religious systems, the suffering victim is placed in the category of a sinner who caused his own fate. Sometimes he is not regarded as a victim at all; he will be more than rewarded on earth or in heaven for his temporary suffering: God is just. The results of two surveys (Quinney, 1964; Lerner & Elkinton, 1970) tend to confirm these observations. People who held fundamentalist religious beliefs were likely to have a "fatalistic" orientation to the world and either to see no victims of injustice in our society or to see people receiving welfare as getting more than they deserve.

Rubin and Peplau (1971) asked people directly about the extent to which they believed in a just world. They found that a person's responses to questions about these beliefs were predictive of his reaction to victims in a variety of contexts. The most compelling finding was that those people who scored high on the "belief in a just world" scale were relatively unsympathetic toward their fellows who were unlucky in the draft lottery. This relationship appeared even though the respondents were themselves draft-age males vulnerable to the same lottery.

Clearly, the most insidious beliefs which shape the way we decide what someone deserves are "stereotypes" learned through socialization. Women, blacks, Jews, poor people, the mentally ill are all "known" to have their special attributes and needs; therefore, a fate that would be inappropriate for us (be unjust) might be viewed as quite appropriate for them: "They don't have the same feelings, goals, values that we do. *They* are a different kind of people. *They* are happy living like that. *They* don't have our worries" (Stein, Hardyck, & Smith, 1965; Allport, 1954).

The dimensions or categories for describing the types of beliefs discussed here, religious fundamentalism, Protestant ethic, belief-in-a-just-world, minority stereotypes, are only some of the more obvious examples of justice-related beliefs. By the time a person reaches adulthood, he has developed sets of assumptions, beliefs, and "truisms," which enable him to come to terms more or less successfully with the world around him. He knows who the good guys and bad guys are. He knows what he and others need to do to make their way in the world. He has developed ways of understanding and dealing with success and failure, and with the pleasurable and the frightening things that can happen to people. According to the theoretical model presented in this chapter, these beliefs will in part be shaped by the person's desire for justice. However, once adopted by the person they will, to a great extent, determine when and how he sees issues of justice and deserving in his world.

B. Forms of Justice

The earlier description of the forms of justice—parity, equity, Marxist, and legal—implied a close link between the particular form elicited in a given encounter and the attitudes of the participants toward each other. In this section we look more closely at the forms of justice and especially the evidence concerning the way the interpersonal attitudes, with the implication of attraction, are a determinant of the criteria employed in deciding what is just and deserved, the form of justice applied.

The most influential theoretical contributions to the social psychology of justice (Adams, 1963; Homans, 1961) have employed a model of justice based on the criterion of investment or "input." A person's outcomes are just if they are proportional to his investment, that is, to the resources he has given up or expended to achieve the outcome. This formula implies a comparison or referent. Each person deserves as much as someone who has provided the same input, but deserves proportionally more or less than other people who have invested more or less. This notion is intuitively compelling and, together with related assumptions, has generated a series of interesting studies (Walster, Berscheid, & Walster, 1973).

On the other hand, people often use criteria other than "investment" in deciding what is deserved. All of us have had the experience of engaging in joint endeavors where the credo of "all for one and one for all—share and share alike" held sway, though not necessarily explicitly. Sampson (1969), in attempting to understand the differences between the "equality" and the "equity" form of justice, suggested that the latter developed from the Protestant ethic philosophy. He provided good evidence that even in bargaining situations, both forms of justice appear, and that it would be "unwise parsimony" to consider equality or the justice of "parity," as we defined it here, as a special case of equity.

Leventhal and Anderson (1970) reported evidence that "parity" tends to be stronger than equity in determining the distribution of rewards by preschool children. The findings of Messe (1971) and Leventhal and Lane (1970) suggested that this preference may change with age so that by adulthood the norm of distributive justice, equity, is more salient in bargaining situations.

The best hunch, however, from common observation is that where there is high attraction among the participants—friends—one is most likely to find the justice of sharing equally, rather than according to some assessment of each person's investment. The data in support of this view, however, are equivocal. For example, Morgan and Sawyer (1967), in a bargaining situation employing pairs of preadolescent boys, found that "equality" of outcomes was much more often preferred to an "equity" solution, regardless of the whether the pair entered the situation as friends or nonfriends. Strict equality was the most desired outcome.

Two other studies directly examined the effect of attraction for the other person on the desired form of justice. Wicker and Bushweiler (1970) employed a questionnaire booklet containing hypothetical situations. They varied the relative value of the work (more, less, or the same) and outcomes in terms of pay (more, less, the same) of the subject and a hypothetical "co-worker," whom he either liked or disliked. The subjects rated the "pleasantness' and "fairness" of the 18 possible combinations. The most one can say on the basis of the rather complex and somewhat confusing findings generated by this design is that, in general, equity considerations predominated in judgments of both pleasantness and fairness. Also, there was a fairly solid main effect of liking for the other on both of these judgments. Certainly there was no confirmation of the hypothesis that equality is preferred over equity among people who like each other.

Benton (1971), on the other hand, provided us with some encouraging evidence. He had one member of a pair of preadolescent youngsters either fail or win the right for both of them to play with a pair of more or less preferred toys. An equity hypothesis would state that the subject who won the opportunity for the pair had invested the most and so the desirability of his outcome should be proportionally greater. Benton found that girls, whether they were "winners" or "losers," preferred equal outcome for themselves and their partners *if* the partner was a friend, or at least neutral in attractiveness. This alternative was also preferred by most of the boys when they were the losers. On the other hand, the winning girls who were paired with nonfriends, and most of the winning males, followed an equity solution. This is rather weak, but provides some support for the hypothesis that attraction—friendship—leads people to prefer, and to see as just, equal outcomes, rather than outcomes based on equity considerations; that is, each person's contributions or costs.

The Marxist form of justice, which ignores a person's investments in favor of his needs in judging what he deserves, has received considerable attention recently from social psychologists, but in another context. Berkowitz (Berkowitz & Daniels,

1963; Berkowitz & Friedman, 1967) and his students have generated an interesting line of research, which has demonstrated that people will expend energy and effort—that is, will work for—others who are dependent upon them for the attainment of a legitimate goal. The greater the dependent other's need, the greater will be the person's efforts on his behalf.

In all fairness, it should be pointed out that this research was designed to illustrate the presence and importance of a "norm of social responsibility." By what right, then, do we consider the findings relevant to questions of justice?

To begin with, there is evidence that the norm of social responsibility is internationalized and does not require an immediate audience to be effective. In other words, there is an "ought" force implied, and it is likely that a person would feel "guilt" for failing to help someone who is dependent upon him for meeting some legitimate need. This moral force, however, does not apply discriminately to all the needs of all others. There is a judgment, usually tacit, concerning the legitimacy of the dependent person's need. If he brought about his own state of need unnecessarily, then he is not likely to be helped (Scholper & Matthews, 1965; Simmons & Lerner, 1968). Or, if he already has received more than he is entitled to, he is less likely to be helped (Simmons & Lerner, 1968). This reasoning resembles the familiar distinction often made between the deserving and undeserving poor.

Reverting again to common observation, this form of justice seems to predominate among people who have an "identification" with one another. The kind of perception of identity usually found among members of a family seems to underly the justice of needs. A variant of this is the kind of identity one can feel with the position another person is in—"that could be me." In our society, this is most often seen outside the family unit in reactions to people who have been stricken through some fortuitous act of nature and who, as a consequence, are unable to participate as members of society and thereby earn and deserve their own outcomes. The awareness of identity with such a stricken or, in the case of a child, undeveloped member implies an obligation to help him reach a state of independence so that he can become a full participant in society. We feel that we owe him this. It is only right and just.

Leventhal, studying the effect of equity considerations in experimental situations, has produced data relevant to this issue. For example, in one study (Leventhal & Weiss, 1971) it was found that when subjects were given the opportunity to divide joint earnings with a co-worker, they gave more money to the partner when his monthly income was relatively low than when it was high. This was based on the perception of comparative need.

In another study (Leventhal & Whiteside, 1971), subjects were given the task of allocating grades as compensation for performance. Predictably, it was found that the better the performance, the higher the grade allocated—justice of equity. However, when the subjects believed that the allocation of grades could serve an important function in helping a deficient student's development, equity considerations were set aside. The poorest performers were given the higher grades, apparently as a form of therapeutic incentive. The major point here is that in these studies the subjects' "helping" behavior was determined primarily by considerations of what the needy person deserved, what he was entitled to have from them.

There is at least one additional form of justice which has an extremely important effect on our behavior. The justice of rules and laws includes by far the most structured and consciously pervasive aspect of justice in our lives. In effect, law and rules provide the framework for each person to pursue his own private interests. Once the rules are established, then each person no longer need be concerned with issues such as needs or investments in determining what another person deserves. Of course, if someone violates the rules, this is an injustice; however, outcomes acquired within the rules are considered deserved and just. The law itself may be judged as unjust, but this position, too, is based upon applying the other forms of justice, (Marxian, parity, equity) to human events which are at that point governed by the justice of the law.

Legalistic justice is often relatively inhuman and unsatisfying in comparison with those forms where the participants' needs or investments are taken into consideration. It is the last alternative before resorting to naked power as a way of deciding who gets what. The hunch offered here, then, is that legalistic justice will be employed most naturally in situations where the participants are strangers or contestants with clear conflict of interest.

There is some evidence, that fits these conjectures. For example, Lerner and Becker (1965) found that when people anticipated entering into a competitive situation in which they or the other person would compete for all the desired resources—only one of them would get everything—they elected to interact with someone who was "different" from them in personality and values, rather than with someone who was similar. When the interaction was to be cooperative and supportive, they chose the similar other. Krauss (1966) also found that high similarity and attraction between participants led to avoidance of a competing strategy in favor of a cooperative one.

One study related fairly directly to the view of justice which most of us employ when faced with a situation where two or more people, with equally legitimate claims, desire the same outcome. The natural law seems to be that of pursuing one's "justified self interest" when it is a "him or me" situation. It is entirely legitimate to do what one can within the rules to get the desired outcome, the promotion, the beautiful woman, the best job, or the only job left. In this experiment (Lerner & Lichtman, 1968) two undergraduate women learned that one of them would have to receive severe electric shocks, while the other would not. One of them then was given the choice of the condition she preferred—via manipulations surrounding a table of random numbers. The vast majority of these women chose the desirable condition for themselves, ascribed responsibility to themselves for their own fortunate fate and the other person's suffering, and yet showed few, if any, signs of guilt. The outcomes were fair and just. As some of them stated, "Anyone would have". Their acts were justified by the justice of legitimate competition, the justice of distributing outcomes according to performance under the rules of laws.

By way of summary, it is reasonably clear that people do apply differing forms of justice in various contexts. The equity form, where a person's outcomes are defined by his relative contribution, appears where an exchange takes place between people who have no particular regard for one another: the market place. The evidence also supported the hypothesis that where there is a perceived identity, tied often to feelings of sympathy and empathy, the Marxian justice of need takes precedence over equity or parity considerations. Less clearly supported is the notion that were positive relationships predominate, as well as a high degree of interdependence such as one finds among team members, the justice of parity will be applied. On the other hand, it does appear that close interdependence for goal attainment when accompanied by negative feelings leads to the adoption of legalistic forms of justice, where the letter of the "law" is followed regardless of the needs and "inputs" of the members.

C. Attribution of Responsibility

The perception of justice or injustice in a situation is closely tied to the process of ascribing causality, or blame, for the fates of the people involved. There is reason to believe that a person's concern with justice and deserving may influence the way he construes the causality of important outcomes in his environment. Most of us would prefer to believe people earn their fates, rather than that they are determined by mysterious or uncontrollable factors. For the sake of our security we may assign blame to fit the outcomes (Chaikin & Darley, 1971; Jenkins & Ward, 1965; Lerner, 1965; Simmons & Lerner, 1968; Walster, 1966; 1967). There are, of course, many factors that influence the way we attribute causality and blame. Fortunately, there are excellent theoretical models and programs of ongoing research which deal directly with the attribution process (see Jones & Davis, 1965; Kelley, 1967); therefore, for the most part, we do not deal with this issue here.

We take up the discussion, instead, at the point where the observer (P) is aware that someone (O) is suffering an undesirable fate. Something has happened to O, or failed to happen, which P identifies as leading to a result he would want to avoid. The major hypothesis is that if P sees O as causally responsible for his own fate—he brought it on himself—considerations of justice and deserving will be minimized, if not eliminated entirely. P's reaction to O, then, will be determined primarily by the instrumental value of the event for P. With consideration of deserving set aside or satisfied, P's reaction to O will be positive, if what O did creates a positive outcome for P; that is, O has exhibited behavior which P values, or has helped P obtain a goal. On the other hand, P's attraction will be lowered if O has violated one of P's values or hindered his achieving a goal. And finally, P will react neutrally, rather indifferently, if there are no direct implications for his goals or values.

There is reasonably good evidence available in support of these hypotheses. Some of the effects were illustrated in a study by Lerner and Matthews (1967). When a person drew a slip which designated that she, rather than the subject, receive electric shocks, her attractiveness to the subject was enhanced. Even though it was clear that she could not have done this good deed intentionally, the "saved" subject seemed to react with a glow of gratitude. However, when their fates were the same as in the previous condition, subject received no shock and other was shocked, but with the difference that the subject drew her own slip and the other drew her shock-designating slip (their fates were noncontingent), the subject's attraction toward the other was unaffected and remained at a neutral point.

The enhancing effect appeared again in a situation that typically elicits the perception of an "innocent victim's" suffering. In this study (Lerner, 1968), subjects were recruited to participate in a experiment to examine the way a person acts under stress. The subjects were instructed to draw slips out of a bowl. They then learned that one of the slips designated the person who was to receive a severe electric shock as part of an experiment said to be related to learning nonsense syllables, while the others would observe. In this case, the victim was seen as having "caused" her own suffering by the act of drawing the "fatal" slip, and, as in the previous experiment, the subject-observers showed an enhanced attraction toward the victim who had saved them from suffering. Apparently, they felt no guilt, and the simplest interpretation is that they felt grateful to the victim.

The lowering of attraction to someone who caused his own deprivation was shown in at least two different experimental paradigms. Schopler and Matthews (1965) found that subject were reluctant to help someone dependent upon them when that person was seen as the careless cause of his state of need. In an experiment reported by Simmons and Lerner (1968), subjects were given the opportunity to work for another person. In some cases they learned that the person had been highly rewarded in a previous task, and in others, that he had received considerably less than the usual reward. Subsequent evidence supported the interpretation that the subjects tended to blame the others for their prior fates. "Winners" were seen as having earned their success and were, therefore, viewed as desirable people, worthy of more help. The losers were seen as unworthy of help.

III. Reactions to Injustice: The Effects on Attraction

A. *Attraction toward the Inflictor*

Edmund Cahn (1949), the noted legal scholar, trying to understand the pervasiveness and strength of the "sense of injustice," described it as:

> ... the sympathetic reaction of outrage, horror, shock, resentment, and anger, those affections of the viscera and abnormal secretions of the adrenals that prepare the human animal to resist attack. Nature has thus equipped all men to regard injustice to another as personal aggression [p. 24].*

*Reprinted by permission of New York University Press from *The Sense of Injustice: An Anthropocentric View of Law* by Edmond N. Cahn. Copyright © 1949 by New York University.

Whatever the underlying psychophysiological processes may be, it is reasonable to expect that people will usually react negatively to someone who has aroused these feelings of "outrage." This reaction can take many forms, including the lowering of attraction to the inflictor of the injustice. After all, he did something that violated our values and beliefs and potentially threatened the achievement of our goals, if not the very basis of our security.

The evidence gathered in the laboratory confirms what appears to happen in the normal course of events. In one experimental paradigm, two partners contributed equally to the earning of a joint payment. When subjects were led to believe that their partner took considerably more than a half share for himself, they rated him as relatively dishonest and not fairminded. The more the distribution diverged from "equal"—the more the partner kept for himself—the more negative were his ratings. (Leventhal & Bergman, 1969).

Ross, Thibaut, and Evenbeck (1971) reported that subjects who felt unjustly deprived because they were given outcomers lower than they felt they deserved reacted by "punishing" their inflictors when given the opportunity. Although the experimenters reported no attraction data, it is reasonable to assume that the victim's retaliation by administering painful noise and withholding desirable outcomes was associated with descreased liking for the inflictors of the injustice.

The most convincing data available on the reaction to persons who violate the justice of "need" was generated by research designed to study the consequences of being made to feel guilty. Freedman, Wallington, and Bless (1967) found that subjects who inadvertently caused harm to, failed to meet the legitimate needs of, someone dependent upon them for help were more willing to engage in unpleasant altruistic acts, that is, to help someone else in need at some cost to themselves. Regan (1971) provided additional support for the "guilt" interpretation of the increased willingness to help by showing that expiation and "confession" eliminated the altruistic response. It is likely that the subjects in these experiments went through the familiar experience of lowering their attraction to themselves, that is, they felt guilty when they perceived themselves as having committed an injustice.

The recent public enthusiasm for "law and order" may reflect the anxiety that a legally privileged elite feels when its victims clamor for justice outside the law. It may also stem quite genuinely from nothing more self-interested than the desire for justice. Lerner and Lichtman (1968) found that undergraduate women reacted negatively to persons who for their own advantage violated or attempted to violate rules laid down by the experimenter. After a "fair" way of deciding which of each pair was to receive electric shocks was employed, some winning subjects were led to believe that their partner had asked for special considerations because of her great fear of shock. In effect, the loser invoked the justice of need *after* having learned the outcome of the stipulated procedure. Interestingly enough, the "winners" usually gave in to the plea, but they showed a significant devaluing of the other. In effect, the other was seen as a poor sport, and/or weakling, worthy of help and pity, but not of respect.

Kaufmann (1970) tapped the way considerations of legal justice affect social judgments. He constructed a series of hypothetical situations in which a bystander failed to intervene to prevent a potentially harmful event. He varied whether the harm actually occurred, or whether it was prevented by a change in situation subsequent to the failure to help, and whether or not there was a law that required a bystander to provide the aid. For our purposes it is important that the bystander was judged to be more worthy of punishment and a less pleasant person if he violated a law by not intervening than if there was no law involved. He was judged to be most undesirable if he failed to comply with the law and the consequences turned out to be serious, rather than trivial.

B. Attraction toward the Victim

There is also a substantial amount of evidence that documents the fact that people often condemn the innocent victim of injustice. Berscheid, Walster, and their colleagues have shown that members of women's church groups devalue others whom they have inadvertently caused to get fewer trading stamps than they presumably deserved (Berscheid & Walster, 1967; Berscheid, Walster, & Barclay, 1969). They also reported that subjects who discovered that they had been in error in publicly condemning another person increased, or at least maintained, their condemnation (Walster & Prestholdt, 1966; Walster, Walster, Abranams, & Brown, 1966). These findings are in line with those of Davis and Jones (1960) and Glass (1964), which suggest that people who cause others harm may derogate their victims, especially if they are not able to correct the injustice.

The person need not be the agent of harm in order to show condemnation of an innocent victim. In a series of related experiments, people observed an experimenter administer severe electric shocks to a subject who quite innocently and unknowingly had agreed to participate in a study of human learning, only to discover that she was to be shocked. The observers were innocent themselves in the sense that they were participating in an entirely separate experiment—looking for cues of emotional arousal—and physically separated from the "event" so that it was impossible to intervene.

When given the opportunity, the vast majority of subjects "voted" to end the victim's suffering and have her compensated. When they had no such power, however, the majority reduced the attractiveness of the "innocent" victim. The degree of condemnation was determined by the amount of injustice they were seeing: the longer the suffering, the greater the condemnation; the more noble and good the victim appeared to be prior to the suffering, the greater the condemnation. If, on the other hand, they believed that the victim would be compensated sufficiently by the experimenter in the end, there was no condemnation (Lerner & Simmons, 1966; Lerner, 1970, 1971).

How generalizable are such findings? The studies reported in this section were conducted with undergraduates and graduate students from the health professions at the University of Kentucky Piliavin and her colleagues (Piliavin, Hardyck, & Vadim, 1967; Simons & Piliavin, 1972) showed similar derogation effects in this experimental situation using high school students in Berkeley, California and University of Pennsylvania undergraduates. Johnson and Dickinson (1971) found that housewives from a low socioeconomic area in one of the Canadian Maritime Provinces also denigrated the innocent victim in this situation.

Experiments employing other situations have yielded comparable results. MacDonald (1971) confronted his subjects with the report of a stabbing. The more innocent he portrayed the victim to be, the less responsible for his suffering, the lower his rated attractiveness. Lincoln and Levinger (1972) found that subjects condemned a black man who was the innocent victim of a policeman's attack. But this occurred only if the subjects were unable to make a public complaint designed to correct the injustice.

C. Condemning the Inflictor and/or Rejecting the Victim

We have looked at evidence indicating that the inflictor of an injustice may be condemned and that the victim may be denigrated. Under what conditions do either or both of these reactions occur?

We can best provide an answer to this question by again examining the process presumed to be taking place in the observer. One assumption has been that each of us would like to believe we live in a just world where we can earn and deserve our fates. We have designed our lives, based our present security and plans for the future on this more or less tentatively held belief. We have also learned and accepted the ideas that justice is good, injustice bad; good people act justly and uphold justice for others. And, of course, we would like to believe we are good people. When we are confronted with an injustice, and become aware of an inflictor and a victim, our security is threatened, and possibly our self-esteem. Our sense of responsibility to maintain justice for others, the good citizen image, may also be made salient.

An easy way to meet these threats and demands is to persuade ourselves that, in fact, no injustice actually occurs. This would be the case if the victim's suffering is deserved, if he is discovered to be a harm doer, a rule violator, or a social "criminal." As it happens, many of the negative attributes and ways of devaluing another person in our culture imply rule-breaking and harmful behavior toward others. Defining another as "immature," "cold," "stingy," "uncooperative," "unfriendly," or "cruel" implies that this person has in the past acted, and is likely to continue in the future to act, in ways that cause other people to suffer. To cause him to suffer, then, is not an injustice, but a punishment appropriate to an inflictor of harm.

An important aspect of this perception or "distortion" of the attributes of the victim (or of any other person) is the relative ease with which it can be accomplished. This is probably because it is partly based on reality. Everyone has at times acted in ways that merit one or more of these harm-doing attributes. All that is required to see the victim's suffering as just is the selective perception of, or emphasis on, particular acts or characteristics which are in part applicable to all of us. The "distortion," then, is less inventive than it is selective emphasis. This process is similar to the strategy by which the fortune teller persuades her customers that she knows them intimately without ever having met them before.

The rejection of the innocent victim has immediate advantages for meeting the observer's concerns about justice. Once the rejection is accomplished, the observer can again rest easy—his world is just, and he need not feel impelled to act to reestablish justice or to maintain his self-esteem. He can resume going about his own business. Obviously, though, this reaction may be quite dysfunctional in the long run. Deciding that threatening agents do not exist in one's world does not, unfortunately, make them go away. German citizens who persuaded themselves that the seemingly innocent persons who were suddenly imprisoned in concentration camps must have been guilty of some crime ultimately paid for avoiding the perception of injustice (Betteleheim, 1943).

Condemning the inflictor follows naturally from the perception of an injustice. This response does not require "distortions" of any sort. It has the advantage of being veridical and prepares the observer to take action that may be valuable to him and the society. It can, however, be relatively costly. Actions taken to correct an injustice require that the person interrupt his normal, everyday activities and interests. They also may cost him valued resources. In the meantime, until justice is reestablished and possibly thereafter, the observer must live with the anger and sense of compassion and threat associated with being aware of an injustice in his world. Even if the inflictor is punished and the victim compensated, the world may never appear quite as safe and secure again. Finally, if the observer discovers that justice will not be reestablished, condemning the inflictor may do nothing to decrease his fear and a sense of threat or outrage.

In virtually all situations, the inflictor and victim will not be blank stimuli, defined only by the nature of their roles in the perceived injustice. They will have other identities, characteristics, and relations to the perceiver. Some of these factors will play an important part, not only in how justice is defined, as discussed earlier in the chapter, but also in the observer's reaction to the injustice.

For example, if the observer is "identified with"—feels he belongs to, likes very much, or is in the "same boat"—one of the participants, it is not likely that he will condemn or reject him. If the observer is identified with the victim, and does not condemn him as a way of reestablishing justice, he will probably devalue the inflictor. The victim has the best chance of being condemned, of course, when the observer is identified with the inflictor.

Available data provide interesting elaborations on these hypotheses. Chaikin and Darley (1971) had subjects witness an event in which a work supervisor "accidently" bumped a table, ruining the product of his worker's good efforts. The experimenters varied the observers's impression as to the seriousness of this "accident" for the worker. In one case, the consequences were severe—they led to the worker's not receiving the payment he had worked for and deserved. In the other, the consequences were milder and not unjust. The experimenters also varied the observers' initial set toward the supervisor and worker by letting half of the subjects believe that they would be supervisors in the next situation and the other half believe that they would be workers. This was done to establish the perceptions of "identity" based on "that could be me."

As one might have expected, subjects who anticipated being workers themselves found the supervisor to be relatively incompetent and blameworthy, especially if the consequences involved a clear injustice for the worker. On the other hand, subjects who anticipated being in the shoes of the supervisor found the supervisor less blameworthy and more competent. This reaction was increased in the condition where the consequences were most severe for the worker. In this instance of clear injustice, supervisor-to-be subjects also condemned the worker as an undesirable person. Once they saw the injustice to the worker, and perceived the inflicting supervisor as innocent and competent, the desire for justice pushed them to find the worker to be an undesirable person who deserved to suffer.

Stokols and Schopler (1973) found similar, but not quite as strong, effects when the observer expected to interact in a cooperative context with the victim. The innocent victim, in this case of rape, was less likely to be devalued if the subject anticipated later interaction with her. Without this basis of "identification," the victim was denigrated, even though seen as clearly innocent. Aderman and Berkowitz (1970) used experimental instructions developed by Stotland (1969) to create in an observer different kinds of identification with a helper or dependent person. They reported that subjects will be differentially influenced in the subsequent responses if they attend to the helper or the supplicant.

Baxter, Lerner, and Miller (1965) offered a modification of the reported tendency for people to "identify with" and to prefer "winners" rather than "losers" (Bandura, Ross, & Ross, 1963). In their study, the subjects were to be taught a new language, Esperanto, by a student instructor. As part of the experiment, they heard the experimenter interview their prospective teacher. The subjects then indicated the degree of similarity in personal attributes between themselves and their future teacher. There were three experimental conditions: (*a*) the subject expected to be shocked for incorrect answers, (*b*) rewarded for correct answers, or (*c*) receive neutral feedback. The subjects were further divided on the basis of self-reports into those who came from authoritarian or relatively nonauthoritarian homes. Subjects from authoritarian homes ascribed the most similarity to the instructor when they were to be shocked. Subjects from nonauthoritarian homes felt this kind of identity with an instructor when they were going to receive positive reinforcements, but not when they were to receive punishment. Whether the underlying mechanism for these findings involves something as complex as "identification with the aggressor" or something as simple as the tendency to expect in the future that which has occurred in the past, the study tells us something about "who" is likely to identify with a victim and who with a victimizer.

The discussion of identification brings us back to the "guilt" and harm-doing literature. When the perceiver sees himself as an inflictor of injury, it is safe to assume that, other things being equal, his prior identifications are fairly solidly with himself. At the least, he prefers to think well of himself, rather than otherwise. A review of the literature concerning the way the harm doer tries to deal with the various contingencies and alternatives, is found in a paper by Walster, Berscheid, and Walster (1970).

It is worth pointing out here, though, that the variable of prior identification with, or attitude toward, the participants can be applied directly to cases where the observer is the inflictor of harm. Glass (1964) has shown that a harm doer will condemn and reject a person whom he caused to suffer severe electric shocks. However, the inflictor will not do this if, prior to the event, his self-esteem has been lowered significantly. In other words, if the person has been led to dislike himself at least temporally, he will not resort to construing his victim an undesirable person who deserves his fate. Presumably, the inflictor, who dislikes himself at this point, will accept his own culpability.

D. Justice and Guilt

We should not conclude the discussion of harm-doing without examining the relation between an observer's reaction—his desire for justice and need to believe in a just world—and the reaction of a harm doer—feeling of guilt, shame, lowered self-esteem, anticipated public sanction, etc. It could be assumed that in some primitive, autistic way, all people feel responsible for everything that happens in their world and that, therefore, the perception of any injustice carries with it a sense of personal responsibility, involvement, and guilt.

Alternatively, the guilt associated with harm-doing can be considered merely a special case of the effect of witnessing an injustice, the only difference being that the observer sees himself as the inflictor. Determinants of his subsequent reaction, such as prior attraction or identification with the inflictor, will be present in greater or lesser degree.

The notion of an omnipresent, pervasive guilt engendered by the suffering of any person does not fit what we know about the behavior of "normal" adults. The evidence indicates that harm doers, as well as innocent witnesses, will not feel guilty or compelled to act as the result of the suffering of any human being. As Tannenbaum and Gaer (1965) illustrated, a person's reaction can vary from elation and joy to indifference or indignation, depending upon whether he believes that the victim *deserved* his fate. The psychology of justice determines who is seen as a victim, what emotional responses follow, and what the participant's reactions will be.

Relevant data emerge from a study by Rawlings (1970), which involved having observers witness a person inflicting severe shock on another person. She found that in the next situation, both the observers and the inflictors were more willing to divide shocks equally with someone else than were subjects who had no prior experience of witnessing harm. The findings, presented as examples of the effect of "reactive guilt" and "anticipatory guilt" on altruistic behavior, failed to confirm the assumption that the subjects felt "guilt" of any sort.

Data collected by Kisch showed that the "altruistic" behavior of those who had witnessed or caused the suffering in this situation probably represented an attempt to be just and fair. Rawling's "altruists" merely divided the shock equally with a partner, whereas the responses of Kisch's subjects [and data from Midlarsky (1971)] showed that if a person were trying to be altruistic or make up for some sense of being a harm doer, he would take considerably more than half of the shock impact in the next situation. Again, his subjects indicated that if they wished to be fair or divide the shock impact according to what would be just, they would take half for themselves, as did Rawlings's subjects.

Regan (1971) looked specifically at the question of whether a harm doer's reaction may be the result of both the arousal of guilt *and* the attempt to bolster his belief in a just world. The imaginative technique she applied to this problem was to give both harm doers and witnesses of harm—the spoiling of a graduate student's research—the opportunity to help a third party in legitimate need. Half of the subjects in both of these conditions were accorded the opportunity to confess and to receive expiation of their responsibility or guilt. Observers gave the most help to the dependent third person, with the magnitude of their response reduced slightly, but not significantly, by a previous guilt-reducing confession. Harm doers, however, helped the third party *only* if they had not first confessed. Confession eliminated their need to help.

The problems that the desire for justice pose for a harm doer apparently are not different in kind from those faced by the innocent observer of an injustice. To be sure, the harm doer primarily will be concerned with his self-esteem, while in most cases, this consideration will be less important for the witness. There is some evidence that intense focusing on one's own needs may preclude, at least momentarily, any concern with the fate of another, including whether his fate is just or not (Berkowitz, 1970). Conceivably there will also be some situations where a harm doer will be so overwhelmed with guilt as to be unconcerned with anything but the saving of his own soul.

E. Additional Consequences of "Identification" with the Victim

Victims of chronic debilitating conditions often acquire a stigma which brands them as relatively inferior beings (Farina & Ring, 1965; Richardson, Hastorf, Goodman, & Dornbush, 1961). Most of us, however, are aware that the majority of these people are innocent victims, usually of forces beyond anyone's control. Given an awareness of the innocence of the victims and the compelling demand of their need, how do we respond?

The combination of our own vulnerability and their clear innocence may promote identification with such victims so that we feel sympathetic toward them, impelled to help, rather than to reject, them. However, the immutability of their condition, as well as the reminder they provide of "that could be us," can make the victims a threat to our security and our belief in a just world, so that we wish to avoid them.

Doob and Ecker (1970) found, for example, that a victim—someone wearing an eye patch—was more likely to get help from people than a nonvictim, if the act of help was "impersonal," in this case completing in private and then mailing a questionnaire. When the act of help required being interviewed by the victim, he then elicited no more help than a nonvictim.

Two studies varied the amount of similarity between the onlooker and the victim. In one study (Novak & Lerner, 1968), students who volunteered to participate in a study of impression formation discovered that another volunteer was either highly similar to them or quite dissimilar in regard to such items as attitudes, background, and aspirations. In addition, half of the subjects within each of these conditions learned that the other person was a former mental patient who was still undergoing treatment. The other half was led to believe the other person was "normal." As might be expected, similar people were viewed as more attractive than dissimilar ones and, in general, the mentally disturbed person was seen as less attractive than the normal person.

Of particular importance for us was the finding that when the subjects were given the opportunity to meet and chat with the other person, they tended to avoid the similar victim more than the dissimilar one, while they wished to avoid a dissimilar normal more than a similar one. On the face of it, this reaction would seem paradoxical, especially since there were no comparable differences in ascribed attributes.

In the second study, with virtually the same experimental situation, the victim was a morphine addict (Lerner & Agar, 1973). The results were somewhat stronger than those for the mental patient. The addict who was highly similar to the subject was avoided, as was the normal who was extremely different. The subjects were much more willing to meet and interact with a normal who was similar to them or an addict who was quite different.

The hypothesis underlying these studies was that the subject's high similarity to the victim constituted a threat. He could not end the victim's suffering, he could not condemn a person who was so similar to him, and it would be difficult for him to decide that he and the similar victim lived in different worlds and were not subject to the same environmental forces. The only alternative available to reduce the implicit threat to his security was to avoid any further discomfort by engaging in alternative, competing activities to blot out awareness of the innocent victim and the frightening implications he represented.

IV. Summary

A person's desire for justice in his "world" and his attraction toward people who populate that world are tied together in a number of ways. In the first place, the way a person construes justice—whether he applies the justice of need, equality, equity, or law—will be determined, in part, by his attitudes toward the people involved. His initial attitudes toward these people will also affect the likelihood of his condemning the inflictor or the victim of an injustice or, in fact, whether he sees any injustice at all. Eventually, if his prior attitudes prevent him from condemning the victim, and he has no other way to reestablish justice, he may have to resort to the primitive response of running away from the event.

References

Adams, S. Toward an understanding of inequity. *Journal of Abnormal and Social Psychology*, 1963, **67**, 422–436.

Aderman, D., & Berkowitz, L. Observational set, empathy, and helping. *Journal of Personality and Social Psychology*, 1970, **14**, 141–148.

Allport, G. *The nature of prejudice*. Reading, Massachusetts: Addison-Wesley, 1954.

Bandura, A., Ross, D., & Ross, S. A. Vicarious reinforcement and imitative learning. *Journal of Abnormal and Social Psychology*, 1963, **67**, 601–607.

Baxter, J. C., Lerner, M., & Miller, J. S. Identification as a function of the reinforcing quality of the model and the socialization background of the subject. *Journal of Personality and Social Psychology*, 1965, **2**, 692–697.

Benton, A. A. Productivity, distributive justice, and bargaining among children. *Journal of Personality and Social Psychology*, 1971, **18**, 68–78.

Berkowitz, L. The self, selfishness and altruism. In J. Macaulay and L. Berkowitz (Eds.), *Altruism and helping behavior*. New York: Academic Press, 1970. Pp. 143–154.

Berkowitz, L., & Daniels, L. R. Responsibility and dependency. *Journal of Abnormal and Social Psychology*, 1963, **66**, 429–436.

Berkowitz, L., & Friedman, P. Some social class differences in helping behavior. *Journal of Personality and Social Psychology*, 1967, **5**, 217–225.

Berscheid, E., & Walster, E. When does a harm-doer compensate a victim? *Journal of Personality and Social Psychology*, 1967, **6**, 435–441.

Berscheid, E., Walster, E., & Barclay, A. The effect of time on the tendency to compensate a victim. *Psychological Reports*, 1969, **25**, 431–436.

Bettelheim, B. Individual and mass behavior in extreme situations. *Journal of Abnormal and Social Psychology*, 1943, **38**, 417–452.

Cahn, E. *The sense of injustice: An anthropocentric view of law*. New York: New York University Press, 1949.

Chaikin, A. L., & Darley, J. M. Victim or perpetrator: defensive attribution of responsibility and the need for order and justice. Unpublished manuscript, Princeton University, 1971.

Davis, K., & Jones, E. E. Changes in interpersonal perception as a means of reducing cognitive dissonance. *Journal of Abnormal and Social Psychology*, 1960, **61**, 402–410.

Doob, A. N., & Eckar, B. P. Stigma and compliance. *Journal of Personality and Social Psychology*, 1970, **14**, 302–304.

Farina, A., & Ring, K. The influence of perceived mental illness on interpersonal relations. *Journal of Abnormal and Social Psychology*, 1965, **70**, 47–51.

Freedman, J., Wallington, S., & Bless, E., Compliance without pressure: The effect of guilt. *Journal of Personality and Social Psychology*, 1967, **7**, 117–124.

Glass, D. C. Changes in liking as a means of reducing cognitive discrepancies between self-esteem and aggression. *Journal of Personality*, 1964, **32**, 520–549.

Homans, G. C. *Social behavior: Its elementary forms.* New York: Harcourt, 1961.

Jenkins, H. M., & Ward, W. C. Judgment of contingency between responses and outcome. *Psychological Monographs,* 1965, **79**, 1–17.

Johnson, R. W., & Dickinson, J. Class differences in derogation of an innocent victim. Unpublished manuscript, St. Francis Xavier University, 1971.

Jones, E. E., & Davis, K. E. From acts to dispositions. In L. Berkowitz (Ed.), *Advances in Experimental Social Psychology.* Vol. 2. New York: Academic Press, 1965. Pp. 219–266.

Kaufman, H. Legality and harmfulness of a bystander's failure to intervene as determinants of moral judgment. In J. Macaulay and L. Berkowitz (Eds.), *Altruism and helping behavior.* New York: Academic Press, 1970.

Kelley, H. H. Attribution theory in social psychology, In D. Levine (Ed.), *Nebraska symposium on motivation, 1967.* Lincoln, Nebraska: University of Nebraska Press, 1967. Pp. 192–238.

Krauss, J. Structural and attitudinal factors in interpersonal bargaining. *Journal of Experimental Social Psychology,* 1966, **2**, 27–41.

Lerner, M. J. Evaluation of performance as a function of performer's reward and attractiveness. *Journal of Personality and Social Psychology,* 1965, **1**, 355–360.

Lerner, M. J. Conditions eliciting acceptance or rejection of a martyr. Unpublished manuscript, University of Kentucky, 1968.

Lerner, M. J. The desire for justice and reaction to victim. In J. Macaulay and L. Berkowitz (Eds.), *Altruism and helping behavior.* New York: Academic Press, 1970.

Lerner, M. J., Deserving versus justice: A contemporary dilemma. Report No. 24, University of Waterloo, 1971. (a)

Lerner, M. J. Justice, guilt, and veridical perception. *Journal of Personality and Social Psychology,* 1971, **20**, 127–135. (b)

Lerner, M. J., & Agar, E. The consequences of Perceived similarity: Attraction and rejection, approach and avoidance. *Journal of Experimental Research in Personality,* 1972, **6**, 69–75.

Lerner, M. J., & Becker, S. W. Interpersonal choise as a function of ascribed similarity and definition of the situation. *Human Relations,* 1962, **15**, 27–34.

Lerner, M. J., & Elkinton, L. Perception of Injustice: An initial look. Unpublished manuscript, University of Kentucky, 1970.

Lerner, M. J., & Lichtman, R. R. Effects of perceived norms on attitudes and altruistic behavior toward a dependent other. *Journal of Personality and Social Psychology,* 1968, **9**, 226–232.

Lerner, M. J., & Matthews, G. Reactions to suffering of others under conditions of indirect responsibility. *Journal of Personality and Social Psychology,* 1967, **5**, 319–325.

Lerner, M. J., & Simmons, C. Observer's reaction to the innocent victim: Compassion or rejection? *Journal of Personality and Social Psychology,* 1966, **4**, 203–310.

Leventhal, G., & Anderson, D. Self-interest and the maintenance of equity. *Journal of Personality and Social Psychology,* 1970, **15**, 57–62.

Leventhal, G. S., & Bergman, J. T. Self-depriving behavior as a response to unprofitable inequity. *Journal of Experimental Social Psychology,* 1969, **5**, 153–171.

Leventhal, G. S., & Lane, D. Sex, Age and equity behavior. *Journal of Personality and Social Psychology,* 1970, **15**, 312–316.

Leventhal, G. S., & Weiss, T. Perceived need and the response to inequitable distributions of reward. Unpublished manuscript, Wayne State University, 1971.

Leventhal, G. S., & Whiteside, H. D. Equity and the use of reward to elicit high performance. Unpublished manuscript, Wayne State University, 1971.

Lincoln, H., & Levinger, G. Observer's evaluations of the victim and the attacker in an aggressive incident. *Journal of Personality and Social Psychology,* 1972, **22**, 202–210.

MacDonald, A. P., Jr. Derogation of a victim: Justice or guilt? Unpublished manuscript, West Virginia University, 1971.

MacDonald, A. P., Jr. More on the Protestant Ethic. *Journal of Consulting and Clinical Psychology,* 1972, **39**, 116–122.

Messe, L. A. Equity in bilateral bargaining. *Journal of Personality and Social Psychology,* 1971, **17**, 187–201.

Midlarsky, E. Aiding under stress: The effects of competence, dependency, visibility, and fatalism. *Journal of Personality*, 1971, **39**, 132–149.

Morgan, W. R., & Sawyer, J. Bargaining, expectations, and the preference for equality over equity. *Journal of Personality and Social Psychology*, 1967, **6**, 139–149.

Novak, D., & Lerner, M. J. Rejection as a consequence of perceived similarity. *Journal of Personality and Social Psychology*, 1968, **9**, 147–152.

Piliavin, I., Hardyck, J., & Vadum, A. Reactions to a victim in a just or non-just world. Paper presented at the Society of Experimental Social Psychology meeting, Bethesda, Maryland, August, 1967.

Quinney, R. Political conservatism, alienation, and fatalism: Contingencies of social status and religious fundamentalism. *Sociometry*, 1964, **27**, 372–381.

Rawlings, E. I. Reactive guilt and anticipatory guilt in altruistic behavior. *Altrusim and helping behavior*. New York: Academic Press, 1970. Pp. 163–177.

Regan, J. W., Guilt, perceived injustice, and altruistic behavior. *Journal of Personality and Social Psychology*, 1971, **18**, 124–131.

Richardson, S. A., Hastorf, A. H., Goodman, N., & Dornbusch, S. M. Cultural uniformities in reaction to physical disabilities. *American Sociological Review*, 1961, **26**, 241–247.

Ross, M., Thibaut, J., & Evenbeck, S. Some determinants of social protest. *Journal of Experimental Social Psychology*, 1971, **7**, 401–418.

Rubin, Z., & Peplau, A. Belief in a just world and reaction to another's lot: A study of the national draft lottery. Unpublished manuscript, Harvard University, 1971.

Sampson, E. E. Studies of status congruence. In L. Berkowitz (Ed.) *Advances in Experimental Social Psychology* Vol. 4. New York: Academic Press, 1969, Pp. 225–270.

Schopler, J., Matthews, M. The influence of the perceived causal locus of partner's dependency on the use of interpersonal power. *Journal of Personality and Social Psychology*, 1965, **4**, 609–612.

Simmons, C. H., & Lerner, M. J. Altruism as a search for justice. *Journal of Personality and Social Psychology*, 1968, **9**, 216–225.

Simons, C. W., & Piliavin, J. A., The effect of deception on reactions to a victim. *Journal of Personality and Social Psychology*. 1972, **21**, 56–60.

Stein, D. D., Hardyck, J. A., & Smith, M. B. Race and belief: An open and shut case. *Journal of Personality and Social Psychology*, 1965, **1**, 281–289.

Stokols, S., & Schopler, J. Reactions to victims: A theoretical and empirical extension of Lerner's paradigm. *Journal of Personality and Social Psychology*, 1973, **25**, 199–211.

Stotland, E. Exploratory investigations of empathy. In L. Berkowitz (Ed.) *Advances in Experimental Social Psychology*. Vol. 4. New York: Academic Press, 1969. Pp. 271–313.

Tannenbaum, P. H., & Gaer, E. P. Mood changes as a function of stress of protagonist and degree of identification in a film viewing situation. *Journal of Personality and Social Psychology*, 1965, **2**, 612–616.

Walster, E. Assignment of responsibility for an accident. *Journal of Personality and Social Psychology*, 1966, **3**, 73–79.

Walster, E. "Second-guessing" important events. *Human Relations*, 1967, **20**, 239–250.

Walster, E., Berscheid, E., & Walster, G. W. The exploited: Justice or justification. In J. Macaulay & L. Berkowitz (Eds.), *Altruism and helping behavior*. New York: Academic Press, 1970.

Walster, E., Berscheid, E., & Walster, G. W. New direction in equity research. *Journal of Personality and Social Psychology*, 1973, **25**, 151–176.

Walster, E., & Prestholdt, P. The effect of misjudging another: Over-compensation or dissonance reduction? *Journal of Experimental Social Psychology*, 1966, **2**, 85–97.

Walster, E., Walster, B., Abrahams, D., & Brown, Z. The effect on liking of underrating or overrating another. *Journal of Experimental Social Psychology*, 1966, **2**, 70–84.

Wicker, G., & Bushweiler, G. Perceived fairness and pleasantness of social exchange situations. *Journal of Personality and Social Psychology*, 1970, **151**, 63–75.

PART V

Romantic Attraction

15

A Little Bit about Love

ELLEN BERSCHEID

Department of Psychology
University of Minnesota
Minneapolis, Minnesota

and

ELAINE WALSTER[1]

Department of Sociology
University of Wisconsin
Madison, Wisconsin

[1]This chapter was prepared while Dr. Walster was at the University of Mannheim, West Germany.

I. The Elusive Nature of Love

Many who have tried to understand the nature of love have concluded in despair that it is impossible to specify in advance who will inspire love, under what conditions, or why. They have resonated to Durrell's (1961) poetic definition of love:

> It may be defined as a cancerous growth of unknown origin which may take up its site anywhere without the subject knowing or wishing it. How often have you tried to love the "right" person in vain even when your heart knows it has found him after so much seeking? No, an eyelash, a perfume, a haunting walk, a strawberry on the neck, the smell of almonds on the breath—these are the accomplices the spirit seeks out to plan your overthrow [p. 106].*

Other writers have tried to explicate *facets* of romantic love. [Delightful essays have been written, for example, by Reik (1943); Beigel (1951); Maslow (1954); Fromm (1956); Goode (1959); and Hunt (1959).] These analysts have often provided compelling—but unnervingly inconsistent—insights into the nature of passionate love.

Contradictions also are found in the voluminous folk sayings addressed to the topic of love. The person who is concerned with predicting the effect of separation upon his romance, for example, will find that folk wisdom has a good deal to say, much of it contradictory: "Out of sight out of mind"; "Absence makes the heart grow fonder"; "Absence lessens half-hearted passions, and increases great ones."

Disagreements such as these led Finck (1891) to the conclusion that "Love is such a tissue of paradoxes, and exists in such an endless variety of forms and shades, that you may say almost anything about it that you please, and it is likely to be correct [p. 244]."

Can scientists do better than those who have provided only fragmentary and contradictory information about the nature of love? Perhaps. But most would agree this is a promise for the future, rather than a feat of the past.

The social scientific journals typically provide little more than an acknowledgment of the absence of an understanding of love. Maslow (1954), for example, offers a sharp criticism of psychological ignorance in this area:

> It is amazing how little the empirical sciences have to offer on the subject of love. Particularly strange is the silence of the psychologists, for one might think this to be their particular obligation. Probably this is just another example of the besetting sin of the academicians, that they prefer to do what they are easily able rather than what they ought, like the not-so-bright kitchen helper I knew who opened every can in the hotel one day because he was so *very* good at opening cans. Sometimes this is merely sad or irritating, as in the case of the textbooks of psychology and sociology, practically none of which treats the subject. . . . More often the situation becomes completely ludicrous. One might reasonably expect that writers of serious treatises on the family, on marriage, and on sex should consider the subject of love to be a proper, even basic,

---

*From the book *Clea* by Lawrence Durrell. Copyright © 1960 by Lawrence Durrell. Published by E. P. Dutton & Co., Inc. and used with their permission.

part of their self-imposed task . . . I must confess that I understand this better now that I have undertaken the task myself. It is an extraordinarily difficult subject to handle in any tradition, and it is triply so in the scientific tradition. It is as if we were at the most advanced position in no man's land, at a point where the conventional techniques of orthodox pyschological science are of very little use. And yet our duty is clear. We *must* understand love . . . [p. 235].

Harlow (1958), too, has declared that, "So far as love is concerned, psychologists have failed in their mission. The little we know about love does not transcend simple observation, and the little we write about it has been written better by poets and novelists [p. 673]."

II. Liking and Loving

Passionate love can be perceived as a variety of *interpersonal attraction*. Interpersonal attraction has been defined by a number of researchers (e.g., Homans, 1950; Newcomb, 1961) as a positive attitude toward another, evidenced by a tendency to approach and interact with him.

Research on interpersonal attraction began early (1884) and has continued at a prodigious rate. Attraction theorists have generally agreed upon the genesis of interpersonal attraction: We are attracted to persons who reward us. The more reward they provide, the more attractive we find them. Reward has been conceived to have so predictable an impact on attraction that Byrne (1971) has even proposed an exact correspondence: "Attraction toward X is a positive linear function of the sum of the weighted positive reinforcements (Number × Magnitude) associated with X [p. 279]."

Although a good deal of evidence has been marshalled to support the reinforcement formulation of attraction, almost all of these data (as well as most data gathered to illuminate the antecedents of attraction) are concerned with one variety of interpersonal attraction, liking. Despite the almost exclusive focus upon this type of attraction, attraction theorists recognize that there are many other varieties. Byrne (1971) has noted, for example, that in addition to liking, interpersonal attraction is composed of a number of other specific response components —such as friendship, parental love, romantic love, sexual attraction, and we would add, companionate, or marital, love. Byrne also warns that the antecedents of these various subcategories of attraction may not be identical.

We agree that "passionate love" (in Byrne's terminology, romantic attraction *and* sexual attraction) is a very special variety of interpersonal attraction and as such is entitled to independent attention. Furthermore, since the antecedents of passionate love seem to differ from liking in several important ways, the prediction of romantic love may demand special knowledge. Some of the ways in which these two phenomena appear to differ are outlined in the following sections.

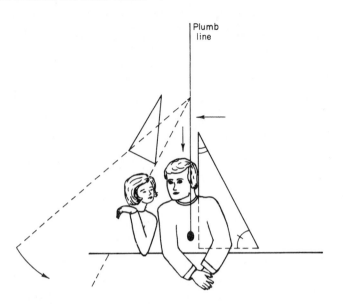

Figure 1   In 1884, Francis Galton (Webb *et al.*, 1966) became convinced that metaphorical expressions often mirror physical reality. He proceeded to investigate "the inclination of one person toward another [p. 151]." On the basis of his observations of people seated next to each other at dinner, Galton concluded that the more attracted dinner partners were toward one another, the more they leaned toward one another. Galton evidently believed that insults could be discreetly traded in an upright position, but that sweeter words are usually spoken at an angle of less than 90°.

A. The Importance of Fantasy

Researchers have generally assumed that it is the actual rewards which are exchanged during interpersonal contact which create liking. It seems doubtful, however, that people are so reality-bound.

When the lover closes his eyes and daydreams, he can summon up a flawless partner—a partner who instantaneously satisfies all his unspoken, conflicting, and fleeting desires. In fantasy he may receive unlimited reward or he may *anticipate* that he would receive unlimited reward were he ever to actually meet his ideal.

Compared to our grandiose fantasies, the level of reward we receive in our real interactions is severely circumscribed. As a consequence, sometimes the most extreme passion is aroused by partners who exist only in imagination or partners who are barely known. Reactions to real-life love objects often seem to be far more tepid.

Theorists interested only in *liking*, then, may possibly afford to focus entirely on the impact actual reward has on liking. In contrast, it seems likely that romantic love theorists will be forced to take into consideration both the rewards a lover receives in fantasy and the rewards he fantasizes he might receive in future interaction with the partner. (Further discussion of the importance of fantasy in generating passionate love is provided by Reik, 1944, and the current state of scientific knowledge of fantasy is reviewed by Klinger, 1971.)

B. *The Effect of Time on Passion*

Passionate love also seems to differ from liking in its fragility. One of the laws of liking, expressed by Homans (1961), is that "... other things equal, the more a man interacts with another, the more he likes him [p. 203]." In stark contrast to this statement is the observation that "The history of a love affair is the drama of its fight against time." Authors of marriage and family texts tend to agree. Williamson (1966), for example, warns that romantic love is a temporary phenomenon and cautions that although intense passion may be a prerequisite for marriage, it is bound to dwindle after lengthy interaction. Reik (1944), too, warns that the very best one can hope for after several years of marriage is an "afterglow."

Over time, then, one's feelings toward another are probably affected less by the infinite rewards one fantasizes he will receive from his ideal, and are affected more by the lesser rewards one can receive from an ordinary mortal. Thus, to the extent that the passionate lover is aroused more by fantasy than fact, the reality information about another, which time usually provides, may erode passionate love. To the extent that liking is based on more realistic grounds, it should not be as vulnerable with continued interaction with the partner.

C. *Liking Is Associated with Positive Reinforcements; Passion Is Associated with a Hodgepodge of Conflicting Emotions*

Liking seems to be a sensible phenomenon. From Aristotle onward, theorists are in agreement: We like those who reward us and dislike those who thwart our desires. Unfortunately, that exotic variety of attraction, passionate love, does not seem to fit as neatly into the reinforcement paradigm. It is true that some practical people manage to fall passionately in love with beautiful, wise, entertaining, and wealthy people who bring them unending affection and material rewards. Other people, however, with unfailing accuracy, seem to fall passionately in love with people who are almost guaranteed to bring them suffering and material deprivation.

Observers disagree, passionately, about the nature of the emotional states which are most conducive to passion. Some insist that passionate love is inexorably entwined with fulfillment and the anticipation of fulfillment. Others insist that passionate love is virtually synonomous with agony. (Indeed, the original meaning of passion was "agony"—as in "Christ's Passion.") College students evidently share the theorists' confusion as to whether passionate love is a joyous state or a painful one. Students at several universities were allowed to ask psychologists one question about romantic love. Among the most frequent questions was: "Can you love and hate someone at the same time?"

III. A Tentative Theory of Passionate Love

It can be argued, then, that passionate love differs from liking in several important ways and that a special approach to this particular variety of interpersonal attraction may be needed. Walster and Berscheid (1971) proposed a tentative theoretical framework to facilitate investigation of romantic love. Following Schachter's general theory of emotion (1964), it was suggested that individuals will experience passionate love whenever two conditions coexist:

1. They are intensely aroused physiologically;
2. situational cues indicate that "passionate love" is the appropriate label for their intense feelings.

A. Schachter's Two-Component Theory of Emotion

In 1964, Schachter proposed a new paradigm for understanding human emotional response. Schachter argued that two factors must coexist if a person is to experience emotion: (*a*) The person must be aroused physiologically; (*b*) it must be appropriate for him to interpret his stirred-up state in emotional terms. Schachter argued that neither physiological arousal nor appropriate emotional cognitions would, by themselves, be sufficient to produce an emotional experience for the individual.

To test the hypothesis that physiological arousal and appropriate cognitions are separate and indispensable components of a true emotional experience, Schachter had to find a technique for separately manipulating arousal and cognition. In their classic study, Schachter and Singer (1962) conceived of a way to do just that.

1. MANIPULATING PHYSIOLOGICAL AROUSAL

The investigators manipulated physiological arousal artificially. A drug—epinephrine—exists whose effects mimic the discharge of the sympathetic nervous system. Shortly after one receives an injection of epinephrine, systolic blood pressure increases markedly, heart rate increases somewhat, cutaneous blood flow decreases, muscle and cerebral blood flow increase, blood sugar and lactic acid concentration increase, and respiration rate increases slightly. The individual injected with epinephrine experiences palpitation, tremor, and sometimes flushing and accelerated breathing. These reactions are identical to the physiological reactions that appear to accompany a variety of natural emotional states.

Schachter and Singer injected volunteers with a substance that they claimed was Suproxin, a new vitamin compound whose effects upon vision was said to be of interest to the experimenters. In reality, one-half of the subjects were injected with epinephrine. By this procedure, Schachter and Singer insured that half of their subjects would experience an exceptionally high degree of physiological arousal, while the other half, those who actually received a saline solution placebo, would be relatively unaroused.

2. MANIPULATING COGNITIONS

The investigators wished to place half of the volunteers in a situation where their aroused or unaroused physiological state could be attributed to a nonemotional cause (the injection). The others were placed in a situation where their aroused or unaroused state could be attributed to an emotional cause.

Thus, in one condition (the nonemotional attribution condition) volunteers were given a complete description of how the shot would affect them. They were warned that in about 15–20 min, the injection of Suproxin would produce palpitations, tremors, flushing, and accelerated breathing. The researchers expected that when the volunteers began to experience these symptoms, they would attribute their stirred-up state to the shot. In another set of conditions (the emotional attribution conditions), subjects were *not* told how the shot would affect them. One group of volunteers was given *no information* about possible side effects of the shot. Another group of volunteers was deliberately *misled* as to the potential side effects of the shot. (They were told that the shot of Suproxin would probably make their feet feel numb, produce an itching sensation over part of their body, and give them a slight headache.)

The experimenters expected that the volunteers who received either *no information* or *incorrect information* about how the shot would affect them, would *not* attribute their aroused state to the shot. Instead, it was expected that these volunteers would attribute their arousal to whatever they happened to be doing when the drug took effect 20 min later.

The experimenters then arranged the situation such that what all volunteers "happened to be doing" was either participating in a gay, happy, social interaction or participating in a tense, explosive interaction. Half of the subjects—those who were to be participating in a gay interaction (the *euphoria* condition)—were asked to wait for 20 min in an adjoining room until the tests of vision could begin. Another student, who was also scheduled to wait in this room for his tests, was actually an experimental confederate; it was his job to make life exciting for the subject. As soon as the experimenter left the room, the confederate doodled briefly on a piece of paper, crumpled it up, and then shot it at a wastebasket. He missed. He constructed a paper airplane, and set it hurtling around the room. A sloppy pile of manila folders caught his eye. He stopped, built a tower of the folders, and then began to shoot paper wads at the tower from across the room. He ended his performance by picking up a hula hoop and dancing wildly.

The remainder of the subjects—those who were to be participating in a tense situation (the *anger* condition)—were asked, along with the confederate, to fill out questionnaires while they waited in a nearby room for the experiment to begin. The confederate was instructed to make life explosive for the subject. The questionnaires started off innocently enough, requesting standard information. Then the questions became more and more insulting. The questionnaire requested such information as who in the subject's family did not bathe or wash regularly and who seemed to need psychiatric care. Another question asked, "With how many men (other than your father) has your mother had extramarital relationships?" The possible responses started with "4 and under." As the confederate and subject worked on these questions, the confederate became increasingly indignant. He criticized the task as a stupid, outrageous waste of time. Finally, in a rage, he threw his questionnaire to the floor and stomped out shouting: "I'm not wasting any more time. I'm getting my books and leaving."

3. ASSESSING THE SUBJECT'S EMOTIONAL RESPONSE

Schachter and Singer predicted that subjects who had received an epinephrine injection, and thus experienced a high degree of physiological arousal, should have stronger emotional reactions in the euphoria or anger settings than should either subjects who had received a placebo (and were not as aroused) or subjects, who had received an epinephrine injection, but had been warned of exactly what physiological changes to expect (and, therefore, should not have attributed their arousal to the emotional cues in the questionnaire situation).

The researchers measured the intensity of the subjects' emotional response in two ways. First, observers stationed behind a one-way mirror assessed the extent to which the subject "caught" the stooge's euphoric or angry mood. Second, subjects were asked to state how euphoric or angry they felt.

The data supported Schachter and Singer's (1962) hypothesis and provided support for the contention that *both* physiological arousal and appropriate cognitions are indispensable components of a true emotional experience; neither component alone appears to create the experiencing of an emotion.

Evidence from Schachter and Wheeler (1962) and Hohmann (1962) has provided additional support for the two-component theory of emotion.

B. The Two-Component Theory and Passionate Love

Walster and Berscheid (1971) speculated that perhaps the two-component theory would be a more useful blueprint than the reinforcement paradigm for assembling the apparent jumble of redundant, inconsistent, and implausible pieces of the passionate love puzzle. Certain puzzle pieces which don't fit into the reinforcement framework seem less awkward in the two-component framework. There is, for example, no longer the problem of explaining why both intensely positive and intensely negative (and presumably unrewarding) experiences can be conducive to love. Both types of experiences may produce physiological arousal. Stimuli which produce "aesthetic appreciation," "sexual arousal," "gratitude," "rejection," "jealousy," or "total confusion" generally produce states of intense physiological arousal. Thus, these positive *and* negative experiences may all have the potential for deepening an individual's passion for another.

What may be important in determining how the individual feels about the person who is apparently generating these intense feelings is how he *labels* his reaction. If the situation is arranged so that it is reasonable for him to attribute this agitated state to "passionate love," he should experience love. As soon as he ceases to attribute his arousal to passionate love, or the arousal itself ceases, love should die.

Does any compelling experimental evidence exist to support the contention that under conditions of physiological arousal, a wide variety of stimuli, properly labeled, may deepen passion? No. Studies have not yet been conducted to test this hypothesis. There are, however, a few investigations designed to test other hypotheses that provide tangential support for the two-component theory of passionate love.

IV. Generating Physiological Arousal: The First Step in Generating Passionate Love

A. Unpleasant Emotional Experiences: Facilitators of Passion?

Negative reinforcements produce arousal in all animals (see Skinner, 1938). For human beings there is some evidence that under certain conditions such unpleasant—but arousing—states as fear, rejection, and frustration may enhance romantic passion.

1. FEAR

When a person is frightened, he becomes intensely physiologically aroused for a substantial period of time (Wolf & Wolff, 1947; Ax, 1953; Schachter, 1957). An intriguing study by Brehm, Gatz, Geothals, McCrommon, and Ward (1970) suggests that fear can contribute to a man's attraction to a woman. Brehm and co-workers tested the hypothesis that a person's attraction to another would be multiplied by prior arousal from an irrelevant event. To test this hypothesis, one group of men was led to believe that they would soon receive three "pretty stiff" electrical shocks. Half of the men in this group ("threat" subjects) were allowed to retain this erroneous expectation throughout the experiment. The other half ("threat-relief" subjects) were frightened, but then were later reassured that the experimenter had made an error; they had been assigned to the control group and would receive no shock. The remainder of the men were told at the start that they had been assigned to the control group; the experimenter did not even mention the possibility that they might receive shock. All of the men were then introduced to a young female college student and asked how much they liked her.

The men in the three groups should vary in how physiologically aroused they were at the time they met the girl. The threat subjects should be quite frightened. The threat-relief subjects should be experiencing both residual fear reactions and vast relief. Both groups of men should be more aroused than the men in the control group. The investigators predicted, as we would, that both threat and threat-relief subjects would like the girl more than would control subjects. These expectations were confirmed. (Threat and threat-relief men did not differ in their liking for the girl.) A frightening event, then, may facilitate attraction.

2. REJECTION

Rejection is always disturbing. When a person is rejected, he generally experiences a strong emotional reaction. Usually one labels his reaction embarrassment, pain, anger, or hatred. It should also be possible, however, under certain conditions, for a rejected individual to label his emotional response as "love."

Some suggestive evidence that love or hate may spring from rejection comes from several laboratory experiments designed to test other hypotheses (Dittes, 1959; Walster, 1965; Jacobs, Berscheid, & Walster, 1971). Let us consider one of these experiments and the way a Schachterian might reinterpret it.

Jacobs and co-workers attempted to determine how changes in the self-esteem of college men affected their receptivity to affection expressed by a female college student. First, the experimenter gave the men a number of personality tests (the MMPI, Rorschach, etc.). A few weeks later he returned a false analysis of their personalities. Half of the men were given a flattering report, stressing their sensitivity, honesty, originality, and freedom of outlook. The other half received an insulting personality report. The report stressed their immaturity, weak personality, conventionality, and lack of leadership ability. This critical report naturally disturbed most of the men.

Soon after receiving their analyses, each man was made acquainted with a young female college student, who in actuality was an experimental confederate. Half of the time the girl responded to the man with a warm, affectionate, and accepting evaluation. The investigators found that the men who had received the critical personality evaluation were *more attracted* to the girl than were their more confident counterparts. Half of the time the girl was cool and rejecting. Under these conditions, a dramatic reversal occurred. The previously rejected men *disliked* the girl more than did their more confident counterparts. Under these conditions, the previously insulted individual's agitation was presumably transformed to enmity. A preceding painful event, then, may heighten the emotional response we feel toward another's expression of affection or disapproval.

3. FRUSTRATION AND CHALLENGE

Khruschev, depicting the Russian character, said:

> When the aristocrats first discovered that potatoes were a cheap way of feeding the peasants, they had no success in getting the peasants to eat them. But they knew their

people. They fenced the potatoes in with high fences. The peasants then stole the potatoes and soon acquired a taste for them [Galbraith, 1969, p. 110].

Theorists seem to agree that the obstacles a lover encounters in his attempt to possess another intensify love.

a. Sexual Frustration.   Sexual inhibition is often said to be the foundation of romantic feelings. For example, Freud (1922) argued: "Some obstacle is necessary to swell the tide of libido to its height; and at all periods of history whenever natural barriers in the way of satisfaction have not sufficed, mankind has erected conventional ones in order to enjoy love [p. 213]." Presumably, when sexual energy is bottled up, it will be sublimated and expressed as romantic longing, rather than sexual longing.

Experimental evidence concerning the impact of other kinds of obstacles to love on the intensity of the lovers' romantic feelings comes from Walster, Walster, Piliavin, and Schmidt (1973) and from Driscoll, Davis, and Lipitz (1972).

b. The Hard-to-Get Girl.   Socrates, Ovid, the Kama Sutra, and "Dear Abby" are in agreement about one thing: A girl who is hard to get inspires more passion than does a girl who "throws herself" at a man.

Socrates (in Xenophon, 1923) advises Theodota, a *hetaera*:

> . . . They will appreciate your favors most highly if you wait till they ask for them. The sweetest meats, you see, if served before they are wanted seem sour, and to those who had enough they are positively nauseating; but even poor fare is very welcome when offered to a hungry man. [Theodota inquires] And how can I make them hunger for my fare? [Socrates' reply] Why, in the first place, you must not offer it to them when they have had enough—be a show of reluctance to yield, and by holding back until they are as keen as can be for then the same gifts are much more to the recipient than when they are offered before they are desired [p. 247].

Ovid (1962) remarks:

> Fool, if you feel no need to guard your girl for her own sake, see that you guard her for mine, so I may want her the more. Easy things nobody wants, but what is forbidden is tempting . . . Anyone who can love the wife of an indolent cuckold, I should suppose, would steal buckets of sand from the shore [pp. 65, 66].

Bertrand Russell (in Kirch, 1960) argues:

> The belief in the immense value of the lady is a psychological effect of the difficulty of obtaining her, and I think it may be laid down that when a man has no difficulty in obtaining a woman, his feeling toward her does not take the form of romantic love [pp. 10–11].

To find authors in such rare accord on an aspect of passionate love is refreshing. Better yet, their observation seems to provide support for the two-component theory. Unfortunately for the theory (but fortunately for easy-to-get men and women), the data suggest that hard-to-get men and women do not inspire especially intense liking in their suitors. (See Walster, Walster, & Berscheid, 1971; and Walster, Berscheid, & Walster, 1973.)

Walster *et al.* (1973) report several experiments designed to demonstrate that a challenging girl will be a more dazzling conquest than a readily available girl. All experiments secured negative results.

In the first set of experiments, college males were recruited for a computer date-match program. The program was ostensibly designed to evaluate and improve current computer matching programs. In an initial interview, men filled out a lengthy questionnaire. They were informed that the computer would *either* provide them with the name of a girl especially matched to their requirements, *or* with the name of a girl randomly selected from the date-match pool. (Presumably, only by comparing men's reactions to matched versus randomly selected girls could it be judged whether or not the matching procedure was effective.)

Two weeks later the men reported to collect the name and telephone number of their date-match. They were asked to telephone her and to arrange a date from the laboratory, so that after the call their first impressions of the date could be assessed. Actually, each man was provided with the telephone number of the same girl—an experimental confederate.

In the *easy-to-get* condition, the girl was delighted to receive his telephone call and grateful to be asked out. In the *hard-to-get* condition, the girl accepted a coffee date with some reluctance. She obviously had many other dates, and was not sure whether or not she really wanted to get involved with someone new.

The results of this and other similar experiments failed to support the "hard-to get" hypothesis; it was found that boys had an equally high opinion of the hard-to-get and the easy-to-get girls.

A further study—a field experiment—also failed to support the hypothesis. In this study, a prostitute serving as the experimenter, delivered the experimental communication while she was mixing drinks for her clients. Half the time she played hard to get. She indicated that she could only see a limited number of clients, and thus, she had to be very selective about whom she could accept as a customer. Half of the time (in the easy-to-get condition) she did not deliver this communication, but allowed the clients to assume that she would accept all customers. She then had sexual intercourse with the clients.

The client's liking for the prostitute was assessed in three ways: (*a*) the prostitute estimated the client's liking for her; (*b*) she recorded how much he paid for the 50-min hour; and (*c*) she recorded how soon he called her for a second appointment.

The hard-to-get hypothesis was *not* supported. Clients appeared to like the selective and unselective prostitute equally well, regardless of the measure of liking used.

Faced with this shower of evidence that a hard-to-get date does *not* seem to inspire more passion than the easy-to-get one, Walster and co-workers reconsidered their hypothesis. First, they systematically considered the advantages and disadvantages a suitor might anticipate from a generally hard-to-get or a generally easy-to-get girl. For example, an "easy-to-get" girl, while perhaps desperate for company because she is unattractive, might be a friendly and relaxing date; a "hard-to-get" girl, while having the advantage of being a challenge, might be unfriendly and ego-crushing. In previous research, each girl's advantages and disadvantages may have balanced one another out. The girls—whether easy or hard to get—had potentially attractive assets and potentially dangerous liabilities. What would the perfect date be like? What kind of a girl would possess most of the advantages, but few of the disadvantages, of both the hard-to-get and the easy-to-get girls? A girl who is crazy about you (she is easy for *you* to get), but is hard for anyone else to get should be maximally rewarding.

Walster and co-workers then tested the hypothesis that the selectively hard-to-get girl would be preferred to a generally hard-to-get girl, to a generally easy-to-get girl, or to a control girl (a person whose general hard-to-getness of easy-to-getness was unknown) in the following way: Men were again recruited for a computer date-match program. They filled out questionnaires, and then waited several weeks for the computer to match them with potential dates. When they reported to the lab for the name of their date, they were told that five girls had been selected by the computer. The men examined biographies of these girls so that they could choose which one they wanted to date. The girls' biographies described their backgrounds, interests, attitudes, etc. Attached to the biography was each girl's evaluation of the dates that had been assigned to her. Each subject, who knew his own code numbers, could thus discover how each girl had rated him and the four other men with whom the computer had matched her. (Presumably, her evaluations were based on the biographies she had been shown.)

These ratings constituted the experimental manipulation. One girl made it evident that she was *generally easy to get*. She indicated that she was "very eager" to date every fellow the computer had assigned to her. A second girl made it evident that she was *generally hard to get*. She indicated that she was willing, but not particularly eager to date the five fellows assigned to her. One of the girls made it evident that she was *selectively hard to get*. Although she was very eager to date the subject, she was reluctant to date any of his rivals. Two of the potential dates were *control* girls. (The experimenter said that they had not yet stopped in to evaluate their computer matches, and, thus, no information was available concerning their preferences.)

These data provided strong support for the revised hypothesis. Men liked the generally hard to get, the generally easy to get, and control dates equally. The selectively hard-to-get girl, however, was uniformly the most popular girl, liked far more than her competitors.

c. Parental Interference.   Driscoll, Davis, and Lipitz (1972) proposed that parental interference in a love relationship intensifies the feelings of romantic love between members of the couple. The authors begin their delightful article by surveying the extent to which parental opposition and intense love have been pitted against one another. They remind readers that Romeo and Juliet's short but intense love affair took place against the background of total opposition from the two feuding families. The difficulties and separations which the family conflict created appear to have intensified the lovers' feelings for each other.

Finally, the authors remind us that DeRougement (1940), in his historical analysis of romantic love, emphasized the persistent association of obstacles or grave difficulties with intense passion. They conclude that an affair consummated without major difficulty apparently lacks zest.

The authors distinguish between romantic love (for example, infatuation, passionate love) and conjugal love. They point out that romantic love is associated with uncertainty and challenge in contrast to the trust and genuine understanding of conjugal love. Conjugal love is said to evolve gradually out of mutually satisfying interactions and from increasing confidence in one's personal security in the relationship.

The authors tested their hypothesis that parental opposition would deepen romantic love (as opposed to conjugal love) in the following way: 91 married couples and 49 dating couples (18 of whom were living together) were recruited to participate in a marital relations project. Some of these couples were happily matched; others were not. The typical married couples had been married 4 years.

All of the 49 dating couples were seriously committed to one another; most of them had been going together for about 8 months.

During an initial interview, all the couples filled out three scales:

Assessment of Parental Interference: This scale measured the extent to which the couple's parents interfered and caused difficulties in their relationship. Participants were asked whether or not they had ever complained to their mate that her (his) parents interfere in their relationship, are a bad influence, are hurting the relationship, take advantage of her (him), don't accept him (her), or try to make him (her) look bad.

Conjugal Love Scale: This scale measured the extent to which participants loved, felt they cared about and needed their partner, and felt that the relationship was more important than anything else.

Romantic Love Scale: The researchers rescored the Conjugal Love Scale in order to obtain "a purified index of Romantic Love." (This index was constructed by partialing out of the Love Scale that portion of variance which could be counted for by trust—a characteristic the authors felt more typical of conjugal love than of passionate love.)

The authors found that parental interference and passion were related, as they expected them to be. Parental interference and romantic love were correlated .50 for the unmarried sample and .24 for the married sample. However, parental interference and conjugal love were also correlated (.36) for the unmarried sample, although not for the married sample (.00). Parental interference and romantic love did seem to be positively and significantly related.

Next, the authors investigated whether *increasing* parental interference would provoke increased passion; 6–10 months after the initial interview, the authors invited all of the couples back for a second interview. During this second interview, the participants once again completed Parental Interference, Conjugal Love, and Romantic Love Scales. By comparing subjects' initial interview responses with their later ones, the authors could calculate whether the participants' parents had become more or less interfering in the relationship, and how these changes in parental interference had affected the couples' affair. The authors found that as parents began to interfere more in a relationship, the couple appeared to fall more deeply in love. If the parents had become resigned to the relationship, and had begun to interfere less, the couples began to feel less intensely about one another. (Changes in parental interference correlated .30 with changes in romantic love and also .34 with changes in conjugal love.)

Since the data from the Driscoll *et al.* study are correlational, rather than experimental, alternative explanations for these findings are, of course, possible. The authors specifically mentioned two other plausible explanations.

First, the results may be due to the selective attrition of participants from the study. A couple with a weak relationship may stop seeing one another as soon as parents voice disapproval. Only couples who are very much in love may be willing to defy strong parental opposition. Thus, parental interference and love may seem to be related only because the sample does not include couples who were low in love and high in parental interferences.

Second, parental interference may not be a *cause* of, but rather a *reaction* to, the couple's commitment to marry. When parents realize that the couple is deeply in love, they may begin to interfere. Thus, it is not interference that deepens love, but deepening love that stimulates worried parents to interfere. The authors attempted to test the validity of these alternative explanations with other available data and concluded that these alternative explanations did not seem probable.

Data indicating that parental interference breeds passion are fascinating. When parents interfere in an "unsuitable" match, they interfere with the intent of destroying the relationship, not of strengthening it. Yet, these data warn that parental interference is likely to boomerang if the relationship survives. It may foster desire rather than divisiveness.

The preceding data lend some credence to the argument that the juxtaposition of agony and ecstasy in passionate love may not be entirely accidental. Although most people assume that agony follows love, it may be that it precedes it and provides the ground in which it can flourish. Loneliness, deprivation, frustration, hatred, and insecurity all appear capable—under certain conditions—of supplementing a person's romantic feelings. Passion demands physiological arousal, and unpleasant experiences are arousing.

B. Pleasant Emotional Experiences: Facilitators of Passion?

1. SEXUAL GRATIFICATION

We previously noted that Freud and others assumed the arousal associated with inhibited sexuality to be the foundation of romantic feelings. Yet both inhibited sexuality and gratified sexuality should be arousing. According to Masters and

Johnson (1966), sexual intercourse induces hyperventilation, tachycardia, and marked increases in blood pressure. According to Zuckerman (1971), during the initial, or excitement, phase of sexual arousal, the physiological reactions exhibited are "not specific to sexual arousal, but may reflect orienting to novelty, or emotions other than sexual arousal [p. 297]." In fact, many of the physiological responses typical of this phase are also characteristic of fear and anger. Zuckerman (1971) argued (on the basis of Kinsey, Pomeroy, Martin, and Gebhard, 1953) that, "In general, only tumescence, vasodilation, genital secretions, and rhythmic muscular movements are characteristic of sexual arousal alone [p. 300]."

In brief, sexual experiences and the anticipation of such experiences are generally arousing. And religious advisors, school counselors, and psychoanalysts to the contrary, sexual gratification has probably incited as much passionate love as sexual frustration has.

Valins (1966) has demonstrated that even the erroneous belief that a woman has excited a man sexually can facilitate his attraction to her. Valins recruited male college students ostensibly to determine how males react physiologically to sexual stimuli. The men were told that their heart rate would be amplified and recorded while they viewed ten semi-nude *Playboy* photographs. The feedback the men received was experimentally controlled. They were led to believe that when they examined slides picturing some of the *Playboy* bunnies, their heart rate altered markedly; when they examined others, they had no reaction. (Valins assumed that men would interpret an alteration in heart rate as enthusiasm for the bunny and no change in heart rate as disinterest.)

The men's liking for the "arousing" and "nonarousing" slides was assessed in three ways: (*a*) they were asked to rate how "attractive or appealing" each pin-up was; (*b*) they were offered a photo of a pin-up in renumeration for participating in the experiment; and (*c*) they were interviewed a month later (in a totally different context) and were asked to rank the attractiveness of the pin-ups. Regardless of the measure of attraction used, men markedly preferred the pin-ups they thought had aroused them to those they thought had not.

2. NEED SATISFACTION

Psychologists have tended to focus almost exclusively on the contribution that sex makes to love, but other rewards are also important. People have a wide variety of needs, and, at any stage of life, many of their needs must remain unsatisfied. When a potential love object meets an important, unsatisfied need, the suitor is likely to have a strong emotional response. Such positive emotional responses should be able to provide the fuel needed for passion.

3. EXCITEMENT

Dangerous experiences are arousing. For some peculiar reason, psychologists almost inevitably assume that the arousal one experiences in dangerous settings is entirely negative. Thus, they typically label the physiological reactions which are provoked by dangerous experiences as "fear," "stress," or "pain." They then focus upon ways individuals can learn to foresee and avoid actual danger, or to overcome unrealistic fears. (They almost seem to equate "excitement seeking" with wickedness. For example, in *Human Sexual Response*, Masters and Johnson (1966) reassured readers that "mere thrill seekers" were scrupulously prohibited from participating in their research. Presumably, one has to be properly respectful about sex before he is entitled to assist in scientific discovery.)

Almost never do psychologists acknowledge that it is sometimes fun to be frightened; that it is enjoyable to have a strong emotional response; that reactions to danger can be labeled in positive, as well as in negative, ways; that excitement is an antidote to boredom. One pioneer, Berlyne (1960), has recognized that "danger and delight grow on one stalk," and has systematically explored the conditions under which novelty and excitement are especially attractive to people.

Nonscientists appear to believe that arousal can be fun. Parachuting, skiing, and sportscar racing are valued by sports enthusiasts for the danger they provide. Passionate affairs are valued by many for their excitement. The individual who realizes that he is on dangerous ground may label the rush of passion that he experiences as "love," as well as "anxiety."

We have proposed a two-factor theory of passionate love. The preceding discussion has focused almost exclusively on one factor. We have discussed the idea that physiological arousal is a crucial component of passionate love, and that the stimuli often associated with fear, pain, and frustration, as well as those often associated with more positive experiences, may contribute to passionate love.

Let us now consider the circumstances that help push individuals to label their tumultuous feelings as "passionate love."

V. The Second Step in Generating Passionate Love: Labeling

What determines how an aroused individual will label his tumultuous feelings? The reinforcement paradigm helps us to pinpoint some of the factors that should affect the way individuals interpret the arousal.

A. Children Are Taught How to Label Their Feelings

An anarchic array of stimuli constantly impinge on a child. The child learns how to categorize these stimuli, to discriminate "important" categories of stimuli from "unimportant" categories. He also learns what reactions different categories of stimuli produce in a person.

Envision, for example, a little boy who is playing with a truck while his mother greets a newly arrived neighbor and her infant daughter. He is rubbing his eyes; he has missed his nap. Soon it will be dinner time; he experiences vague hunger pangs. While absorbed in the visitor's movements, he accidently runs his truck over his hand; it hurts. He watches his mother talking and gesturing to the visitor and her little girl. Her voice seems unusually high and animated. They all look at him. His nose tickles.

In response to this *complex* of factors, the boy becomes momentarily overwrought. He hides his face in his mother's skirt for a few seconds; and then peers out. What caused him to hide his face? What emotion is he feeling? Is he jealous of the little girl? Is he afraid of strangers? Is he playing a game? Is he angry because the truck hurt his hand? Is he trying to get attention?

His mother provides an answer for him. She says, "Don't be shy, John. Susan won't hurt you. Come out and meet her." His mother reduces a chaotic jumble of stimuli to manageable size. She instructs him that it is Susan's appearance that has caused his emotional agitation. She informs him that when one has an emotional reaction in the presence of strangers it is called "shyness." She also communicates that the other stimuli, his sore hand for example, are not responsible for his aroused state.

By the time one reaches adolescence, he has learned cultural norms concerning categories of stimuli (situations) that produce specific emotions. He has been painstakingly taught what the common emotions "feel" like. He may base his identification on: (*a*) the perception that he is generally aroused *plus* his knowledge of the situation; or (*b*) the perception that he is *generally* aroused *plus* his knowledge of the situation *plus* the perception that he is physiologically aroused in a *special* way. (Physiologists have not yet identified the extent to which each emotion is associated with unique and readily recognized physiological cues.) In any case, by adolescence, individuals are well trained in what stimuli go with what emotions.

B. Some Emotions Are Better Articulated Than Others

Children undoubtedly have clear perceptions as to what hate, embarrassment, jealousy, and joy are supposed to feel like. They get little practice in learning to discriminate more esoteric emotions, such as bliss, loathing, and contempt.

"Passionate love" is undoubtedly a poorly articulated emotion. Children receive little instruction as to the conditions under which "passionate love" is an appropriate label for one's feelings versus the conditions under which the passionate love label is inappropriate. Most parents assume that children are incapable of experiencing passionate love; they consider passion to be an adolescent phenomenon.

The fact that children are given only glimmerings of information as to the situations conducive to passion, and what passion is supposed to feel like, probably accounts at least in part for the fact that so many teenagers seem confused about the nature of love. "Dear Abby" frequently receives concerned letters asking, "How can I tell if I'm really in love?" Inevitably, she fails to provide an answer. Her stock reply is, "When you're in love, you'll know it; you won't have to ask." Perhaps "Dear Abby" doesn't know either.

Popular songs provide some instructions to teenagers concerning what love should feel like: "When your heart goes bumpety, bump . . . that's love, love, love" they are informed. [The notion that love can be identified by the presence of physiological arousal, at least as evidenced by a quickened heart rate (or even, in severe cases, by cardiac arrest) is common in folklore—if new to social science.] The fact that adolescents often have only very general and somewhat vague notions about how to identify love suggests that situational factors should have a profound impact on whether they label a wide variety of states of generalized arousal as love or as something else.

C. Sometimes Individuals Experience a Mixture of Emotions

People sometimes have difficulty labeling their feelings because a number of potential labels could reasonably describe their aroused state. Consider, for example, the soldier who reports that when he received his first mail from home, he became extremely agitated. He is at a loss to explain just why the package had upset him. Was he feeling homesick? Perhaps the package was upsetting because it was a tangible reminder of how much he longed to be back home. Was he feeling lonesome? His girlfriend had sent the package; perhaps he hadn't realized how much he missed her. Was he feeling resentful? The package reminded him that people back home were free while he was stuck in foreign combat. Or was he worried? His girlfriend's accompanying letter mentioned problems with his car and with his application for admission to college.

When a myriad of labels are potentially appropriate labels for one's feelings, we might again expect social influences to have an unusually great impact on one's choice of label.

D. Determinants of Labeling in Ambiguous Situations

Schachter stated that individuals will label their emotional responses with the "most plausible" label available to them. Are there rules which help us predict what label will seem "most plausible" to the individual? The presence and salience of certain stimuli previously associated with a particular label undoubtedly play a role. But there are undoubtedly other factors which influence "plausibility." Many have argued that reinforcement principles pervade and influence all of human behavior. Walster, Berscheid, and Walster (1973) among other investigators have hypothesized that individuals will try to maximize their outcomes (where outcomes equal rewards minus costs). We would suggest that cost considerations influence one's choice of emotional labels, as well as other behaviors. The label that is likely to be socially approved, for example, would be more likely to be chosen over those which are not.

E. Everyone Loves a Lover: The Cultural Encouragement of Love

In our culture it is expected that almost everyone eventually will fall in love. Individuals are strongly encouraged to interpret a wide range of confused feelings as love. Linton (1936) made this point in a harsh observation:

All societies recognize that there are occasional violent emotional attachments between persons of the opposite sex, but our present American culture is practically the only one which has attempted to capitalize on these and make them the basis for marriage. The hero of the modern American movie is always a romantic lover, just as the hero of an old Arab epic is always an epileptic. A cynic may suspect that in any ordinary population the percentage of individuals with capacity for romantic love of the Hollywood type was about as large as that of persons able to throw genuine epileptic fits [p. 175].*

F. Cultural Norms Specify Whom It Is Reasonable to Love

1. I TOOK ONE LOOK AT YOU AND THEN MY HEART STOOD STILL

"It's not true that only the external appearance of a woman matters. The underwear is also important [Firestone, 1971, p. 134]." In our culture, people assume that passionate fantasies are inspired only by attractive human beings. If one admits that he is sexually attracted to a hunchback, an octogenarian, or a man with no nose, he is branded as sick or perverse.

The evidence suggests that most individuals docilely accept the prescription that beauty and sexual and romantic passion are inexorably linked. The best evidence we have suggests that teenagers and young adults are more enamored by the physical attractiveness of their dating partners than by the partners' intelligence, personality, or similarity.

In a typical study, Berscheid, Dion, Walster, and Walster (1971) took Polaroid snapshots of college males and females. Judges categorized each photo as attractive or unattractive. The experimenters then secured a dating history from the student. The physical attractiveness of female subjects was strongly related to their actual dating popularity. Attractive females had more dates within the past year ($r = .61$), the past month ($r = .50$), and the past week ($r = .44$). There was slight (but insignificant) relationship between the males' physical attractiveness and his dating frequency (past year $r = .25$; month $r = .21$; and week $r = .13$).

Byrne, Ervin, and Lamberth (1970) conducted a field study to determine the extent to which beauty and romantic attraction were related. Students were told that the study involved computer dating and that they had been matched by the computer with a partner who was similar or dissimilar in attitudes to themselves. During this initial interview, the experimenter unobtrusively evaluated the man and woman's physical attractiveness. The partners were introduced to one another and asked to spend the next 30 min on a coke date in the student union. They were told they should then return to the experimental room so that the experimenter could ask them about their first impressions of one another. Each subject indicated how sexually attractive his partner seemed, how much he thought he would enjoy dating him or her, and how much he would like this person as a spouse.

The physical attractiveness of both the male and the female were strongly associated with how desirable they were as a date. The more handsome a male, for example, the higher his partner evaluated his sexuality (.69), his datability (.59), and his marriageability (.59).

Walster, Aronson, Abrahams, and Rottmann (1966) assessed the physical attractiveness of 752 college freshmen. (A panel of college sophomores rated them; they had only 5 sec or so in which to rate the freshmen's attractiveness.) A good deal of data concerning the freshmen's intelligence, personality, and attitudes were also assembled in subsequent university-wide testing. Freshmen were then randomly assigned a date for a large computer dance. During intermission, the freshmen were asked to say how satisfied they were with their computer date. The authors discovered that the sole determinant of how much students liked their date, how eager they were to date their partner again, and how often they subsequently asked their partner out for a date (it was determined later) was simply the physical attractiveness of the partner. The more physically attractive the date, the more he or she was liked and the more he or she was pursued. Efforts to find additional factors that would influence attraction failed. For example, students with exceptional social skills and intelligence levels were not liked any better than were students less fortunate in this regard. It seems, then, that it is helpful to be beautiful if you wish to inspire passion in your contemporaries.

2. LOVE AND MARRIAGE ... GO TOGETHER LIKE A HORSE AND CARRIAGE

Winch (1952) has also argued that one's culture dictates whom one can or cannot love. He maintains that cultural norms legislate that for each person only a strictly prescribed subsample of the population is lovable or "marriageable." This acceptable group is called "the field of eligibles." Young, unmarried adults soon learn that if they fall in love with the right person—someone in their field of eligibles—they can marry and merit social approval. If they should fall in love with the wrong person, they must expect to encounter stinging social disapproval. In American culture, the "field of eligibles" consists of partners who are of the opposite sex, who are single, who are similar to oneself in age (marriages between elderly women and young boys are subject to more disdain than marriages between elderly men and young girls, however), similar in other social background variables, who have known one another for some time, and who desire one another sexually. (See Chapter 3 of this volume.)

Cultural influences are generally effective in determining whom one should love. (See Chapter 4 of this volume.) If parents try to impose additional restrictions on their children's choices, they may not be effective in guiding their children's selections. We recall that "unjustified" parental interference was found by Driscoll *et al.* not to deter the formation of romantic bonds.

3. INFATUATION VERSUS LOVE

In a poll conducted at three universities, college students were asked what one thing they most wished they knew about romantic love. A surprisingly frequent question was: "What is the difference between infatuation and love? How will I know when I am really in love and not just infatuated?" We have become increasingly skeptical that infatuation and passionate love differ in any way—*at the time one is experiencing them.* Data provided by Ellis and Harper (1961), for example, suggest that the difference between infatuation and romantic love is merely semantic. Ellis reported that young adults use the term "romantic love" to describe relationships with the opposite sex that are characterized by strong positive affect and that *are still in progress.* They use the term "infatuation" to describe relationships with the opposite sex that were characterized by strong positive affect and that, for a variety of reasons, *were terminated.*

It appears, then, that it may be possible to tell infatuation from romantic love only in retrospect. If a relationship flowers, one continues to believe he is experiencing true love; if a relationship dies, one concludes that he was merely infatuated. We need not assume, then, that at the time one experiences the feeling, "true love" differs in any way from the supposed "counterfeit," infatuation.

If an individual relabels his feelings as infatuation, rather than love, it may have important consequences for his subsequent behavior. In our culture, "romantic love" tends to be the *sine qua non* for marriage. Kephart (1967) found that in his sample, 65% of the college men would *not* marry a woman they did not love—even though she possessed every other characteristic they desired in a wife. (Women did not associate "love" with "marriage" to the same extent as did men. Only 24% of the women said that they would *not* marry a desirable man simply because they did not love him.)

Since romantic love is likely to lead to marriage in our culture, parents are eager to insure that young people label their feelings as "love" only if they are directed toward "right" people. When their children are attracted to the wrong sort—to someone outside their field of eligibles—the parents may try to persuade their children to label their attraction as "infatuation" and thereby decrease the likelihood that the children will marry unsuitable partners.

G. Cultural Reinforcements Determine Appropriate Labels

When an individual is experiencing arousal which he can reasonably label in a variety of ways, we speculated earlier that he will prefer to label his feelings in whatever way he anticipates will be most rewarded by others and will avoid labeling his feelings in ways that he can anticipate will provoke punishment. When one systematically applies such reinforcement principles to predicting how individuals will label their reactions there are some interesting ramifications. For example, at one period in American history (and perhaps even today), the "double standard" for sexual behavior was commonly accepted (see Reiss, 1960). This standard insisted that "nice" girls must not have sexual intercourse before marriage. If, however, they were "in love," especially if they were engaged, and particularly if they married soon after, transgression was forgivable. These restrictions did not apply to men. Men were supposed to have some sexual experience before marriage. In fact, in many circles a man who had made many sexual conquests was held in high regard.

How would we expect these inconsistent sex-specific, social norms to affect the way men and women labeled sexual arousal? Cost considerations would predispose men and women to choose quite different labels for precisely the same type of physiological reaction. When a man became aroused in a sexual context, he could afford to frankly label his reaction as "sexual excitement." A woman could not. She had most to gain from convincing herself that passion equaled love since such a label allowed her to have both sexual relations and self-respect.

Given such a reward structure, it is not surprising that people soon came to believe that men are sexier than women, and that it is women who are the romantics.

H. Individual Expectations

We have argued that whether or not an individual is susceptible to "falling in love" will depend on the expectations and reward structure of his culture and his reference group. An individual's own expectations should also determine how likely he is to experience love.

1. SELF-PERCEPTIONS AND LOVE

The individual who thinks of himself as a nonromantic person should fall in love less often than an individual who assumes that love is an inevitable and recurring experience. The nonromantic may experience the same feelings that the romantic does, but he should code them differently.

2. SELF-ESTEEM AND LOVE

A person who assumes he is unlovable should have a difficult time finding love. An individual conveys his expectations in subtle ways to others; these expectations should influence the way his partner labels *her* reactions. The insecure man who habitually complains to his girlfriend: "You don't love me, you just think you do; if you loved me, you wouldn't treat me this way," and then itemizes evidence of her neglect, may—by interpreting his girlfriend's actions for her and in a damaging way—alter her feelings for him. Alternately, a man with a great deal of self-confidence, may by his unconscious guidance induce an unreceptive woman to agree that her feelings for him should be labeled love.

3. BACKGROUND FACTORS AND LOVE

Wide variations exist in the feeling states individuals associate with "passionate love." The boy brought up on the sunny lyrics of: "What a day this has been. What a rare mood I'm in. Why it's almost like being in love ..." is likely to assume that love is a positive experience. For him love is likely to be associated predominately with esthetic reverence, sexual ecstasy, excitement, and joy.

An individual brought up on a diet of: "Can't help loving dat man....," "I should hate, yet I love you ...," "You've got me in between the devil and the deep blue sea . . .," or "Bill Bailey, won't you please come home . . ." is likely to assume that love is a negative experience—a state inexorably linked to sexual deprivation, longing for appreciation, and the shame of rejection and neglect.

4. ATTITUDES TOWARD DEPENDENCY AND LOVE

Dependency is an important theme in much of the romantic love literature. When one imagines the flawless partner, or is lucky enough to find in real life a person who can satisfy many of one's desires, an awareness of the extent to which one could be dependent on that other, how much one needs the other, is a frequent concomitant. But when lovers realize they are about to become or have become dependent on the loved one, they may experience conflicting reactions.

On one hand, their awareness of how much joy the loved one may bring them should cause lovers to further appreciate each other. On the other hand, their awareness of dependency may be upsetting: First, the more the benefits the loved one provides, the more the dependent lover has to fear should the loved one no longer love him. Second, adults are supposed to be independent; weak, dependent adults are scorned. One prominent theorist, Maslow (1954), exemplified the subtle way we cast aspersions on a person who reveals his dependency. Maslow argued that there are two types of love: (*a*) an inferior type of love characteristic of "nonactualized," ordinary mortals—D *love*, or deficiency love, where one loves another for what the other can do for them; and (*b*) that rare and superior type of love characteristic of "self-actualized" people—B *love*, or love for the other's being.

Because dependency is both delightful and disturbing, most individuals are intensely ambivalent about becoming dependent on another. A number of romantic love theorists have commented upon this ambivalence. For example, Blau (1964) noted that in romantic love, dependency "has a frightening aspect." Reik (1963) and Klein and Riviere (1953) associated "anxiety of dependency" and "fear of dependency" with love. Thibaut and Kelley (1959) ascribed the "ambivalence which frequently dominates heterosexual love relationships" to the threat to independence which a person tries to delay "before it overwhelms him [p. 66]."

Those individuals who associate romantic love with dependency, and who have learned to fear deep reliance upon another person should be less vulnerable to passionate love.

VI. Summary

Psychologists know very little about passionate love. Thus, our chapter has had two goals: (*a*) To describe some of the sparse experimental laboratory data that exist on the topic of passionate love; (*b*) To marshall evidence that supports the two-component theory, which seems to handle the complex and elusive phenomenon of passionate love. According to this theory, two conditions—physiological arousal and appropriate labeling—are necessary if an individual is to experience a "true" emotional response. It was suggested that a wide variety of arousing experiences may have the potential to fuel passion. What may be crucial in determining what emotion the person will experience is how the individual labels his aroused state. A number of cultural and personality factors should affect whether individuals label their feelings as passionate love, or as something else. A great deal of research must be done before this approach gains the status of even a tentative theory of romantic love. At the present time, however, the two-component theory seems to be an effective way to organize the little we know about love.

Acknowledgments

Preparations of this paper was facilitated in part by NIMH grant MH 16661, and NSF grants GS 35157X and GS 30822X.

References

Ax, A. F. Fear and anger in humans. *Psychosomatic Medicine,* 1953, **15**, 433–442.

Beigel, H. G. Romantic love. *American Sociological Review,* 1951, **16**, 326–334.

Berlyne, D. E. *Conflict, arousal and curiosity.* New York: McGraw-Hill, 1960.

Berscheid, E., Dion, K., Walster, E., & Walster, G. W. Physical attractiveness and dating choice: A test of the matching hypothesis. *Journal of Experimental Social Psychology,* 1971, **7**, 173–189.

Blau, P. M., *Exchange and power in social life.* New York: Wiley, 1964.

Brehm, J. W., Gatz, M., Geothals, G., McCrommon, J., & Ward, L. Psychological arousal and interpersonal attraction. Mimeo. Available from authors, 1970.

Byrne, D. *The attraction paradigm.* New York: Academic Press, 1971.

Byrne, D., Ervin, C. R., & Lamberth, J. Continuity between the experimental study of attraction and real-life computer dating. *Journal of Personality and Social Psychology,* 1970, **16**, 157–165.

DeRougemont, D. *Love in the western world.* (Translated by M. Belgion.) New York: Harcourt, 1940.

Dittes, J. E. Attractiveness of group as function of self-esteem and acceptance by group. *Journal of Abnormal and Social Psychology,* 1959, **59**, 77–82.

Driscoll, R., Davis, K. E., & Lipitz, M. E. Parental interference and romantic love: The Romeo and Juliet effect. *Journal of Personality and Social Psychology,* 1972, **24**, 1–10.

Durrell, L. *Clea.* New York: Dutton, 1961.

Ellis, A., & Harper, A. *Creative marriage.* New York: Stuart, 1961.

Finck, H. T. *Romantic love and personal beauty: Their development, causal relations, historic and national peculiarities.* New York: Macmillan, 1891.

Firestone, S. *The dialectic of sex.* New York: Bantam, 1971.

Freud, S. *Group psychology and the analysis of the ego.* (Translated by J. Strachey.) New York: International Psychoanalytic Press, 1922.

Fromm, E. *The art of loving.* New York: Harper, 1956.

Galbraith, J. K. *The ambassador's journal.* Boston, Massachusetts: Houghton, 1969.

Goode, W. J. The theoretical importance of love. *American Sociological Review,* 1959, **24**, 38–47.

Harlow, H. F. The nature of love. *American Psychologist,* 1958, **13**, 673–685.

Hohmann, G. W. The effect of dysfunctions of the autonomic nervous system on experienced feelings and emotions. Paper presented at the Conference on Emotions and Feelings at New School for Social Research, New York, 1962.

Homans, G. C. *The human group*. New York: Harcourt, 1950.

Homans, G. C. *Social behavior: Its elementary forms*. New York: Harcourt, 1961.

Hunt, M. M. *The natural history of love*. New York: Knopf, 1959.

Jacobs, L., Berscheid, E., & Walster, E. Self-esteem and attraction. *Journal of Personality and Social Psycology*, 1971, **17**, 84–91.

Kephart, W. M. Some correlates of romantic love. *Journal of Marriage and the Family*, 1967, **29**, 470–474.

Kinsey, A., Pomeroy, W., Martin, C., & Gebhard, P. *Sexual behavior in the human female*. Philadelphia, Pennsylvania: Saunders, 1953.

Kirch, A. M. (Ed.). *The anatomy of love*. New York: Dell, 1960.

Klein, M., & Riviere, J. *Love, hate and reparation*. London: Hogarth Press, 1953.

Klinger, E. *Structure and functions of fantasy*. New York: Wiley, 1971.

Linton, R. *The study of man*. New York: Appleton, 1936.

Maslow, A. H. *Motivation and personality*. New York: Harper, 1954.

Masters, W. H., & Johnson, W. E. *Human sexual response*. Boston, Massachusetts: Brown, 1966.

Newcomb, T. M. *The acquaintance process*. New York: Holt, 1961.

Ovid. *The art of love*. (Translated by Rolfe Humphries.) Bloomington, Indiana: University of Indiana Press, 1962.

Reik, T. *Need to be loved*. New York: Farrar, Straus & Co., 1943.

Reik, T. *A psychologist looks at love*. New York: Farrar & Rinehart,, 1944.

Reiss, L. *Premarital sexual standards in America*. New York: Free Press, 1960.

Schachter, S. The interaction of cognitive and physiological determinants of emotional state. In L. Berkowitz (Ed.), *Advances in experimental social psychology*. Vol. 1. New York: Academic Press, 1964.

Schachter, S. Pain, fear and anger in hypertensives and normotensives: A psycho-physiological study. *Psychosomatic Medicine*, 1957, **19**, 17–24.

Schachter, S., & Singer, J. F. Cognitive, social and physiological determinants of emotional state. *Psychological Review*, 1962, **69**, 379–399.

Schachter, S., & Wheeler, L. Epinephrine, chloropromazin, and amusement. *Journal of Abnormal and Social Psychology*, 1962, **65**, 121–128.

Skinner, B. F. *The behavior of organisms: An experimental analysis*. New York: Appleton, 1938.

Thibaut, J. W., & Kelley, H. H. *The social psychology of groups*. New York: Wiley, 1959.

Valins, S. Cognitive effects of false heart-rate feedback. *Journal of Personality and Social Psychology*, 1966, **4**, 400–408.

Walster, E. The effect of self-esteem on romantic liking. *Journal of Experimental Social Psychology*, 1965, **1**, 184–197.

Walster, E., Aronson, V., Abrahams, D., & Rottmann, L. The importance of physical attractiveness in dating behavior. *Journal of Personality and Social Psychology*, 1966, **4**, 508–516.

Walster, E., & Berscheid, E. Adrenaline makes the heart grow fonder. *Psychology Today*, 1971, **5**, 47–62.

Walster, E., Berscheid, E., & Walster, G. New directions in equity research. *Journal of Personality and Social Psychology*, 1973, **25** (2), 151–176.

Walster, E., Walster, G., & Berscheid, E. The efficacy of playing hard-to-get. *Journal of Experimental Education*, 1971, **39**, 73–77.

Walster, E., Walster, G., Piliavin, J., & Schmidt, L. "Playing hard-to-get": Understanding an elusive phenomenon. *Journal of Personality and Social Psychology*, 1973, **26**(1), 113–121.

Webb, E. J., Campbell, D. T. Schwartz, R. D., & Sechrest, L. *Unobtrusive measures: Nonreactive research in the social sciences*. Chicago, Illinois: Rand McNally, 1966.

Williamson, R. C. *Marriage and family relations*. New York: Wiley, 1966.

Winch, R. F. *The modern family*. New York: Holt, 1952.

Wolf, S. & Wolff, H. G. *Human gastric function.* (2nd ed.) London and New York: Oxford University Press, 1947.

Xenophon. *Memorabilia III.* (Translated by E. C. Marchant.) London: Heinemann, 1923.

Zuckerman, M. Physiological measures of sexual response in the human. *Psychological Bulletin,* 1971, **75**, 297–329.

16

From Liking to Loving: Patterns of Attraction in Dating Relationships

ZICK RUBIN

Department of Psychology
and Social Relations
Harvard University
Cambridge, Massachusetts

I. Introduction

Although liking and loving are closely related varieties of interpersonal attraction, psychologists who have been interested in liking and those who have been concerned with loving have taken distinctly separate paths. Abundant attention has been given to each of the two sentiments, but only rarely are the two mentioned in the same sentence, the same journal, or the same spirit. It is more than a matter of professional specialization. Rather, the literatures on liking and on loving seem to represent fundamentally different approaches to the understanding of interpersonal attraction. The liking researchers are determined data gatherers. By means of hundreds of experimental studies they have uncovered a great deal of information on the wide range of factors that lead one person to like—or, at least, to say that he likes—another person. For all their energetic data-gathering, however, the liking researchers have spent remarkably little time debating what liking is. Its conceptual meaning is generally left to the realm of "common understanding." The love watchers, on the other hand, are of a less experimental and more theoretical stripe. From Plato to Freud to present-day theorists such as Fromm, Maslow, and May, the psychology of love has always been a prime topic of discourse and debate. Creative definitions of love are plentiful. But very few behavioral scientists have conducted empirical research on love. "So far as love or affection is concerned," one experimental psychologist—Harlow (1958)—has written, "psychologists have failed in their mission[p. 673]."

Whatever its causes, the split between the liking researchers and the love watchers has led to the unnatural segregation of two closely related aspects of interpersonal relations. This chapter reports an attempt to build a bridge between the two by examining romantic love empirically. The adjective "romantic" is not meant to connote all of the trappings of the medieval romantic ideal, but simply to distinguish the sort of love which may exist among unmarried, opposite-sex partners from such other related forms as love between children and their parents, close friends, and men and God. The research to be reported attempted to combine some of the insights of the love watchers with some of the empirical tools of the liking researchers. An important focus of the research strategy was to distinguish the concepts of liking and loving and to measure them in the same relationships.

II. Conceptual Beginnings

In accord with a strategy of construct validation, the attempts to conceptualize and to measure liking and loving are seen as integral parts of a single endeavor (see Cronbach & Meehl, 1955). Whereas such a psychometric approach has occasionally been taken with regard to liking, psychologists have not yet seen fit to apply such an approach to love. The attempt is not really at odds with even the most poetic temperament, however. "How do I love thee? Let me count the ways," Elizabeth Barrett Browning wrote, thereby alluding to the most basic form of measurment. The difficult question is to decide which ways to count.

A survey of the prodigious literature on love encounters widely divergent, proposed answers to this question. What Shakespeare defined as "a spirit all compact of fire" has been defined by others as a "centrifugal act of the soul" (Ortega y Gasset), "a state of perceptual anesthesia" (H. L. Mencken), and "not ever having to say you're sorry" (Erich Segal). For Freud, love is a push from behind, produced by the sublimation of overtly sexual impulses. For Plato it is a pull from ahead, engendered by the search for the ultimate good. Among these and hundreds of other conceptions, two themes stand out as central. These are the conceptions of love as *needing* and as *giving*.

The conception of love as a physical or emotional need can be traced back at least as far as the sixth century B.C., when the poetess Sappho set forth a symptomatology of lovesickness, which was used as a diagnostic aid by Greek physicians for centuries thereafter and which sometimes seems valid even today. It included heart palpitations, flushing, auditory disturbances, profuse sweating, and muscle tremors, followed by faintness and pallor. As the Supremes put it in a song of the 1960s, "Love is like an itching in my heart." The defining features of love, in terms of this conception, are powerful desires to be in the other's presence, to make physical contact, to be approved of, to be cared for. In its most extreme form the love need appears as a passionate desire to possess another person, corresponding to what the Greeks called *eros*. In milder and more contemporary psychological terms, we can identify the need conception of love with "attachment," as exemplified by the bonds formed between infants and their parents (see Bowlby, 1969; Harlow, 1958).

In apparent contrast to the conception of love as a cluster of needs is the conception of love as giving to another person. This is the conception of love emphasized in the New Testament, epitomized by St. John's declaration that "God is love." Contemporary psychological definitions also depict the lover as the ultimate altruist. For Fromm (1956): "Love is the active concern for the life and the growth of that which we love [p. 26]." According to Sullivan (1953): "When the satisfaction or the security of another person becomes as significant to one as is one's own satisfaction or security, then the state of love exists [pp. 42−43]." Love as giving corresponds to what the Greeks called *agape* and to what I will refer to as "caring."

The argument can be made that attachment is a less mature form of love than caring. Whereas infant primates develop strong attachments toward their parents, for example, caring is a phenomenon that does not typically appear until somewhat later in life. (In Sullivan's view, people first learn to care about others in the context of childhood friendships.) The developmental sequence from attachment to caring is made explicit in Maslow's (1955) analysis of love. Maslow, a guiding spirit of the "humanistic revolution" in modern psychology, associated attachment with people's "deficiency needs" for acceptance and approval. He suggested that "love hunger is a deficiency disease exactly as is salt hunger or the avitaminoses [p. 26]," and as such is an immature form of love. People who have reached a higher state of "self-actualization," in Maslow's framework, have already satisfied their need for love. D-love (D for "deficiency") is replaced by B-love (B for "being"), which is less needful and dependent, and more autonomous and giving.

Maslow's analysis of love implies that needing and giving stand opposed to one another, and that the more there is of one, the less there will be of the other. But it is doubtful that such an opposition corresponds to the actual nature of love relationships. It seems more likely that as a couple's relationship becomes increasingly close, it will be associated with both increased attachment and increased caring. Orlinsky (1972) suggested, for example, that attachment and caring merge to form a "dual feeling-impulse," which may be equated with love.

The theologian Paul Tillich (1957) also discussed love as ideally being a merger of attachment and caring, as expressed by the Greek conceptions of *eros* and *agape*:

> *Eros* is described as the desire for self-fulfillment by the other being, *agape* as the will to self-surrender for the sake of the other being. . . . No love is real without a unity of *eros* and *agape*. *Agape* without *eros* is obedience to moral law, without warmth, without longing, without

reunion. *Eros* without *agape* is chaotic desire, denying the validity of the claim of the other one to be acknowledged as an independent self, able to love and to be loved. Love as the union of *eros* and *agape* is an implication of faith. [pp. 114–15].

Rather than equating love with attachment or with caring, therefore, I would consider both to be basic components of love. Both attachment and caring remain essentially *individual* conceptions, however. They refer to entities within one person's mind or heart. But love may also be viewed as an inherently dyadic phenomenon, as well as an individual one. Two people who love one another establish an intimate bond which may be attributed to the relationship between them, rather than to the two parties individually. Martin Buber (1970) made this point when he talked about the "I–Thou" relationship:

> Love does not cling to an I, as if the You were merely its "content" or object; it is *between* I and You. Whoever does not know this ... does not know love ... [p. 66, my italics].

It seems useful, therefore, to postulate a third component of love which refers to the bond or link between two people. This third component, which I will call "intimacy," should be manifest most clearly by close and confidential communication between two people, through both verbal and nonverbal channels.

When we turn from loving to liking, we encounter a wealth of operational definitions, mostly of the self-report variety. Byrne's two-item index, for example, combines an experimental subject's answers to the questions, "How much do you feel that you would like this person?" and "How much do you believe that you would like working with this person in an experiment?" (see Byrne, 1971). Other measures call for the subject to rate another person on sets of evaluative bipolar adjectives, such as "warm–cold," "mature–immature," and "intelligent–unintelligent." Conceptually, liking is generally regarded as a more or less undifferentiated positive attitude toward another person. The evaluative component of liking is usually given greatest emphasis. A "likable" person is one who is viewed as good or desirable on a number of dimensions. The focal evaluative dimensions tapped in measures of liking are often, although not exclusively, "task-related" ones. We like people who are intelligent, competent, and trustworthy—the sorts of people with whom we prefer to work in experiments and for whom we vote in elections (for example, "I Like Ike"). The pervasive finding that we like others whose attitudes resemble our own (see Byrne, 1971) may be interpreted in terms of such a task-related conception of liking. We are apt to view another person's agreement with our own opinions as evidence of his intelligence, maturity, and good judgment—and, accordingly, of his "likability."

What would we expect to be the empirical relationships between one person's love and his liking for another person? In most instances one would expect at least a moderately positive evaluation of another person to be a prerequisite for the development of attachment, caring, and intimacy. Thus, it would be surprising if liking and loving were not at least moderately correlated with one another. But, whereas liking and loving may have much in common, we would hesitate to equate the two phenomena. People often express liking for a person whom they would not claim to love in the least. In other instances they may declare their love for someone whom they cannot reasonably be said to like very well. "As much as I can't stand how crazy he is half the time," one student recently told an interviewer, "I love him more than anything and couldn't live without him." Folk wisdom suggests, moreover, that the bases of the two phenomena may sometimes differ. Whereas we are predisposed to like others who are similar to ourselves, it has been proposed that we are drawn to love others who "complement" or "complete" ourselves (see Reik, 1944). And whereas it is well documented that we are most apt to come to like people to whom we are frequently exposed (see Festinger, Schachter, & Back, 1950; Zajonc, 1968), in the case of love it seems that absence at least sometimes makes the heart grow fonder.

III. Measuring Liking and Loving

On the basis of the above considerations, the starting assumption in my attempt to develop self-report scales of liking and loving was that they should represent moderately correlated, but nevertheless distinct, dimensions of one person's attitude toward another person. With this starting assumption, my study consisted of three stages. First, I constructed parallel self-report scales of liking and loving, which met the requirements of the starting assumption. Second, I examined the ways in which people's scores on each of the two scales related to a variety of other self-report measures, including their plans for marriage. Third, I proceeded to assess the usefulness of the love scale in predicting people's subsequent behavior and the course of their relationships.

The first step in scale construction was to make up a large number of items reflecting aspects of one person's attitudes toward a particular other person. The items spanned a wide range of thoughts, feelings, and behavioral predispositions— for example, "How much fun is _____ to be with?", "How much do you trust _____ ?", "To what extent are you physically attracted to _____ ?", "How much does _____ get on your nerves?" To check on my own initial intuitions as to which items were more relevant to "liking" and which to "loving," I asked a number of friends and acquaintances of both sexes to sort the items into "liking" and "loving" sets, based on their own understanding of the meaning of the two terms. After making revisions suggested by these raters' judgments, I presented a new pool of 70 items to 198 undergraduates at the University of Michigan and asked them to respond to each in terms of their feelings toward their boyfriend or girlfriend (if they had one), and in terms of their feelings toward a platonic friend of the opposite sex. Factor analysis of these responses led to the specification of two 13-item scales, one of "love" and the other of "liking" (see Table 1).[1]

[1]Details of the scale-development procedure are presented by Rubin (1969, Chapter 2).

TABLE 1

Love-Scale and Liking-Scale Items

LOVE SCALE

1. If _____ were feeling badly, my first duty would be to cheer him (her) up.
2. I feel that I can confide in _____ about virtually everything.
3. I find it easy to ignore _____'s faults[a].
4. I would do almost anything for _____ .
5. I feel very possessive toward _____ .
6. If I could never be with _____ , I would feel miserable.
7. If I were lonely, my first thought would be to seek _____ out.
8. One of my primary concerns is _____'s welfare.
9. I would forgive _____ for practically anything.
10. I feel responsible for _____'s well-being.
11. When I am with _____ , I spend a good deal of time just looking at him (her).
12. I would greatly enjoy being confided in by _____ .
13. It would be hard for me to get along without _____ .

LIKING SCALE

1. When I am with _____ , we almost always are in the same mood.
2. I think that _____ is unusually well-adjusted.
3. I would highly recommend _____ for a responsible job.
4. In my opinion, _____ is an exceptionally mature person.
5. I have great confidence in _____'s good judgment.
6. Most people would react favorably to _____ after a brief acquaintance.
7. I think that _____ and I are quite similar to one another.
8. I would vote for _____ in a class or group election.
9. I think that _____ is one of those people who quickly wins respect.
10. I feel that _____ is an extremely intelligent person.
11. _____ is one of the most likable people I know.
12. _____ is the sort of person whom I myself would like to be.
13. It seems to me that it is very easy for _____ to gain admiration.

Note: Psychometric data on the two scales can be found in Rubin (1970). In my current research I am making use of 9-item versions of the two scales, omitting love items 1, 3, 5, and 11 and liking items 1, 7, 8, and 10.

[a]This item proved to be more highly correlated with total liking scores than with total love scores. The data presented in Table 2 are based on the original 13-item versions of both scales. In all other analysis presented in this chapter, the love score is based on a 12-item version, omitting this item.

The content of the scales corresponds closely to the conceptions of liking and loving outlined in the previous section. The love scale includes items directed at the postulated components of attachment ("If I were lonely, my first thought would be to seek _____ out"); caring ("If _____ were feeling badly, my first duty would be to cheer him (her) up"); and intimacy ("I feel that I can confide in _____ about virtually everything"). The items on the liking scale focus on favorable evaluation of the other person on several dimensions—including adjustment, maturity, good judgment, and intelligence—and on the associated tendency to view the other person as similar to oneself. The close fit between the scale items and the preceding conceptual discussion is by no means accidental. Rather, my working definitions of liking and loving were to a large extent given focus by the results of the scale-development procedure.

Specification of liking and love scales with some degree of face validity is but a small step in the enterprise of construct validation, however. The task that remained was to assess the utility of the scales in the description of ongoing interpersonal relationships. With this goal in mind, I proceeded to administer the scales, with their component items interspersed, to a volunteer sample of 182 dating couples[2] at the University of Michigan in the fall of 1968. The modal couple consisted of a junior man and a sophomore woman who had been dating for about a year. Each respondent individually completed the scales with respect to his or her dating partner, and with respect to a close same-sex friend. The respondent indicated how much he agreed or disagreed with each item by placing a check on a continuous scale, which was later converted to a score from one to nine. On the same questionnaire, the respondents were asked for further information about themselves and their relationship. Six months later, a follow-up report about the movement of their relationship toward greater or lesser "intensity" was obtained from the respondents.

Coefficient alpha, an index of internal consistency, was greater than .80 for each scale among both men and women. For the scales to have discriminant validity, however, it was also necessary for them to be only moderately correlated with one another (see Campbell, 1960). This proved to be the case. The correlation between men's love and liking scores for their girlriends was .56, and the correlation between women's love and liking for their boyfriends was .36. The finding that love and liking were more highly related to one another among men than among women was unexpected, but perhaps not inexplicable. Parsons and Bales (1955) have suggested that in most societies men tend to be the "task specialists," while women tend to be the "social-emotional specialists." Perhaps by virtue of their specialization, women develop a more finely tuned and more discriminating set of interpersonal attitudes than do men. Men may be more likely to blur such subtle distinctions as the one between liking and loving, while women may be more likely to experience and express the two sentiments as distinct.

Further insight into the nature of love and liking for men and for women was derived from a comparison of their mean scores on the two scales. Table 2 shows that the average love scores of men for their girlfriends and of women for their boy-

---

[2]By 1968–69, when I conducted the study, it had already become somewhat outmoded for college students to "date." Continuing and casual contacts between the sexes, often facilitated by residential proximity in apartments or dormitories, have to a considerable extent replaced the traditional pattern in which boy phones girl days or weeks in advance to invite her to accompany him to a movie, football game, or fraternity party. In spite of the decline of the date, however, exclusive or semiexclusive relationships between unmarried men and women still thrive on American campuses. One of the major functions of these relationships, although it is not universally subscribed to, continues to be the selection of marriage partners. For lack of a better word ("opposite-sex relationships" is too pedantic, "boy–girl relationships" too patronizing), I continue to refer to these liaisons as "dating relationships" and to the principals as "dating couples."

TABLE 2

Love and Liking for Dating Partners and Same-Sex Friends

	Women		Men	
	Mean	SD	Mean	SD
Love for partner	89.46	15.54	89.37	15.16
Liking for partner	88.48	13.40	84.65	13.81
Love for friend	65.27	17.84	55.07	16.08
Liking for friend	80.47	16.47	79.10	18.07

Note: Based on responses of 158 couples. Data for 24 engaged couples were not included.

friends were almost identical. But women *liked* their boyfriends significantly more than they were liked in return. Cultural expectations related to male and female roles seem to provide the explanation. The liking scale is "sex-biased" in that it asks the respondent to size up his or her partner on such stereotypically male characteristics as maturity, intelligence, and good judgment. It is doubtful that the men in our sample were in fact more mature, more intelligent, or endowed with better judgment than their girlfriends. Nevertheless, it is generally considered to be more appropriate for men, than for women, to excel on these predominantly "task-related" dimensions.

Table 2 also shows that when the respondents evaluated their same-sex friends, there was no tendency for men to be liked more than women. Thus, the data do not support the conclusion that men are generally more "likable" than women, but only that they are liked more in the context of dating relationships. Rather than obliterating stereotypical differences between the sexes, the dating relationship may perpetuate them. The findings seem to be in accord with the feminist critique of traditionally structured male–female relationships as fortifying the favored position of the male and reemphasizing the inferior position of the female.

The data presented in Table 2 also indicate that women tended to love their same-sex friend more than men did. This difference may reflect substantive differences in the nature of men's and women's same-sex friendships. Survey evidence suggests that although women do not tend to have more friends than men, their friendships tend to be more intimate, involving more spontaneous joint activities and more exchanging of confidences (see Booth, 1972; Douvan & Adelson, 1966; Jourard & Lasakow, 1958). The male role, for all its task-related "likability," may limit the ability to love (see Jourard, 1964, Chapter 6). Loving for men may be channeled exclusively into a single opposite-sex relationship, whereas women may be able to experience and express attachment, caring, and intimacy in other relationships, as well.

Another approach toward assessing the construct and discriminant validity of the measures of love and liking involved comparing their empirical links to other variables. One of the questionnaire items was "Would you say that you and _____ are in love?", to be answered by checking "Yes," "No," or "Uncertain." Slightly more than two-thirds of both men and women answered affirmatively, with only about 10% of each sex reporting that they were not in love, and the remaining 22% of each sex pleading uncertainty. The correlation between love scores and the "in love" index was reasonably high: .61 for women and .53 for men. The correlation between liking scores and the "in love" index was considerably lower: .29 for women and .36 for men. These data indicated that the love scale (which nowhere included the word "love" itself) tapped a sentiment that is distinctively related to the respondents' own categorization of their dating relationships.

The students were also asked to estimate the likelihood "that you and _____ will marry one another," on a probability scale ranging from 0–10% to 91–100%. The average estimate was about 50% for women and 45% for men. The correlations between love scores and estimates of marriage likelihood were substantial: .60 for women and .59 for men. The correlations between liking scores and marriage likelihood estimates were substantially lower: .33 for women and .35 for men. Once again the pattern of correlations seems reasonable. In societies like our own with a "love pattern" of mate selection (see Goode, 1959), the link between love and marriage is strongly emphasized by parents, mass media, and other socializing agents. The link between liking and marriage, on the other hand, is too often a well-kept secret.

Based on our conceptualization of the two sentiments, it is also possible to make a prediction about the relative degree of mutuality of liking and of loving. Since liking is defined in terms of one person's unilateral evaluation of another, there is no necessary reason to expect a high correlation between A's liking for B and B's liking for A in the context of a dating relationship. The conception of love, on the other hand, specifically postulates a component of intimacy which characterizes the dyad as a whole. Thus, we might predict that boyfriends' and girlfriends' love for one another will be more highly intercorrelated than their liking for one another will be. The data bear out this expectation, but only weakly—the intracouple correlations are .43 for love and .28 for liking.

IV. Loving and Looking

It is a well-known folk wisdom that people who are in love spend inordinate amounts of time gazing into each others' eyes. Not all such truisms are in fact true, but there is reason to believe that this one may be. Sociologists, as well as song writers, have noted that eye contact plays, as Goffman (1963) put it, "a special role in the communication life of the community [p. 92]." Eye contact serves as a mutually understood signal that the communication channel between two people is open. The actions of either party while eye contact is sustained are automatically defined as relevant to both of them. As a result, Goffman noted, people will studiously avoid making eye contact with others when they wish to minimize the possibility that any interaction will ensue between them. Strangers who find themselves in the same elevator typically stare blankly into space, and the harried waitress takes pains to prevent prospective customers from catching her eye.

Georg Simmel eloquently described the sociological function of eye contact in his *Soziologie*:

> Of all the special sense-organs, the eye has a uniquely sociological function. The union and interaction of individuals is based upon mutual glances. This is perhaps the purest and most direct reciprocity that exists anywhere.... So tenacious and subtle is this union that it can only be maintained by the shortest and straightest line between the eyes, and the smallest deviation from it, the slightest glance aside, completely destroys the unique character of this union.... The totality of social relations of human beings, their self-assertion and self-abnegation, their intimacies and estrangements, would be changed in unpredictable ways if there existed no glance of eye to eye. This mutual glance between persons, in distinction from the simple sight or observation of the other, signifies a wholly new and unique union between them (Simmel, cited in Park & Burgess, 1924, p. 358).*

Social scientists have speculated about the developmental and evolutionary origins of the social functions of eye contact. Eye contact has been identified by students of infant behavior as a critical element in the development of mother–infant attachment. One researcher concluded that "not physical, but visual contact is at the basis of human sociability" (Rheingold, 1961). Another investigator reported that "The nature of the eye contact between a mother and her baby seems to cut across all interactional systems and conveys the intimacy or 'distance' characteristic of their relationship as a whole" (Robson, 1967, p. 18). On the evolutionary level, Konrad Lorenz (1952) has, in his characteristic analogical style, noted convergences between the functions of eye contact among human beings and among lower animals:

> As he makes his proposal, the male [jackdaw] glances continually toward his love but ceases his efforts immediately if she chances to fly away; this however she is not likely to do if she is interested in her admirer.... He casts glowing glances straight into his loved one's eyes, while she apparently turns her eyes in all directions other than that of her ardent suitor. In reality, of course, she is watching him all the time, and her quick glances of a fraction of a second are quite long enough to make her realize that all his antics are calculated to inspire her admiration: long enough to let "him" know that "she" knows [pp. 156–157].†

Whatever its origins, eye contact clearly provides a channel through which intimate feelings can be directly expressed. As a result, when two people do not feel close to one another, eye contact is extremely difficult to sustain. To the extent that two people love one another, on the other hand, we would predict that they would not only tolerate, but in fact welcome, the opportunities provided by eye contact as a vehicle for intimate communication.

A laboratory test of this prediction was conducted by unobtrusively observing

---

*Reprinted from *Introduction to the Science of Sociology*, 2nd edition, edited by R. E. Park and E. W. Burgess, by permission of the University of Chicago Press. Copyright © 1924 by the University of Chicago.

†From *King Solomon's Ring* by Konrad Z. Lorenz, Copyright 1952 by Thomas Y. Crowell company. With permission of the publishers.

the amount of time couples spent making eye contact during a fixed interval, while they were waiting for an experiment to begin. As predicted, "strong love" couples (those in which both partners had scored above the median on the love scale) made significantly more eye contact than "weak love" couples (those in which both partners had scored below the median). This finding was certainly not a surprising one. But it added considerably to my confidence that the love scale measured something that went beyond mere questionnaire-checking to other modes of interpersonal behavior. Importantly, the difference between "strong love" and "weak love" couples did not emerge with respect to the sheer quantity of looking-at-the-other by the two partners, but rather with respect to its cooccurrence. "Weak love" boyfriends and girlfriends were relatively more likely to look at one another unilaterally, while "strong love" boyfriends and girlfriends were more likely to look at one another simultaneously.

Eye contact was also measured in two additional experimental conditions. These conditions again compared "strong lovers" and "weak lovers," but subjects were paired with other people's boyfriends and girlfriends instead of their own. The additional conditions investigated the possibility that "strong lovers" are the sort of people who find it easy to maintain eye contact, not only with their partners, but with other people in general. Such a possibility is suggested by Fromm's (1956) analysis of love: "Love is not primarily a relationship toward a particular person. It is . . . an *orientation of character* which determines the relatedness of a person to the world as a whole, not toward one 'object' of love . . . . If I truly love one person I love all persons, I love the world, I love life [pp. 38–39]." Thus, one might conjecture that when two "strong lovers" encounter one another, even though they have never before met, they still might find it easier to communicate intimately and to maintain eye contact than "weak lovers."

But this suggestion was not supported by the obtained data. When the dyads consisted of opposite-sex strangers, the "strong lovers" did not make significantly more eye contact than did those who were "weak lovers." Therefore, the pattern of results was more congruent with a conception of love as an attitude toward a particular person than as an orientation toward all mankind. There may still be considerable truth in Fromm's analysis; but its behavioral implications may be offset by the fact that when two people are in love with one another they have fewer emotional resources left for others. The latter point was emphasized by Freud (1955), who maintained that "two people coming together for the purpose of sexual satisfaction, in so far as they seek solitude, are making a demonstration against . . . the group feeling. The more they are in love, the more completely they suffice for each other . . . [p. 140]."[3] Or, as the popular song has it, "I only have eyes for you."

[3] The obtained findings on eye contact are not directly relevant to the distinction I have drawn between love and liking. There are, in fact, experimental findings which indicate that in interactions among strangers the amount of eye contact engaged in is directly related to sentiments of liking (see Exline, 1971). To the extent that love and liking are directly related to one another, we would expect liking to be related to eye contact among dating couples, as well. Further research on behavioral correlates of love is reported by Rubin (1973, pp. 225–228).

V. Similar Attitudes and Different Religions

The question of what factors produce love between two people is an enormously complicated one. There are probably at least as many reasons for loving as there are people who love. In each case there is a different constellation of needs to be gratified, a different set of characteristics that are found to be rewarding, and a different ideal to be fulfilled. Moreover, the precipitating events are different from one case to another. People may sometimes be impelled to love by the death of a parent or by the break-up of a previous relationship. But there are also people who are most likely to fall in love after a victory, when their self-esteem is at a peak. Yet in spite of all of these variations, it may be possible for social scientists to advance our understanding of the factors precipitating love by taking small pieces of the picture at a time.

On one level, the question of what precipitates love concerns the factors which make it likely for a particular man and woman to encounter one another and to consider one another "eligible" for at least a trial period. The fact that all of the couples in my sample were students at the same campus helps to account for the fact that they found one another. I found, in addition, that there was a remarkably large correlation between boyfriends' and girlfriends' scores on a measure of authoritarianism ($r = .51$). Attitude similarity on this dimension seemed to have exerted considerable influence in getting particular people together.[4]

But given this sort of "prefiltering," what general factors can begin to distinguish between those couples who fell deeply in love and those who did not? One part of the answer concerned the religious composition of the couples. In 62% of the cases in which both partners listed one of the three major religions as his or her "religious background," the two partners were of the same religion. In the remaining 38% of the cases, however, the religions of the two partners differed. Given that a young man and woman are going together and that they are serious enough to volunteer to fill out a questionnaire about their relationship, how might we expect their religious similarity or dissimilarity to affect their degree of love? My prediction was that members of interfaith couples would love one another more.

There are several rationales for this prediction. There are often strong pressures,

---

[4]An alternative interpretation of the same data is that the couples were not attracted to one another on the basis of attitudinal similarity, but that their views became more similar *after* they had selected one another, as a result of their interaction. A more detailed analysis of the data rendered this alternative explanation less plausible, however. The correlation between boyfriends' and girlfriends' authoritarianism scores turned out to be just as great among those 40 couples who has been dating less than 4 months (.58) as among those 60 couples who had been dating for 18 months or more (.53). The correlations were of the same order of magnitude among the 4–11 month and 12–17 month groups as well (.47 and .57). If the partners' attitudes became more similar as a consequence of their interaction, we would have expected the correlation to increase as a function of the length of time the couple had been dating. Since the size of the correlation was extremely stable, it is more reasonable to conclude that attitude similarity on this dimension plays an important role in the initial selection or very early filtering of dating partners.

especially from parents, against marrying or even dating a person of a different religious background from one's own. It seemed likely, therefore, that these pressures would be defied only if the partners felt a particularly strong degree of love. Festinger's (1957) theory of cognitive dissonance makes a similar prediction, but reverses the causal sequence. Assume that two students of different religions have found one another attractive and started dating. It may well be dissonant for a member of such a couple to believe that: (*a*) I am going with someone of another faith, in defiance of my early training and my parents' wishes and (*b*) I don't even love him (her) very much. To reduce the inconsistency one might resort to either of two quite different tactics. One tactic would be to break off the relationship. Those interfaith couples who had already hit upon this solution were not, of course, represented in my sample. Another solution, however, would be to decide that "I must really love him after all."

Driscoll, Davis, and Lipetz (1972) outlined another reason for making the same prediction, the possibility that parental opposition may directly increase the partners' love for one another. They call this "the Romeo and Juliet effect":

> [In *Romeo and Juliet*,] the short but intense love affair took place against the background of total opposition from the two feuding families. The family conflicts did, in several parts of the play, force the lovers to decide whether their primary allegiance was to each other or to their families, and created difficulties and separations that appear to have intensified the lovers' feelings for each other [p. 2].

The Roman myth of Pyramus and Thisbe is also based on this theme: ". . . they longed to marry, but their parents forbade it. Love, however, cannot be forbidden. The more the flame is covered up, the hotter it burns [Hamilton, 1942, p. 101]." A general principle that has frequently been noted by students of intergroup behavior is that external opposition to a group or nation tends to increase ingroup solidarity (see LeVine & Campbell, 1972). Parental opposition may well play an analogous role in unifying young couples.

Driscoll and his co-workers obtained some support for the operation of the Romeo and Juliet effect in a study of dating and married couples in Boulder, Colorado. They found positive correlations between a measure of "parental interference," as perceived by the partners, and a measure of love, which was somewhat similar to my love scale. My own results, comparing the same-religion and different-religion couples, provided further corroboration of the effect. But the data suggested that the effect may be operative only among relatively *short-term* couples. Among those couples who had been dating up to 18 months, the love scores of members of different-religion couples were significantly higher than the love scores of same-religion couples. But among those 54 couples who had been dating for longer than 18 months, including the majority of the engaged couples in the sample, the pattern reversed itself. For these long-term couples love scores were higher if the two partners were of the same religion.

Especially since I did not obtain any direct measure of parental opposition, it is difficult to interpret this reversal among the long-term couples. One possibility is, as Driscoll and his colleagues have suggested, "if such [parental] interference continues without resolution, it is likely to undermine the overall quality of the relationship [p. 9]." The relationships of the long-term interfaith couples may have been subjected to *too much* external pressure to fan the flames of love. As a result, their relationships may have been in the process of weakening. This interpretation is a speculative one, however, and I have no additional evidence to back it up. What seems most clear is that external obstacles, of the sort which may often prevent or destroy a relationship, can under some conditions have the effect of fostering romantic love.

VI. Love, Liking, and Mate Selection

The link between love and marriage has been viewed by some anthropologists as a peculiarity of the American courtship system. Lindon (1936) has observed that, "All societies recognize that there are occasional emotional attachments between members of the opposite sex, but our present American culture is practically the only one which has attempted to capitalize on these, and make them the basis for marriage [p. 175]." Rosenblatt's recent research, as reported in this volume (Chapter 4), suggests that Linton may have overstated his position. In fact there are several non-Western societies in which elements similar to "romantic love" are central features of the mate-selection process. Nevertheless, it is true that contemporary American society has exhibited the "love pattern" of mate selection to an unusually large degree (see Goode, 1959).

The current American view of love has been influenced by the "romantic ideal" derived from the games of courtly love played by members of the European nobility in the Middle Ages. Its distinguishing features include the beliefs that love is fated and uncontrollable, that it strikes at first sight, consumes the lovers with single-minded passion, transcends all social boundaries, and lasts throughout life. Whereas courtly love was always extramarital, however, the Americanized version of the ideal has been transposed to the context of dating and marriage. This Americanized version is faithfully transmitted by an ever-popular and pervasive genre of movies, television serials, magazines, and comic books.

In the novel and movie *Love Story*, for example, the son of an aristocratic Boston family and the daughter of an Italian-American baker from Providence meet in the Radcliffe library, fall in love shortly thereafter, and marry despite his father's vehement objections. In the movie "Guess Who's Coming to Dinner?" a rich white girl and a brilliant black physician meet in Hawaii, fall in love at first sight, and in the subsequent week manage to break down their parents' opposition, get married, and fly off to what promises to be a lifetime of bliss in the doctor's jungle hospital. A recent saga from *Young Romance* comics begins with Samantha, a waitress at the exclusive Carlton Colony Club, considering marriage to a wealthy lawyer whom she does not love. As she sits under a tree comtemplating all the beautiful things he would buy for her, a handsome busboy named Sandy walks up and says "Hi." (*"It started with a single word."*) It is love at first sight. (*"It had struck like a flash of lightning, blinding us to everything else in the world . . . shocking our senses so that we were conscious only of one sensation of bittersweet pain . . . ."*) After some vacillation, Samantha decides to marry the poor busboy instead of the rich lawyer and they walk off hand in hand toward what the knowledgeable reader can safely assume will be years of perfect happiness.[5]

The socialization of young Americans for love begins, in fact, even before they are old enough to attend the movies and read the comic books:

> The telling of the myth is begun in the nursery with fairy tales: Cinderella, Sleeping Beauty, Snow White, Frog Prince, and half a hundred less famous stories. Hardly a child *believes* the tales, but they all have the same message: A handsome prince overcomes obstacles to marry the poor maid with whom he has fallen in love; they are married and live in bliss. Alternately, the handsome but poor peasant boy overcomes obstacles to marry the princess, with whom he has fallen in love; they are married and live in bliss. Always beauty, always obstacles, always love, always a class barrier (presumably changing from frog to human leaps an ethnic barrier), always married bliss. The unsaid last line of each story is "some day this may happen to you." Parents set the proper example for their children by relating to the child their own prince-and-beauty story. "Why did you marry Daddy?" "Because we fell in love" [Udry, 1971, p. 163].

This intensive socialization for love undoubtedly has some impact on the course of dating relationships. Although they may "know better," many people are beneath it all convinced that there is only one "true love" for a person, and that once it is found it will last throughout life, most probably in marriage. Not all young people wholeheartedly accept these tenets of the romantic ideal, however. Many are keenly aware of the importance of "nonromantic" factors in mate selection, including considerations of economic and social status. There is also an emerging view that love should be enjoyed only while it lasts, rather than being embedded in a permanent relationship or institutionalized in marriage (see Carey, 1969). These differing ideological positions give rise to specific hypotheses about the role of love in the development of dating relationships. For individuals who are "romantic," love for one's partner should predict progress toward a more intense or enduring relationship. For individuals who are "nonromantic," on the other hand, there should be little or no such predictability.

To test these hypotheses, I used an already existing Romanticism Scale (Hobart, 1958) to categorize members of dating couples with respect to their romantic ideology. The scale consists of nine statements to which respondents indicated their degree of agreement or disagreement. Agreement with items such as "To be truly

---

[5]This story, entitled "A Price on My Love," was published in *Young Romance* comics, June–July, 1970. I am indebted to Lynn Mary Karjala for bringing this and other such sagas to my attention in an insightful paper on "'Love Comics' and the Romantic Ideal."

in love is to be in love forever" and "A person should marry whomever he loves regardless of social position" was scored as "romantic"; agreement with items such as, "Most of us could sincerely love any one of several people equally well" and "Economic security should be carefully considered before selecting a marriage partner" was scored as "nonromantic." There was considerable variation among respondents in their degree of romanticism. Interestingly, boyfriends proved to be significantly more romantic than their girlfriends, corresponding to the results of several previous studies (see Hobart, 1958; Kephart, 1967). Mate selection still seems to be a more serious matter for women than for men in our society. Hence the male may find it easier to hold onto his romantic illusions, while the female finds it more necessary to revise or abandon hers in favor of more "rational" considerations.

On the basis of their scores on the Romanticism Scale, I divided both the men and the women in the sample into romantic and nonromantic subgroups. I then proceeded to examine the correlations between individual love scores and a follow-up index of the couple's progress toward a more "intense" relationship obtained 6 months later.[6] The top row of Table 3 shows support for the hypotheses. In the romantic subgroups, love scores were substantially related to the reported movement of relationships toward greater intensity. Among couples in which *both* partners were romantic, the degree of predictability from love to progress was even greater—the correlations were .41 for women and .52 for men. Among the nonromantic subgroups, on the other hand, love scores were entirely unrelated to progress. When both partners were nonromantic, in fact, the correlations between love and further involvement became slightly negative: −.16 for women and −.10 for men.

The implication that love propels young romantics toward marriage will be received with knowing frowns by some social critics. De Rougemont (1949) has contended that men and women, especially in the United States, are seduced by the romantic ideal to ignore practical considerations—including those of social class, education, religion, and outlooks on the future—which in past eras helped to insure successful marriages. De Rougemont attributed the soaring divorce rates of the first half of the twentieth century in large measure to this seduction. He writes, "We are in the act of trying out—and failing miserably at it—one of the most pathological experiments that a civilized society has ever imagined, namely, the basing of marriage, which is lasting, upon romance, which is a passing fancy

---

[6]Follow-up reports were received from 317 of the 364 initial respondents (87.1%) and from at least one member of 179 of the 182 couples (98.4%). Boyfriends' and girlfriends' responses to the question about progress were highly correlated ($r = .88$), and a single index of progress was constructed by combining the responses of the two partners. When only one member of a couple returned the follow-up questionnaire, the index was based on his or her response alone. The index had three points, ranging from "less intense" (21% of the couples, most of whom had discontinued their relationship) to "no change" (19% of the couples) to "more intense" (60% of the couples). The index of progress was substantially correlated with the degree to which respondents' estimates of the likelihood of marrying their partner were revised upward from October to April ($r = .63$ for women and $r = .56$ for men).

TABLE 3

Correlations between Individual Love and Liking Scores (October) and Couple's Progress (April) for Romantic and Nonromantic Respondents

	Women		Men	
	Nonromantic (N = 95)	Romantic (N = 84)	Nonromantic (N = 87)	Romantic (N = 92)
Love and progress	−.02	.41**	−.01	.37**
Liking and progress	.12	.30*	−.00	.33*

*p < .01.   **p < .001.

Note: Based on 179 couples in which at least one member returned follow-up questionnaire.

[p. 325]." Waller (1938) offered similar advice in his classic textbook on marriage:

> It is possibly very unfortunate that people must make one of their most important decisions on the basis of certain delusive emotions of adolescence. There is truth in the ancient proverb, *Amantes amentes*, lovers are mad. And the persons who have the power to excite this madness in others are by no means always the persons with whom it is possible to live happily after the knot is tied [p. 208].

Other observers would be more sanguine about our data. Beigel (1951) has maintained, for example, that "seen in proper perspective, [love] has not only done no harm as a prerequisite to marriage, but it has mitigated the impact that a too-fast-moving and unorganized conversion to new socio-economic constellations has had upon our whole culture, and it has saved monogamous marriage from complete disorganization [p. 333]."

I have no data with which to settle this issue. But it is illuminating—and, perhaps, encouraging—to discover that among the romantic subgroups in my sample, *liking* scores were virtually as powerful predictors of movement toward a more intense relationship as were love scores (Table 3, bottom row). You will recall that in the sample as a whole, love scores were considerably more highly related than liking scores to the respondents' estimates of the likelihood that they would marry their dating partner. This pattern of correlations was obtained within both the romantic and the nonromantic subgroups. When it comes to tracking the progress of the relationship over time, however, liking is almost as effective a predictor as love. It is not possible to make precise causal statements about the precipitants of progress among the new romantics on the basis of the data at hand.[7] But the pattern of correlations suggests that the romantic ideal undergoes modification in the translation from myth to reality. The romantic is not propelled toward marriage by blind, unthinking love, in the manner of Samantha and Sandy. The progress of the relationship seems to depend quite as much upon the ways in which the partners evaluate one another's intelligence, maturity, and good judgment as upon their initial feelings of attachment, caring, and intimacy. Liking may even serve as one subjective index of the loveworthiness of a dating partner.

[7]I am currently conducting more extensive longitudinal research that will hopefully shed light on possible causal processes.

VII. Conclusion

The foregoing results surely raise many more questions than they answer. What factors, for example, account for the fact that some people are more "romantic" than others? If neither liking nor loving predicts progress toward more intimate relationships among "nonromantics," then what does? What are the causal, sequential links between liking and loving? Under what specific conditions does each facilitate the development of the other? And on and on.

Perhaps a question that is logically prior to all of these is whether or not taking an empirical approach to romantic love is a proper or useful way of expanding our knowledge in this area. The approach is not without its dangers. In *Love and Will*, the existential psychologist Rollo May (1969) argued that statistical studies of sexual behavior have had damaging effects upon interpersonal relationships:

> It is an old and ironic habit of human beings to run faster when we have lost our way; and we grasp more fiercely at research, statistics and technical aids in sex when we have lost the values and meaning of love ... [p. 15].

> Couples place great emphasis on bookkeeping and timetables in their love-making—a practice confirmed and standardized by Kinsey. If they fall behind schedule they become anxious and feel impelled to go to bed whether they want to or not ... [p. 43].

> The computer hovers in the stage wings of the drama of love-making the way Freud said one's parents used to [p. 44].

It is likely that May would have similar reservations about my computerized study of love. The opposing point of view, which I must admit to holding, is that it is only by getting a firmer grasp on the elusive nature of love that we can ultimately hope to learn and to teach others, as Bennis (in Bennis & Slater, 1968) put it, "how to get love, to love, and to lose love." The statistical way is surely not the only way to this goal. But it is one way, and I persist in my efforts to put love on a scale in the hope that it may bring us just a bit closer to it.

Acknowledgments

The research reported in this paper was supported by a predoctoral fellowship from the National Institute of Mental Health and by a grant-in-aid from the Society for the Psychological Study of Social Issues. I am grateful to Theodore M. Newcomb for his guidance in the conduct of the initial research and to J. Patrick Berry for assistance with data analysis. An expanded version of the material in this chapter is presented by Rubin (1973, Chapters 9 and 10).

References

Beigel, H. Romantic love. *American Sociological Review*, 1951, **16**, 326–334.
Bennis, W. G., & Slater, P. E. *The temporary society.* New York: Harper, 1968.
Booth, A. Sex and social participation. *American Sociological Review*, 1972, **37**, 183–192.

Bowlby, J. *Attachment and loss.* Vol. 1. New York: Basic Books, 1969.

Buber, M. *I and Thou.* New York: Scribner's, 1970.

Byrne, D. *The attraction paradigm.* New York: Academic Press, 1971.

Campbell, D. T. Recommendations for APA test standards regarding construct, trait, and discriminant validity. *American Psychologist,* 1960, **15**, 546—553.

Carey, J. T. Changing courtship patterns in the popular song. *American Journal of Sociology,* 1969, **74**, 720—731.

Cronbach, L. J., & Meehl, P. E. Construct validity in psychological tests. *Psychological Bulletin,* 1955, **52**, 281—302.

De Rougemont, D. The crisis of the modern couple. In R. N. Anshen (Ed.), *The family: Its function and destiny.* New York: Harper, 1949.

Douvan, E., & Adelson, J. *The adolescent experience.* New York: Wiley, 1966.

Driscoll, R., Davis, K. E., & Lipetz, M. E. Parental interference and romantic love: The Romeo and Juliet effect. *Journal of Personality and Social Psychology,* 1972, **24**, 1—10.

Exline, R. Visual interaction: The glances of power and preference. In J. K. Cole (Ed.), *Nebraska Symposium on Motivation, 1971.* Lincoln, Nebraska: University of Nebraska Press, 1971.

Festinger, L. *A theory of cognitive dissonance.* Stanford, California: Stanford University Press, 1957.

Festinger, L., Schachter, S., & Back, K. W. *Social pressures in informal groups.* New York: Harper, 1950.

Freud, S. Group psychology and the analysis of the ego. In *The standard edition of the complete psychological works of Sigmund Freud.* Vol. 18. London: Hogarth, 1955.

Fromm, E. *The art of loving.* New York: Harper, 1956.

Goffman, E. *Behavior in public places.* New York: Free Press, 1963.

Goode, W. J. The theoretical importance of love. *American Sociological Review,* 1959, **24**, 38—47.

Hamilton, E. *Mythology.* New York: New American Library of World Literature, 1942.

Harlow, H. F. The nature of love. *American Psychologist,* 1958, **13**, 673—685.

Hobart, C. W. The incidence of romanticism during courtship. *Social Forces,* 1958, **36**, 363—367.

Jourard, S. M. *The transparent self.* Princeton, New Jersey: Van Nostrand Reinhold, 1964.

Jourard, S. M., & Lasakow, P. Some factors in self-disclosure. *Journal of Abnormal and Social Psychology,* 1958, **56**, 91—98.

Kephart, W. M. Some correlates of romantic love. *Journal of Marriage and the Family,* 1967, **29**, 470—479.

LeVine, R. A., & Campbell, D. T. *Ethnocentrism: Theories of conflict, ethnic attitudes, and group behavior.* New York: Wiley, 1972.

Linton, R. *The study of man.* New York: Appleton, 1936.

Lorenz, K. *King Solomon's ring.* New York: Crowell, 1952.

Maslow, A. H. Deficiency motivation and growth motivation. In M. R. Jones (Ed.), *Nebraska Symposium on Motivation, 1955.* Lincoln, Nebraska: University of Nebraska Press, 1955.

May, R. *Love and will.* New York: Norton, 1969.

Orlinsky, D. E. Love relationships in the life cycle: A developmental interpersonal perspective. In H. A. Otto (Ed.), *Love today: A new exploration.* New York: Association Press, 1972.

Park, R. E., & Burgess, E. W. *Introduction to the science of sociology.* (2nd ed.) Chicago, Illinois: University of Chicago Press, 1924.

Parsons, T., & Bales, R. F. *Family, socialization, and interaction process.* Glencoe, Illinois: Free Press, 1955.

Reik, T. *A psychologist looks at love.* New York: Rinehart, 1944.

Rheingold, H. L. The effect of environmental stimulation upon social and exploratory behavior in the human infant. In B. M. Foss (Ed.), *Determinants of infant behavior.* Vol. 1. New York: Wiley, 1961.

Robson, K. S. The role of eye-to-eye contact in maternal-infant attachment. *Journal of Child Psychology and Psychiatry,* 1967, **8**, 13—25.

Rubin, Z. *The social psychology of romantic love.* Ann Arbor, Michigan: University Microfilms, 1969, No. 70—4179.

Rubin, Z. Measurement of romantic love. *Journal of Personality and Social Psychology,* 1970, **16**, 265—273.

Rubin, Z. *Liking and loving: An invitation to social psychology.* New York: Holt, 1973.

Sullivan, H. S. *Conceptions of modern psychiatry.* (2nd ed.) New York: Norton, 1953.

Tillich, P. *The dynamics of faith.* New York: Harper, 1957.

Udry, J. R. *The social context of marriage.* (2nd ed.) Philadelphia, Pennsylvania: Lippincott, 1971.

Waller, W. *The family: A dynamic interpretation.* New York: Dryden, 1938.

Zajonc, R. B. Attitudinal effects of mere exposure. *Journal of Personality and Social Psychology, Monograph Supplement,* 1968, **9**, No. 2, Part 2.

Author Index

Numbers in italics refer to the pages on which the complete references are listed.

A

Abelson, R., 12, *25*
Abrahams, D., 17, *28*, 104, *120*, 178, *192*, 342, *351*, 375, *380*
Adams, J. S., 21, *25*, 333, 335, *349*
Adelson, J., 390, *401*
Aderman, D., 345, *349*
Agar, E., 348, *350*
Alexander, I. E., 325, *329*
Allport, G. W., 144, *165*, 335, *349*
Altman, I., 17, *25*, *28*, 122, 123, 125, 127, 130, 131, 132, 135, 136, 137, *138, 139, 140, 141, 142,* 277, *283*
Amir, Y., 186, *189*
Ammons, H., 37, *57*
Ammons, R., 37, *57*
Anderson, D., 336, *350*
Anderson, N. H., 12, 13, *25, 27,* 102, *119,* 149, 151, 164, *165, 167,* 179, 189, *189,* 292, 303, *304, 306*
Andres, D., 296, *304*
Aponte, J. F., 173, 186, *191*
Argyle, M., 131, 133, 134, 135, *139*
Aronson, E., 6, 7, 12, 16, *25, 26,* 156, 163, *165,* 171, 173, 176, 177, 180, 181, *189, 190, 191,* 205, *213,* 240, 244, 259, 265, 268, 269, 271, 272, 274, 276, 277, *280, 281, 282,* 294, 302, 303, *304, 306,* 314, 315, 317, 325, *328*
Aronson, V., 17, *28*, 104, *120*, 178, *192,* 375, *380*
Arrowood, A. J., 177, *190*, 251, *280,* 322, *328*
Asch, S. E., 102, *119*
Austin, M. C., 49, *57*
Ausubel, D. P., *57*
Ax, A. F., 363, *379*

B

Back, K. W., 115, *120*, 135, *140*, 387, *401*
Backman, C. W., 221, *230*, 242, 243, *280*

Baer, D. M., 24, *26*
Baldridge, B., 157, 159, *166*
Bales, R. F., 8, 25, 237, 242, 251, *280*, 389, *401*
Bandura, A., 152, *165*, 345, *349*
Banks, F., 63, 67, *77*
Barclay, A., 342, *349*
Barefoot, J. C., 185, *189*
Barker, R. G., 135, *139*
Baron, R. A., 16, *25*, 300, *304*
Barth, J., 224, *225, 229*
Barton, R. F., 90, *94*
Baskett, G. D., 8, 16, *26*, 147, 164, *165, 168,* 298, 300, *304*
Batchelor, T. R., 183, *189*, 293, *304*
Baxter, J. C., 345, *349*
Beach, F. A., 10, 13, *26,* 87, 92, *94*
Beam, L., 228, *230*
Bean, F., 73, *77*
Becker, F. D., 136, *142*
Becker, S. W., 287, 306, 338, *350*
Beigel, H. G., 356, *379*, 399, *400*
Belenky, M., 39, 42, 45, *58*
Bell, L., *281,* 294, *306*
Bell, N., 256, *282*
Bell, R. R., 69, 74, *76*
Bem, D. J., 180, *190,* 203, *212,* 255, 256, 264, *281*
Benedict, B., 86, *94*
Bennis, W. G., *400*
Benton, A. A., 336, *349*
Bergman, J. T., 341, *350*
Berkowitz, H., 270, *280*
Berkowitz, L., 194, 209, *212, 213,* 246, *281,* 287, *304,* 336, 337, 345, 347, *349*
Berkowitz, N. N., 8, 28, 206, *215*
Berkowitz, W. R., 181, *189*
Berlyne, D. E., 371, *379*
Bernard, J., *71,* 72, *76*
Bernot, L., 84, *94*
Bernstein, A., 132, *140*

403

Subject Index

A
B
C
D
E
F
G
H
I
J